COLOR ATLAS OF THE AUTOPSY

COLOR ATLAS OF THE AUTOPSY

Scott A. Wagner

CRC PRESS

Boca Raton London New York Washington, D.C.

The sole purpose of this book is instructional. No permission will be given to use the photographs for any reason other than education. All care has been taken to maintain the anonymity of the persons shown.

Library of Congress Cataloging-in-Publication Data

Wagner, Scott.
Color atlas of the autopsy / Scott A. Wagner.
p. ; cm.
Includes bibliographical references and index.
ISBN 0-8493-1520-4 (alk. paper)
1. Autopsy—Atlases. 2. Forensic sciences—Atlases.
[DNLM: 1. Autopsy—Atlases. W 617 W135c 2003] I. Title.
RB57 .W34 2003
616.07′59—dc22 2003055692

Direct all inquiries to CRC Press LLC, 2000 N.W. Corporate Blvd., Boca Raton, Florida 33431.

Visit the CRC Press Web site at www.crcpress.com

No claim to original U.S. Government works
International Standard Book Number 0-8493-1520-4
Library of Congress Card Number 2003055692
Printed in the United States of America 1 2 3 4 5 6 7 8 9 0
Printed on acid-free paper

Preface

Finally, there is a book that takes the reader through the autopsy procedure in a stepwise fashion, just as though the reader were at the autopsy. The chapters and the information in this book are revealed in layers, just like opening the body at autopsy. The aim is not only to show *what* is done in an autopsy, but *why* and *how* it is done. Many similar books have been written for pathologists or other physicians, but not for those who must work with pathologists. Death investigators, law enforcement officials, and other professionals need to know about the "strange" things pathologists do as well as how and why they do them. This book is dedicated to and written for those patient souls who must interact with pathologists before, during, and after the autopsy.

The primary purpose of this book is to introduce the process and principles of the autopsy procedure to the new and uninitiated. Because the autopsy is primarily a visual study of the diseases and injuries of the human body, images are essential to explain the process. Images are used in the book to tell the story of how the forensic pathologist develops opinions of the cause and manner of death.

This book is written as a natural extension of 15 years of teaching and demonstrating the autopsy to medical students, paramedics, flight nurses, nursing students, death investigators, law enforcement officials, firefighters, conservation officers, and other similar professionals and students of these professions. Many such professionals are involved with the practice of medicine and are eager to see the autopsy. For some, viewing an autopsy is an educational requirement. I have found it difficult to demonstrate an autopsy for all those professionals who need to see the procedure because the demand to see an autopsy exceeds the number of autopsies being performed. Also, the time for teaching during the $1^1/_2$-hour standard autopsy is limited. For me, it was difficult to orient the visitor to what I was doing. I finally realized that the professionals and students who came to my autopsy suite left with more questions than they had when they arrived.

I began looking for videos and other teaching aids to orient those uninitiated to the autopsy. I found that little or nothing was available, especially in the video medium. To fill this void, I produced the video, *The Autopsy, Chapter One: Unraveling Life's Mysteries,* in the year 2000. This video serves to teach and demonstrate visually the basic principles and practices of the autopsy. It allows the viewer to see three autopsies, with narrative explanations. Response to the video has been fantastic. Since its release, we have had numerous requests for written material to support and supplement the video medium. This book is largely a response to those requests. With narrative and over 500 still pictures, this book expands greatly on each aspect of the autopsy.

The reader should keep in mind that this is a basic book on the autopsy. The intent is not to teach one how to do an autopsy, but to show the process and principles used in the basic forensic autopsy. Those who are interested in learning more details about anatomy, physiology, pathology, forensic pathology, and other disciplines touched upon here should consult the suggested reading list at the back of the book. The methods demonstrated in this book are not meant to advocate only one way to perform the procedures. They simply indicate one way to do each procedure. The aim is to present a practical approach to the autopsy, with interesting findings presented along the way. One should think of this book as spending a few days at the author's autopsy table.

It is my intention that the information and images in this book be used only by professionals and students in fields related to law enforcement, death investigation, medicine, and law, or by funeral directors. Improper use of these images can be a violation of the law, and using these photographs in a salacious manner violates the basic ethics the author and his colleagues uphold. The first lesson to learn about the autopsy is reverence for the deceased and their families. It is in keeping with this reverence that I honor the deceased and use these images only to educate future and seasoned death investigators, detectives, nurses, paramedics, and other professionals. This is done to better our understanding of diseases and injuries, with the aim of benefiting the whole of humankind.

Scott A. Wagner

Acknowledgments

The author would like thank the following:
My lovely wife Suzanne, whose advice and patience are unmatched, daughters Amanda and Natalie, and my entire family for excusing me while working; my colleagues, Robert Gutekunst, M.D. (thanks for proofreading the manuscript), J. Tom Lucas, M.D., and all the pathologists of Indiana Pathology Consultants, Inc.; my staff of assistants, Alex Workman, Michelle Minnick, and Kimberly Hoeffler; John Pless, M.D., Dean Hawley, M.D., Michael Clark, Ph.D., M.D., and Richard Haruff, M.D., for the inspiration; Jim and John Brune for help with the graphics; authors Dawn Dunn and Ann Rule for the advice; Jon Brandenberger, M.D., and C.R. "Dick" Alfeld for the support; the late Phillip O'Shaugnessy, D.D.S., and family; and also David Brandt, Jack Brady, Terry Brazzel, John Brazzel, Randy Fox, Frank Jagoda, Barbara Julian, Leslie Cook, Sgt. Mike Trittipo, Sgt. Mike Burris, and Ofc. Chris Miehls.

About the Author

Scott A. Wagner, M.D., is the director of the Phillip E. O'Shaugnessy Northcast Indiana Forensic Center in Fort Wayne, IN, and an assistant clinical professor of pathology at Indiana University School of Medicine. Dr. Wagner loves to share his fascination with pathology and forensic pathology with colleagues, students, coroners, nurses, law enforcement, first responders, and others. He has developed a video series, *The Autopsy, Chapter One: Unraveling Life's Mysteries,* and is currently producing the second video in this series.

Introduction

The study of the autopsy begins with two basic assumptions: 1) the life of the individual is of the highest value, and 2) the deceased is to be treated with reverence. Our society holds the life of an individual above all else. If our culture had no reverence for life, we certainly would not care about death. Autopsies obviously do not benefit the dead; they benefit the living, and that is the focus of our study.

This book was written to fill a gap in information about the autopsy. Books on the autopsy are normally written for physicians or experts in the fields of pathology and forensic pathology. While these books are essential for physicians and other experts in the field, no accessible books are available that show the process of the autopsy to those who interface with pathologists. It is often difficult for paramedics, crime scene investigators, firefighters, law enforcement officials, nurses, and students of these fields to observe an autopsy. Even when an autopsy can be viewed, the pathologist has limited time to explain the theories behind, and the purposes of, the autopsy procedure. Some professionals never see or experience an autopsy until they are on the job. Pathologists benefit when they interact with professionals who understand something about the autopsy, i.e., what an autopsy can and cannot do.

This book is not a comprehensive study of the autopsy procedure. Anatomy, physiology, and histology are touched upon, but they are not the focus of the book. Forensic medicine and principles are introduced. However, the reader is advised to consult the bibliography for encyclopedic information on diseases and injuries. We depict routine autopsy procedures done in a convenient, practical way. There are many ways to approach and perform an autopsy, and we certainly do not mean to imply that our methods are the only ones, or even the best. Our aim is to expose the reader to the principles, common findings, and practices of the adult autopsy.

Contents

Chapter 1 Approach to the Autopsy: Purpose and Philosophy 1

What Is an Autopsy? 1
Types of Autopsies: Hospital and Medical–Legal 1
What Is the Purpose of the Autopsy? 2
Cases That Usually Require an Autopsy 2
Natural Deaths 3
Unnatural Deaths 3
Homicides 3
Suicides 4
Accidents 4
The Autopsy: Assembling a Puzzle 4
What Is a Forensic Pathologist? 5

Chapter 2 Circumstantial and Medical History 7

Identify the Problem and "Chief Complaint" 7
Identification of the Body 7
Direct Identification by Family Members 7
Personal Features 7
Objects in the Body 8
Higher-Order Identification 8
Fingerprints 8
Dental Identification 8
Deoxyribonucleic Acid 8
Investigative Questions 8
Basic Demographic Questions 8
Question of Occupation 8
Question of Medical History 8
Question of Medications 9
Question of Mental Health History 9
Question of Illicit Drug Use 9
Question of Ethanol Use 9
Question of History with Law Enforcement or Incarceration 9
Other Investigative Questions 9

Chapter 3 External Examination: The Preliminary Examination 15

Suiting Up: Universal Precautions 15
Opening the Body Bag 15
Clothing and Valuables 15
Body Storage 16
Trace Evidence 16
Four Signs of Death 16
Rigor Mortis 16
Algor Mortis 16
Livor Mortis 16
Decomposition 17
Focus on What Is Not Obvious 17

Documenting Traumatic Injuries: Diagrams and Descriptions 17
Radiology and Imaging 18
Photography and Video as Documentation Tools 18
Scars, Tattoos, and Other Unique Marks 18
Artifacts of Medical Intervention 19

Chapter 4 External Examination: Specific Injuries 37

Forensic Injuries and Definitions 37
Blunt Force Injuries 37
Laceration 37
Abrasion 37
Contusion 37
Avulsion 37
Sharp Force Injuries 38
Stab Wounds 38
Incised Wounds 38
Defense Wounds 38
Puncture Wounds 38
Chopping Wounds 38
Gunshot Wounds 38

Chapter 5 External Examination: Specific Body Areas 51

Overall “Gestalt” 51
Skin 51
Hair 51
Scalp 51
Face 51
Eyes 51
Nose 52
Mouth 52
Neck 52
Chest 52
Breasts 52
Abdomen 52
Extremities, Hands, Fingers, Nails 52
Back 52
Genitalia 53
Rectum/Anus 53

Chapter 6 Internal Examination: Opening of Body Cavities and Initial Assessment 67

Dissection of the Skin and Opening of the Chest and Abdomen 68
Survey of Chest Tissues and Organs 79
Survey of Abdominal Organs 87
Collecting Blood, Urine, Bile, and Vitreous Specimens for Toxicology 95

Chapter 7 Organ and Tissue Removal 99

Heart Excision 100
Lung Excision 103
Liver Excision 106
Spleen Excision 111
Small and Large Bowel Excision 113

Adrenal Gland and Kidney Removal ... 123
Aorta Examination ... 131
Uterus Removal ... 137
Bladder Removal ... 138
Neck Dissection ... 140

Chapter 8 Individual Organ Examination ... 147

Heart ... 148
Lung ... 163
Neck Organs: Epiglottis, Vocal Cords, Trachea, Thyroid, Cartilage, Strap Muscles, Hyoid Bone ... 173
Liver ... 183
Spleen ... 188
Urinary Tract: Kidneys, Bladder, Ureter, Prostate ... 190
Esophagus and Stomach ... 197
Uterus and Ovaries ... 200

Chapter 9 Examination of the Head, Skull, Brain, and Spinal Cord ... 203

Scalp Examination and Excision of the Brain ... 204

Chapter 10 Microscopic Examination ... 221

Chapter 11 Postmortem Laboratory Analysis of Drugs, Chemicals, and Microorganisms ... 229

The Scene and the Body ... 229
Specimens to Obtain at Autopsy ... 230
Blood ... 230
Urine ... 230
Vitreous Humor ... 230
Gastric Contents ... 230
Bile ... 230
Tissues and Other Specimens ... 230

Chapter 12 Review Questions: Putting It All Together ... 235

References and Suggested Reading ... 239

Index ... 241

1 Approach to the Autopsy: Purpose and Philosophy

"To the living we owe respect, but to the dead we owe only the truth."

Voltaire

WHAT IS AN AUTOPSY?

The autopsy answers the final question: Why did life pass from a specific human body? It is a question we have all asked when a loved one, friend, coworker, or even a public figure dies. The more untimely the death, the more tragic it seems, so many more questions arise. A wife asks why her healthy husband suddenly collapses and is unresponsive. Coworkers are puzzled as they watch a young bricklayer cry out in pain and fall to his death from a great height. An entire country wants to know how its president was assassinated. The autopsy serves to answer these and many other questions.

The autopsy is a complete evaluation of an individual's death and the circumstances surrounding that death. It includes a full examination of the body, and the autopsy has been called "the ultimate physical examination." This examination includes:

- A complete evaluation of the medical history and the events leading to death
- The collection and documentation of trace evidence on and around the body
- The photographing and cataloging of injuries
- A detailed external examination from head to toe
- An internal examination, including the dissection of organs and tissues
- A microscopic examination of organs and tissues
- Laboratory and toxicologic examinations of body tissues and fluids
- A written report detailing the pertinent findings, negative findings, and conclusions, including the cause and manner of death

A common misconception is to think of the autopsy as simply a dissection of organs. Yes, the autopsy involves dissecting organs, but it is a much more comprehensive study of a person's death. The dissection portion of the autopsy is only a part of the complete examination a pathologist performs. More than a simple medical procedure, the autopsy is a comprehensive consultation with the pathologist and part of a complete death investigation. Your family doctor takes the same approach. For example, you may go to your doctor because you are tired all the time and want to find out why. You know your doctor will listen to your heart and lungs, but you want him to do more because your sluggishness might not be caused by a heart or lung problem. You want the doctor to use any means available to find out why you are so tired. He might have to perform blood tests or x-rays or take a detailed history from you. The pathologist approaches the autopsy in the same fashion, finding all the medical facts, whether they lie in the medical history, dissection, or toxicology results. The facts obtained in the study of the problem are used to form opinions. The key opinions are usually the cause and manner of death.

The body of the deceased is treated with the same respect the pathologist would show his or her own loved ones. Except in unusual circumstances, the autopsy does not alter any viewable portions of the body. Only rarely are visitors to the funeral service able to recognize that an autopsy has been performed. One misconception is that the body is mutilated during an autopsy. This book will show that the autopsy is a precisely performed examination and dissection.

TYPES OF AUTOPSIES: HOSPITAL AND MEDICAL–LEGAL

There are two types of autopsies: hospital and medical–legal. Hospital autopsies are performed on inpatients of hospitals, upon the requests of families. Physicians cannot order these autopsies without permits signed by the next of kin. Autopsy permits often grant physicians permission to study only those body parts that might help answer a specific medical question or determine the mechanism of death. Most hospital autopsies are done in teaching hospitals, where the examinations are often quite detailed and are performed for institutional research and the education of medical residents.

Hospital autopsies are less common today than in the past for a number of reasons. The approximate $1500 to $2000 cost is not covered by Medicare or private insurers, so the expense is borne by the hospital or family. Hospital regulatory agencies no longer require autopsy quotas for accreditation, and more hospital deaths have come under the purview of the coroner and medical examiner systems.

Previously, physicians eagerly sought autopsies to gauge the quality of medical care and to gain medical knowledge. In today's legal climate, some physicians fear an autopsy might elicit facts that could be used in lawsuits against them. In the author's experience, the reverse is true — an autopsy generally demonstrates that the patient died of causes unrelated to the standard of care. Not performing an autopsy in this situation can lead to the worst assumptions, i.e., that poor medical care caused the death and that this substandard care is being covered up.

Medical–legal autopsies are performed at the behest of the medical examiner or coroner, who is required to investigate all suspicious and unnatural deaths (see the section "Unnatural Deaths"). In most states a board-certified pathologist must perform these autopsies. The aim of medical–legal autopsies is to obtain the cause and manner of death (see the following bulleted lists). Because medical–legal autopsies are comprehensive examinations that include a study of the central nervous system, they exceed hospital autopsies in scope. As medical science is increasingly able to prolong the lives of victims of severe trauma, more and more hospital deaths are coming under the jurisdiction of the coroner or medical examiner. Victims who, in past times, would have died at the scene or in the emergency room now either recover or die after a long hospital course. Since such traumatic deaths are considered unnatural, these cases fall under medical–legal jurisdiction.

The different aims of hospital and medical–legal autopsies are illustrated in the following example. A 92-year-old woman with significant cardiac disease falls down her steps and suffers a hip fracture. While convalescing in the hospital, she dies suddenly, 3 days after her accident and admission.

A hospital autopsy would focus on answering these medical questions:

- Did she suffer a myocardial infarction or a pulmonary embolus (mechanism of death)?
- If her hospital care had been different (e.g., if anticoagulants had been given more aggressively), could her death have been prevented?
- If she was given a new anticoagulant under a research protocol, was this new drug effective? (This involves evaluating new drug protocols.)

The medical–legal investigation and autopsy would focus on:

- The injury (cause of death).
- The hip fracture.
- How the injury occurred (manner of death): Did she trip (accident), or did she have a myocardial infarction before falling down the steps (natural)? If she were pushed down the steps, the manner of death would be homicide.

If it was shown that this woman slipped and fell down the steps, sustained a hip fracture, and developed blood clots that embolized to the lung after 3 days of hospitalization, the death certificate would read as follows — Cause of Death: pulmonary embolus due to fracture of the hip; Manner of Death: accident.

When pathologists are asked to do an autopsy, they use any means available or known to them to answer the questions posed by the death investigation. A major part of this examination is the autopsy procedure itself. This book will show that the autopsy is a complex and comprehensive investigation into the causes and circumstances of death. The investigation of death and the autopsy can take the pathologist into virtually any field of medicine, engineering, science, law, law enforcement, and many other disciplines.

WHAT IS THE PURPOSE OF THE AUTOPSY?

The fundamental function of the jurisdictional authority investigating the death, i.e., the medical examiner or the coroner, is also the basic purpose of the autopsy: to establish the cause and manner of death. An autopsy is done mainly to complete a death certificate and to register the vital statistics. The cause of death is the disease or injury that sets into motion the chain of events leading to the death. The manner of death is a classification system for deaths (natural, homicide, suicide, accident, and undetermined). A treating physician, coroner, medical examiner, or health officer can certify death without an autopsy. Autopsies are expensive, so the jurisdictional authority in charge of the investigation must be selective about choosing cases for autopsy. A coroner, medical examiner, judge, and in many areas the public health officer can order an autopsy without the consent of next of kin.

Autopsies are usually not required when the patient has been under the regular treatment of a physician for a potentially terminal illness, and in such cases the treating physician can certify the death. However, when a person dies suddenly, unexpectedly, or under suspicious circumstances, even while under documented treatment of a physician, an autopsy is usually required. Listed below are cases that nearly always require an autopsy. As one can see, virtually any death can come under medical–legal jurisdiction.

CASES THAT USUALLY REQUIRE AN AUTOPSY

These include the following:

- Homicides
- Suicides
- Accidents that occur on the job

- Drivers in single-car accidents (could be a suicide)
- Sudden, unexpected deaths of children
- Deaths of pilots in aircraft crashes
- Natural diseases that might impact the community (e.g., meningitis)
- Fire deaths
- Accidents caused by the negligence or reckless behavior of others
- Deaths of persons in custody of the State or other agency
- Accidents that occur without a witness
- Accidents in which natural disease is a factor
- Sudden, unexpected deaths of apparently healthy persons (usually younger than 75 years)
- Deaths in which the manner of death is not readily apparent
- Deaths in which litigation is reasonably expected
- Hospital deaths in which the quality of care is an issue
- All suspicious deaths

Natural Deaths

When a disease, a syndrome, or a combination of diseases is the primary cause of death, the manner of death is categorized as natural. Investigating natural deaths is significant to the coroner and medical examiner for at least two reasons. First, infectious diseases such as meningitis, human immunodeficiency virus (HIV), or hepatitis can be discovered and those who had contact with the deceased can be evaluated and treated. Second, inherited diseases can be diagnosed, so living and future descendants of the deceased may be helped if they have correctable medical conditions.

Natural is the most common manner of death. Apparent accidental deaths are often natural deaths, such as in cases when the driver of a vehicle suddenly swerves off the road and is found dead after only a minor crash. Myocardial infarction is a common cause of death in this situation. Finding a natural disease by autopsy in this situation is important for a number of reasons. First, the cause of the automobile crash is needed for accident reconstruction purposes. Second, life insurance policies often pay double indemnity if the manner of death is an accident. Third, alcohol and substance abuse are ruled out as causes of the crash. In the investigation of sudden, unexpected death, most individuals also are found to have died of natural causes, usually cardiac in nature.

Some deaths, such as from cirrhosis of the liver, are classified as natural, even if the cause is chronic alcoholism and even though the person willingly drinks alcohol and knows cirrhosis can result. This classification is done both by convention and presumably because the alcohol-induced cirrhosis develops over 10, 20, or more years. If a smoker with severe emphysema continues to smoke and dies from respiratory failure, this death would also be classified as natural. But if a person takes arsenic chronically, that death would be classified as a suicide.

Victims of homicides also have natural diseases. These diseases can accelerate death in some cases. In fact, an elderly man with severe heart disease might not survive the same gunshot wound that a young, healthy person would. Blood loss from a leg wound would be easily tolerated by a healthy 20-year-old, but an elderly man with cardiac disease might not survive the stress on his cardiovascular system and could develop a myocardial infarction. Since pathologists make no assumptions, we treat the cases of the elderly man and the younger man equally, and the manner of death is homicide in both. We do not blame or hold the victim accountable for his existing cardiovascular disease. The gunshot wound set into motion a chain of events that resulted in death. Even though the cardiac disease contributed to the death, the cause of death is the gunshot wound.

Unnatural Deaths

Autopsies are necessary in most unnatural deaths including homicides, suicides, accidents, and those deaths in which the manner of death cannot be classified with the available information (often termed undetermined, unclassified, or could not be determined). Unnatural death is not a manner of death, per se. In an unnatural death, even though the cause and manner of death might appear obvious at the scene, an autopsy is usually performed. In an accident, finding the cause of the accident is essential, and an autopsy is often a large part of that investigation. In an apparent suicide, *intent* to kill oneself must be demonstrated. In a homicide, evidence must be collected and injuries must be documented. Autopsies are always performed in homicides or apparent homicides.

Homicides

A homicide is the killing of another human being, either by commission or omission. Murder, manslaughter, and reckless homicide are legal terms referring to the degree of action in the homicide. Certifying a case's manner of death as homicide does not mean the perpetrator committed murder or will even face legal charges. Shootings and stabbings are the obvious homicides, but a policeman shooting a school sniper is an example of "justifiable" or "police action" homicide. A common question is, "Why, in the case of a witnessed homicide involving a single gunshot wound to the head, is an autopsy necessary?" Here are but a few reasons for an autopsy in such a case:

- To confirm the cause and manner of death; that which appears as "obviously" true to a layperson occasionally proves to be false upon examination by an expert
- To provide photographic evidence for court proceedings
- To obtain the bullet and match it to a purported gun
- To track a bullet through the body, e.g., the bullet might not have entered the brain, and the person was strangled instead by a second perpetrator
- To obtain trace evidence
- To obtain independent confirmation of statements because witnesses might die or change statements
- To obtain specimens from the deceased for toxicology studies
- To gather medical data for expert medical testimony
- To allow the forensic pathologist to explain direct observations, such as injuries, to the court and thereby act as a witness for the deceased
- To correlate the injuries and other observations on the body and the evidence with witness statements
- To generate a report for the defense and its experts to review
- Because the court and the jury expect that such an exam should take place, i.e., performing a complete autopsy in homicide cases is a legal and medical standard in the U.S.

For the above reasons and others, it is the duty of the forensic pathologist to conduct a full medical–legal autopsy so that no reasonable investigative question remains unanswered. A thorough job must be done even though the cause of death might seem obvious.

Suicides

Suicide is the independent, willful taking of one's own life. A suicide usually requires an autopsy. One good reason for an autopsy is to rule out a possible homicide that has been made to look like a suicide. A frequent theme in movies, television shows, and books, this unlikely possibility can seem like a real explanation to friends and relatives, who may find the suicide of a loved one to be a devastatingly emotional event. These well-meaning people can cling to alternative theories to explain the death, such as homicide or an unusual accident. The religious implications of suicide are so powerful in some faiths that families might never agree with the ruling of suicide. Families and friends have been known to remove important evidence from the scene, presumably to prevent the conclusion that the death is a suicide.

A common theme in all suicides is the intent to kill oneself. Demonstrating this intent can be difficult. Scene investigation involves a search for evidence of this intent, such as a rope constructed for hanging, the wired trigger of a gun, or a suicide note.

Accidents

Accidents also typically require autopsies. A fatal accident that happens on the job should have a full investigation, including an autopsy. Deaths at the workplace are usually investigated by the Occupational Safety and Health Adminstration (OSHA). Insurance companies might require an autopsy before paying benefits. In the death of a law enforcement officer on duty, an autopsy is an absolute requirement for the investigation and for the family to receive certain death benefits. An accident involving alcohol or drugs has criminal implications and should receive a full investigation, including an autopsy. Accidents resulting from negligence should also be investigated.

Occasionally, accidents can appear to be suicides, such as in autoerotic asphyxia. In this accidental form of death, the victim uses a ligature to enhance sexual arousal. The ligature compresses the jugular veins, stopping venous return to the heart and cutting off oxygen to the brain. If the victim slips or becomes unconscious, death can ensue within minutes, due to asphyxia. Also, intoxicated people can accidentally ingest an overdose or a lethal combination of drugs. Ultimately, it can be difficult to determine if the intent was suicide in such cases.

THE AUTOPSY: ASSEMBLING A PUZZLE

The essence of the autopsy involves working backward from one undeniable fact: a death has occurred. Forensic pathologists look back in time to the point when a disease or injury set into motion a chain of events that were ultimately, and tragically, fatal. An old axiom in forensic pathology is "one takes the victim as one finds him." This simply means that the pathologist starts at the beginning of the death investigation, with a deceased victim, and makes no other assumptions. Facts are determined based on the examination of the specific victim, with his or her unique set of circumstances, medical conditions, and injuries.

Forensic pathologists do not work in a vacuum, however. While collecting information from various sources, they interact with crime scene investigators and law enforcement, review statements of witnesses, examine the scene, and follow leads that the scene provides. Analysis of this information sets the foundation for the autopsy procedure and the final opinions of the pathologist including the cause and manner of death.

A comprehensive medical–legal autopsy has three phases:

1. Premorgue analysis
2. Morgue analysis, or the autopsy per se
3. Postmorgue analysis

Premorgue analysis involves assessing the facts of the death scene (including environmental conditions), witness statements, and the known circumstances surrounding the death. Morgue analysis includes examination of the body and the associated trace evidence. Postmorgue analysis occurs over the ensuing weeks to months and includes analysis of microscopic slides of tissues sampled during the autopsy procedure. Toxicologic, microbiologic culture, chemical, and other laboratory results are also reviewed in this phase and special forensic tests such as DNA identification are performed. Often, additional investigative information is acquired during this time period.

The facts obtained from all three phases of analysis are assembled like the pieces of a puzzle to form a picture of the person just before death. The forensic pathologist views this picture of assembled facts to render an opinion, most importantly the cause and manner of death. The pertinent assembled facts and opinions are included in a written autopsy report. Occasionally, pieces of the puzzle are missing. In such cases, the forensic pathologist must use his or her experience and training to fill in the missing pieces and render an opinion.

Since an opinion is formed by the facts at hand, if the facts change, so can the opinion. For example, initially a gross autopsy in a case of sudden, unexpected death might show severe coronary disease. Days later, when the toxicology analysis is reported and high levels of multiple drugs are found, the cause of death must be changed to multiple drug toxicity. Thus, the opinion given by the pathologist is based only on the known facts. If the facts are insufficient, the pathologist may have no opinion, and the cause and manner of death are ruled to be undetermined.

WHAT IS A FORENSIC PATHOLOGIST?

In the U.S., a forensic pathologist is a physician (M.D. or D.O.) who is board certified in pathology and forensic pathology. Board-certified pathologists have studied 4 to 5 years after medical school and have passed a board certification exam. Most forensic pathologists are board certified by the American Board of Pathology. Today, all forensic pathologists must take an additional fellowship year to study forensic pathology before sitting for the exam. For those of you who aspire toward a career in forensic pathology, that is 4 years of medical school, 4 to 5 years of residency, and an additional year of fellowship before you can begin the practice of forensic pathology.

A pathologist is a physician who specializes in the study of the laboratory diagnosis of diseases. For example, if your aunt had a breast biopsy for cancer, that biopsy was read under the microscope and the diagnosis was made by a pathologist. If you had a cholesterol analysis, a pathologist supervised that test and might have interpreted the result for your family doctor.

Forensic pathologists work in several settings. Most work for county, state, or federal governments in medical examiner jurisdictions. Medical examiners are often, but not always, forensic pathologists who are either appointed or elected to their positions. In some jurisdictions, coroners are legally compelled to perform the death investigations. Coroners are usually elected and may or may not be forensic pathologists, pathologists, or even physicians. The background and training of coroners across the country varies greatly. Nonpathologist coroners commonly include physicians, nurses, and funeral directors; they may have extensive backgrounds and experience, or no training or qualifications at all. The quality of these elected coroners, as with all elected officials, can vary from highly competent and experienced to inexperienced. In most states, these nonpathologist coroners must employ a pathologist to perform the autopsy portion of the death investigation. These pathologists are generally contracted to do the autopsy. This book will not explore the merits or problems with the death investigation system in the U.S. See the references for sources on that topic. In any event, the majority of autopsies in the U.S. are performed by either a pathologist or a forensic pathologist.

Courtroom testimony is an important facet of forensic pathology. The pathologist who has performed an autopsy on a homicide victim will undoubtedly receive a subpoena to testify in court. In such cases, the forensic pathologist is an expert witness. An expert witness is much different than a fact witness. A fact witness, for example, testifies about what he or she observed and gives the date and time this observation. Fact witnesses are not allowed to give opinions. Expert witnesses are allowed to give opinions to the court and to explain their answers. The pathologist must be qualified as an expert by the court. As an expert witness, a pathologist should be honest, speak loudly, and answer the questions the attorneys ask. The pathologist should remember that the goal is to explain his or her opinion to the jury, not to take sides or try to help the prosecutor or the defense. The pathologist is, in a sense, the "witness for the truth," or a witness for the deceased.

2 Circumstantial and Medical History

IDENTIFY THE PROBLEM AND "CHIEF COMPLAINT"

Doctors are trained to focus on the major problems or chief complaints that patients present. A chief complaint is the main reason a patient visits a doctor, and the patient wants the complaint investigated and cured. Shortness of breath and chest pains are common chief complaints. To investigate a complaint, a physician takes the patient's medical history, performs a physical exam, orders tests, and arrives at a final diagnosis. At this point, the chief complaint can be treated and solved.

In medical–legal death investigations, forensic pathologists focus on specific problems in much the same way. For example, consider the case of a person found with a gunshot wound to the neck. The major problem or chief complaint raised by detectives is, "Does this case represent a homicide or suicide?" Initially, direct examination of the wound might suggest a contact gunshot wound (Figure 2.1), supporting the theory of suicide. Yet, before the cause and manner of death can be opined, the forensic pathologist must gather and integrate information from the scene, the detectives, and the other investigators (similar to a doctor taking a patient's medical history). In addition, a complete physical exam (autopsy) and lab testing (of toxicology and microscopic slides) must be performed. The "doctor–patient" relationship has begun.

In order to address the complaint (diagnose the cause and manner of death), the pathologist must start by obtaining detailed facts about the circumstances surrounding the death. This information is known as the circumstantial history. The pathologist will talk to detectives to find out what witnesses, such as friends, family, or bystanders, saw or knew about the deceased and how he or she died. Detectives might discover that the deceased was under treatment for depression and had attempted suicide previously. The scene might reveal other facts consistent with a self-inflicted wound, such as the gun remaining in the hands of the deceased. A suicide note might be present. Soot and injuries from the gun mechanism might be on the hands and fingers (Figure 2.2). The pathologist uses this background information, history, and the examination of the body to render an opinion (final diagnosis) about the cause and manner of death. In this case, the history, scene investigation, and examination of the body allow the forensic pathologist to render the diagnosis — Cause of Death: gunshot wound; Manner of Death: suicide.

IDENTIFICATION OF THE BODY

Proper identification is essential for many reasons. For one, the death certificate is a legal document required for burial and obtaining death benefits. Also, since a death certificate is required to prosecute an offender in murder and related crimes, the identification must withstand a legal challenge. Correct identification is essential in homicide investigations for another reason: incorrectly identifying homicide victims can bring undue anguish to the victims' loved ones.

The highest order of identification is scientific, including DNA and fingerprint analysis. Dental identification is highly reliable as well. These and other means of body identification are described in the following.

Direct Identification by Family Members

Direct identification of the body by family members is not always reliable. Uneasy relatives might not take a good look at the body while in the morgue and may sheepishly agree to the identification. Family members simply may not recognize the body, as people look different dead, compared with the way they appeared when alive. The investigator commonly uses a photograph of the deceased to make an identification and also notes if the individual was found in familiar surroundings, such as his or her house or car. Although viewing the face in the morgue is a common method of identification, pathologists find it much more effective to have a friend or family member view a photograph or video of the deceased's body. People tend to be more comfortable looking at a photograph in an office than at a body in the morgue. They are also less likely to take a cursory glance of the face and make an erroneous identification.

Personal Features

Personal features serve to back up the identification. The deceased might have deformities, scars, tattoos, or piercings. Unusual dental appliances can be useful as well (Figure 2.3). Hair length, color, and style; eye color; height; weight; clothing; and personal effects are commonly used to make an identification. Personal effects found in the pockets, for example, can help confirm an identification (Figure 2.4).

Objects in the Body

Many people have metallic or other objects in their bodies that can be seen on radiographs. If comparison films are available, these objects can be useful in establishing identification. The more unique an object is, the more it facilitates a convincing identification. For example, bodies commonly contain a few staples around the appendix; but chest wires from open heart surgery are rarer and can establish identity more effectively, especially if the number of wires and their configuration match an individual's medical records (Figure 2.5). Large orthopedic rods in the back, particularly if the serial numbers on the rods are confirmed in the patient's medical records, can also be used to make a reasonable identification (Figure 2.6).

Higher-Order Identification

Higher-order identification is often needed when the deceased's appearance is altered in some way, such as from fire, decomposition, a mass-transit accident, and the like.

Fingerprints

Fingerprints are commonly used for identification, but finger ridges might be decomposed or burned away in the scenarios mentioned. Many of us have fingerprints on file somewhere; soldiers, veterans, law enforcement officials, gun permit holders, and those who have been arrested commonly have fingerprints on file. The Automated Federal Identification System is a nationwide computerized network that recently has made fingerprint identification easier and faster. The problem, of course, is that the unidentified individual's prints must be in the system.

It is essential to obtain fingerprints in homicides for several reasons. First, the identification must stand up to a legal challenge (Figure 2.7A, Figure 2.7B). Also, especially if the deceased's prints are not on file, the known prints of the deceased must be compared to those found at the scene. The scene prints could be from the victim or from the perpetrator. Failure to take the victim's prints leaves at least two unknowns: the victim and at least one perpetrator.

Dental Identification

Dental identification is the next step of identification if ridged skin on the fingers is gone or if the person does not have prints on file. The investigator must search for any dental records of the deceased. This is sometimes difficult, especially if the deceased had not seen a dentist in a while (or ever). Also, teeth might have fallen out over time or been extracted. Postmortem x-rays (Figure 2.8) or findings from direct examination of the teeth are compared with dental films (Figure 2.9) or other records (Figure 2.10) of the deceased created during his or her lifetime. These comparisons are made by a forensic odontologist, a dentist specializing in making identifications for medical–legal purposes.

Deoxyribonucleic Acid

Deoxyribonucleic acid (DNA) is a unique molecular fingerprint that can identify an individual with a certainty estimated at one in the billions. DNA is a powerful tool if used correctly and proper procedure is followed. The sample must be collected so that there is no question of contamination. In decomposed bodies, bone marrow from teeth, ribs, or vertebrae often, but not always, yields useable DNA. There must be other DNA to compare it with, either from the deceased, a sibling, a child, or another relative. DNA or fingerprints from the deceased can be obtained from personal items, such as a hairbrush.

INVESTIGATIVE QUESTIONS

The investigation of death begins a process of answering key pertinent questions. These are questions asked by the state, courts, law enforcement, doctors, families, society, and many others. Questions not answered in the initial investigation might be answered by the autopsy. The autopsy, or evidence collected at the autopsy, usually spurs further investigation. Some questions are easily answered, some are difficult to answer, and at times some go unanswered.

Basic Demographic Questions

The following demographic information is collected:

- Full name
- Date of birth
- Social security number
- Sex
- Date of birth
- Address

Question of Occupation

It is important to know the occupation of the deceased before death, particularly in accidental deaths; for example, if an apparently electrocuted man was a certified electrician or a weekend repairman (Figure 2.11).

Question of Medical History

Knowing the medical history of the deceased is essential not only in natural deaths, but in all manners of death. Apparent accidents could be determined to be natural if disease was the cause of death, for example. Family members, friends, caretakers, and doctors are often most helpful in providing medical information. Examining medications at the residence is helpful, particularly when no other information is available. Since most deaths are natural, coroners' and medical examiners' offices spend a lot of time gathering medical information. Medical records provide a wealth of information in many death investigations (Figure 2.12).

Question of Medications

Medications are often the key to finding the cause of death. Many diseases can be lethal when the patient stops taking medication. Epilepsy, diabetes mellitus, and unstable angina are common conditions that can become quickly fatal if one does not take medication properly. Conversely, medication overdoses (accidental or intentional) are also common causes of death. At the beginning of the investigation it is helpful to obtain all medication vials, check the dates prescriptions were filled, and then determine if the number of pills missing matches the prescription instructions (Figure 2.13).

Question of Mental Health History

Psychiatric history should be actively sought. Previous suicide attempts, a history of severe mental illness, and medications might explain suicidal or bizarre behavior. For example, schizophrenics who do not take their antipsychotic medications can become overtly psychotic and exhibit dangerous, even fatal behavior.

Question of Illicit Drug Use

Drug use and drug-seeking behavior place individuals at high risk for violent death. A history of abuse of a specific drug helps direct autopsy toxicology. Cocaine, for example, has a short half-life in the blood, but traces can be found in bile for a longer time. A special bile cocaine test can be ordered if cocaine use is suspected.

Question of Ethanol Use

As the reader probably knows, a large proportion of cases that fall under the purview of the coroner or medical examiner involve a history of ethanol use. Acute alcohol toxicity is death from drinking excessive alcohol in one sitting (the blood alcohol concentration is greater than 0.40% or as low as 0.25 to 0.30% if the individual survived as comatose for some period; see Di Maio and Di Maio, 1989). Chronic alcoholism causes cirrhosis of the liver, and death often results from bleeding esophageal varices or other medical complications. In chronic alcoholics, a halt in the intake of alcohol can cause delirium tremens, seizure, and death. Alcohol intoxication decreases judgment, reaction time, and other mentation; it also diminishes motor skills. These effects of alcohol are often a factor in all types of deaths — homicide, suicide, accident, or natural.

Question of History with Law Enforcement or Incarceration

Law enforcement officials will usually provide this history to the pathologist, if the information is available. Past incarceration for drug charges, for example, can be helpful. Previous incarceration means that fingerprints and photographs are available, which are useful in confirming the identification. Outstanding arrest warrants might help explain a suicide.

Other Investigative Questions

Through the investigation and the subsequent autopsy, the goal is always to answer the numerous other questions that arise, including the following:

- What was the date and time of death?
- What was the location of death?
- When and where was the deceased last seen alive?
- When and where was the deceased injured?
- What was the location and position of the body at death?
- How was the deceased injured and killed?
- What killed the deceased?
- Who killed the deceased?

At times, the questions are only partially answered.

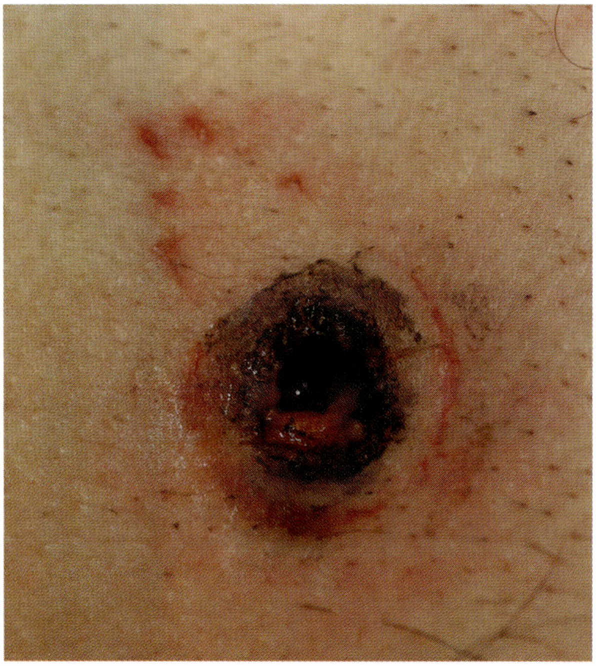

FIGURE 2.1 Hard contact entrance gunshot wound. The patterned abrasion at 10 o'clock and the red abrasion ring around the wound were produced by the gun barrel and sight contacting the skin when the gun was fired. Around the wound is heavy soot, the black material. The finding of a hard contact wound on the chest of this individual supports the theory of suicide.

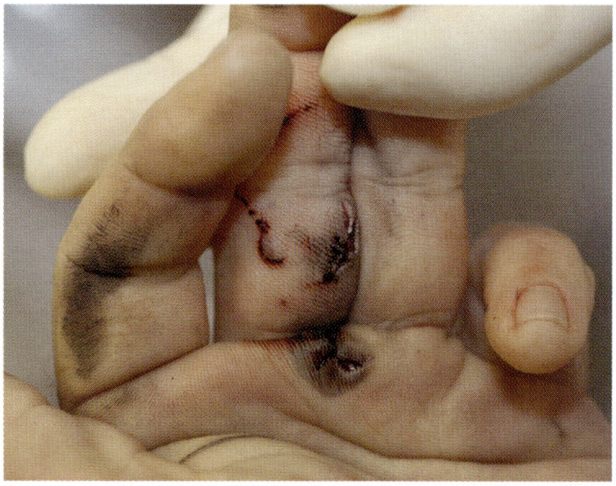

FIGURE 2.2 Gun-induced laceration and soot deposition on the hand. The mechanism of the pistol produced a laceration of the hand. Soot was also deposited on the hand and fingers. These findings indicate that the gun was in the hand of the victim and supports the theory of suicide.

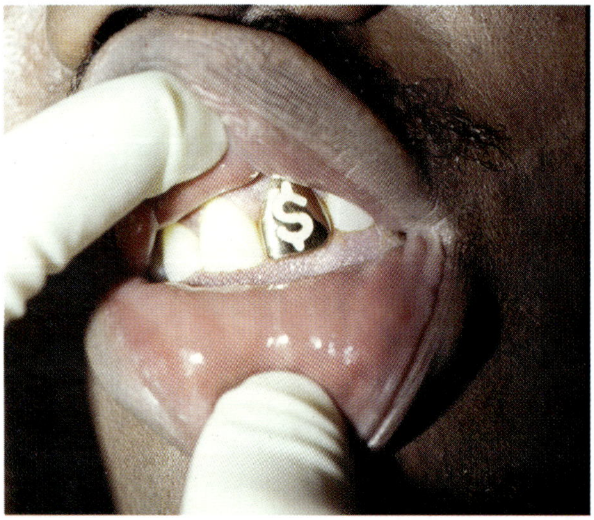

FIGURE 2.3 Dental cap. Unique dental appliances are often useful in helping confirm the victim's identity.

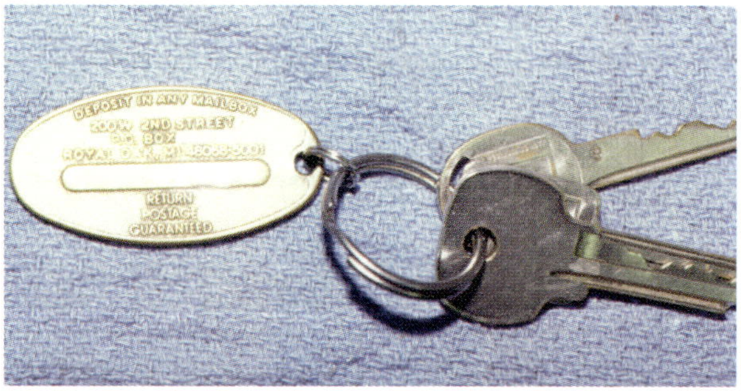

FIGURE 2.4 Keys found in victim's pocket. Personal effects that are unique can help confirm identity. These keys were marked with a unique serial number, registered to the individual (numbers were sanitized).

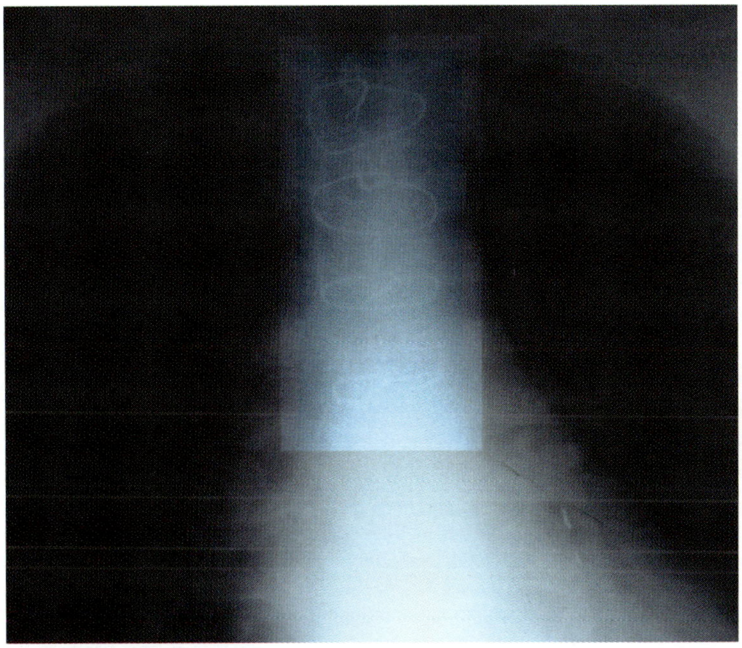

FIGURE 2.5 Radiograph of surgical sternal wires. Surgical wires and devices, when somewhat unique, can aid in identification when old comparison films are available.

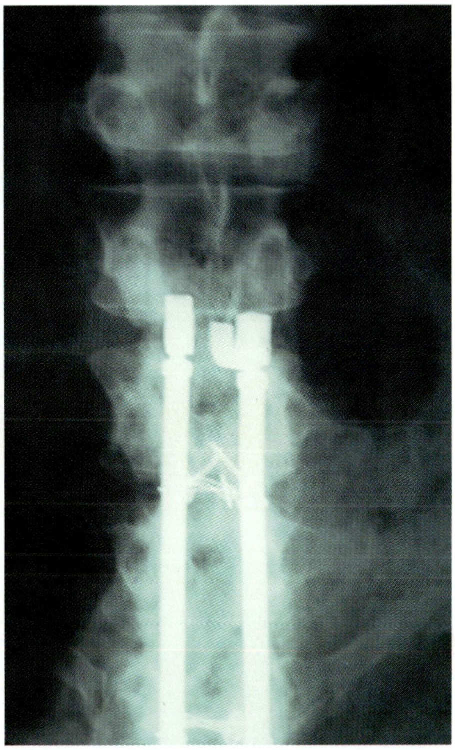

FIGURE 2.6 Radiograph of spinal rods. Unique surgical appliances are useful in making an identification. Radiographs of the body can be made for comparison. Also, serial numbers on the devices can be compared with previous medical records.

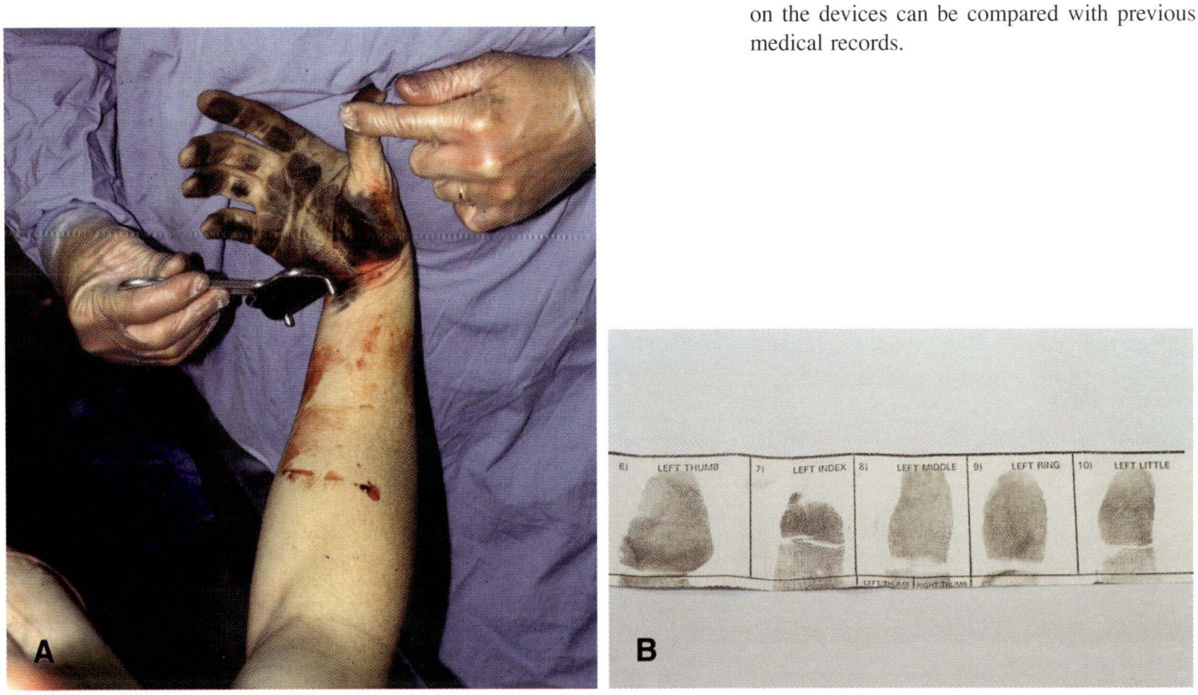

FIGURE 2.7 (A), (B) Postmortem fingerprints. It is essential that experienced technicians obtain postmortem fingerprints in all homicides or potential homicides.

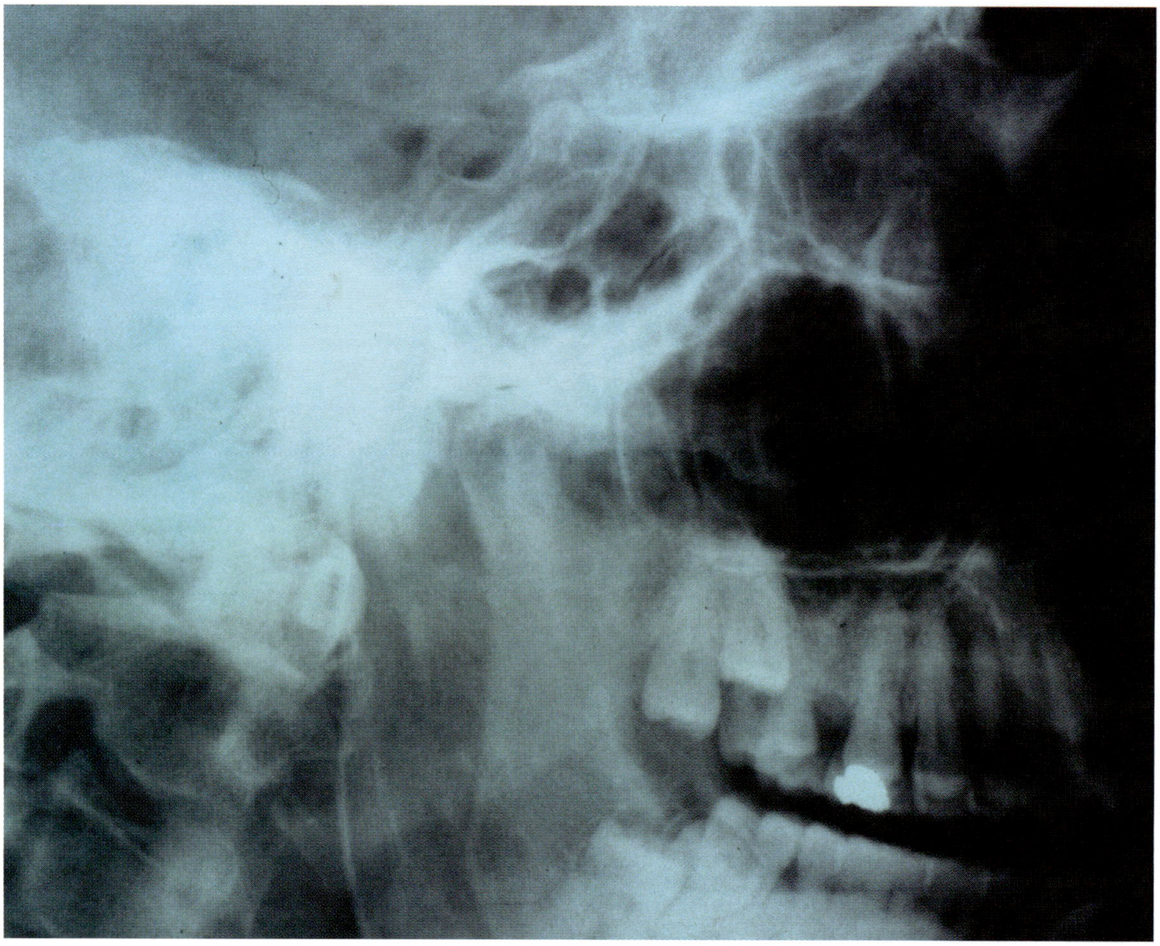

FIGURE 2.8 Skull radiograph with dental amalgam. A lateral skull film, as shown, or multi-angle "panorex" films can be compared to premortem films. Such a comparison and identification are the exclusive purview of the forensic odontologist.

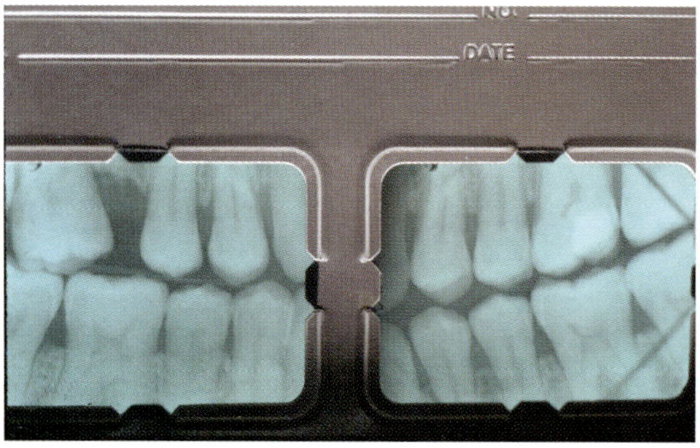

FIGURE 2.9 Premortem dental radiographs. Premortem radiographs obtained from the dentist of the purported victim are compared with autopsy dental radiographs.

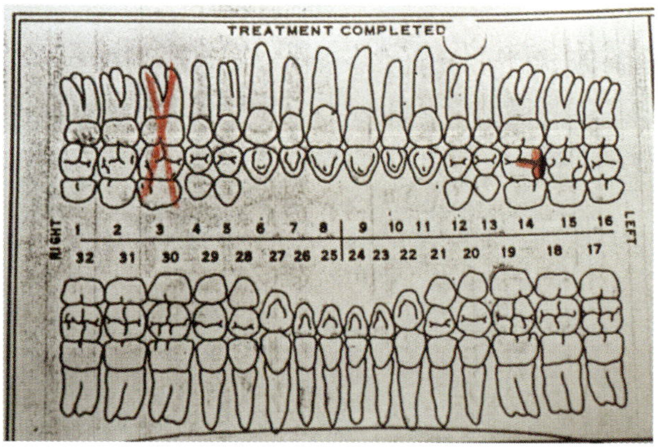

FIGURE 2.10 Premortem dental charts. Premortem dental charts can be compared with the teeth at autopsy to make an identification.

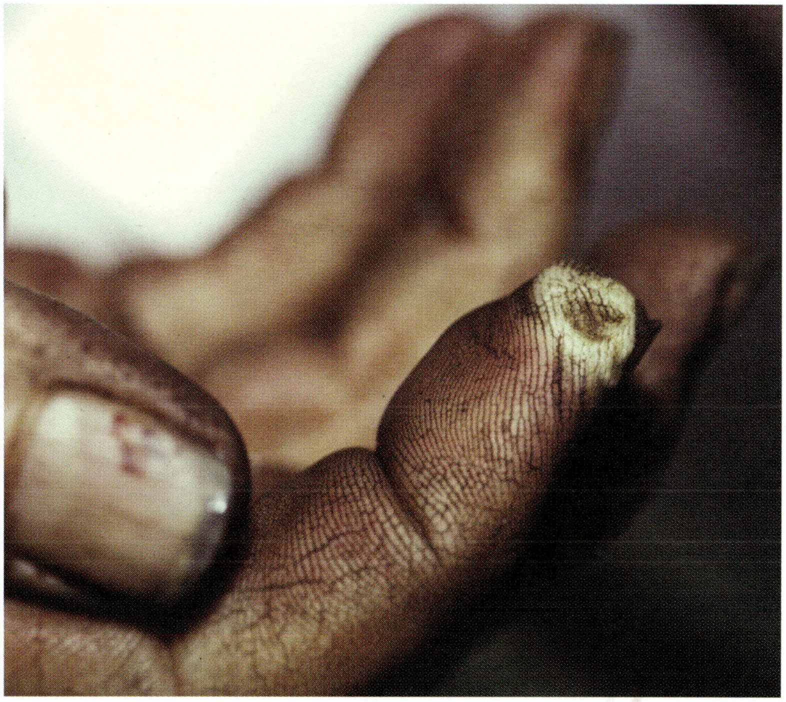

FIGURE 2.11 Electrical injury, fingertip. The point of entry or exit of electrical current traveling through the body is often burned. A history of an electrician working on electrical equipment can prompt a search for such an injury. The sole of the foot is another common site of electrical injury.

FIGURE 2.12 Medical records. The time spent studying medical records is not wasted. One learns a great deal about the deceased and his or her medical problems. Medications, allergies, previous surgery, social history, and other "pearls" are there to direct the investigator or the pathologist in finding the cause of death.

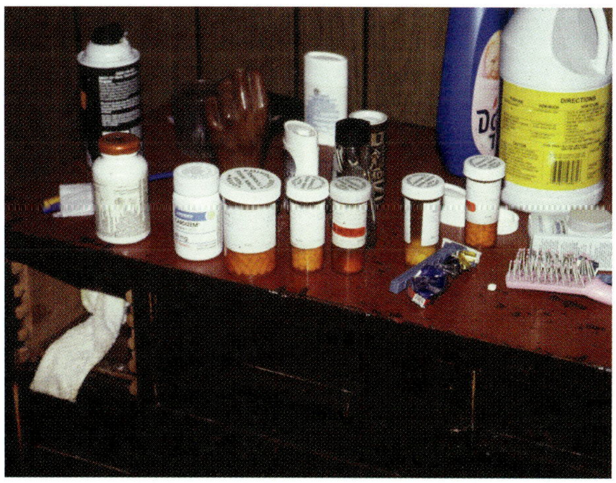

FIGURE 2.13 Medications at a death scene. The prescription medications at a death scene can tell a story of an individual's medical history. Diltiazem and medications to lower high blood pressure indicate hypertension and ischemic heart disease. Theophylline and other related respiratory medications suggest chronic obstructive lung (pulmonary) disease (COLD or COPD); a recently filled broad-spectrum antibiotic indicates a recent infection.

3 External Examination: The Preliminary Examination

SUITING UP: UNIVERSAL PRECAUTIONS

Protection of the pathologist, autopsy assistants, investigators, and medical personnel at the autopsy is not just a good idea — it is required by Occupational Safety and Health Administration (OSHA) regulations. The required methods of protection are called universal precautions. To perform an autopsy, the pathologist and the assistant wear hats, masks, gowns, shoe covers, mesh gloves, and latex gloves (Figure 3.1). Some facilities use vacuum-assisted saws to gather bone dust from skull and rib sawing. All cases are treated as potentially infectious from bloodborne pathogens. Although pathologists handle those cases known to be infectious with care, they must not be casual about the routine case that can harbor a latent hepatitis virus or human immunodeficiency virus (HIV), for example. All cases need to be treated as potentially infectious.

OPENING THE BODY BAG

Once everyone is properly suited up for protection from bloodborne pathogens, the body bag may be opened. Identification tags are placed on the body and the bag at the scene. Tags placed on the outsides of bags can be lost, so tagging the body directly is essential. The body is placed in a clean plastic body bag (Figure 3.2). Some pathologists recommend that the body be wrapped in a clean white sheet, since trace evidence can be lost in the large body bag. This sheet is carefully examined at the autopsy.

The hands of the deceased are also bagged (preferably with paper bags) at the scene in suspicious deaths. Trace evidence has a higher chance of being on the hands, presumably because the victim grabs or contacts the perpetrator in some way that transfers trace evidence, such as hair, skin, or grass, to the victim's hands (Figure 3.3). In practice, successful retrieval of useful trace evidence from the bagged hands is not very common. However, the one case of many that yields a DNA match or fiber match makes bagging the hands in every case worthwhile. Also, bagging the hands is usually expected by juries and courts. If the hands are not bagged, defense attorneys can use this omission to cast doubt on the thoroughness of the entire death investigation.

CLOTHING AND VALUABLES

The clothing of the deceased is also evidence and may contain additional trace evidence. To protect all evidence from contamination or loss, and for practical reasons, the clothing is not removed in the uncontrolled environment of the scene. An exception to this rule is made in rare cases when moisture could alter a substance on the clothing; for example, condensation may form in the body bag when the body is placed in a cooler.

The clothing can be quite helpful in a death investigation, since it is intimately associated with the body. For example, the range of fire in a gunshot wound is often determined from a shirt the victim was wearing when shot. Unburned particles from the weapon will tattoo the bare skin. If clothing intervenes between the weapon and the skin, the majority of the unburned particles form a pattern on the clothing, with very few particles going through the clothing to the skin (Figure 3.4). This clothing can be analyzed by a forensic scientist, who can estimate the range of fire of the weapon and the width and configuration of the pattern correlated to the distance of the shirt from the weapon. With rare exception, clothing should not be altered, removed, or cut at the scene, and it should not be cut at all in a homicide case. Clothing can contain unusual evidence (Figure 3.5), and therefore should be carefully removed in a controlled environment.

To save the life of an individual, clothing is often cut, altered, or removed at the scene of a violent death by first responders, such as paramedics. Removing the clothing is part of the routine examination of the patient, especially a victim of trauma. If the body is removed from the scene and taken to the hospital, the body is often fully undressed, possibly irreversibly altering, losing, or contaminating any trace evidence. Hospital personnel must save the clothing so that the death investigation agency can retrieve it. Even if cut, removed clothing can be valuable in determining gunshot distance, for example. First responders to the medical emergency must be careful not to destroy evidence when suspicion of violent death or injury exists. Obvious bullet holes or other significant evidence on clothing should not be cut or altered if possible. Figure 3.6 shows a cut in the middle of a garment made by first responders who appropriately avoided the gunshot wounds.

BODY STORAGE

The body must be stored in a secure cooler, preferably under lock and key (Figure 3.7). Only a limited number of individuals should have the key. A complete log sheet of the body arrival time and all encounters with the body should be maintained indefinitely. This log should include all valuables found on or with the body. Any personal item that is not considered to be evidence should be logged, described, and retained for the family. Items that appear to have no value to the investigator might have value to the family, so care of these items is recommended. Once lost, cheap trinkets can become "expensive jewelry" (Figure 3.8). Valuables can also become evidence. The watch in Figure 3.9 was broken by a golf club used to attack the victim. It was thought to have been broken at the time of the assault, a rare occurrence that makes the watch a valuable piece of evidence.

TRACE EVIDENCE

For the purpose of the autopsy, trace evidence is any visible or invisible substance, material, or object that is present on, in, or around the body and has potential value as evidence. Obvious trace evidence that might be lost in transport can be collected at the scene. Common objects collected at the scene include hair, small fibers, or paint flakes that could easily be lost. Since scene lighting is often poor and the setting inappropriate, trace evidence is best taken at the autopsy suite (Figure 3.10). One method of preparing the body for transport is to drape a clean sheet over the body and then place it in a clean body bag.

FOUR SIGNS OF DEATH

Rigor Mortis

Rigor mortis is the temporary stiffening of muscles after death. The muscle proteins actin and myosin lock together, making the muscles stiff. This process is an irreversible chemical reaction. Immediately after death, the muscles become limp or flaccid. Generally within 30 minutes to 1 hour, the muscles begin to stiffen. Rigor mortis starts in all muscles at the same time. However, because muscle groups vary widely in size and mass, rigor mortis is noticed in the smaller muscles first, namely the jaw and the fingers. Within 3 hours, rigor mortis is noticed in nearly all muscles. Full rigor mortis, the peak stiffness of all muscles, can take up to 10 to 12 hours to develop in an average-sized adult at a temperature of about 70°F (Figure 3.11). Rigor continues for 24 to 36 hours until decomposition starts to loosen the muscles.

Environmental conditions greatly influence the rate of rigor mortis onset. Warm temperatures accelerate rigor, while coldness retards it. Decedents with high body temperature or fever at death show accelerated rigor. In fact, vigorous exercise, emotional rage, and some drug toxicities such as with cocaine abuse are associated with fast or nearly instant rigor mortis.

Once the muscle is stiffened, it will remain so until the rigor mortis is broken by manipulation of the muscle or until decomposition occurs. Breaking the rigor is most commonly demonstrated by straightening the arm or leg of the body.

Observing rigor mortis can be useful if a body has been moved after death. For example, a decedent who was killed in a sitting position, left in that position for 3 hours, and then moved will retain the stiffened sitting position. Also, rigor mortis can be used along with the other signs of death to estimate the time of death.

Algor Mortis

Algor mortis is the cooling of body temperature after death. During life, our metabolism holds the core body temperature constant at about 98.6°F. Death and the loss of metabolism allow the body to eventually assume the temperature of the environment. Therefore, if the outside temperature is 110°F, the body temperature will increase. In forensic pathology, it is generally accepted that at the standard temperature of 70°F between about 2 and 12 hours after death, the body cools at a rate of 1.5 degrees per hour. After about 12 hours, the body temperature equals that of room temperature. It is more difficult to predict the time of death at the scene, however, because these ideal conditions are not always present.

Core temperature can be taken rectally or by inserting a probe-type thermometer into the liver. These practices require full-time death investigators, not often available in small jurisdictions. In many jurisdictions, an experienced investigator can evaluate the body for warmth to the touch, a method often more practical at a busy crime scene (because the body usually is dressed and the body wall is not punctured to reach the liver). Conditions in the field are rarely those of standard temperature and humidity. Factors such as air temperature, clothing, body mass, and premortem hyperthermia or hypothermia can alter the rate of cooling. If the environment is warmer than the premortem body temperature, the core temperature can increase.

Livor Mortis

Livor mortis is the gravity-dependent settling of blood into the blood vessels and soft tissues after death. When blood is no longer pumped by the force of the heart, it follows the force of gravity and pools in the dependent areas of the body. Vascular tone is lost after death as well, causing the blood to leach out of the small vascular channels and into the surrounding tissues. Since most decedents are placed in a supine position (on their backs), the livor mortis settles in the posterior surface of the body (Figure 3.12). Areas that touch the autopsy table show a clearing of the livor. Generally, livor mortis first becomes visible between 20 and 30 minutes after death; it can shift or be cleared for about 8 to 12 hours. These times can vary widely. Since livor is observed visually as blood in the tissues, anemic individuals or those who have died from severe hemorrhage may have little or no livor. In dark-skinned individuals, livor mortis can be difficult to see. In such cases, internal organs such as the lungs can be used to assess livor.

Livor mortis that is not "fixed" can be cleared with manual pressure (Figure 3.13A, Figure 3.13B). Any object resting against the downward portion of the body can form a pattern in the livor mortis (Figure 3.14). If a body is moved before the livor is fixed, the livor can shift, forming a second pattern. Two livor patterns on a body can be useful in predicting the movement of a body after livor mortis has formed (Figure 3.15A, Figure 3.15B).

"Fixed" livor mortis cannot be cleared with manual pressure. Between about 10 and 24 hours after death, the blood stains the tissues and is increasingly difficult to clear. Livor can shift after 10 hours, but this shifting is more difficult to see. A body found in water often has no livor mortis pattern since the body was in a zero-gravity situation and was moving and tumbling frequently.

Decomposition

Decomposition is the late advancement of postmortem tissue breakdown. Once released by dying cells, enzymes begin the autolysis process, causing mostly a liquefaction of the tissues. Bacteria, mostly from a nonsterile area of the body like the gastrointestinal tract, multiply rapidly, producing gas and further consuming the devitalized tissue.

Early in decomposition, the skin becomes a discolored purplish-green and might blister and "slip" (Figure 3.16). Blood in the vessels stains the soft tissues (Figure 3.17), creating what is referred to as "venous marbling." The hair begins to slip as well. Discolored tissues begin to swell due to the formation of gas produced by bacteria in the tissue. The odor from this gas is putrid and unmistakable. The discolored tissues can be mistaken for injuries by the untrained eye (Figure 3.18). This "gas bloating" can be quite remarkable when a body found in water is removed (Figure 3.19).

Decomposition is very dependent on environmental conditions. Bodies that are frozen can be preserved for a long time. Because cold temperatures preserve tissues, bodies are stored in the morgue cooler at about 38 to 42°F, and decomposition can be slowed for days to weeks. Warm temperatures hasten decomposition, as does high humidity. Hot, dry conditions cause mummification, or the drying out of tissues (Figure 3.20).

Insects, carnivores, and other invaders can speed up the decomposition process. Forensic entomology is the study of insects as they relate to death investigation. For example, fly larvae can be obtained at the death scene, identified, and reared in incubators. The postmortem interval (time of death) can be estimated based on the fixed-time growth cycles of the fly larvae (Figure 3.21).

FOCUS ON WHAT IS NOT OBVIOUS

The external examination of the deceased is a focused head-to-toe examination of the body. This exam is similar to a physical exam one might get from a physician. All parts of the body are examined, from the hair on top of the head to the toenails. The pathologist spends as much time on the external exam as on the internal exam and is always looking for trace evidence on the skin and clothing and in wounds or orifices of the body. The logical tendency would be to focus first on the obvious gunshot wound or gaping laceration, but the pathologist focuses on the other areas of the body first and then on the obvious injury. Most pathologists use a systematic examination process to make a detailed survey of all systems, being careful not to overlook any area of the body (Figure 3.22).

When examining an organ, a tissue, or a region of the body, the pathologist looks for:

- Traumatic injuries, both old and new
- Natural disease processes, such as tumors or atherosclerosis
- Congenital defects or deformities
- Toxicologic, thermal (burns), and chemical injuries
- Trace evidence
- Infectious disease processes
- Anything abnormal, unusual, or unexpected

DOCUMENTING TRAUMATIC INJURIES: DIAGRAMS AND DESCRIPTIONS

Documenting injuries is one of the principal goals of the forensic autopsy. The body is assessed from head to toe. The injury is examined from the outside of the body to the inside and is photographed, measured, diagrammed, and described. The autopsy records must accurately depict an injury, both in a written, descriptive manner and in visual form. Diagrams and sketches are generally drawn when notes are taken; however, since most pathologists are not artists, photography is the professional standard in documenting significant injuries (Figure 3.23). It is essential that the significant injuries are well documented, both by descriptions in the report and by photography. Because another expert will likely review the pathologist's documentations in court, the forensic pathologist has an ethical duty to accurately document his or her observations. Failure to document can also cause potential difficulties in court, since defendants are legally allowed to examine the evidence against them.

RADIOLOGY AND IMAGING

In the autopsy suite, radiographs are primarily used in routine cases to:

- Evaluate gunshot wounds to locate and enumerate bullets, bullet fragments, and other metallic objects (Figure 3.24, Figure 3.25).
- Examine stab wounds or puncture wounds. Occasionally a portion of a knife, scissor, or other sharp metallic object will break off when bone is struck (Figure 3.26, Figure 3.27).
- Identify the deceased. Jaw radiographs are compared with dental records of the purported victim. Unique metallic implants, such as rods in the back, can aid identification (Figure 3.28).
- Investigate possible child or elder abuse by looking for subtle or healed fractures (Figure 3.29).
- Find evidence in unusual deaths, such as those from explosions or plane crashes (Figure 3.30).
- Examine severely charred or decomposed remains for hidden objects like bullets and clues to identification (Figure 3.31, Figure 3.32).
- Document characteristic fractures, such as a "nightstick fracture" of the forearm, a classic blunt force injury sustained as the victim holds up his or her arm to block a nightstick attack (Figure 3.33, Figure 3.34, Figure 3.35).

The autopsy is much more sensitive than the radiograph in exposing fractures of certain areas, such as the skull, ribs, or hyoid bone, because the bone is directly visualized during autopsy. When viewed during autopsy, hemorrhage resulting from a fracture enhances the visibility of the fracture (Figure 3.35). The radiograph is simply a tool to supplement the autopsy. Radiographs and other methods of imaging have many more uses in forensic pathology; see the references for further information.

PHOTOGRAPHY AND VIDEO AS DOCUMENTATION TOOLS

As mentioned, in addition to describing findings in a detailed written report, the pathologist must visually document pertinent injuries in cases of medical–legal significance. Over the last several decades, 35-mm photography of key injuries like gunshot wounds has been the gold standard documentation tool. Today, digital photography is accepted by many courts. Generally, to be accepted by the courts, the photographs must be true and accurate representations of what was seen during the autopsy examination.

In homicide cases, pictures are taken of nearly every step of the autopsy, from opening the bag to documenting the last injury. Injuries are photographed both before and after the wounds are cleaned. It is crucial to clean the wounds to remove blood or debris. Only then can the true configurations of the wounds be revealed (Figure 3.36, Figure 3.37). Also, the wounds must be clearly demonstrated for another pathologist-expert to review. A jury will probably view the photographs, and a key job of the pathologist is to explain injuries to the jury. Pictures that display the injuries poorly do not aid in this communication. Bloody, unclear, or unnecessarily grotesque photographs will probably not be admitted into evidence by the court.

Although commonly used in crime scene investigations, videotapes of the autopsy have not been used widely in the past, mainly because of the poor resolution of VHS and other common videotaping systems. High-resolution digital video shows much better detail. Still pictures of good quality can be produced from the footage, and the quality will continue to improve as high-definition digital video becomes widely available. Three CCD (charge-coupled device) high-quality video is a useful documentation tool in complex cases with many injuries (Figure 3.38). The cameras are light, inexpensive, and do not require special lighting. Many of the images in this book are three CCD video still photographs (e.g., Figure 3.1). If video of a forensic autopsy is taken, shots of evidence and injuries should be of the same type as those taken with a 35-mm camera, but should also include multiple perspectives. Shots from many different angles are very useful to the viewer when there are many or complex injuries. Videotape of the entire autopsy, however, is not a useful tool, in the author's experience.

SCARS, TATTOOS, AND OTHER UNIQUE MARKS

The skin bears many marks, some unique and some not. These marks can tell us a great deal about an individual. A scar in the middle of the chest (Figure 3.39) can indicate a patient with severe coronary artery disease that required cardiac bypass grafting. A scar in the midline abdomen may indicate previous exploratory surgery (Figure 3.40A and Figure 3.40B). Specific finger, leg, arm, or other deformities can help identify an individual (Figure 3.41). Unique tattoos or those in a certain location or combination can also be helpful in identification (Figure 3.42).

ARTIFACTS OF MEDICAL INTERVENTION

Medical devices can give the pathologist an idea about resuscitative or interventional procedures that have been performed on the deceased. Although these devices can move or become dislodged during transport of the body, they should be left in place by the nursing staff and others who are responsible for preparing the body. Incisions made for chest tubes, for example, could be misinterpreted as stab wounds once the tubes are removed (Figure 3.43). Needle puncture sites from intravenous (IV) therapy can be difficult to differentiate from IV drug abuse sites or fresh "tracks" (Figure 3.44). Therefore, the pathologist must review the medical record and compare it with what is found on the body.

Sometimes medical devices reveal information about the impacts of resuscitation attempts that is not written in medical records. These medical devices and their impacts on a body may affect the findings of an autopsy. For example, central intravascular lines can be responsible for vascular tears and pneumothorax; endotracheal tubes can be placed in the esophagus, causing tears; feeding tubes can become dislodged, causing serious or fatal injury (Figure 3.45).

The role of the pathologist is to document the location of a medical device. If the placement or performance of the device had negatively affected the deceased while he or she was a patient, the pathologist should report this fact to the trauma or nursing service in the interest of improving future quality of patient care.

Common medical therapeutic or diagnostic devices and related problems can include:

- IV lines — placement can cause an artifact of hemorrhage
- Electrocardiogram (ECG) pads — can cover wounds
- Cricothyroidotomy — done to produce an emergency airway; causes problems when performed improperly (Figure 3.46)
- Surgery — done emergently to save the life, but bullet and stab wounds might be altered
- Bandages — might cover key wounds (Figure 3.47)
- Sutures — must be removed to show wound configurations (Figure 3.48A, Figure 3.48B)
- Arterial and large venous lines — because of their size, more likely to cause complications like hemorrhage than small venous lines
- Defibrillators — can cause burns on the chest and be mistaken for premortem burns

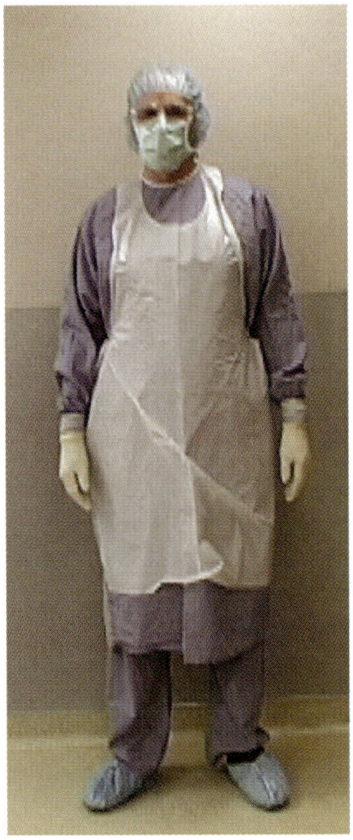

FIGURE 3.1 Universal precautions. Proper protection of the pathologist and all assistants from infectious diseases is essential. Eye protection, mouth and nose protection, double and cut-resistant gloves, a waterproof barrier, and a long-sleeve gown keep potential infectious agents away from the prosectors (those who cut) of the autopsy.

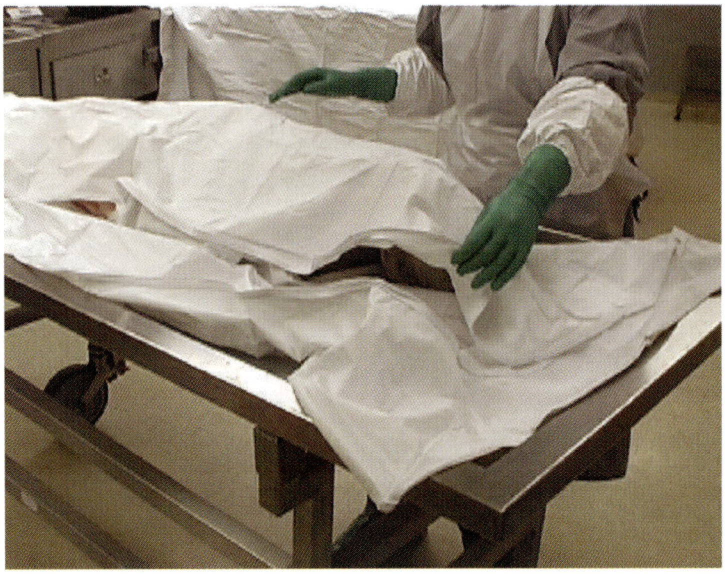

FIGURE 3.2 Opening the body bag. The body is placed in a clean, white body bag. Some wrap the body in a clean white sheet to help contain potential trace evidence.

FIGURE 3.3 Trace evidence on bagged hands. The hands are bagged in all homicides. This allows more careful examination of trace evidence at the autopsy. This individual has a "death grip" on some trace evidence.

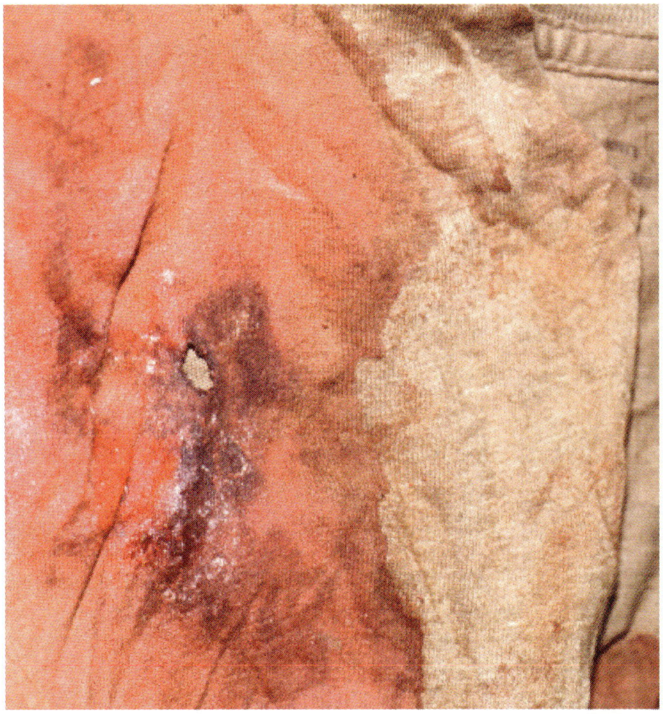

FIGURE 3.4 Gunshot hole in a shirt. The presence of an intervening object, such as clothing, between the gun barrel and skin can alter the soot pattern on the skin. Dark soot can be seen on and around the gunshot hole. Although it is not the duty of the forensic pathologist to issue a report on examination of clothing, the clothing should be surveyed to better understand the wound on the body.

FIGURE 3.5 Bullet in a sweater. Some articles of clothing can trap bullets. For this reason, the clothing should be x-rayed and carefully searched, so as not to lose a bullet or other trace evidence.

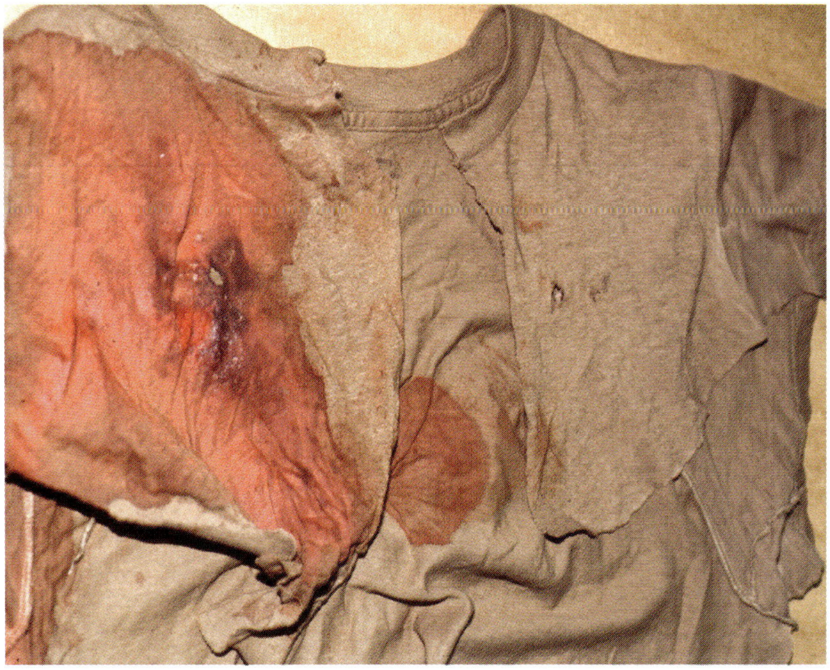

FIGURE 3.6 Cut shirt with gunshot holes. Ideally, clothing should not be cut in a homicide or potential homicide. If the clothing must be cut to aid in rapid resuscitation, cuts should be made to avoid the gunshot holes in the shirt, as shown in this figure.

FIGURE 3.7 Lockable cooler. Bodies should be kept in a lockable cooler, and a registry of all valuables should be maintained. All activity in and out of the cooler should be logged. Cooler temperature is kept between about 38 and 42˚F.

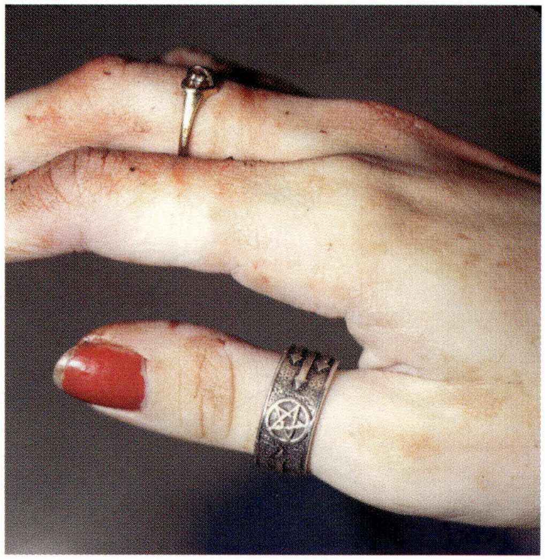

FIGURE 3.8 Rings on the fingers. All valuables and personal effects, no matter how insignificant, must be catalogued and returned to the family.

FIGURE 3.9 Broken watch. Valuables can become evidence, such as this watch that was broken during an assault. The victim (and the watch) received many blunt force injuries, a few of which were from a golf club.

FIGURE 3.10 Trace evidence on the buttocks. In sexual assaults, trace evidence might be as fine as a single hair, as seen on the buttock here. This small, fine evidence can be lost during transfer of the body and is one exception to not taking evidence from the body at the scene. Pubic hair from the body can be analyzed with the suspect's, as was done in this case, producing an identification match.

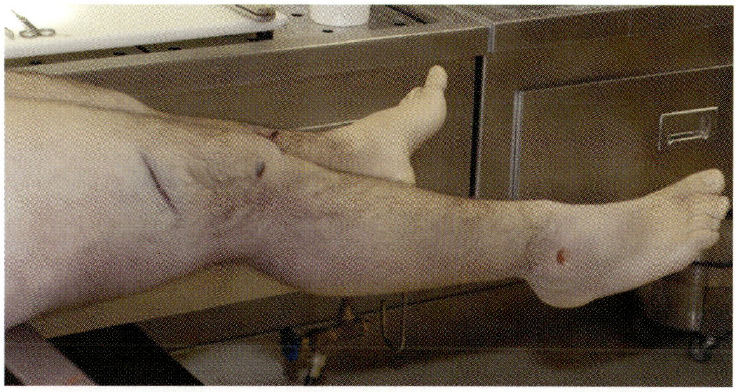

FIGURE 3.11 Rigor mortis. Rigor mortis is the temporary stiffening of muscles after death. The stiffening is often quite strong. The legs shown here are stiff enough to support their own weight when hanging completely off the table.

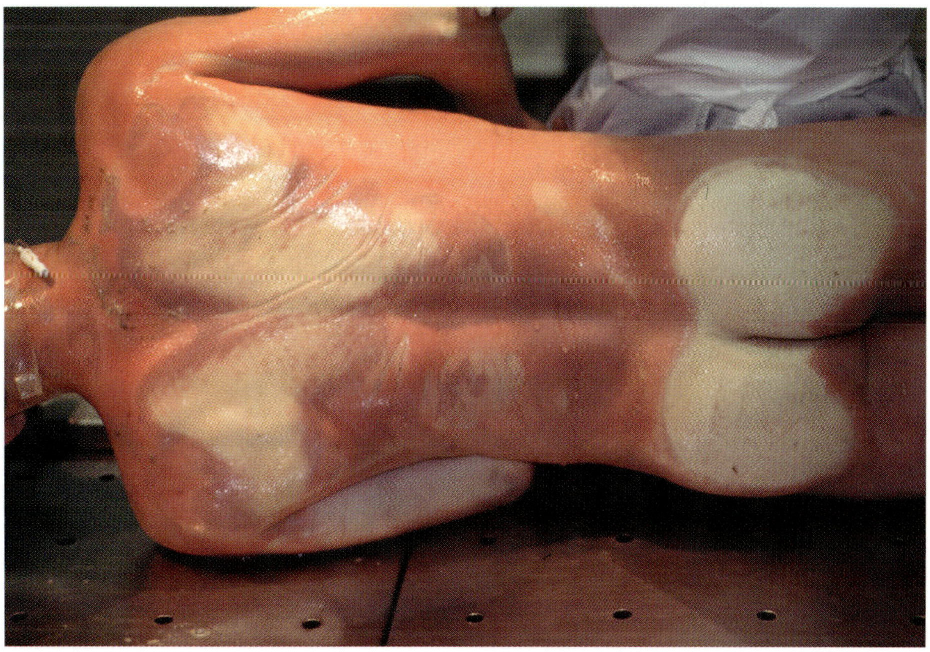

FIGURE 3.12 Livor mortis. The distribution of livor mortis is a function of gravity. The purplish-red areas depict livor mortis. The pale areas are "cleared" where the body contacted the table.

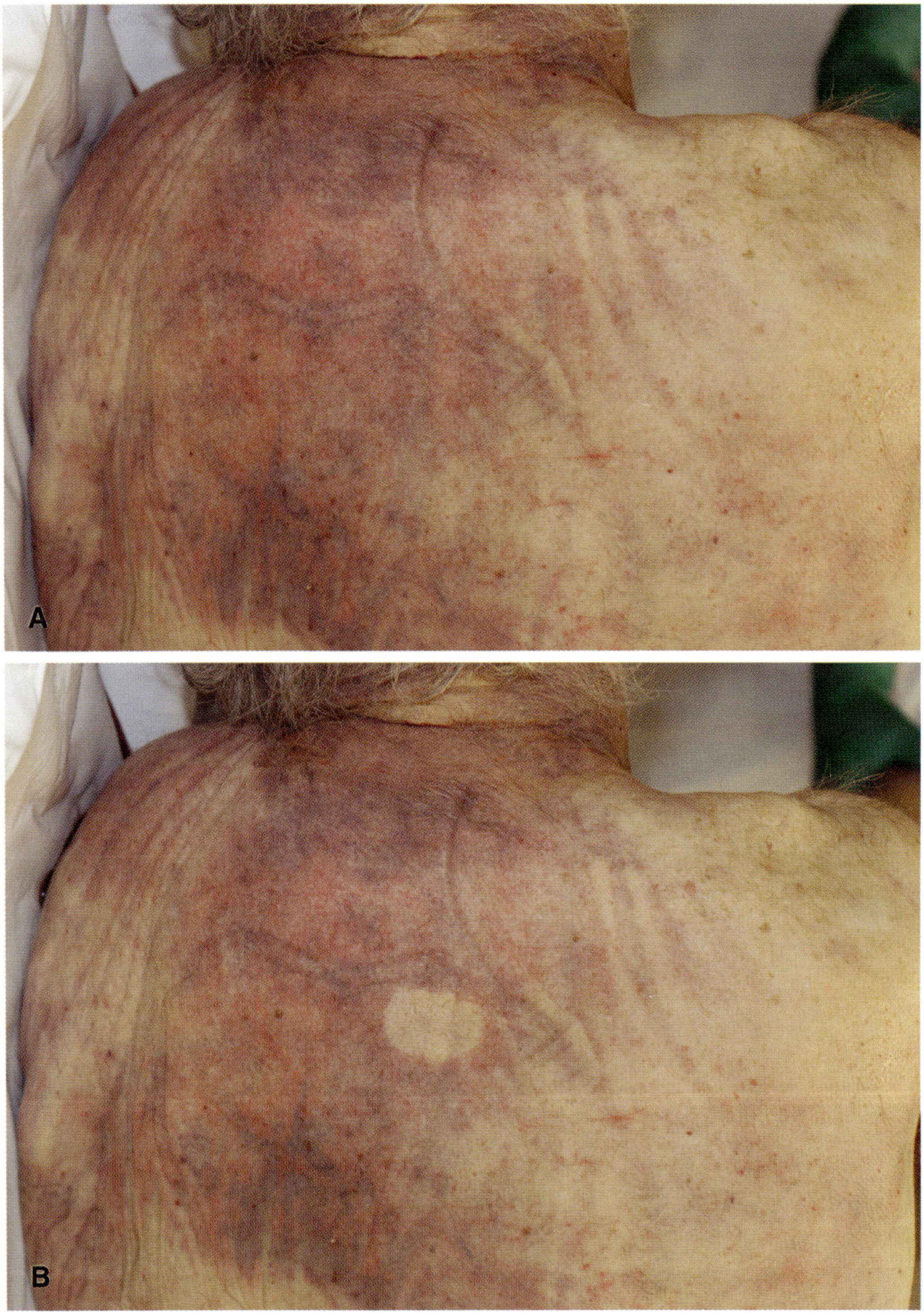

FIGURE 3.13 Pressure clearing of livor mortis. (A) Livor mortis can be seen on the back, on which the recently deceased victim was lying. (**B**) The pathologist has checked for pressure clearing of the livor mortis by pressing a finger on the back. The livor mortis has cleared.

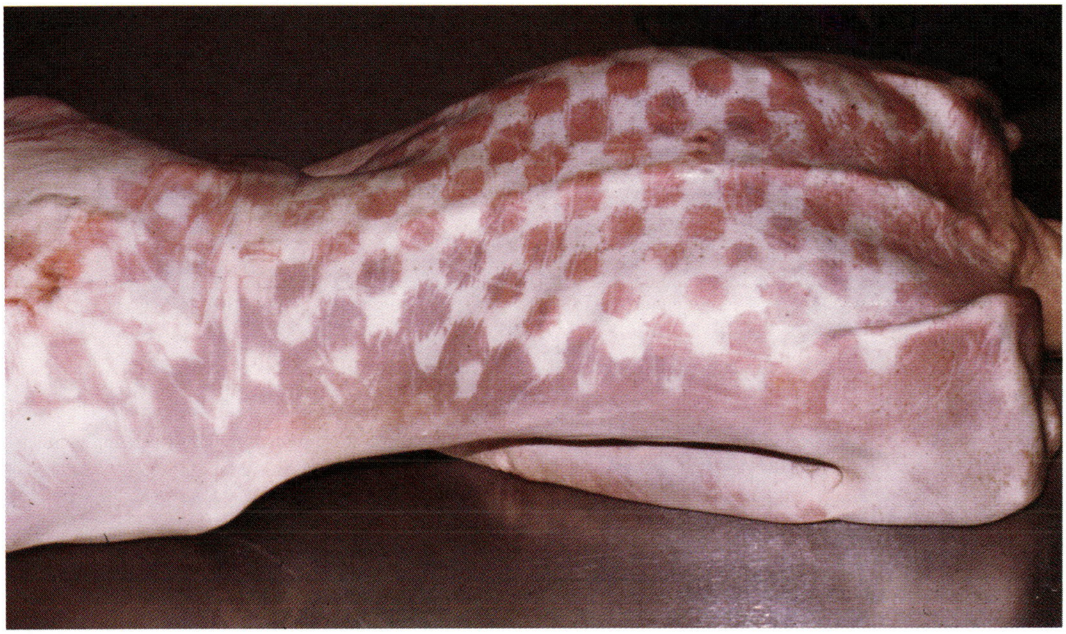

FIGURE 3.14 Patterned livor mortis. Since livor mortis can be cleared with pressure, objects pressing against the skin when livor forms can cause a pattern. This individual was lying on an "egg crate" foam mattress. The foam tips of the mattress touched the skin and cleared the livor, while the cups of the mattress allowed the livor to form.

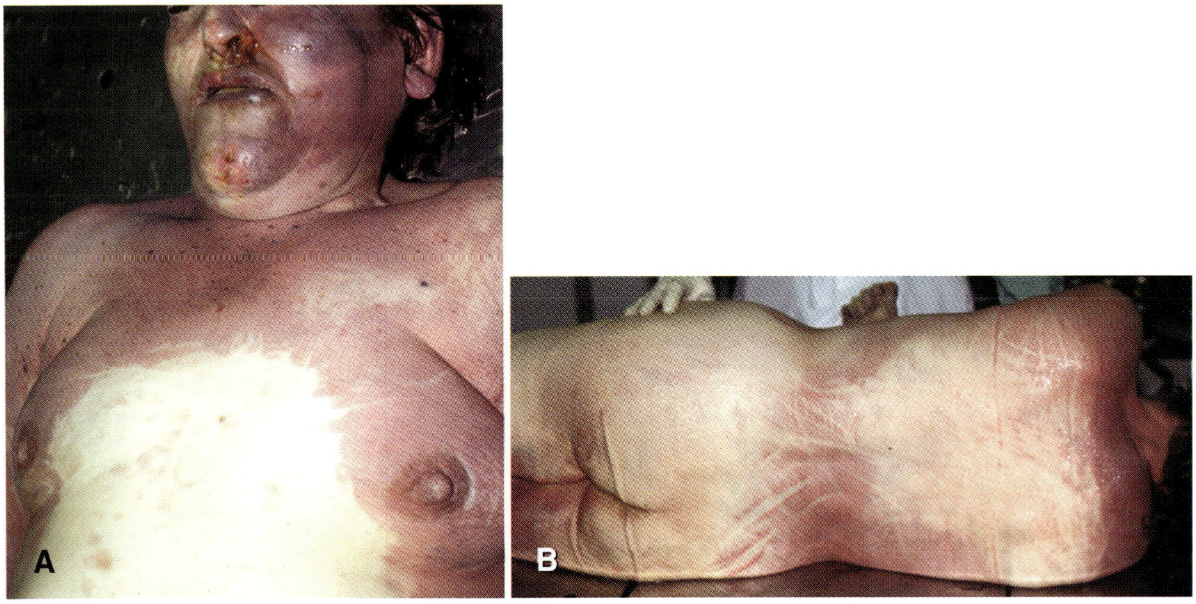

FIGURE 3.15 (A), (B) Two livor mortis patterns. This individual was found dead in a prone position (face down). As is commonly done, the body was turned over so that the individual was lying on the back. Generally livor mortis can still shift, as shown, about 12 hours after death. In suspicious deaths, two livor mortis patterns at the scene indicate moving of the body, or even that there are two crime scenes.

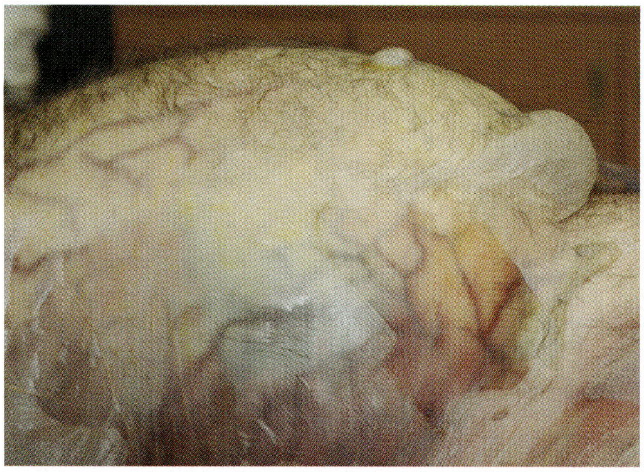

FIGURE 3.16 Decomposition: Skin marbling, blistering, and venous marbling. These signs of decomposition, depending on environmental conditions, generally begin to appear about 24 to 36 hours after death. A putrid odor usually accompanies these signs of decomposition.

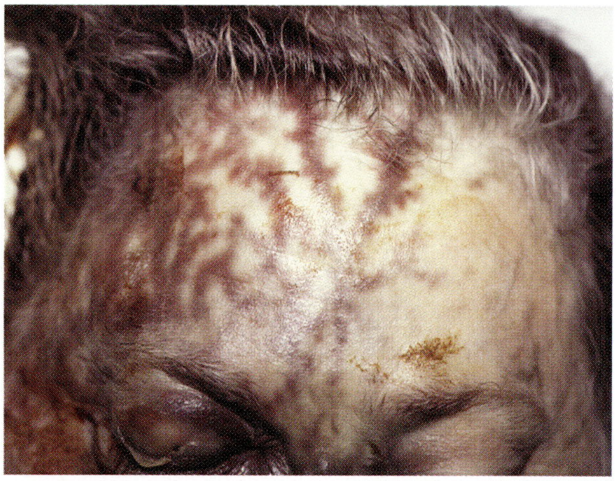

FIGURE 3.17 Decomposition: Venous marbling and discoloration of tissues. As blood in the blood vessels begins to hemolyze and decompose, the red-purple pigments stain the tissues, at times in the pattern of a blood vessel.

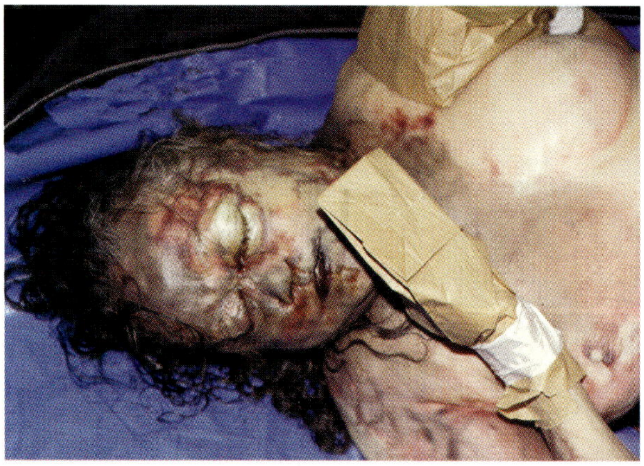

FIGURE 3.18 Decomposition: Discoloration and swelling of tissues of the face, mimicking blunt force injury. Postmortem production of gas by bacteria causes swelling and discoloration of tissues. To the untrained eye, these signs can resemble blunt force injuries. In this case, scene investigators were suspicious that this individual was killed by blunt force injuries of the head, so the hands were bagged and the case was handled as a homicide. The cause of death was natural.

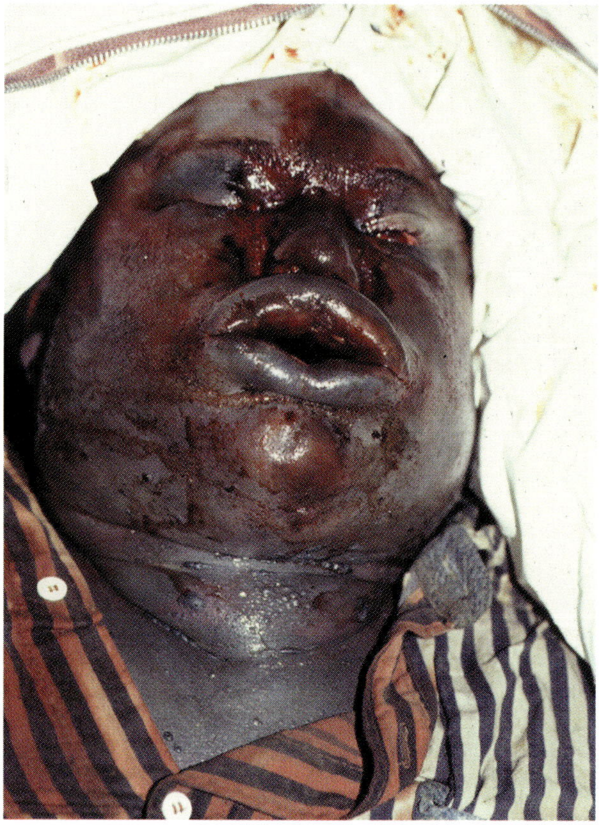

FIGURE 3.19 Decomposition: Extreme tissue discoloration and gas formation in a body removed from water. Bodies removed from water show excessive gas production and tissue discoloration owing to explosive bacterial gas production. The gas causes the bodies to bloat excessively, which can cause an explosion in the abdomen.

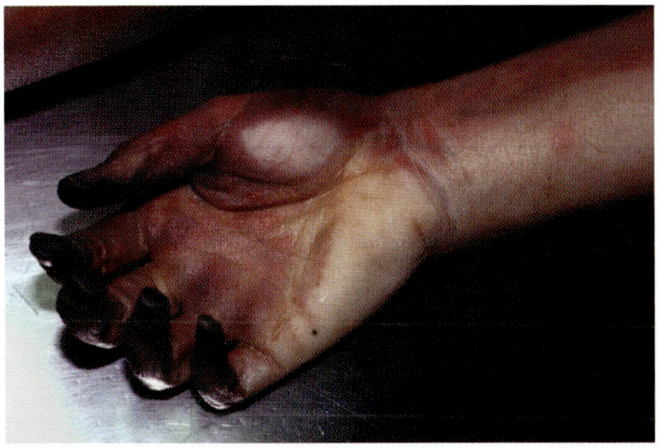

FIGURE 3.20 Mummification. Hot and dry conditions with low humidity can dry out tissues, causing a dark, leathery appearance. Desert climates as well as the heated indoors (non-humidified) can create conditions in which mummification can occur. This individual was killed in a house in the winter in which the heat was turned up maximally, presumably to speed up decomposition.

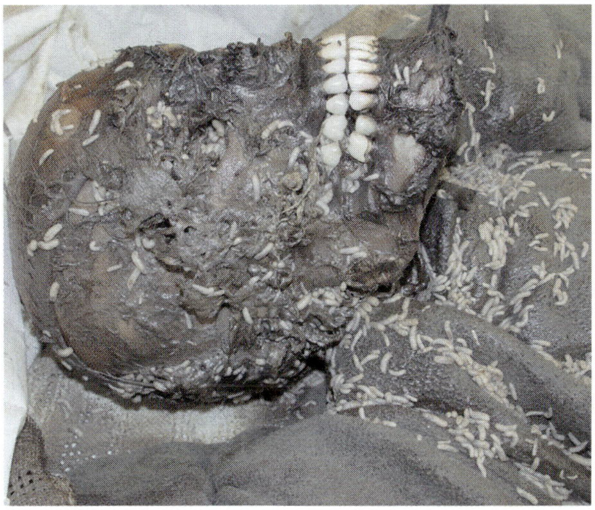

FIGURE 3.21 Decomposition: Fly larvae. These larvae speed up decomposition by consuming soft tissue. The larvae will greatly diminish and then leave when all the soft tissue has been consumed.

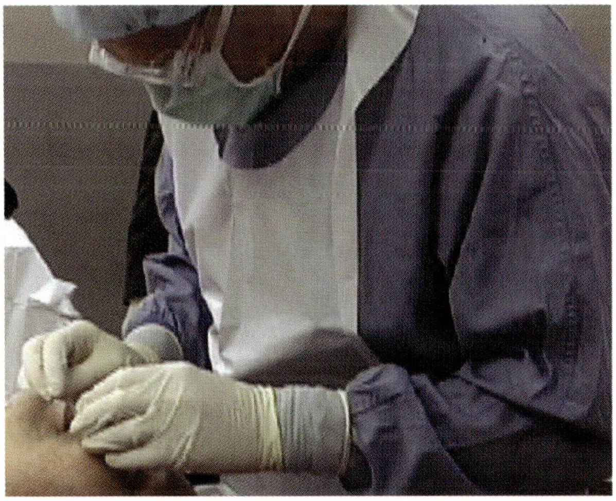

FIGURE 3.22 Examination of the mouth. The pathologist must perform a detailed and systematic exam of the entire body, being careful not to overlook any body system. During the external exam, the focus is taken off the obvious injury.

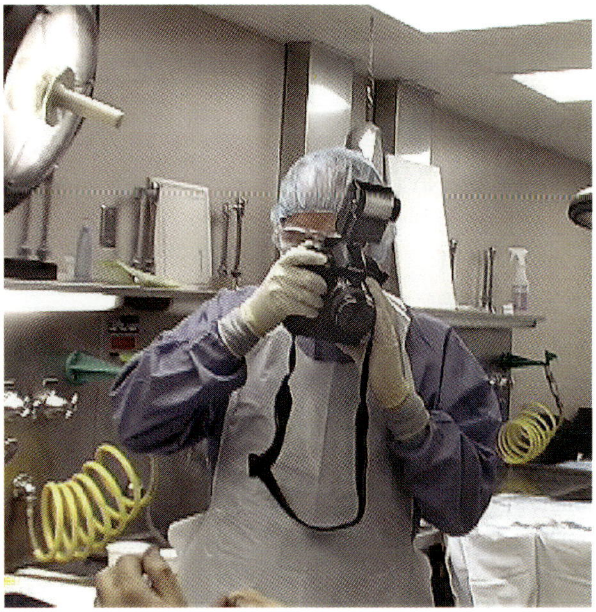

FIGURE 3.23 Documentation by photography. Photographing injuries is an essential part of the autopsy.

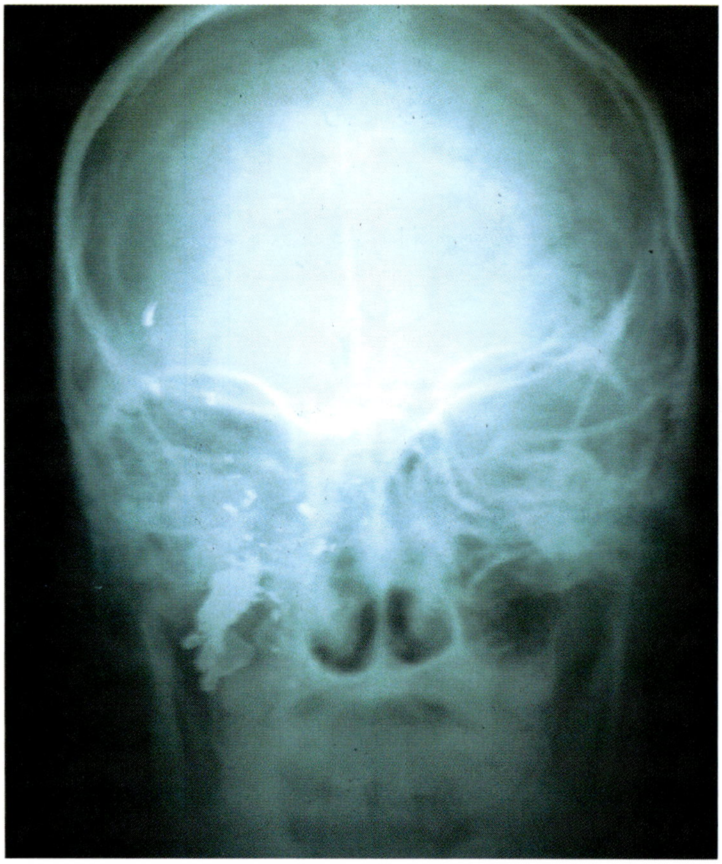

FIGURE 3.24 Radiograph of a skull with a fragmented bullet. On the left side of the figure, just below the eye, is a fragmented bullet. X-rays are most helpful in locating bullets for removal (see Figure 3.25).

FIGURE 3.25 Bullet on removal. This bullet is seen on x-ray in Figure 3.24. Upon removal, bullets are photographed and placed in a unique evidence box for later identification. Some pathologists mark bullets, being careful not to alter any unique markings that the firearms examiner will need to perform firearms examinations.

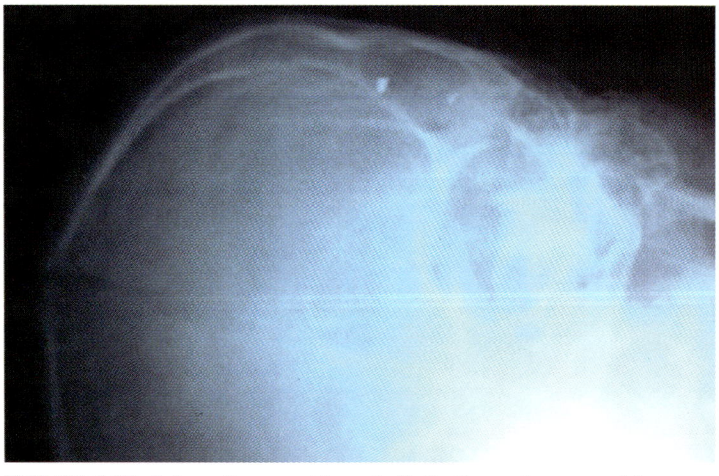

FIGURE 3.26 Scissor fragment in a skull. Radiographs are used for more than just examining gunshot wounds. In this x-ray of a stabbing victim, a small metallic fragment can be seen in the middle of the figure, with a white dot near the top. This victim was stabbed with a scissor, part of which broke off in the skull. The small fragment was removed at the autopsy (see Figure 3.27). Knife tips can also break off when hitting bone. The broken fragment can be matched to a purported weapon.

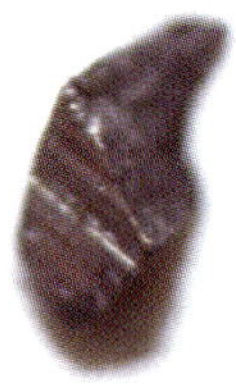

FIGURE 3.27 Metallic fragment removed at autopsy. This is the removed scissor fragment, as described in Figure 3.26.

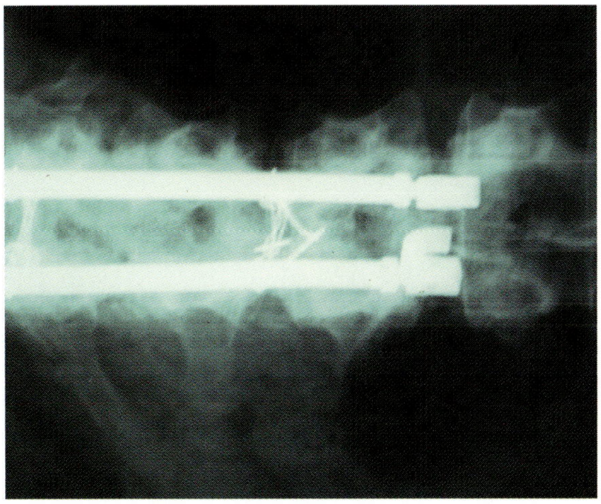

FIGURE 3.28 **Radiograph of spinal rods.** Unique prosthetic devices in the body are useful in making an identification.

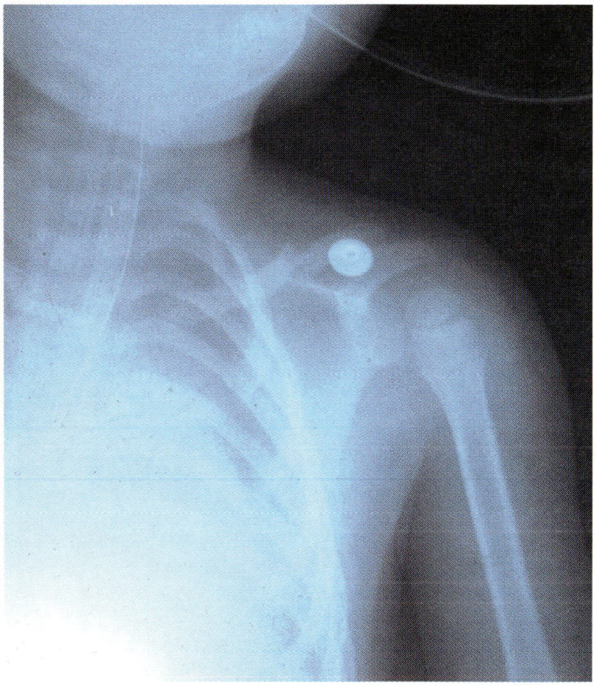

FIGURE 3.29 **Fractured clavicle on radiograph.** Full-body radiographs are taken in cases of suspected child abuse. This fractured clavicle (just left of the white circular dot left by the electrocardiograph pads) was unexpected, being found in a child who also had suffered an abusive skull fracture.

FIGURE 3.30 **Screening remains from a mass disaster.** Large bomb-scanning units or airport scanners have been used to screen the large quantity of remains found in mass disasters, such as plane crashes.

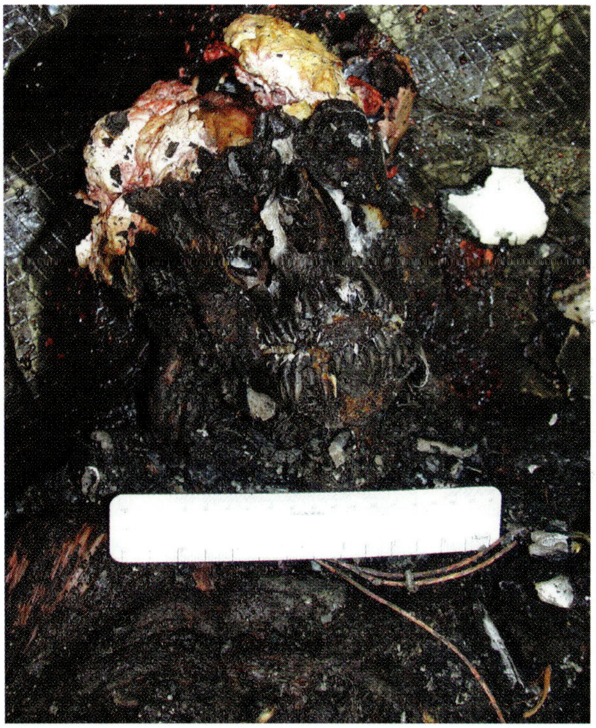

FIGURE 3.31 **Charred remains.** This figure depicts the torso and head of an individual with extreme thermal burns and charring. The yellow material at the top of the figure is the brain. Since the individual was obviously burned beyond recognition, dental identification was performed.

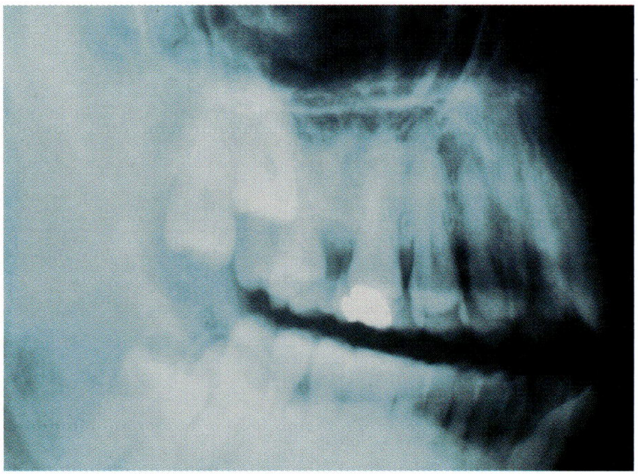

FIGURE 3.32 Skull film with dental filling. Comparison of postmortem radiographs with premortem dental records can be used to make an identification at the hands of a forensic odontologist.

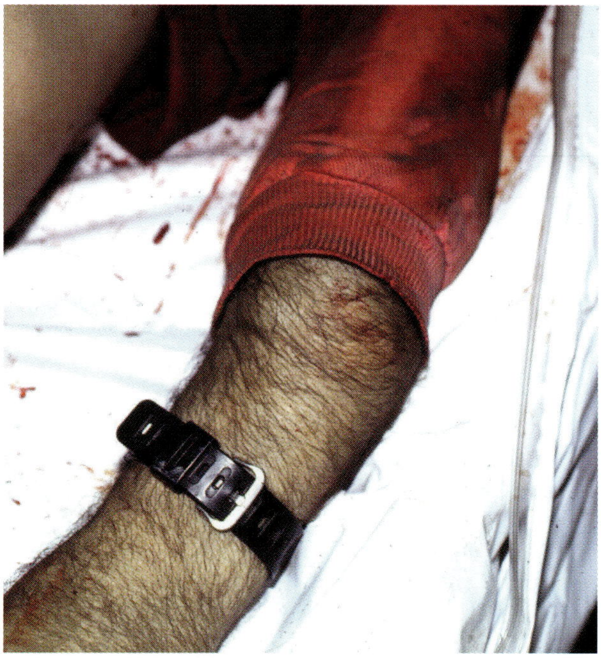

FIGURE 3.33 Forearm fracture. External exam of this forearm reveals a somewhat obvious deformity. The question is which bone is fractured — the radius, the ulna, or both? The x-ray is seen in Figure 3.34.

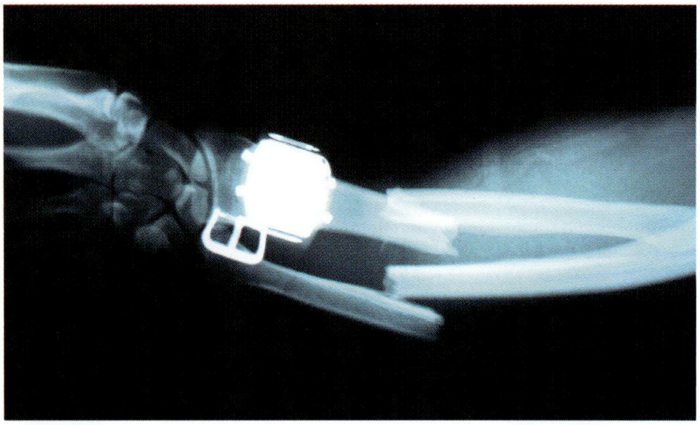

FIGURE 3.34 Radiograph of forearm fracture (see Figure 3.33). The x-ray shows a fracture-dislocation of the left forearm. This injury (also referred to as a "nightstick fracture") was most likely caused by a baseball bat when the victim used his arm to shield the blows. The victim also suffered a fatal skull fracture, most likely from the baseball bat.

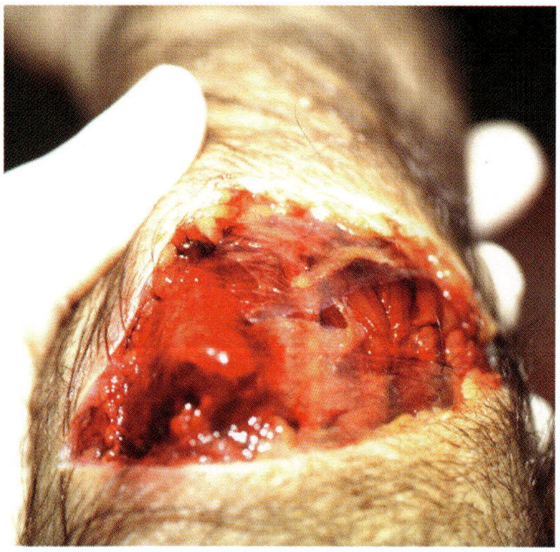

FIGURE 3.35 Incision of left forearm fracture (see Figure 3.33, Figure 3.34). Incision into the fracture reveals acute hemorrhage. This confirms that the fracture was premortem. Viewing fractures directly at autopsy, especially in the skull, is more sensitive than viewing them in x-rays.

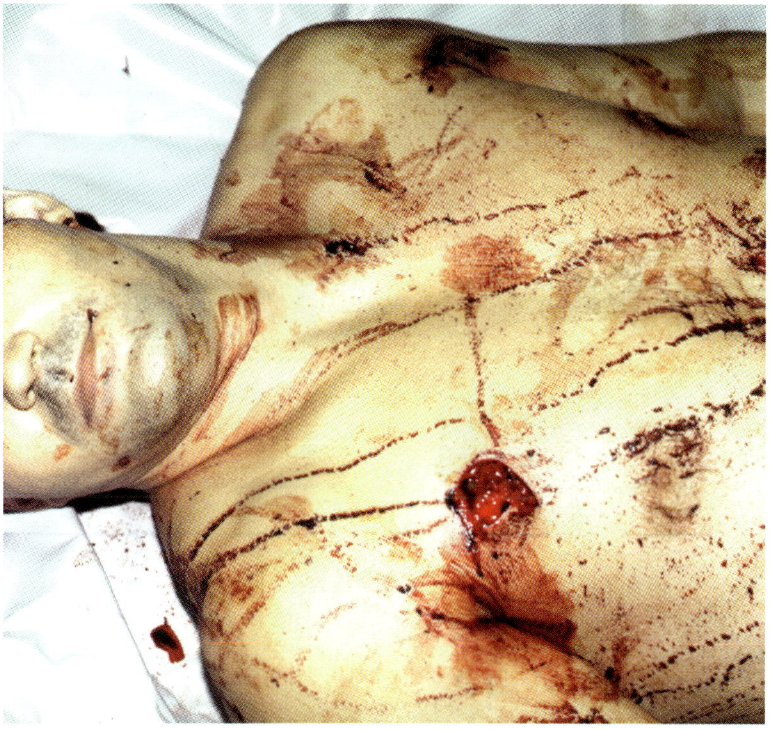

FIGURE 3.36 Stab wounds of chest. When the body is first examined, blood covers the injuries. Blood spatter and drainage patterns are important to document and study, so these are photographed. The body must then be cleaned so the wounds can be studied.

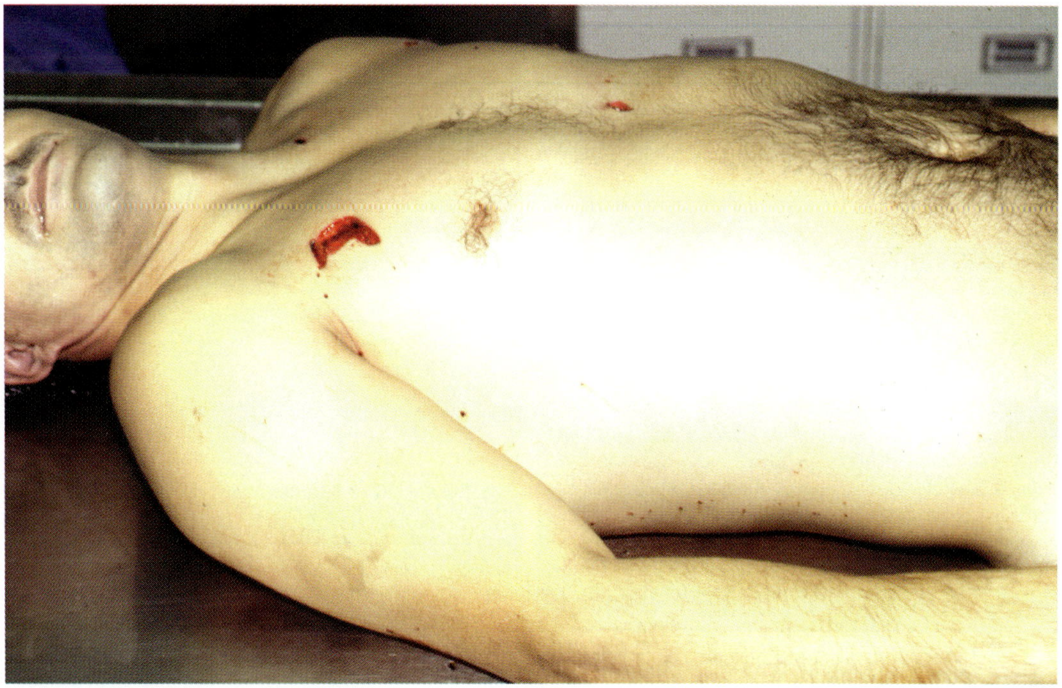

FIGURE 3.37 Stab wounds of chest after washing away the blood (see Figure 3.36). The stab wound configurations can be seen clearly now that the blood has been cleaned away from the chest and trunk.

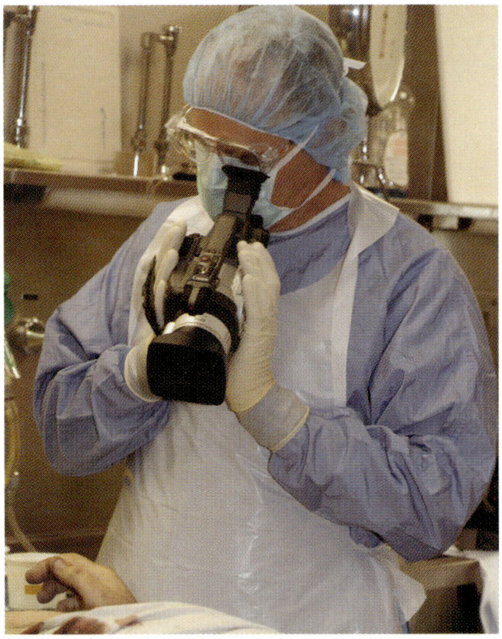

FIGURE 3.38 Digital video documentation. Documentation of injuries and other pertinent findings by digital video allows viewing of the subject from many different angles. Three CCD and the high-definition digital video now available have sufficient resolution to derive high-quality still pictures from the footage.

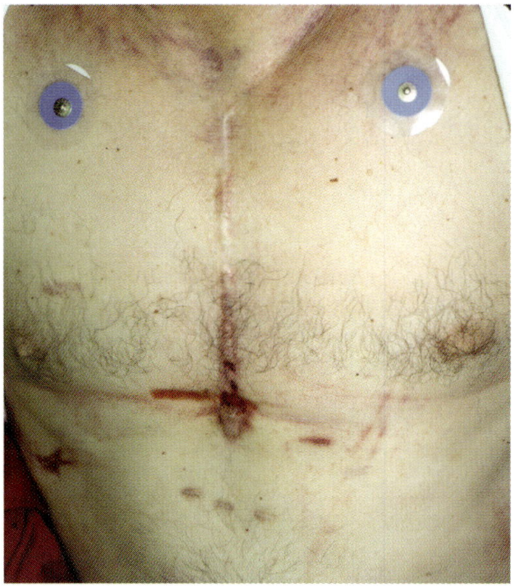

FIGURE 3.39 Midline chest scar. This scar suggests to the pathologist that this person has had cardiac surgery. Especially since the wound appears to be fairly recent, this finding will direct the pathologist to inquire more about the medical history. Also, the pathologist will look internally at the chest for coronary artery disease, cardiac valve disease, and other cardiac disorders.

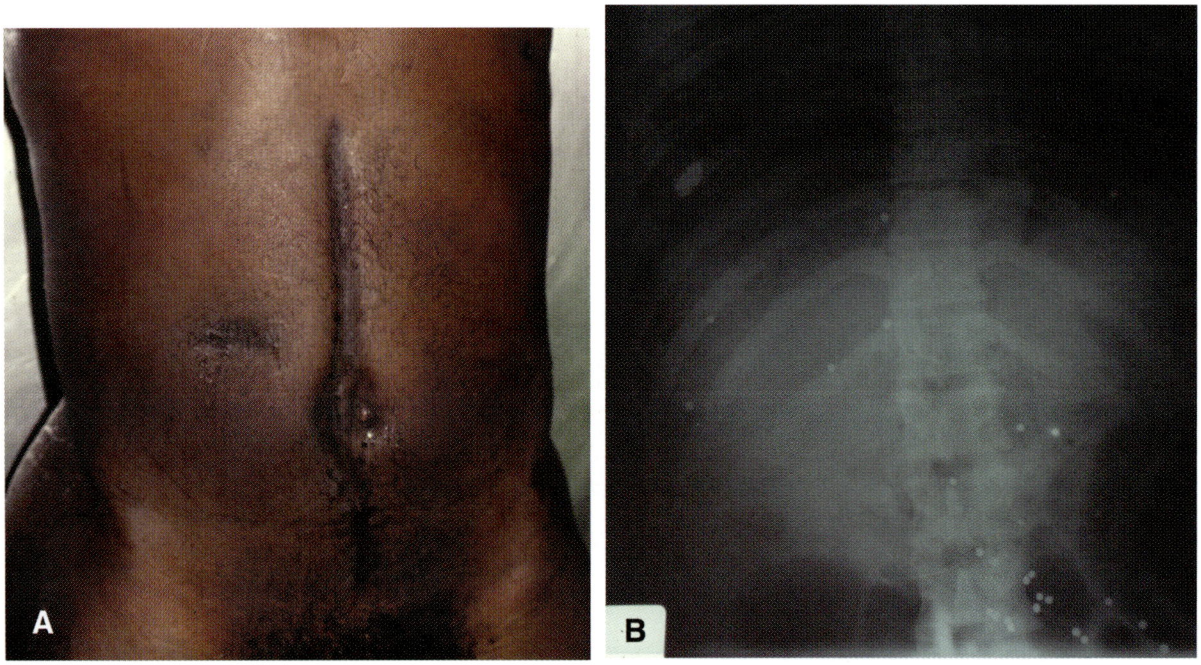

FIGURE 3.40 (A) Midline abdominal scar. The presence of this long, midline abdominal scar indicates previous abdominal exploratory surgery. The deceased was the victim of homicide by a handgun. **(B) Reason for the previous emergency surgery.** In addition to the bullet in the upper left rib cage area, multiple buckshots can be seen in the lower half of the figure. The deceased had been shot by shotgun in a previous assassination attempt.

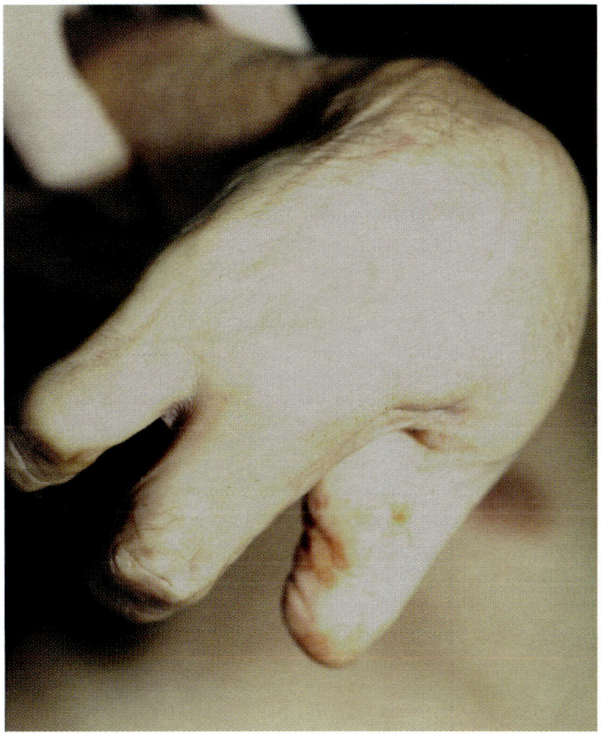

FIGURE 3.41 Hand deformity. Limb and body deformities are useful in identifying an individual and also speak to the medical history.

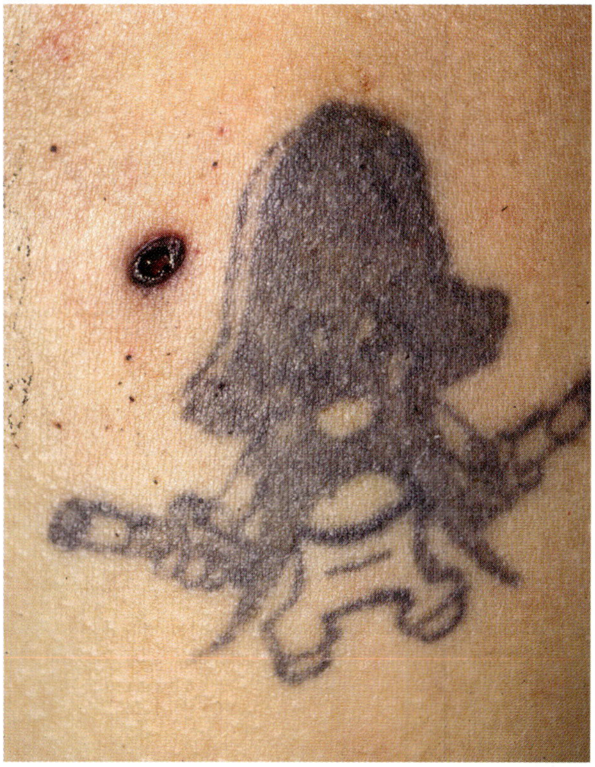

FIGURE 3.42 Unique tattoo. Unique tattoos, along with tattoo location on the body, can be helpful in identification. Descriptions of tattoos, for example, are available in arrest records.

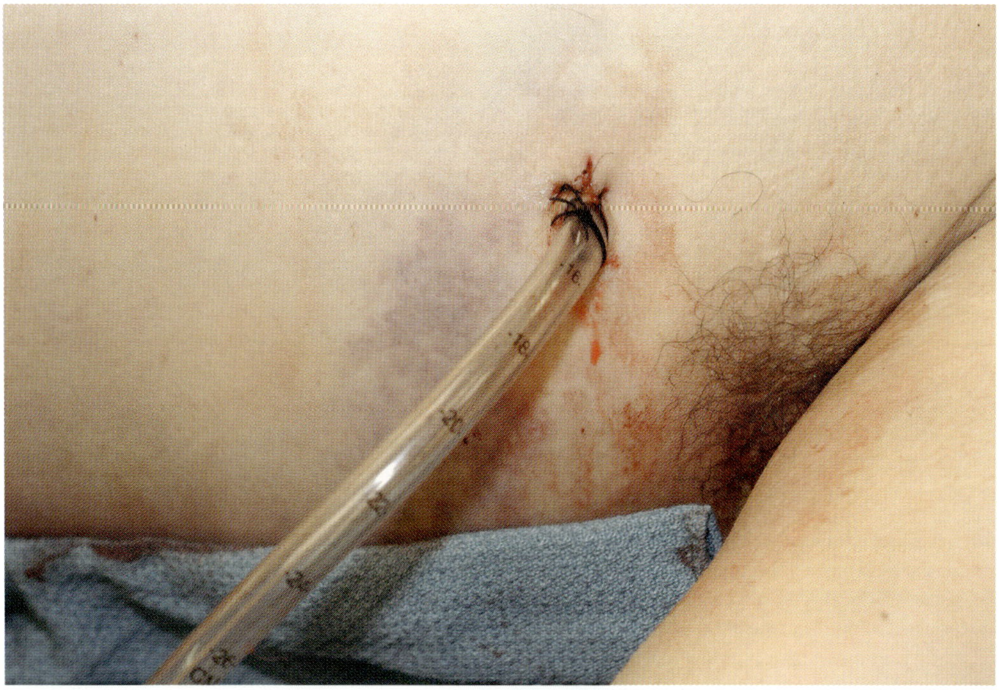

FIGURE 3.43 Chest tube. The location of chest tubes should be documented in the record and by photography. Once removed, the chest tube incision can look very much like a stab wound.

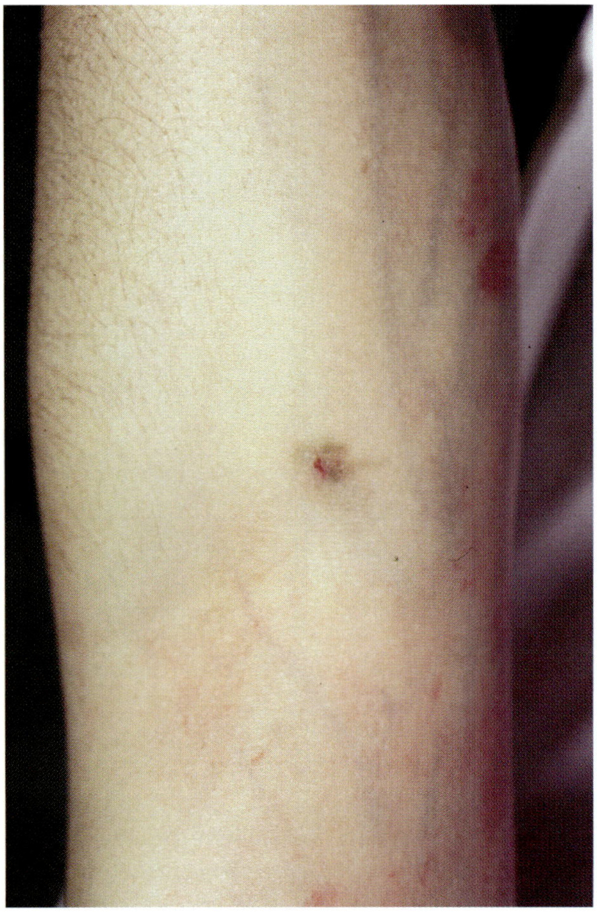

FIGURE 3.44 IV drug abuse site. The forearms and legs must be carefully examined for signs of IV drug abuse. These sites can look very much like therapeutic IV sites. In such cases, examining medical records or questioning treating personnel can be helpful. Cutting into the site should reveal acute hemorrhage and foreign material microscopically.

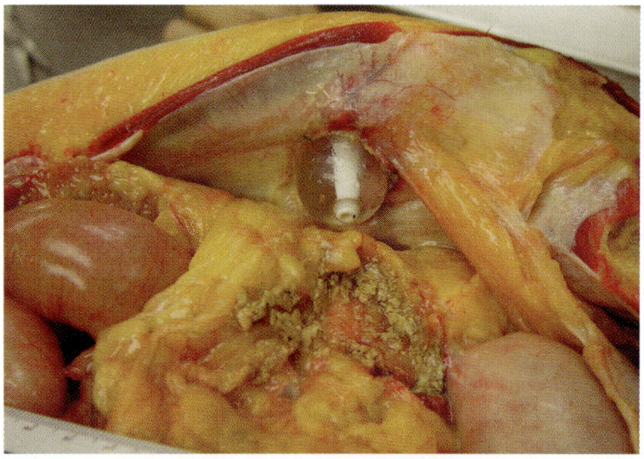

FIGURE 3.45 Gastric tube dislocated from the stomach. Medical devices can become accidentally dislodged and, if not soon discovered, can cause severe, sometimes fatal complications. This individual developed fatal peritonitis because the gastric tube had been dislodged, probably for several days. Medical personnel had continued to put feedings in the tube during this period of time.

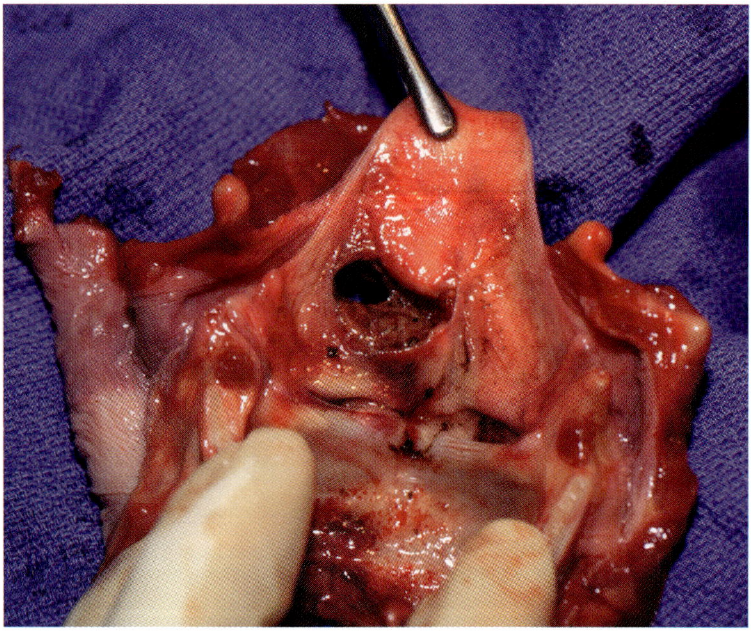

FIGURE 3.46 Misplaced cricothyroidotomy. When a patient in the field has respiratory failure and cannot be successfully bagged or intubated, an emergency cricothyroidotomy must be performed. The cricothyroid membrane is below the thyroid cartilage, or "Adam's apple." Improperly placed cricothyroidotomies can save the life, but can also cause vocal cord damage or other problems, if the patient survives.

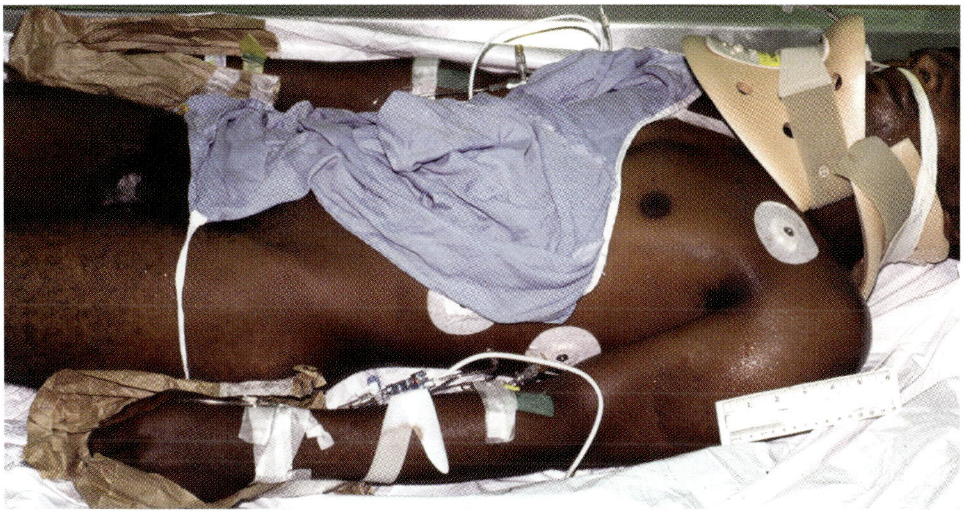

FIGURE 3.47 Medical treatment devices. After the placement of each device is documented, the devices are removed. All bandages must be removed to expose all wounds. In the confusion of resuscitation, key gunshot wounds might be covered with a simple bandage.

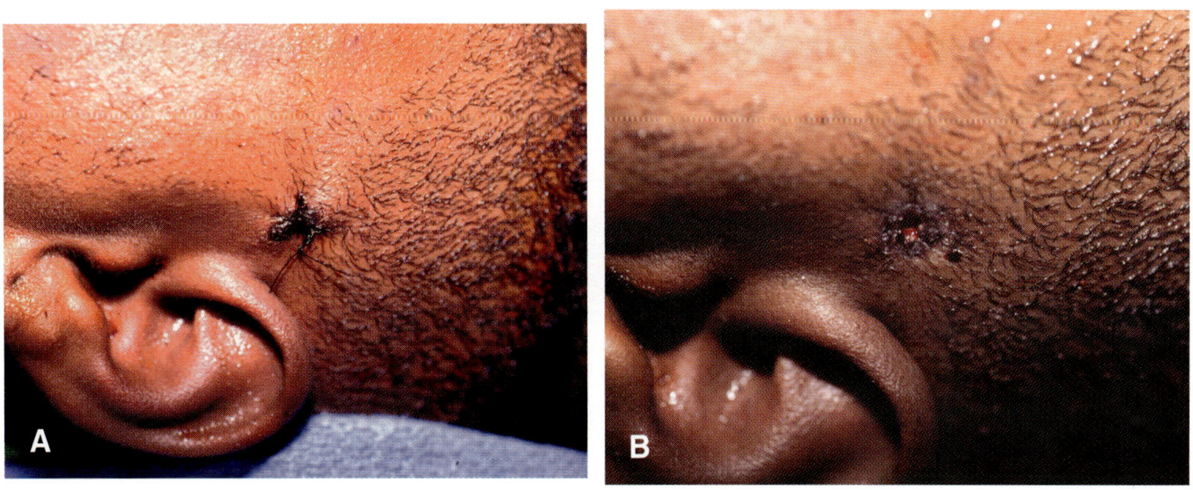

FIGURE 3.48 (A) Sutured gunshot wound. This gunshot wound was quickly sutured, obviously to stop the profuse bleeding during resuscitation. **(B) Contact gunshot wound.** The wound is easily recognized as a contact gunshot wound. If any significant healing had occurred, the wound would have been more difficult to examine.

4 External Examination: Specific Injuries

FORENSIC INJURIES AND DEFINITIONS

In the discipline of forensic pathology, injuries must be described precisely. The words used to describe these injuries have exact meanings. For example, a laceration is the tearing or splitting of tissue by blunt force. An autopsy report describing a laceration brings a visual picture of the injury to any forensic pathologist because of the descriptive language used. Also, many injury descriptions are based on the object causing the injury. For instance, a laceration is caused by a blunt object. The forensic pathologist who sees a large laceration in a homicidal head injury can therefore tell the police to look for a blunt object, not a knife (Figure 4.1A, Figure 4.1B). Described below are some common injuries, with illustrations. See the "References and Suggested Reading" section for more in-depth studies of forensic injuries.

Blunt Force Injuries

Laceration

A laceration is the tearing or splitting of skin by a blunt force object carrying force. Lacerations show at least three characteristics (Figure 4.2):

1. Undermined margins
2. Tissue bridging
3. Abraded margins

Lacerations can be straight or jagged in shape. A common error is to call a straight laceration a cut. A cut is really an incised wound, which is a sharp force injury, i.e., the tissue is cut, not torn (as described in the section "Sharp Force Injuries"). The laceration in Figure 4.3 is classified as such because it has undermined margins, tissue bridging, and marginal abrasions. The laceration is straight because the victim fell against the sharp edge of a table during a seizure.

Abrasion

An abrasion is the denuding of skin or tissue caused by a blunt or rough object. An abrasion is commonly known as a "scrape." There are four major types of abrasions:

1. A usual abrasion or scrape is due to an object contacting skin or tissue parallel to its surface (Figure 4.4A).
2. A sliding abrasion is more linear than a usual abrasion and is caused when movement or sliding is involved. The abrasion lines show the direction of sliding (Figure 4.4B).
3. A pressure abrasion is due to a heavy or forcefully projected blunt object contacting or compressing skin or soft tissue in a perpendicular fashion (Figure 4.5).
4. A pattern abrasion is the combination of usual and pressure-type abrasions, usually forming a pattern reminiscent of the blunt object that forcefully contacted the skin (Figure 4.6).

Lacerations and abrasions are often seen together in blunt force injuries. Occasionally, the objects causing these injuries leave behind pattern abrasions (Figure 4.7A, Figure 4.7B).

Contusion

A contusion, commonly known as a bruise, is a hemorrhage into skin or tissues caused by a blunt force tearing blood vessels. The leaking blood discolors the tissues. This purplish-red or dark-red hemorrhage can usually be seen by the naked eye. Contusions can also show patterns when the object producing the blunt force has a complex surface, such as an automobile bumper (Figure 4.8).

Multiple contusions and abrasions can be seen in the neck and base of the jaw in manual strangulation (Figure 4.9).

Avulsion

An avulsion is the tearing away of skin and/or tissue, usually as a result of blunt force. An avulsion can have characteristics of contusions, lacerations, and even sharp force injuries if the avulsing object has a sharp edge. Avulsions are important to recognize because a portion of skin or tissue is likely present at the scene or on the weapon. Avulsion injuries are characteristic of high-speed (and therefore high-energy) transportation crashes, such as airplane crashes (Figure 4.10).

Sharp Force Injuries

Sharp force injuries are caused by a sharp object cutting the skin or tissue. "Cutting" is a key distinction from blunt force injuries, which tear tissues. Therefore, when one refers to a cut, he or she is talking about a sharp force injury. There are two major types of sharp force injuries, stab wounds and incised wounds.

Stab Wounds

Stab wounds are generally deeper than they are long. They can be caused by knives or other sharp objects. Since stab wounds can cut deep arteries and veins and organs with large vessels, the mechanism of death in these cases is often hemorrhage (Figure 4.11).

Incised Wounds

Incised wounds are generally longer than they are deep. For example, classic incised wounds are hesitation cuts, seen in suicides or suicide attempts (Figure 4.12). In hesitation cuts, the victim tries to cut the blood vessels of the wrist, but lacks the knowledge of anatomy to make an incision in the proper spot. The victim stops cutting because these wrist cuts are painful. Then the victim gathers more nerve and cuts deeper, usually into superficial tendons, not the more distant blood vessels. Often, the victim gives up this method of suicide and either seeks medical care or resorts to another method of suicide.

Defense Wounds

Defense wounds (cuts) are special types of incised wounds received when victims attempt to defend themselves from knife attacks (Figure 4.13). Characteristically, the wounds are seen on the hands, wrists, and forearms. Defense wounds can also be stab wounds. The term "defense wound" does not necessarily rule out the recipient, or "victim," as the aggressor.

Puncture Wounds

Puncture wounds are special sharp force wounds that are much deeper than they are wide. These wounds are round or punctuate (pointlike), being caused by such objects as ice picks and nails (Figure 4.14).

Chopping Wounds

Chopping wounds are caused by objects with a sharp edge and substantial weight, such as an ax or a machete. In these injuries, cutting and tearing are seen. Bones can be broken, especially in the case of an ax (Figure 4.15A, Figure 4.15B).

Gunshot Wounds

Gunshot wounds are usually produced from four main types of weapons in North America: revolver, pistol, rifle, and shotgun. The revolver, pistol, and rifle produce a single entrance wound under normal circumstances. The shotgun can produce a single entrance wound if a slug is the type of round used or multiple entrance wounds if buckshot is fired (Figure 4.16).

In the study of gunshot wounds, as in every other aspect of forensic pathology, the pathologist is part of a team. The pathologist is responsible for describing the wounds on the body, collecting bullets or bullet fragments, and performing other duties. Based on the examination of these wounds, the pathologist is asked to render an opinion on the range of fire. The presence or absence of gunpowder stippling patterns is described, and patterns are measured by the pathologist. The firearms examiner compares these measurements and descriptions with test patterns produced by firing the purported gun. The information gathered by comparing known patterns at known distances with the unknown pattern on the body allows the range of fire to be estimated.

The pathologist is responsible for removing the bullets, which are handled as evidence. The firearms examiner compares test-fired bullets from the purported gun to those found at the autopsy. The pathologist must be careful not to damage the bullets on removal. Bullet removal is best documented by photographing and/or marking the bullets and placing them into a unique, labeled container.

Gunshot wounds are studied by forensic pathologists to determine entrance and exit wounds. From this examination, pathologists can assist in determining the following:

- Direction of fire
- Range of fire
- Type of weapon
- Position of victim at the shooting scene, e.g., behind a door
- Direction of the bullet traveling through the body and the organs involved

These listed findings are often helpful to investigators reconstructing the shooting event. The study of gunshot wounds and their classification takes extensive training. Gunshot wounds should be officially classified only by a forensic pathologist.

There are four qualitative range-of-fire determinations a forensic pathologist makes:

- *Hard contact gunshot wound:* The barrel of the gun is held tightly against the skin. Unburned material from the gun barrel, or soot, is deposited down into the wound. The gases produced from firing the round cannot escape, so they dissect down into the wound, sometimes tearing the tissues. An imprint or "stamp" of the muzzle can often be seen (Figure 4.17A, Figure 4.17B). The exit wound is more irregular in shape and sometimes stellate (star-shaped; Figure 4.17C). This is a typical wound caused by a .22-caliber rifle (Figure 4.17A).
- *Contact gunshot wound:* The barrel of the gun is held loosely to the skin or is very near the skin. Heavy soot is seen around the wound (Figure 4.18). Contact wounds and hard contact wounds are the only gunshot wounds that allow the pathologist to opine the distance of the gun barrel from the wound.
- *Intermediate-range wound:* The gun barrel is held from a few inches to about 2 to 3 feet from the wound. Unburned gunpowder and other material tattoo the skin in a pattern called "stippling" (Figure 4.19).
- *Undetermined- or distant-range gunshot wound:* No powder or stippling pattern is seen; therefore, the wound cannot be classified (Figure 4.20).

If an intervening target is between the gun barrel and the skin, the aforementioned patterns can be altered. This is why it is important for the pathologist to report only what is seen on the body. The approximate distance of the fire can be estimated only by a firearms expert (except for contact wounds) by firing the purported gun with similar ammunition at various ranges. The test patterns are compared to the stippling pattern measured by the pathologist.

The configuration of the wound and the pattern (or absence) of gunpowder residue are examined. The path the bullet takes through the body is determined. The trail the bullet leaves behind is assessed. For example, when a bullet travels through the skull, it leaves behind a bevel or wedge, much like a BB gunshot of a windshield (Figure 4.21). Inward beveling tells the pathologist that he or she is looking at an entrance wound of the skull.

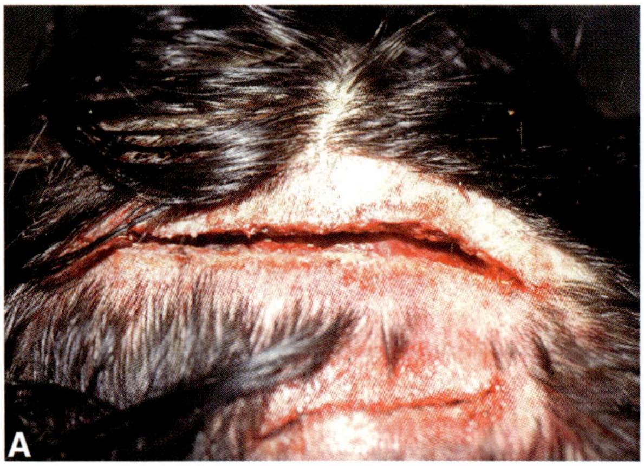

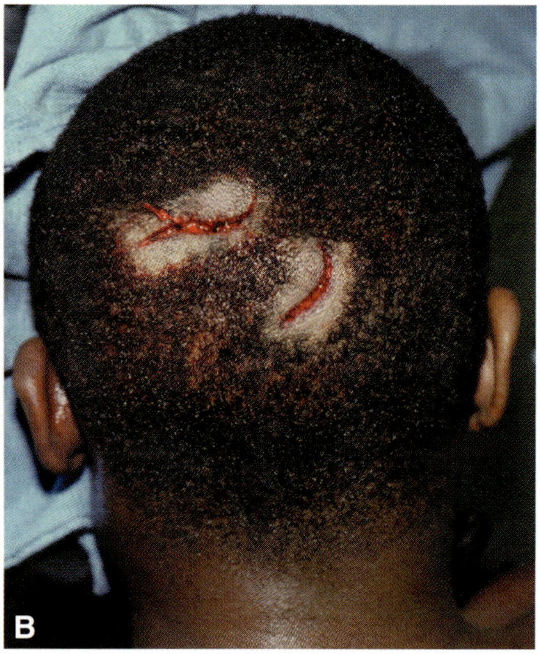

FIGURE 4.1 (A), (B) Lacerations of the scalp. Lacerations are often erroneously called cuts. When the skin contacts a blunt object or surface with a sufficient force, the skin is torn or ripped. This tearing produces distinct configurations in the wound. Cutting the skin with a sharp object produces clean margins.

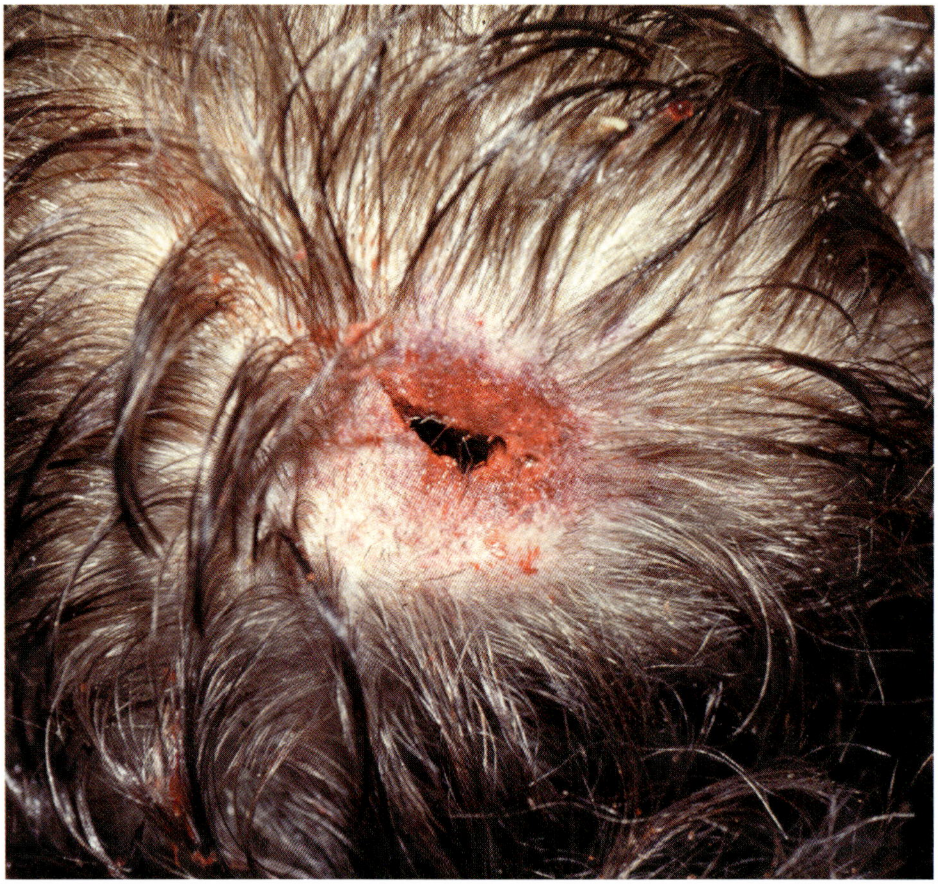

FIGURE 4.2 Laceration of the scalp with marginal abrasion. Blunt force striking the skin with sufficient force tears the skin, resulting in tissue bridging, undermined margins, and a marginal abrasion.

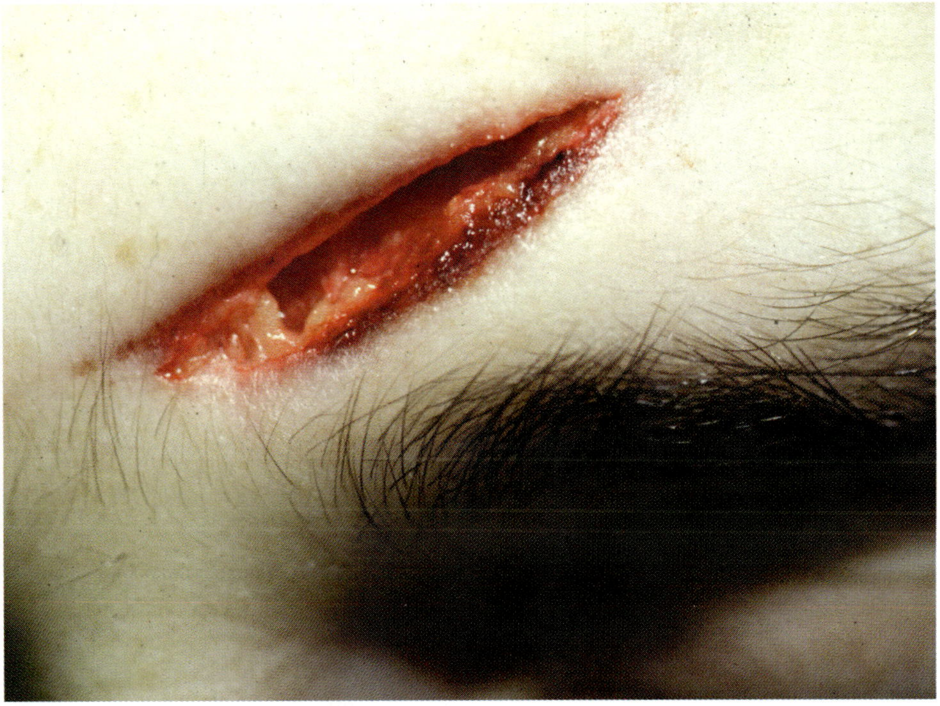

FIGURE 4.3 Laceration of the forehead. This laceration may look like a cut because it is straight. Careful observation, however, reveals tissue bridging, undermined margins, and marginal abrasion.

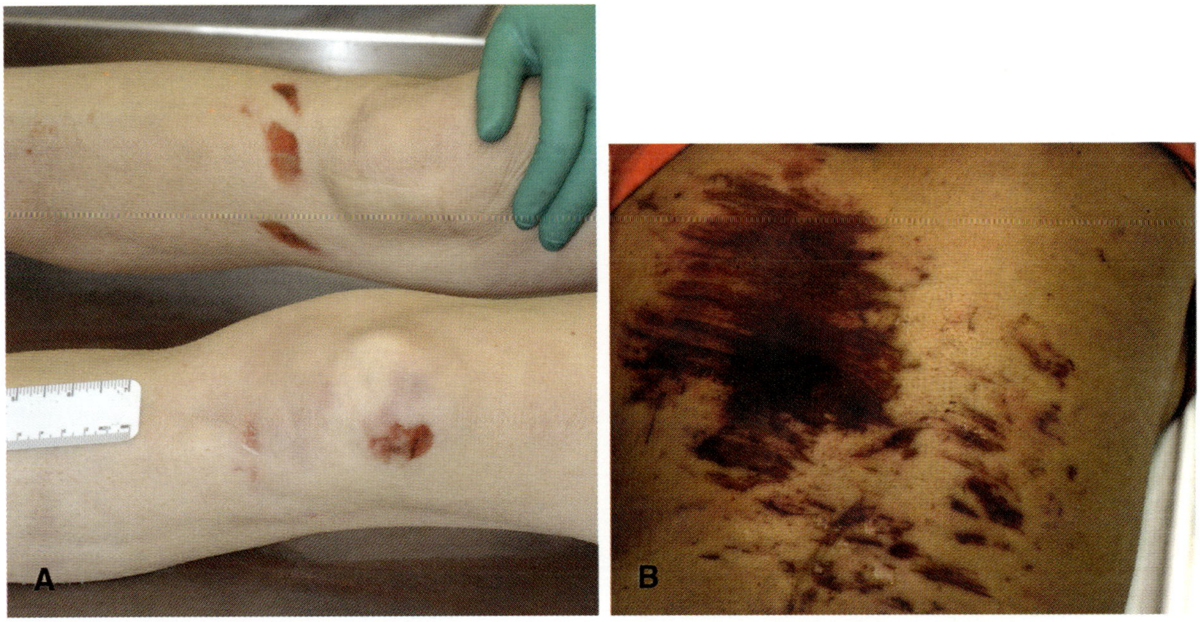

FIGURE 4.4 (A) Usual abrasions. Abrasions are patterns in the skin caused by blunt objects denuding the skin. This victim of a motor vehicle crash shows usual abrasions on the knees, commonly known as "scrapes." **(B) Sliding abrasions.** This victim was thrown out of a moving vehicle. The long axis of the abrasions shows the direction in which the body moved across the pavement.

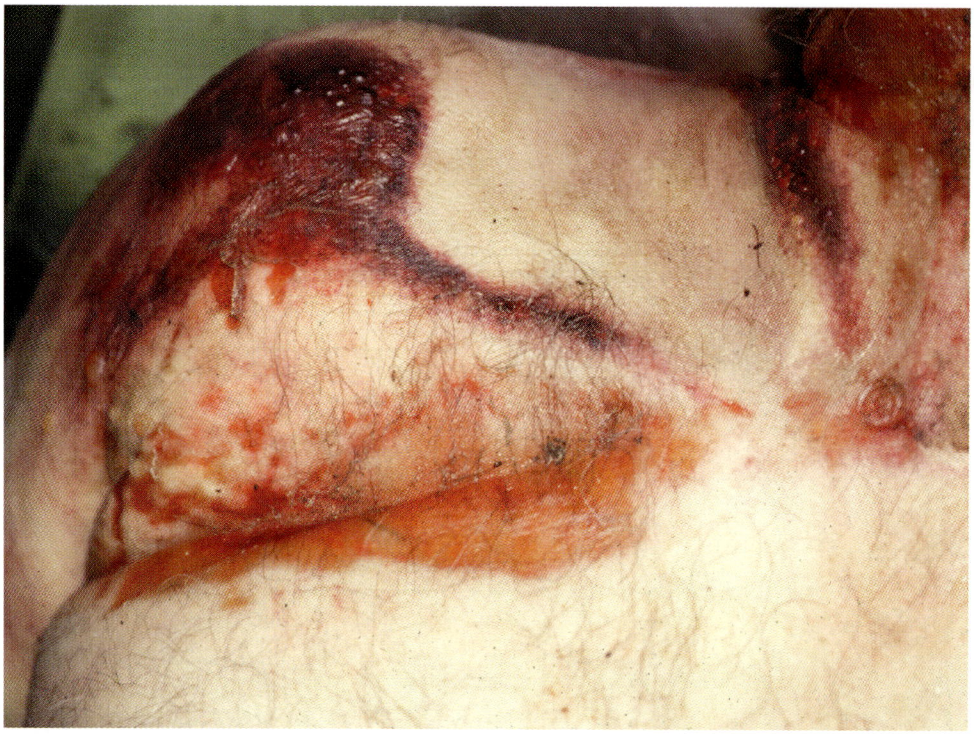

FIGURE 4.5 Pressure abrasion. The shoulder shows a yellow indentation below a purplish thermal burn. This victim's shoulder was wedged in a roller mechanism. The sheer force crushed the shoulder. The pressure flattened and thinned the skin so that the fat beneath shows through. The mechanism was also hot and produced the thermal burn on the upper part of the shoulder.

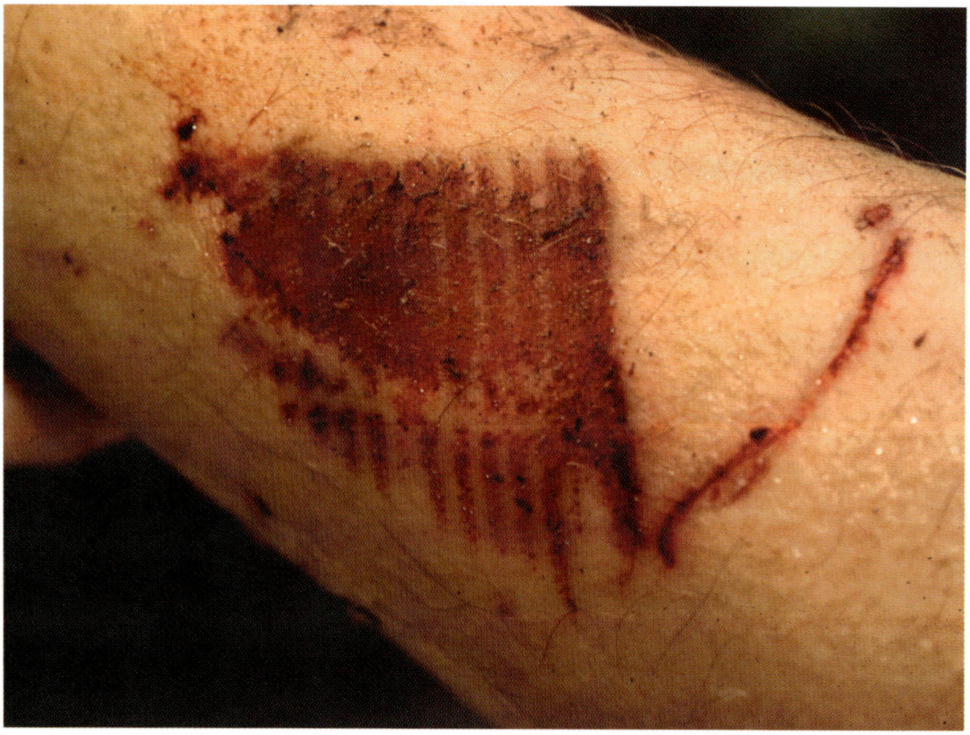

FIGURE 4.6 Patterned abrasion. This individual struck a solid object in his vehicle at a high rate of speed, causing this patterned abrasion of the leg. Automotive aficionados will recognize the pattern as that of a a brake pedal made by General Motors. The study of patterned abrasions can be useful because they can leave an outline of the object that caused the injury.

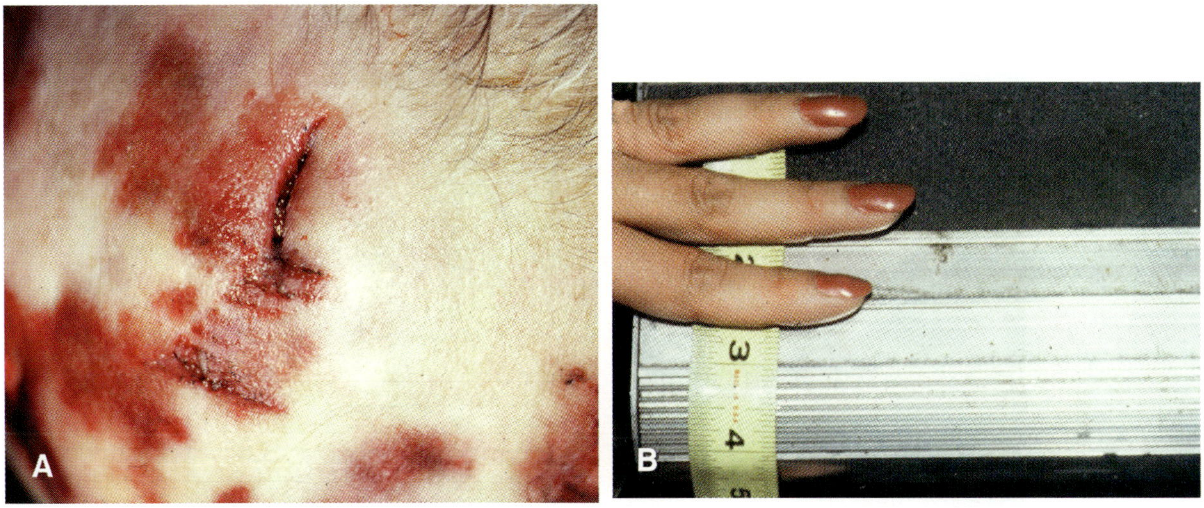

FIGURE 4.7 **(A) Patterned abrasions with a flanking contusion.** Objects with complex surfaces often cause complex injuries. Regular, periodic, linear abrasions can be seen below the central laceration. **(B) Truck floorboard.** One probable explanation for these patterned abrasions and laceration is that the head was propelled against this truck floorboard found at the scene, since the ridges of the floorboard match up to the abrasions seen in the injury.

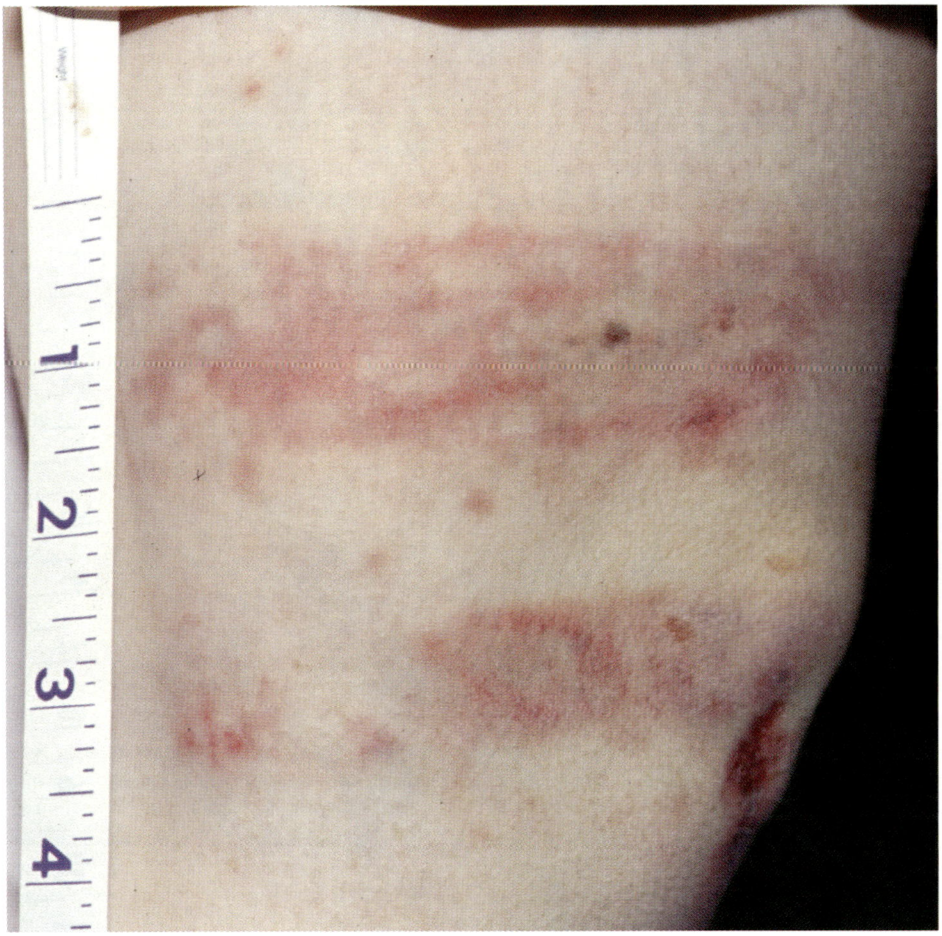

FIGURE 4.8 **Patterned bumper contusions.** This individual was killed by being struck with an automobile multiple times. This figure shows two linear contusions of the knee, caused by the bumper striking the victim while walking. The height of these injuries can be measured from the ground and compared to the vehicle. Also, the configurations of the contusions can be compared to the bumper of the vehicle. Other tests can be performed on the vehicle, such as inspecting it for blood and tissue.

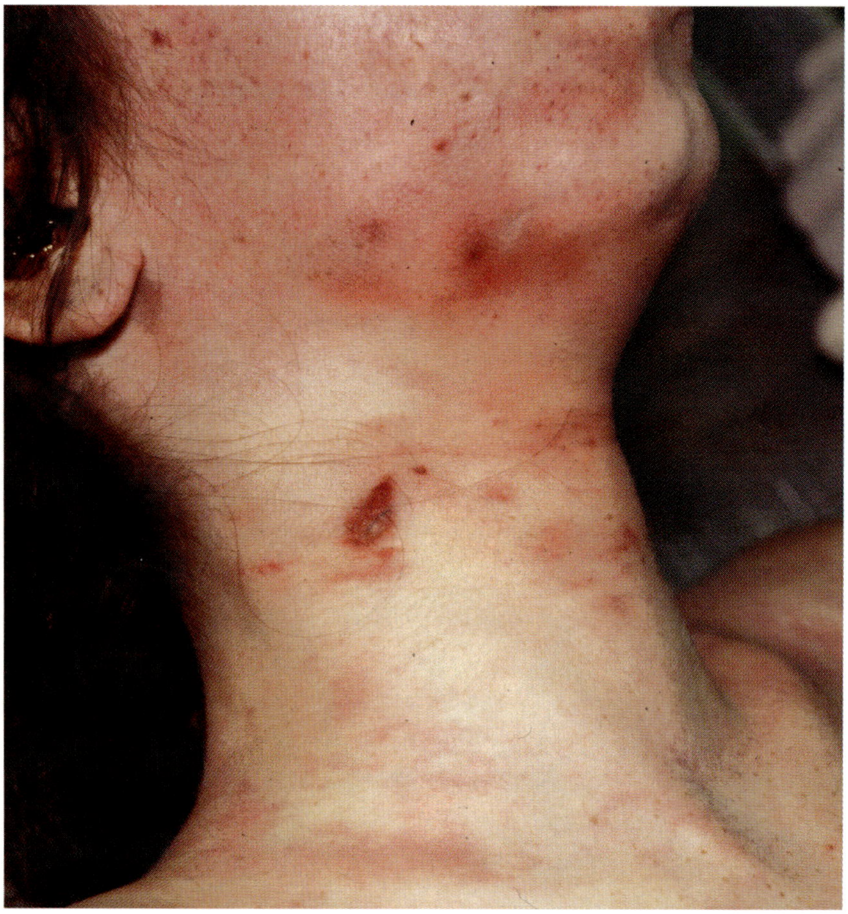

FIGURE 4.9 Contusions of the neck. This individual was the victim of manual strangulation. Multiple contusions (and a few abrasions) are seen, especially at the midline of the neck and the base of the jaw.

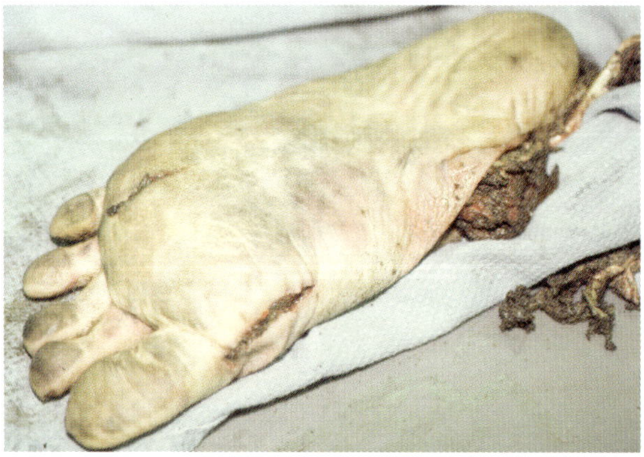

FIGURE 4.10 Avulsion of the foot. Airplane crashes impart tremendous force to tissues, causing shearing and shredding of the entire body. Intact body parts can be difficult to find in high-speed airplane crashes.

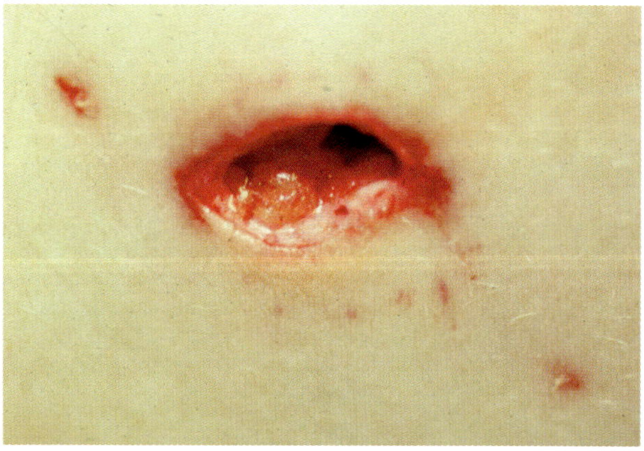

FIGURE 4.11 Stab wound with hilt mark. Stab wounds are deeper than they are long. This stab wound demonstrates that the full length of the knife was thrust into the body. The abrasion on the wound and the radial marks surrounding the wound were caused by the hilt, or end, of the knife. The two outside abrasions were caused by the finger guards of the knife. These characteristic marks could be used to exclude or include unknown knives in an investigation.

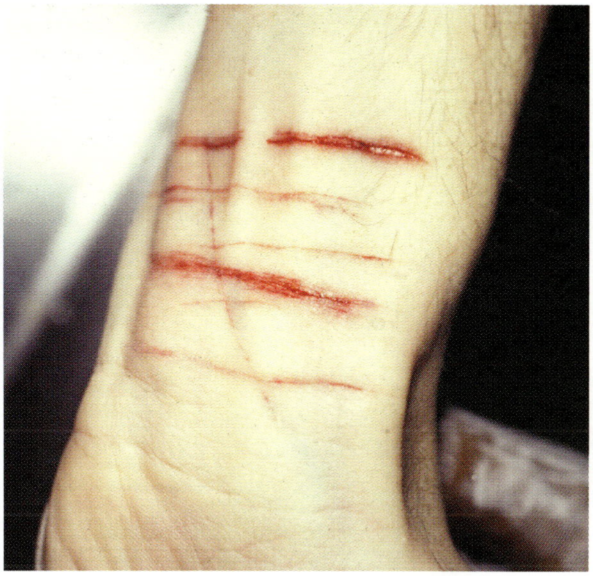

FIGURE 4.12 Incised wounds of the wrist (hesitation cuts). Incised wounds are longer than they are deep. These characteristic incised wounds of the wrist, seen in suicide attempts, are also called hesitation cuts.

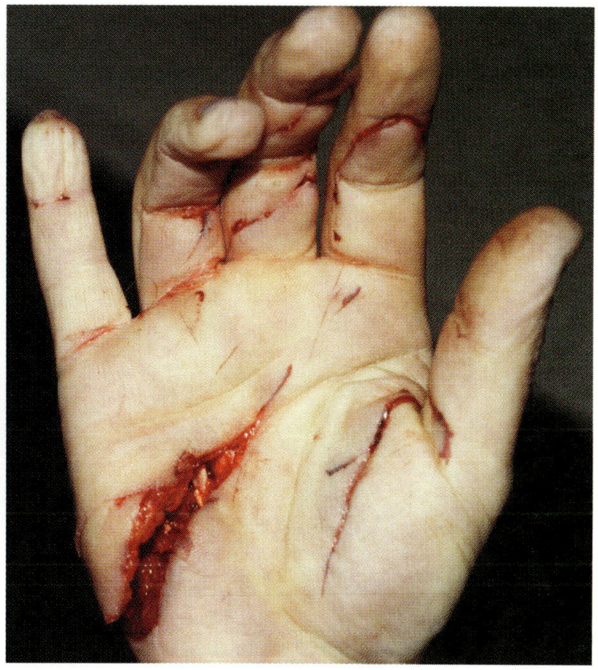

FIGURE 4.13 Incised wounds of the hand (defense cuts). Defense cuts are special types of incised wounds encountered when victims have attempted to fight off knife attacks. The deep cuts seen here tell us the story of the violence inherent in the attack and the determination of the victim to prevent the attack.

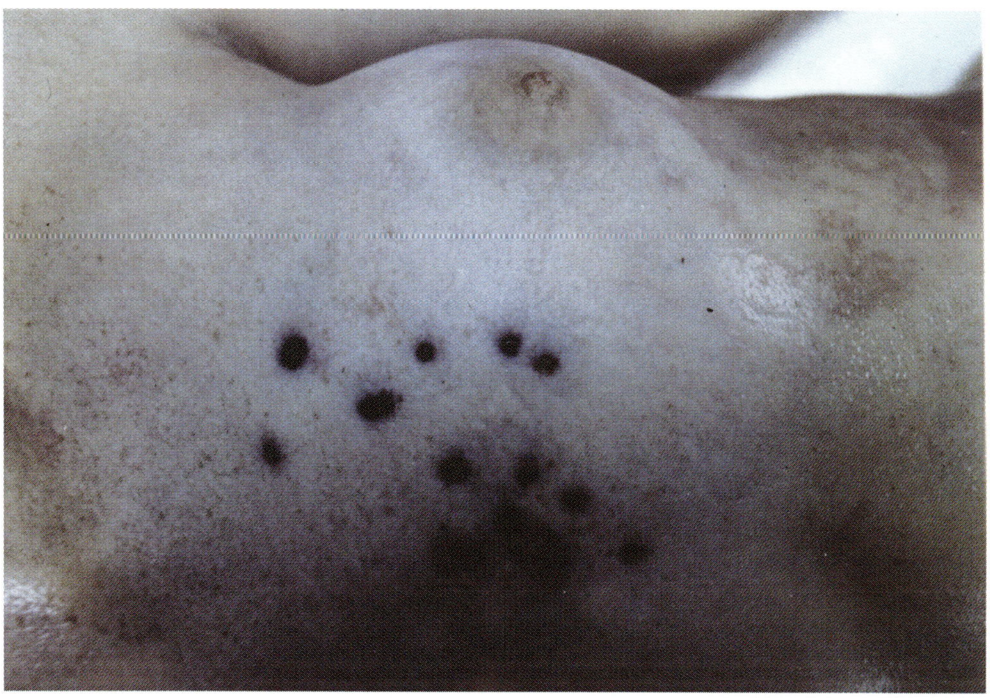

FIGURE 4.14 Puncture wounds of the chest. The victim was killed with an ice pick. The multiple stab wounds are located around the heart. The purposeful placement of the ice pick wounds around the heart display the determination of the perpetrator, i.e., these are not randomly placed puncture wounds.

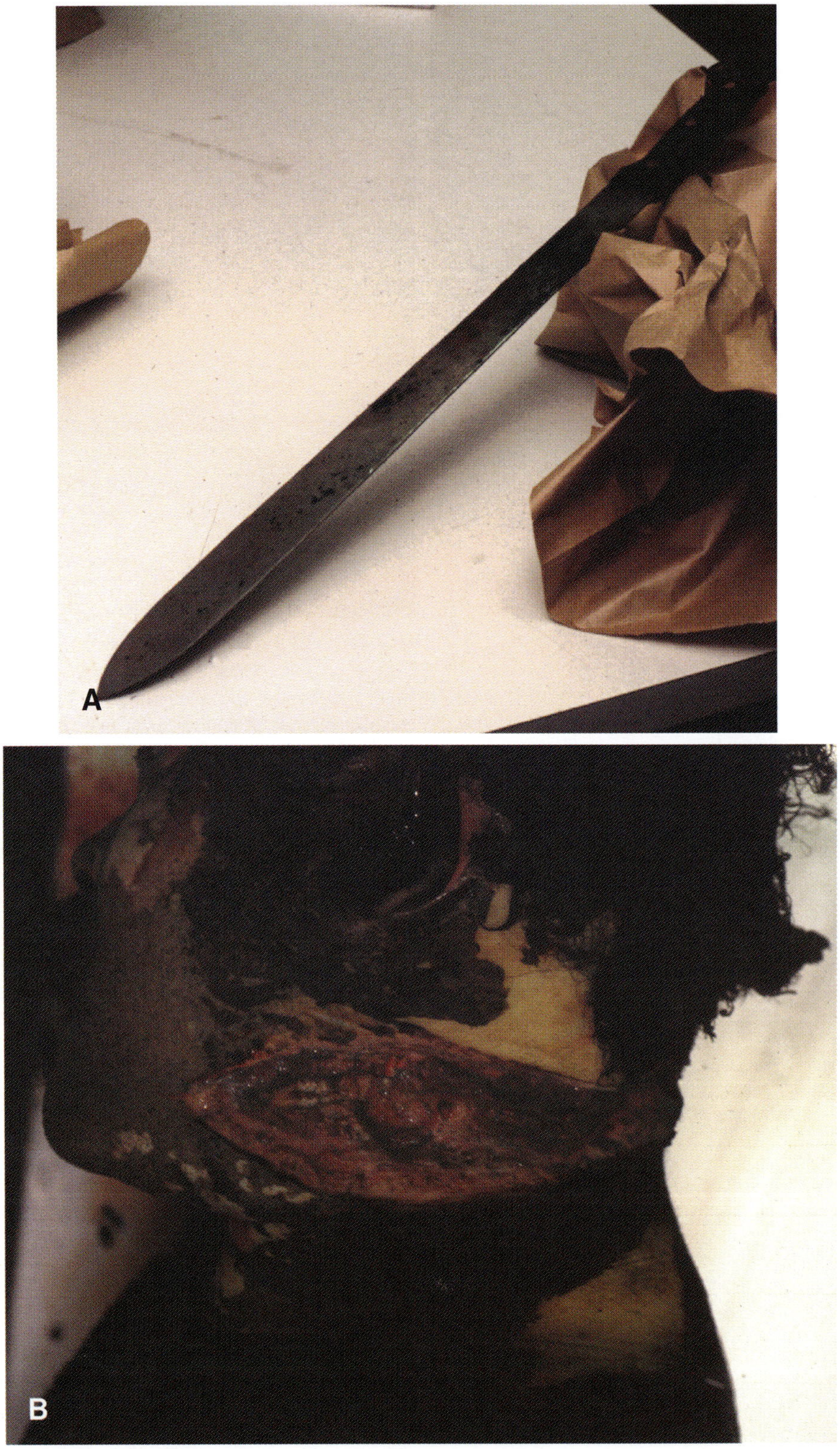

FIGURE 4.15 **(A) Machete.** Axes, swords, machetes, and other such weapons have sharp edges and weight. These weapons can cut, tear, and break bones. **(B) Sharp force wound.** These cuts are often long and deep. After being cut with the machete, this victim was set afire, which caused the dark, charred skin.

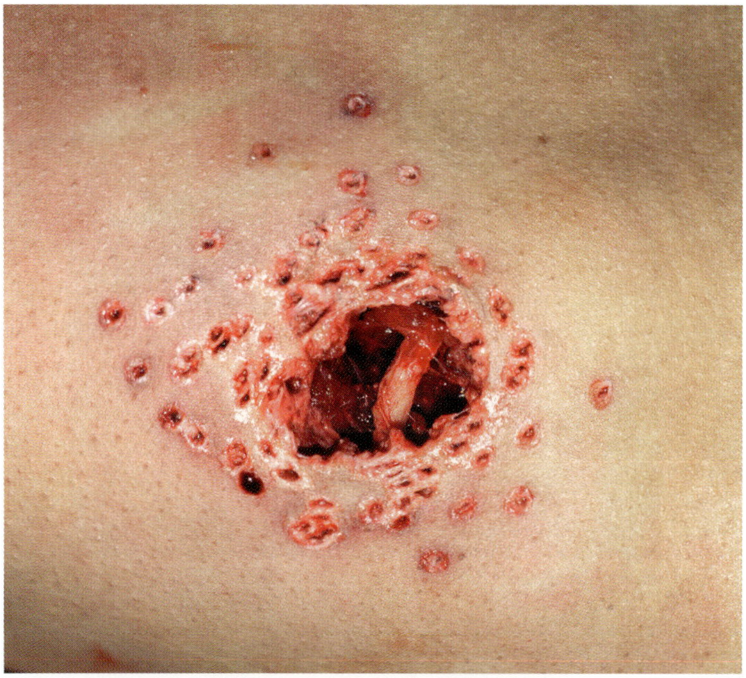

FIGURE 4.16 Shotgun wound. Shotgun shells contain multiple small "BBs," called shot. As the shot comes out of the barrel of the gun, it stays together for several feet, and then starts to separate. As individual shot break up and hit the skin, characteristic individual satellite shot injuries can be seen around the main hole.

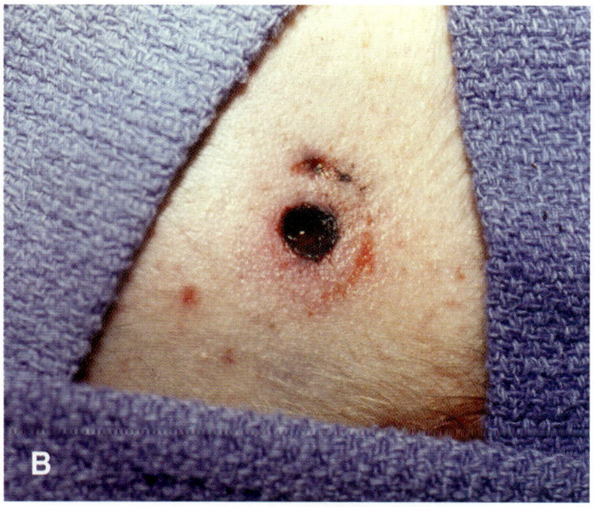

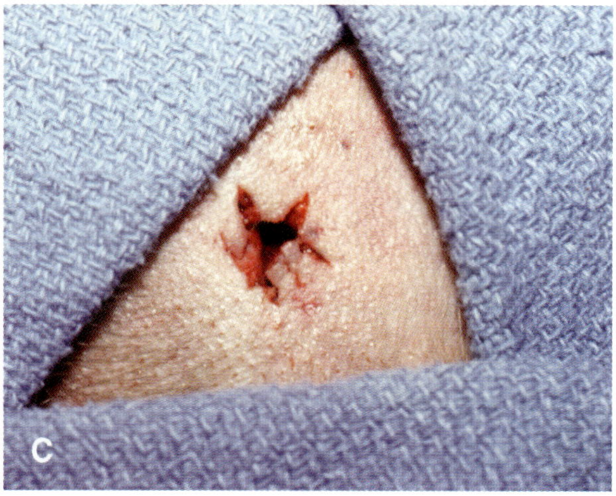

FIGURE 4.17 **(A) .22-caliber rifle.** This rifle was held tightly above the skin by the victim and caused a suicidal gunshot wound. **(B) Hard contact entrance wound**. Dark soot can be seen in the center of the wound. The circular abrasion surrounding the wound was caused by the round muzzle and is often called a "muzzle abrasion." This injury is referred to as a hard contact wound since all the soot is inside the wound. **(C) Exit wound.** The exit wound is stellate in configuration. No soot or abrasion can be seen around it.

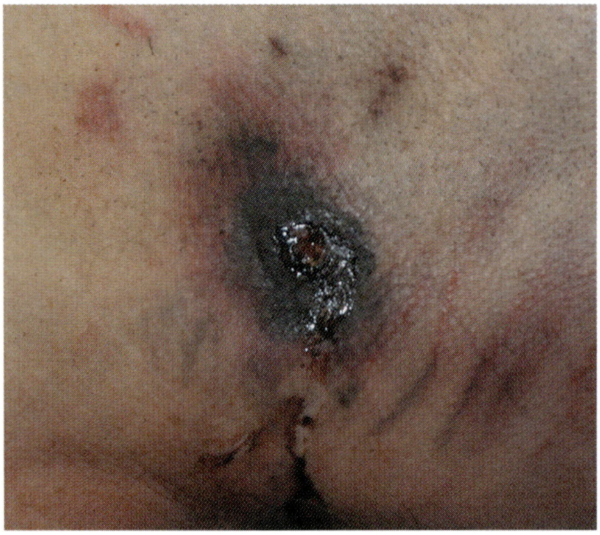

FIGURE 4.18 Loose contact wound. The gun muzzle held slightly away from the skin causes the black soot to go both in and around the wound.

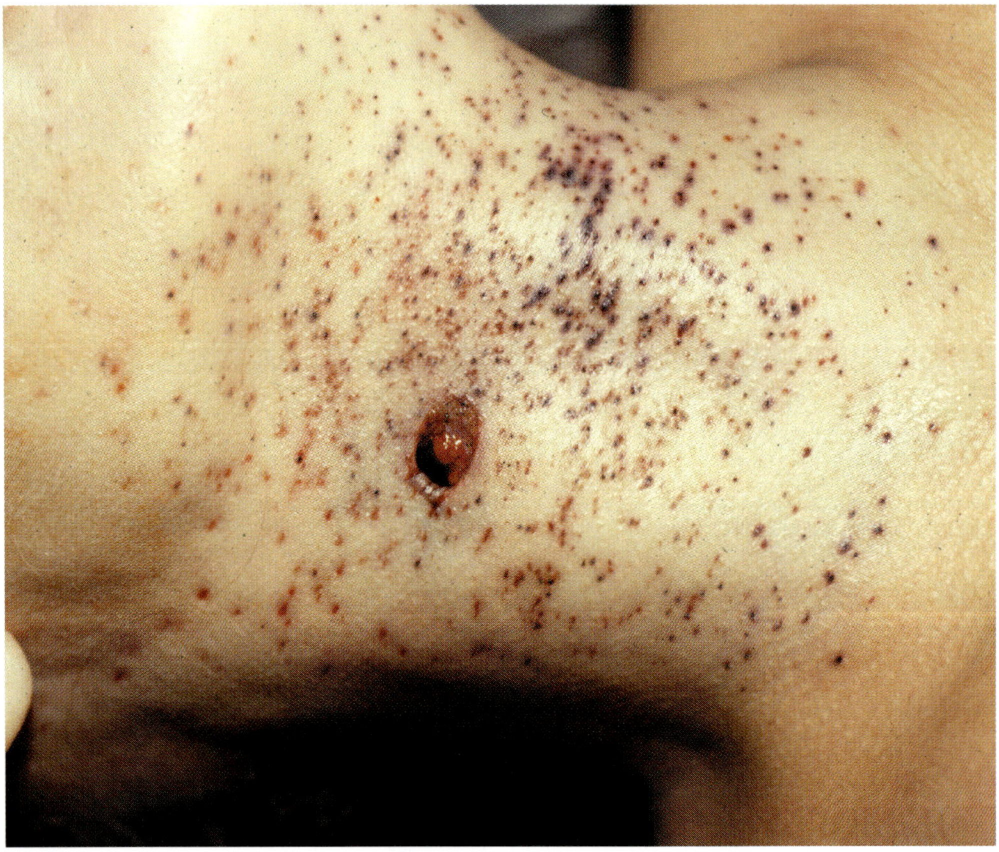

FIGURE 4.19 Intermediate-range gunshot wound. This refers to any gunshot wound with stippling (small dots surrounding the wound). Unburned portions of gunpowder tattoo the skin. The stippling must be measured in all directions. The firearms examiner can then fire test patterns with the same gun and ammunition at known distances. These patterns can be compared to the unknown pattern on the body, and the distance can be estimated.

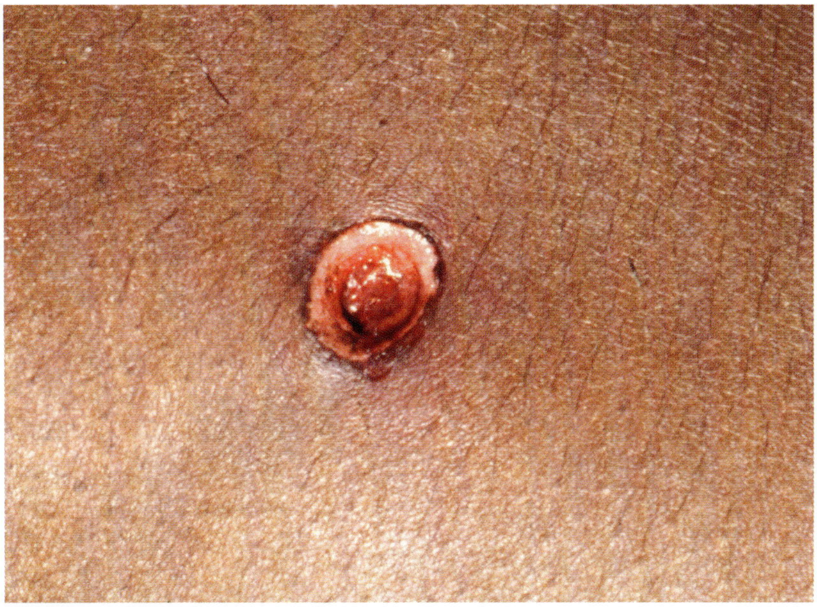

FIGURE 4.20 Undetermined-range gunshot wound. This gunshot wound has no surrounding soot or stippling; therefore, the range cannot be determined.

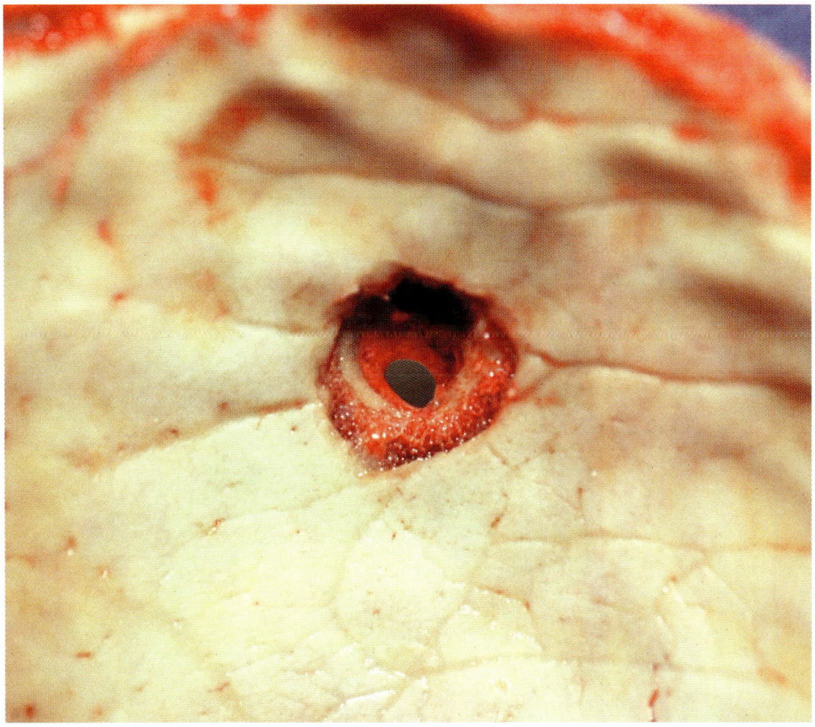

FIGURE 4.21 Entrance wound of the skull. The bullet path began behind the page and moved toward the reader. The bullet cored out a wedge of bone in front of it as it traveled. The pointed end of the wedge occurred at the point of entry, and the base was produced as the bullet exited the skull.

5 External Examination: Specific Body Areas

OVERALL "GESTALT"

After the body has been undressed and carefully cleaned, the pathologist steps back from the body and looks at the overall position or shape of the body (habitus). Is the body symmetrical? Is there morbid obesity, or is the frame extremely thin (indicative of cachexia)? Is there an overall deformity? For example, is the body in a fetal position? Is there something amiss or out of place? This is also a good time for the pathologist to reflect on what has been done to this point and what is about to be done.

SKIN

The skin is technically an organ per se. It is the organ that is most carefully assessed during the external examination. The skin acts as an outward sentinel or "red flag" for deep injuries or diseases within the body. The skin of the individual in Figure 5.1A shows a brown pigmentation in the axilla ("armpit"), a condition known as *acanthosis nigricans*. Also on the trunk are multiple brown, greasy-looking benign moles, known as seborrheic keratoses (Figure 5.1A, Figure 5.1B). Observation of this number of lesions alerts the pathologist to look for an internal cancer, usually of the gastrointestinal tract. In fact, this unfortunate individual had carcinoma of the colon (Figure 5.1C).

HAIR

Hair color is noted for identification. Hair roots can be used for DNA identification; at least 100 hairs must be pulled, not cut. Hair can contain trace evidence or gross evidence, such as the knife used to murder this individual (Figure 5.2A, Figure 5.2B). Toxicologic analysis of hair is useful for diagnosing chronic drug use or poisoning.

SCALP

An injury of the scalp is often the sentinel to deeper injuries, like skull fractures, brain contusions, and hematomas. Hair can cover injuries, particularly those that do not bleed, so a careful examination must be undertaken. Small-caliber gunshot wounds are notoriously difficult to find in thick hair. Scalp injuries on the back of the head can be easily overlooked (Figure 5.3). In order to see a scalp wound and photograph it properly, the hair around the wound is carefully shaved (Figure 5.4). The wound in Figure 5.3 is a laceration with an abrasion of the margin. The skull below this area in the same individual revealed a fracture in the back of the head, or occipital bone (Figure 5.5). The opposite part of the brain, or frontal lobe, shows contusions, indicating that the person fell backward and was not struck in the head. Figure 5.6 shows that this is a contrecoup injury (also see Chapter 9).

FACE

The face is dissected only in rare cases, e.g., to retrieve a bullet or other evidence. Every attempt should be made not to cut or alter the face, both out of respect for the individual and in consideration of viewing at the funeral service.

Facial injuries can be important in determining who was driving when multiple individuals, usually unbelted, die in a motor vehicle crash. Identifying the driver can be important if the vehicle was operated unlawfully, e.g., the driver was under the influence of alcohol. Automotive side glass is tempered, not laminated like the windshield. When it breaks, automotive side glass shatters into many small cubes that tend to cause small cubic cuts and abrasions on the face. Hence, the driver tends to have side glass injuries on the left side of the face. These injuries, as always, do not prove who was the driver or passenger and must be looked at in the context of the entire case (Figure 5.7).

EYES

The eye (iris) color is recorded, and the eyes are examined for hemorrhage. Small punctuate (pointlike) hemorrhages in the conjunctiva (white part of the eye) often suggest an asphyxial cause of death (Figure 5.8). Yellow conjunctiva (jaundice) might indicate liver disease or hemolysis, a disorder of many different causes in which the blood cells are broken apart in the body. The soft tissues around the eye (orbit) are very vascular. Blunt force to the area can easily cause contusion (a "black eye"), relative to many other areas of the body. Orbital soft tissue hemorrhage can also be seen in skull fractures involving the base of the frontal bone, in particular (Figure 5.9). This point illustrates the aim of the external exam: the outward hemorrhage directs the pathologist to look inward for a cause.

NOSE

The nasal cartilage can be fractured in traumatic injuries; therefore, palpation and increased range of motion can indicate fracture. Drug residues can be seen in the nares. The chronic snorting of drugs can damage the nasal mucosa.

MOUTH

The mouth can be tightly clenched due to rigor mortis. In such cases it is difficult to open. Examination of the mouth after rigor is released is much easier. The teeth are examined, and visible teeth are catalogued (Figure 5.10A). Unusual teeth or dental appliances can be used to make an identification. Dental caries (cavities) are noted. Drug residue may be seen, such as in cases of drug abuse or overdose. In sexual assault cases, oral examination and swabs are taken to look for spermatozoa. In suffocation and strangulation cases, there are often injuries in the mouth (Figure 5.10B). These injuries can occur when the perpetrator forcibly holds the mouth closed.

NECK

The skin of the anterior neck is examined for contusions or abrasions that might suggest manual or ligature strangulation (Figure 5.11A). The thyroid gland is palpated in the lower lateral neck (Figure 5.11B). The neck is manually examined for tumor masses and enlarged lymph nodes (Figure 5.11C). The neck's range of motion is checked. A highly flexible range of motion is abnormal during rigor mortis and reminds the pathologist to look for a fracture during internal examination.

CHEST

The chest is examined for symmetry and size (Figure 5.12A). Patients with emphysema and other chronic diseases often have an expanded, or "barrel," chest. Crepitus, or a crackling sound, indicates subcutaneous air from a pneumothorax. Rib fractures can be palpated as well. In severe chest injuries, such as from a high-speed motor vehicle crash, the chest can appear collapsed (Figure 5.12B).

BREASTS

The skin and nipple are observed for masses and ulcerations. The breast is palpated for masses and tumors (Figure 5.13A). The axilla, or armpit, is examined for enlarged lymph nodes. Breast cancers commonly spread to these axillary lymph nodes (Figure 5.13B, Figure 5.13C).

ABDOMEN

The abdomen is visually examined for distention, or bloating. Victims who have had cardiopulmonary resuscitation often have distention in the epigastric area. This is a result of air going into the stomach. The abdomen can also become distended (Figure 5.14A) due to hemorrhage or ascites (Figure 5.14B). Ascites is the accumulation of fluid in the abdomen, occurring in conditions like cirrhosis of the liver. Distention can also be seen due to bowel rupture and extensive inflammation, alerting the pathologist to take microbiologic cultures when opening the abdomen.

The abdomen is a common place for scars. The pathologist should search for scars including gallbladder, appendectomy, and other surgical scars. The presence or absence of scars can be used to make an identification.

EXTREMITIES, HANDS, FINGERS, NAILS

The pathologist must focus on the extremities, hands, fingers, and nails. These areas are easily forgotten, probably because their examination rarely elicits the cause of death. However, these areas are often rich in trace evidence and in clues to the cause and manner of death. For example, the extremities bear the brunt of knife attacks. Victims often grab the knife and hold their hands in a defensive position to ward off the attack. These wounds are often referred to as defense wounds (Figure 5.15A). The hands, nails, and fingers can carry trace evidence from a weapon or a perpetrator, such as wood fragments, hair, and skin. For this reason, the hands must be carefully examined and the fingernails scraped. Careful examination could show a portion of a missing nail. The death scene could then be searched for this torn nail fragment (Figure 5.15B).

Clues to natural disease processes can be seen in the hands and fingers. In Figure 5.15C, splinter hemorrhages in the fingernail beds are an outer sign of vegetations on the aortic valve, a condition called bacterial endocarditis. In this condition, bacteria-laden thrombi break off the valve and travel in the arterial system to the ends of the fingers and, more ominously, to the brain (Figure 5.15D), causing an abscess.

BACK

Since bodies are not easy to turn over, examination of the back is sometimes overlooked. In order to prevent this, the back is examined ritualistically at the same point in every autopsy. The back is a large area covering the back of the chest, the back of the abdomen, and even the posterior portions of the neck and abdomen. If many or key injuries are seen while the body is in the supine position, the body is carefully turned prone (face down) for documentation and examination of these injuries. Occasionally, the anterior, or front portion, of the body is free of injuries, while the back contains a serious injury (Figure 5.16A, Figure 5.16B).

GENITALIA

The male genitalia are assessed for evidence of circumcision. This observation can be helpful in identification. The testes are assessed for tumors. Rarely, an undescended testis is noted. Injuries, such as abrasions or bite marks, can be seen in a sexual assault. If the penis has been traumatically severed, the resultant blood loss can be fatal.

The female genitalia are examined for tumors or developmental anomalies. In unnatural deaths, the female genitalia are examined for injuries from sexual assault. The sexual assault protocol includes an initial external examination for trace evidence such as hair. The vaginal area and rectum are examined for injuries (Figure 5.17A). The vagina, rectum, and surrounding areas are swabbed for semen or other secretions. The underpants and clothing are collected. The author has found commercially available sexual assault kits to be convenient since they contain more than enough material to do the examination (Figure 5.17B).

RECTUM/ANUS

Like the genitalia, the anus of both sexes is examined for sexual assault. Tumors and ulcerations are common findings in this region. In the bedridden, the sacral region, buttocks, and lateral ankles should be examined for pressure sores. The presence of such injuries might indicate elder abuse. Inflammatory bowel diseases, such as Crohn's disease, can be seen from inspecting the anus (Figure 5.18).

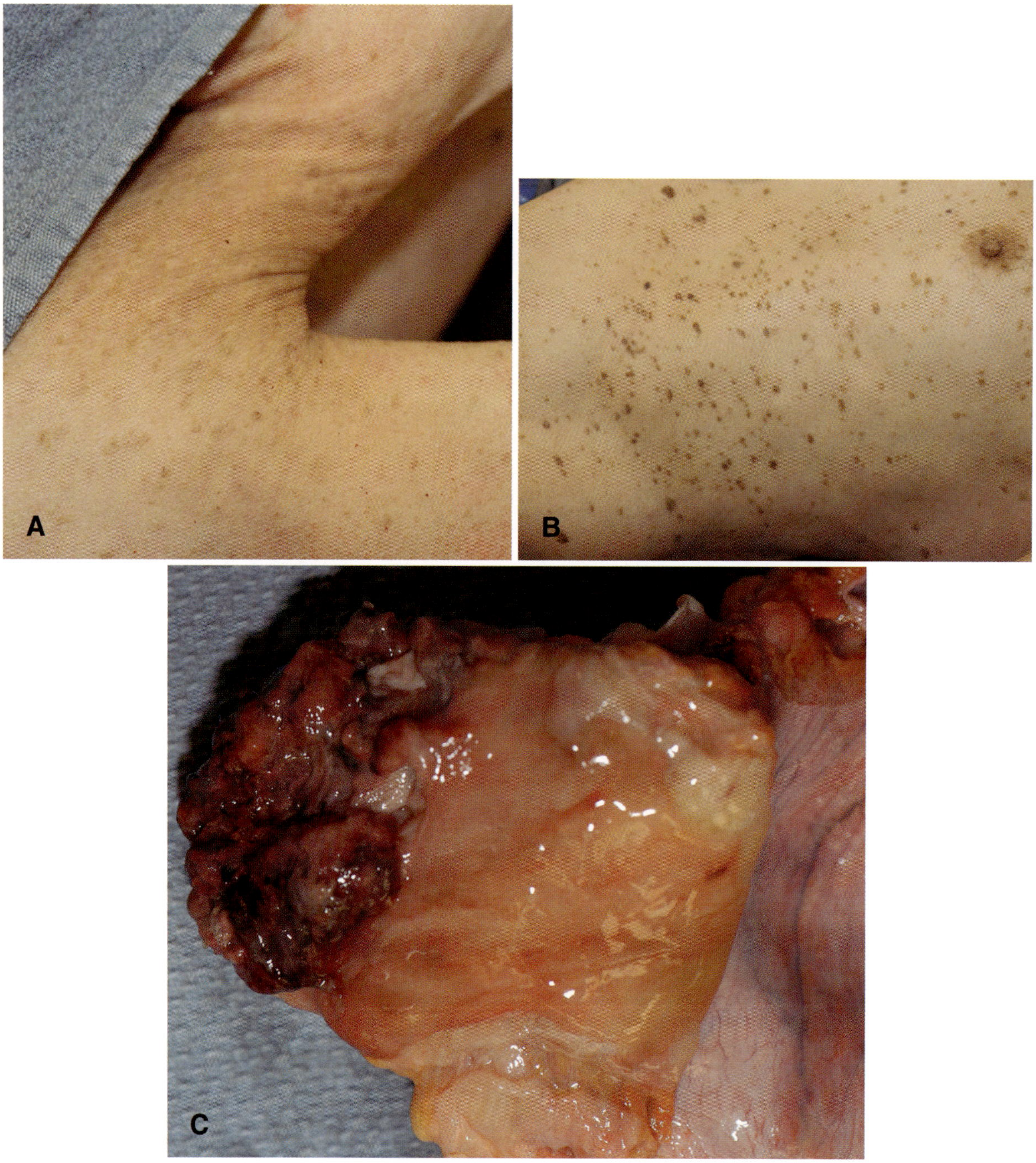

FIGURE 5.1 (A) *Acanthosis nigricans*. (B) Seborrheic keratoses. (C) Carcinoma of the colon. Dark pigmentation of the skin and multiple "greasy" keratoses on the body alert the pathologist to look internally for a visceral cancer. In the rectal-sigmoid colon of this patient, a carcinoma was found.

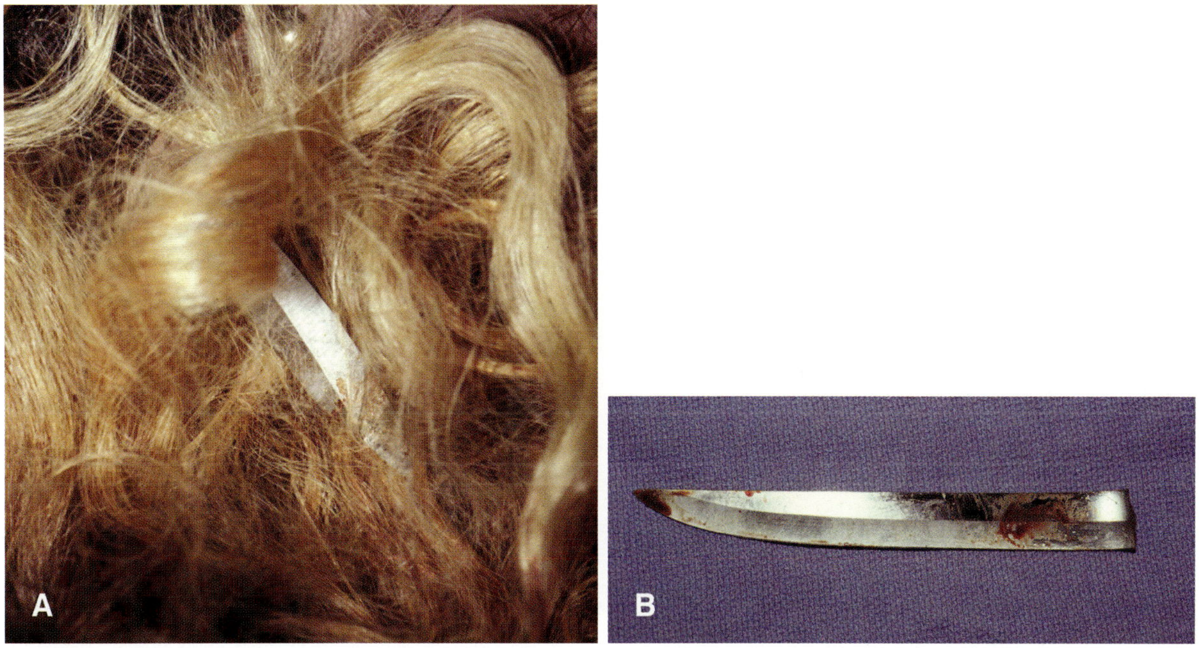

FIGURE 5.2 Broken knife found in the hair. **(A)** The hair must be carefully examined for evidence. **(B)** The murder weapon, a broken kitchen knife, was found in the hair of this victim.

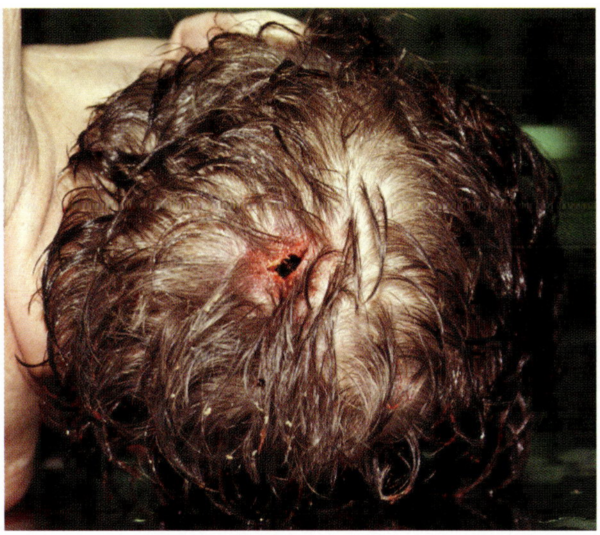

FIGURE 5.3 Laceration of the scalp. The blood has been washed out of the hair, exposing what appears to be a laceration. One cannot be sure until the hair around the wound is shaved and the wound more closely examined (see Figure 5.4).

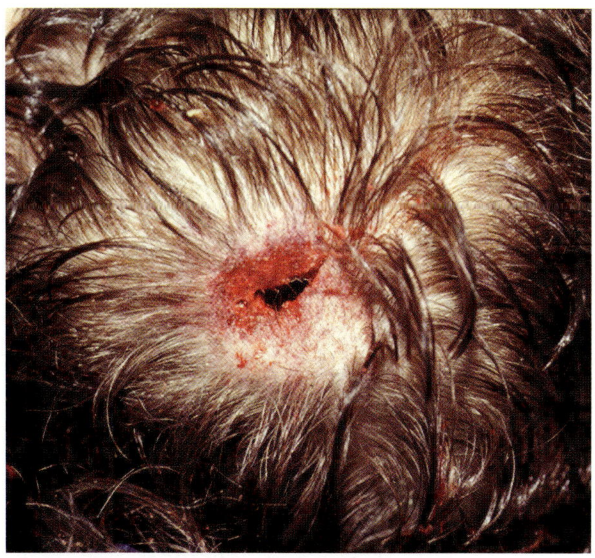

FIGURE 5.4 Close-up of laceration of the scalp. The hair around the wound has been shaved and the wound more carefully cleaned. One can see marginal abrasion, undermined margins, and tissue bridging. These findings, now clearly seen, demonstrate a laceration.

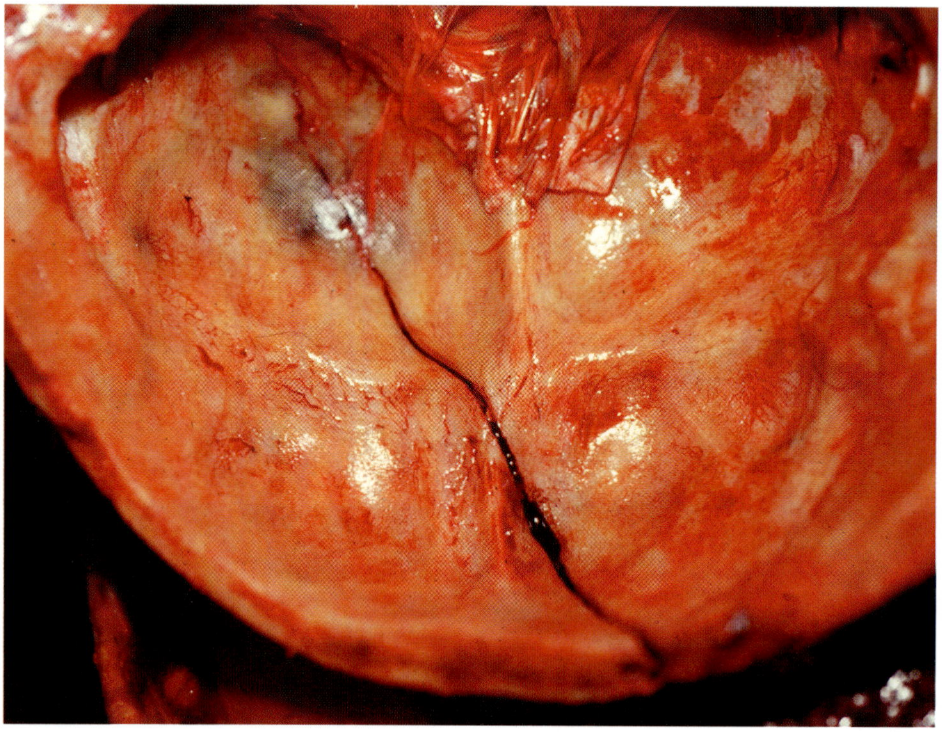

FIGURE 5.5 Fracture of the occipital bone of the skull. This fracture was discovered below the laceration shown in Figure 5.3 and Figure 5.4. One must conclude that this is a blunt force injury. The question remains: Was this person struck with a blunt force object, or was there a fall (see Figure 5.6)?

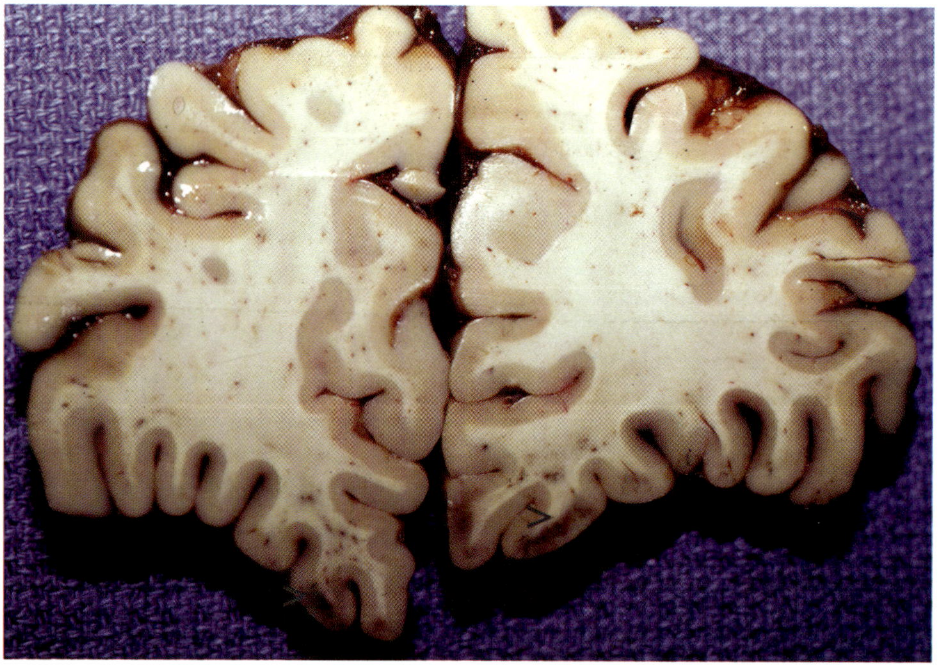

FIGURE 5.6 Contrecoup injury in the frontal lobe. Contusion hemorrhages can be seen at the arrows, near the bottom of the specimen. Their position indicates a contrecoup injury, meaning the victim fell backward, striking and fracturing the occipital bone. The brain is moveable inside the skull; when the skull is impacted, the moving brain can slap against the frontal skull base, producing contusion hemorrhages such as these.

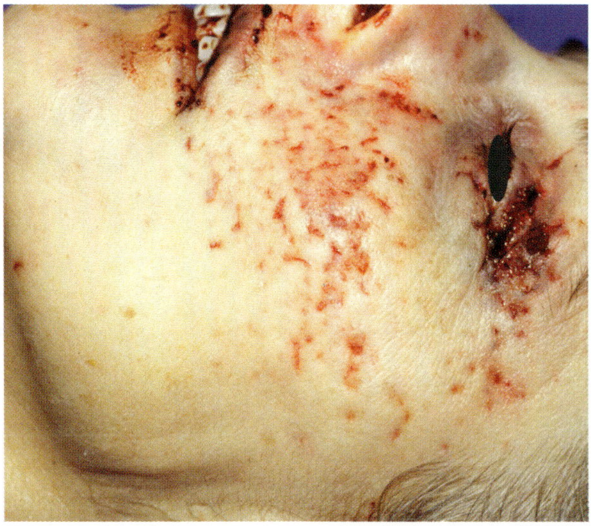

FIGURE 5.7 Side glass abrasions/lacerations. The face exam can be helpful in determining the driver in a motor vehicle crash. Since side glass is tempered, not laminated like windshield glass, it breaks up into small cubes upon impact, dicing the face. Often, but not always, injuries on the left side of the face indicate the driver, and those on the right side of the face indicate a passenger.

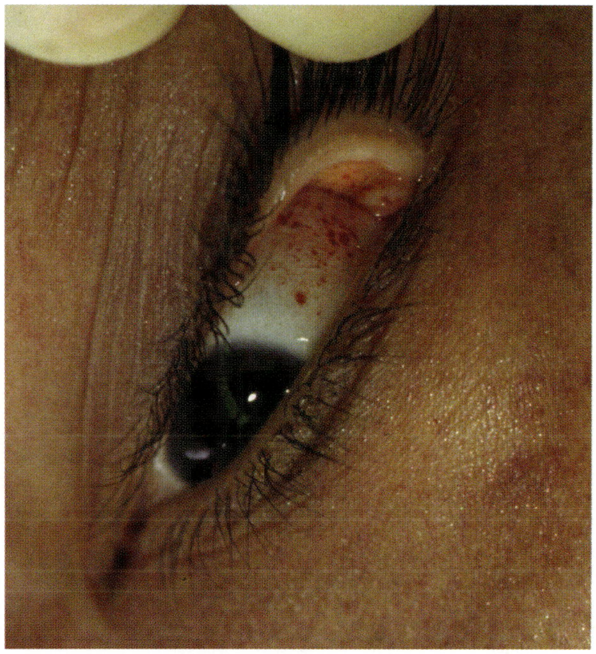

FIGURE 5.8 Conjunctival petechiae. Small pointlike hemorrhages in the conjunctiva, or clear membrane of the eye, are often seen in asphyxial deaths. These petechiae are due to hemorrhage of small vessels in the conjunctiva, caused by the increased vascular pressure associated with asphyxia.

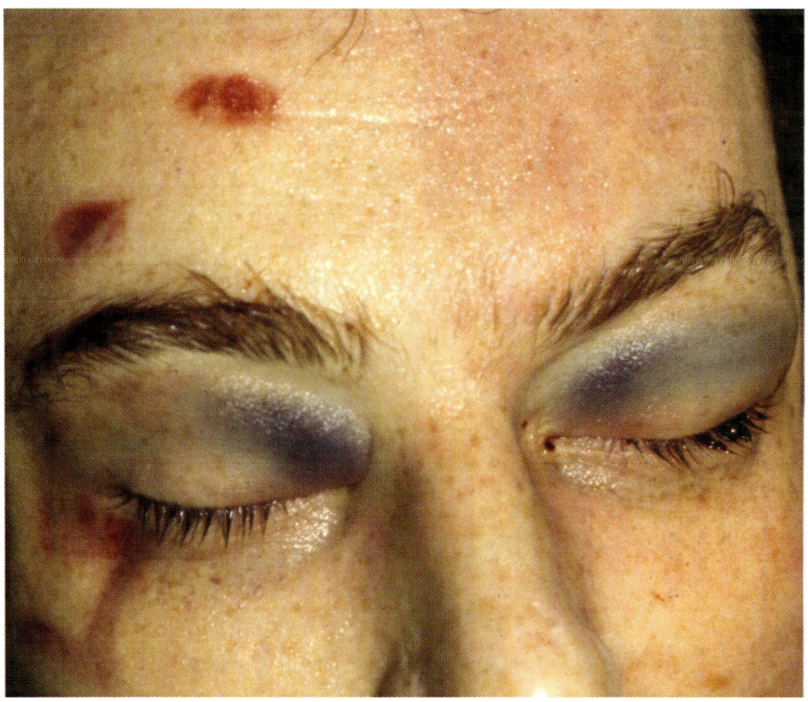

FIGURE 5.9 Orbital ecchymoses or "raccoon eyes." The darkening of the soft tissue around the eyes is due to blood accumulating in these soft tissues. This finding alerts the pathologist to search for fractures in the base of the skull, most likely the frontal bone or orbital roofs.

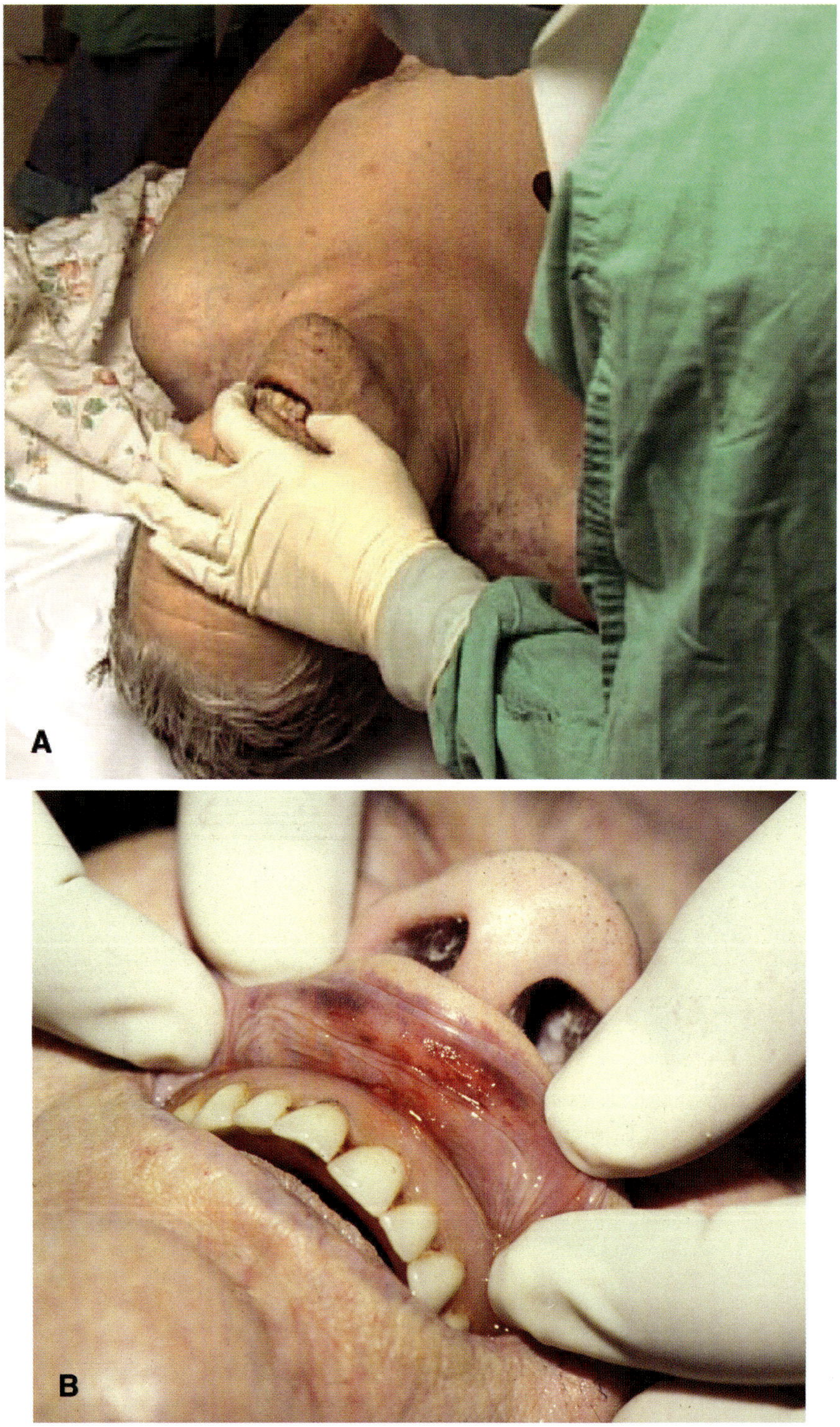

FIGURE 5.10 Examination of the mouth. **(A)** The mouth and teeth are examined for injuries and foreign material. The mouth is difficult to open in most autopsies because the jaw muscles are tightly clenched due to rigor mortis. **(B)** The upper lip shows contusion and abrasion in a victim who was strangled and suffocated. This injury was produced by external pressure on the mouth.

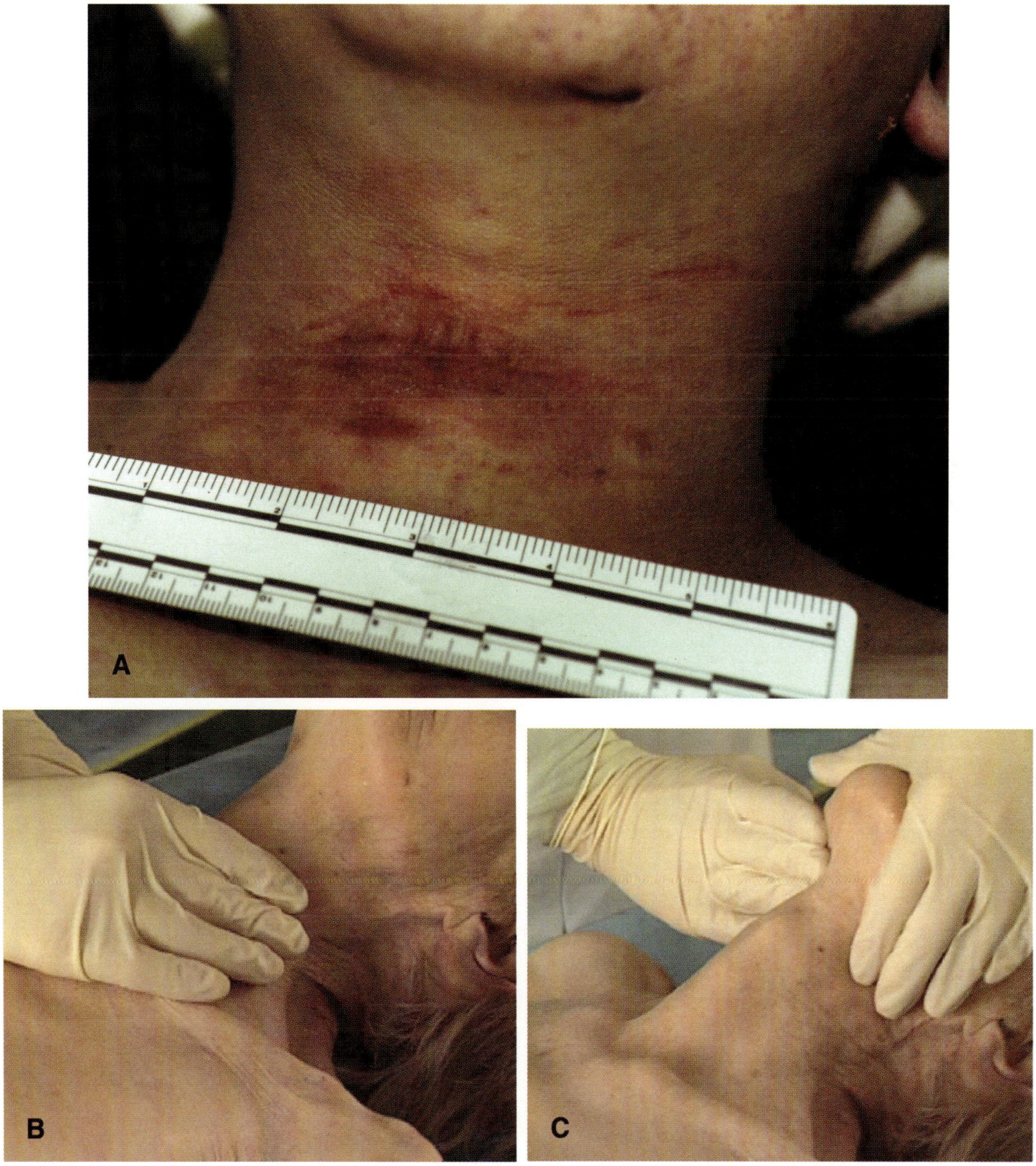

FIGURE 5.11 **(A) Neck abrasions and contusions in strangulation.** Multiple abrasions and contusions of the anterior neck are usually seen in strangulation injuries. Also, searching for internal injuries of the neck is essential to opine that these injuries are due to strangulation. **(B), (C) Examination of the neck.** The neck is palpated for masses, enlarged lymph nodes, and thyroid abnormalities. Tracheal deviation can indicate air in the chest or neck (pneumothorax and pneumomediastinum).

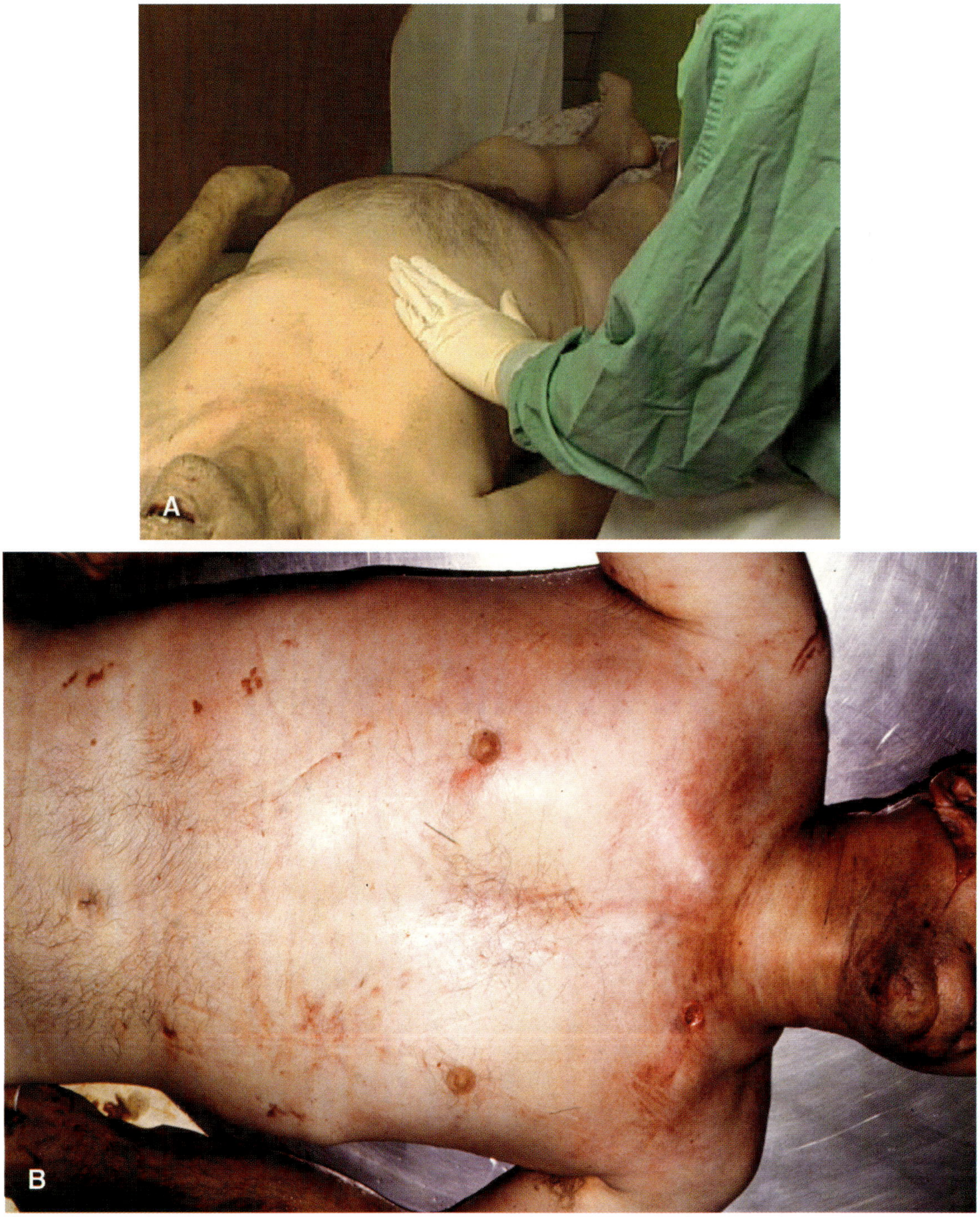

FIGURE 5.12 Examination of the chest. (A) The chest is examined for injuries, like rib fractures or crepitus due to air in the soft tissues. **(B)** The chest is flattened due to fracture of all the ribs anteriorly during a high-speed crash in excess of 100 mph; the airbag failed and the chest wall was crushed upon impact.

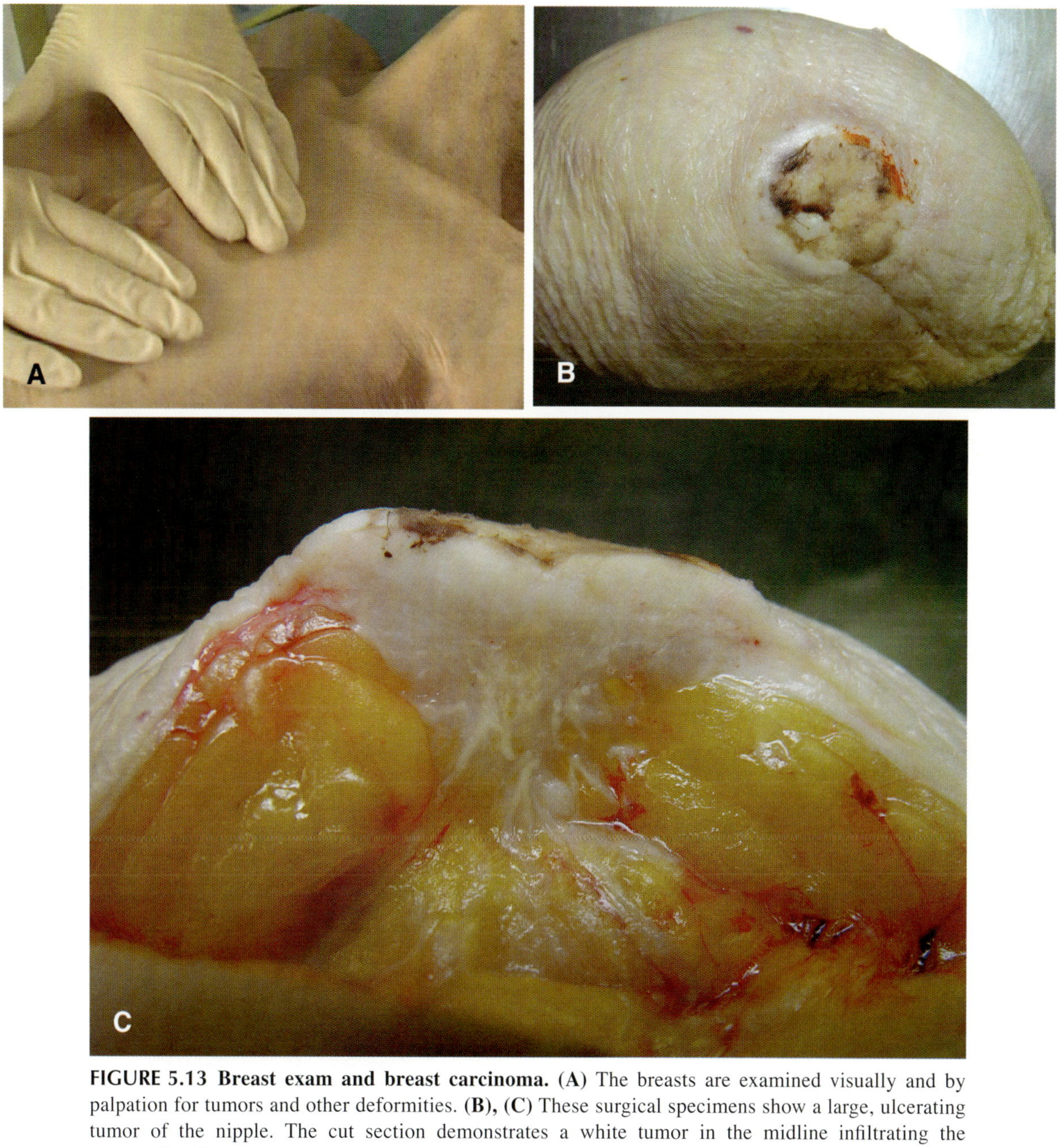

FIGURE 5.13 Breast exam and breast carcinoma. **(A)** The breasts are examined visually and by palpation for tumors and other deformities. **(B), (C)** These surgical specimens show a large, ulcerating tumor of the nipple. The cut section demonstrates a white tumor in the midline infiltrating the surrounding fat.

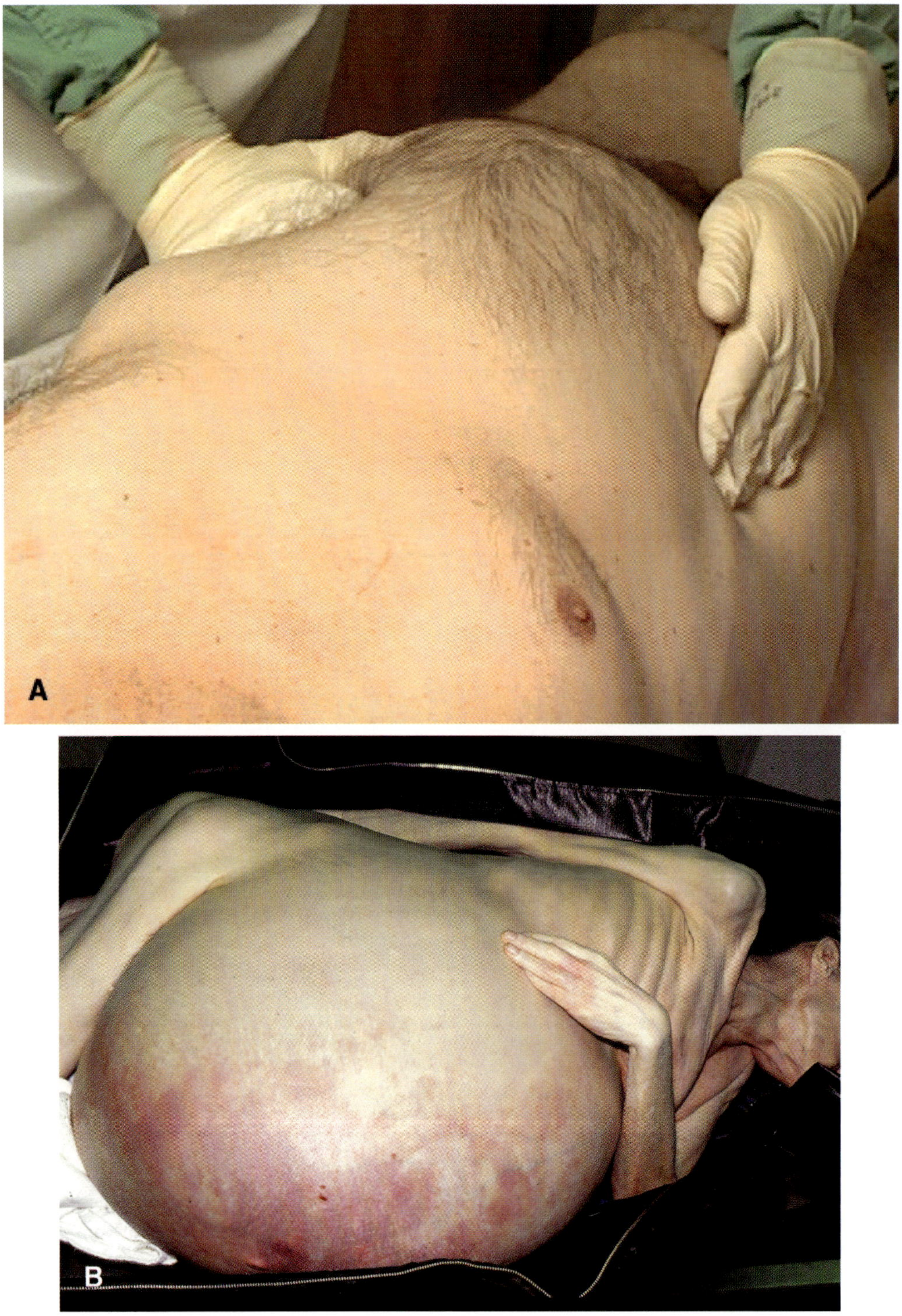

FIGURE 5.14 Abdominal examination. (A) The abdomen is visually examined for distention and other abnormalities. The abdomen is palpated for solid masses and enlargement of the spleen and liver. **(B)** The patient died from carcinoma of the ovary. The extremely distended abdomen is the result of excessive fluid in the abdominal cavity.

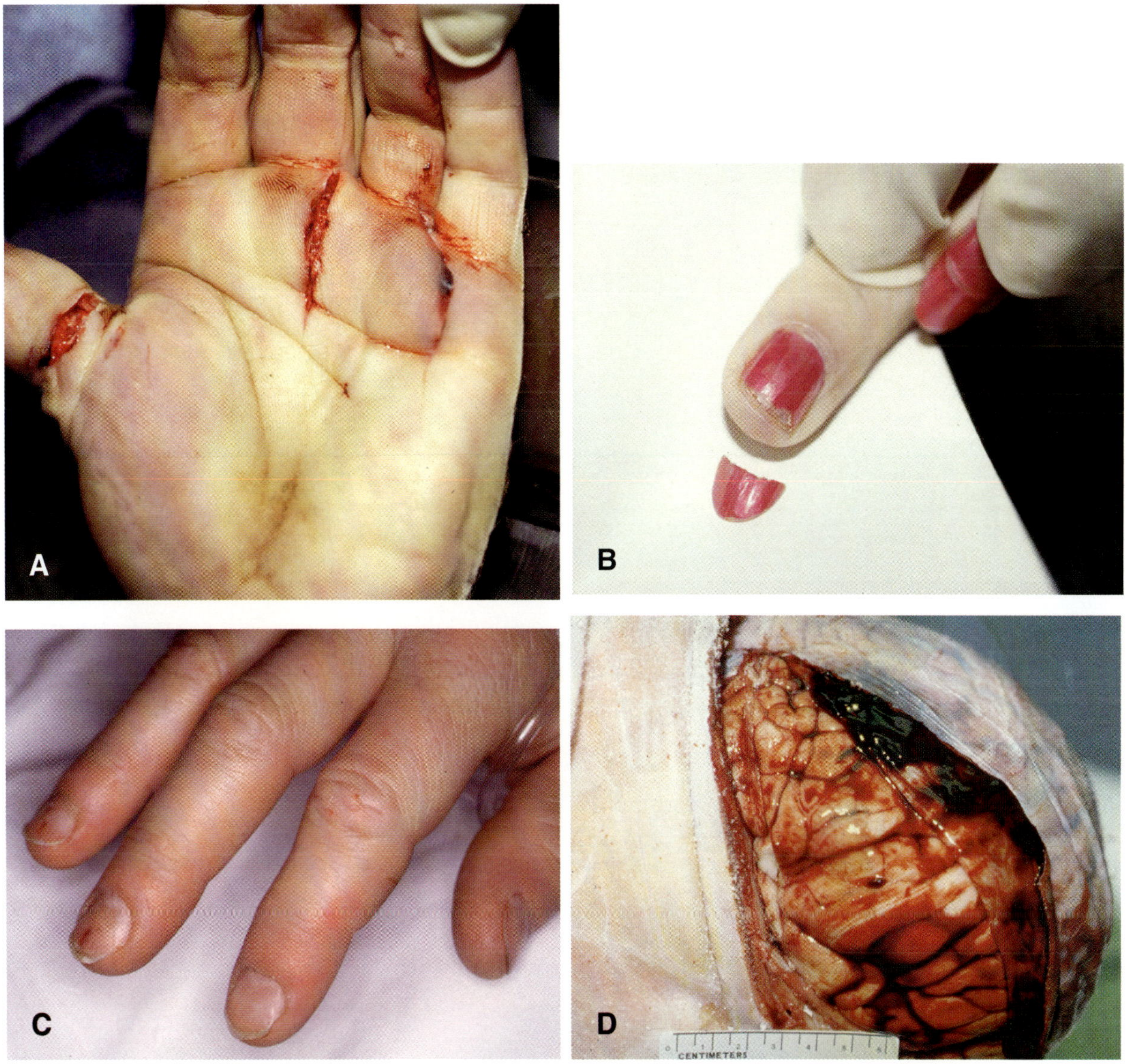

FIGURE 5.15 Examination of the hands and fingers. Examination of the hands is useful in both forensic and medical cases. The hands usually must be opened for examination, since rigor mortis often causes them to clench. **(A)** This figure shows defense cuts on the palmar surface of the hand, wounds obtained from defending against a knife attack. **(B)** The image depicts a finger and broken nail from a homicide victim. The broken nail was found at a second crime scene, where the victim was most likely assaulted. Finding and matching this missing nail implicated a suspect in this strangulation homicide. **(C)** The splinter hemorrhages in the middle and ring finger nail beds are signs of bacterial endocarditis and vegetations on the mitral or aortic heart valves. In this condition, small bacteria-laden emboli are disseminated throughout the arterial system into the nail beds, kidneys, and brain. **(D)** The brain shows hemorrhage from septic infarct, abcess, and stroke.

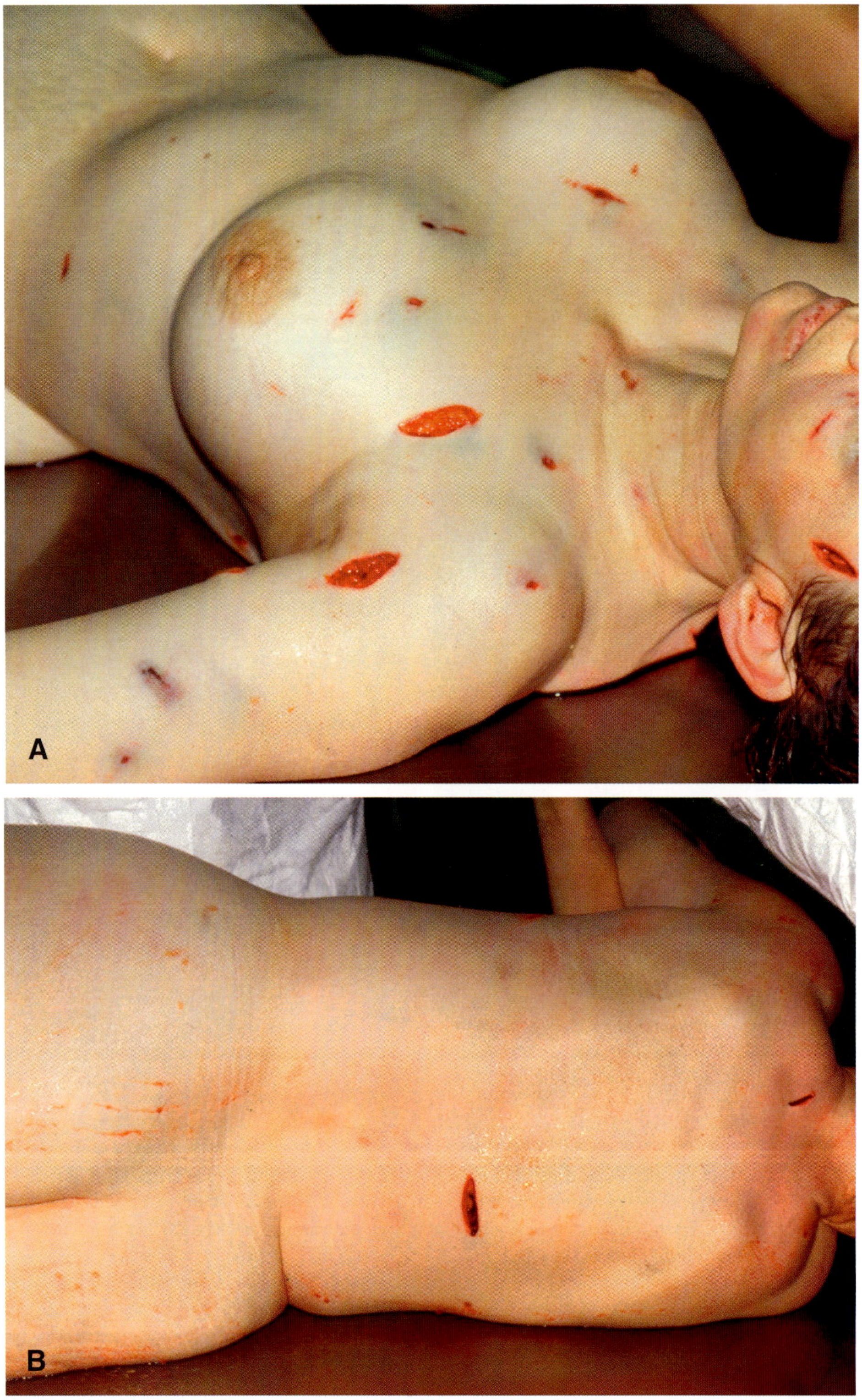

FIGURE 5.16 (A), (B) Stabs wounds found upon examination of the back. Bodies are difficult to turn over, so there is a natural tendency to forget to look at the back. Autopsy protocols are designed so that the back exam is not overlooked; in the case depicted, one would miss at least two stab wounds.

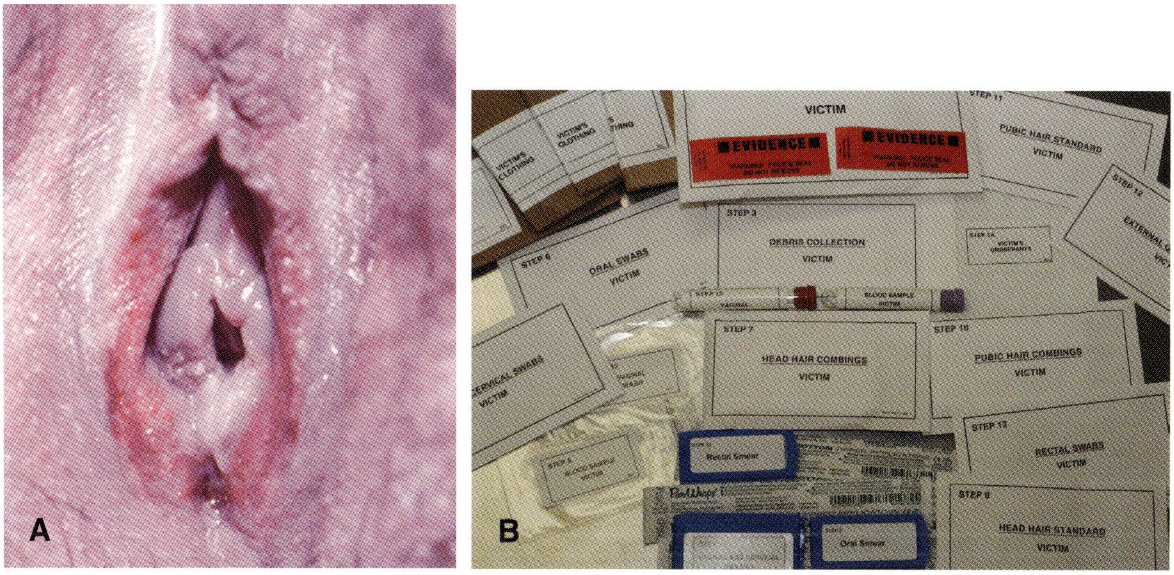

FIGURE 5.17 (A) Abrasions found upon vaginal examination. Examination for sexual assault is essential in suspicious deaths. Excessive abrasion, laceration, or contusion of the genitalia usually indicates assault. The labia here show a great deal of abrasion. **(B) Sexual assault kit.** A full sexual assault kit was obtained during this case, further confirming the assault. The victim was strangled to death during the assault.

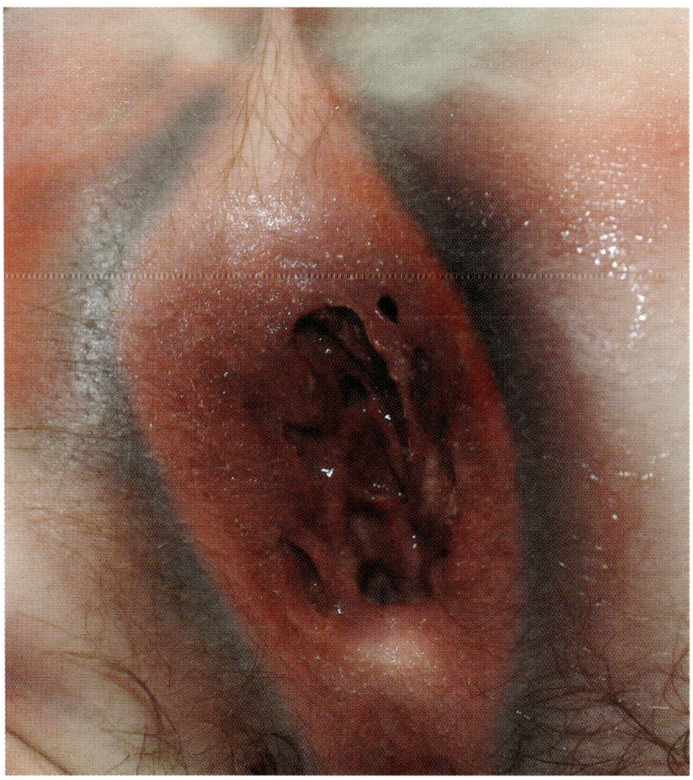

FIGURE 5.18 Inflammatory bowel disease found upon anal examination. The anus is examined for assault and for medical conditions. The injury depicted shows multiple ulcerations and fistulae caused by inflammatory bowel disease, most likely Crohn's disease. Inflammatory bowel disease causes ulcerations in the bowel wall and mucosa. If untreated, this disease can cause peritonitis and death.

6 Internal Examination: Opening of Body Cavities and Initial Assessment

As has been shown, the external exam provides clues about what the pathologist can expect to find inside the body. During the internal exam, these leads are investigated. As with any investigation, some findings are completely unexpected. This means that the pathologist must examine all tissues carefully and objectively. Going into an autopsy with preconceived notions about potential findings can cause the pathologist to overlook the unexpected. For this reason, each internal exam includes, at minimum, an examination of the following:

- Heart, including coronary arteries and heart valves
- Chest cavity and mediastinum
- Lungs and lung hilum
- Liver and gallbladder
- Spleen
- Stomach and esophagus
- Small and large intestines
- Bowel mesentery
- Peritoneal cavity
- Body walls
- Aorta and its branches
- Kidneys and adrenal glands
- Bladder
- Prostate
- Uterus and ovaries
- Neck organs, including larynx and thyroid gland
- Vertebral column
- Skull
- Brain and its coverings

This is a general list. Special cases or circumstances might require a more focused study of a specific tissue or organ system.

During the internal exam, the pathologist looks continuously for injuries and diseases with every cut of the knife. All of the senses, except taste, are used. Tumors are often hard and can be palpated with the fingers. Hemorrhage can be seen in tissues that have deep, traumatic contusions. A smell of bitter almonds might indicate cyanide poisoning. Delicate crackles heard in the chest and mediastinal tissues indicate air in the tissues, or pneumothorax. The dissection is a careful, stepwise examination of the tissues and organs, usually performed in the same way so that nothing is forgotten. Most pathologists use their own routine protocols for dissection for this reason.

The reader should follow the figures page by page to experience the actual steps that are taken during the autopsy dissection.

DISSECTION OF THE SKIN AND OPENING OF THE CHEST AND ABDOMEN

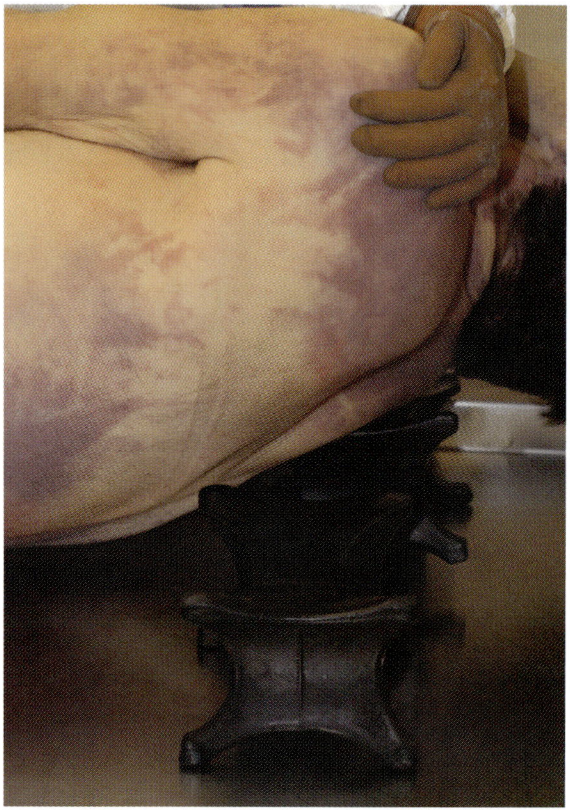

FIGURE 6.1 Placing the body on blocks. The shoulder region of the body is placed on rubber blocks. This freely exposes the neck. Also, the shoulders naturally spread apart in this position.

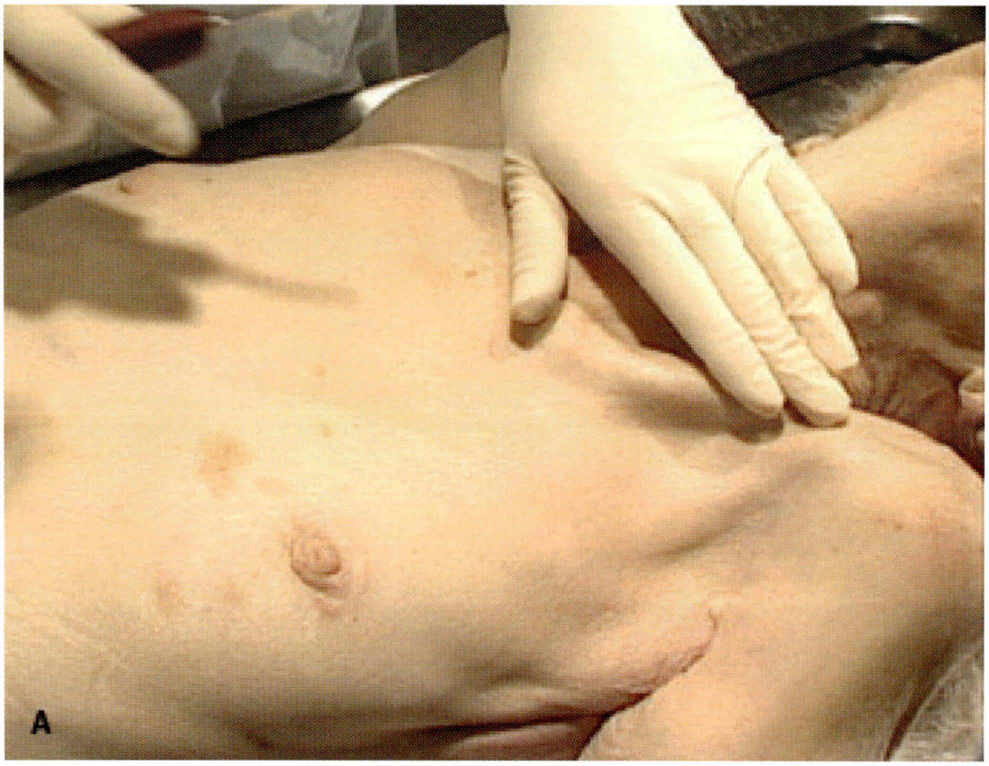

FIGURE 6.2 (A)–(C) Initial "Y" incision. The body is opened with a Y-shaped incision extending from one shoulder to the other. The yellow subcutaneous fat is exposed.

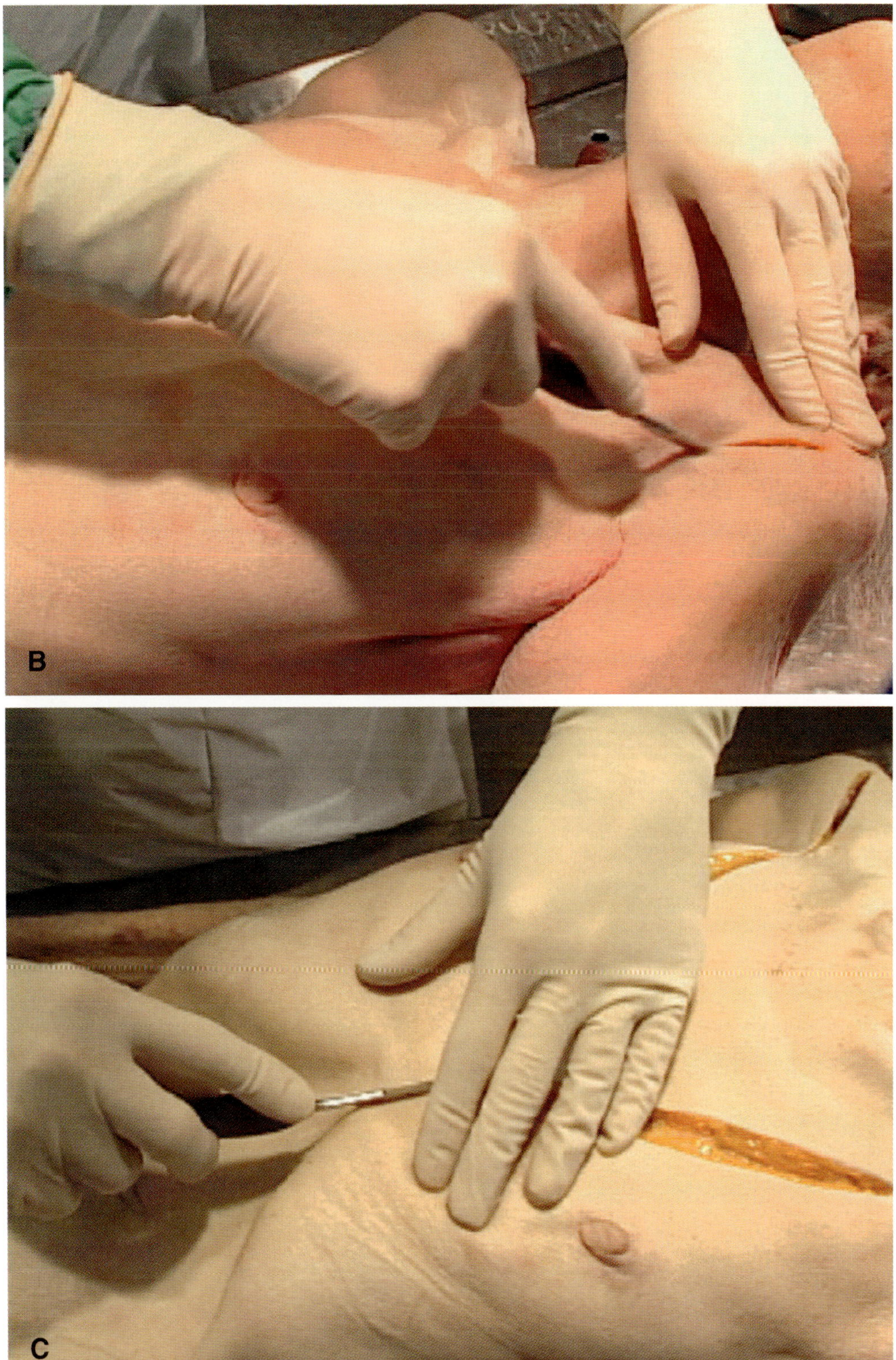

FIGURE 6.2 (CONTINUED) **Initial "Y" incision.** The body is opened with a Y-shaped incision extending from one shoulder to the other. The yellow subcutaneous fat is exposed.

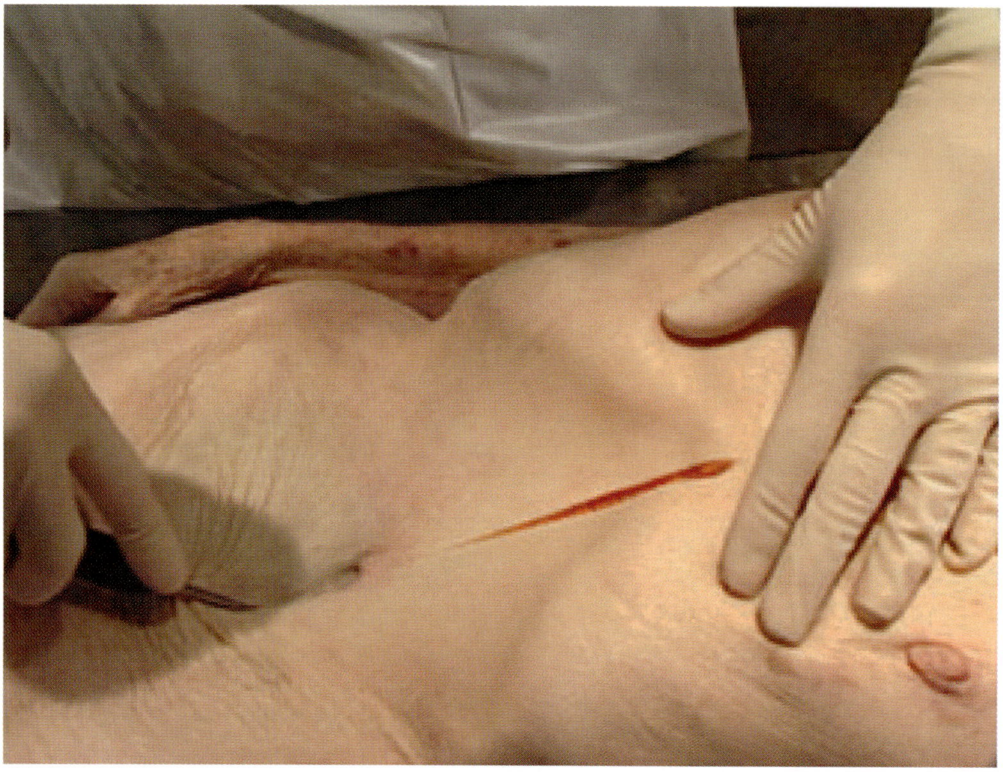

FIGURE 6.3 Midline incision. The incision is extended to the midline abdomen, down to the midline of the pubic bone (pubic symphysis).

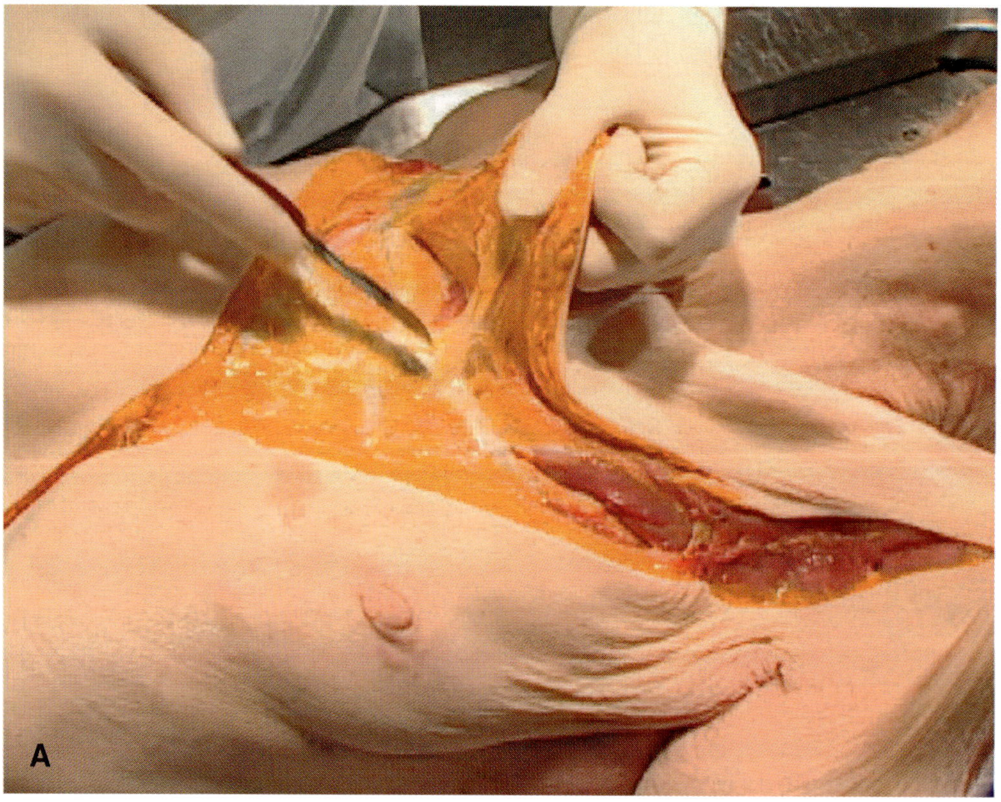

FIGURE 6.4 (A)–(C) Dissection of chest skin and soft tissue. The skin and subcutaneous tissue are dissected back to expose the underlying muscle and bone. The natural yellow color of the subcutaneous fat can be seen here. The soft tissue at the base of the neck can be seen in Figure 6.4C.

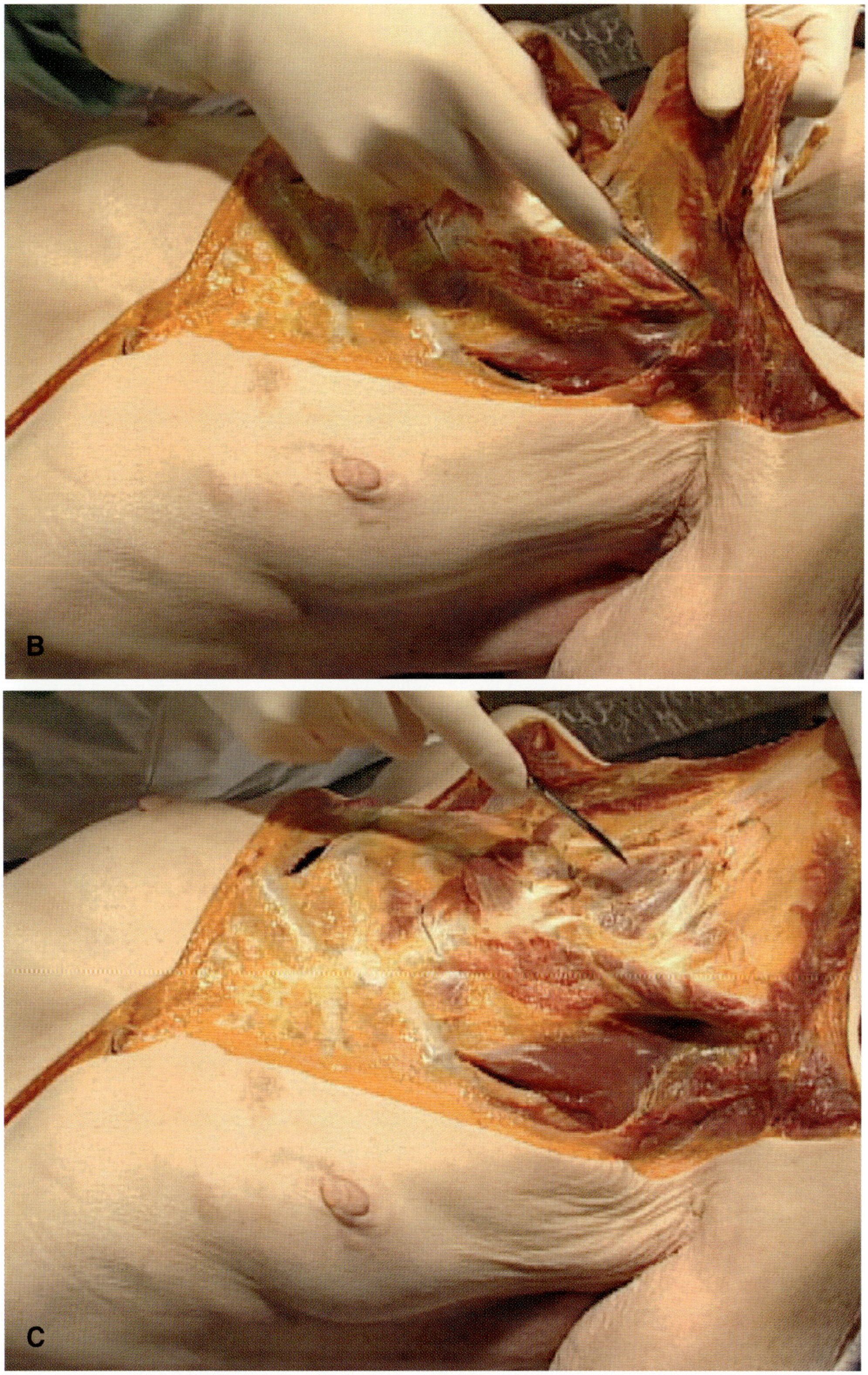

FIGURE 6.4 (CONTINUED) (A)–(C) Dissection of chest skin and soft tissue. The skin and subcutaneous tissue are dissected back to expose the underlying muscle and bone. The natural yellow color of the subcutaneous fat can be seen here. The soft tissue at the base of the neck can be seen in Figure 6.4C.

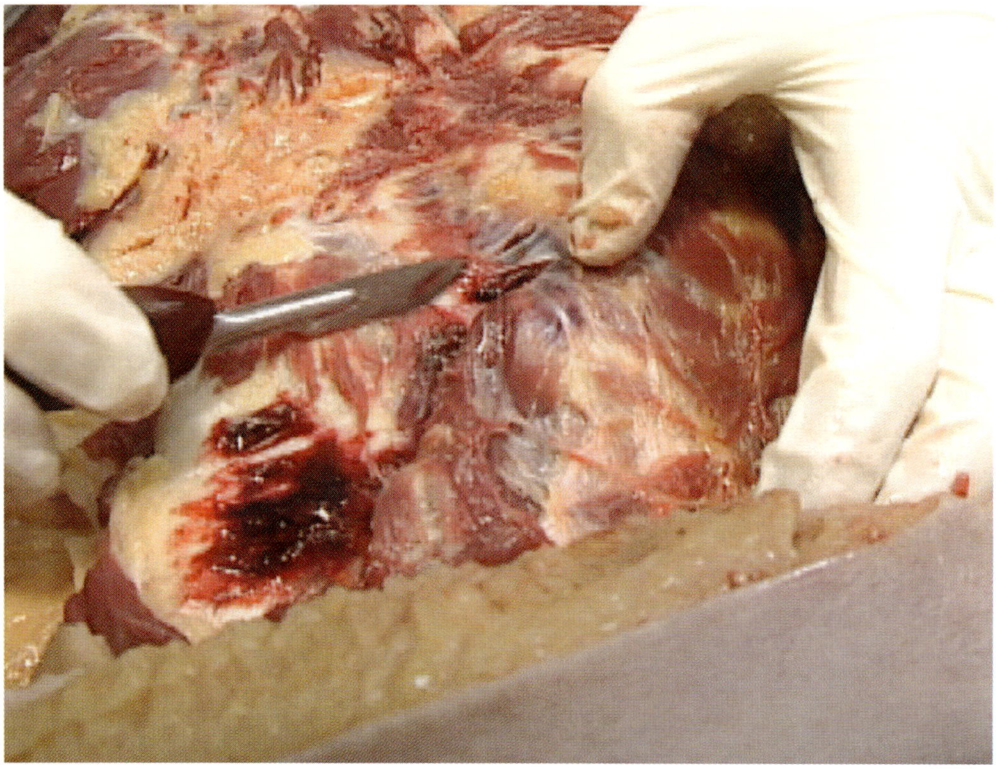

FIGURE 6.5 CPR fracture of the ribs. The pathologist is constantly looking for injuries. This minimal focal hemorrhage is a result of rib fracture due to cardiopulmonary resuscitation. Fracture of these ribs during life would yield extensive, not focal, hemorrhage.

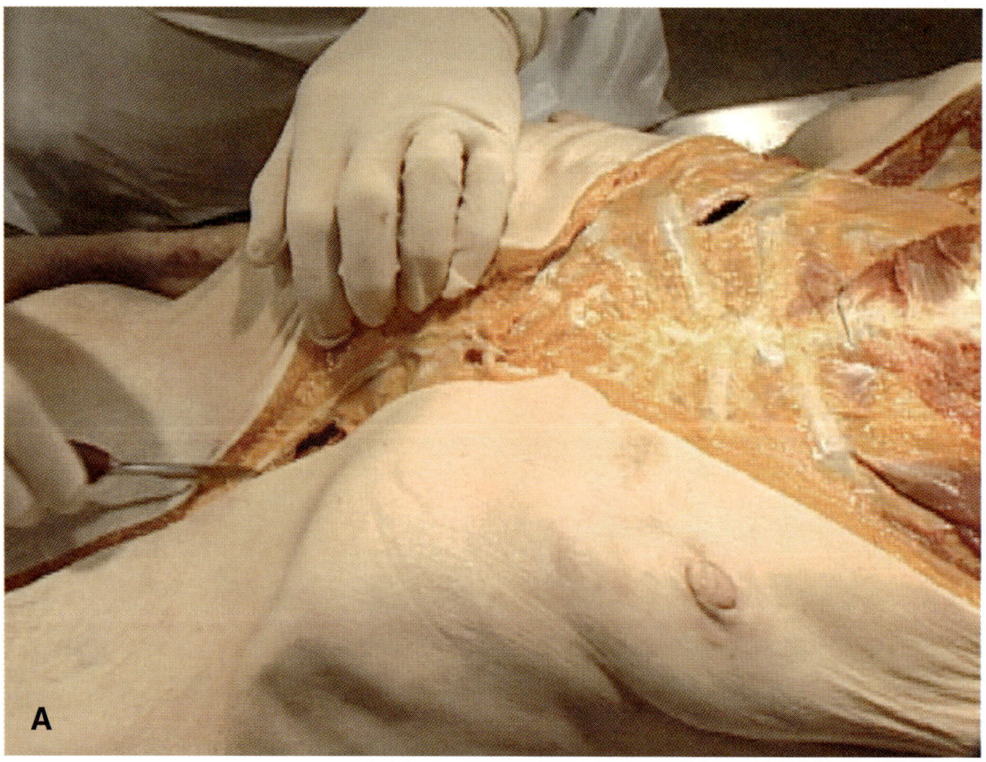

FIGURE 6.6 (A)–(C) Opening of the abdominal cavity. The abdomen is opened, exposing the underlying viscera. The pathologist is constantly looking for fluid, hemorrhage, or signs of inflammation in the abdominal cavity.

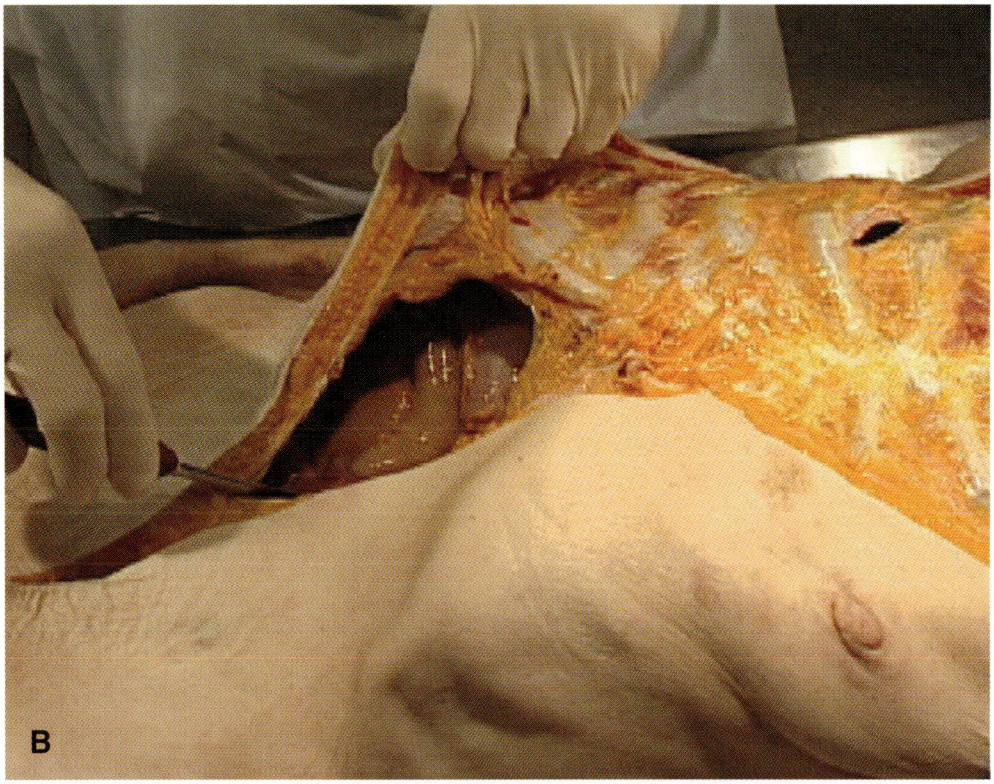

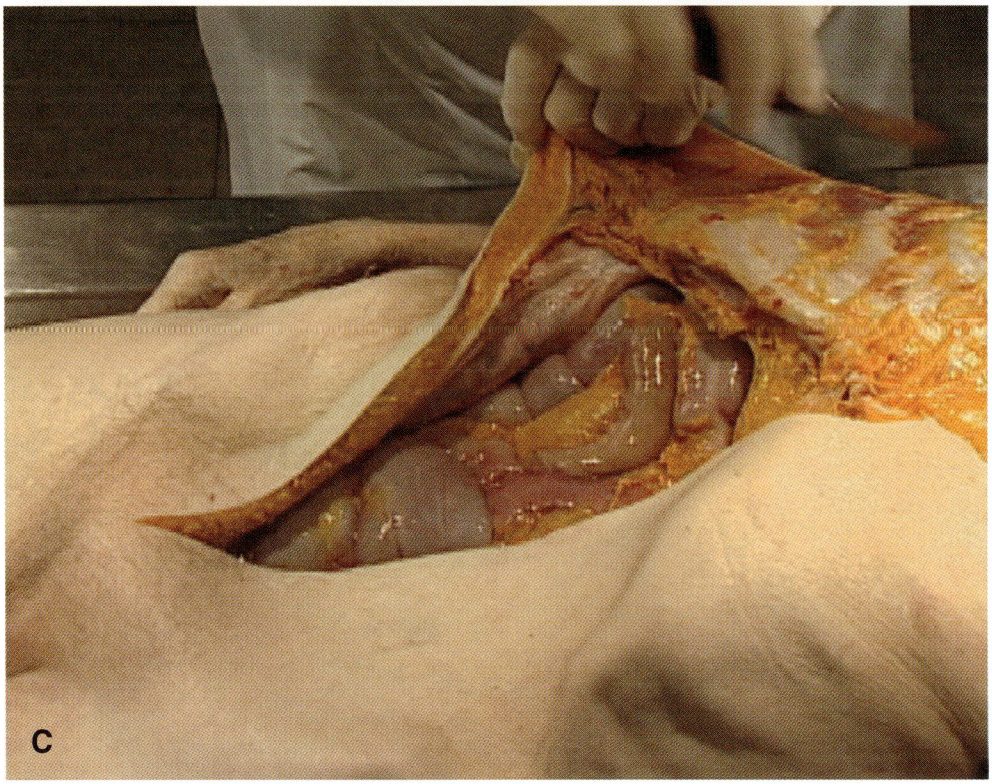

FIGURE 6.6 (CONTINUED) (A)–(C) Opening of the abdominal cavity. The abdomen is opened, exposing the underlying viscera. The pathologist is constantly looking for fluid, hemorrhage, or signs of inflammation in the abdominal cavity.

FIGURE 6.7 Pus in the abdomen. This figure shows yellowish pus, a sign of peritonitis. Microbiologic cultures can be taken to diagnose the source of infection. Also, the abdomen will be searched for an anatomical source of this fluid, such as a perforated stomach ulcer.

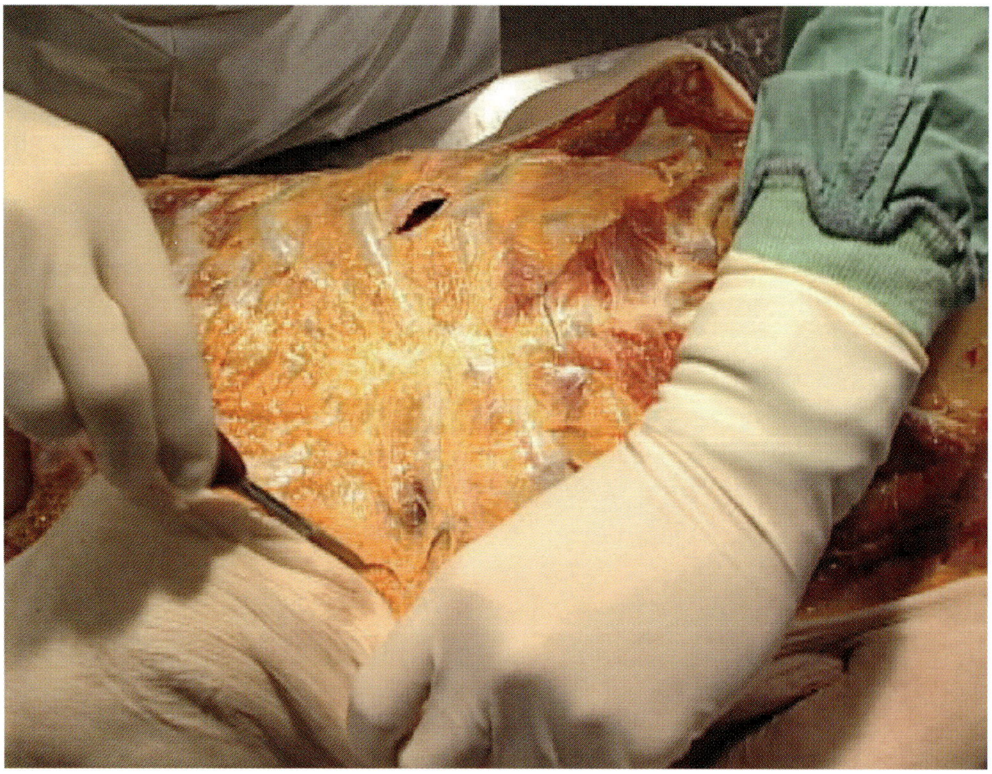

FIGURE 6.8 Marking the ribs. The ribs are marked for sawing.

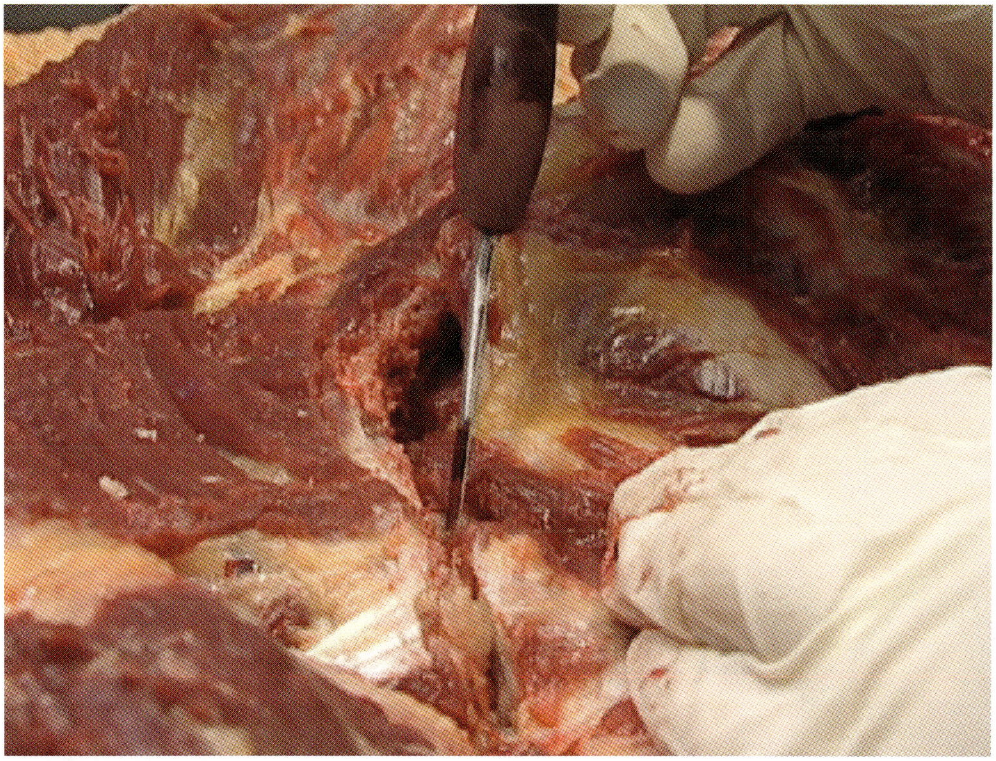

FIGURE 6.9 Sternoclavicular joint cut. The sternoclavicular joint is often cut because the thick joint can be difficult to saw.

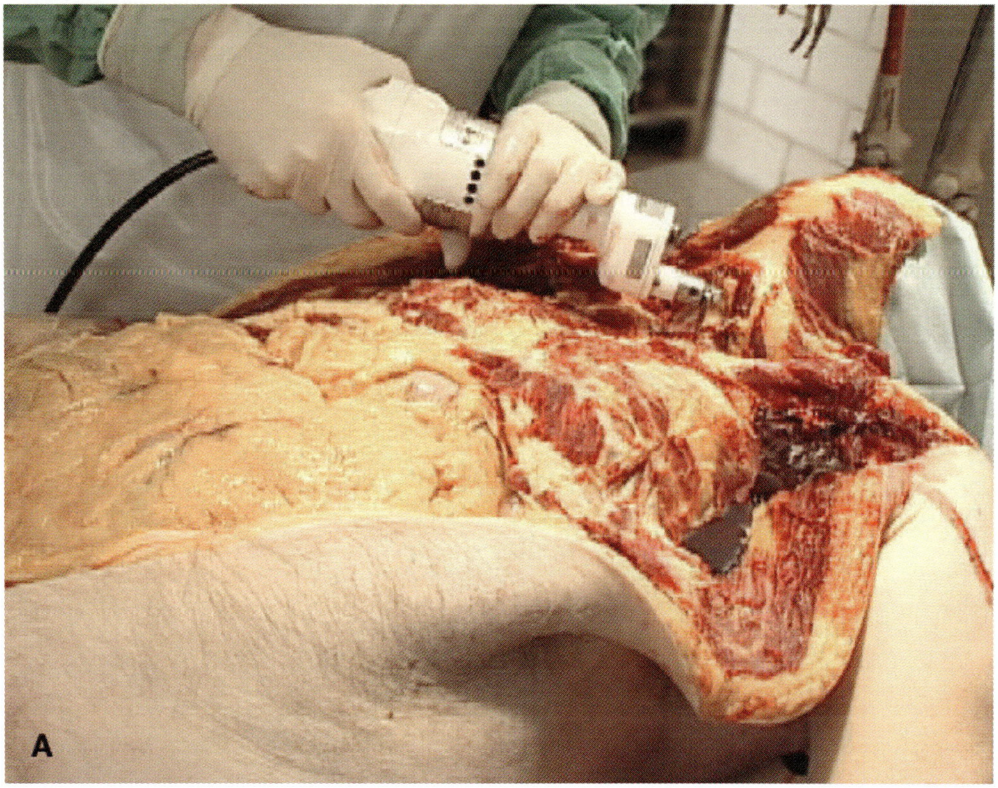

FIGURE 6.10 (A)–(C) Opening of the ribs with a bone saw. The ribs are sawed and opened with wide arcs to facilitate access to the chest organs and tissues.

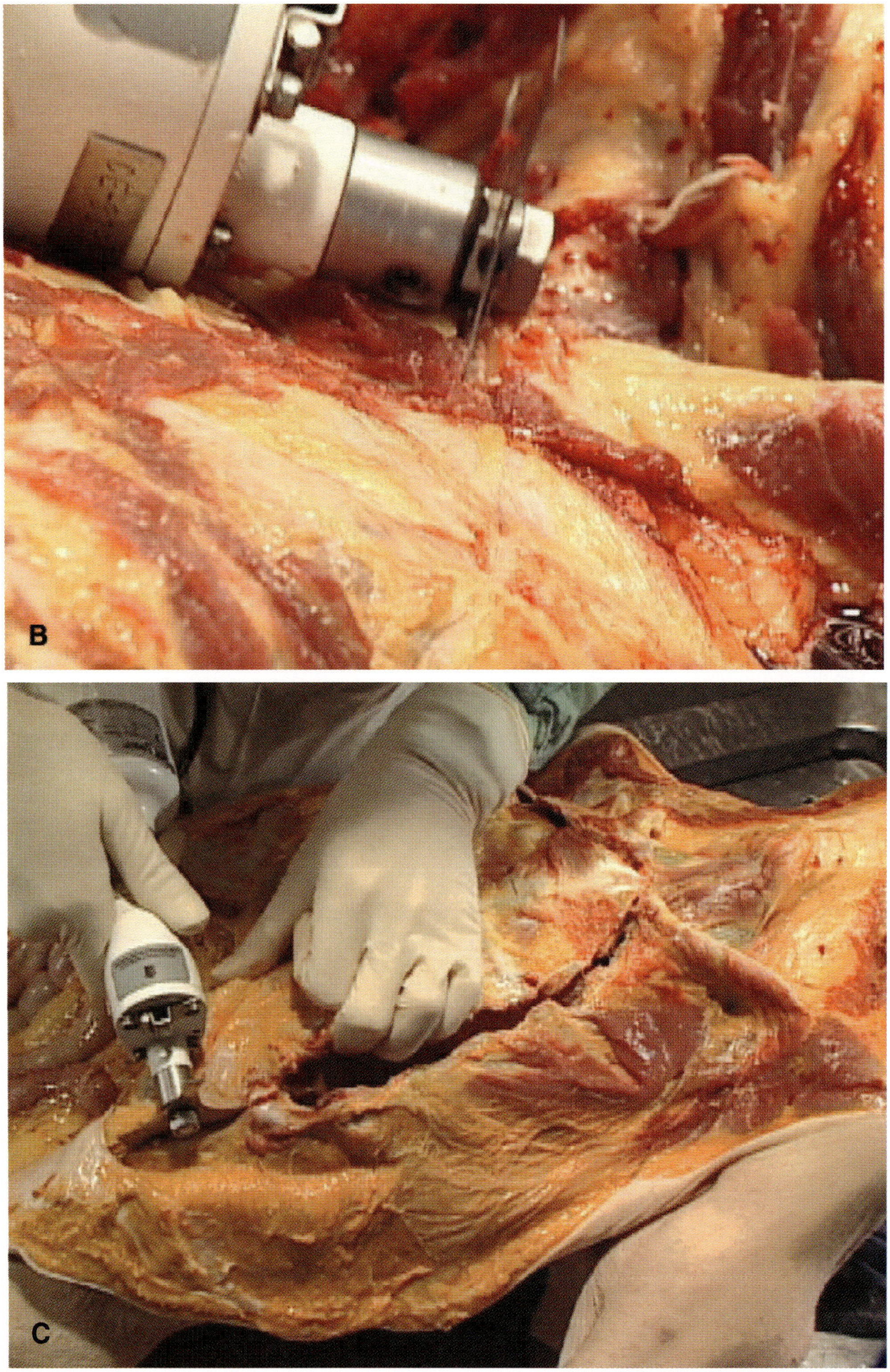

FIGURE 6.10 (CONTINUED) (A)–(C) Opening of the ribs with a bone saw. The ribs are sawed and opened with wide arcs to facilitate access to the chest organs and tissues.

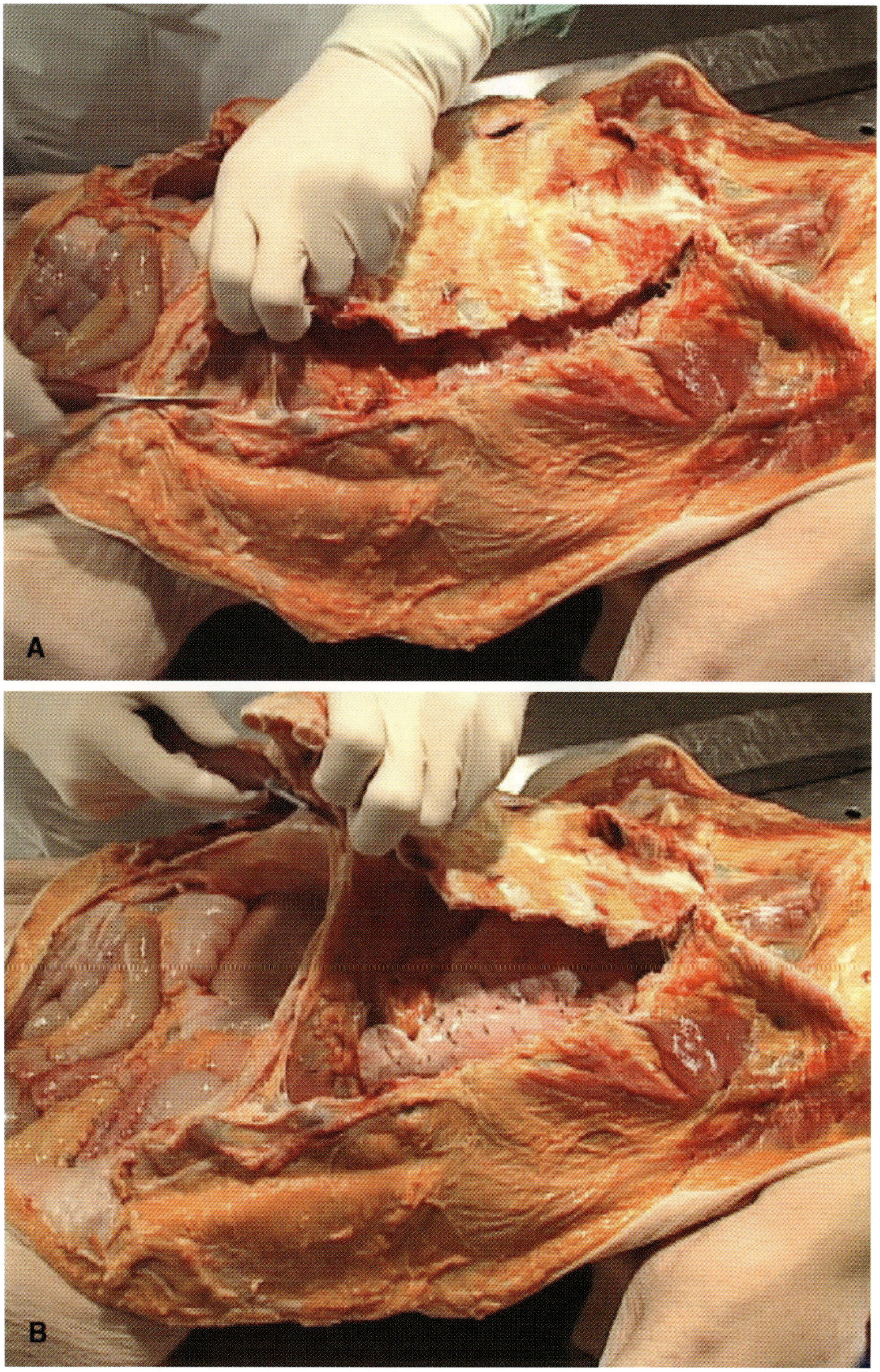

FIGURE 6.11 (A)–(D) Removing the "chest plate." The anterior diaphragm, uncut soft tissue, and soft tissue of the mediastinum are cut as the chest plate, or sternum, and ribs are lifted off.

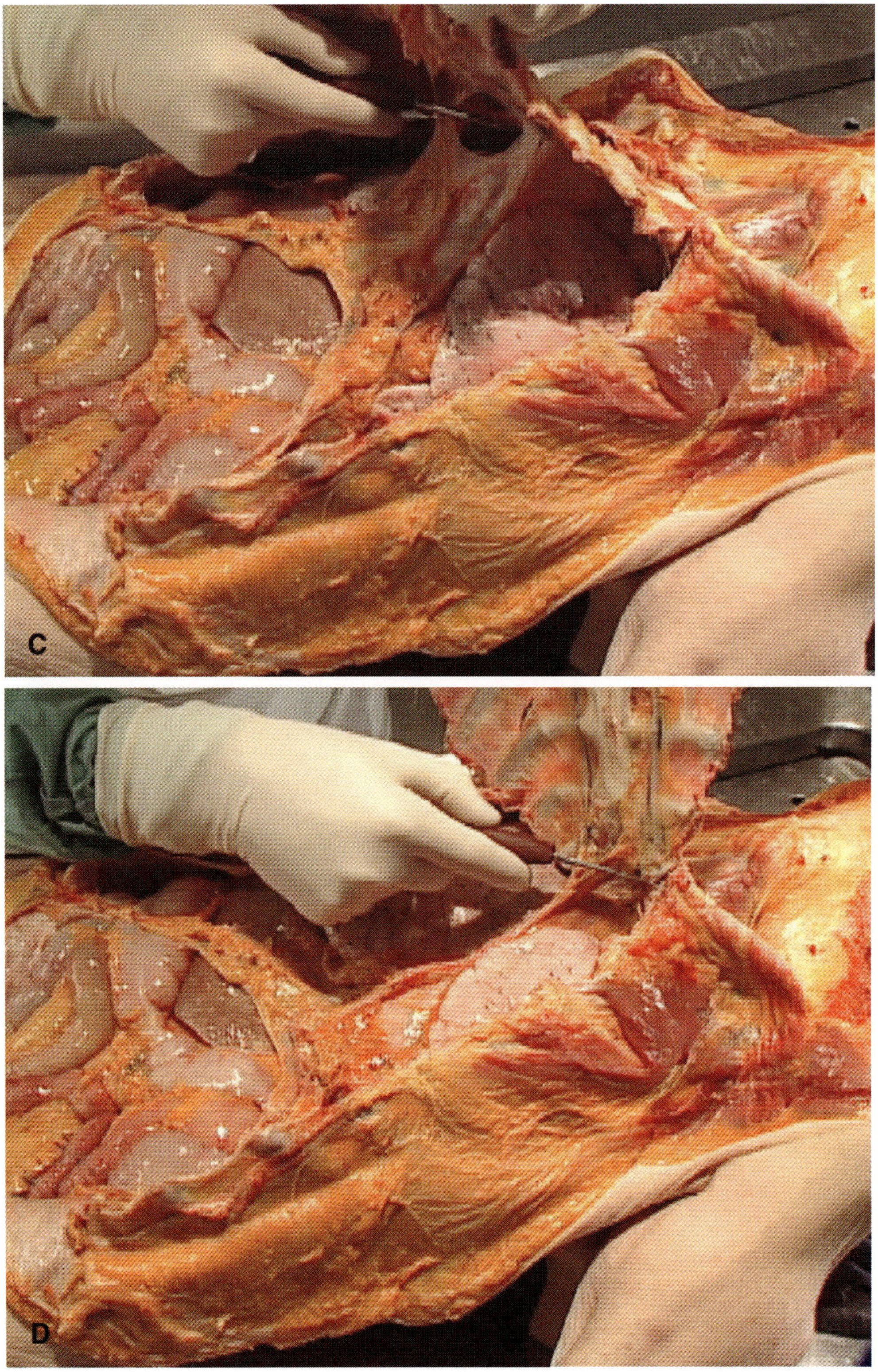

FIGURE 6.11 (CONTINUED) (A)–(D) Removing the "chest plate." The anterior diaphragm, uncut soft tissue, and soft tissue of the mediastinum are cut as the chest plate, or sternum, and ribs are lifted off.

SURVEY OF CHEST TISSUES AND ORGANS

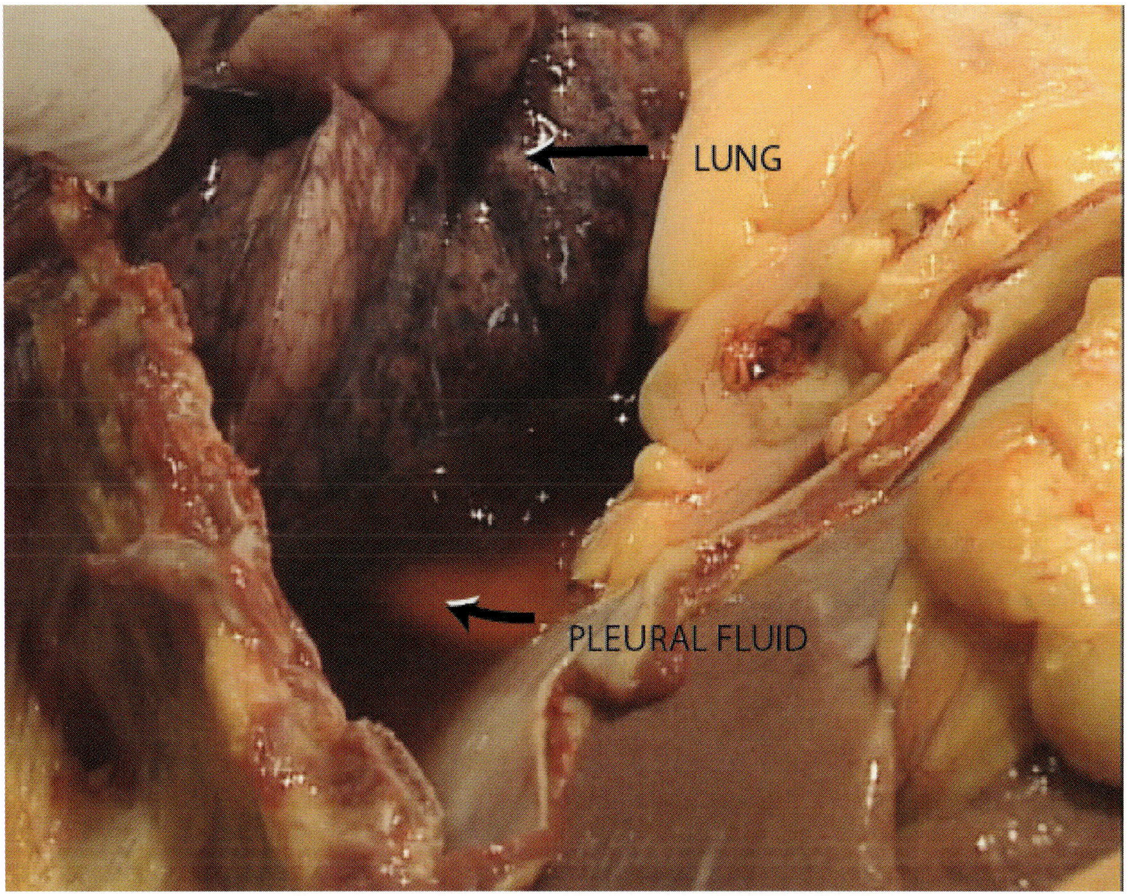

FIGURE 6.12 Fluid in the pleural cavity. Just as the sawed ribs are lifted up, inspection of this right chest cavity reveals serous fluid. The chest fluid here is the result of congestive heart failure. This failure of the heart as a pump results in fluid backing up in the lungs and chest. All fluids encountered are measured or closely estimated.

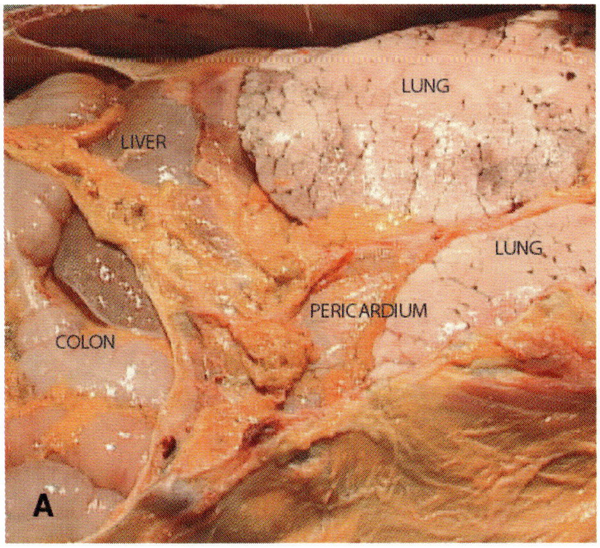

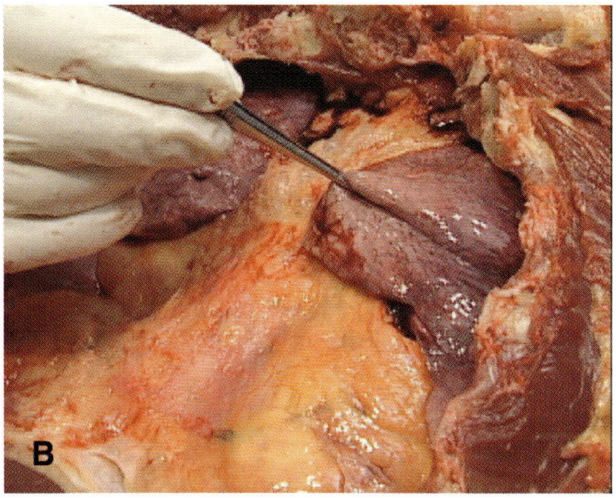

FIGURE 6.13 Survey of the lungs. (A) After the chest plate is removed, the lungs are examined *in situ*. The lungs here are situated normally in the chest. **(B)** The lung is held by the forceps.

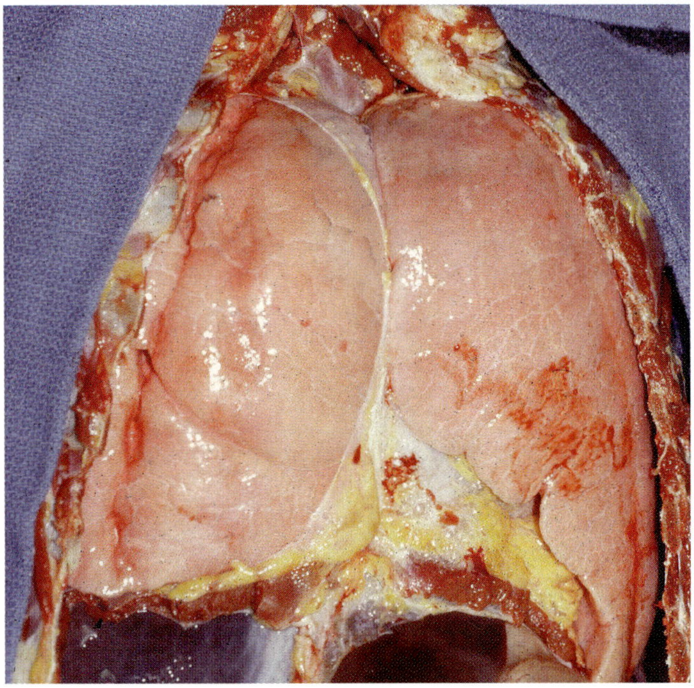

FIGURE 6.14 Hyperinflated asthmatic lungs. The lungs here show hyperinflation due to trapping of air. This patient died of a sudden asthma attack (*status asthmaticus*), during which bronchial spasm and mucous plugging hamper breathing, causing air to be trapped.

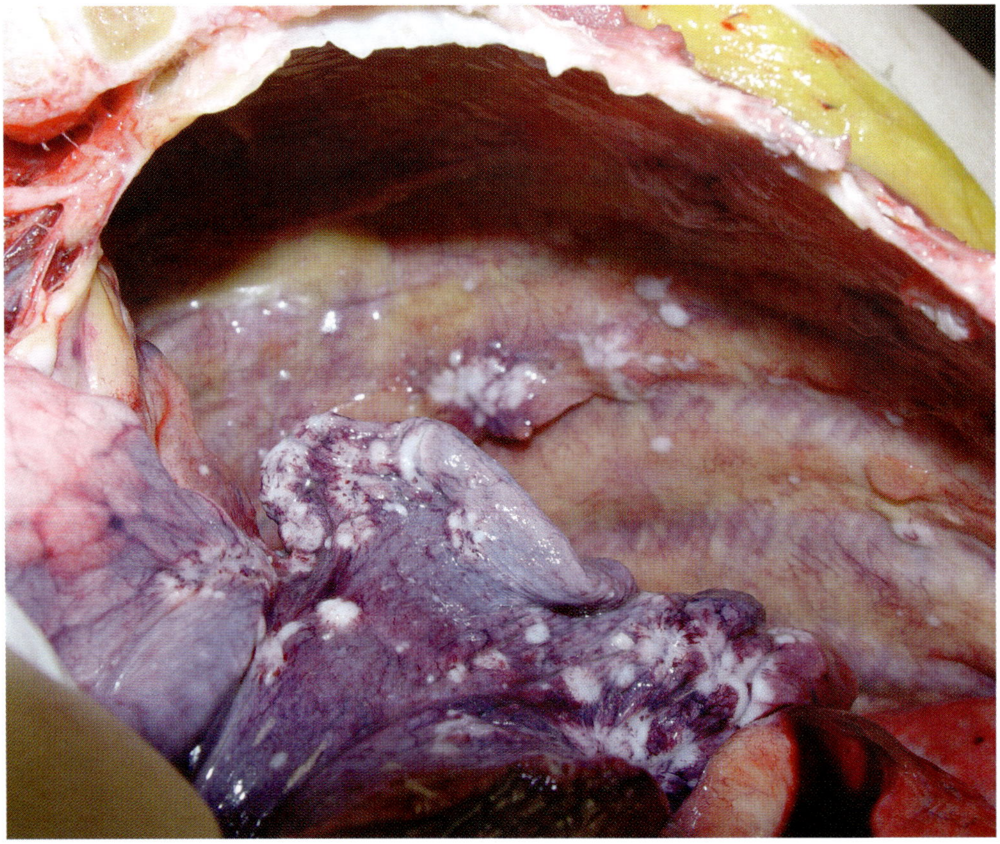

FIGURE 6.15 Metastatic carcinoma of the lung. Multiple white nodules on the lung pleura (covering) are from a carcinoma of the lung that has spread from the primary site (metastasized).

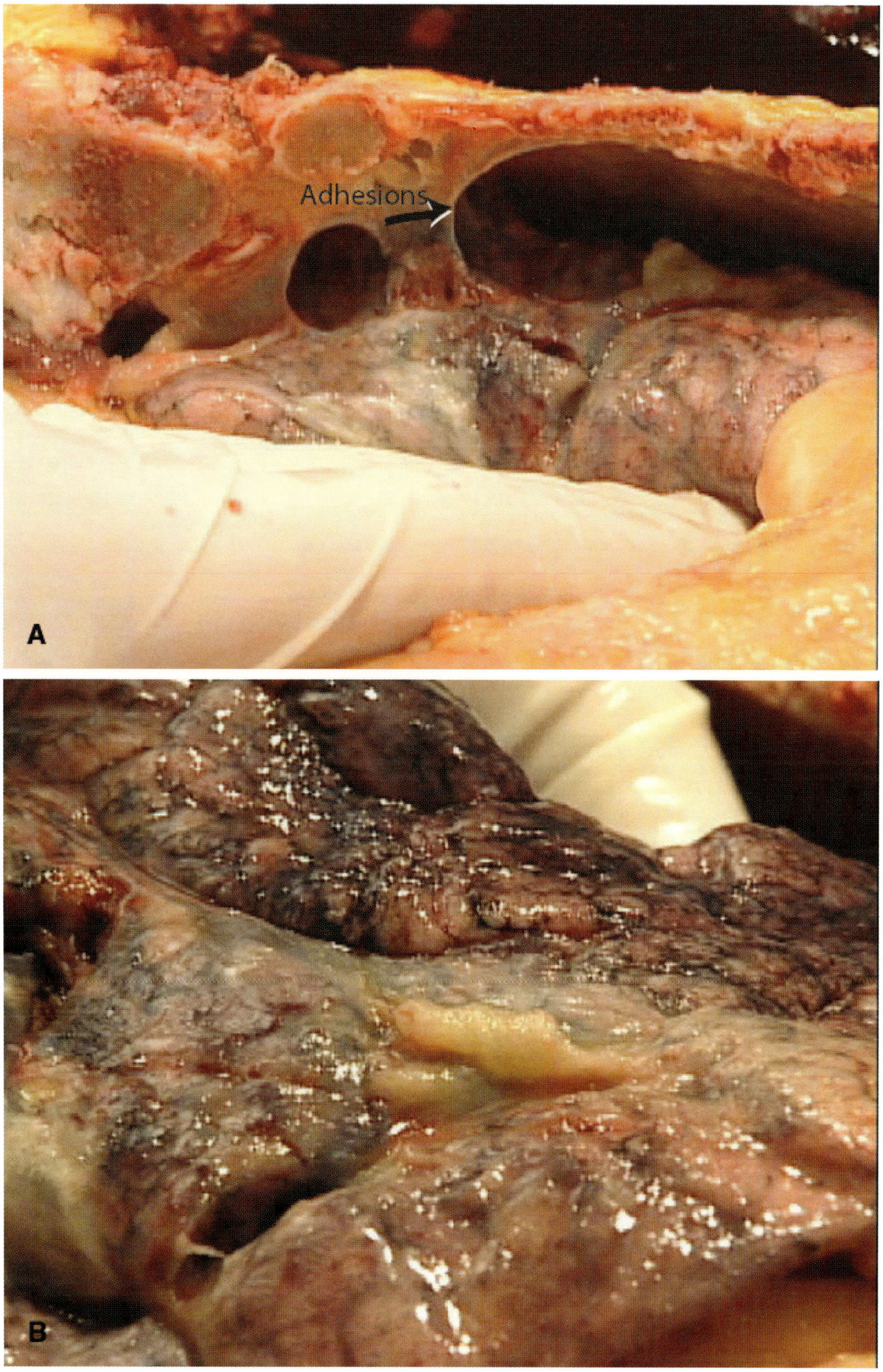

FIGURE 6.16 Lung and pleural adhesions. (A) Adhesions can be seen just below the cut ribs. **(B)** The covering of the lung, or pleura, shows a yellow exudate (center) also, suggesting an inflammation of the lung and pleura, such as pneumonia.

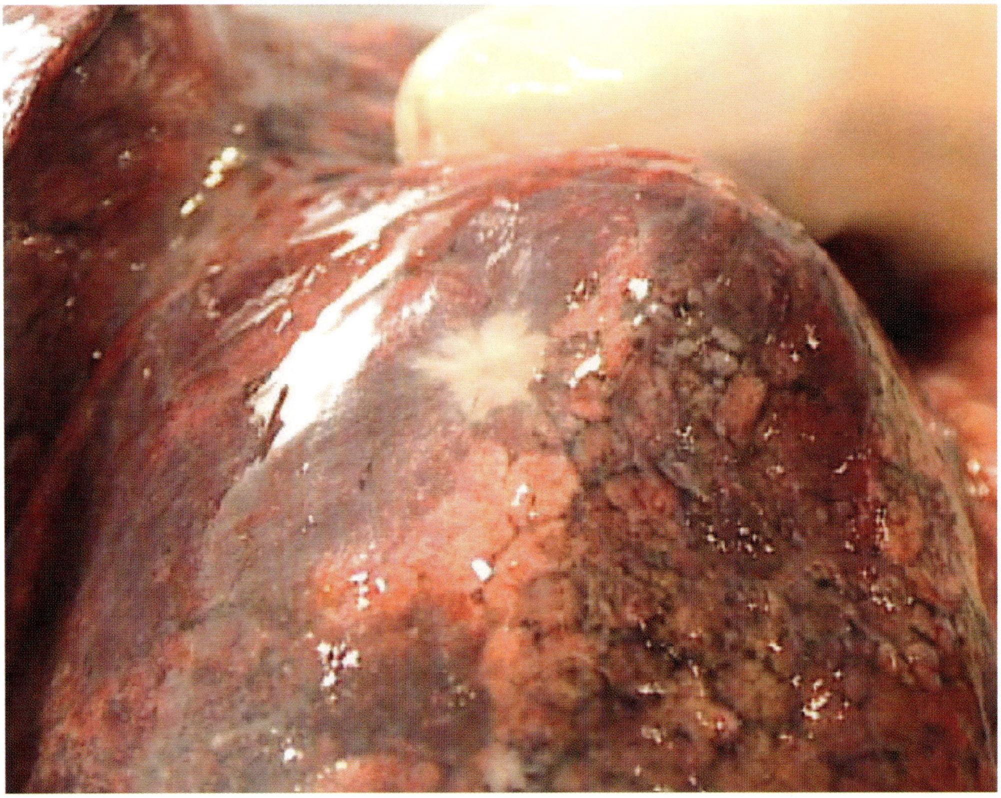

FIGURE 6.17 Pleural scar of the lung. Initial exam of this lung shows a whitish scar on the pleura. This is likely a healed focus of inflammation.

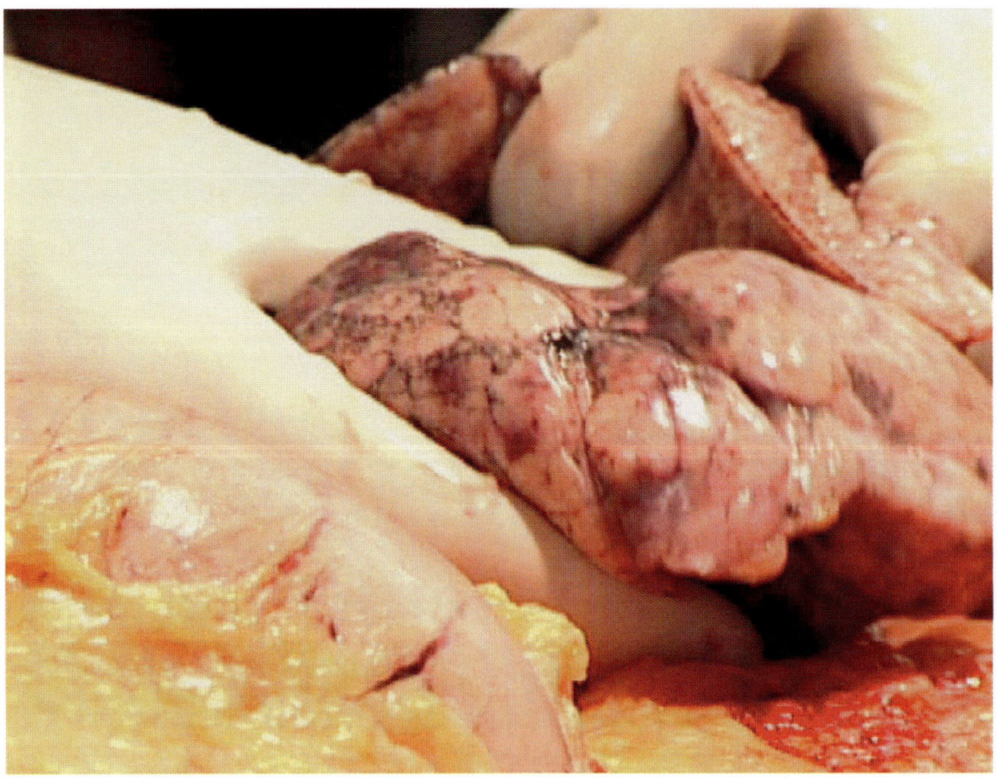

FIGURE 6.18 Palpation of mass in the left lung. The pathologist uses the sense of touch to feel for masses. Tumors are commonly firm to the touch. The pathologist is palpating a tumor between the thumb and forefinger. This tumor will be dissected later in the organ exam (see Figure 8.37).

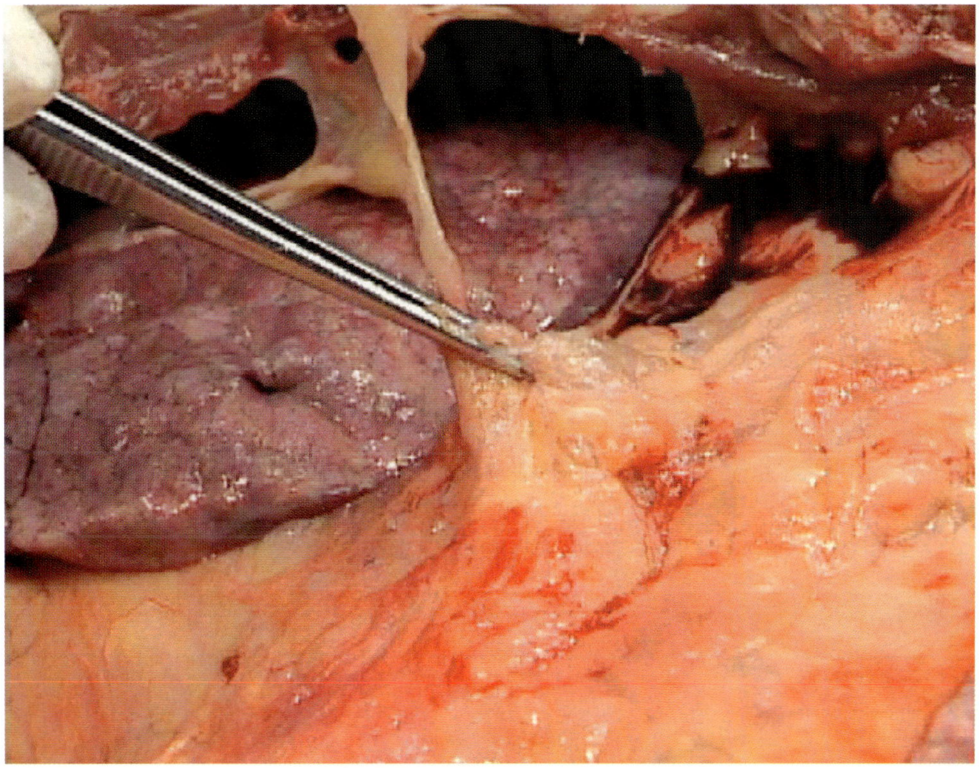

FIGURE 6.19 Pericardial air bubbles. Small "bubbles" in the tissue, as seen here between the forceps, indicate dissection of air from the lung into the chest cavity and surrounding soft tissue of the chest (pneumothorax). The cause of pneumothorax in this figure is a rib fracture from cardiopulmonary resuscitation.

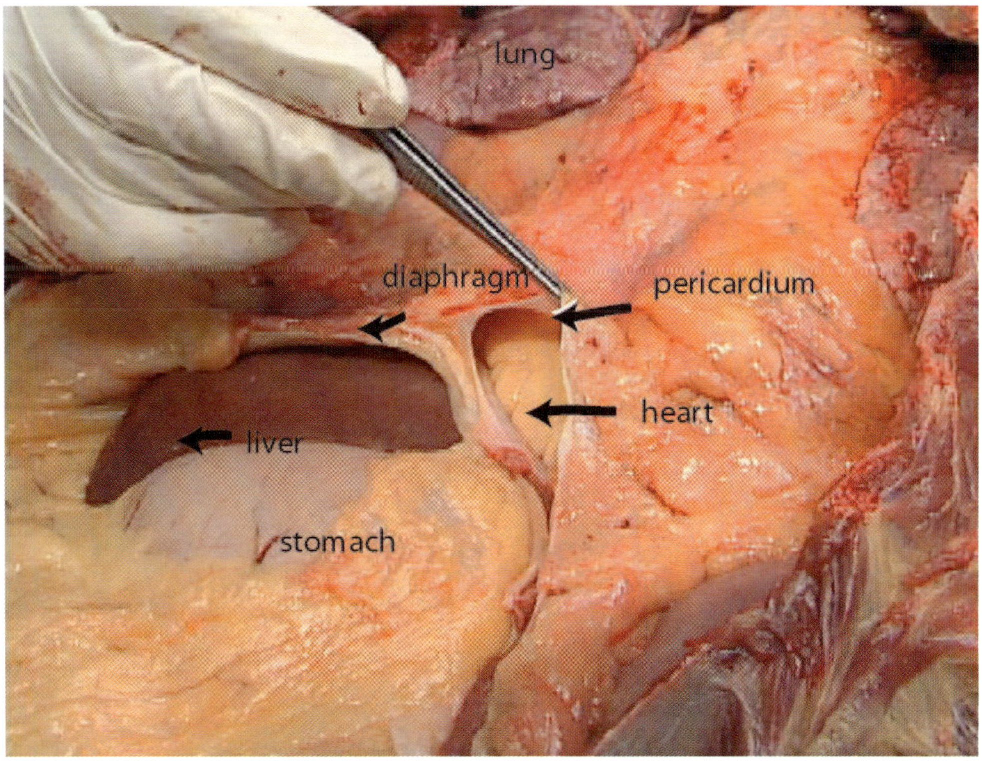

FIGURE 6.20 Pericardium displayed. The pericardium (heart lining) has been opened and is lifted up by the forceps. The heart is contained within. The fat-covered tip of the heart can be seen. The liver is dark brown, just below, resting on the stomach.

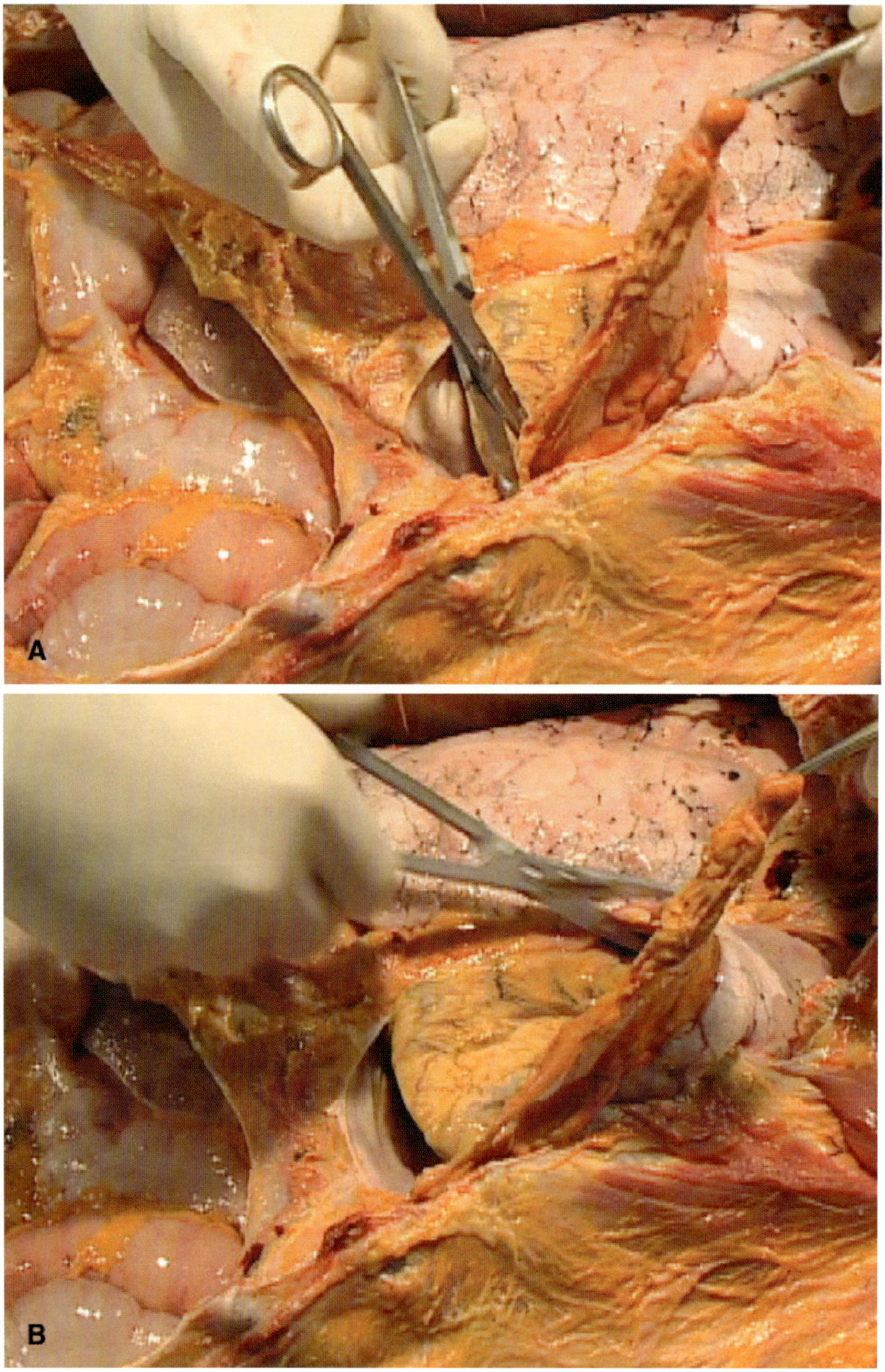

FIGURE 6.21 (A), (B) Opening of the pericardium. The pericardium is opened to look for fluid and inflammation.

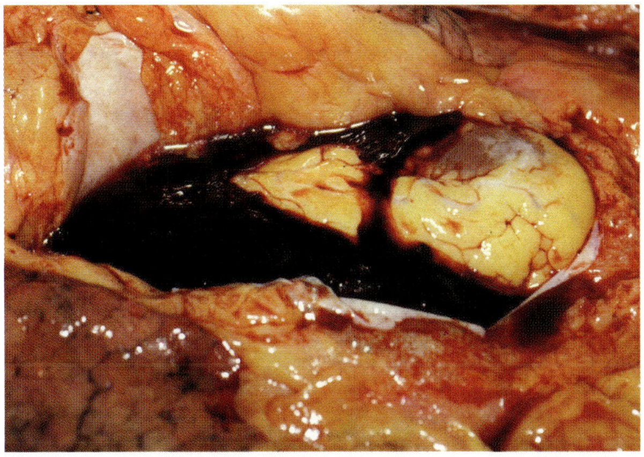

FIGURE 6.22 Hemopericaridum. Blood can be seen filling the pericardium. This patient had suffered a myocardial infarction about 5 days previously. The infarcted (dead) heart tissue burst open, allowing for hemopericardium. The blood in the pericardium interferes with the contraction of the heart (cardiac tamponade) and can cause cardiac arrest.

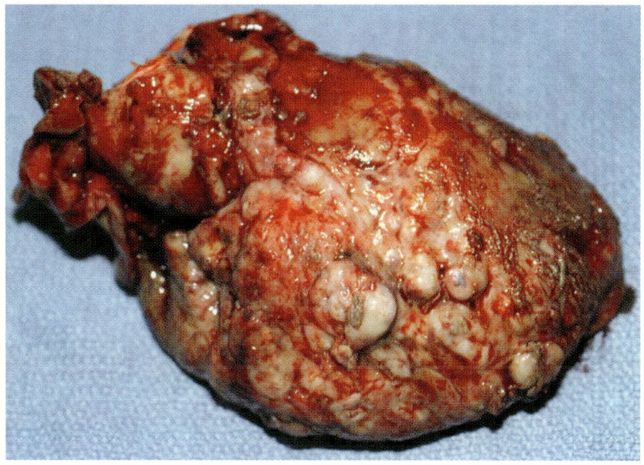

FIGURE 6.23 Metastatic carcinoma of the heart. The epicardium (outer surface of the heart) is covered with metastatic tumor nodules. The diagnosis of carcinoma will be confirmed by microscopic exam (see Figure 10.6).

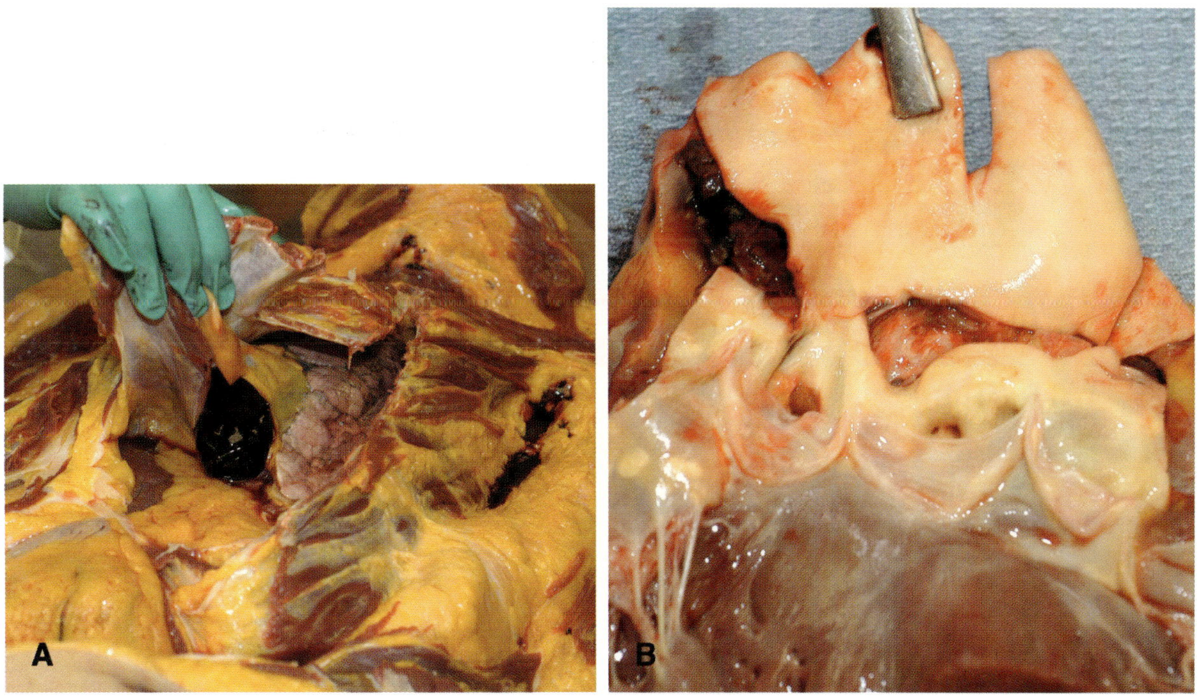

FIGURE 6.24 (A) Hemopericardium. A large, about 200-cc hemopericardium is seen. **(B) Aortic laceration.** Once the clot is evacuated and the heart removed, the source of the blood is found to be an aortic dissection near the aortic valve. Since this part of the aorta is within the pericardial sac, the blood is found here.

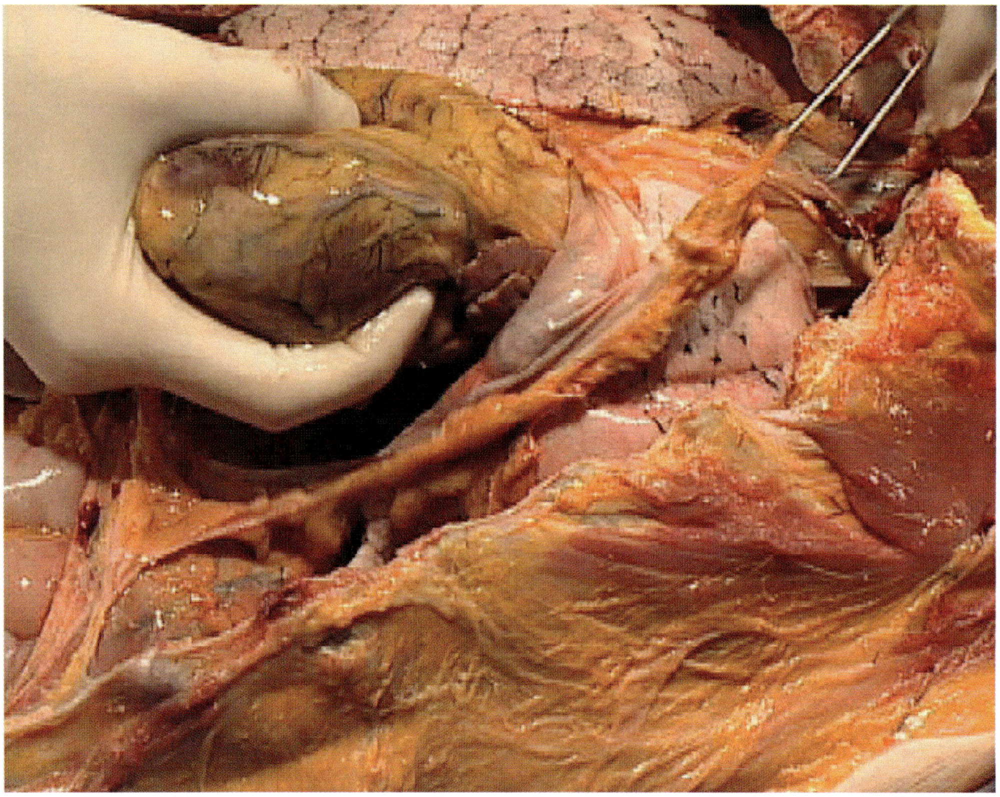

FIGURE 6.25 Palpation and examination of the heart *in situ*. The heart is palpated and visually examined *in situ*. Soft areas in the heart may indicate infarction. A diffusely soft heart might indicate myocarditis.

SURVEY OF ABDOMINAL ORGANS

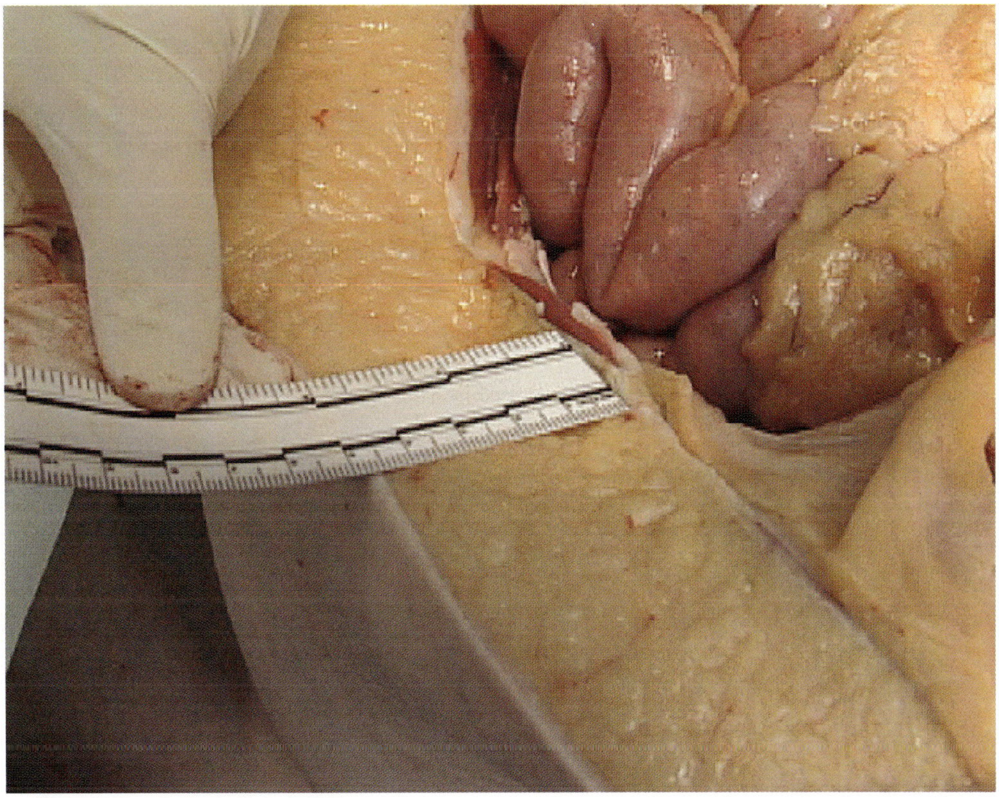

FIGURE 6.26 Abdominal panniculus. The abdominal panniculus (fat pad) is measured and recorded. The panniculus is greatly thickened in obesity and razor-thin in malnutrition.

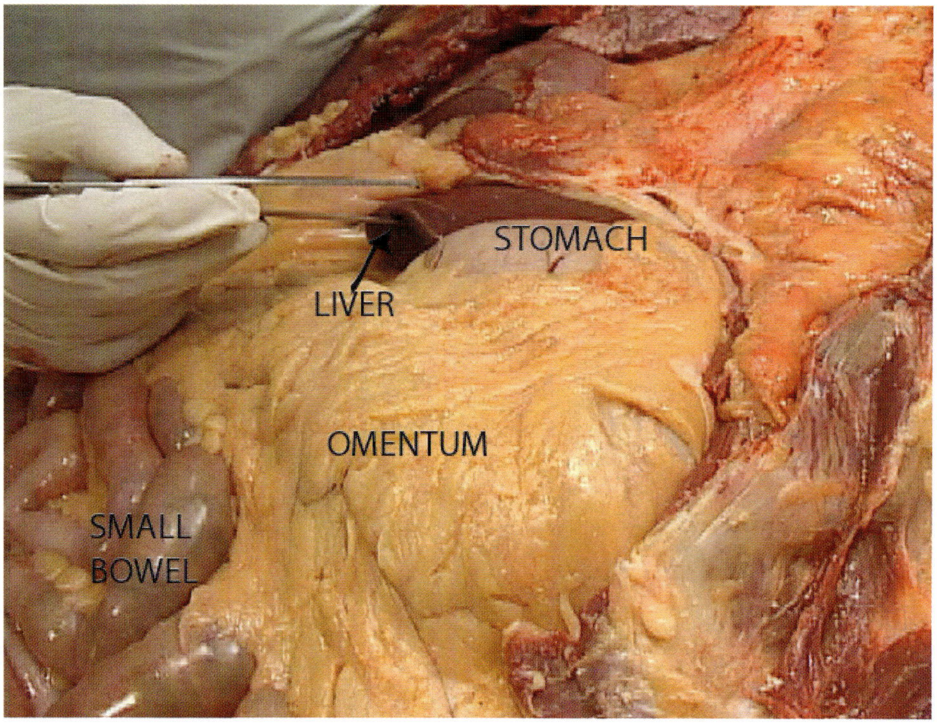

FIGURE 6.27 Upper abdominal organs. The liver is lifted up with the forceps as it rests on the stomach. The omentum (protective fat layer) is seen below the stomach, partially covering the bowel.

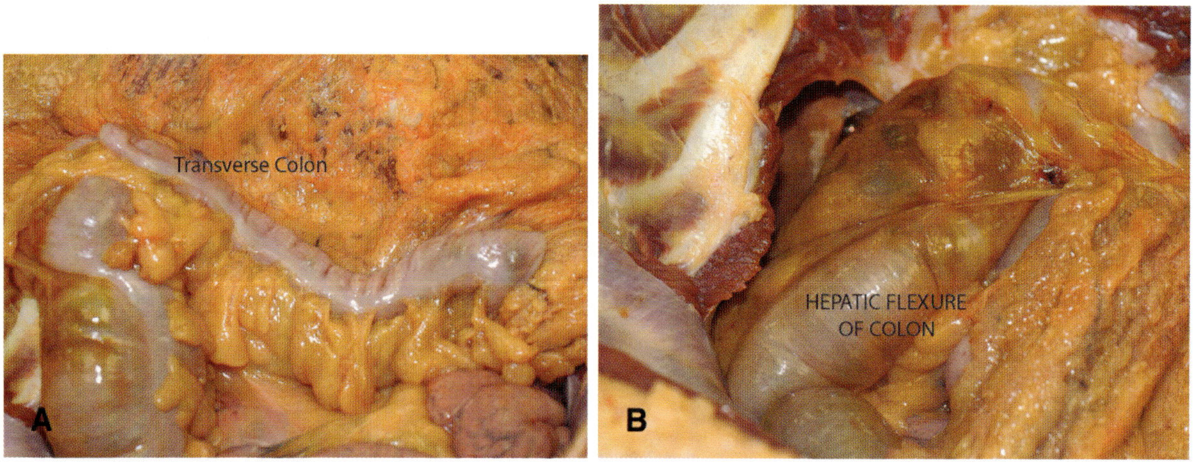

FIGURE 6.28 Omentum and colon. **(A)** If the omentum is reflected back, the transverse colon is exposed. **(B)** The hepatic flexure of the colon can be seen just below the rib cage. This is the point where the ascending colon turns into the transverse colon at the liver.

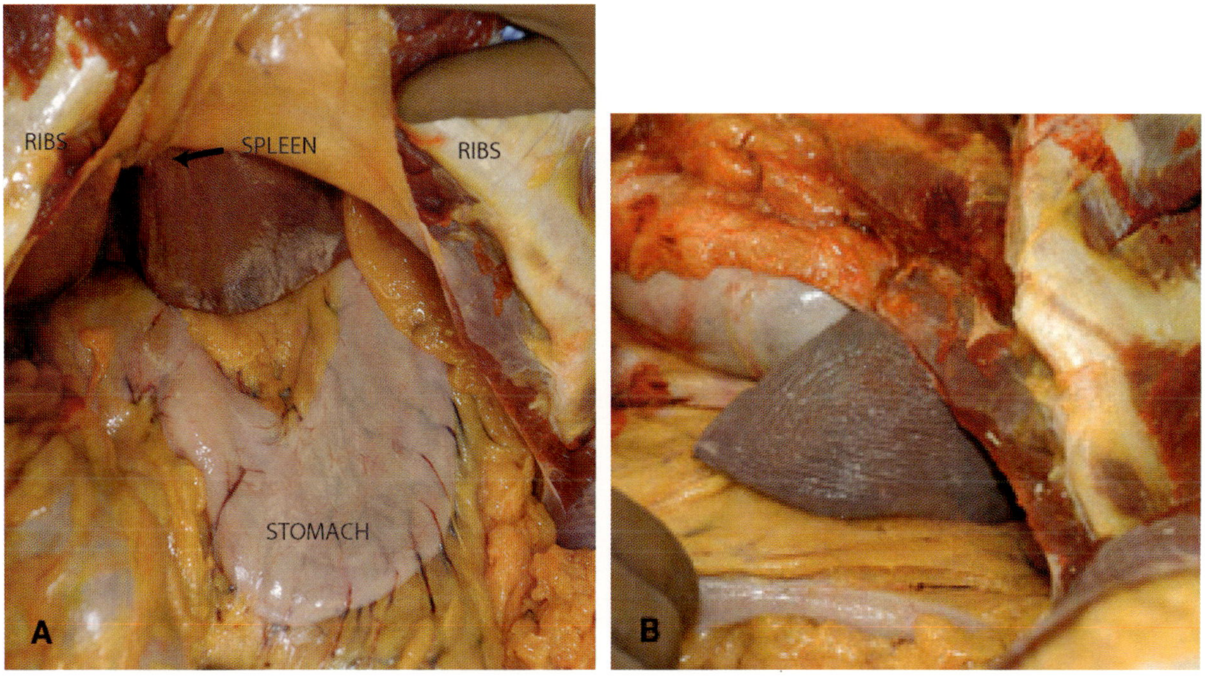

FIGURE 6.29 Spleen *in situ*. (A) The dark brown spleen can be seen in the upper part of the picture just above the stomach. This spleen is free of laceration. Laceration is common in severe blunt trauma to the abdomen. **(B)** The spleen is in the middle of the picture, and the whitish descending colon is at the bottom of the figure. Anatomically, the spleen is located in the left upper quadrant of the abdomen under the rib cage.

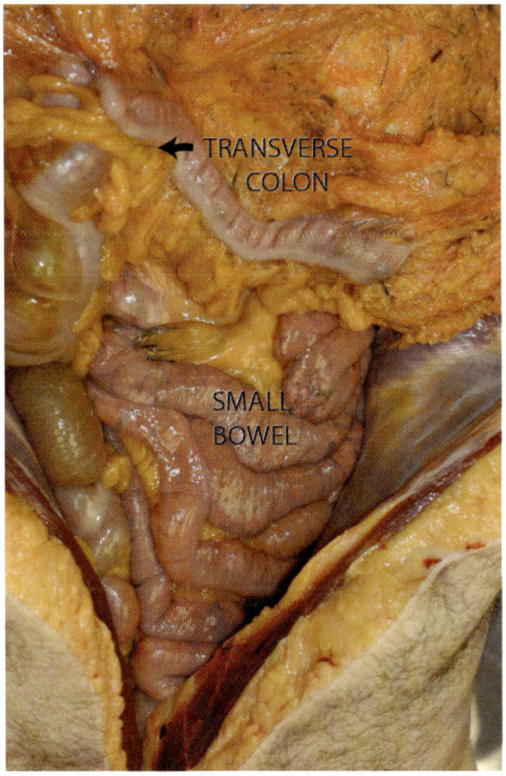

FIGURE 6.30 Transverse colon and small bowel *in situ*. The normal bowel is in the proper location, extending transversely across the abdomen. The transverse colon is surrounded by connective fat at the top of the figure, and the small bowel is bunched together in a zigzag fashion on the bottom.

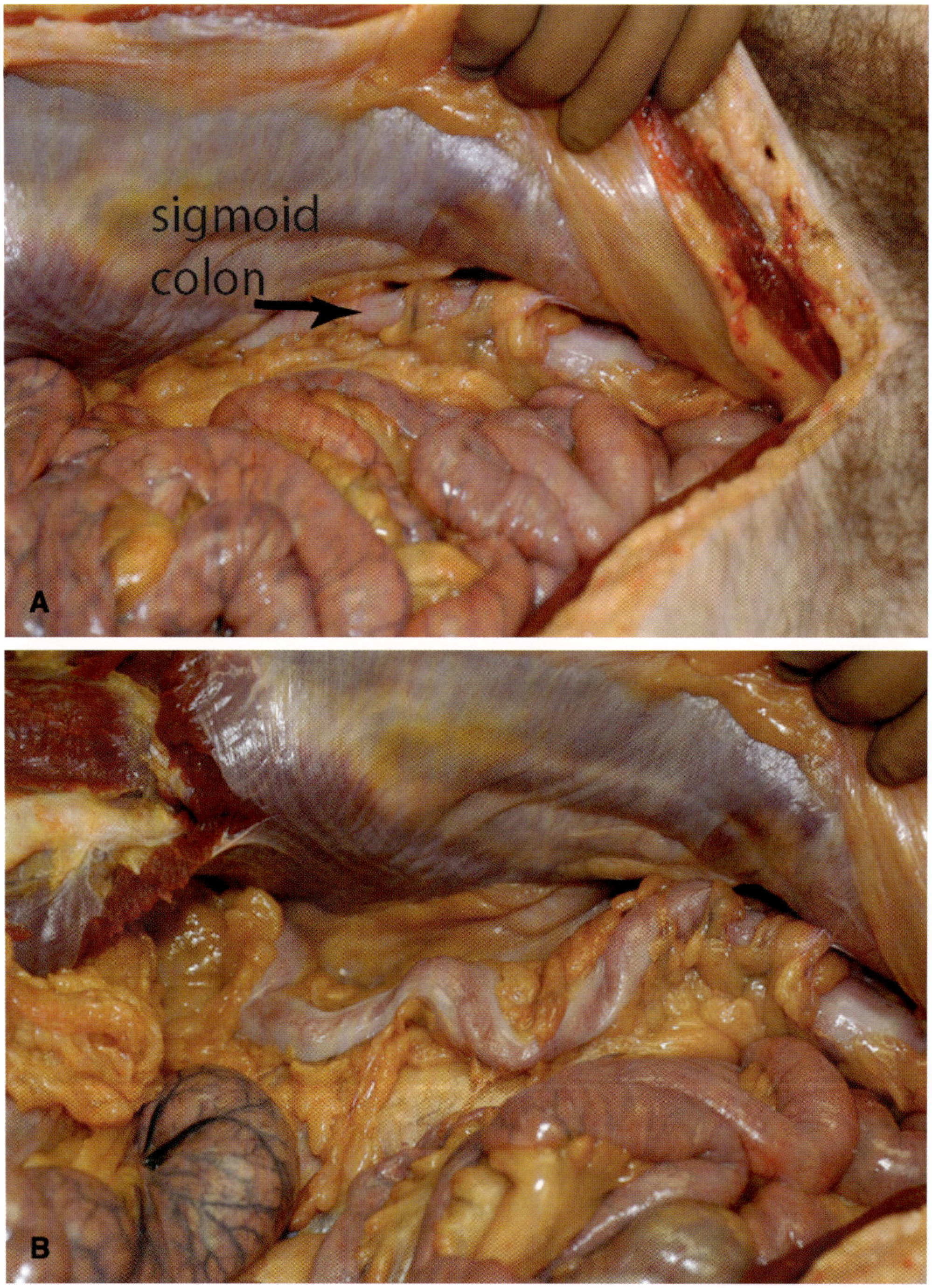

FIGURE 6.31 Sigmoid colon. **(A)** The whitish sigmoid colon is behind the reflected abdominal wall, amid the small bowel in the foreground. **(B)** The bowel is pulled out slightly, exposing its course.

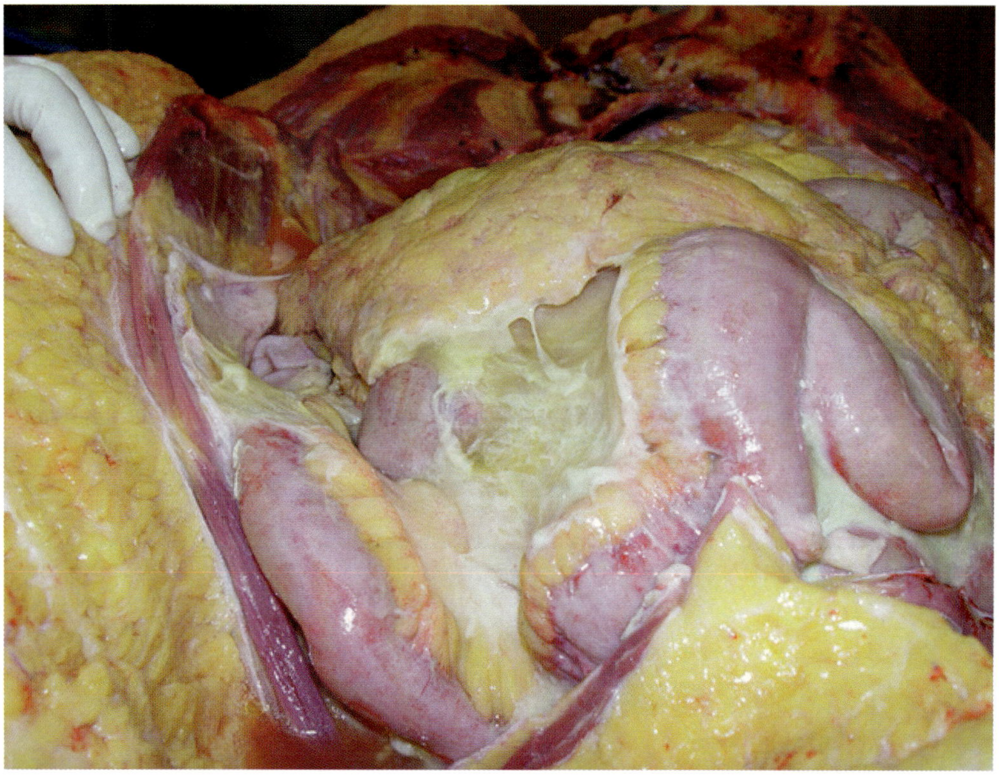

FIGURE 6.32 Inflammation of the abdomen and bowel. Survey of the bowel in this case reveals a whitish-yellow (fibrinopurulent) exudate, indicating an ongoing (subacute) infection of the abdominal cavity. Notice how reddened (erythematous) the bowel appears. This erythema indicates inflammation.

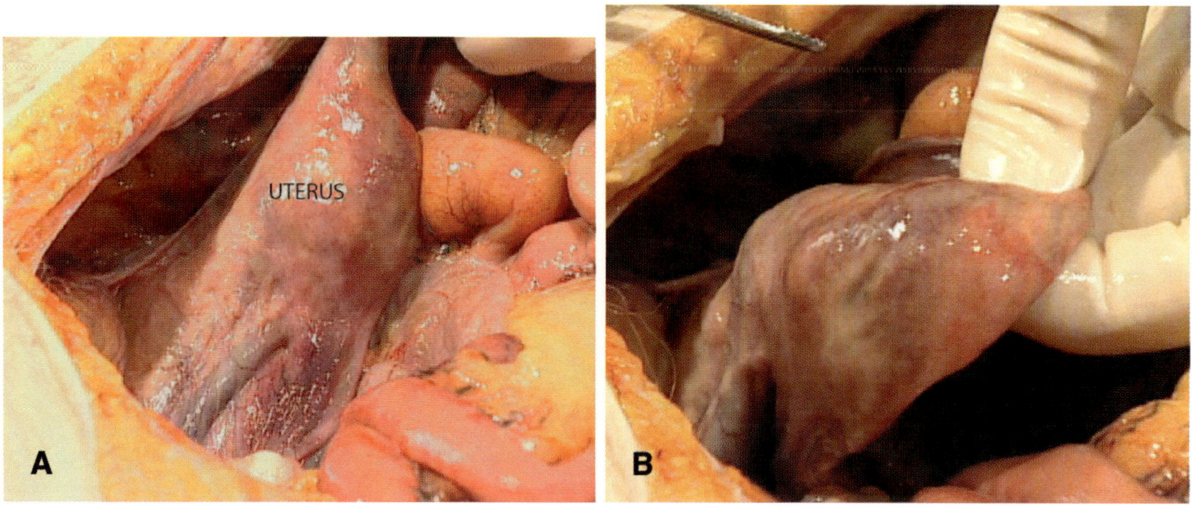

FIGURE 6.33 Uterus *in situ*. **(A)** The uterus is in the midline of the pelvis. **(B)** No lesions are seen as it is examined *in situ*.

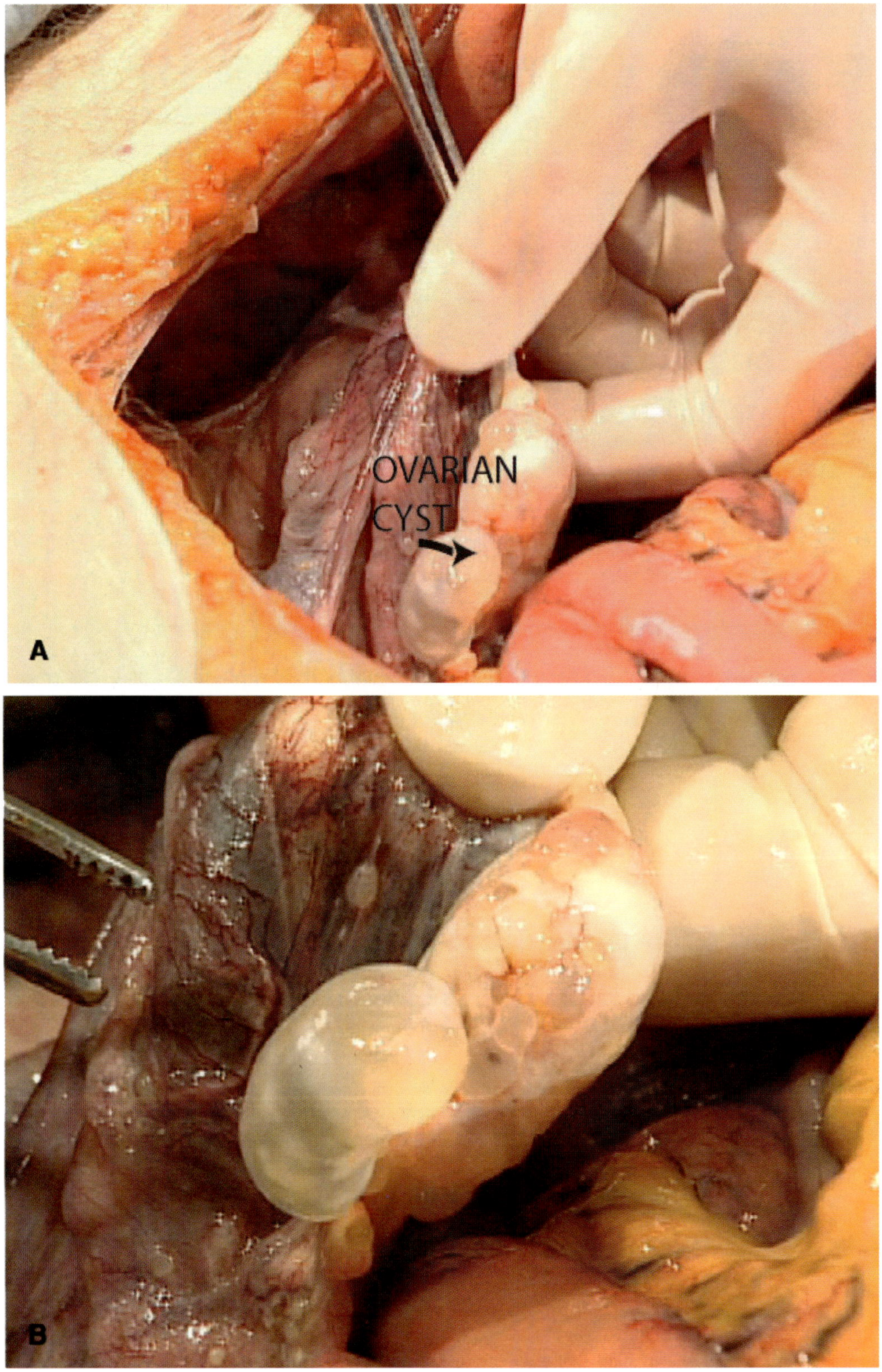

FIGURE 6.34 Small ovarian cyst. (A) A small ovarian cyst can be seen on this left ovary. **(B)** It is better seen when pulled out.

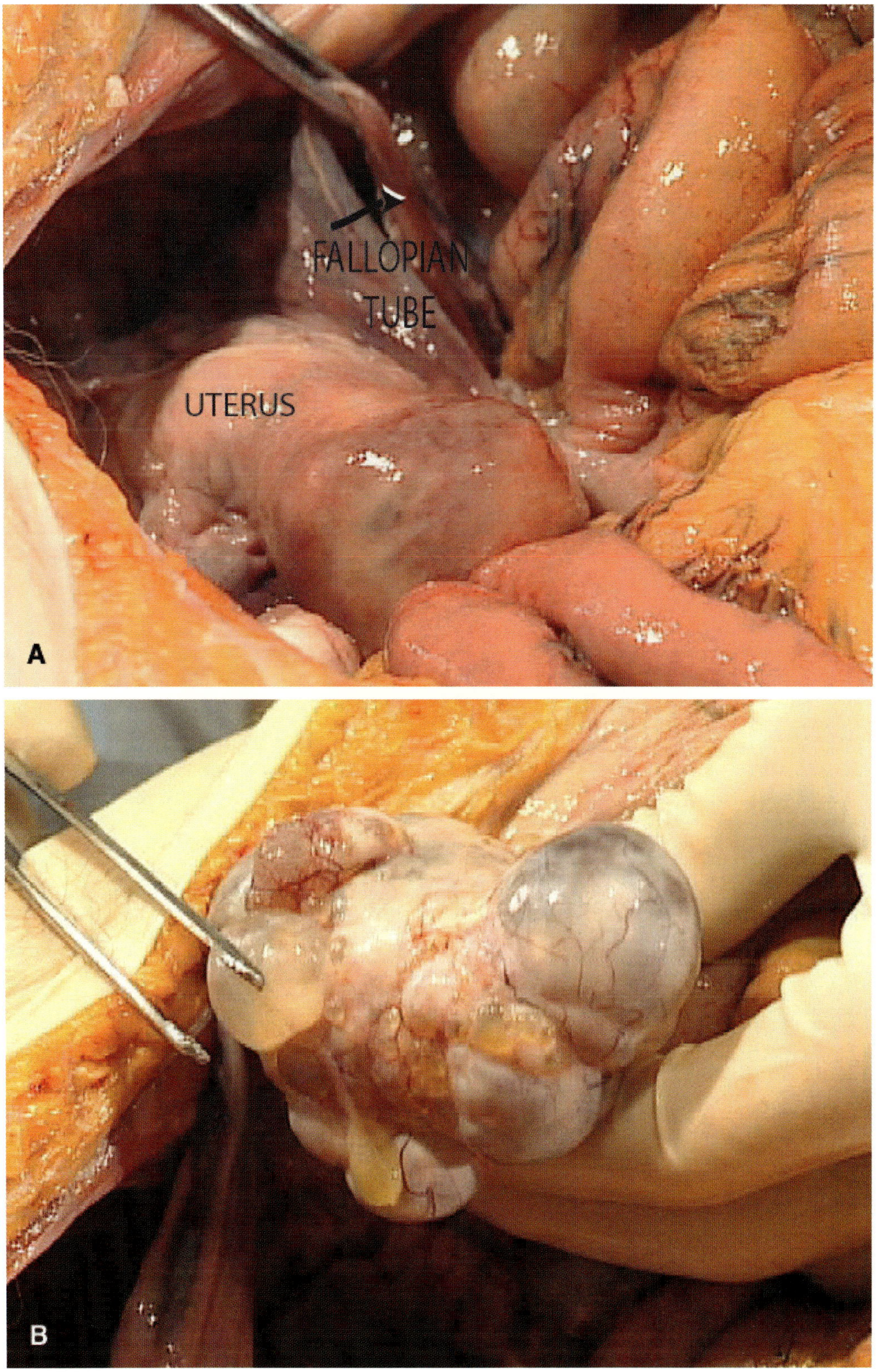

FIGURE 6.35 (A), (B) Large ovarian cyst. Pulling on the left fallopian tube reveals a much larger cyst of the right ovary.

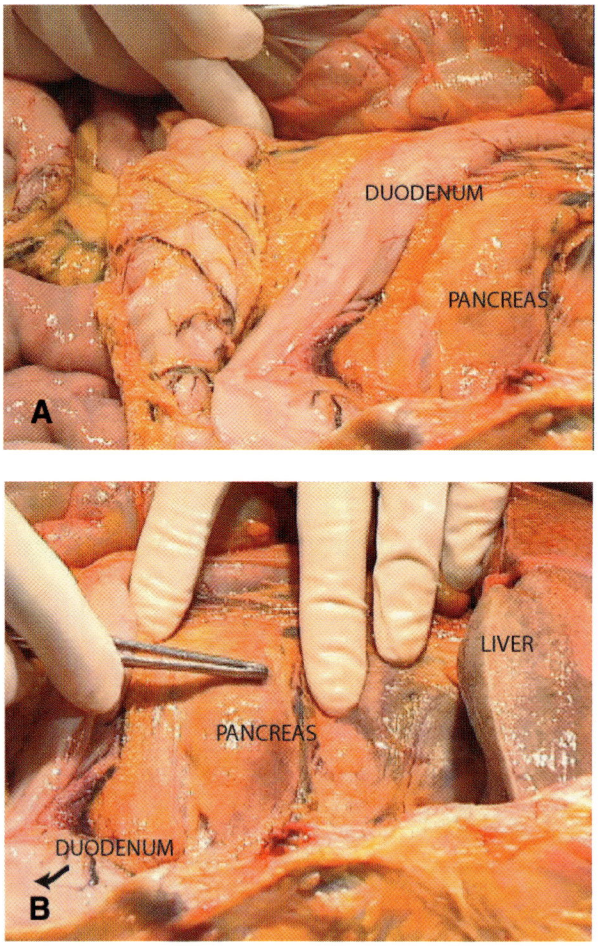

FIGURE 6.36 Pancreas and duodenum. (A) The duodenum is the L-shaped segment of the small bowel, cradling the pancreas to the immediate right. **(B)** The pancreas is pointed out by the forceps tip.

COLLECTING BLOOD, URINE, BILE, AND VITREOUS SPECIMENS FOR TOXICOLOGY

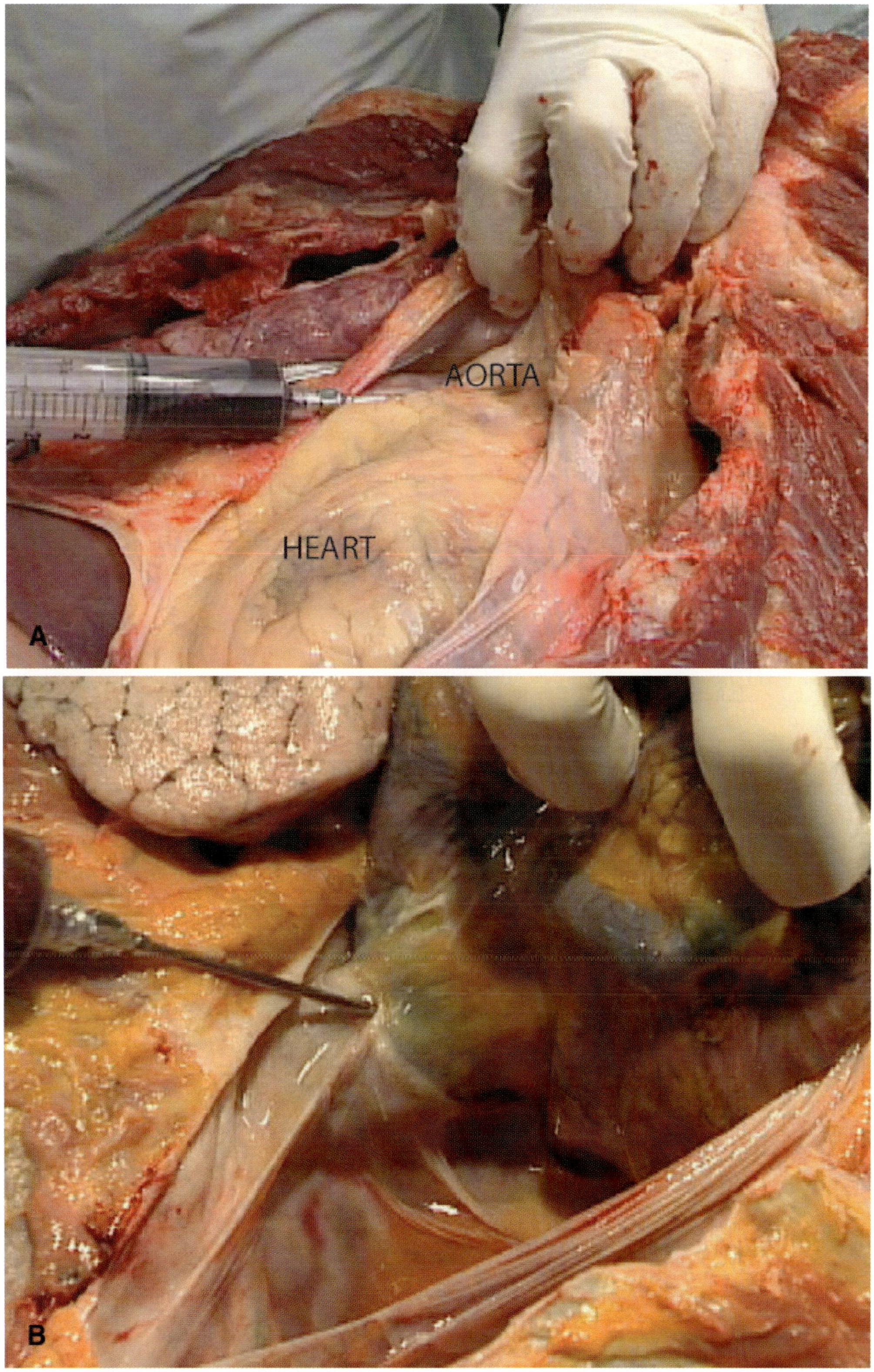

FIGURE 6.37 **(A) Taking blood from the aorta.** Routinely, blood is removed from the aorta. **(B) Taking blood from the inferior vena cava.** Blood screening is usually preferable when the concentration of a specific drug must be known, e.g., alcohol or carbon monoxide.

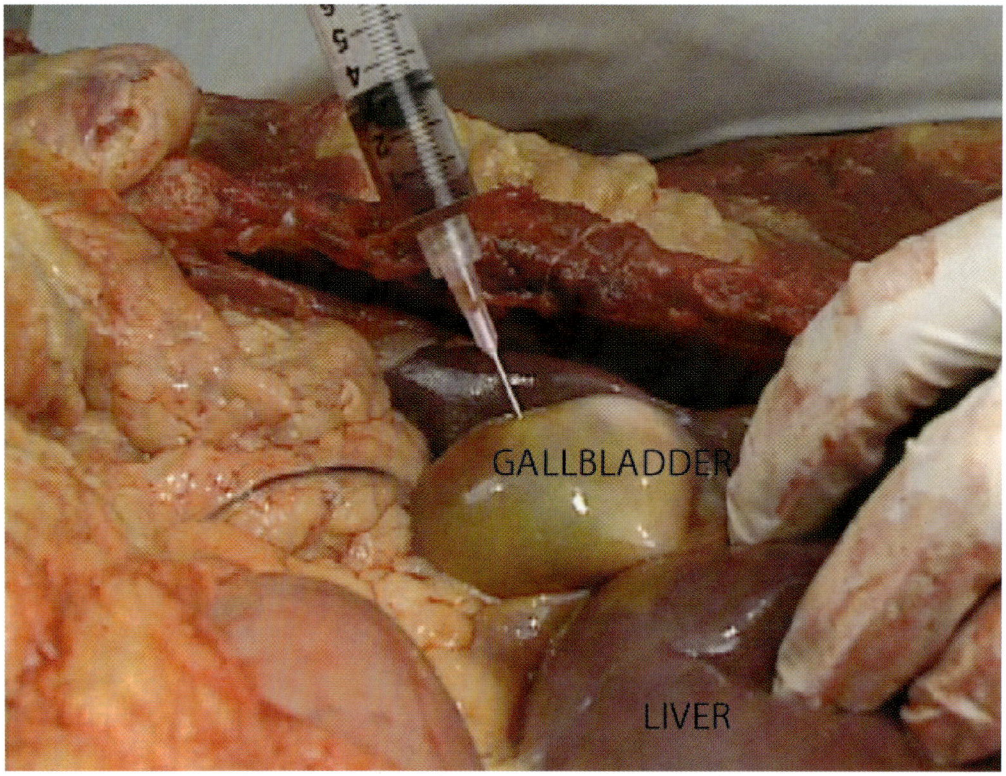

FIGURE 6.38 Obtaining bile from the gallbladder. Cocaine and other narcotics concentrate in the bile. Because cocaine has a short half-life in the blood, testing bile can confirm the presence of cocaine in cases where cocaine abuse is suspected and blood levels are negative.

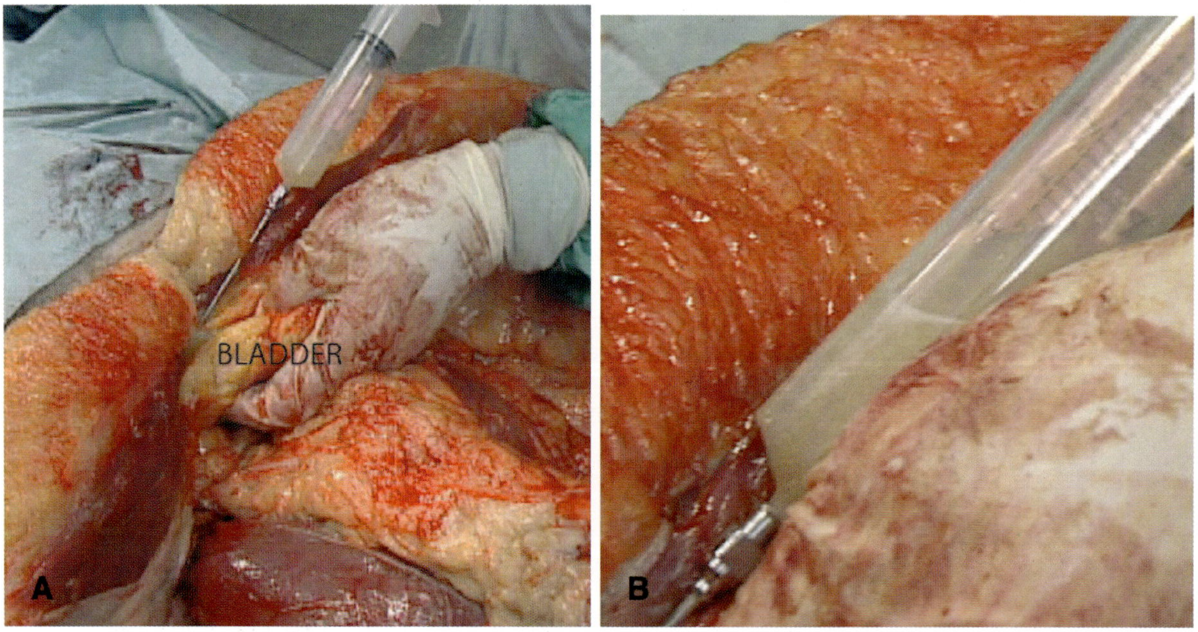

FIGURE 6.39 (A), (B) Removing urine from the bladder. At least 7 cc of blood is preferred when screening for most drugs, toxins, and poisons. Urine is the preferred body fluid when screening for the most commonly abused drugs. When testing for the presence of some drugs and toxins, tissues such as brain, muscle, fat, hair, liver, kidney, bone, and nails are preferred. For example, arsenic is best found in the hair and nails.

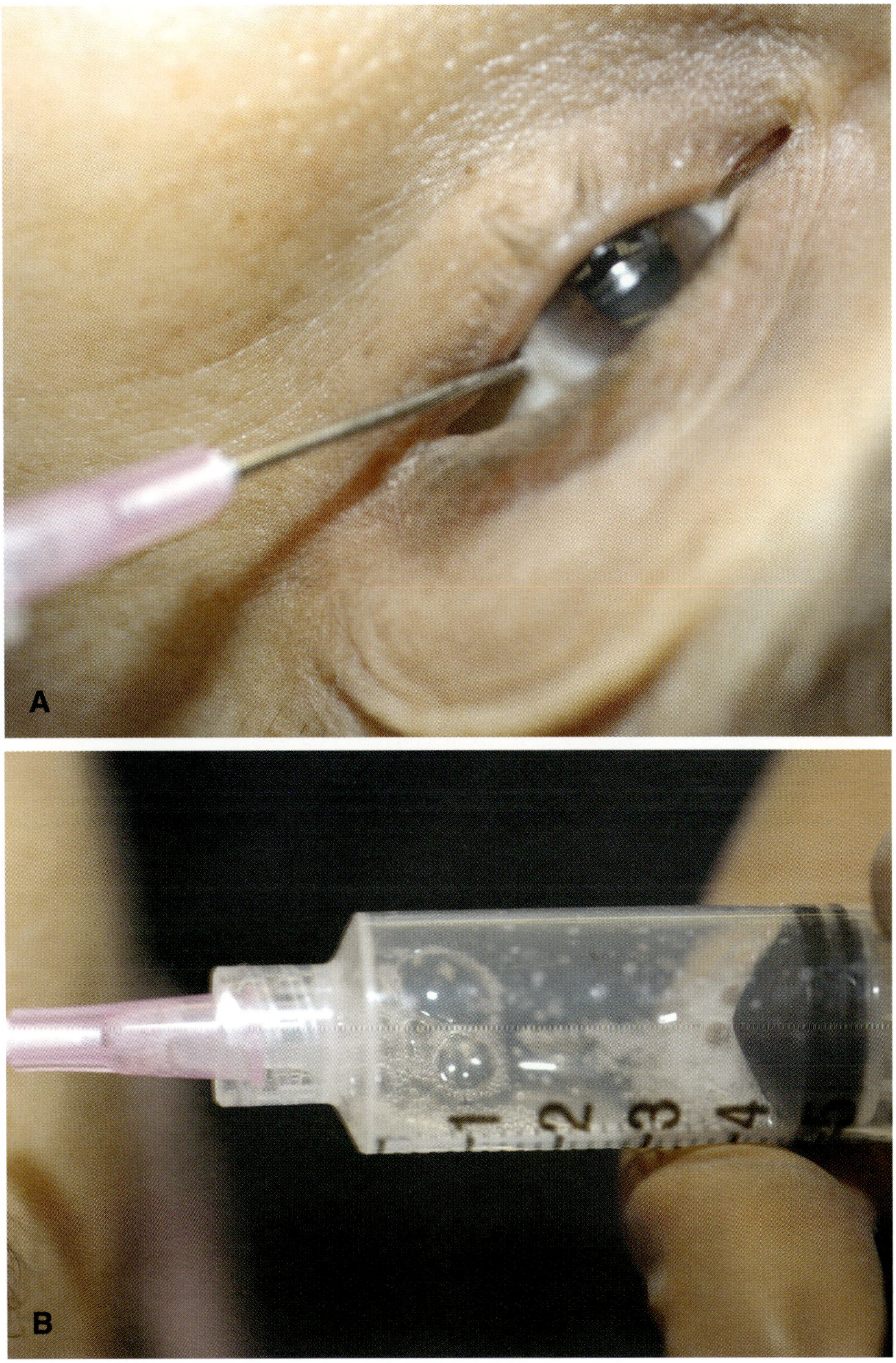

FIGURE 6.40 (A), (B) Obtaining vitreous humor from the eye. Vitreous humor, or clear liquid fluid in the eye, is obtained routinely. Since the vitreous humor tends to concentrate drugs and other analytes, testing is useful in a number of cases. For example, blood glucose is not reliable postmortem. A very high postmortem vitreous glucose can aid in the diagnosis of diabetic hyperglycemia (high blood sugar).

7 Organ and Tissue Removal

In the Virchow autopsy method, the organs are removed one after another in an organized and logical fashion, i.e., the neck organs are removed after the viscera to negate the artifactual appearance of hemorrhage often produced by congestion. Other organ removal methods include the Gohn, Letulle, or modified Rokitansky methods, in which the organs are removed *en bloc* (all together). This type of removal allows the internal viscera to be examined while they are still connected together. Some pathologists always remove organs *en bloc*. The author has found the Gohn method useful when examining infants with multiple cardiac and other birth defects. There is no right or wrong method of dissection; the aim is simply to perform a complete autopsy and to provide a detailed description of that autopsy.

HEART EXCISION

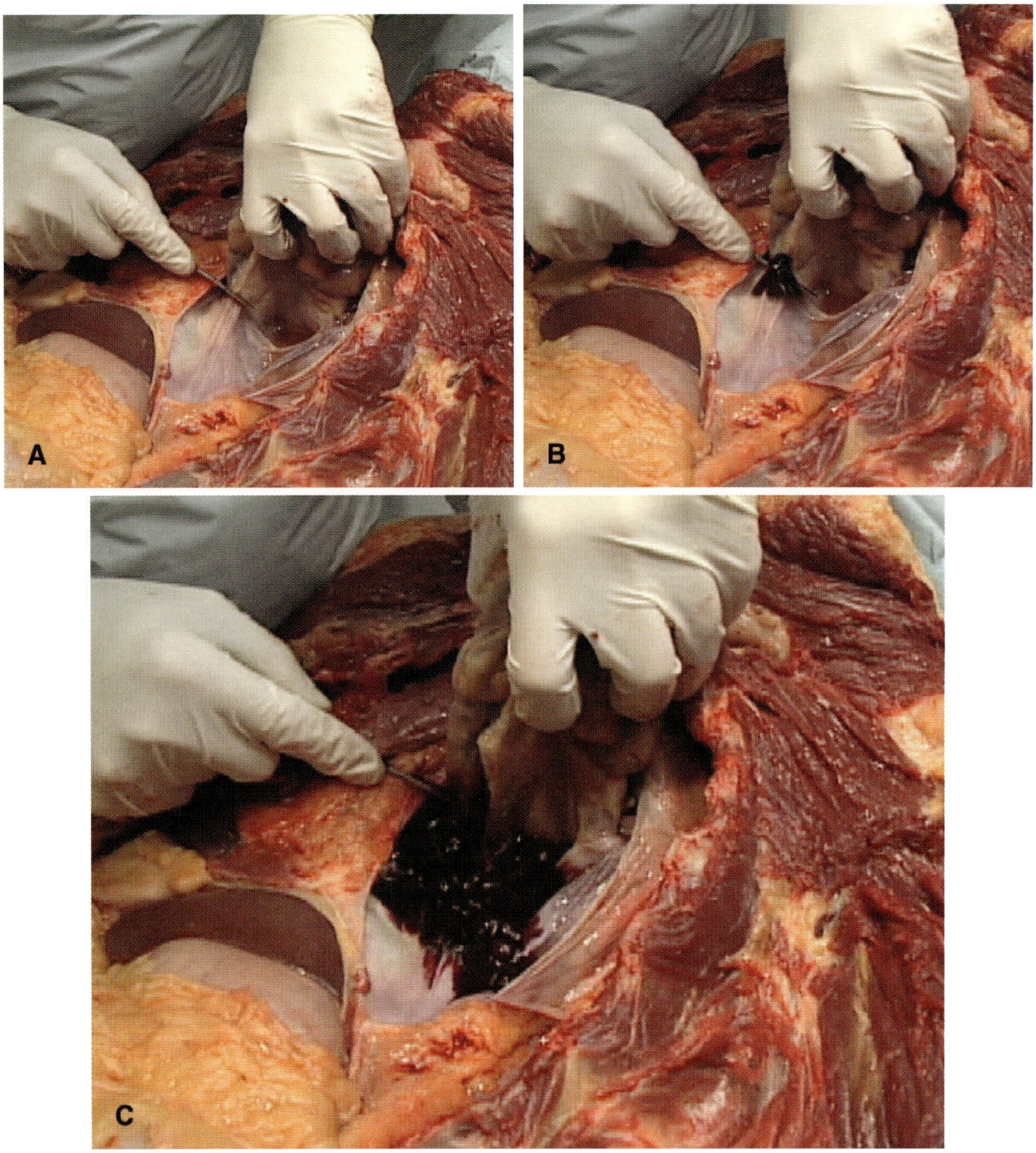

FIGURE 7.1 (A)–(C) Heart removal, cutting the inferior vena cava. The inferior vena cava is cut, as are the pulmonary veins, pulmonary arteries, and aorta. The heart is held in the left hand in these figures. Blood flows from the cut vessels if the blood is not clotted, decomposed, or mostly absent from the body. In cases of severe hemorrhage, there is a notable absence of blood at this moment of the autopsy.

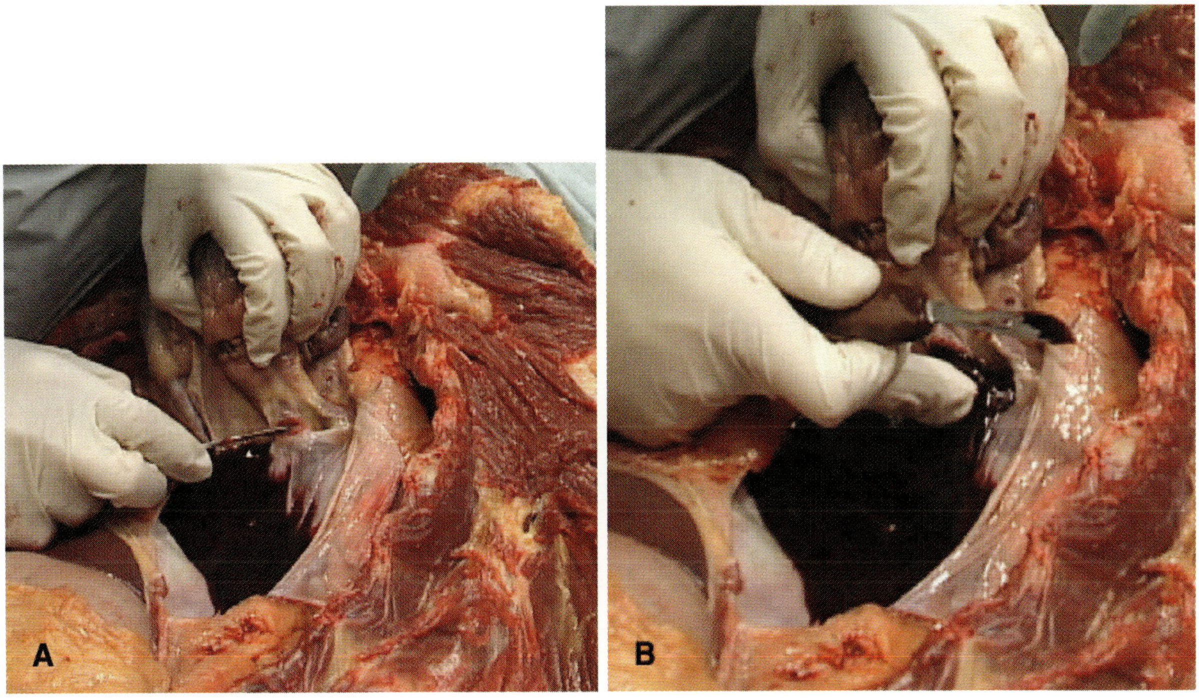

FIGURE 7.2 **(A) Cutting the pulmonary artery**. The left pulmonary artery is cut as is the left pulmonary vein. **(B) Checking for pulmonary embolus.** The pulmonary artery is checked for a clot (thromboembolus).

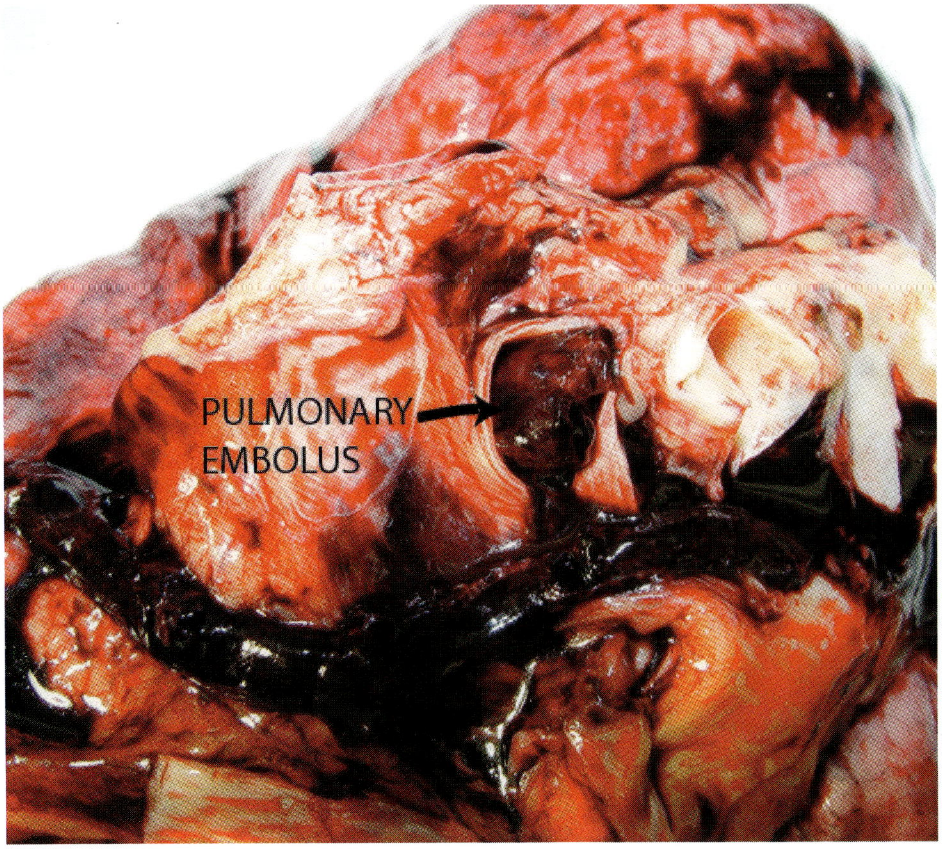

FIGURE 7.3 **Pulmonary embolus.** The long blood clot depicted was taken from the inferior vena cava. A large pulmonary embolus is seen in the pulmonary artery as well. These clots (emboli) can move up from the lower leg veins, or less commonly, from the pelvis or upper arm veins to the right heart, and then out to the pulmonary arteries. If these thromboemboli are large enough, they can cause immediate cardiac arrest.

FIGURE 7.4 (A), (B) Weighing the heart. The heart, like all organs, is weighed. Increased weight of the heart can indicate hypertensive heart disease or numerous other conditions that cause heart failure, like cardiomyopathy. The heart is a specialized muscle that increases in size and weight as more work is required of it. High blood pressure causes the heart to increase in weight and thickness because of the increased pressure the heart must maintain. The average heart weighs about 350 g in a 190-lb man. A hypertensive heart might weigh more than 500 g. This particular heart weighs about 620 g, due to hypertensive heart disease.

LUNG EXCISION

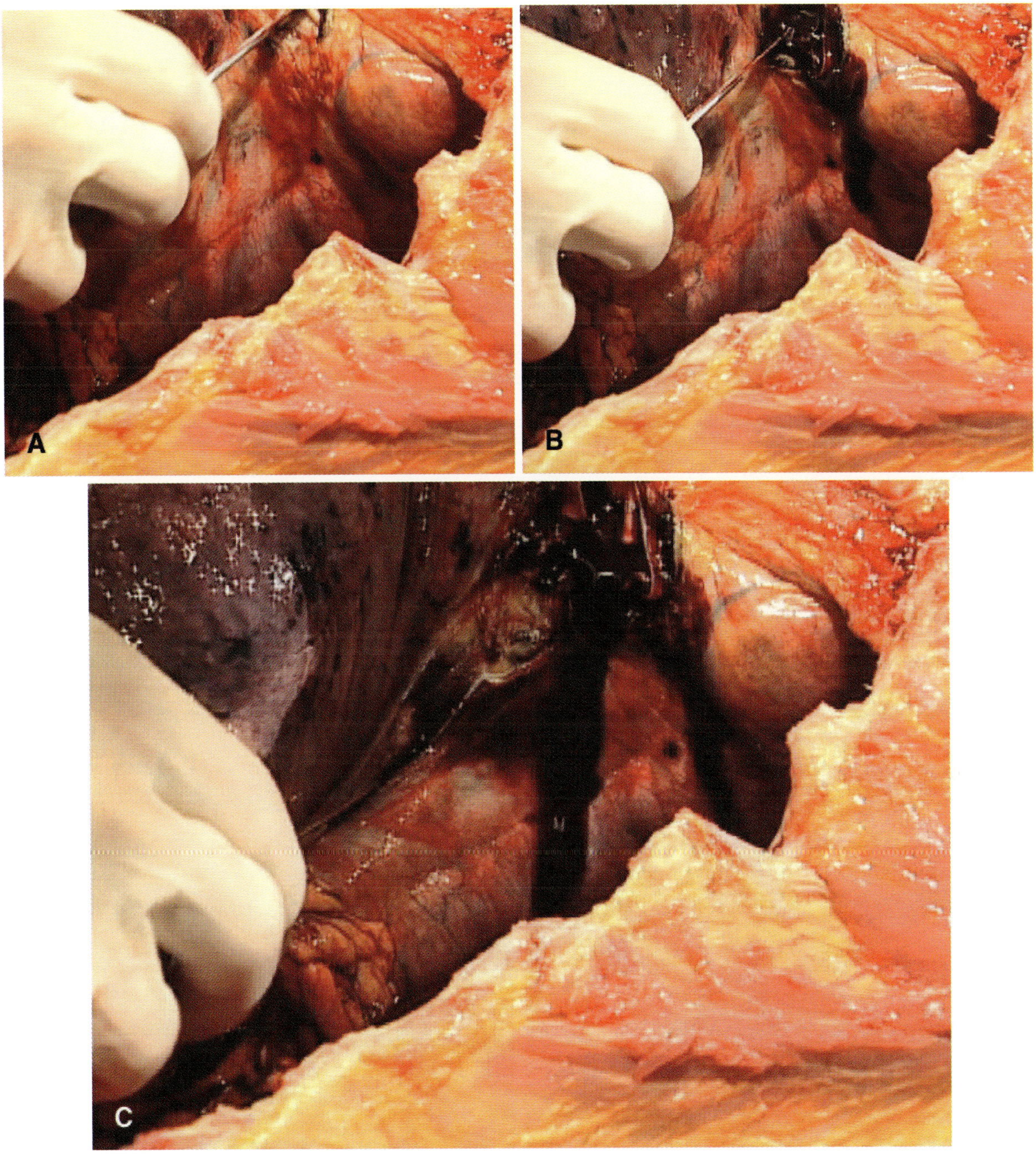

FIGURE 7.5 (A)–(C) Excision of the lungs. The lungs are removed at the hilum, or center of attachment.

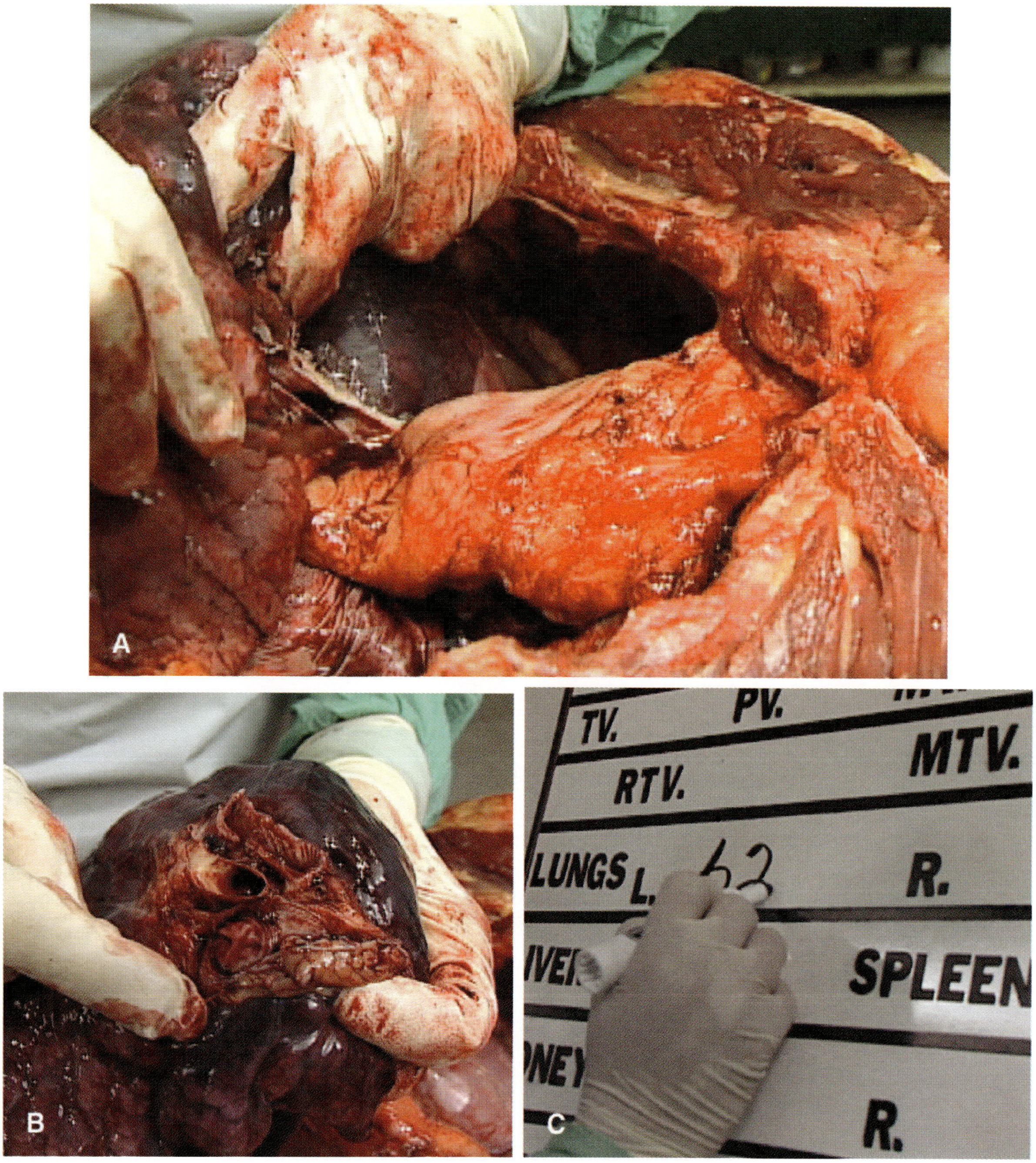

FIGURE 7.6 (A)–(C) Exam of the hilum. As this right lung is removed, the hilum is quickly examined for tumors or infection. The lung is weighed. Heavy lungs are commonly seen in pneumonia and heart failure (associated with pulmonary edema).

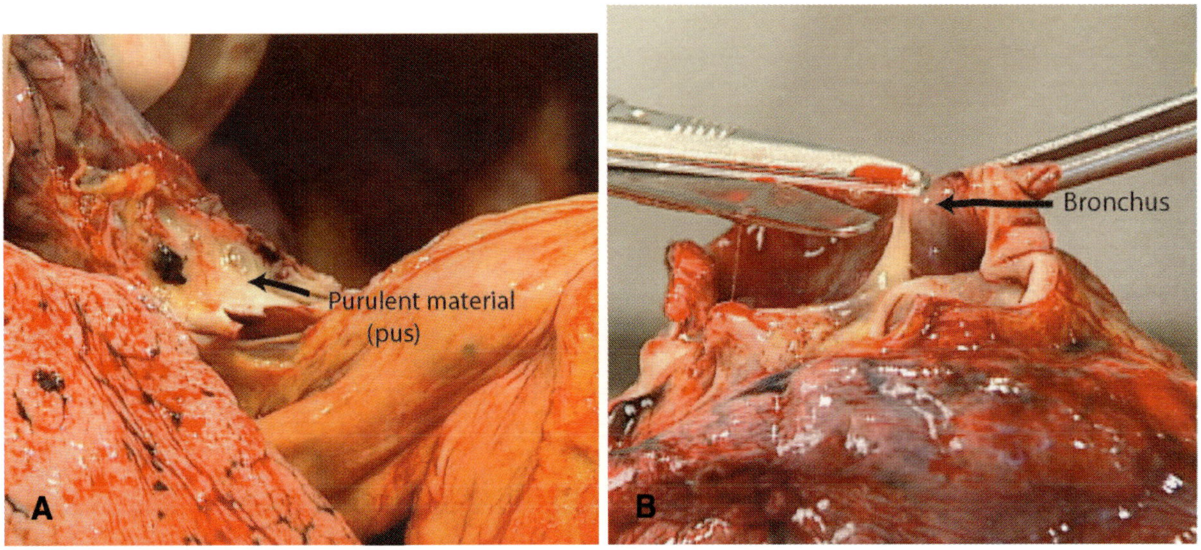

FIGURE 7.7 Bronchial pneumonia. (A) Examination of this hilum shows pus in the bronchus bubbling through the bronchial artery. **(B)** The pus an be seen at the tip of the scissor. The pus is a sign of bronchopneumonia.

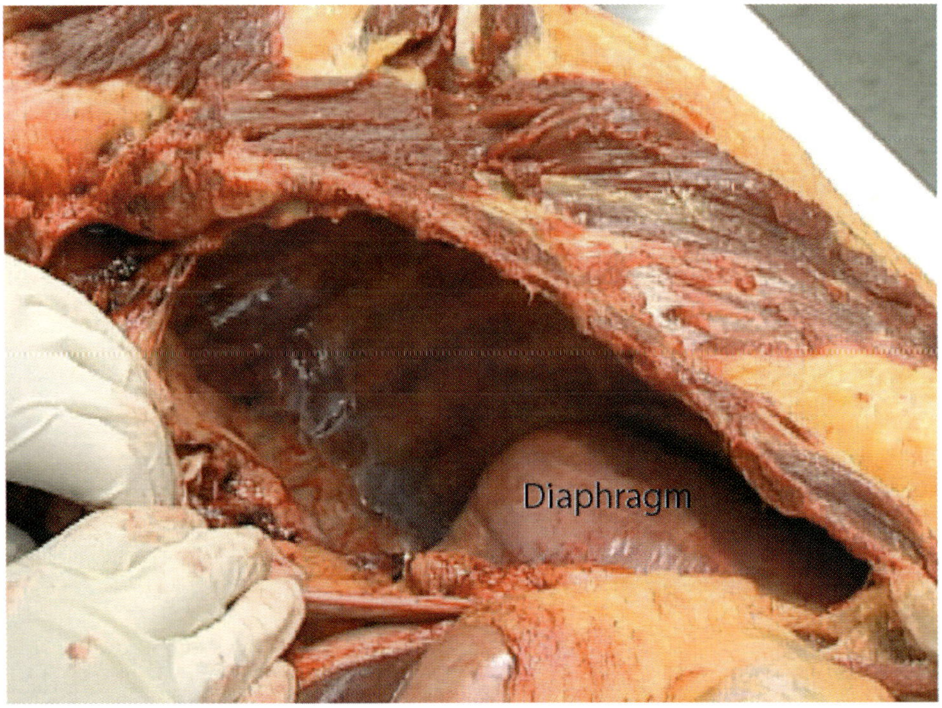

FIGURE 7.8 Chest cavity exam. The chest cavity and ribs are examined for tumors, rib fractures, and contusions, among other conditions. The diaphragm is the dome-shaped structure in the lower center of the picture.

LIVER EXCISION

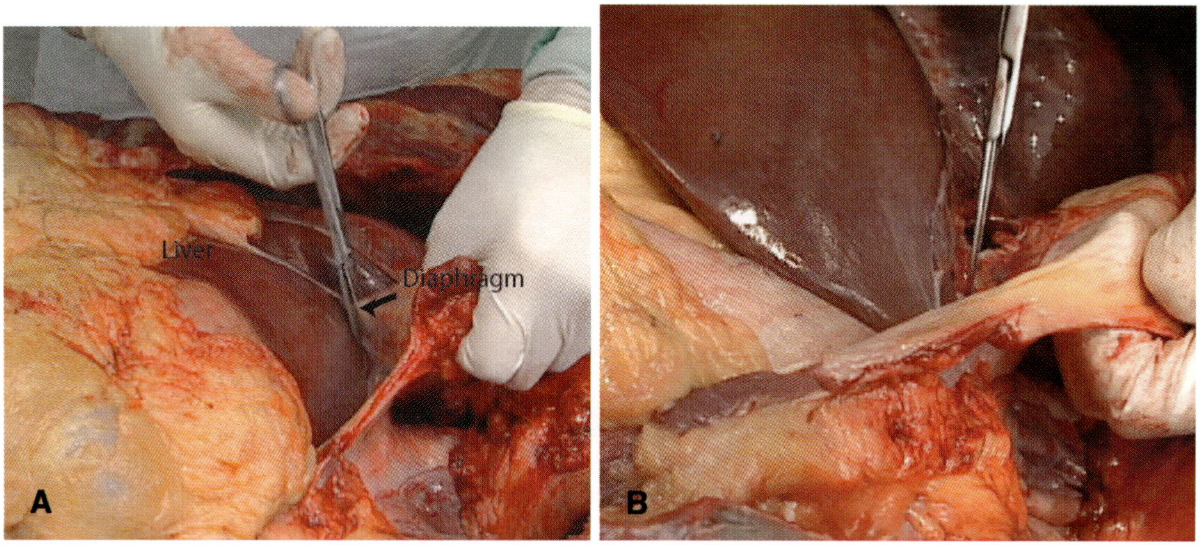

FIGURE 7.9 (A), (B) Freeing the liver from the diaphragm. The liver is freed from the diaphragm, ligaments, and other attachments.

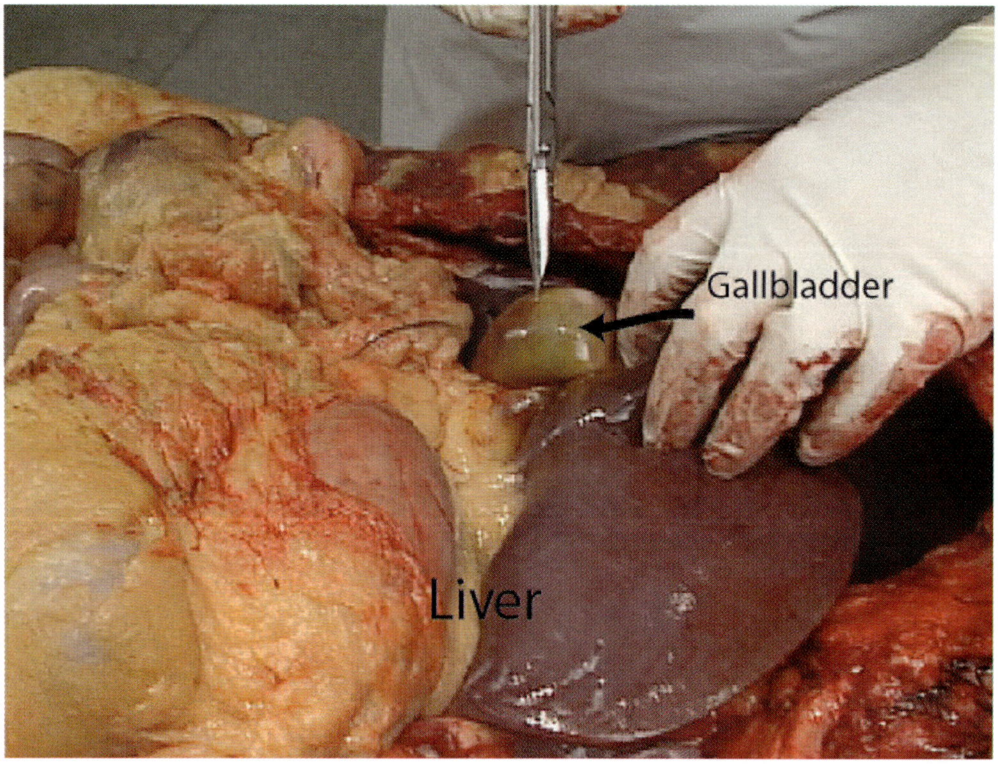

FIGURE 7.10 Liver and gallbladder. The gallbladder is seen *in situ*. The diaphragm has been cut away and the liver is turned up toward the head. The gallbladder is removed with the liver.

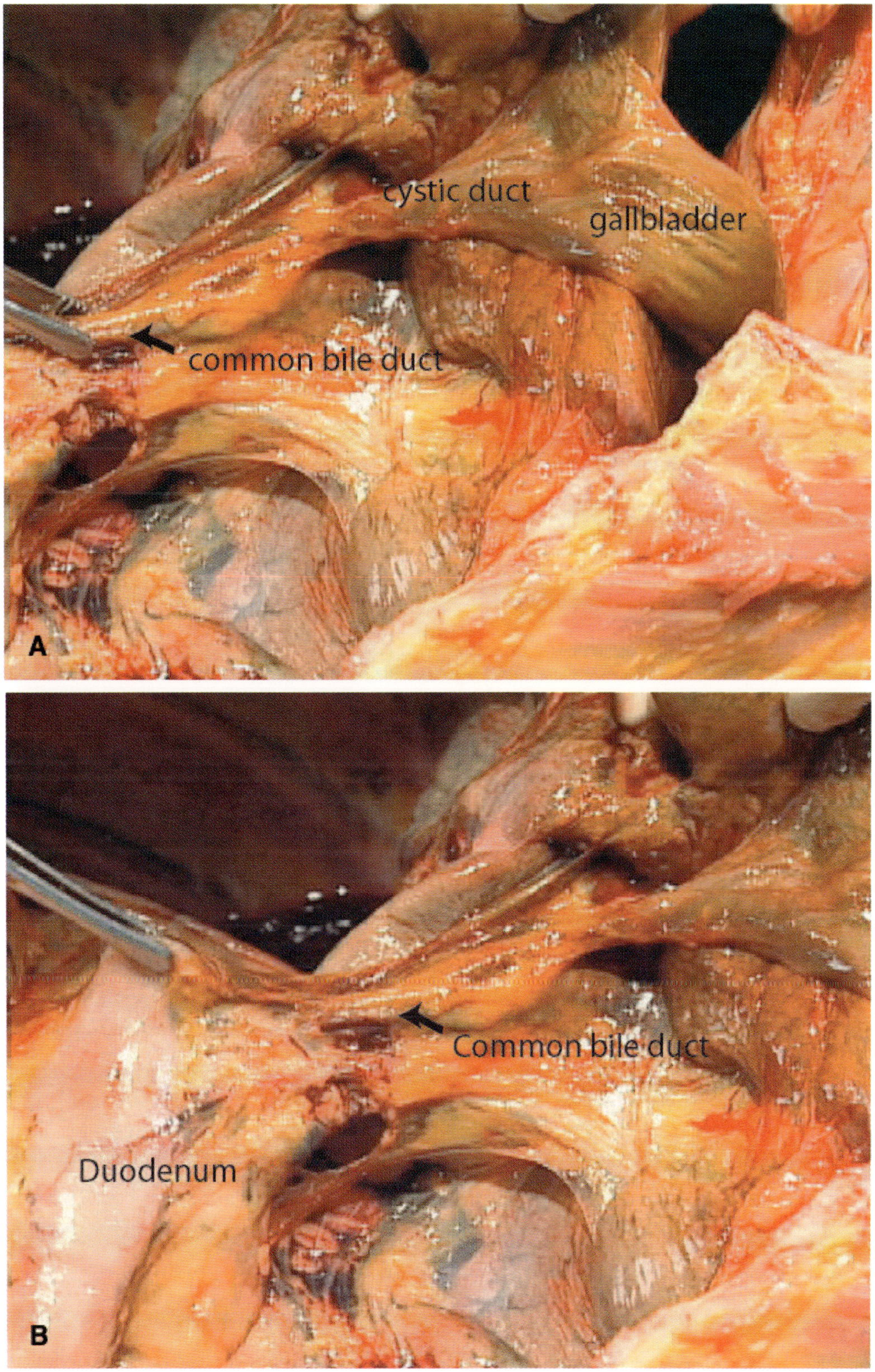

FIGURE 7.11 (A)–(D) Common bile duct and duodenum. The common bile duct is displayed as it empties bile into the duodenum. In Figure 7.11B, the duodenum is held up by the forceps. The common duct is cut and examined for stones also. Gallstones or other stones can plug up the duct, preventing bile from draining from the liver, and resulting in jaundice in the patient.

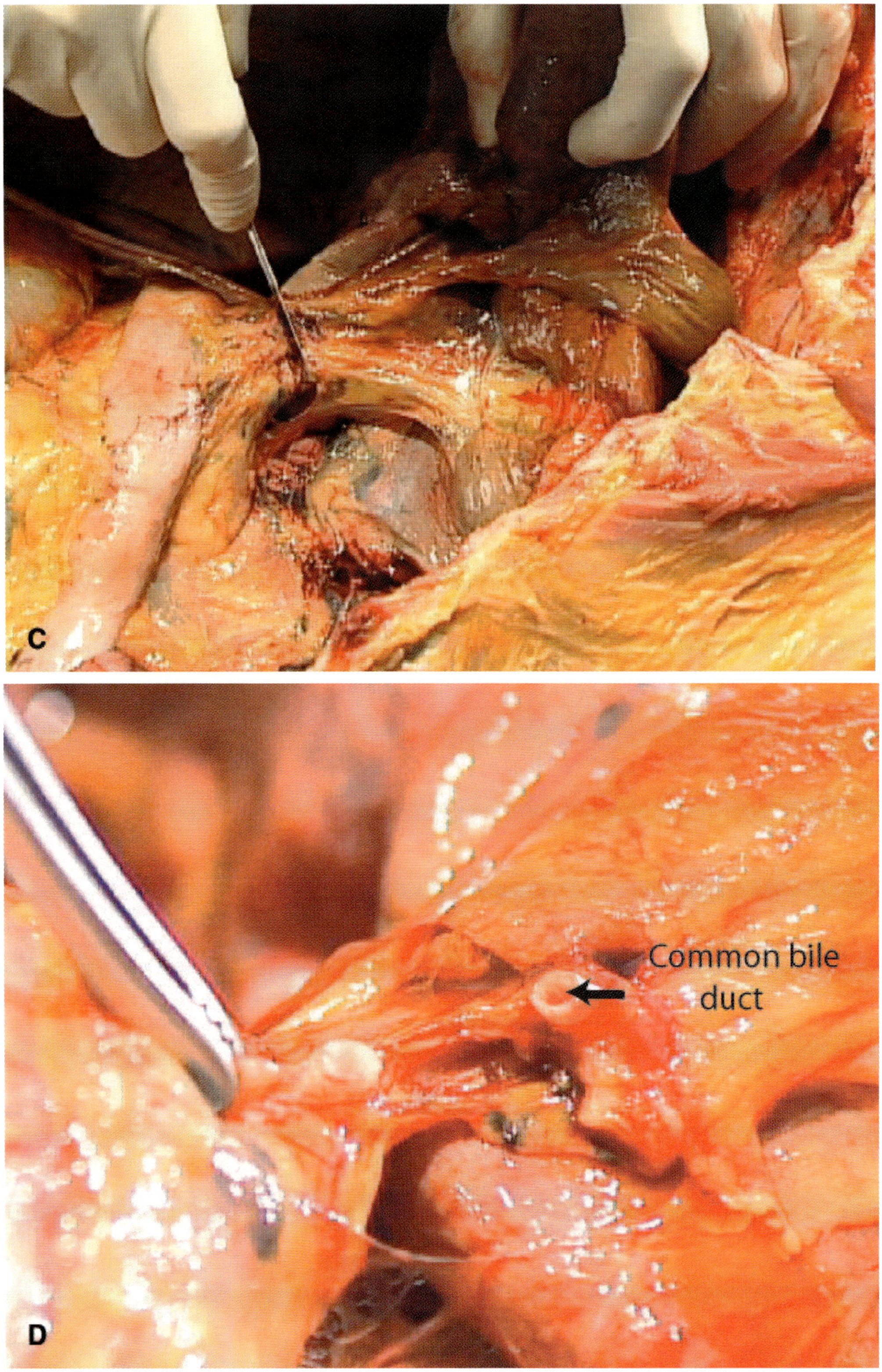

FIGURE 7.11 (CONTINUED) (A)–(D) Common bile duct and duodenum. The common bile duct is displayed as it empties bile into the duodenum. In Figure 7.11B, the duodenum is held up by the forceps. The common duct is cut and examined for stones also. Gallstones or other stones can plug up the duct, preventing bile from draining from the liver, and resulting in jaundice in the patient.

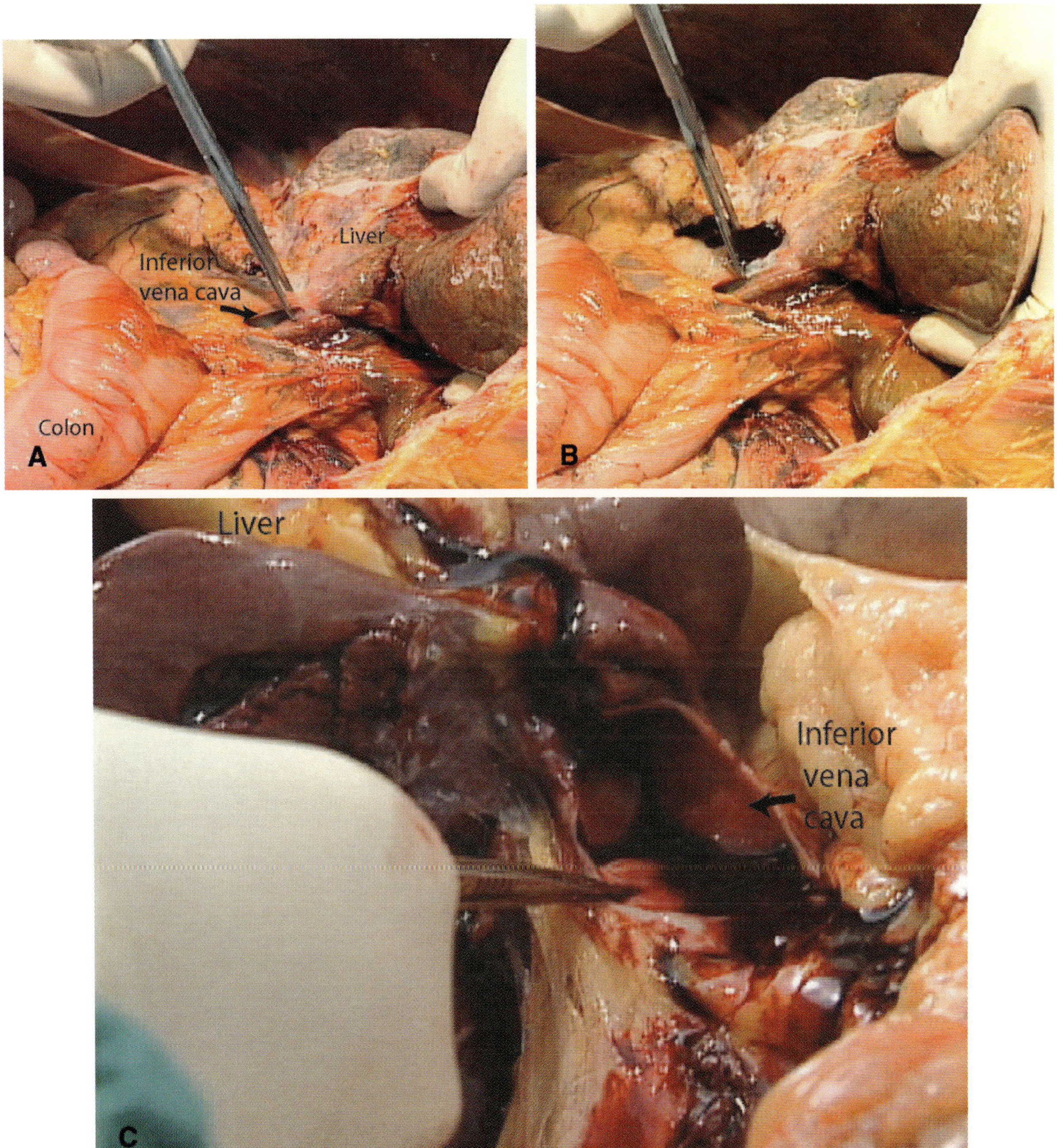

FIGURE 7.12 Cutting the inferior vena cava. **(A), (B)** The inferior vena cava is cut as it enters the dorsal surface of the liver. **(C)** This figure shows the large diameter of the inferior vena cava when opened.

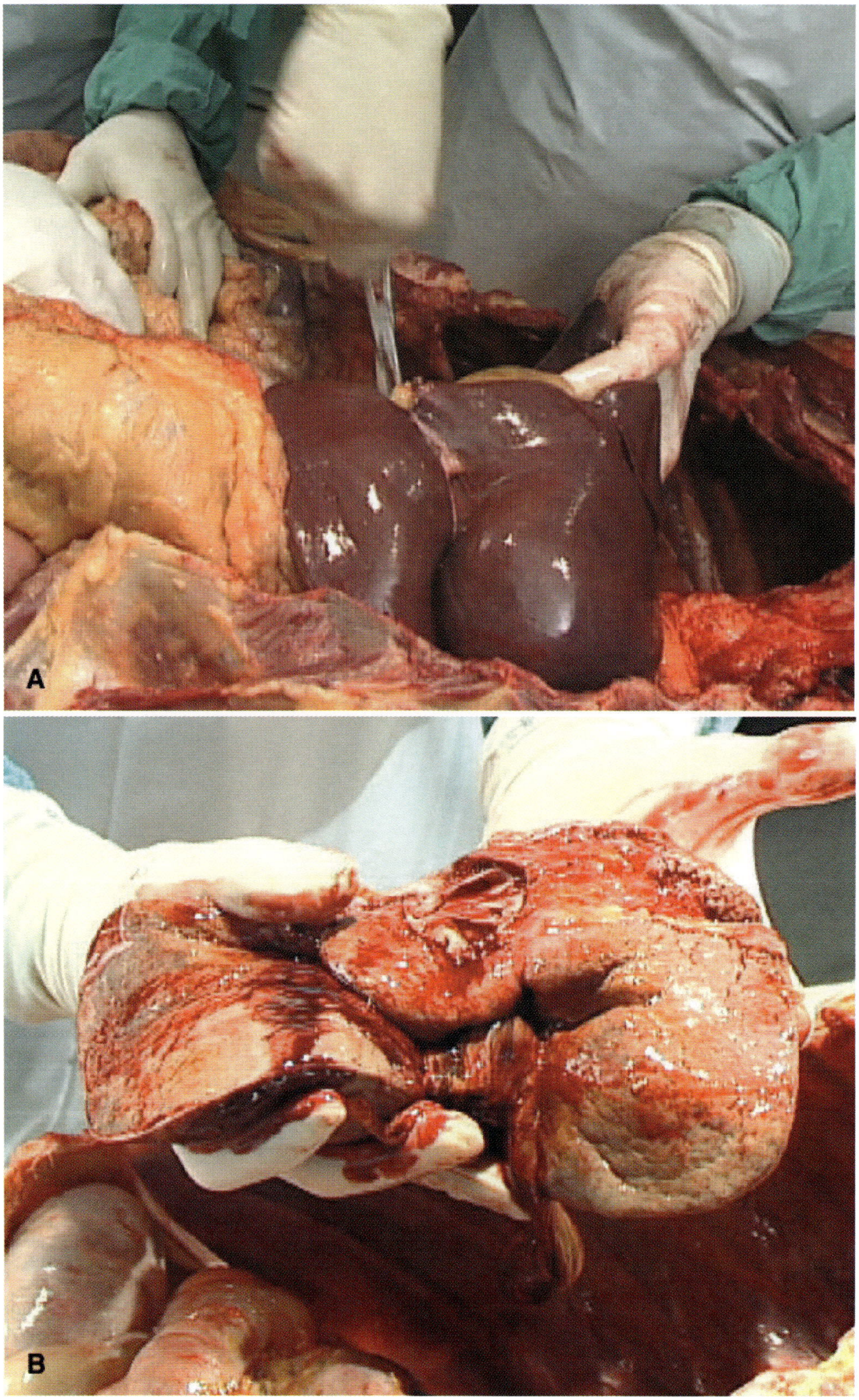

FIGURE 7.13 (A), (B) Removing the liver. Once the liver is completely cut away, it is lifted out of the body for weighing. Those who see the liver for the first time are astonished at its size and weight. The average liver weighs about 1930 g, or about 4.5 lb, in a 170-lb man.

SPLEEN EXCISION

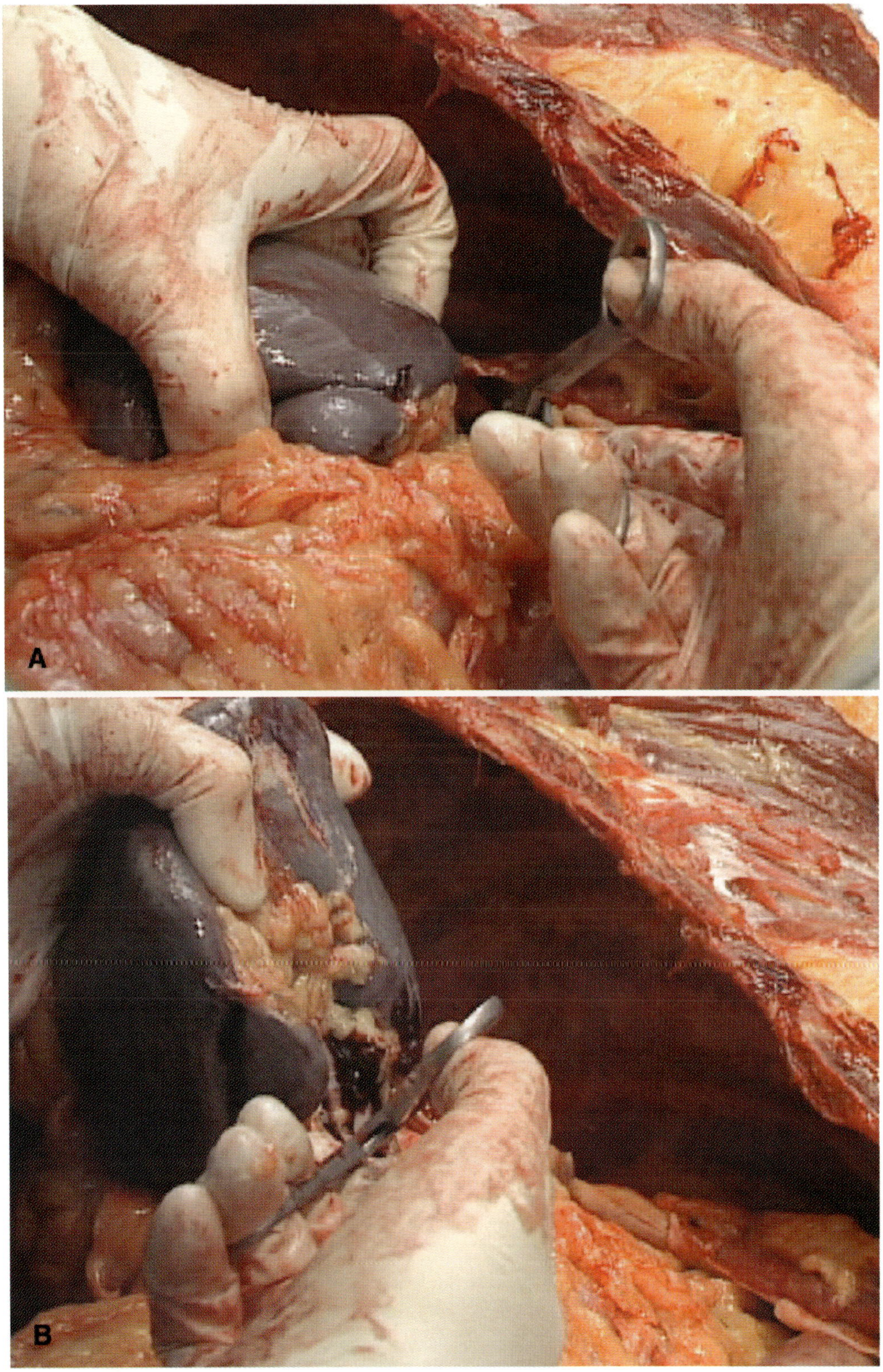

FIGURE 7.14 (A), (B) Removing the spleen. The spleen is removed by cutting the vessels away from the hilum, checking carefully for lacerations because the capsule (covering) of the spleen can be easily torn on removal.

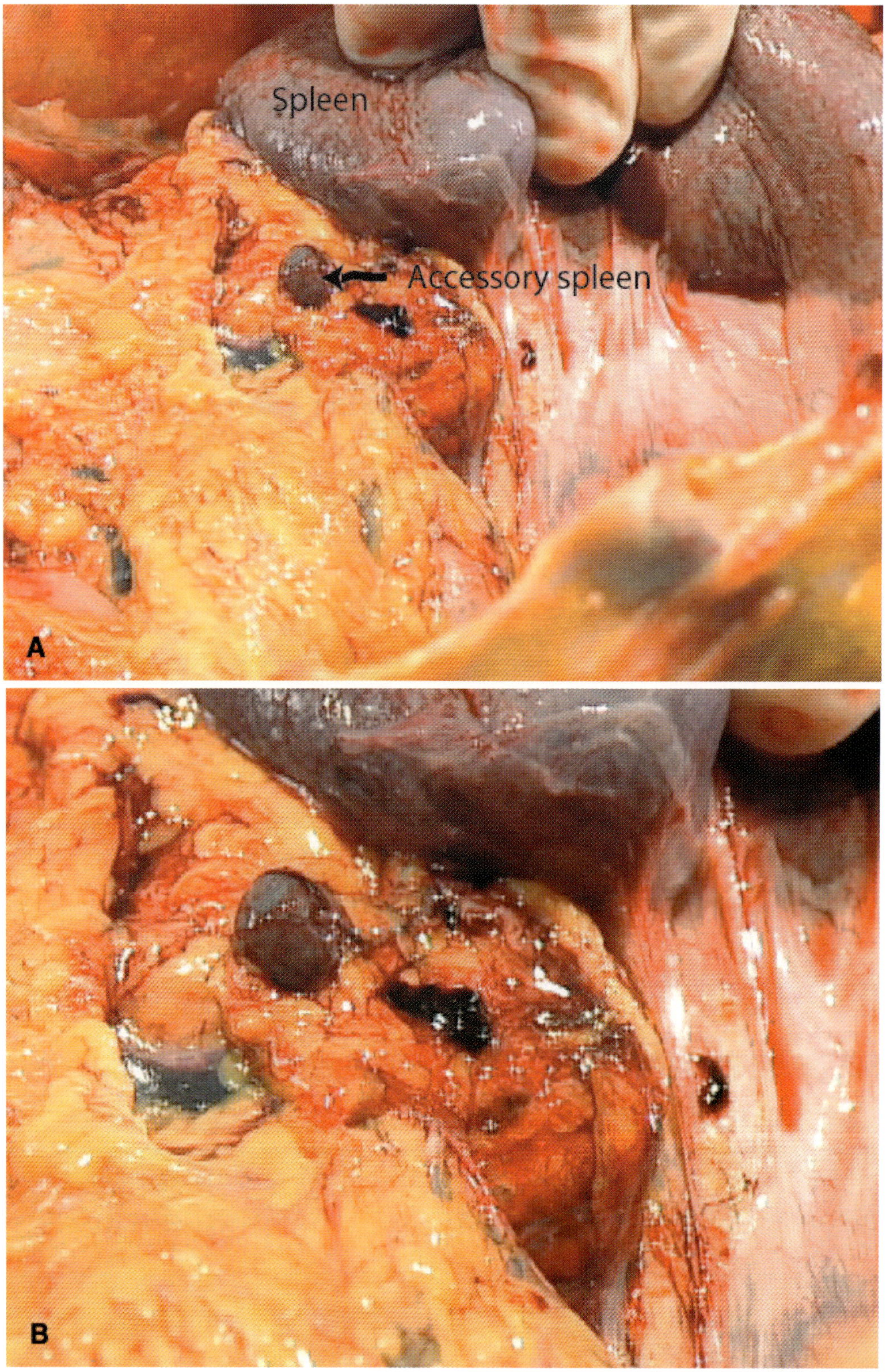

FIGURE 7.15 **(A), (B) Accessory spleen.** Adjacent to this spleen is a small accessory spleen. Accessory spleens can become quite large if the main spleen is removed. This can be problematic in a condition called hypersplenism, in which the spleen pathologically destroys red blood cells. The accessory spleen, if not removed, can enlarge and cause the hypersplenism to return.

SMALL AND LARGE BOWEL EXCISION

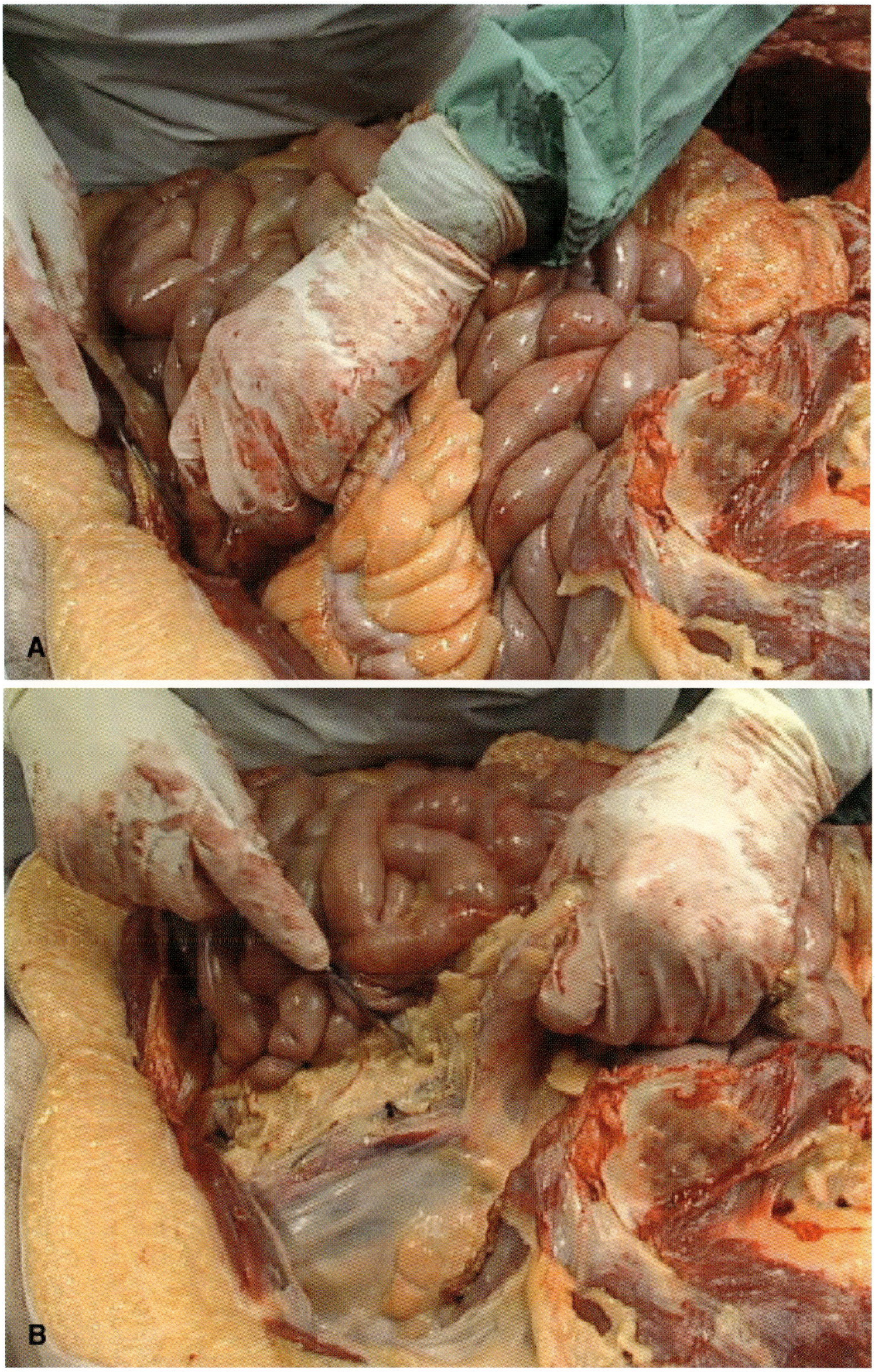

FIGURE 7.16 (A), (B) Bowel excision. In this removal method, the excision starts at the rectum and progresses upward toward the sigmoid colon in the left part of the abdomen.

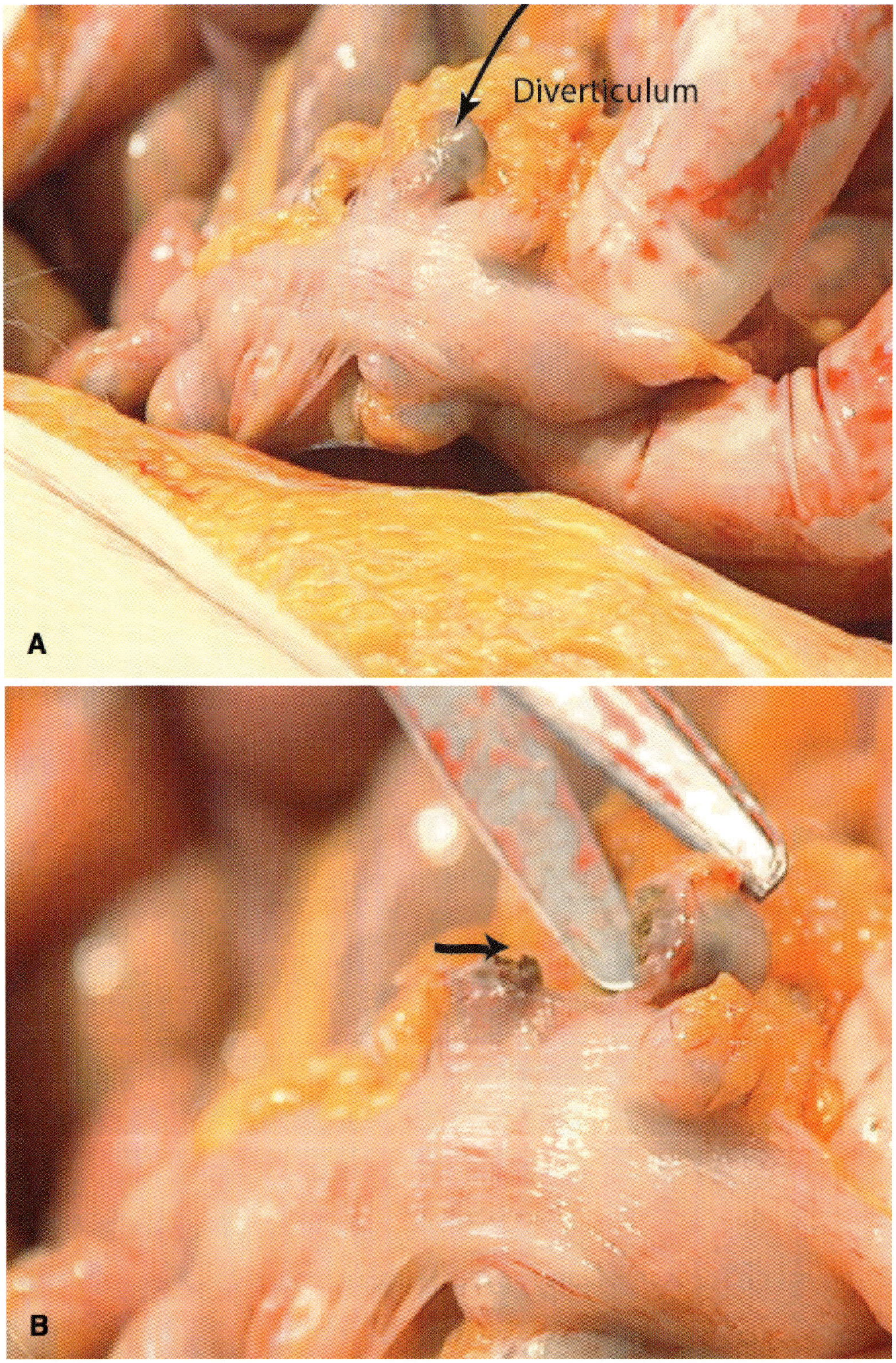

FIGURE 7.17 Diverticuli of the sigmoid colon. (A) The sigmoid colon is prone to forming diverticuli, often seen in middle-aged to older patients. In this condition, the mucosa herniates through weak points in the muscular colon wall. **(B)** Fecal matter, seen on cutting (see arrow), can plug up these diverticuli and cause inflammation (diverticulitis).

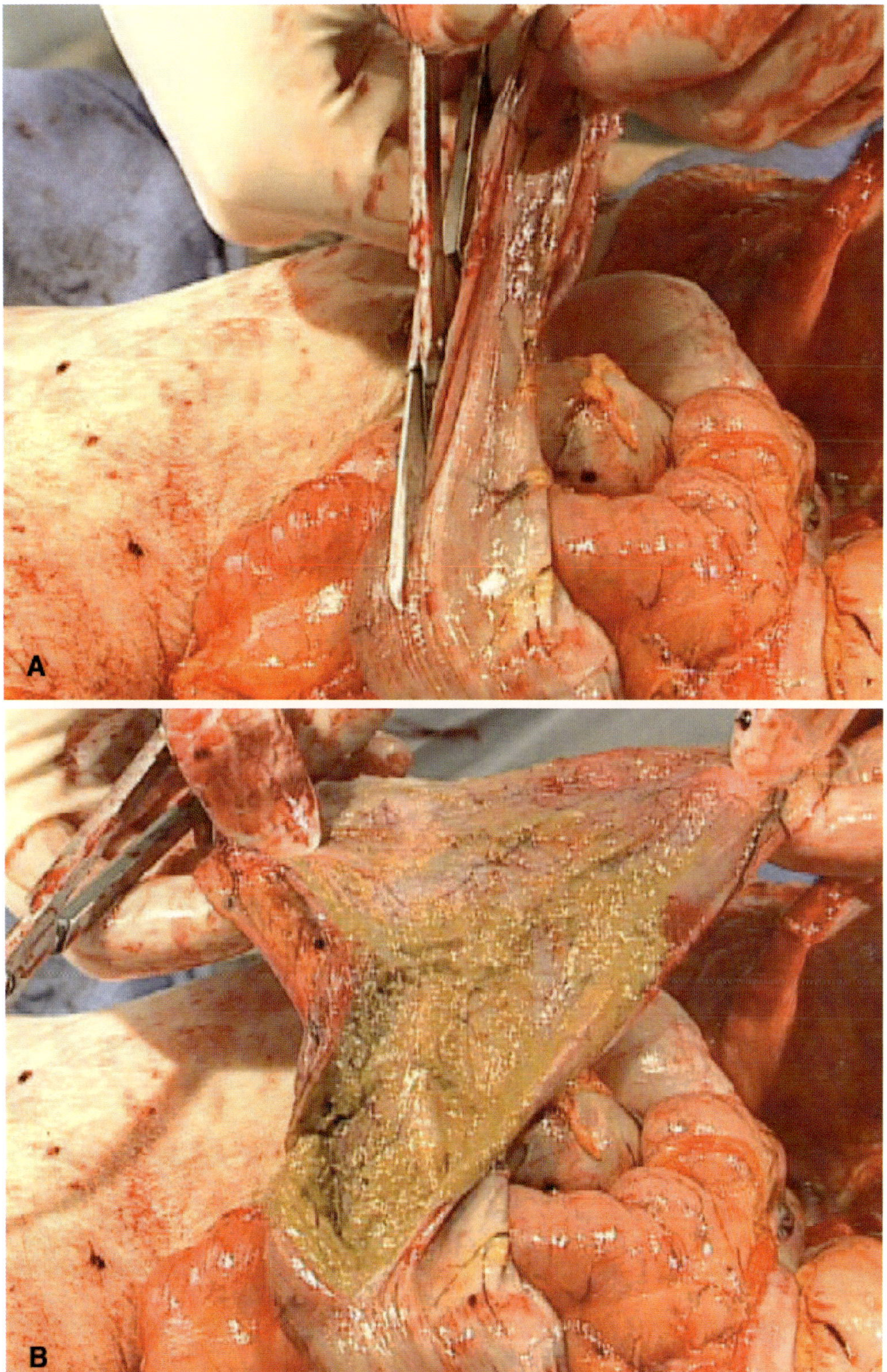

FIGURE 7.18 (A), (B) Opening or "running" the bowel. The bowel is opened completely and examined for tumors, diverticuli, and other lesions.

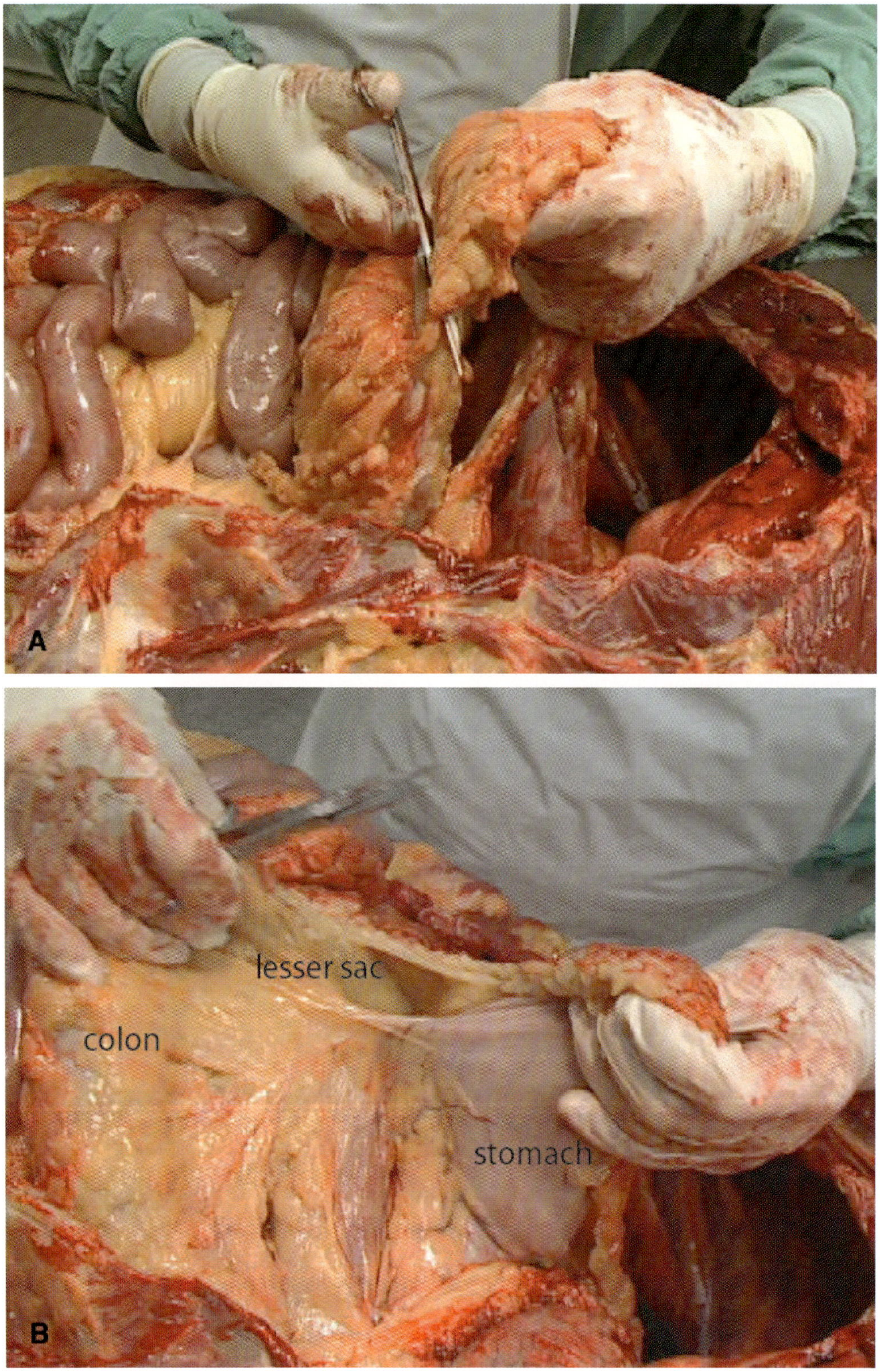

FIGURE 7.19 (A), (B) Cutting the gastrocolic ligament. The gastrocolic ligament, between the stomach and transverse colon, is cut, opening the lesser sac.

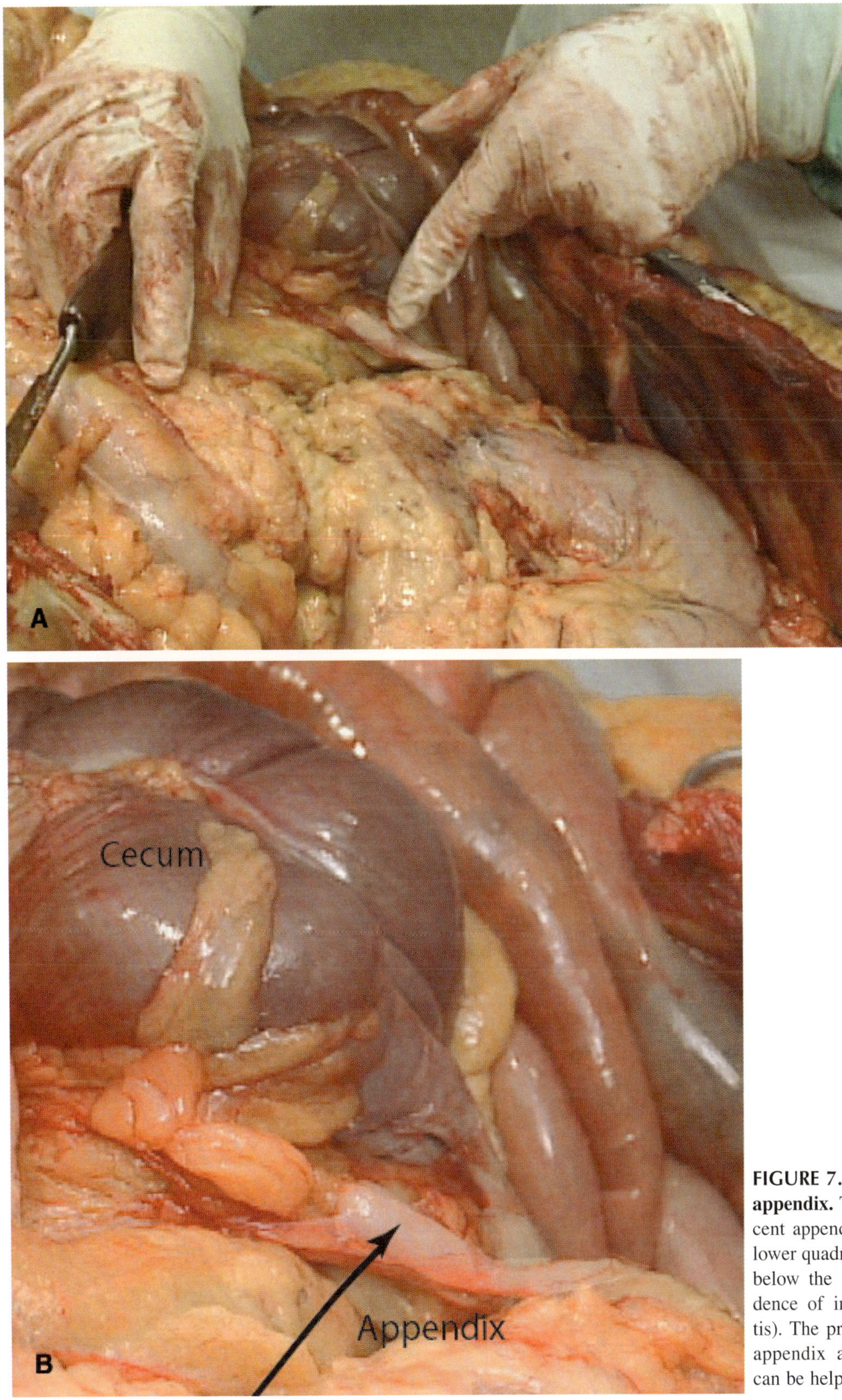

FIGURE 7.20 (A), (B) Cecum and appendix. The cecum and the adjacent appendix are seen in the right lower quadrant of the abdomen, just below the finger. There is no evidence of inflammation (appendicitis). The presence or absence of an appendix and accompanying scar can be helpful in identification.

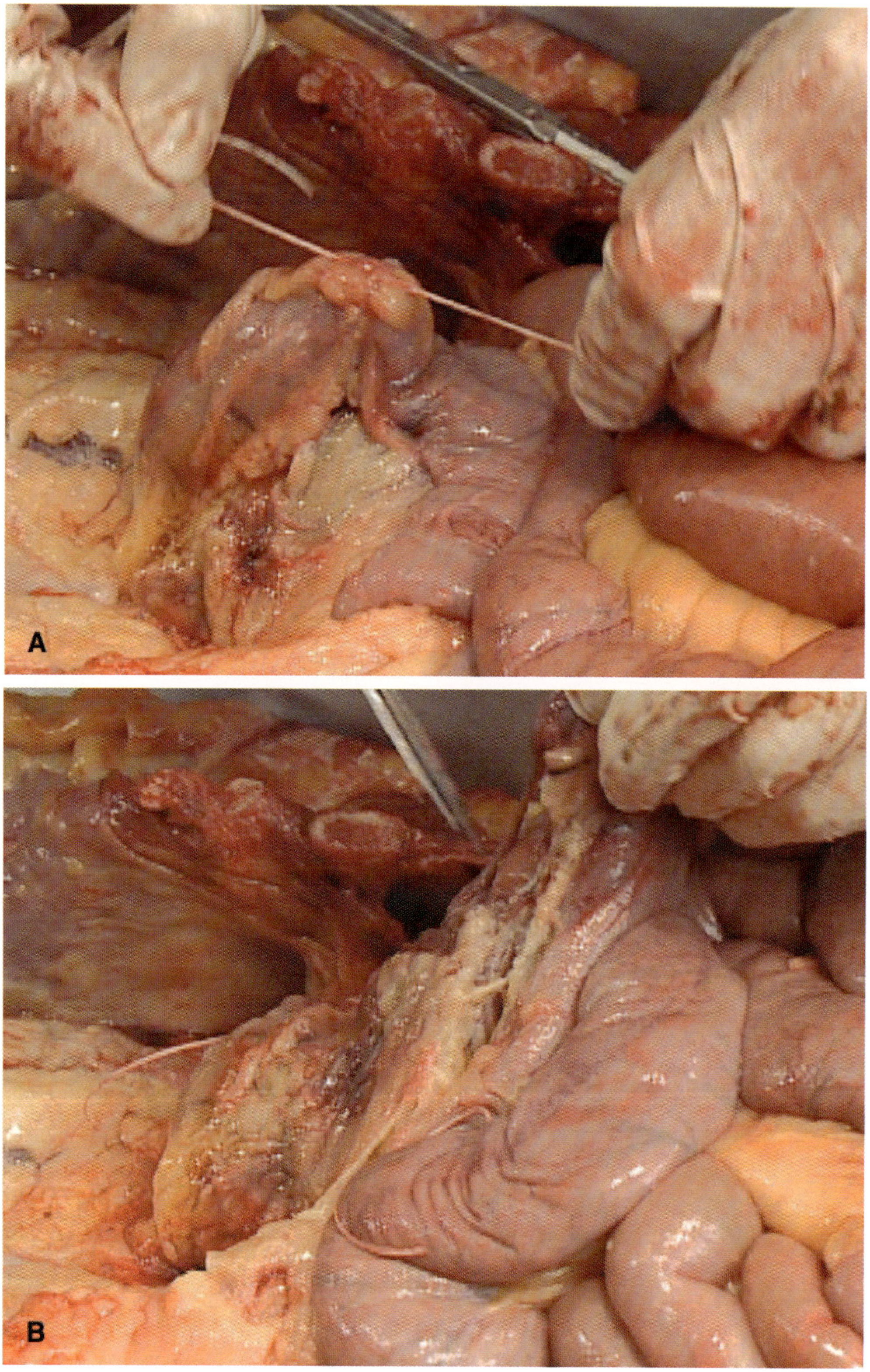

FIGURE 7.21 (A), (B) **Tying and cutting of the duodenum.** The duodenum is tied. This is done to prevent gastric contents from leaking out when the duodenum is cut for removal.

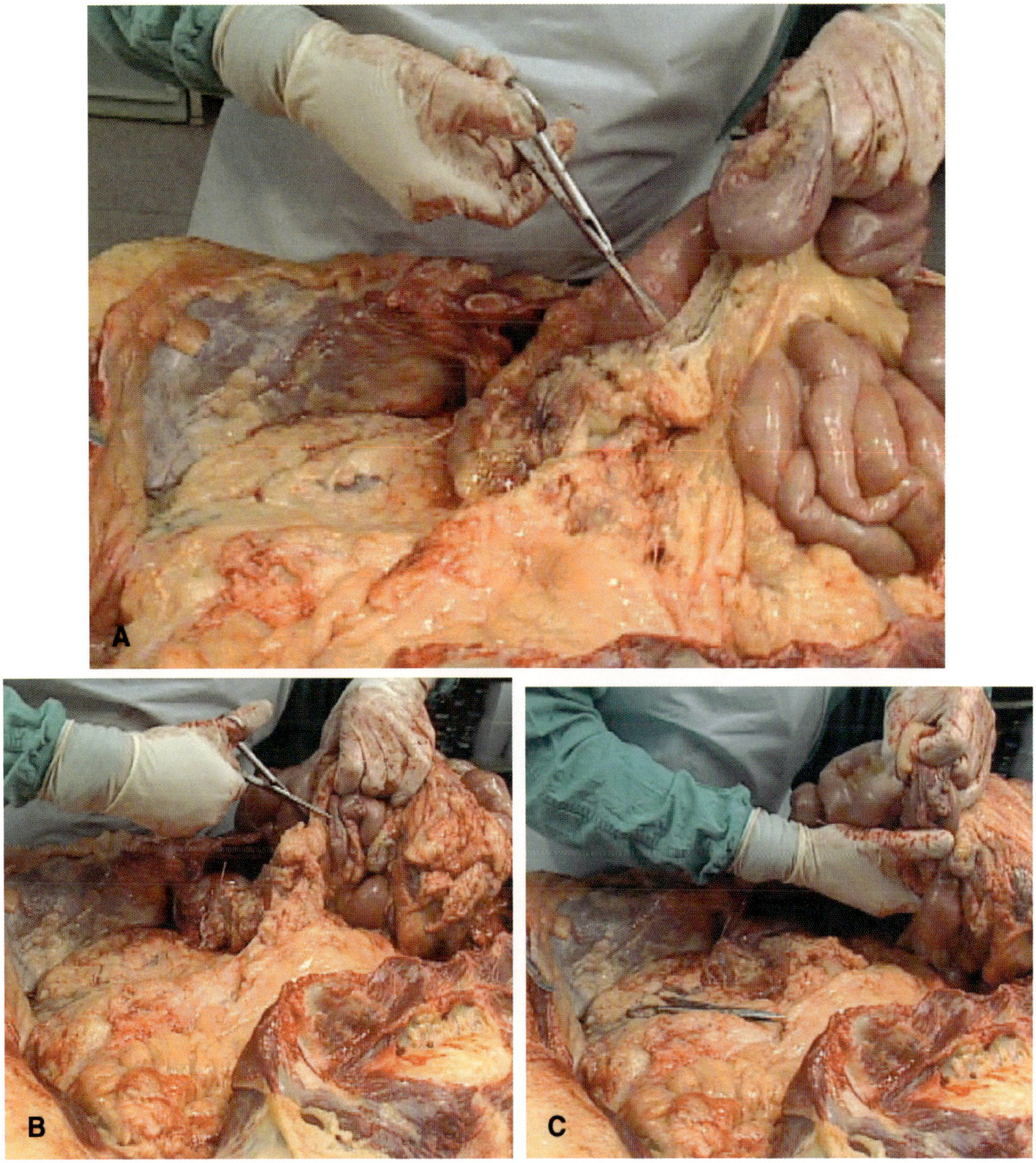

FIGURE 7.22 (A)–(C) **Removal of the small and large bowels.** The large and small bowels are removed as the mesentery is cut. Traction is applied to the bowels as the soft tissue is cut.

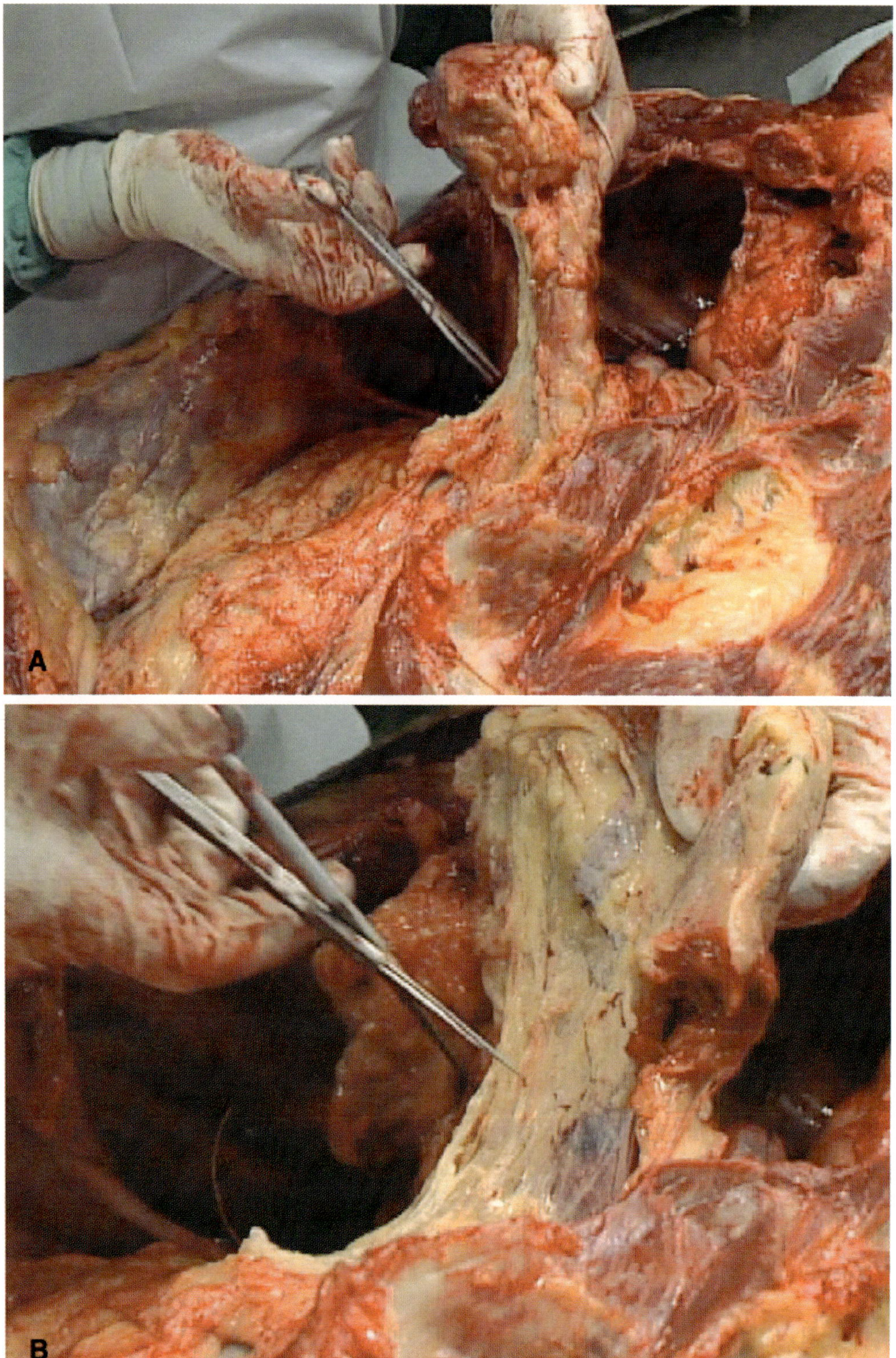

FIGURE 7.23 (A), (B) Excising the pancreas and duodenum. The pancreas and duodenum are held in the left hand, as the soft tissue is cut by the right hand.

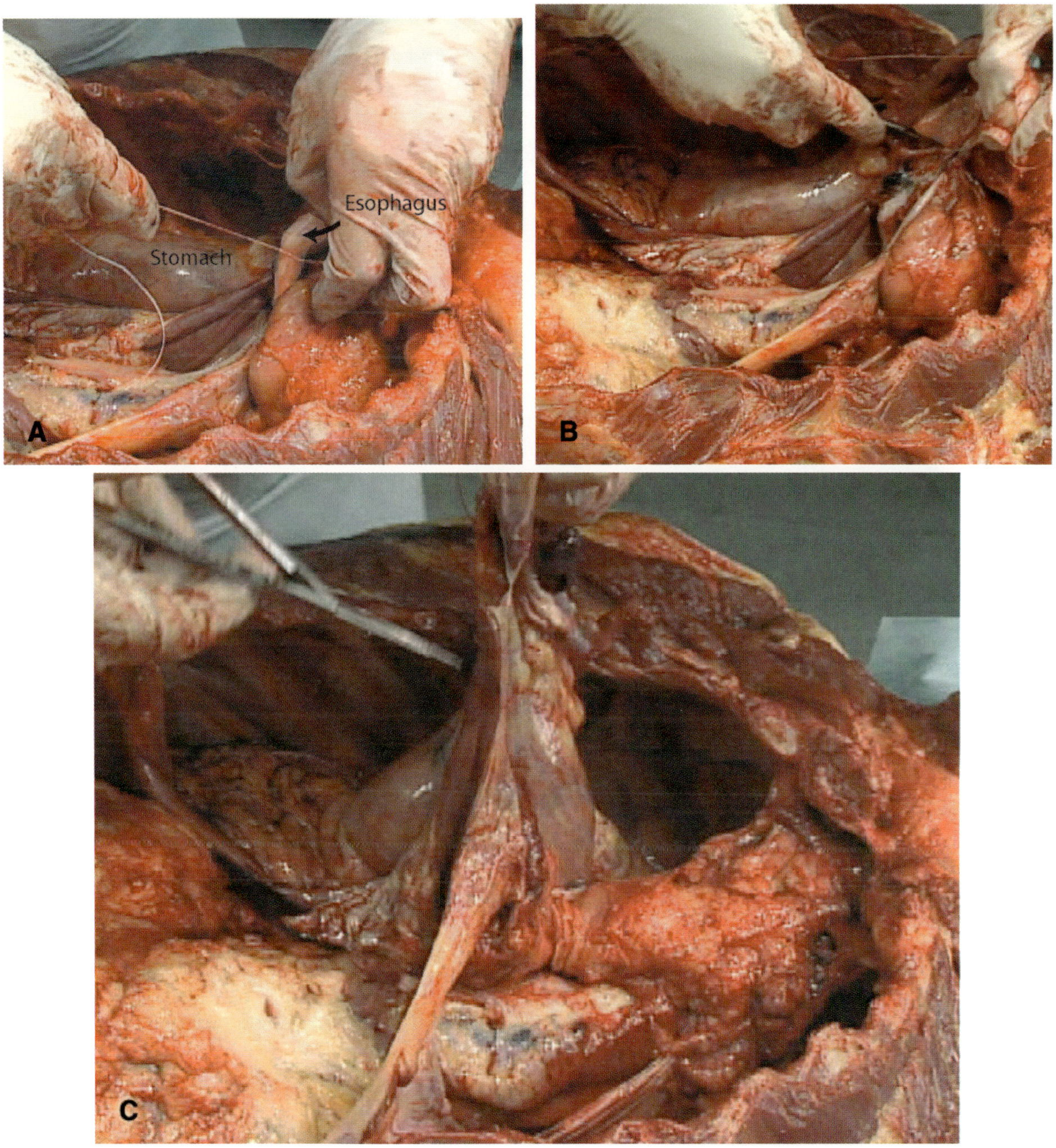

FIGURE 7.24 **(A)–(C) Removing the esophagus and stomach.** The esophagus is tied to prevent loss of gastric contents while the stomach is cut and removed.

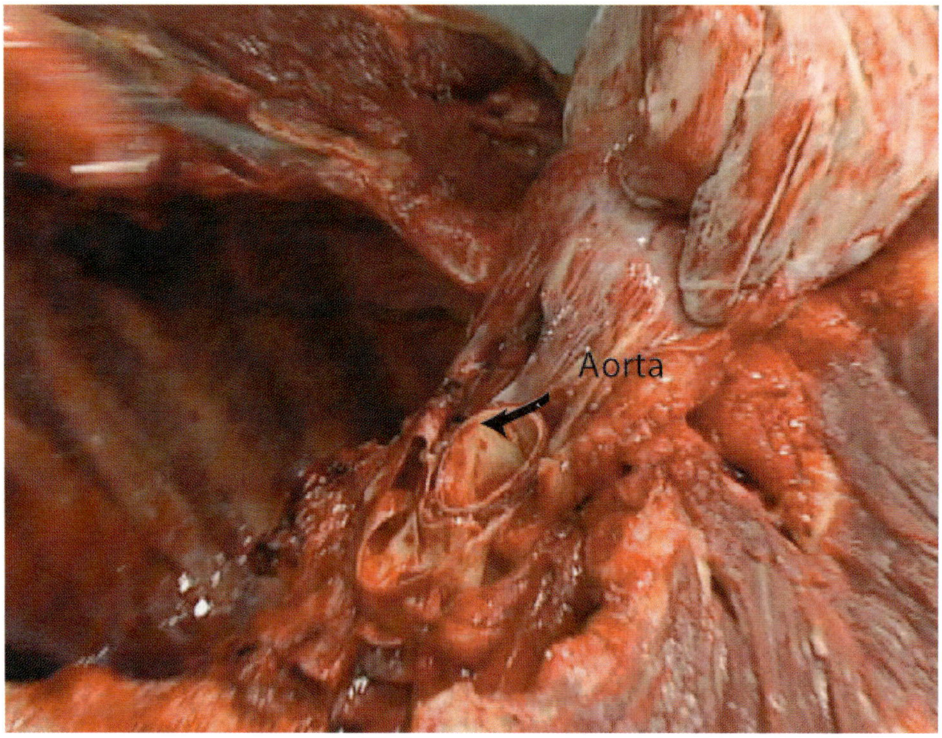

FIGURE 7.25 Mediastinum exam. The mediastinum is examined for tumors and a thymus. The thymus is usually small after about age 25. Lung tumors and other malignancies, such as lymphomas, often spread or "metastasize" to the mediastinum. The aorta is seen in the center.

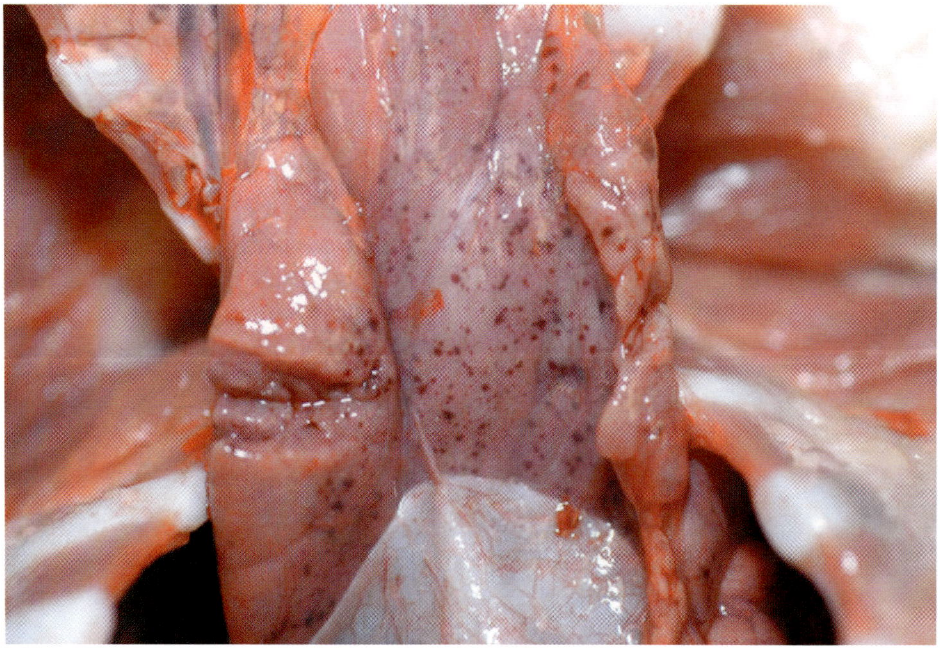

FIGURE 7.26 Thymus with petechiae. This thymus from a sudden infant death syndrome (SIDS) case shows multiple petechiae. The cause of SIDS is essentially unknown. Many cases are thought to be asphyxial deaths.

ADRENAL GLAND AND KIDNEY REMOVAL

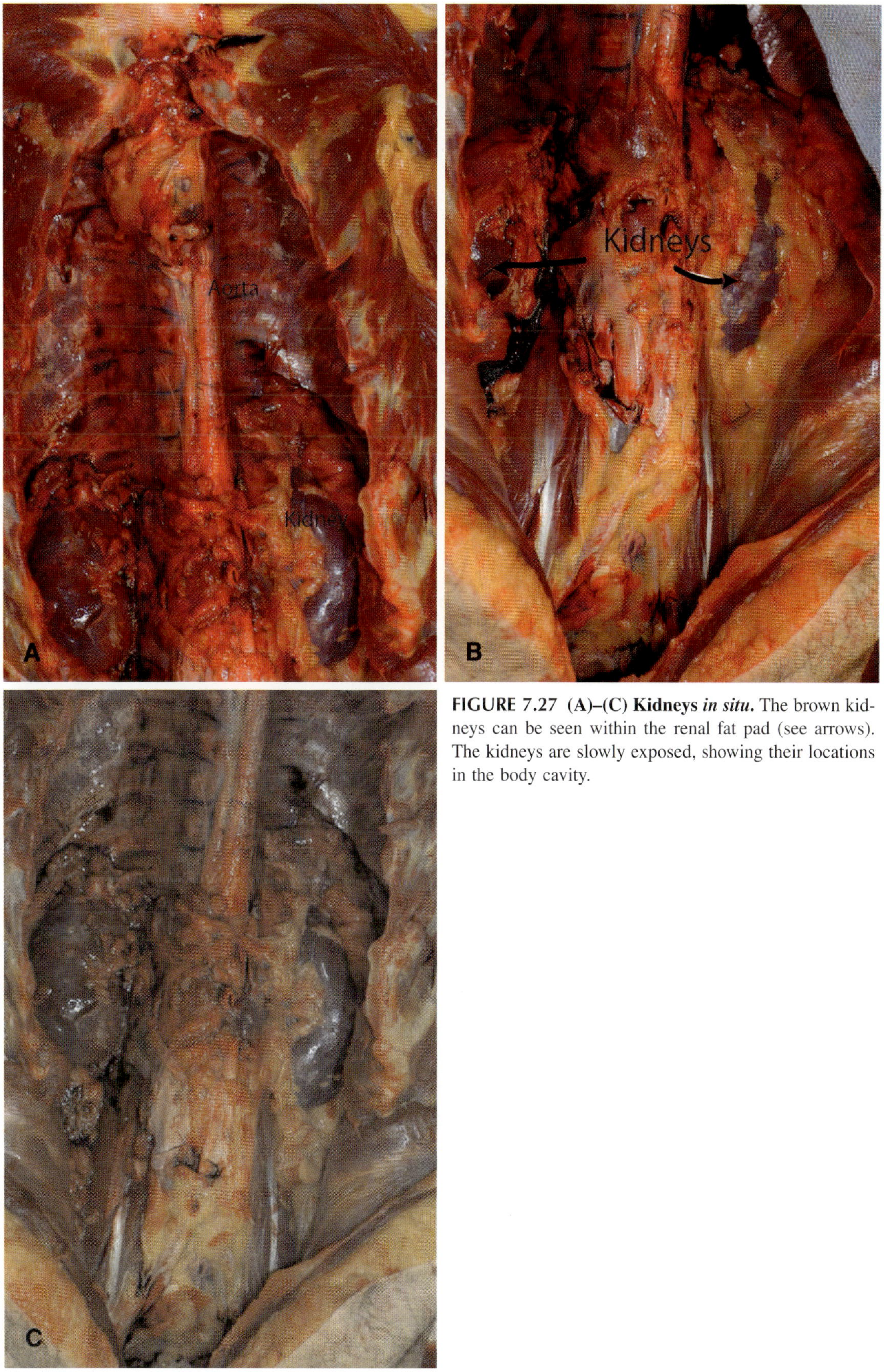

FIGURE 7.27 (A)–(C) Kidneys *in situ*. The brown kidneys can be seen within the renal fat pad (see arrows). The kidneys are slowly exposed, showing their locations in the body cavity.

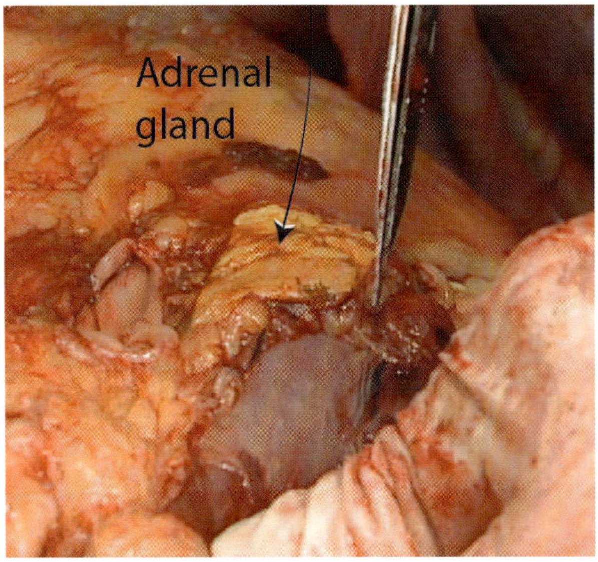

FIGURE 7.28 Adrenal gland *in situ*. The adrenal gland is to the left of the scissor, and the kidney is hidden below, under the renal fat pad.

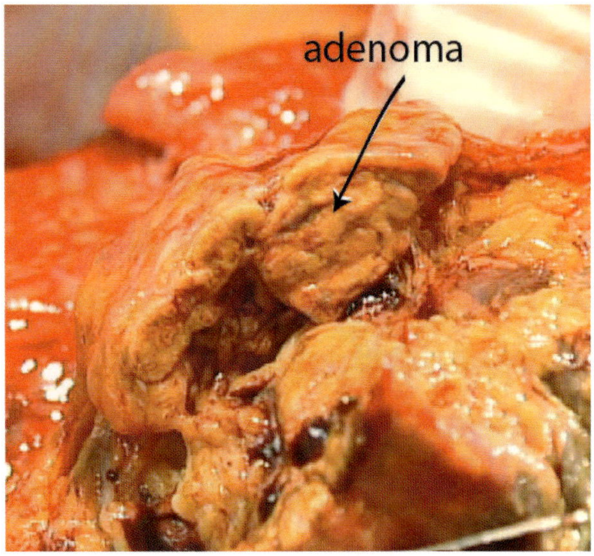

FIGURE 7.29 Adrenal cortical adenoma. The adrenal gland is cut here. The bright yellow cortex contains an adenoma, or nodule. These nodules can be associated with hypertension.

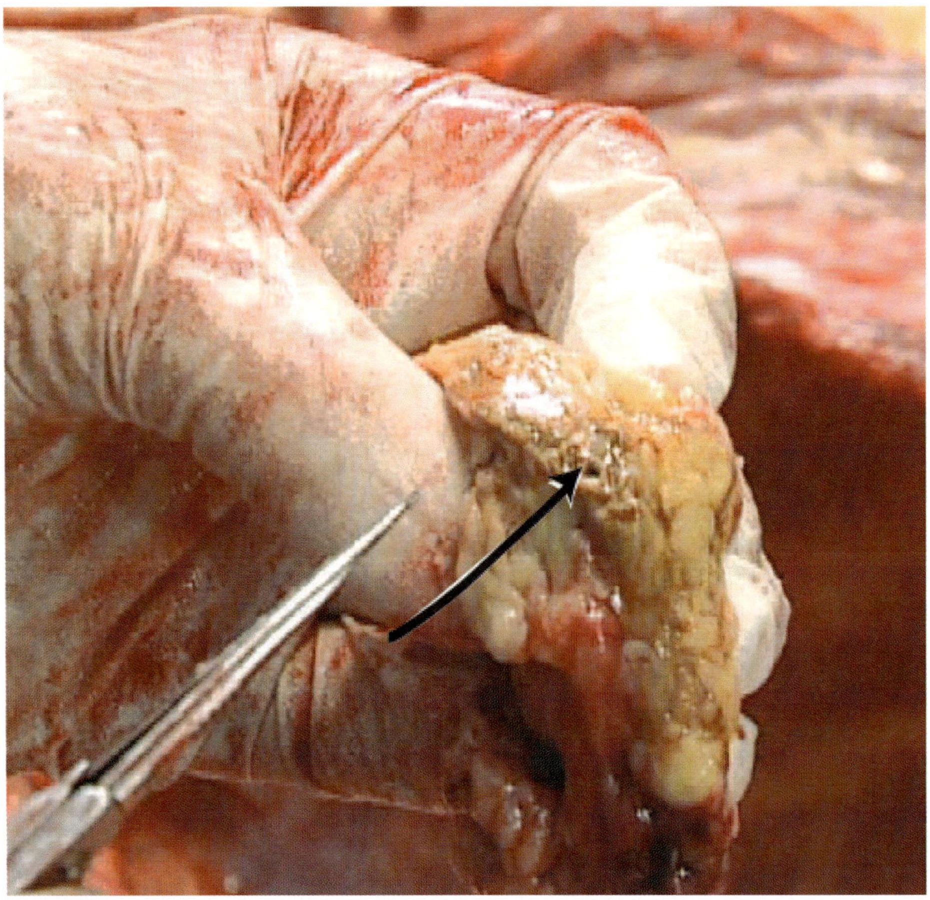

FIGURE 7.30 Adrenal gland autolysis. The adrenal gland here shows autolysis of the cortex. The adrenal gland is one of the first tissues to autolyze visibly after death.

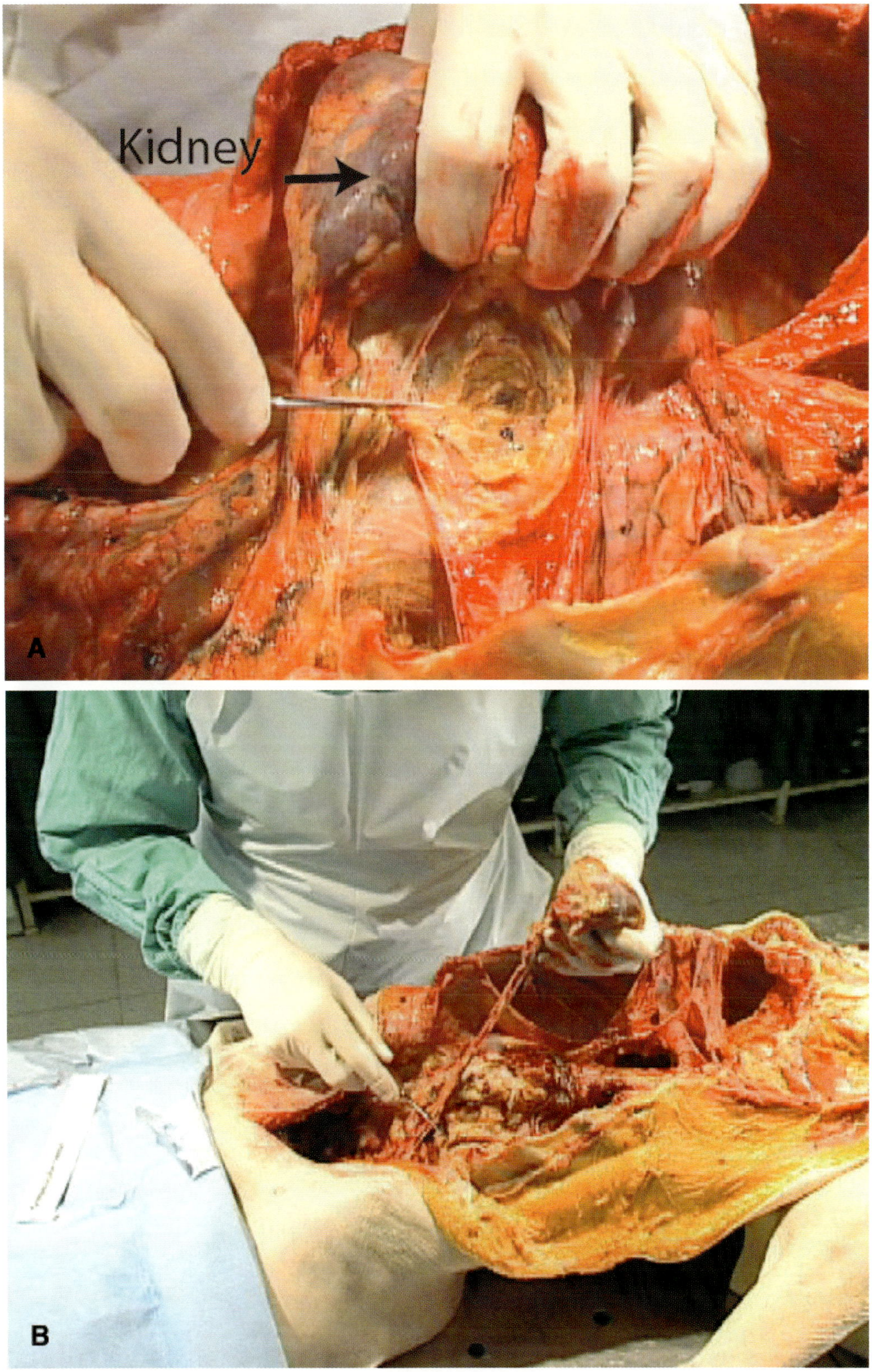

FIGURE 7.31 **(A) Removal of the kidney.** The kidney is removed along with the ureter. **(B) Removal of the ureter.** The kidney is in the left hand, and the ureter is being cut.

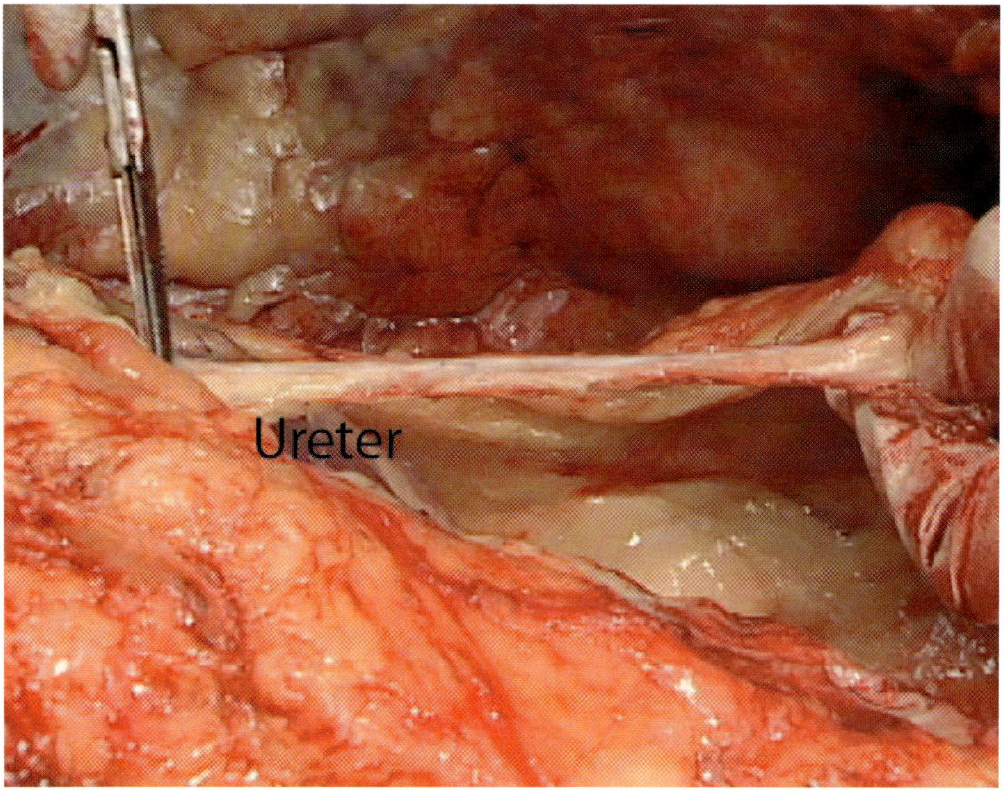

FIGURE 7.32 Ureter. The ureters are identified as they extend downward to the bladder. The ureters can contain tumors or stones (kidney stones).

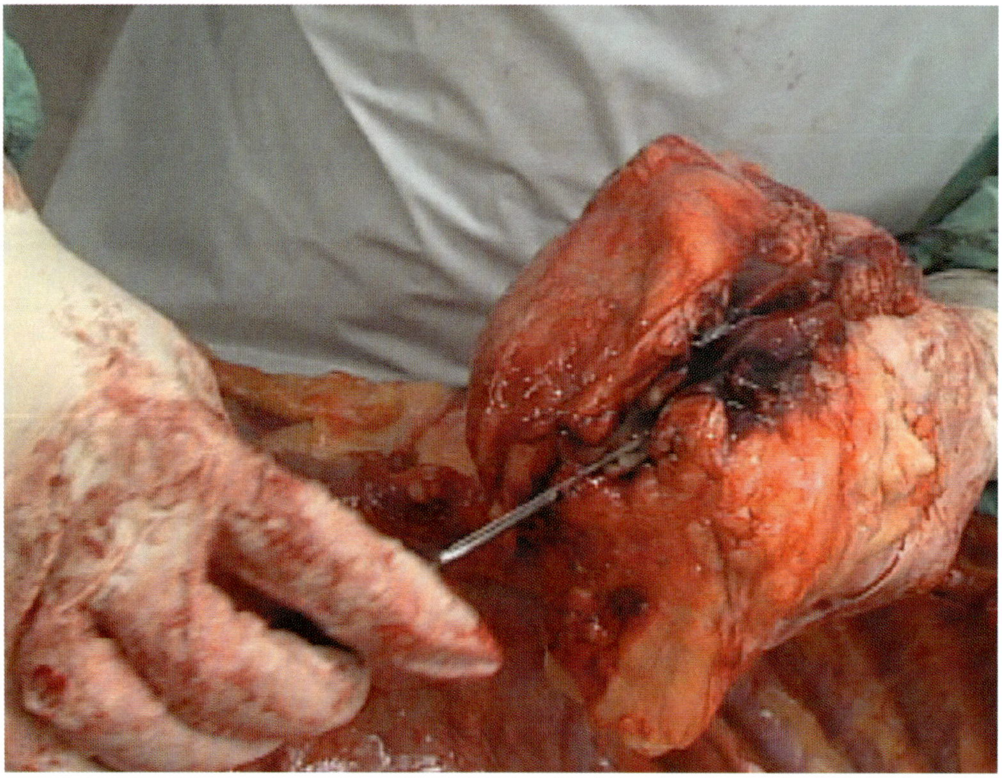

FIGURE 7.33 Perirenal fat. The kidney is shown as the renal fat pad that surrounds the kidney is cut.

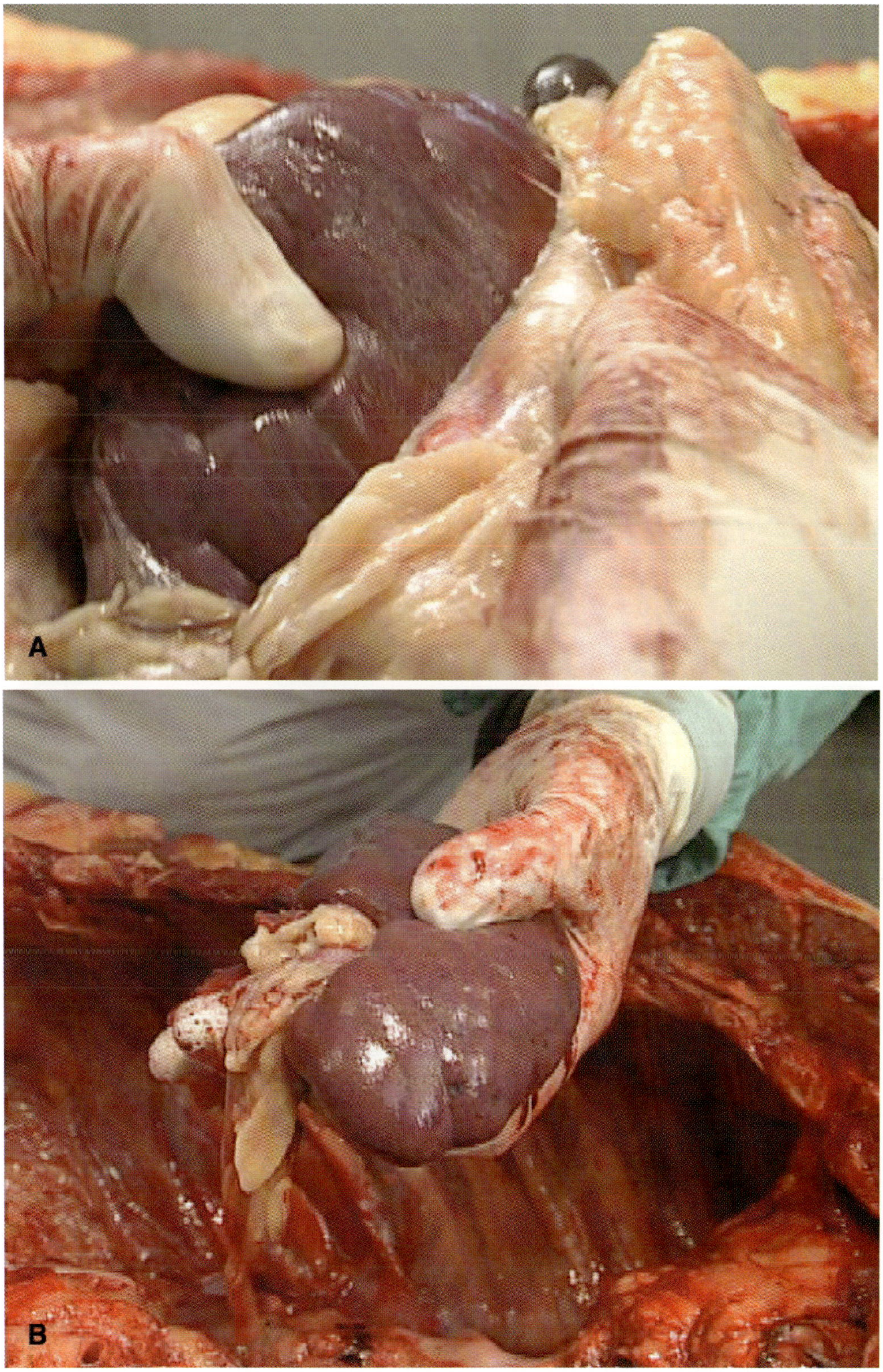

FIGURE 7.34 (A), (B) Removing perirenal fat. The renal fat pad is stripped away, revealing the kidney beneath.

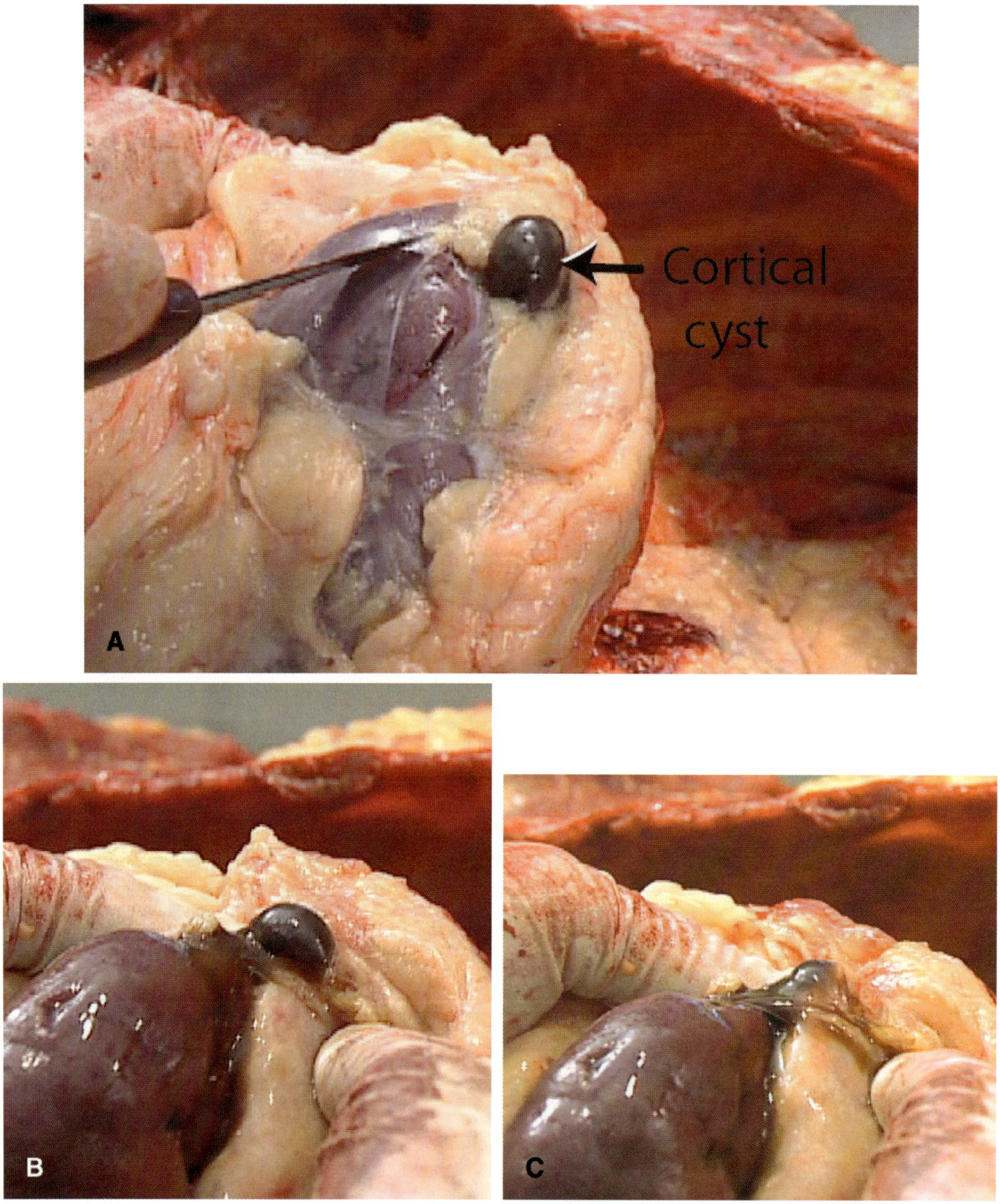

FIGURE 7.35 **(A)–(C) Renal cortical cyst.** After removing the renal fat pad, a cyst is uncovered in the cortex (outer layer) of the kidney. Often, these cysts are very thin and rupture easily upon removal, as happened in this case.

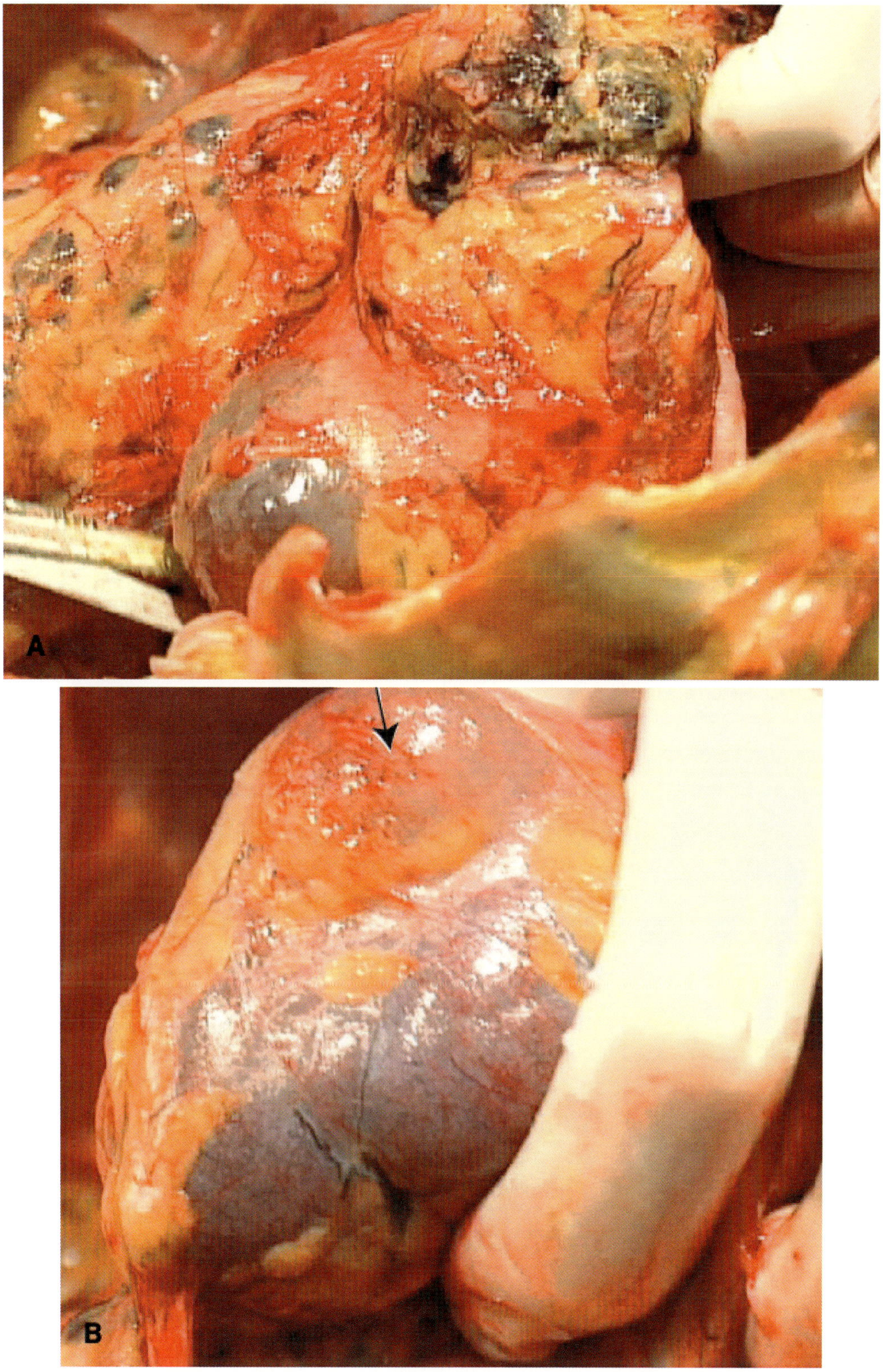

FIGURE 7.36 (A), (B) Renal cortical cyst, large. This cyst (see arrow) is very large and thick-walled, staying intact upon removal. This cyst will be opened during the individual organ examination.

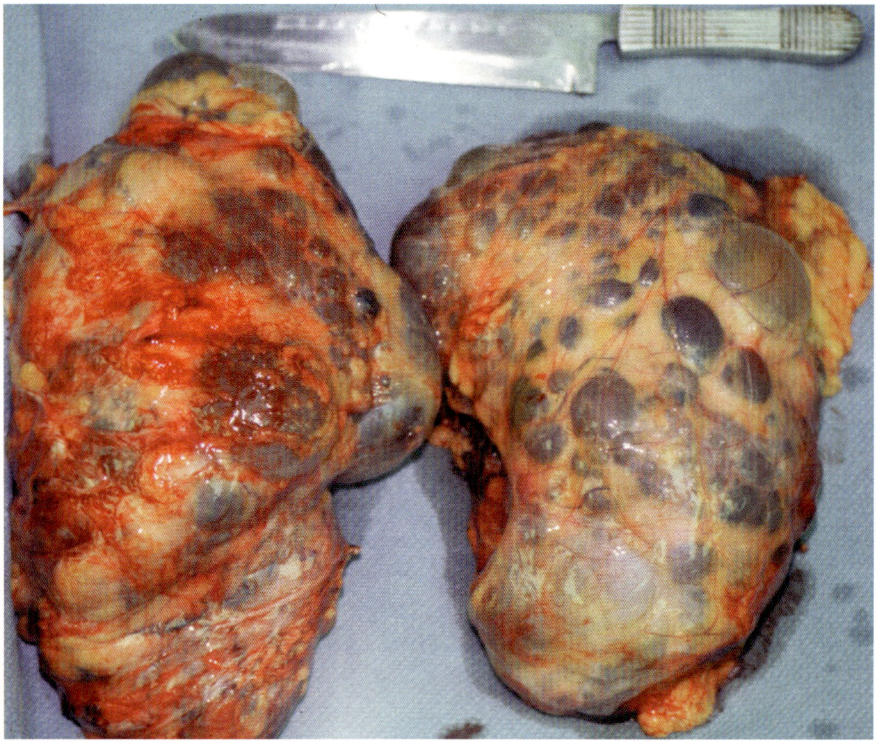

FIGURE 7.37 Polycystic kidneys. Rarely, the entire kidney is replaced with cysts in a condition called polycystic kidney disease. These patients experience renal failure in their thirties and forties. The knife in the picture is about 1 ft long, so these kidneys are over twice the normal size.

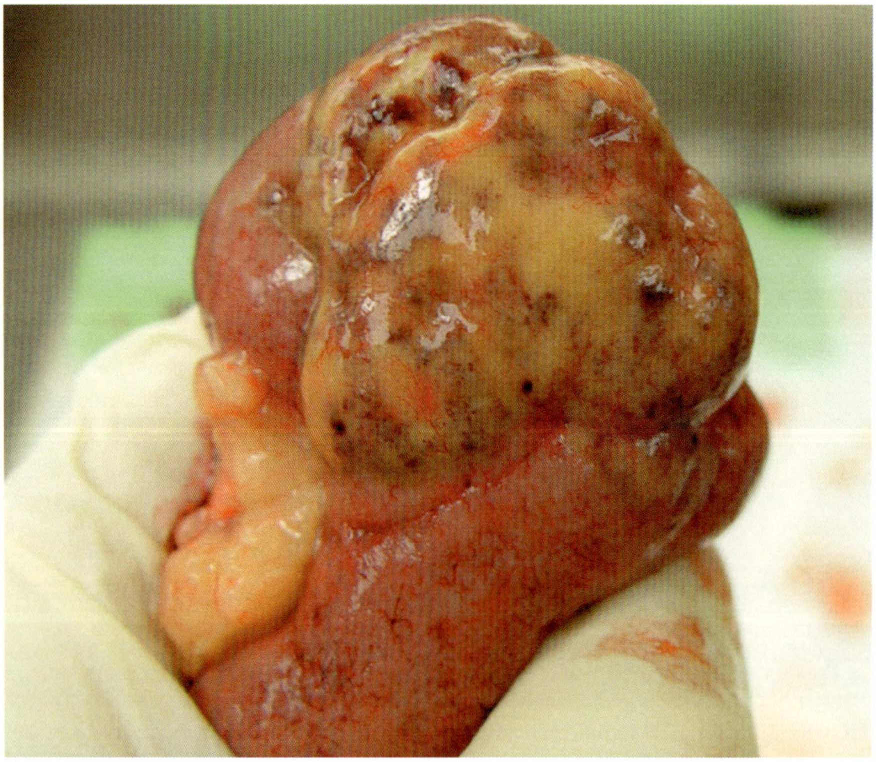

FIGURE 7.38 Renal cell carcinoma. Large tumors can be encountered upon removing the kidneys. This yellowish, rounded tumor is a renal cell carcinoma, a common malignant tumor of the kidney.

AORTA EXAMINATION

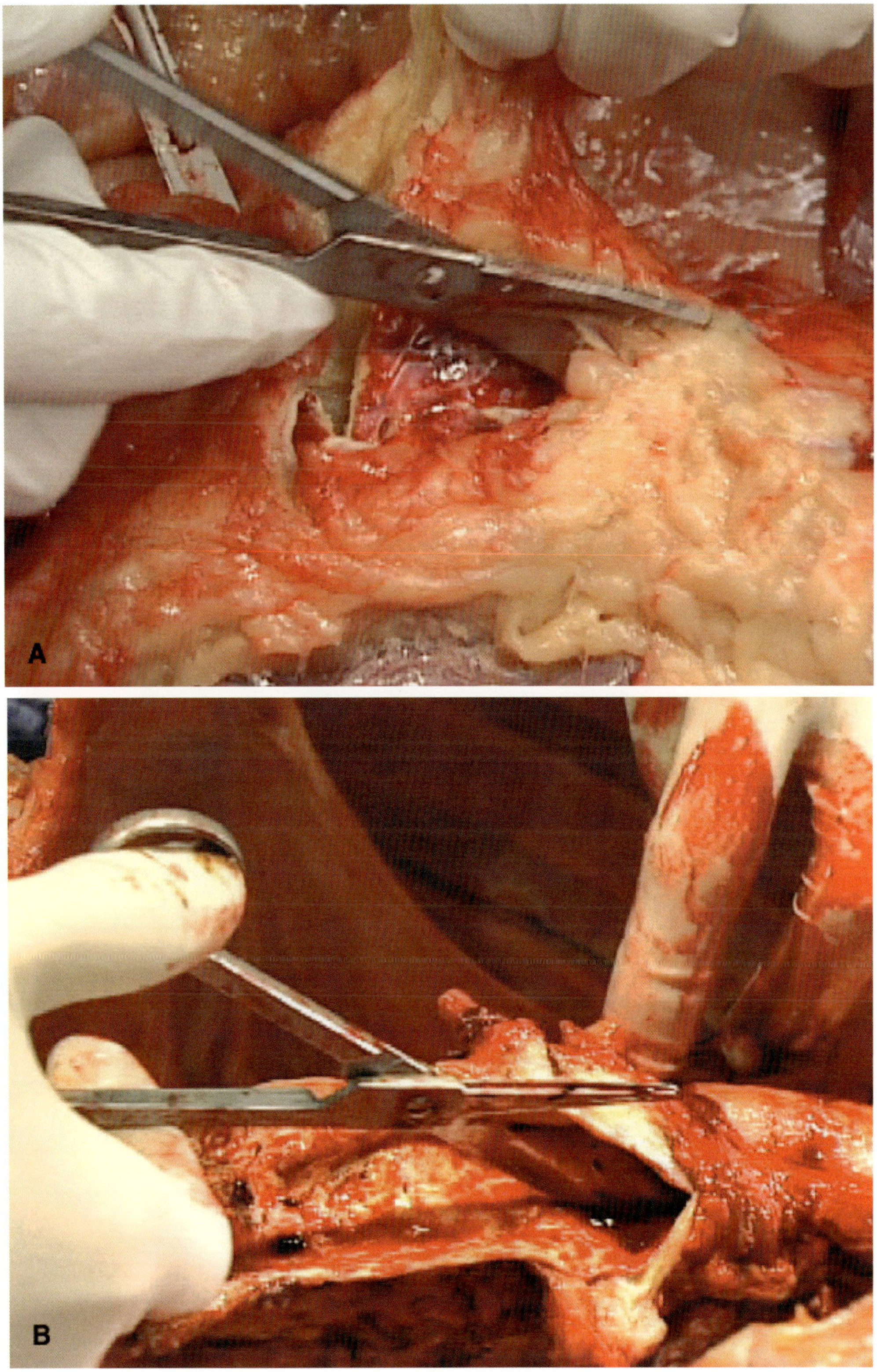

FIGURE 7.39 Opening the aorta. (**A**)–(**C**) The aorta is opened from the iliac bifurcation up to the ascending aorta. (**D**) The abdominal aortic anatomy is displayed.

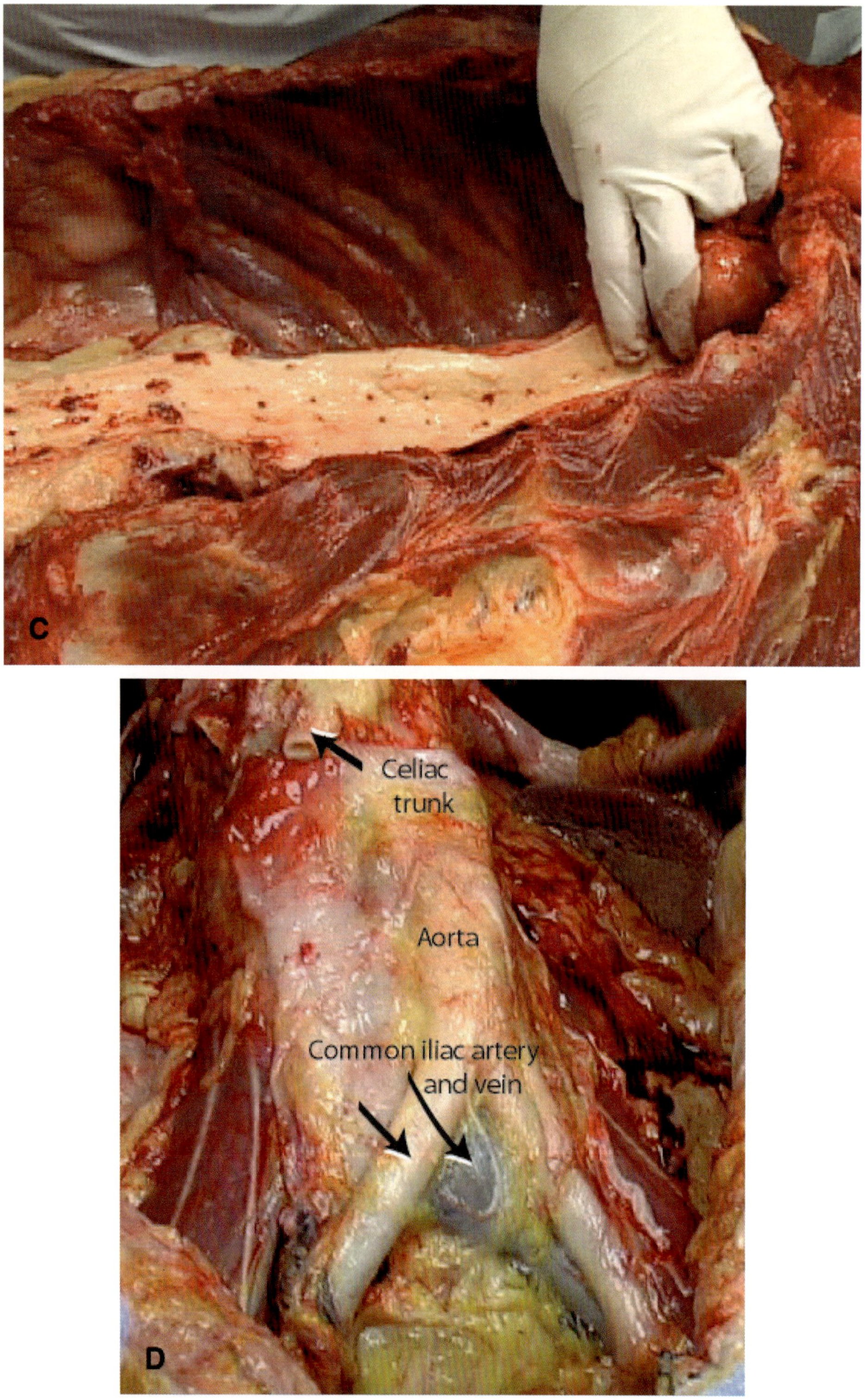

FIGURE 7.39 (CONTINUED) Opening the aorta. (A)–(C) The aorta is opened from the iliac bifurcation up to the ascending aorta. **(D)** The abdominal aortic anatomy is displayed.

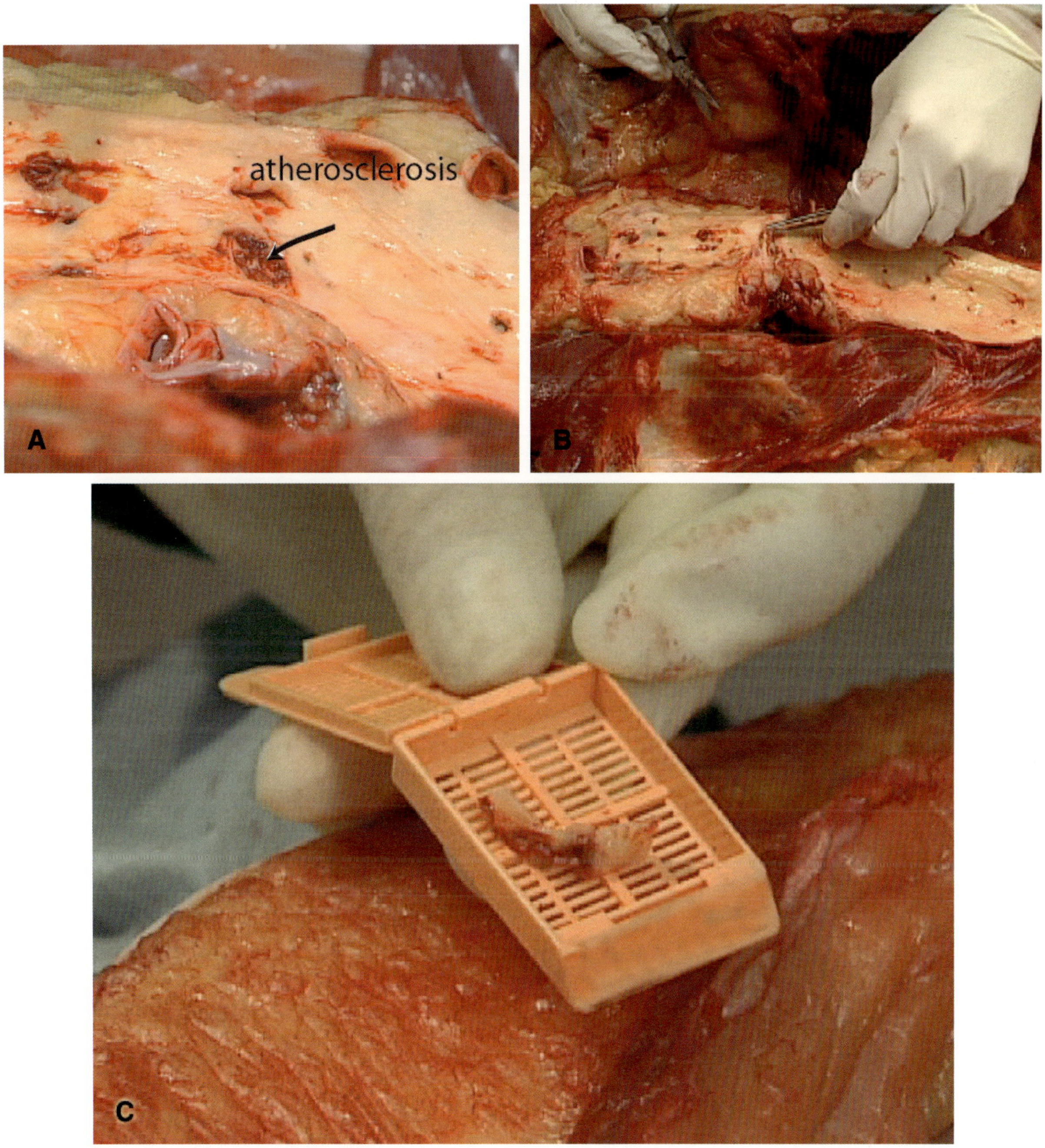

FIGURE 7.40 Aortic atherosclerosis. (A), (B) An atherosclerotic ulcer is seen in the middle of the image. **(C)** A section of this plaque is submitted in a histology cassette so it can be processed to a glass slide and reviewed under the microscope.

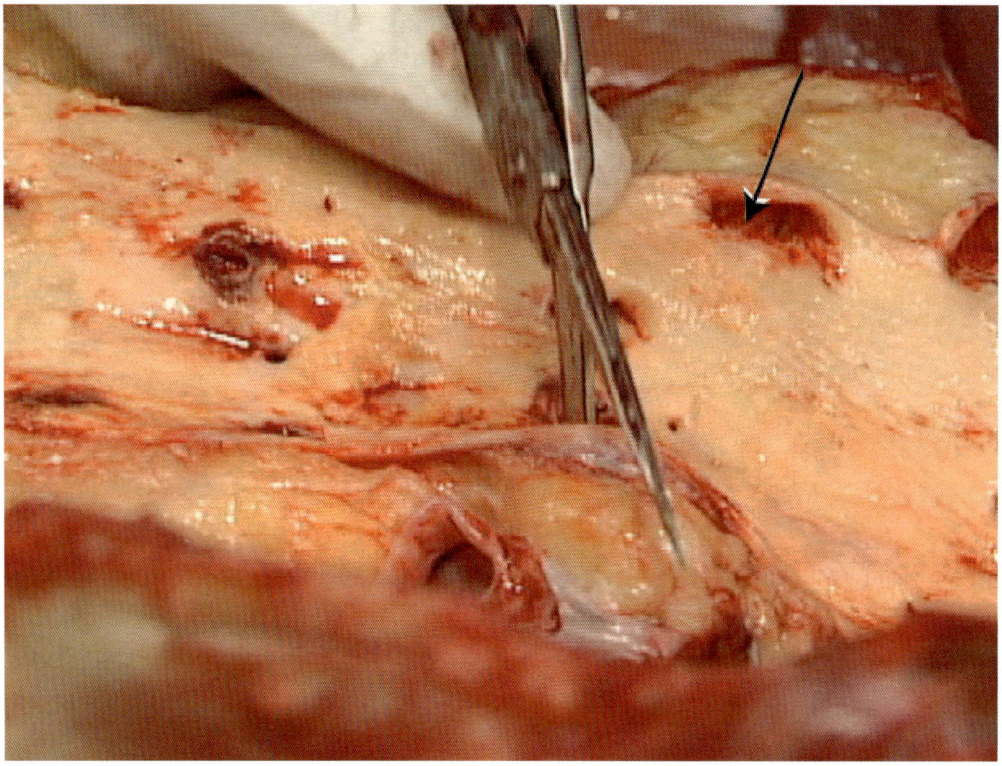

FIGURE 7.41 Renal artery. The scissor is in the renal artery. This artery is opened to check for stenosis of the artery, one of the clinical causes of hypertension. The other renal artery is indicated by the arrow.

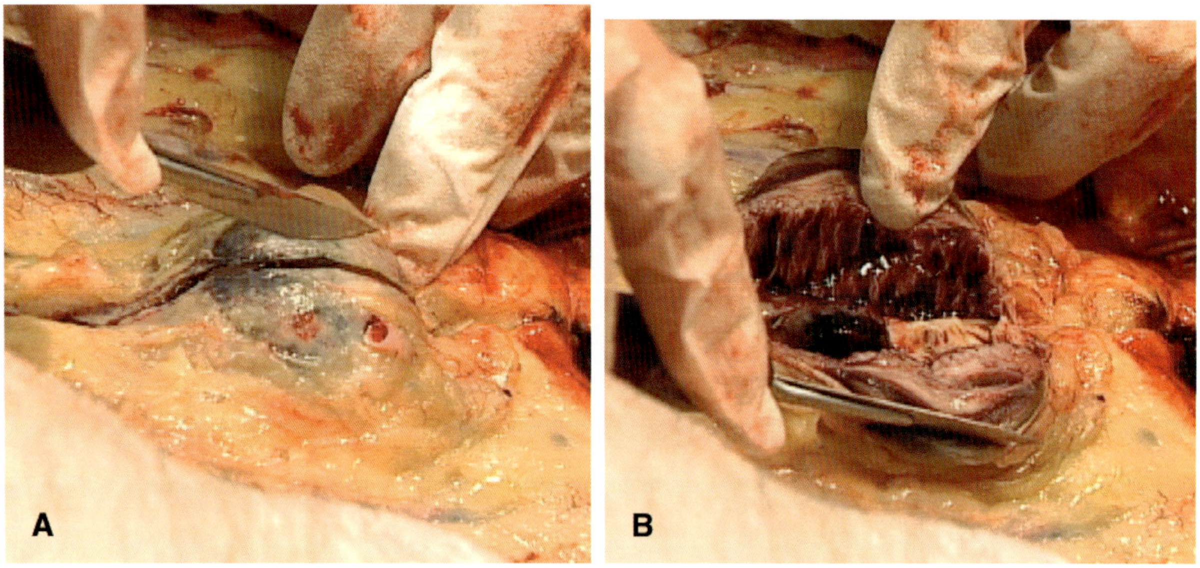

FIGURE 7.42 Abdominal aortic aneurism. (A) The scalpel points to a bluish-purple knob in the region of the abdominal aorta, partially obscured by retroperitoneal fat. **(B)** The aneurism is incised to reveal the thick aneurismal wall.

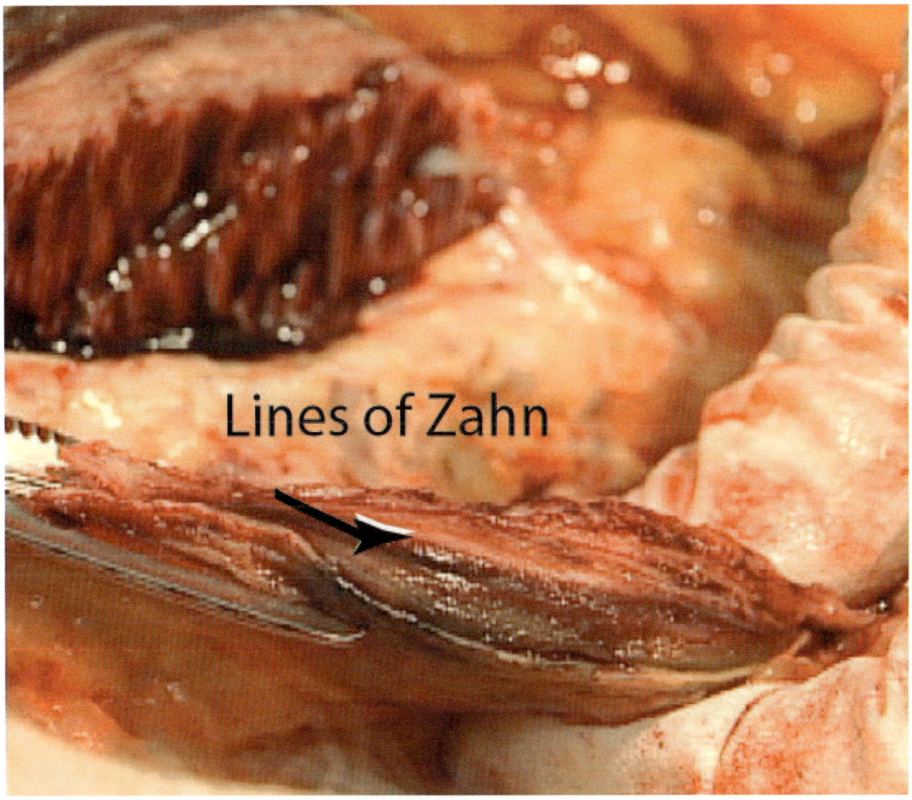

FIGURE 7.43 Aortic aneurism wall, showing lines of Zahn. An aneurism is an outpouching of a blood vessel wall, in this case caused by atherosclerosis. The aneurism is exposed, and the wall is cut open to reveal a thick, layered wall. The alternating light and dark lines demark layers of white blood cells (light) and red blood cells, fibrin, and platelets (dark).

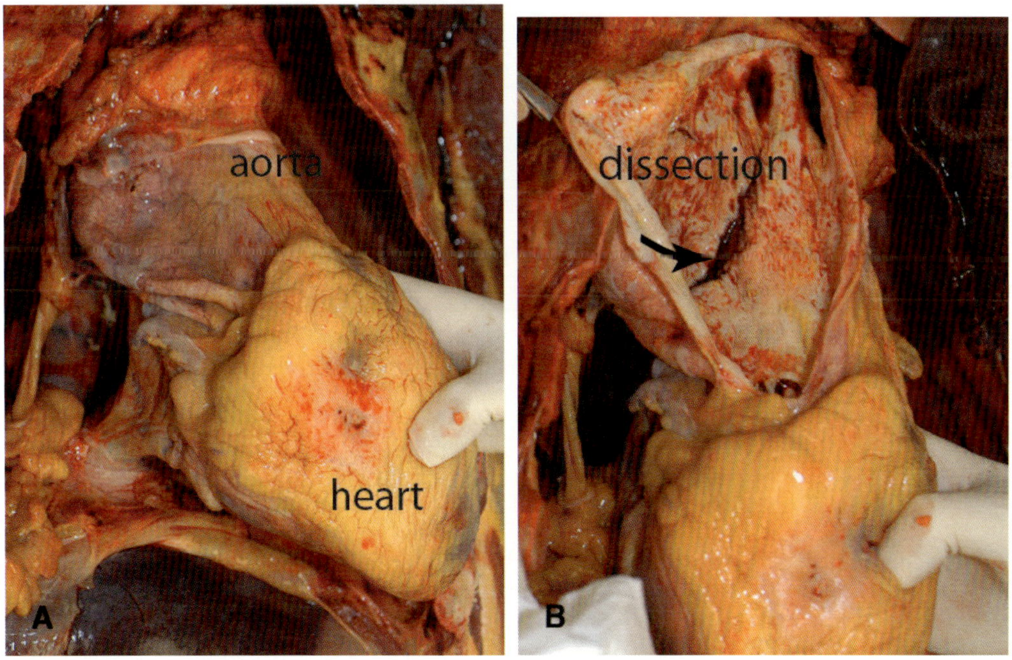

FIGURE 7.44 (A) Ascending aortic aneurism. Another type of aneurism is seen near the heart, involving the aortic root. The broad structure shown by the arrow is the aorta. This individual was suspected to have Marfan's syndrome, a connective tissue disease associated with the weakening of blood vessel walls. **(B) Aortic dissection.** This figure shows the opened aorta, which contains a large tear. The thin aneurism can tear spontaneously, allowing blood to dissect outside the aorta, resulting in an aortic dissection.

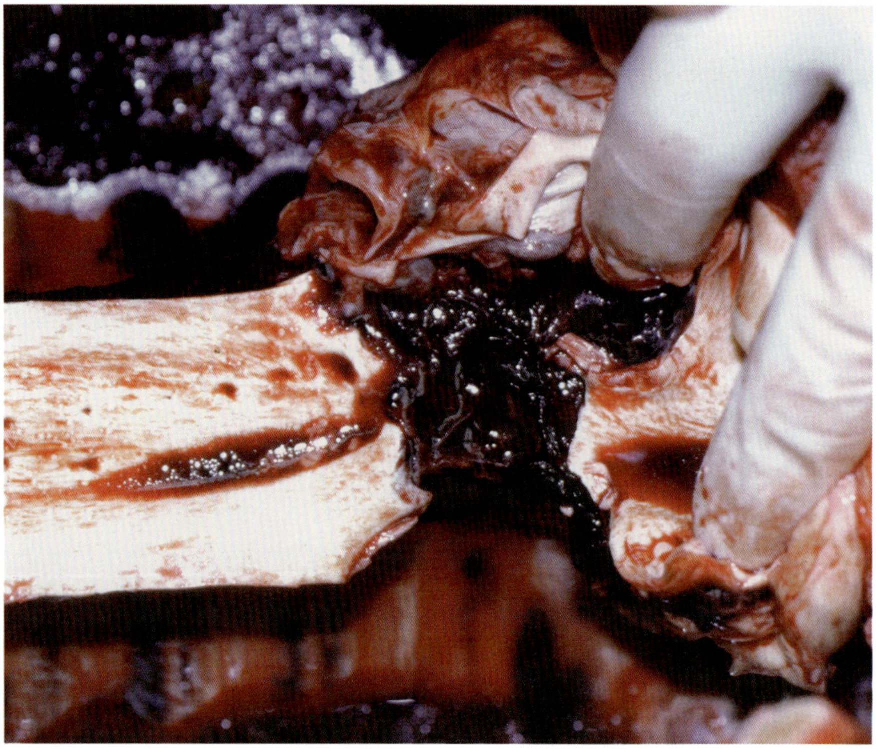

FIGURE 7.45 Laceration of the aorta. In a severe trauma, such as one caused by a motor vehicle crash, the aorta can be lacerated or completely transected as seen here.

UTERUS REMOVAL

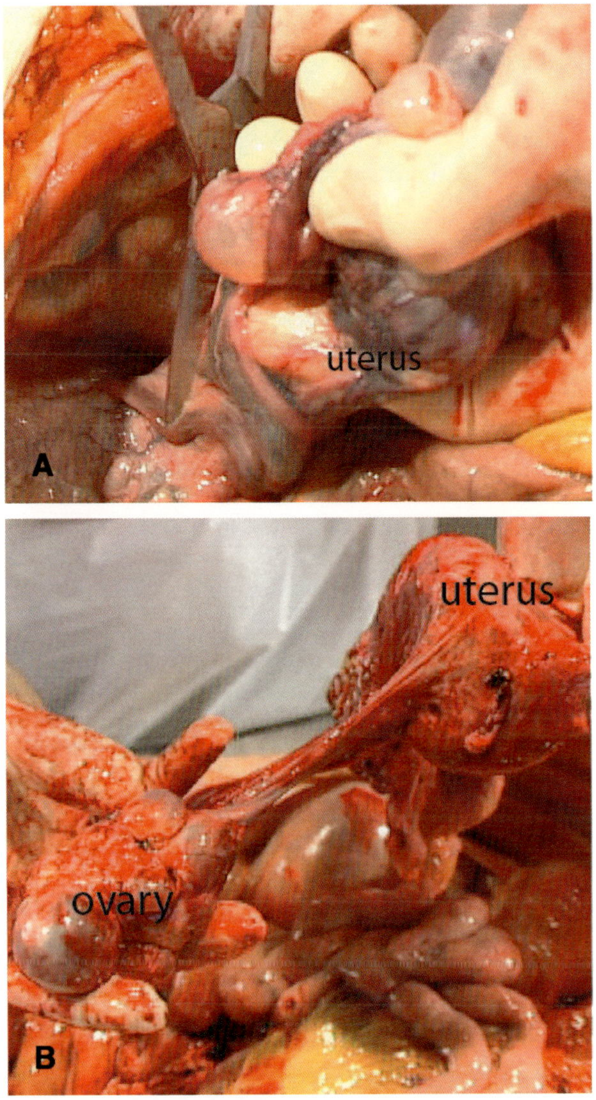

FIGURE 7.46 Removal of the uterus and ovaries. (**A**) The uterus is excised from the lower pelvis and is removed separately from or with the bladder. The uterus is displayed with two attached ovarian cysts. (**B**) A large cyst can be seen on the left side of the figure (also see Figure 6.35A, Figure 6.35B). Upon removal of these and other organs, the natural appearance of the tissues is often partially obscured by blood. This blood can easily be washed off, as is done when the tissues are examined in the individual organ examination portion of the autopsy.

BLADDER REMOVAL

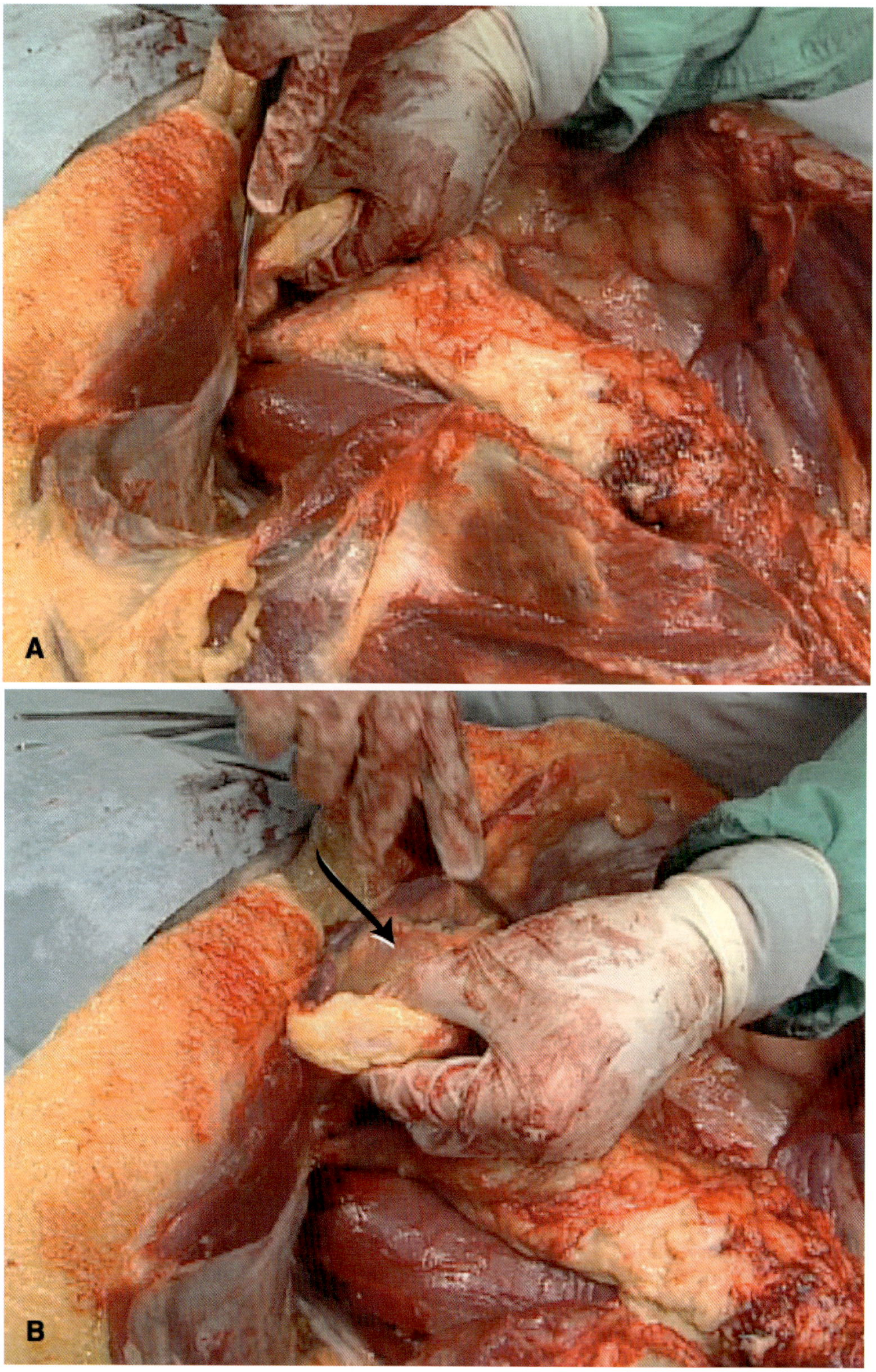

FIGURE 7.47 (A)–(D) Removal of the bladder. The pathologist dissects the bladder from the lower pelvis in the male, being careful to include the prostate gland. The bladder is held in the left hand (see arrows). The pathologist must be careful not to empty urine from the bladder. If only a small amount of urine is present at the initial aspiration for toxicology, a small amount of additional urine can often be obtained by carefully opening the bladder.

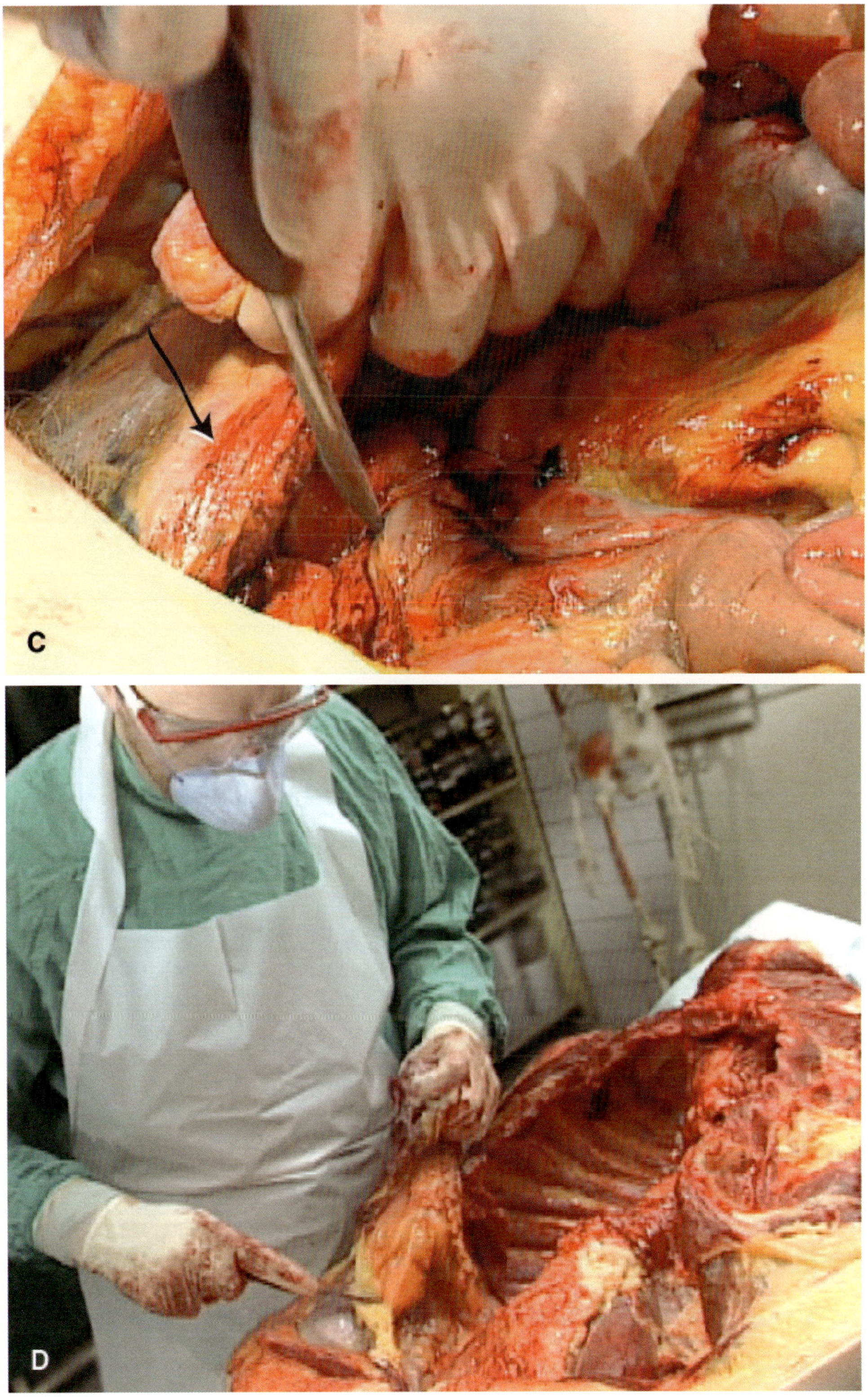

FIGURE 7.47 (CONTINUED) **(A)–(D) Removal of the bladder.** The pathologist dissects the bladder from the lower pelvis in the male, being careful to include the prostate gland. The bladder is held in the left hand (see arrows). The pathologist must be careful not to empty urine from the bladder. If only a small amount of urine is present at the initial aspiration for toxicology, a small amount of additional urine can often be obtained by carefully opening the bladder.

NECK DISSECTION

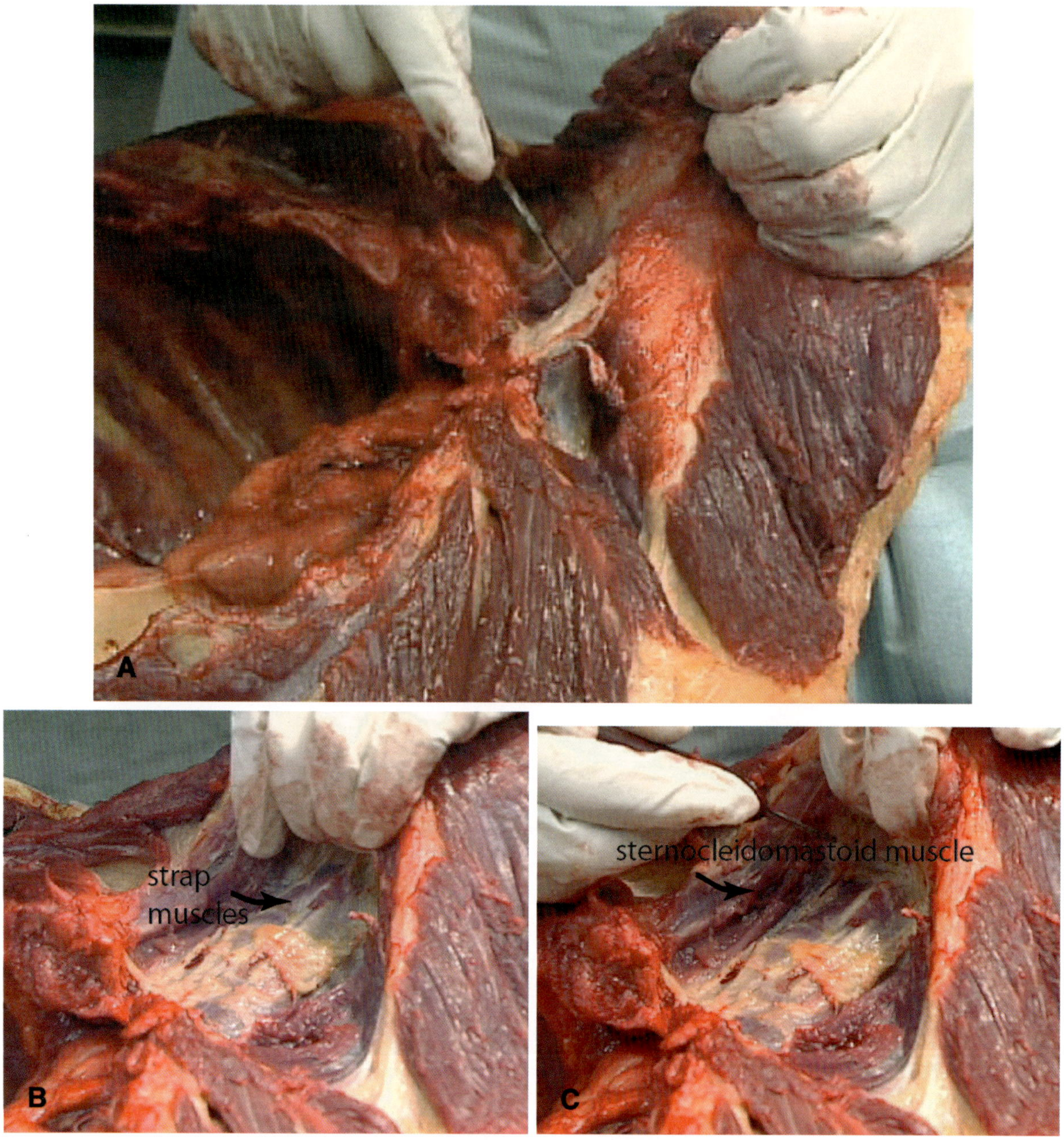

FIGURE 7.48 (A)–(C) Neck dissection, exposing muscles. The neck is dissected after the viscera have been removed. While applying traction to the upper chest skin and soft tissue flap, the "strap" muscle group (midline) and sternocleidomastoid (lateral) are revealed during careful dissection. The main focus of the dissection is to look for hemorrhage. If hemorrhage is discovered at any step, the dissection is photographed as it progresses. Suspected strangulation cases are imparted an even more detailed dissection than depicted here.

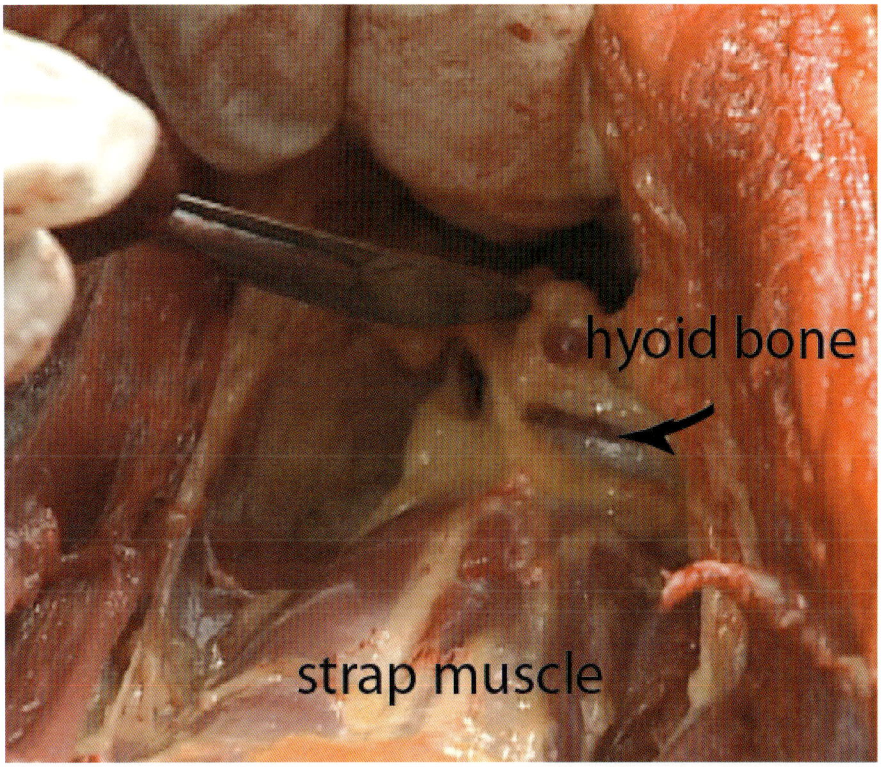

FIGURE 7.49 Neck dissection, cutting above the hyoid bone. The dissection is carried up high into the neck, and a cut is made in the muscle above the hyoid bone, a horseshoe-shaped bone that can be broken during strangulation. The tongue is removed with the other neck organs in certain cases, such as strangulation, or when the tongue needs to be examined directly. Some pathologists remove the tongue in all autopsies. The forensic autopsy is incomplete without at least the complete removal of the hyoid bone with the neck organs.

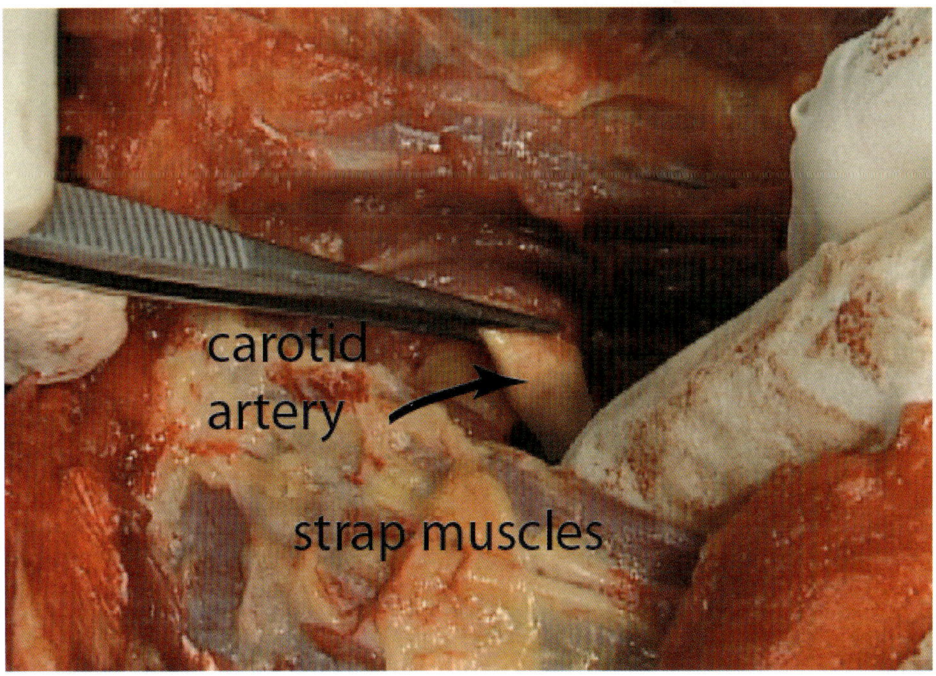

FIGURE 7.50 Neck dissection, exposing the carotid artery. The lateral soft tissue of the neck is cut away, revealing the carotid artery.

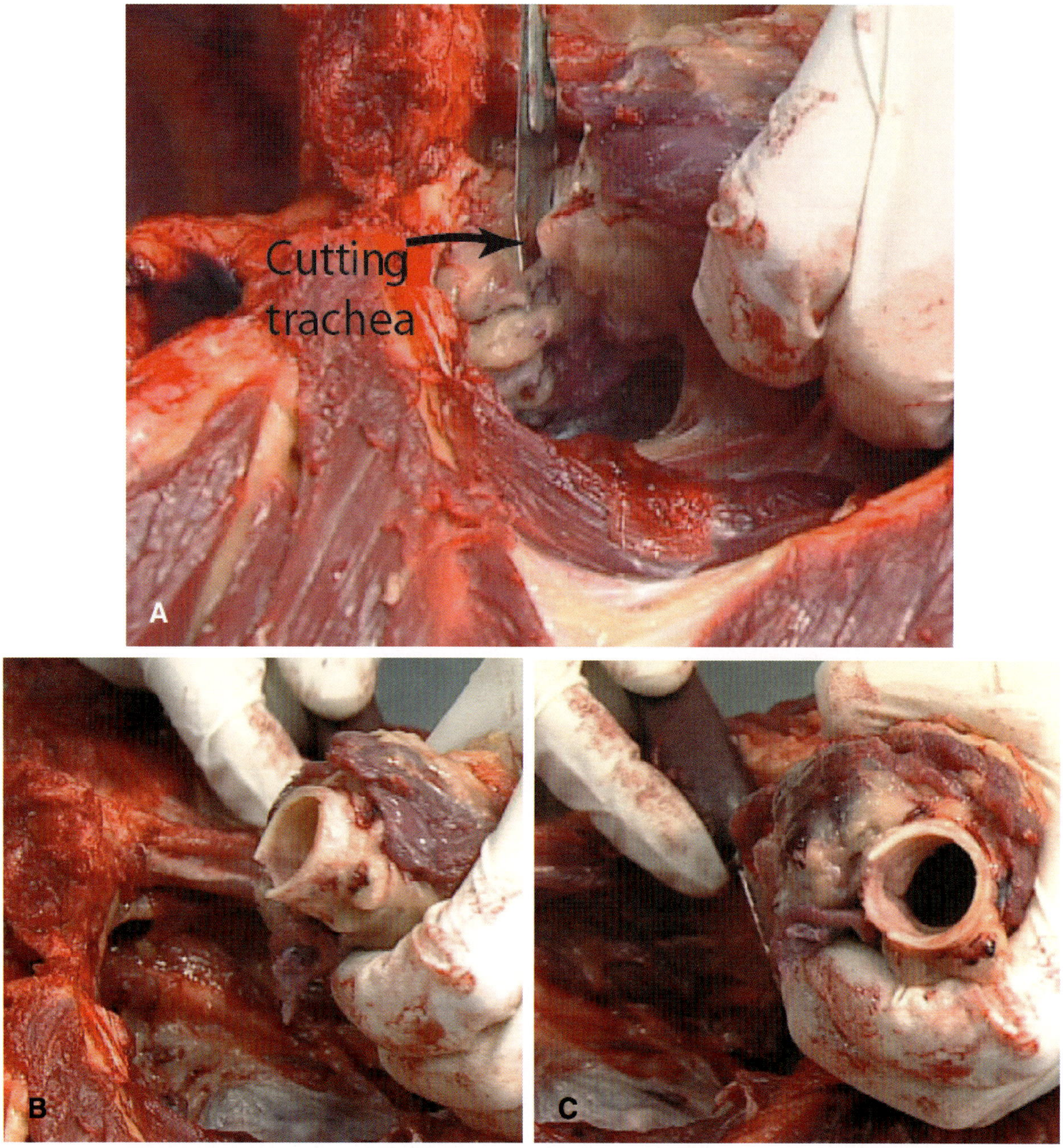

FIGURE 7.51 (A)–(C) Neck dissection, cutting the trachea. The trachea and esophagus are cut, while traction is placed with the left hand. The pathologist is careful to cut away the tissue without cutting the carotid arteries, since the embalmer uses the carotid arteries to embalm the head. Cutting the carotids makes them difficult for the embalmer to find.

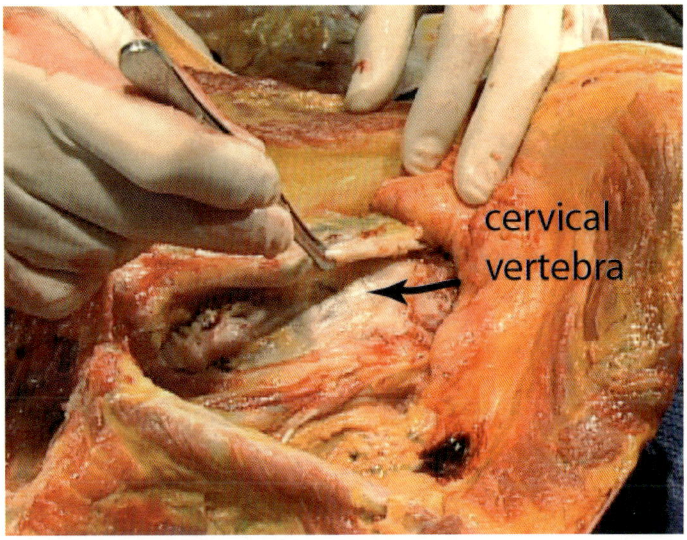

FIGURE 7.52 Carotid artery relationships. The carotid artery is shown by the forceps. The neck organs have been removed. The cervical vertebrae are just below the artery. Significant hemorrhage or fracture of the cervical vertebrae can be seen at this stage of the dissection (see Figure 7.53).

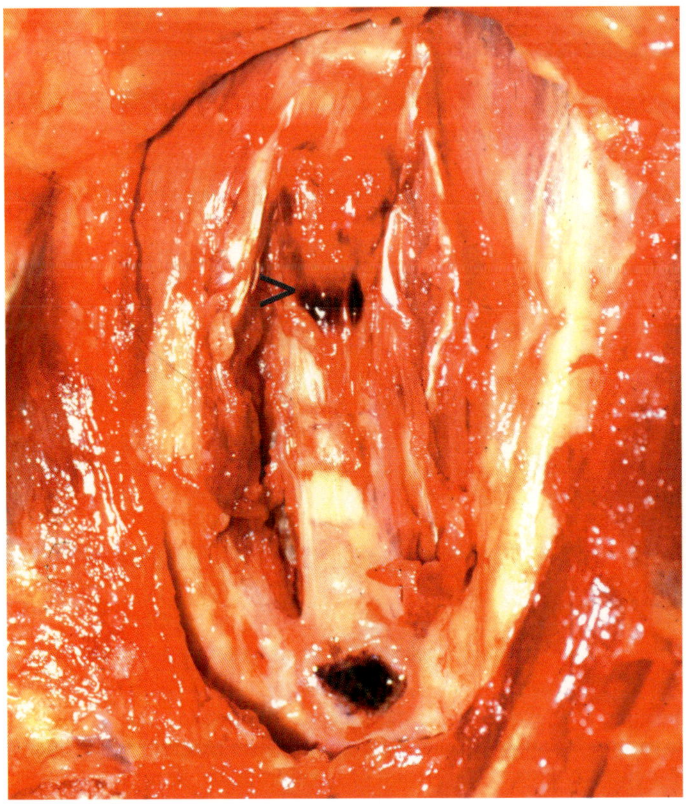

FIGURE 7.53 Cervical vertebra fracture. Removal of the neck shows hemorrhage due to the fracture of a vertebral body in the neck (see arrow). This victim suffered this and other blunt force injuries while being murdered. Fracture of the cervical vertebrae often results in swelling and hemorrhage of the spinal cord. The higher the injury is on the spinal cord, the more severe the effect on the victim. Damage of the spinal cord at levels 3, 4, and 5 can cause paralysis of the diaphragm, for example, resulting in respiratory failure. An x-ray can be helpful if obvious fracture or hemorrhage is not seen during examination.

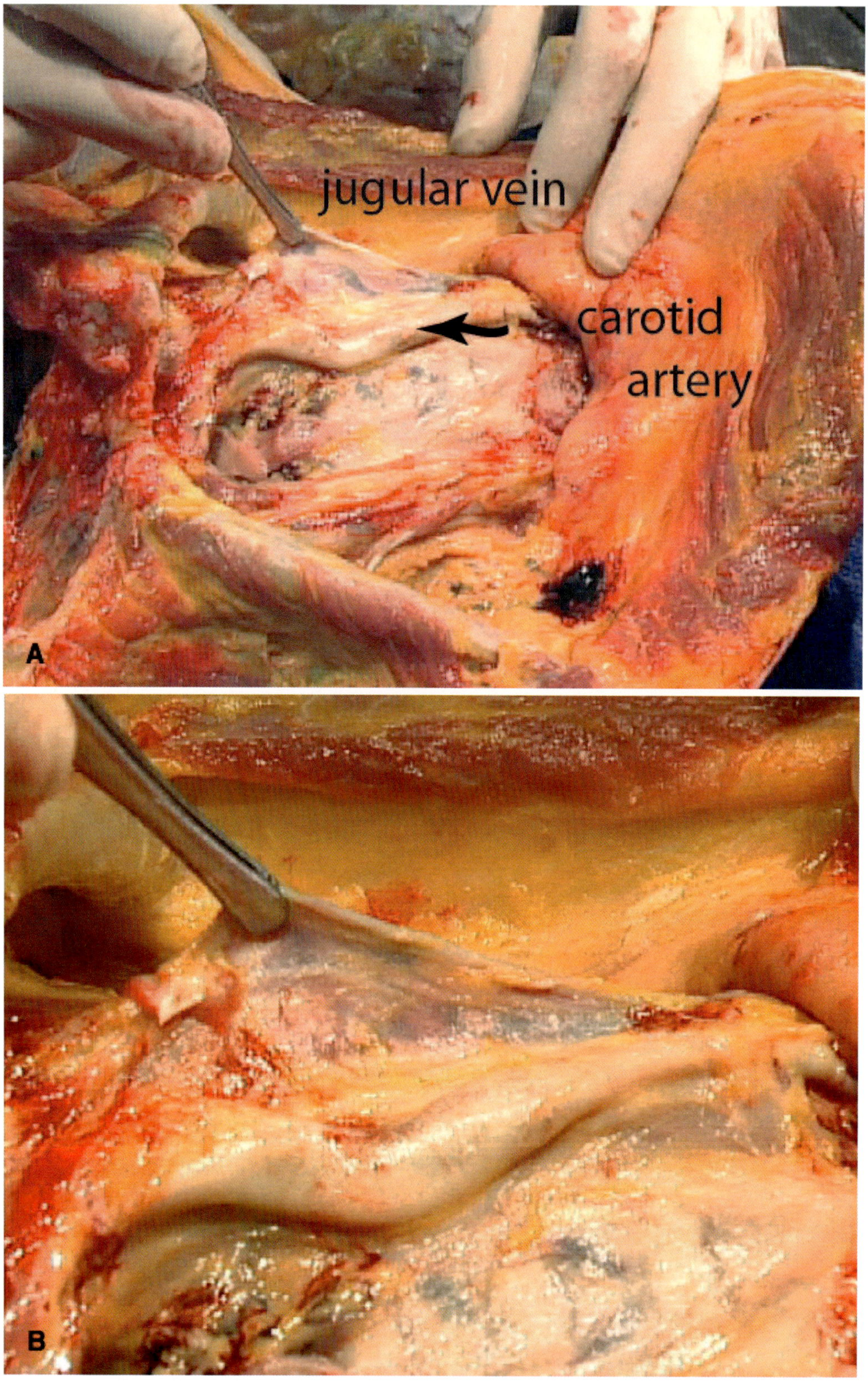

FIGURE 7.54 (A), (B) Jugular vein relationships. The jugular vein is the collapsed, thin-walled vein displayed by the forceps. The jugular veins are easily compressed by choking, classic ligature hanging, or strangulation. The compressed jugular veins significantly limit venous return of blood from the veins of the head and neck to the heart. Blood is pumped into the brain, but cannot return to the heart. The result is hypoxia of the brain, unconsciousness, and death.

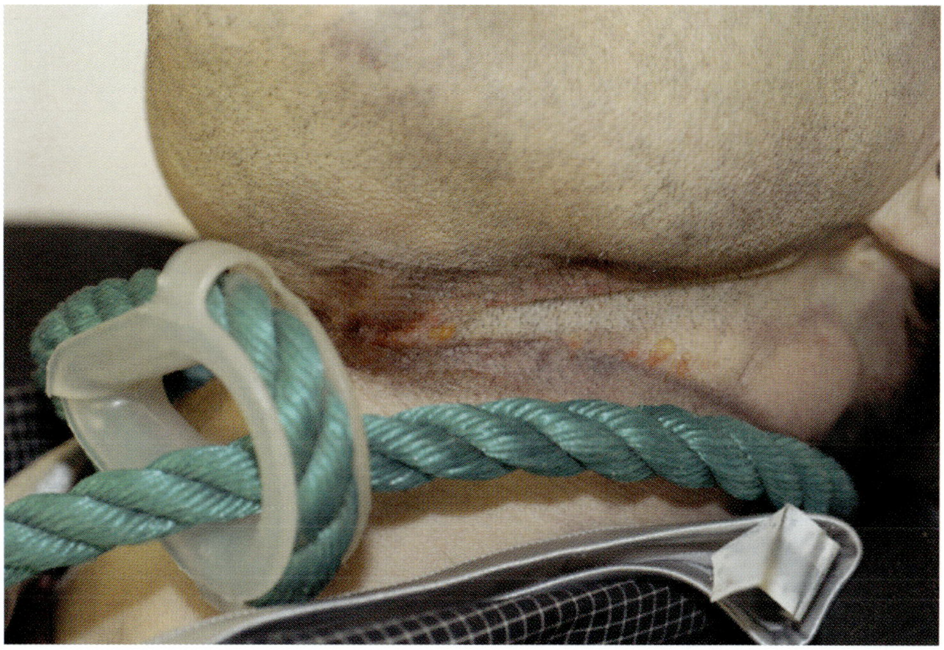

FIGURE 7.55 Hanging by ligature. This victim of a suicidal hanging was suspended by the depicted rope. The impression left by the ligature, or ligature furrow, shows that the ligature compressed the area of the jugular vein, not the trachea; still, death by asphyxia resulted.

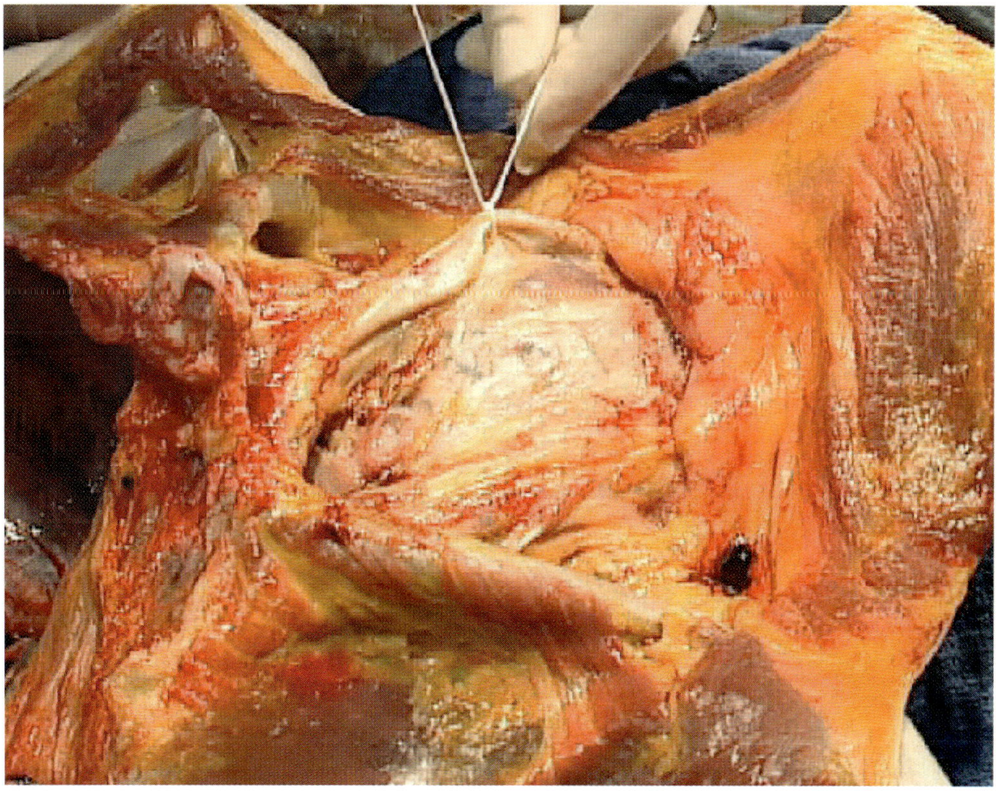

FIGURE 7.56 Carotid tie. The carotid is tied to help the embalmer find the vessels for injection of tissue preservatives.

8 Individual Organ Examination

Generally, the pathologist examines each organ and tissue from the outside to the inside: first observing its "gross" or macroscopic appearance, then dissecting it, and finally studying its microscopic features. The objectives are to:

- Examine and observe the diseases or injuries of each organ or tissue in a systematic, complete fashion.
- Make diagnoses and form opinions about the etiologies of the diseases or injuries. This is done by examining the gross organ on the day of the autopsy and then looking at microscopic sections of the organ or tissue at a later date (see Chapter 10).
- Describe the diseases, disorders, or injuries, and make a record of these observations. This allows other experts to review the report and to draw independent conclusions about the data provided.
- Document pertinent diseases or injuries using photography or other media.
- Preserve pertinent tissues either in a fixative or paraffin, so that additional studies can be performed later. For example, hemorrhagic soft tissue of the neck is often retained in strangulation cases.

HEART

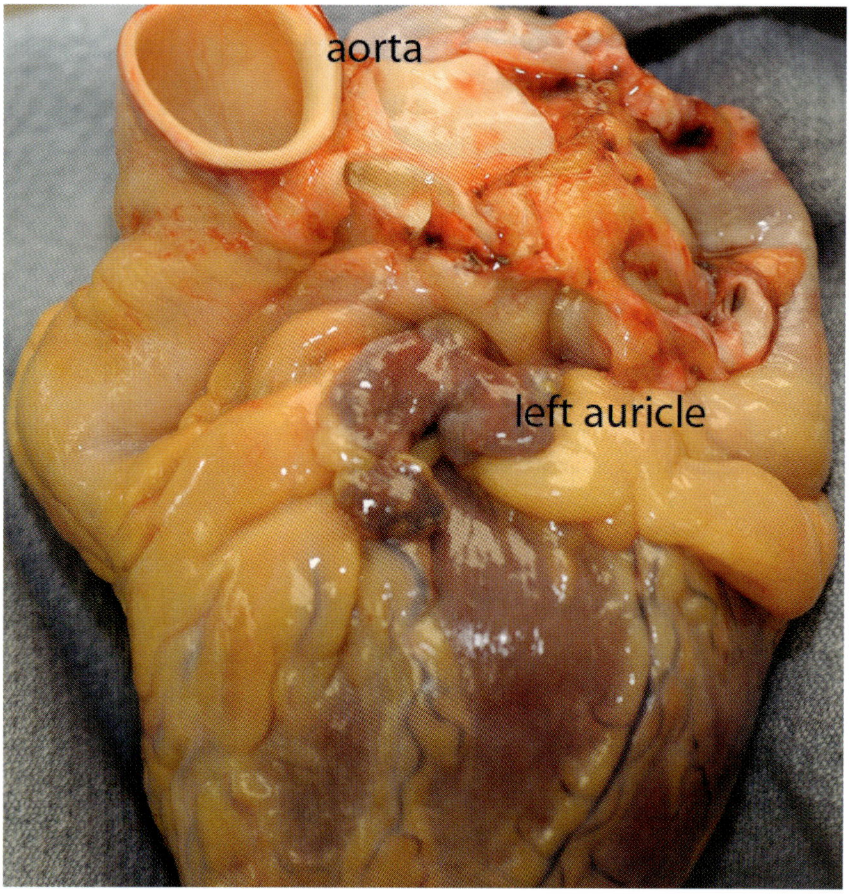

FIGURE 8.1 Anterior view of the heart. The normal heart is viewed after its removal, showing the open aorta and smaller auricle, or "ear," of the left atrium.

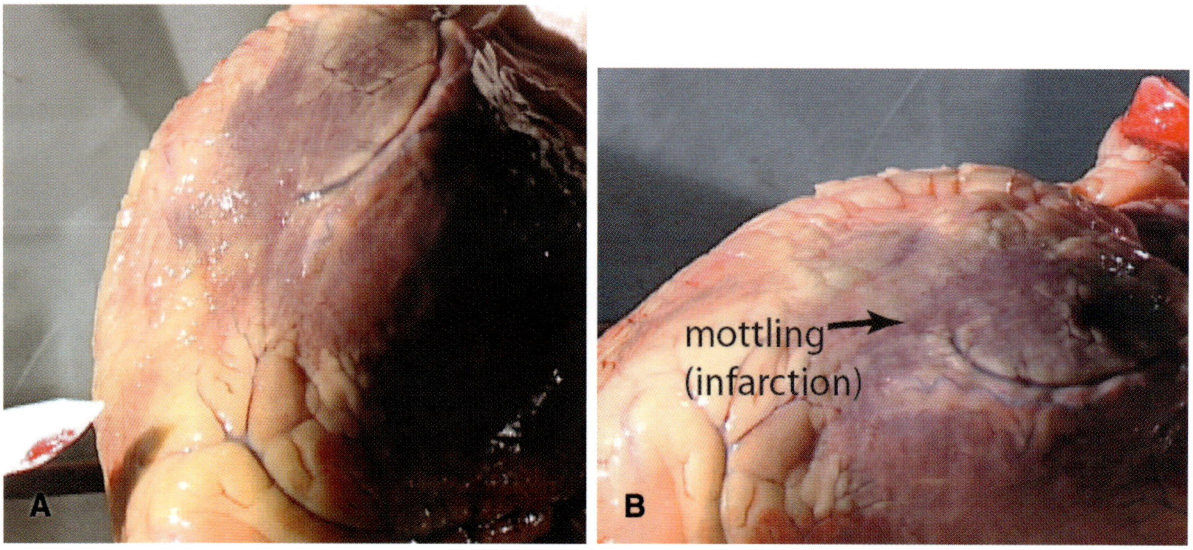

FIGURE 8.2 (A), (B) Mottling, due to myocardial infarction. The outside of the heart, or epicardium, is examined revealing a discoloration or mottling as shown by the arrow (also see Figure 8.17A and Figure 8.17B).

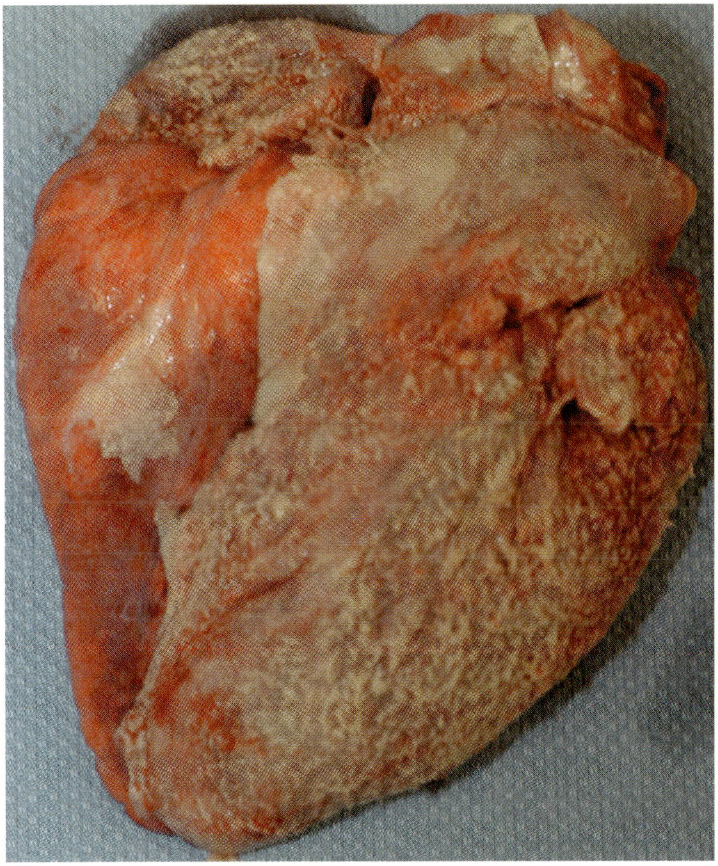

FIGURE 8.3 Pericarditis. Bacterial inflammation of the heart leaves a "crust," or exudate, often referred to as "bread and butter" pericarditis.

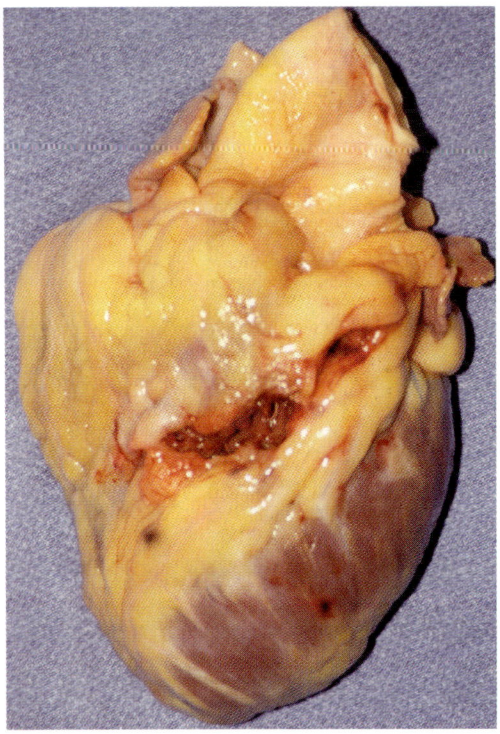

FIGURE 8.4 Cardiac laceration. A severe blunt trauma to the chest, such as that occurring in a high-speed motor vehicle crash, can cause cardiac laceration.

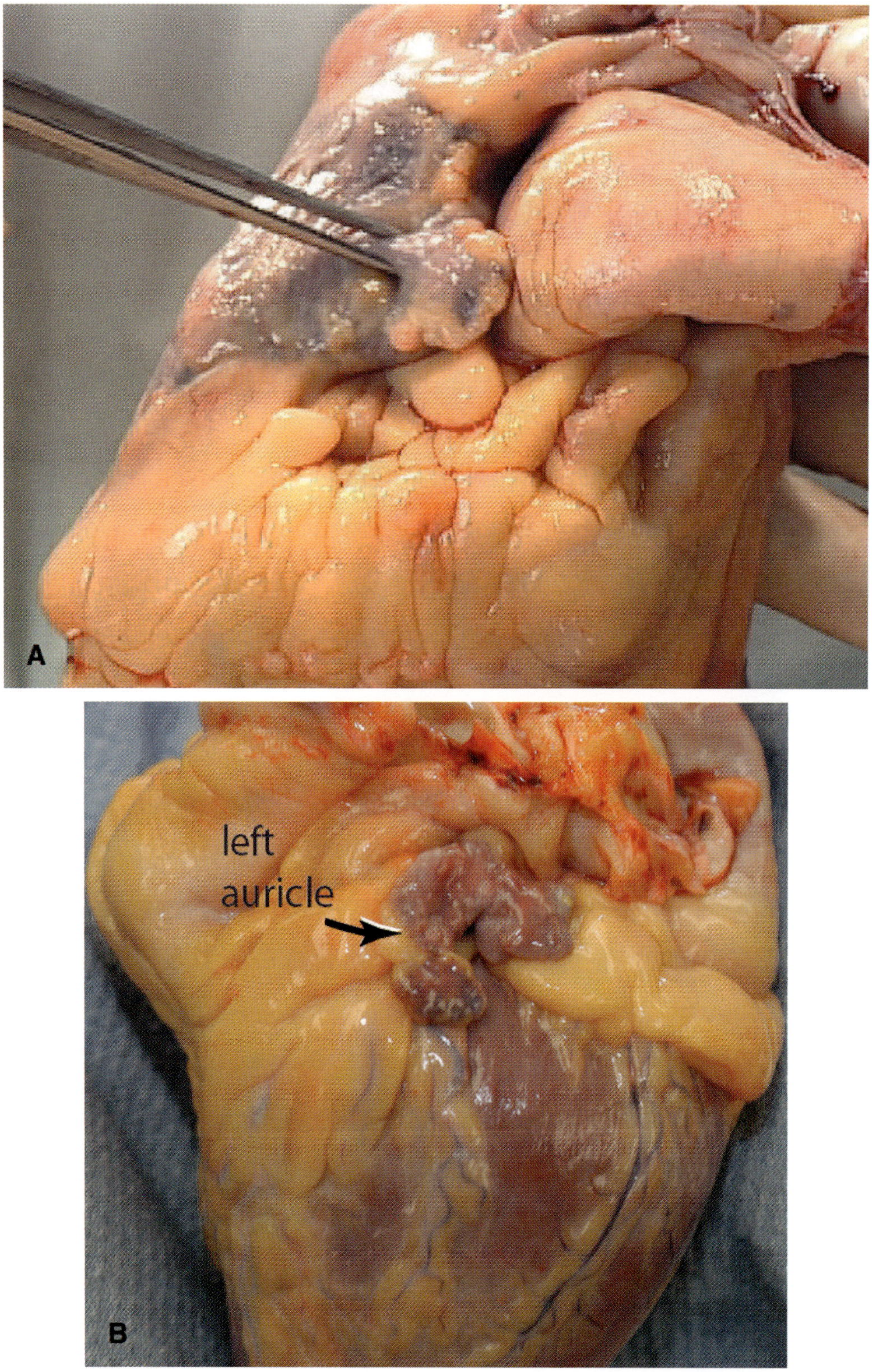

FIGURE 8.5 **(A) Right auricle**. The heart has two auricles, or "ears," a right and a left. The right auricle is shown by the forceps. **(B) Front view of the heart.** The left auricle is shown by the arrow. When the coronary artery anatomy is normal, the right main coronary artery can be found by lifting up the right auricle of the right atrium. The left main coronary is found under the left auricle.

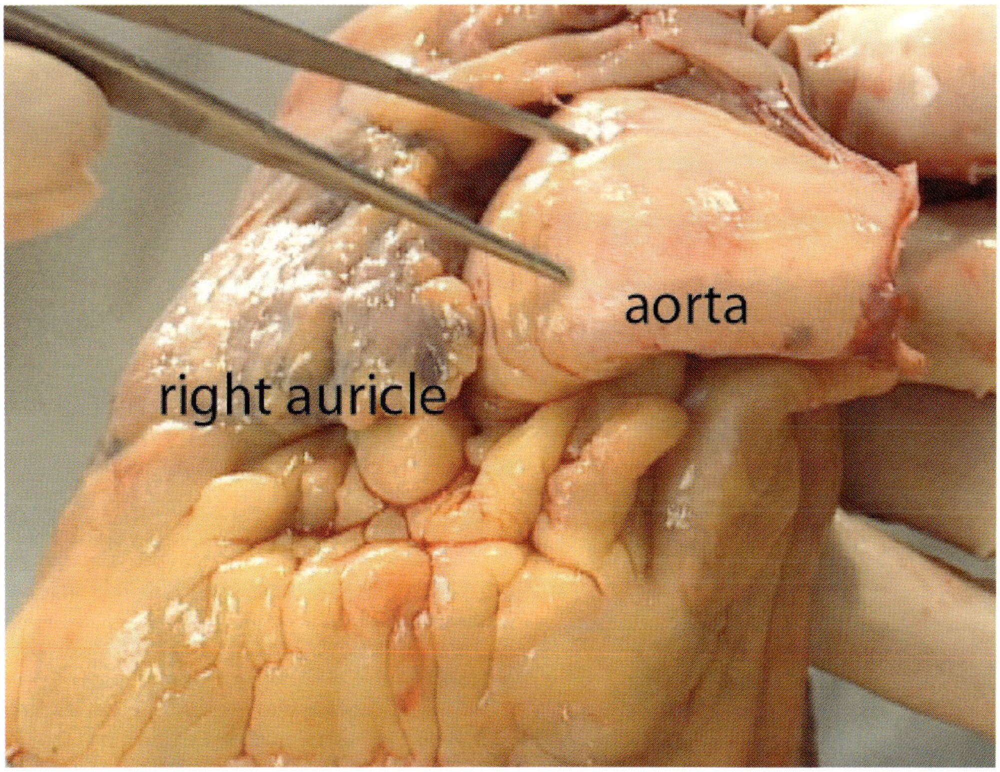

FIGURE 8.6 Aorta and right atrial auricle. The aorta is the curved structure indicated by the forceps.

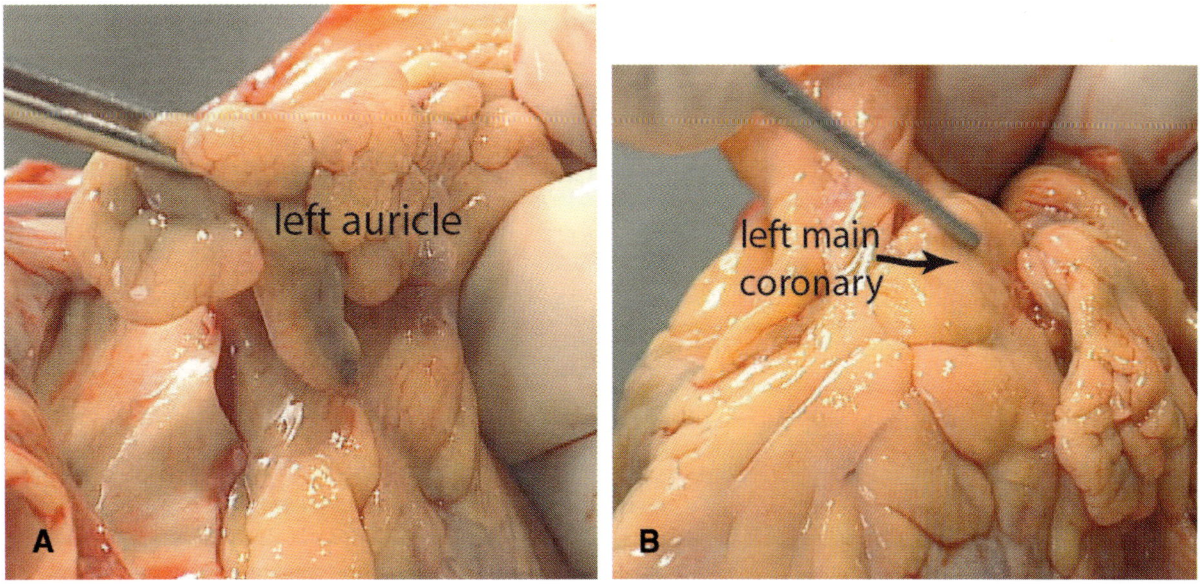

FIGURE 8.7 (A) Left auricle. The left auricle is held up by the forceps. The left auricle is somewhat smaller than the right. **(B) Left main coronary artery relationships.** The left main coronary artery runs beneath the auricle, generally the area indicated by the forceps.

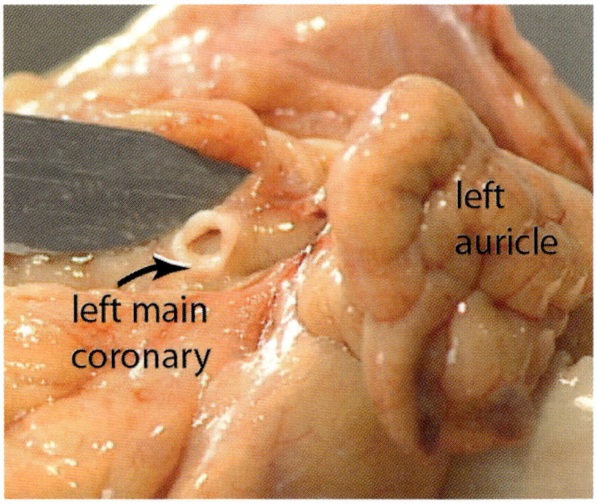

FIGURE 8.8 Cutting the left main coronary artery. The left auricle is lifted and cuts are made into the left main coronary artery and the left anterior descending branch of this artery. In this method, cuts are made to the artery in order to look for atherosclerotic plaque, thrombi (blood clots), or aneurisms (ballooning of the vessel wall).

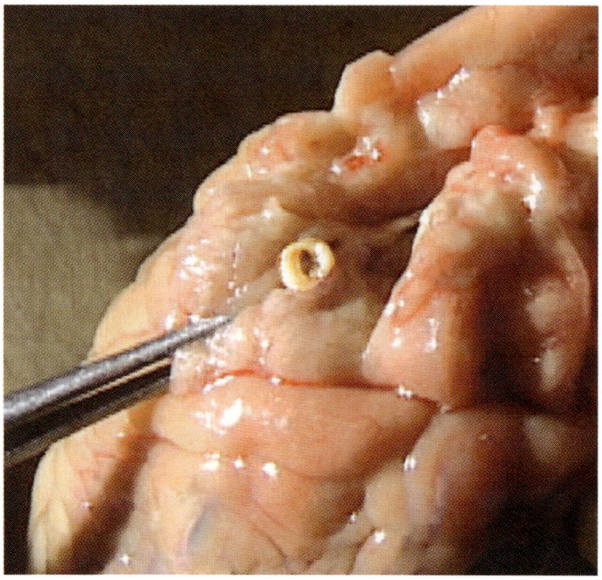

FIGURE 8.9 Left coronary artery thrombosis. This cut of the left main coronary artery shows nearly complete occlusive atherosclerosis. A small, dark thrombus occludes the lumen (seen near the tip of the forceps). Occlusion of the artery results in loss of blood flow to the region of the left ventricle of the heart that the artery supplies. Lack of blood flow results in lack of oxygen (hypoxia) to the tissues. If the thrombus or blocking plaque continues to occlude the vessel wall, the lack of oxygen results in cell death. Widespread cell death in the heart results in myocardial infarction, commonly known as a heart attack.

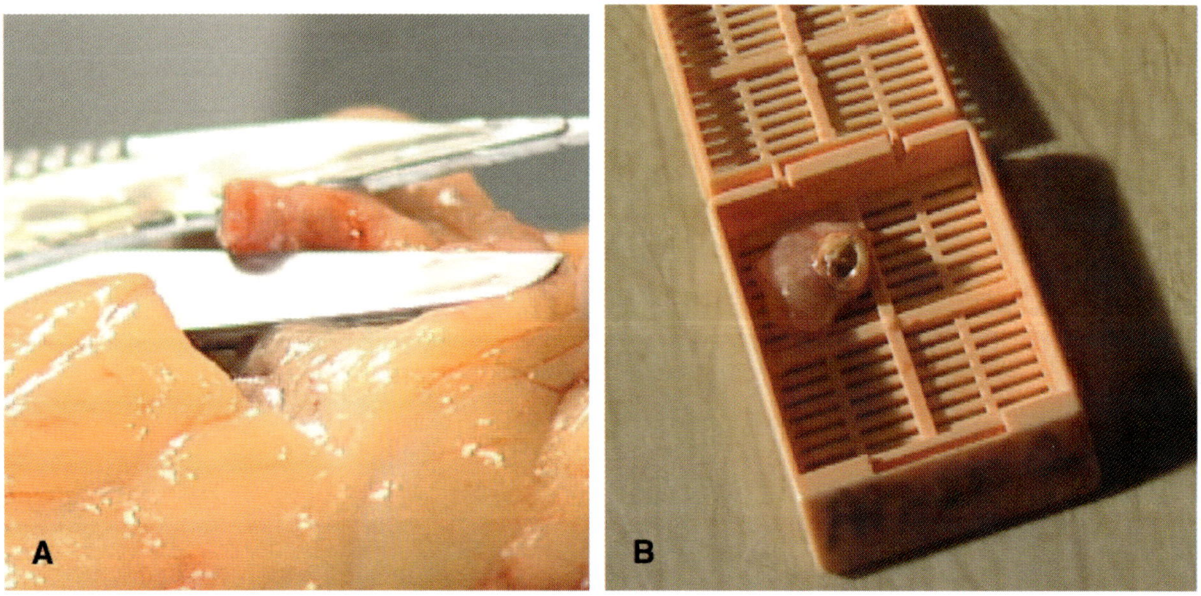

FIGURE 8.10 (A) Cutting a coronary artery. This artery is difficult to cut because it is affected with atherosclerosis. **(B) Placing the section for microscopic examination.** A section of the artery is cut and placed in a histology cassette. The tissue will be processed, cut into thin sections, placed on glass slides, and stained for review under the microscope (see Figure 10.3A). In the center of the specimen is a dark-colored thrombus.

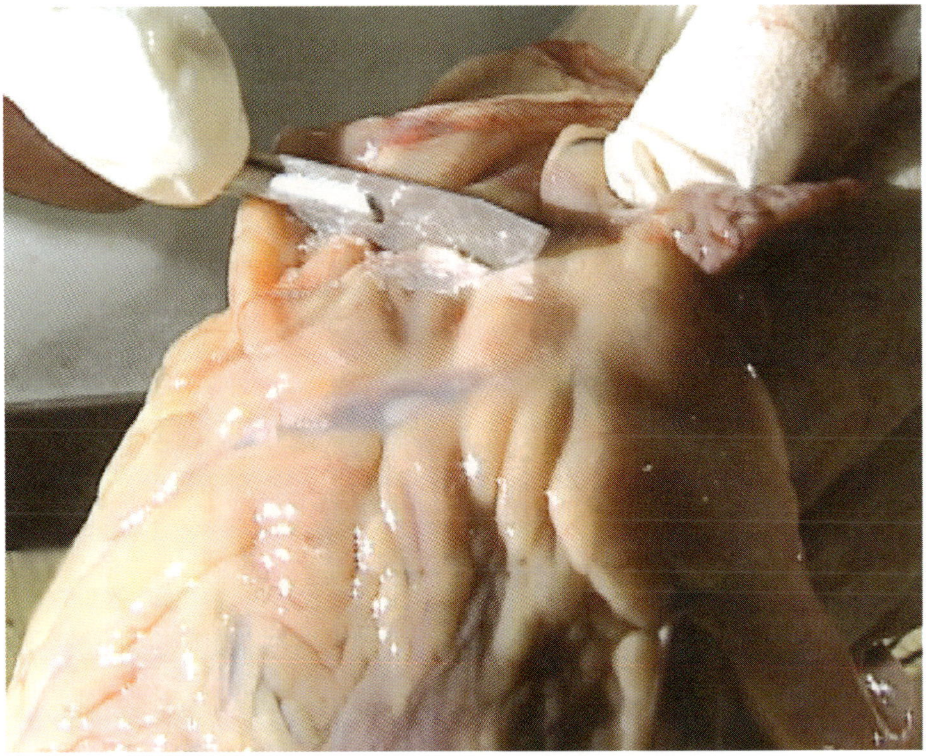

FIGURE 8.11 Cutting the left anterior descending coronary artery. A series of cuts are made along the entire length of the left anterior descending branch of the left coronary artery, usually the largest coronary artery of the heart. The artery must be examined from its origin, called the coronary ostium, so as not to overlook a focal thrombus or coronary disease.

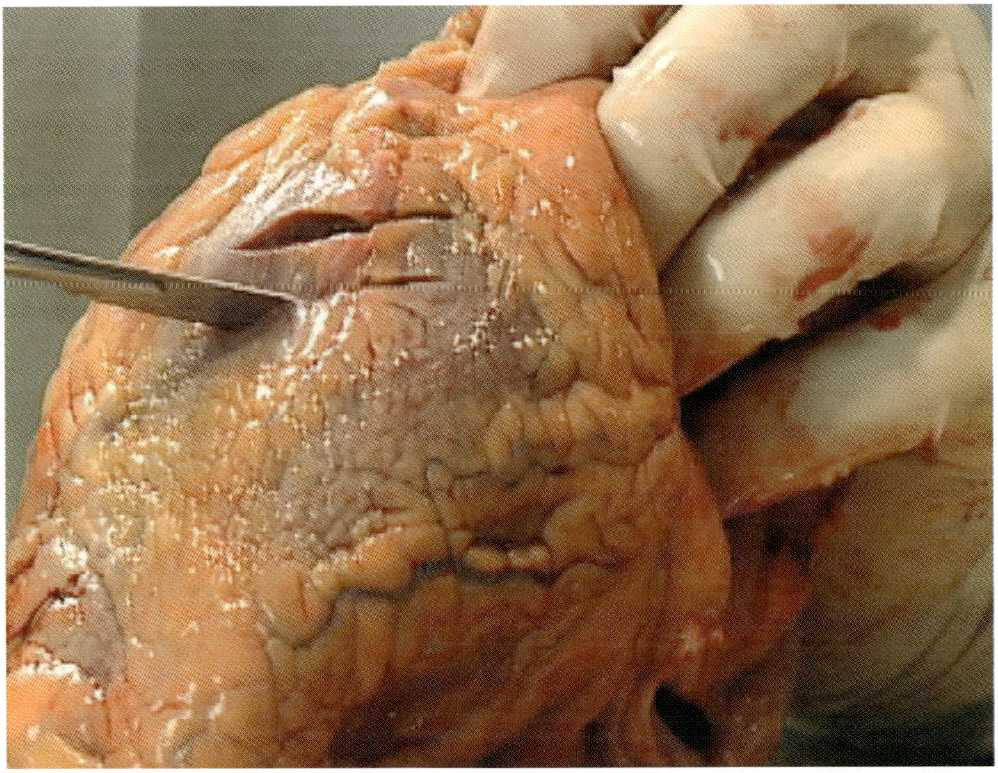

FIGURE 8.12 Cutting the first diagonal branch of the left coronary artery. Smaller left coronary artery branches are also examined.

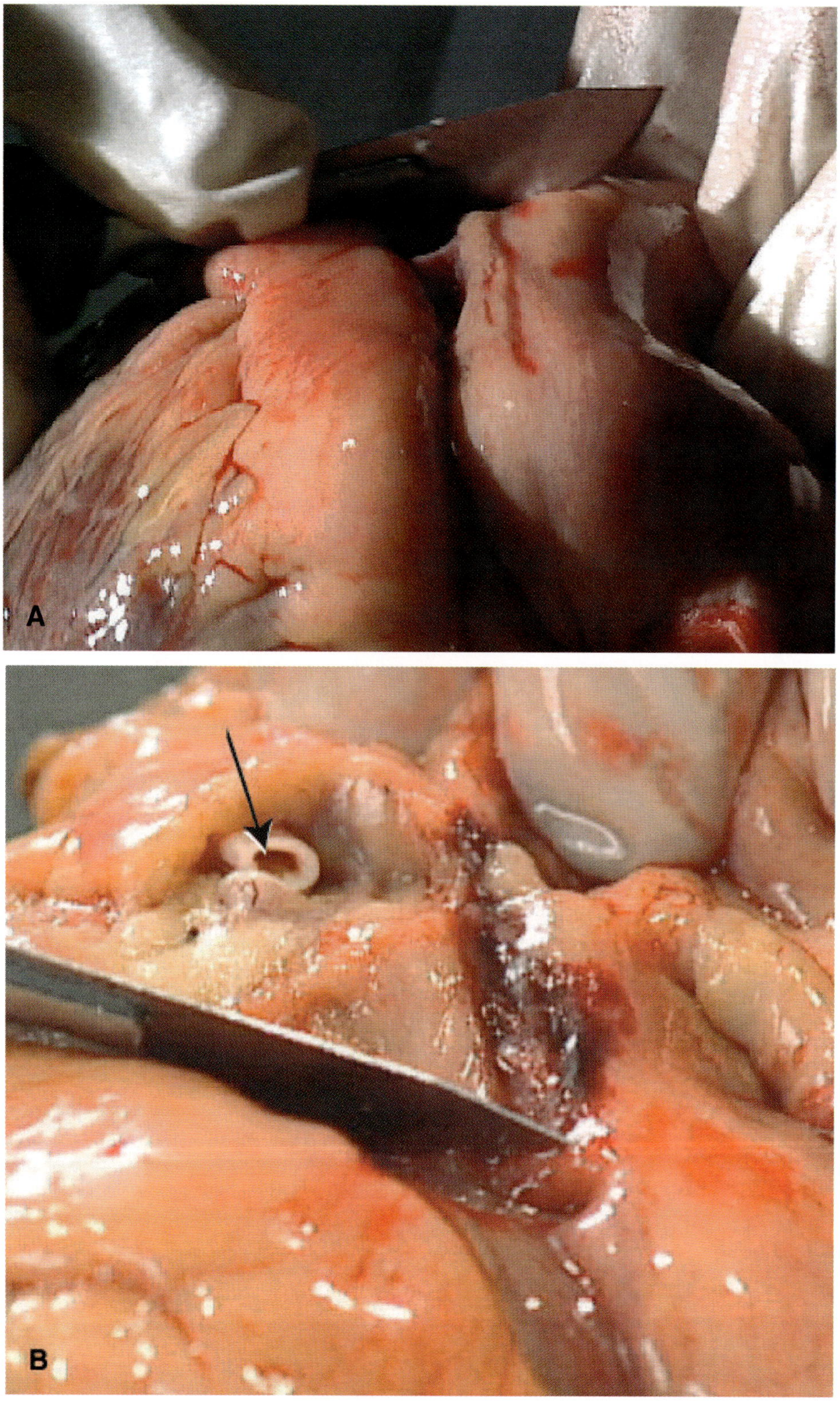

FIGURE 8.13 Cutting the circumflex coronary artery. **(A)** The circumflex artery usually branches off the left main coronary artery. More rarely, it can originate from the aorta. The circumflex artery turns sharply left, running above the upper margin of the left ventricle of the heart. **(B)** The cut artery is shown by the arrow.

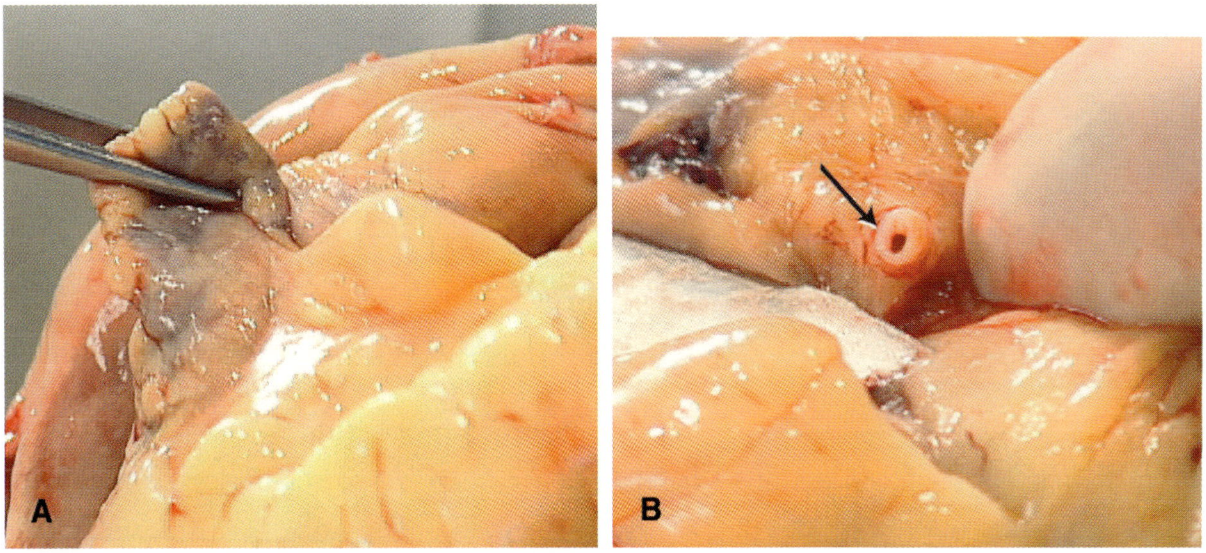

FIGURE 8.14 Cutting the right coronary artery. (A) The right auricle is shown by the forceps. **(B)** As the cut is made, a mostly patent right coronary artery cross section is visible (see arrow). This artery is larger than the circumflex artery in most people because it supplies the posterior septum (back of the heart).

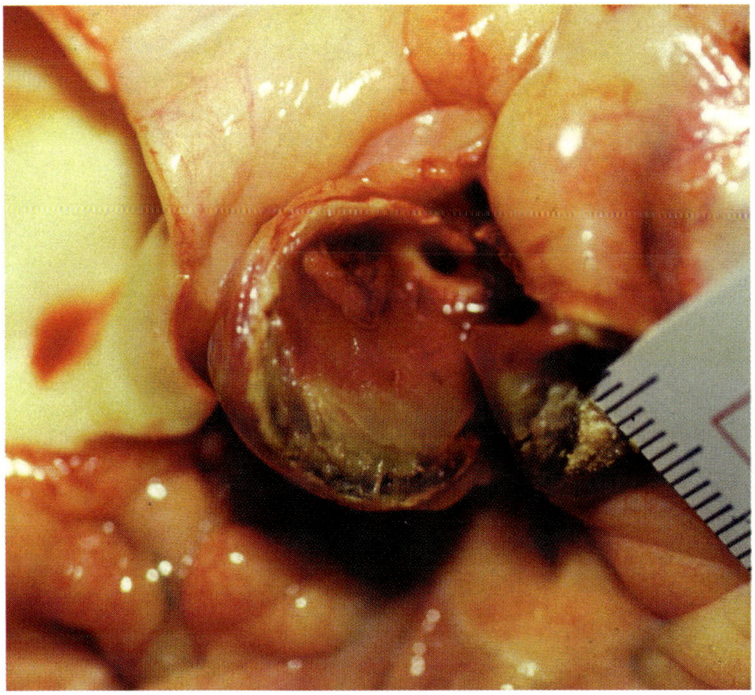

FIGURE 8.15 Coronary artery aneurism with atherothrombotic occlusion. The cross section of this coronary artery shows a dilated (aneurismal) artery filled with atherosclerotic plaque and thrombus. This person was the victim of a motor vehicle crash, and the heart disease was not related to the crash. This case illustrates that even with severe coronary artery disease, many people can function relatively normally. The scale shown is in centimeters.

FIGURE 8.16 (A)–(C) "Breadloafing" the ventricles of the heart. The heart can be opened in many different ways. For example, the heart is cut in the direction of blood flow when developmental abnormalities are seen. Since myocardial infarction is suspected in this heart, cuts will be made in the ventricles perpendicular to the long axis of the heart, referred to as "breadloafing."

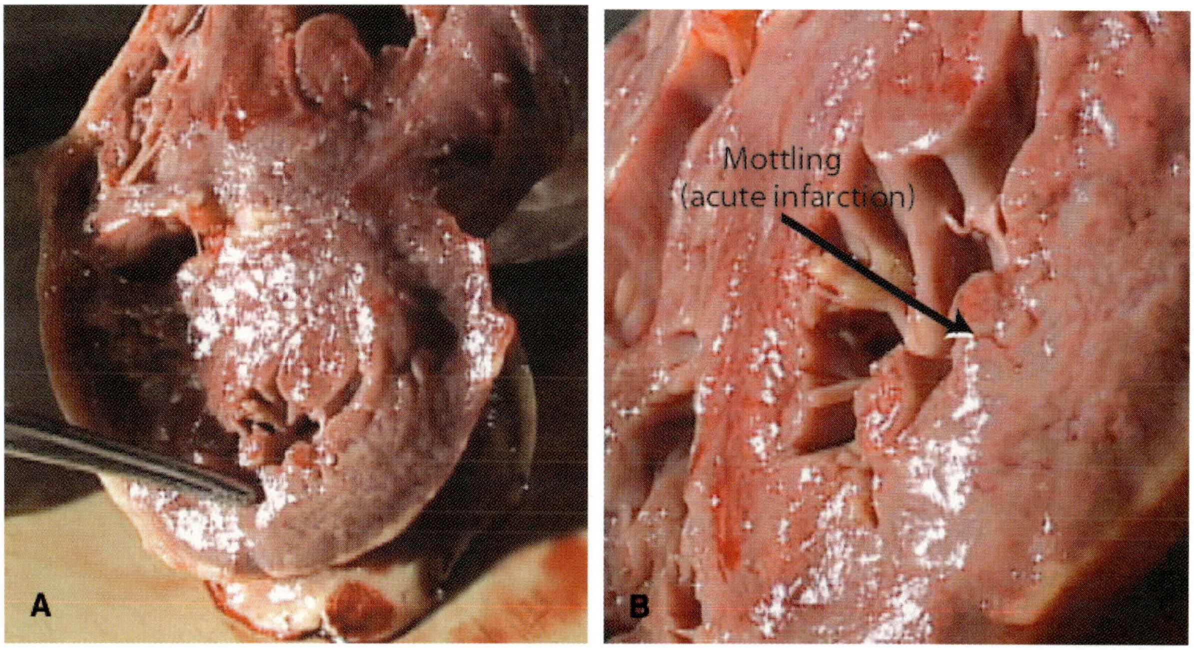

FIGURE 8.17 Mottling of cut myocardium due to acute myocardial infarction. This myocardial section shows mottling in the lateral left ventricular wall, suggesting early myocardial infarction. Infarction will be confirmed by examining tissue sections with the microscope (also see Figure 8.2A, Figure 8.2B, Figure 10.2A, and Figure 10.2B).

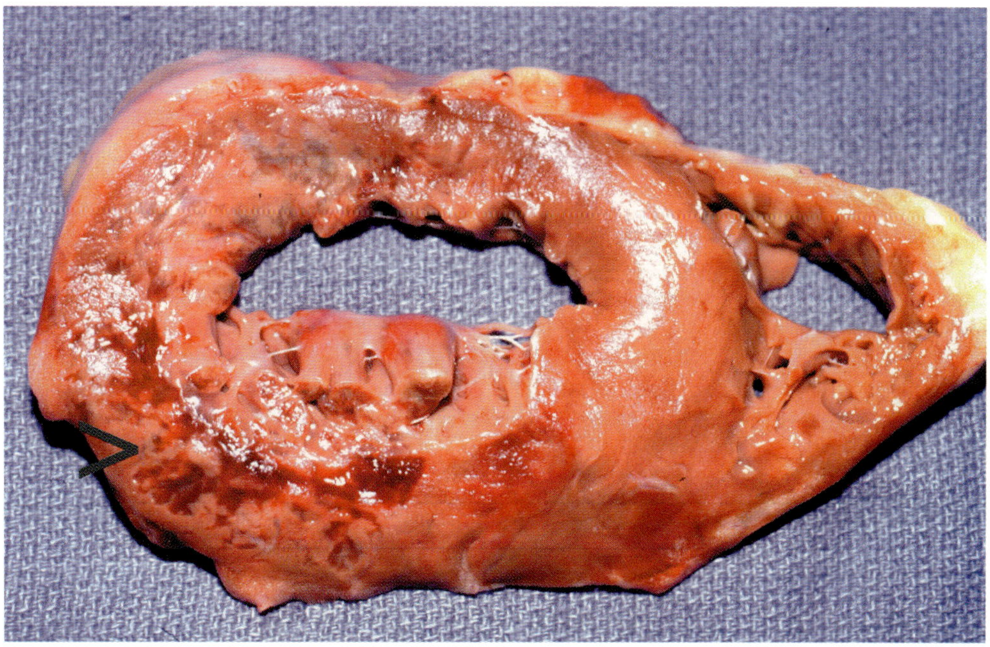

FIGURE 8.18 Acute myocardial infarction. Marked mottling can be seen on the anterior left ventricular wall, at the bottom of the figure.

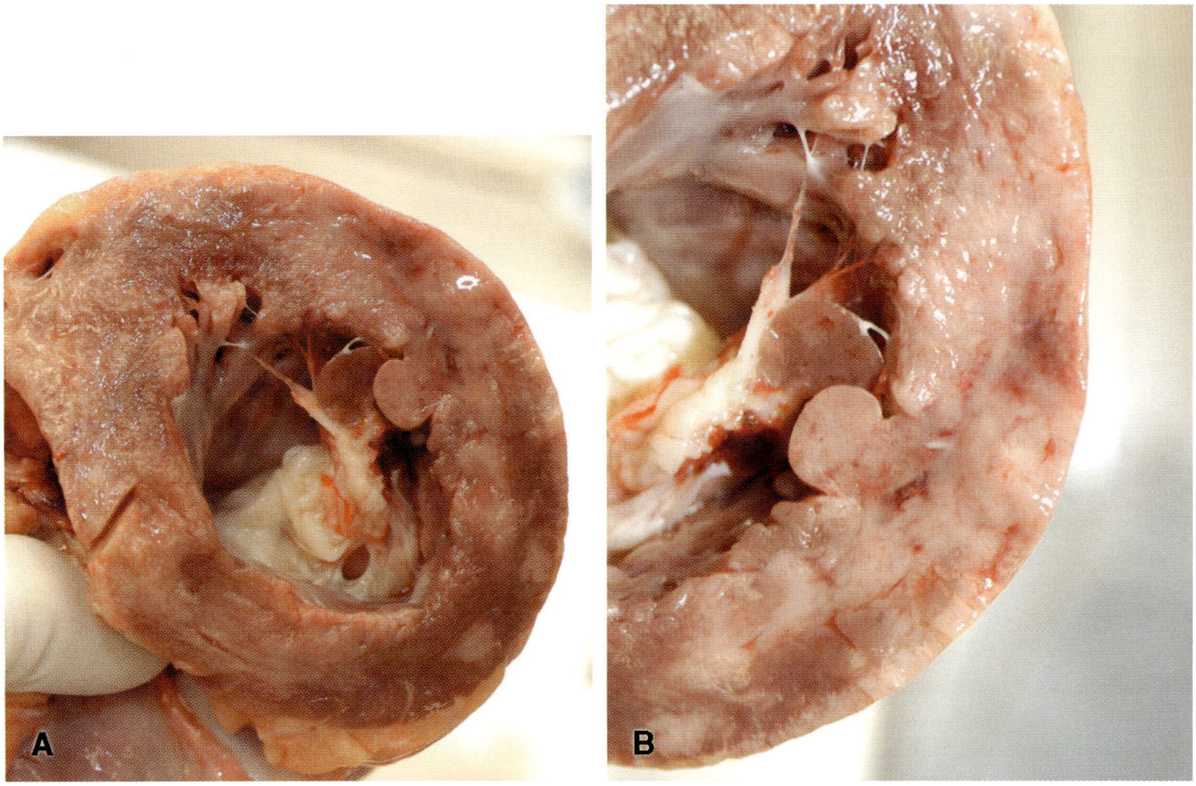

FIGURE 8.19 (A), (B) Myocarditis. The cross section of this heart shows blotches and streaks of white myocarditis throughout the normal brown myocardium. This patient had severe myocarditis, resulting in heart failure and death. The causes of myocarditis can be bacterial (Lyme disease), fungal, viral (Coxsackie B virus is common), and drug reactions. The cause of myocarditis is not found in many cases (see Figure 10.4A and Figure 10.4B for microscopics).

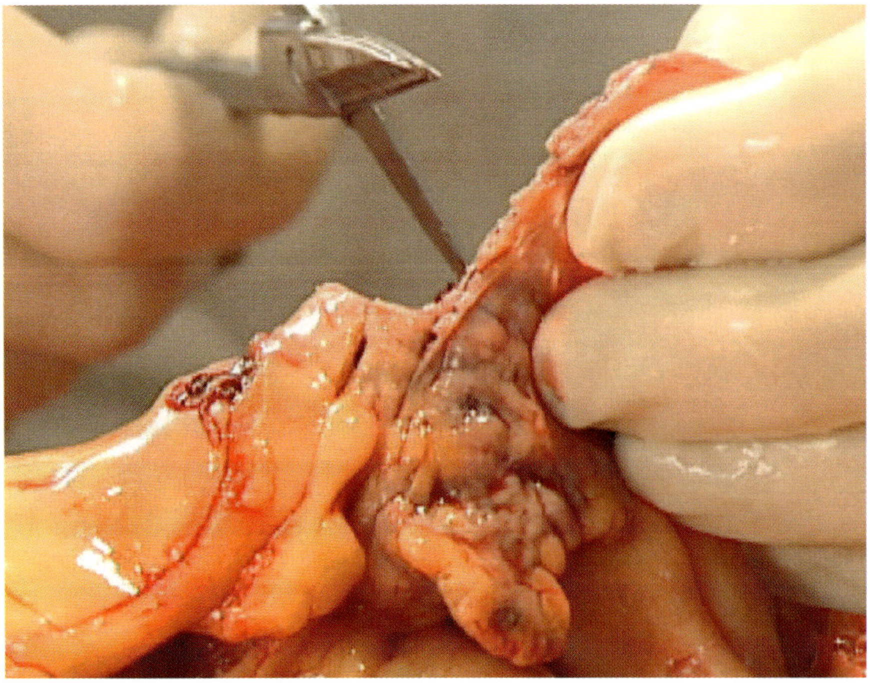

FIGURE 8.20 Opening the right atrium. Now that the right and left ventricles have been cut, the atria and the heart valves are opened in the direction of blood flow. Venous blood with low oxygenation is returned from the body and enters the right atrium. Blood is then pumped through the tricuspid valve to the right ventricle. From the right ventricle, blood is pumped through the pulmonic valve to the lungs for oxygenation. Oxygenated blood is returned to the heart via the pulmonic veins and enters the left atrium. Then, through the mitral valve, blood is pumped into the left ventricle. Finally, blood is pumped from the left ventricle through the aortic valve and into the aorta and systemic circulation, carrying oxygen to the tissues of the body.

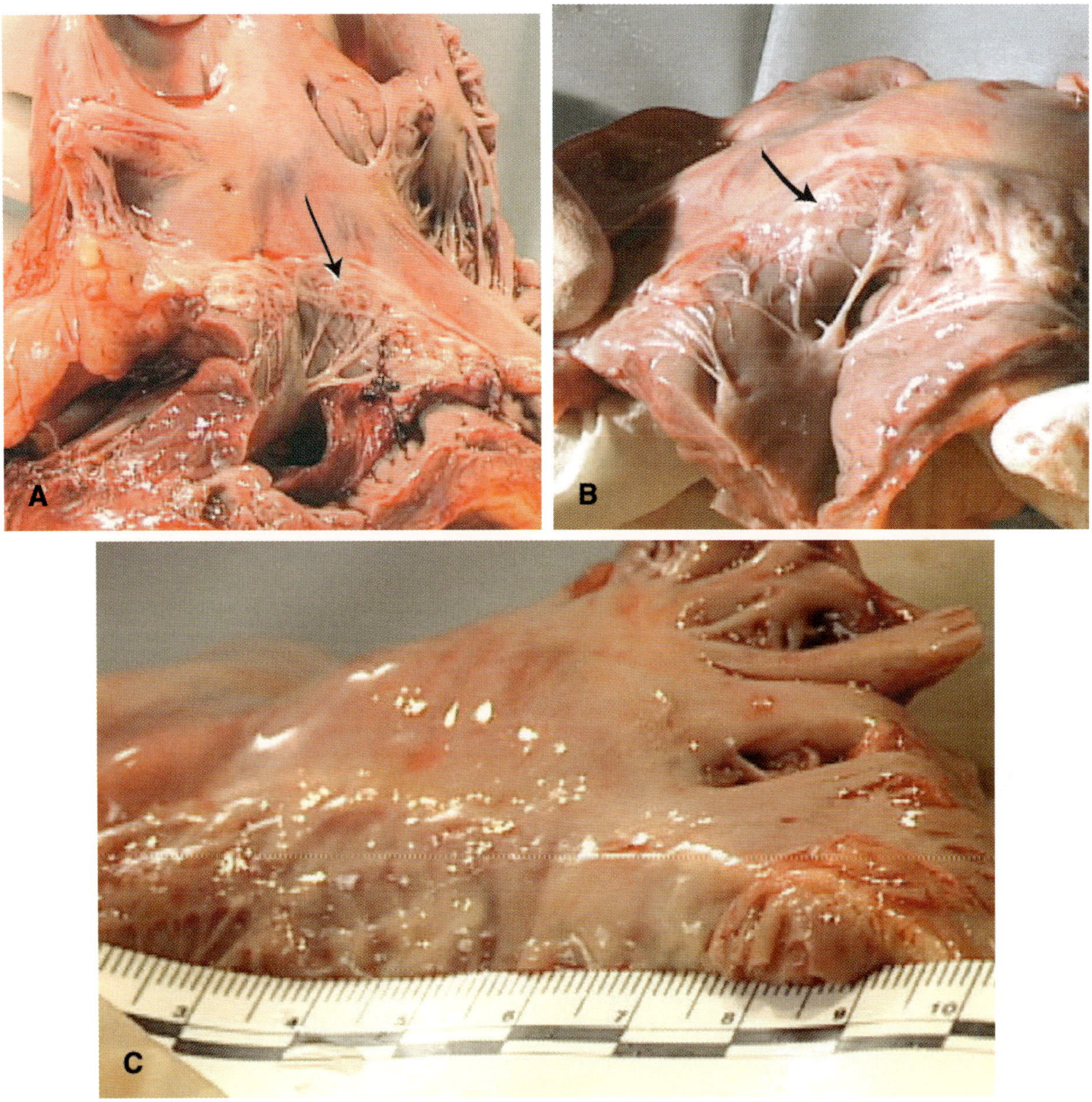

FIGURE 8.21 Right atrium and tricuspid exam. (A), (B) The right atrium is opened (see tops of figures), exposing the tricuspid valve, shown by the arrows. **(C)** The valve circumference is measured. Enlarged hearts, especially in right heart failure, can have large, incompetent valves.

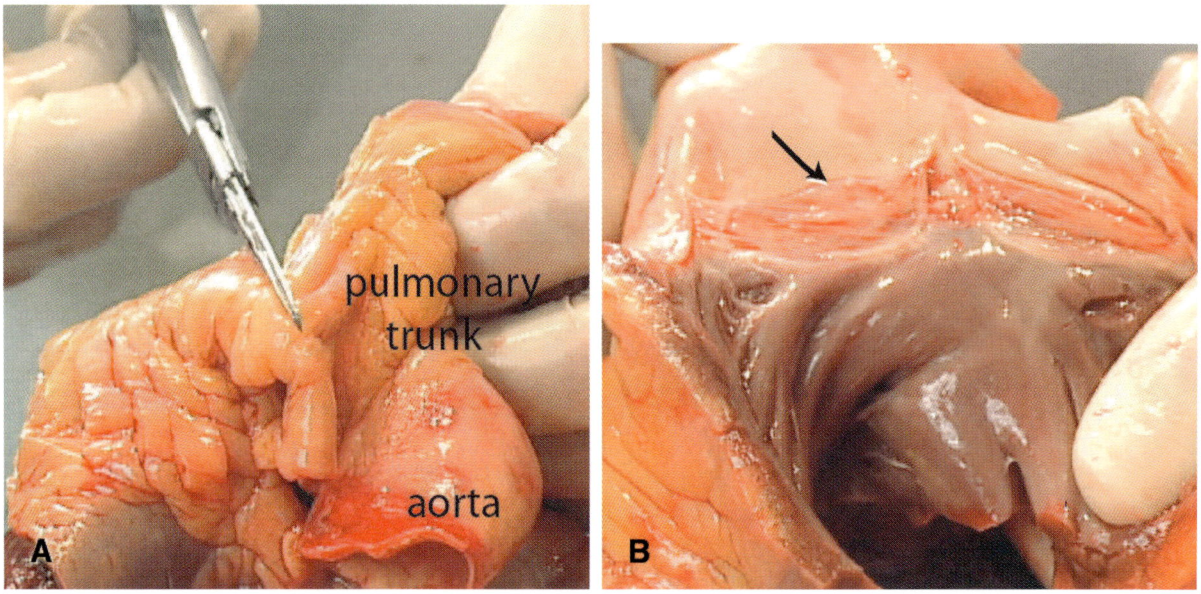

FIGURE 8.22 (A), (B) Opening and examining the pulmonic valve. The pulmonary trunk is opened to reveal a valve with three cusps. The pathologist checks carefully for thrombi (blood clots) or vegetations.

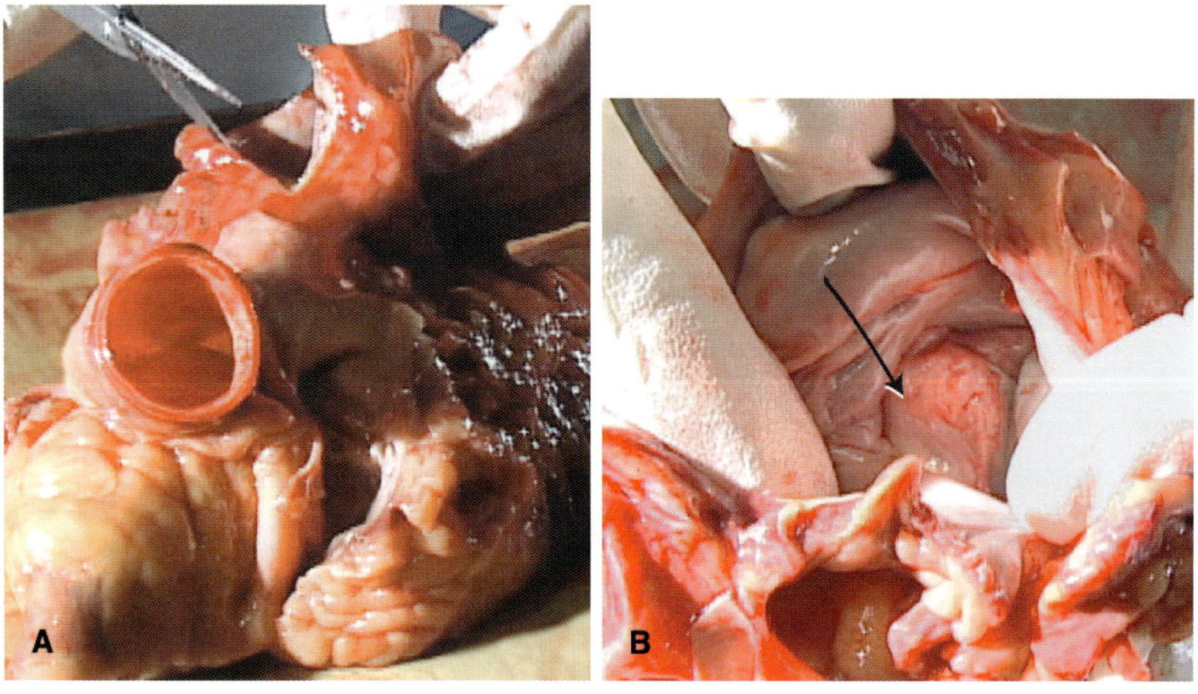

FIGURE 8.23 (A), (B) Opening the left atrium and exposing the mitral valve. The left atrium is opened to expose the mitral valve (see arrow).

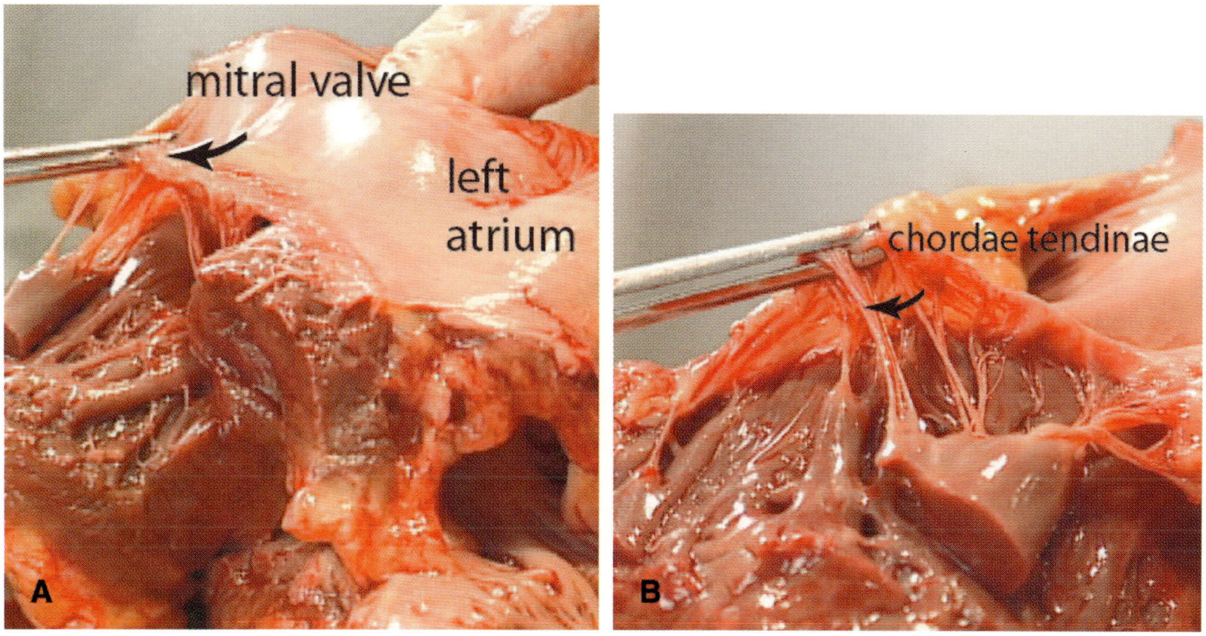

FIGURE 8.24 (A), (B) Mitral valve opening and examination. The mitral valve is opened. The thick, tendon-like structures that tether the valve are called chordae tendinae. The mitral valve has two leaflets, anterior and posterior.

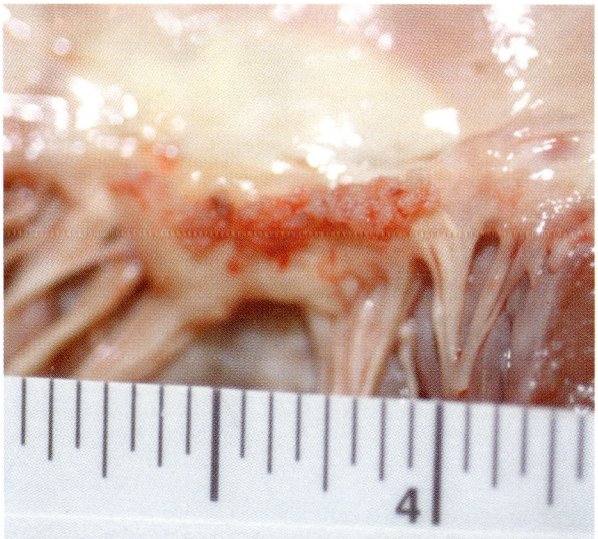

FIGURE 8.25 Mitral valve vegetations. The mitral valve edge is examined for vegetations. These are deposits of fibrin, clots, and bacteria in some cases that stick to the free edge of the valve leaflets. These vegetations can break loose, move into systemic circulation, and travel to organs and tissues, causing abscess (infection) in the brain, for example (see Figure 5.15C and Figure 5.15D).

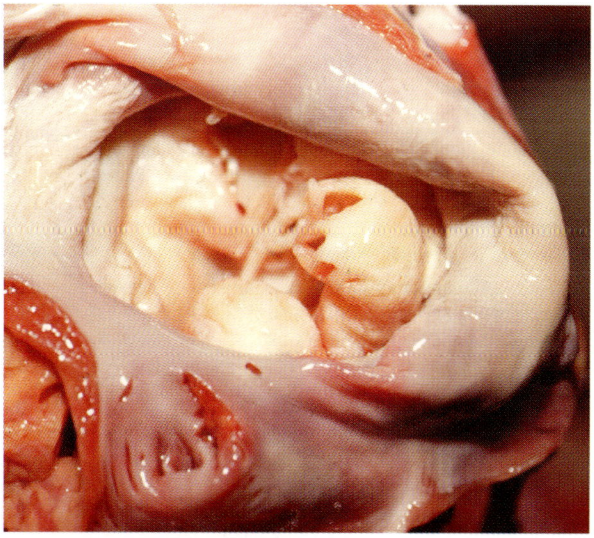

FIGURE 8.26 Floppy mitral valve. These valve leaflets are floppy, i.e., they are redundant and project upward when viewed from the open left atrium. This abnormal valve can cause a murmur, a condition associated with sudden cardiac death.

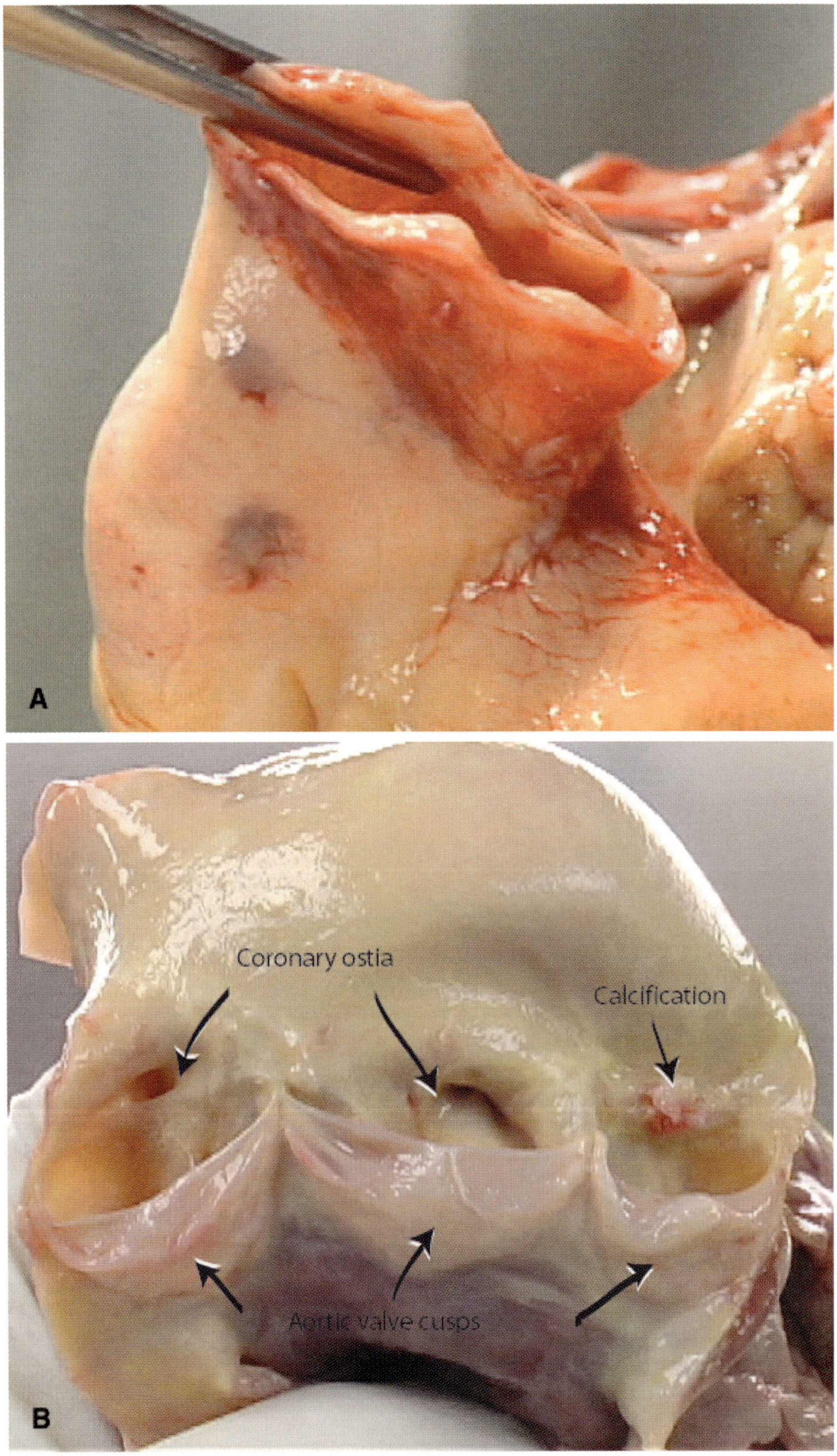

FIGURE 8.27 Opened aortic valve. (A) The aortic valve is opened to display three cusps. A common disorder in this region is calcification, which can cause bacteria or blood clots to form there. These bacteria or clots can travel or embolize throughout the body. **(B)** The coronary ostia, as depicted by the arrows, are the origins of the coronary arteries. The ostia are carefully examined because they are prone to occlusion by atherosclerotic plaque. The ostia should be "sighted," or looked through, to be sure no occlusion exists.

LUNG

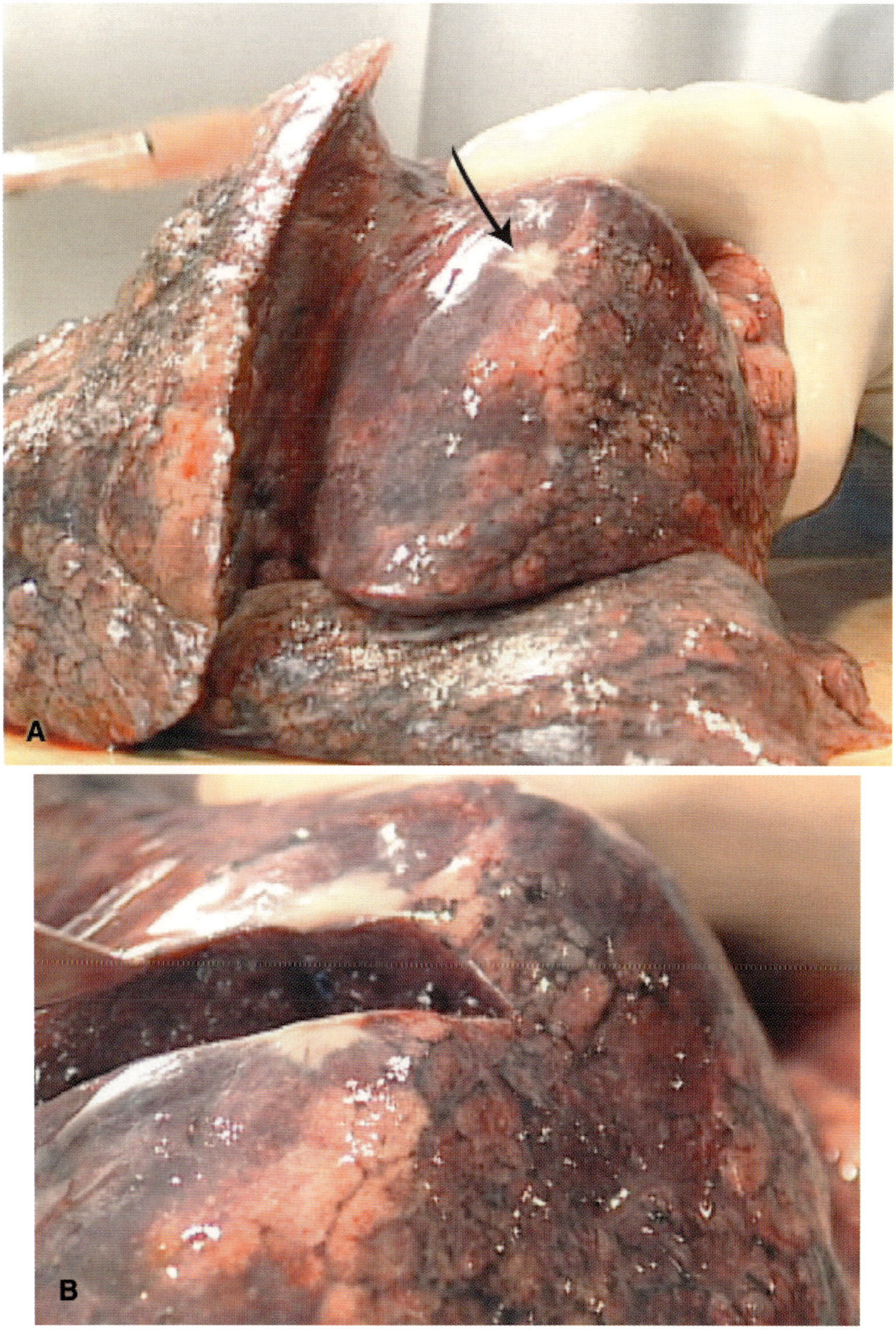

FIGURE 8.28 Lung examination and scar. (A) Examination of the pleura, or outer covering of the lung, reveals a whitish stellate scar (see arrow). **(B)** Upon closer examination and incision, it appears to be a thin surface scar, probably the result of a healed injury or infection of the area.

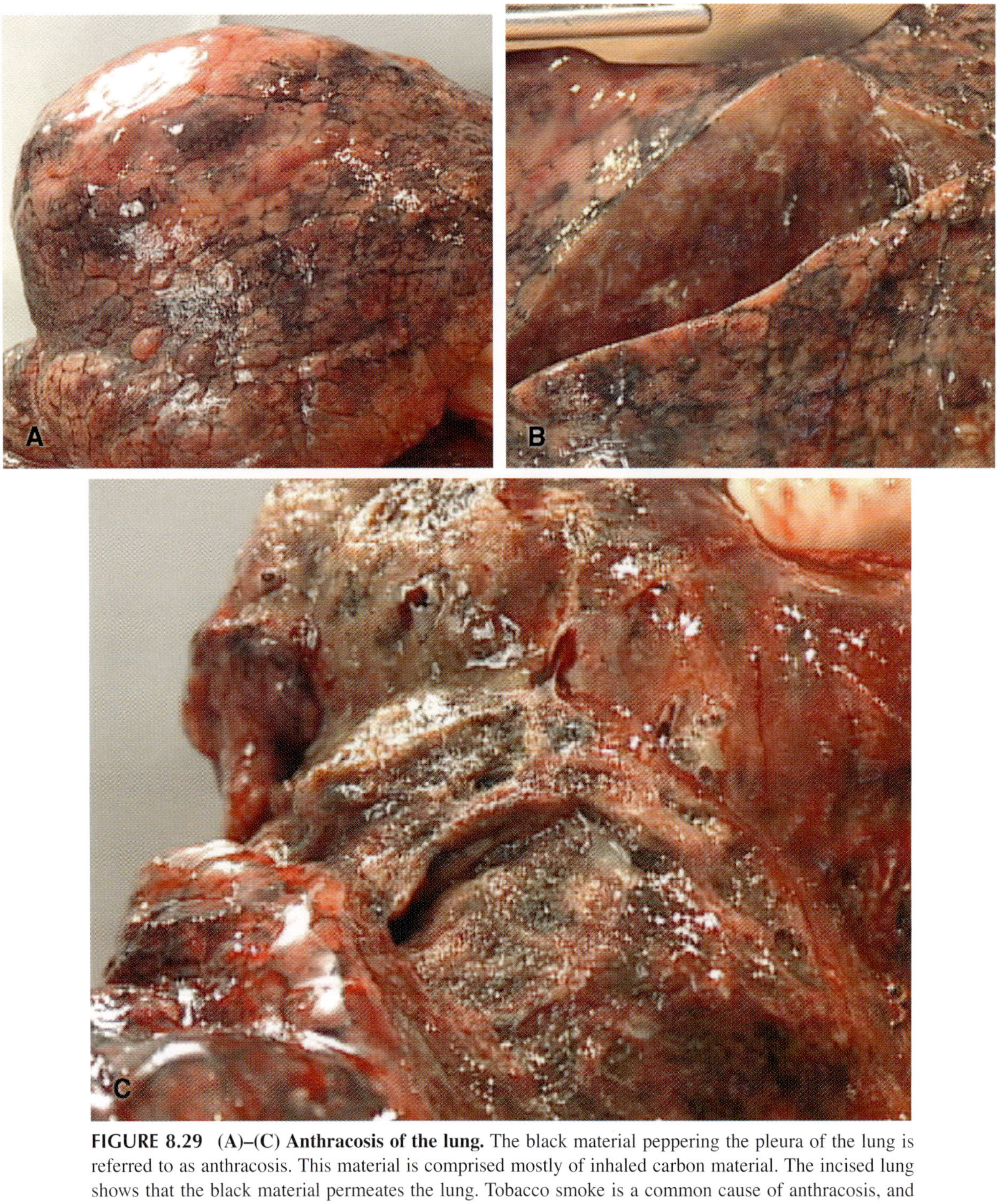

FIGURE 8.29 (A)–(C) Anthracosis of the lung. The black material peppering the pleura of the lung is referred to as anthracosis. This material is comprised mostly of inhaled carbon material. The incised lung shows that the black material permeates the lung. Tobacco smoke is a common cause of anthracosis, and smokers' lungs tend to be laden with anthracotic material. However, people can inhale carbon due to other activities, and there are many other causes of anthracosis. Coal miners and coal furnace workers, for example, can develop anthracosis.

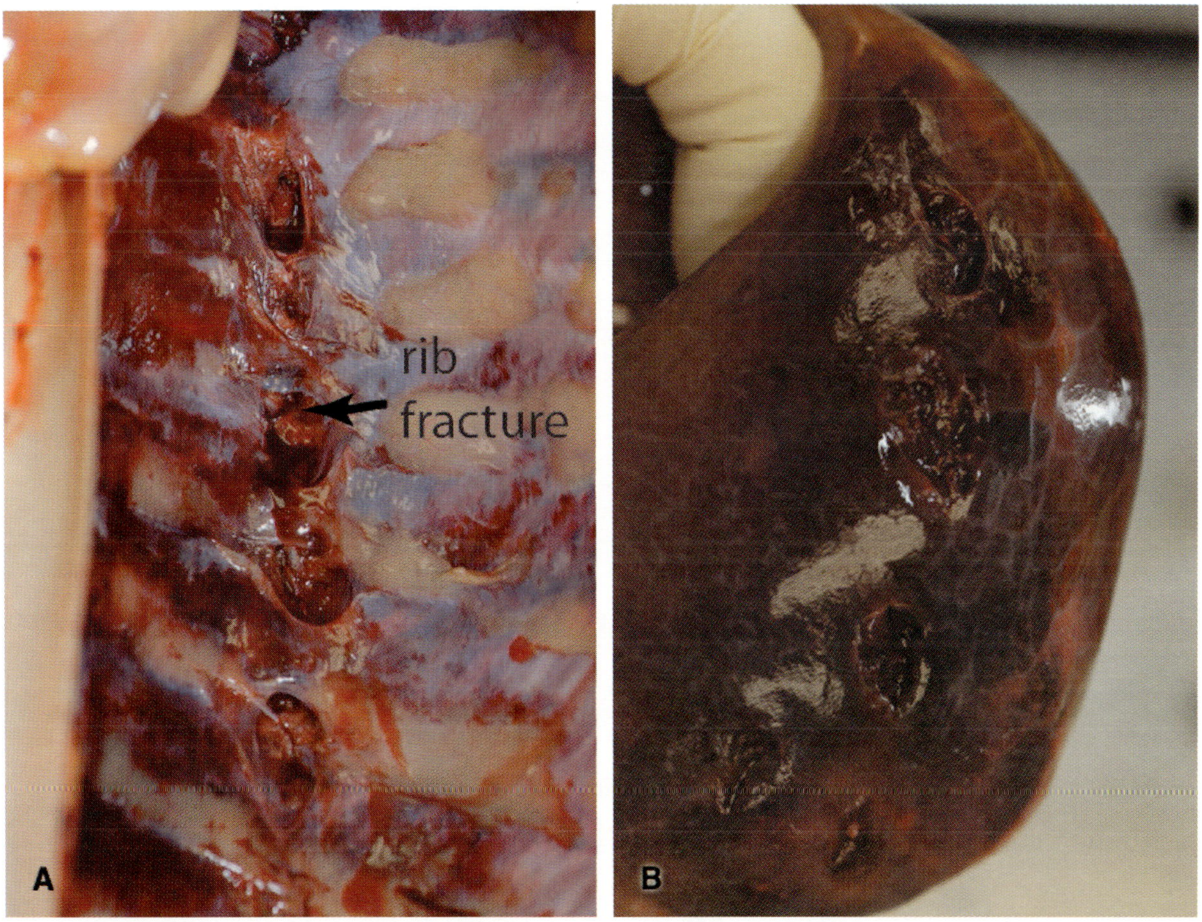

FIGURE 8.30 Rib fractures and corresponding lung lacerations. **(A)** The chest, ribs, and underlying lungs are susceptible to significant blunt trauma, such as that experienced in a motor vehicle crash. **(B)** The rib fractures in Figure 8.30A are responsible for these regular, periodic lacerations of the lung.

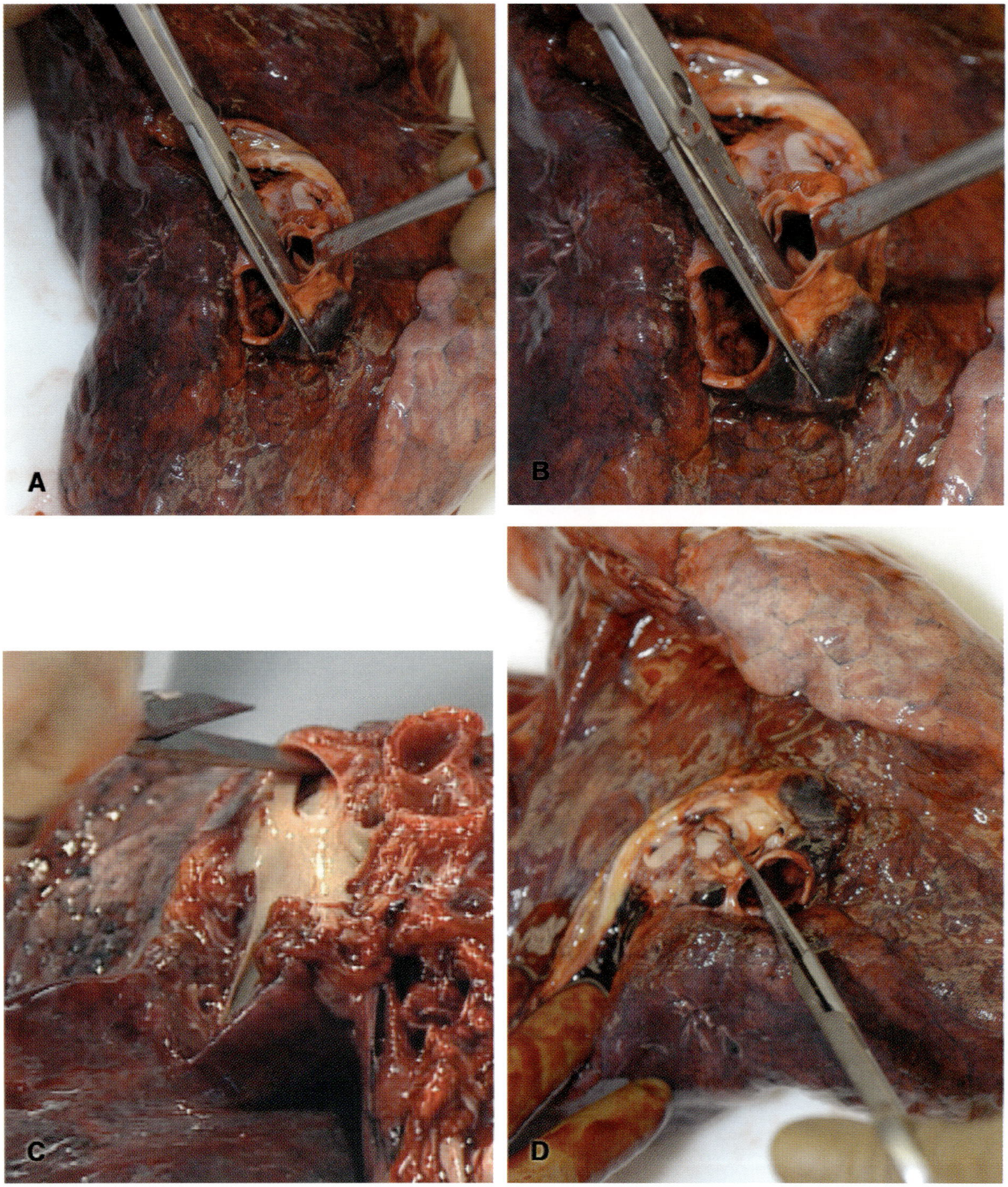

FIGURE 8.31 (A)–(D) Dissection of the pulmonary arteries. Starting at the hilum, or attachment point of the lung, the main bronchi are opened to look for inflammation and tumors, among other things (Figure 8.31D). The pulmonary arteries and branches are opened to search for emboli. The lymph nodes at the hilum can be examined at this time as well.

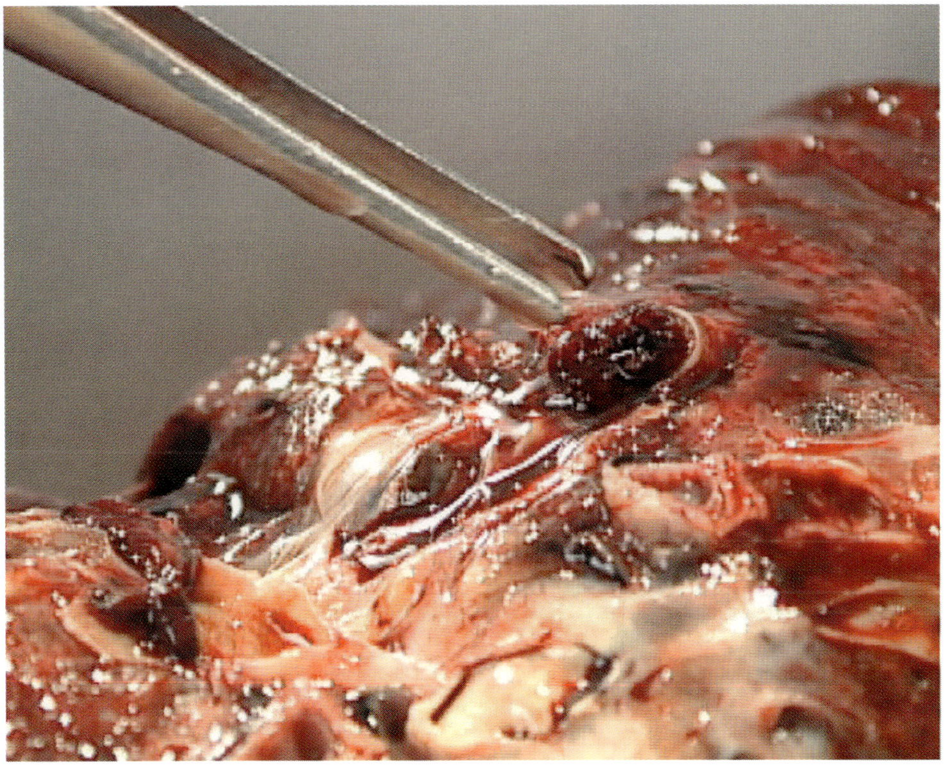

FIGURE 8.32 Large pulmonary embolus *in situ*. Dissection of this lung revealed a large thromboembolus (blood clot) in the pulmonary artery branch. These clots usually migrate or "embolize" from the lower extremities where, through the venous system, they become wedged in the large pulmonary arteries or the smaller branches, depending on the size. If large enough, these thromboemboli can cause immediate cardiac standstill and sudden death. Smaller thromboemboli cause chest pain and an infarction of a small segment of lung. Pulmonary embolus is the most common cause of death in the hospitalized patient.

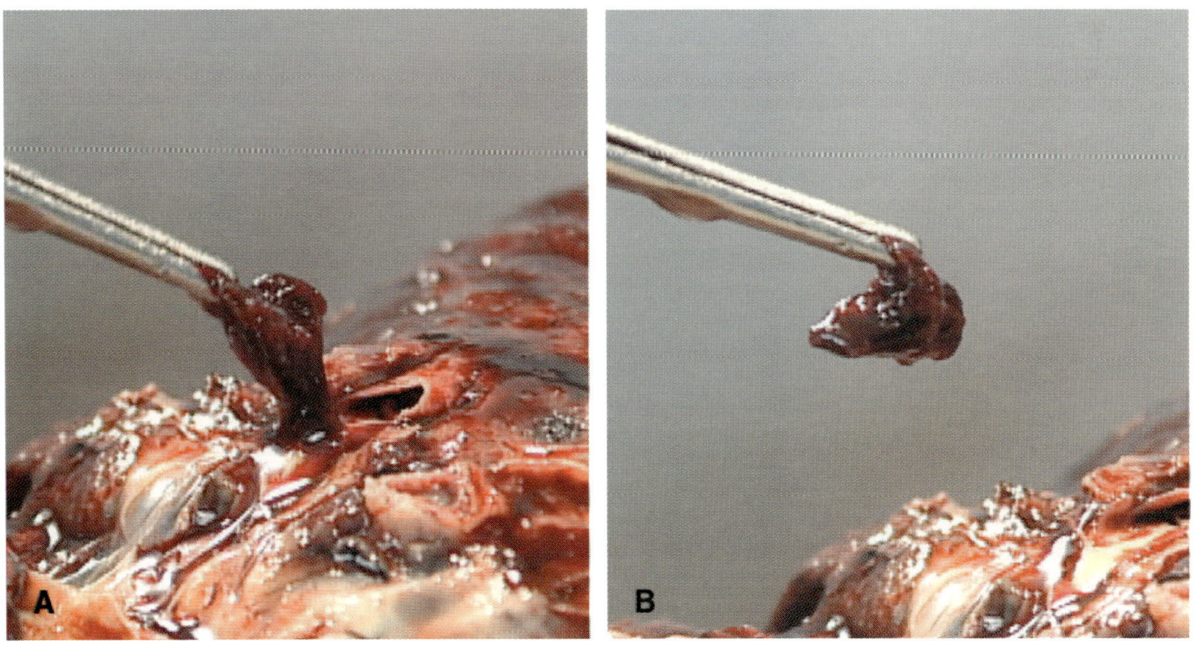

FIGURE 8.33 (A), (B) Large thromboembolus removed. If thromboemboli are gently tugged on, their true morphology can be determined. As this clot is removed it is slightly adherent to the vessel wall, forming a cast of the vessel. Thromboemboli must be distinguished from postmortem clots, which are common throughout the vascular system after death.

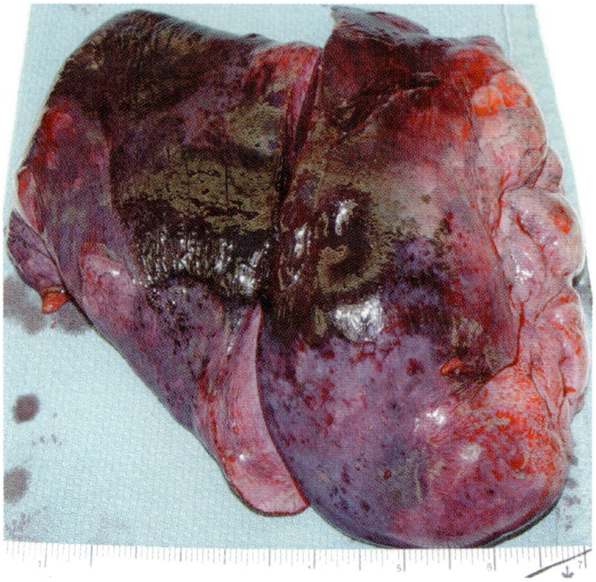

FIGURE 8.34 Pulmonary infarction. This lung shows a broad, dark-purple area of infarction (top and middle of the figure), which stands out from the pink parenchyma of the overall lung. Pulmonary infarction is the result of a clot large enough to cause tissue necrosis of the lung.

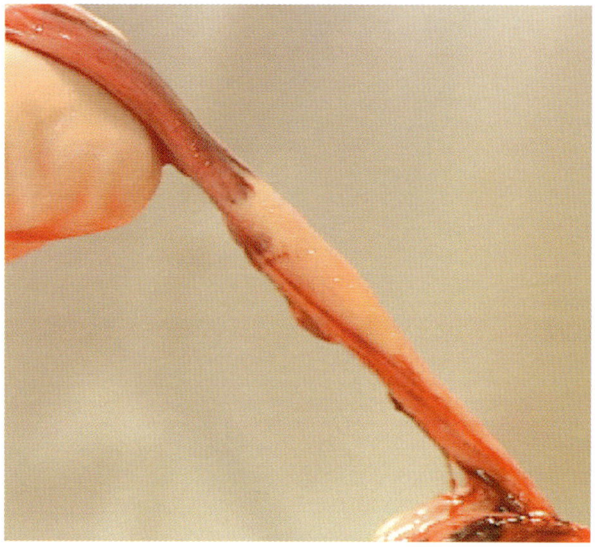

FIGURE 8.35 Postmortem blood clot. This stringy postmortem clot is being pulled out of a blood vessel. It does not form a cast of the vessel like premortem clots do. Postmortem blood clots are a mixture of two separate areas: a purple, soft, "currant jelly" area with a yellow, harder, "chicken fat" area. It is important for the pathologist to recognize the difference between a premortem thromboembolus and a postmortem blood clot. These two clots can look very similar. If the postmortem clot is mistaken for a premortem clot, the cause of death could be determined erroneously as pulmonary thromboembolus.

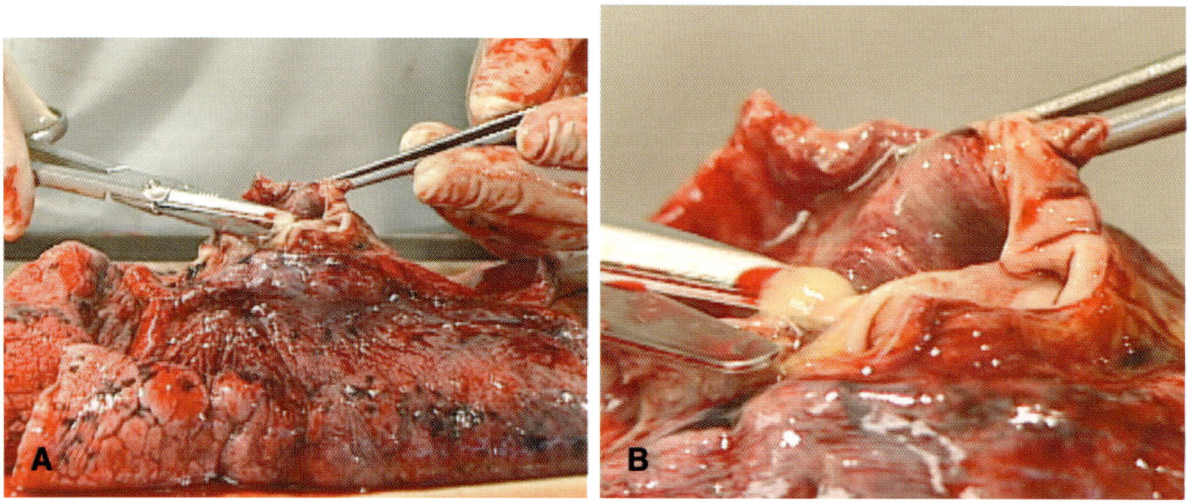

FIGURE 8.36 Bronchial inflammation. (A) Upon dissecting this bronchus from the hilum, or center of attachment of the lung, a yellow mucoid substance is noted at the tip of the scissors. **(B)** The bronchus is erythematous (red), and pus can be seen on the scissor. These findings suggest bronchitis or bronchopneumonia.

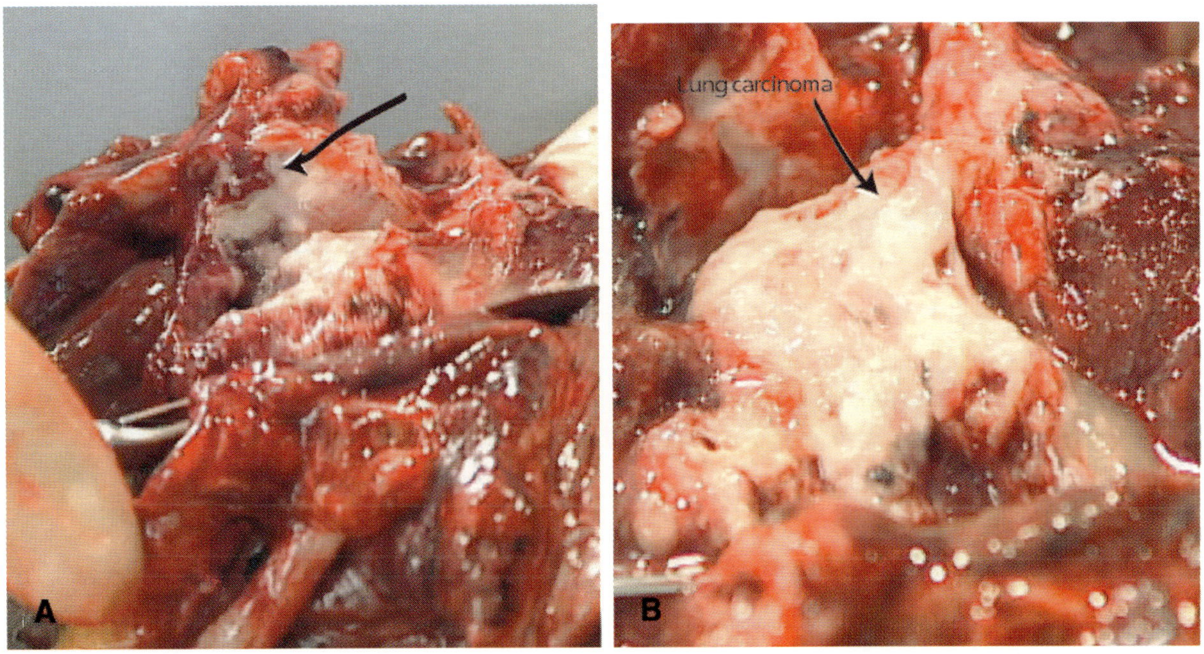

FIGURE 8.37 (A), (B) Carcinoma in the lung hilum. Bronchial dissection at the hilum reveals a whitish tumor, as displayed by the arrows. Cancers grow quickly and tend to outgrow their blood supplies, causing tissue death, or necrosis. This tumor will be sectioned for microscopic examination to determine the type of tumor or cancer.

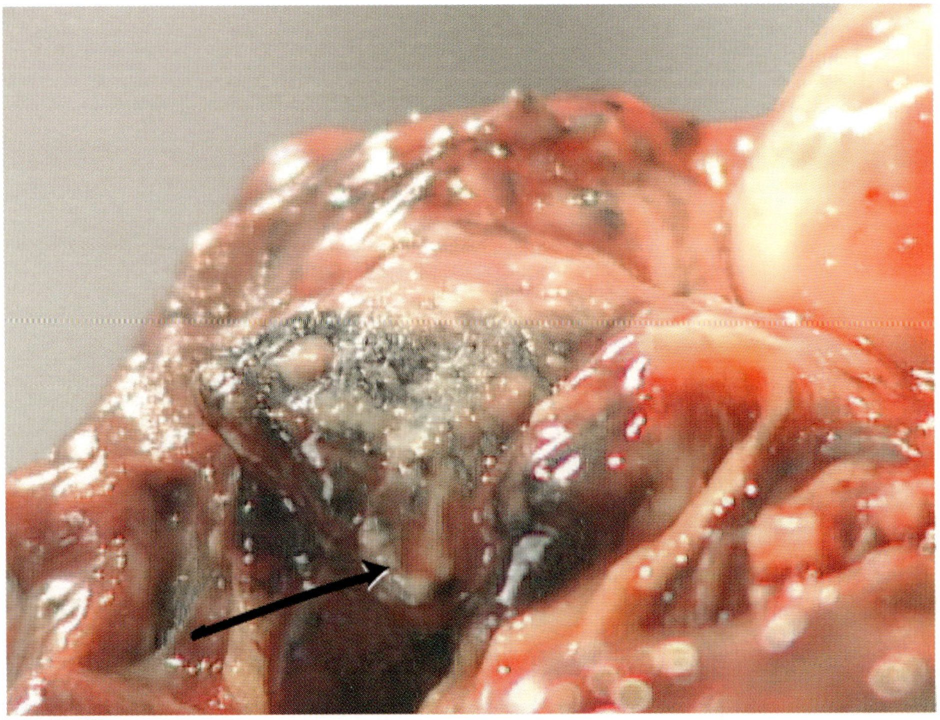

FIGURE 8.38 Cancer in an anthracotic lymph node. The tumor displayed has metastasized (spread) to the hilar lymph nodes, which are abundant in the hilum of the lung. Anthracosis (black pigment, likely from smoking in this case) is also seen in the lymph node. This tumor, after microscopic review, was determined to be a squamous cell carcinoma, which is found almost exclusively in smokers.

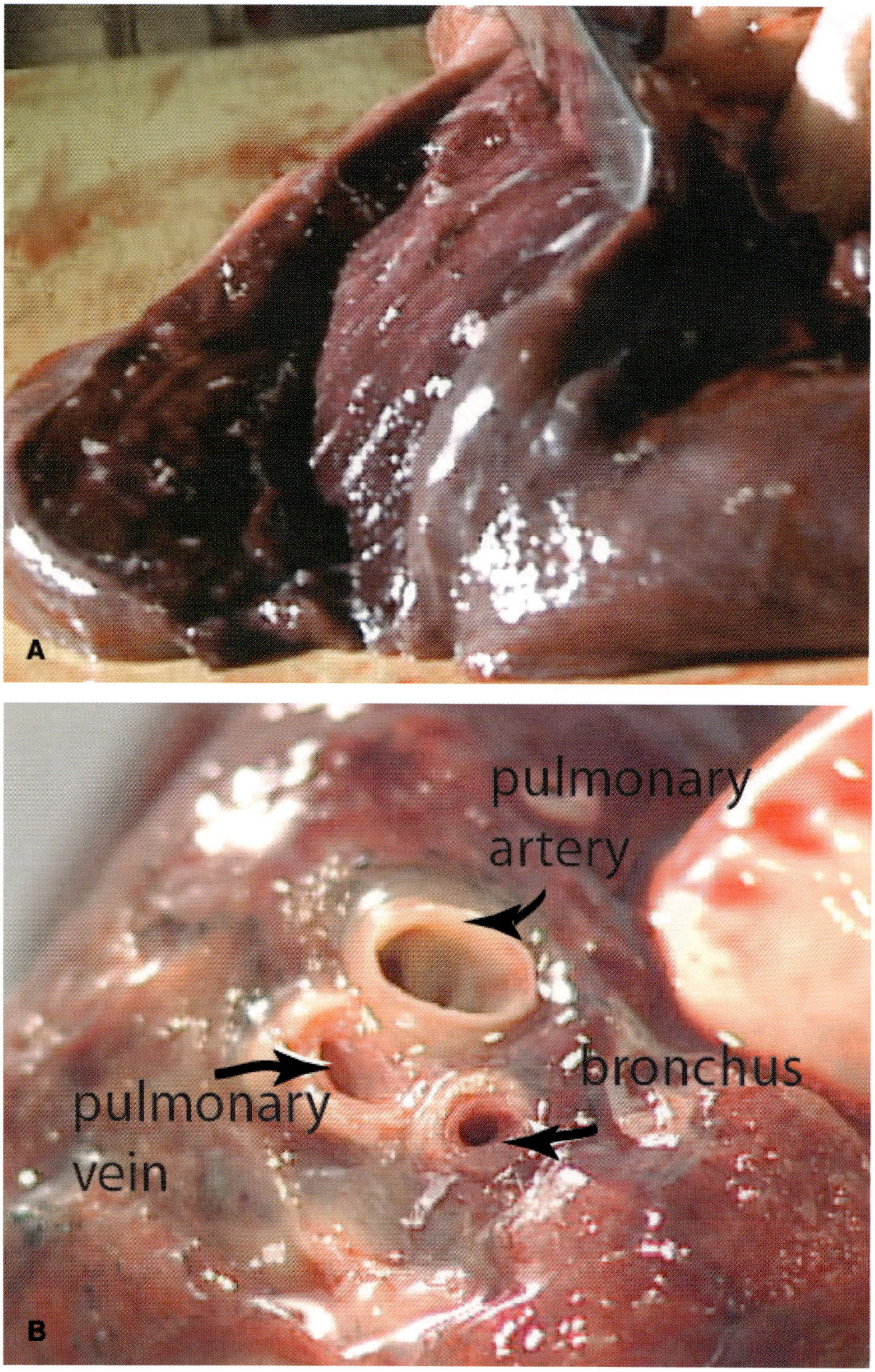

FIGURE 8.39 Sectioning of the lung. **(A)** The lung is serially sectioned, revealing the lung parenchyma. **(B)** The figure shows a normal pulmonary artery vein and a bronchus.

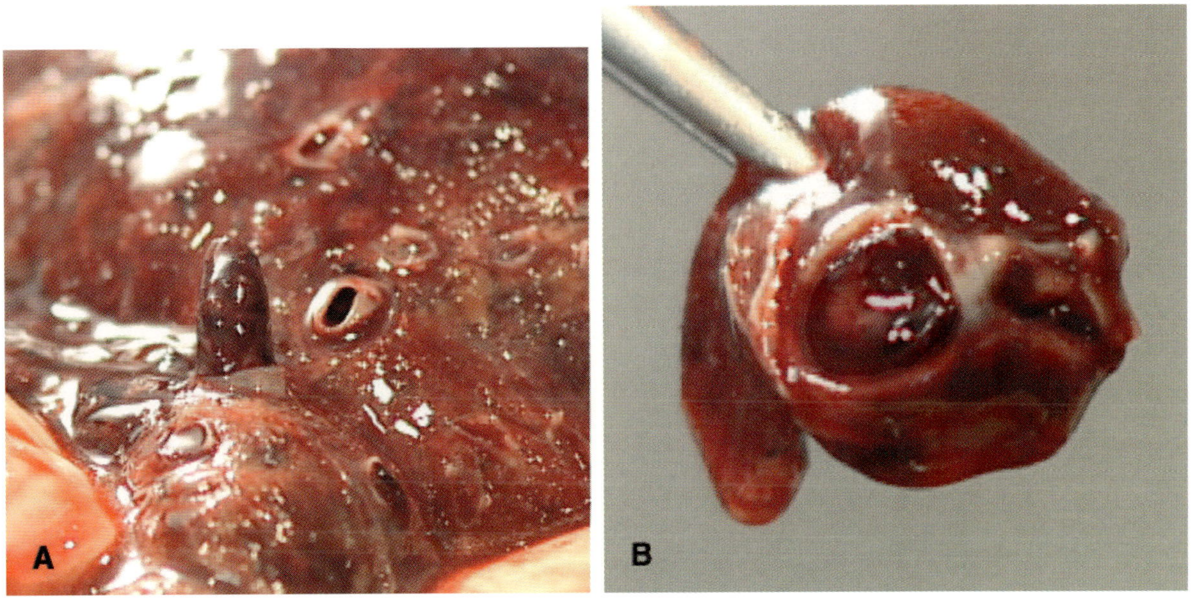

FIGURE 8.40 Small pulmonary emboli. **(A)** Further sectioning of this lung shows pulmonary emboli in the smaller pulmonary vessels. These emboli protrude from the vessel wall when cut, as opposed to postmortem clots, which are stringier. **(B)** This adherent clot from the center of the vessel will be submitted for microscopic examination to provide further proof that the clot is premortem.

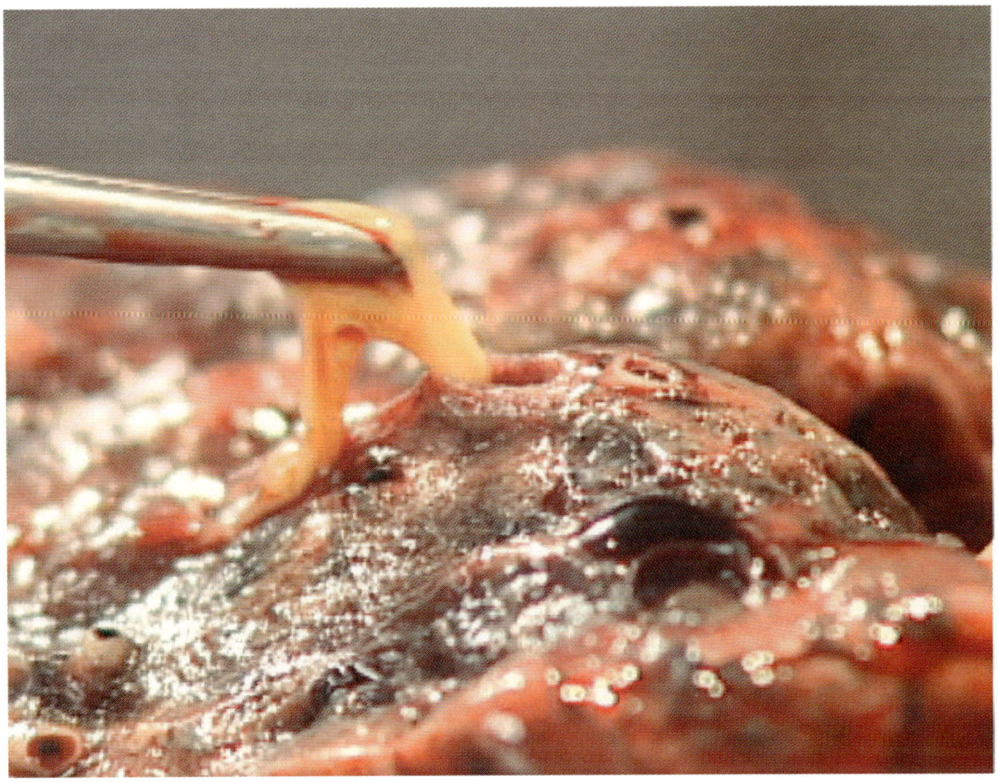

FIGURE 8.41 Purulent material in the smaller bronchus. Further sectioning of this lung shows yellowish, mucoid pus in the bronchi, indicating bronchopneumonia.

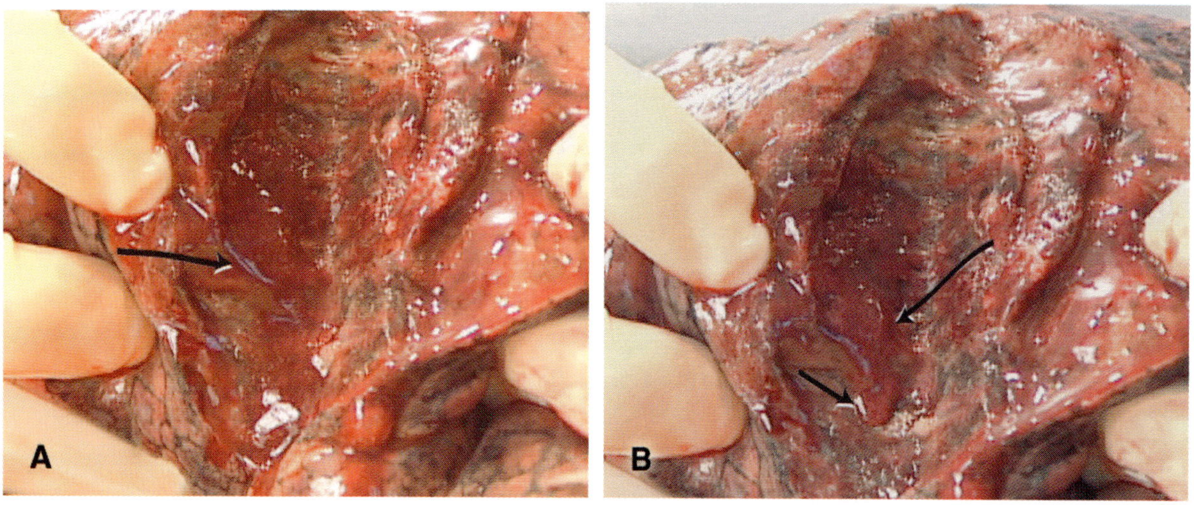

FIGURE 8.42 (A), (B) Pulmonary congestion. Fluid freely flows or cascades from the cut section of lung, indicating congestion (see arrows). The congested lung weighs up to twice the normal average weight of about 400 g. The normal lung is soft and puffy, still containing air even at autopsy. This lung has a boggy, full feeling. The capillaries, large blood vessels, and tissues are filled with fluid. Lung congestion is a nonspecific finding and generally results from a slow stoppage of the heart.

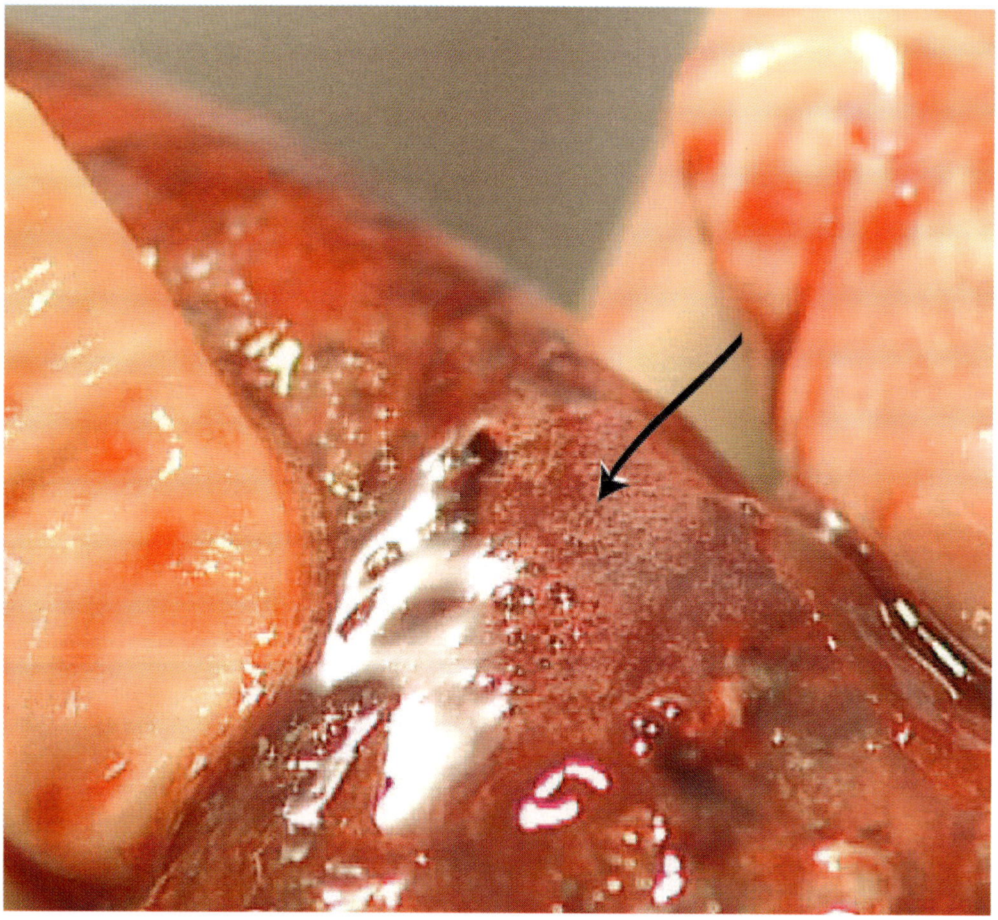

FIGURE 8.43 Pulmonary edema fluid. This lung section shows edema fluid characterized by fluid exuding from the air-filled spaces, producing bubbles (see arrows). Common causes of pulmonary edema include heart failure, drug overdose, and central nervous system pathology. Fluid engorges the vascular system and exudes into the air spaces, where it mixes with air to form a foamy, bloody fluid (see Figure 10.7 for a microscopic view).

NECK ORGANS: EPIGLOTTIS, VOCAL CORDS, TRACHEA, THYROID, CARTILAGE, STRAP MUSCLES, HYOID BONE

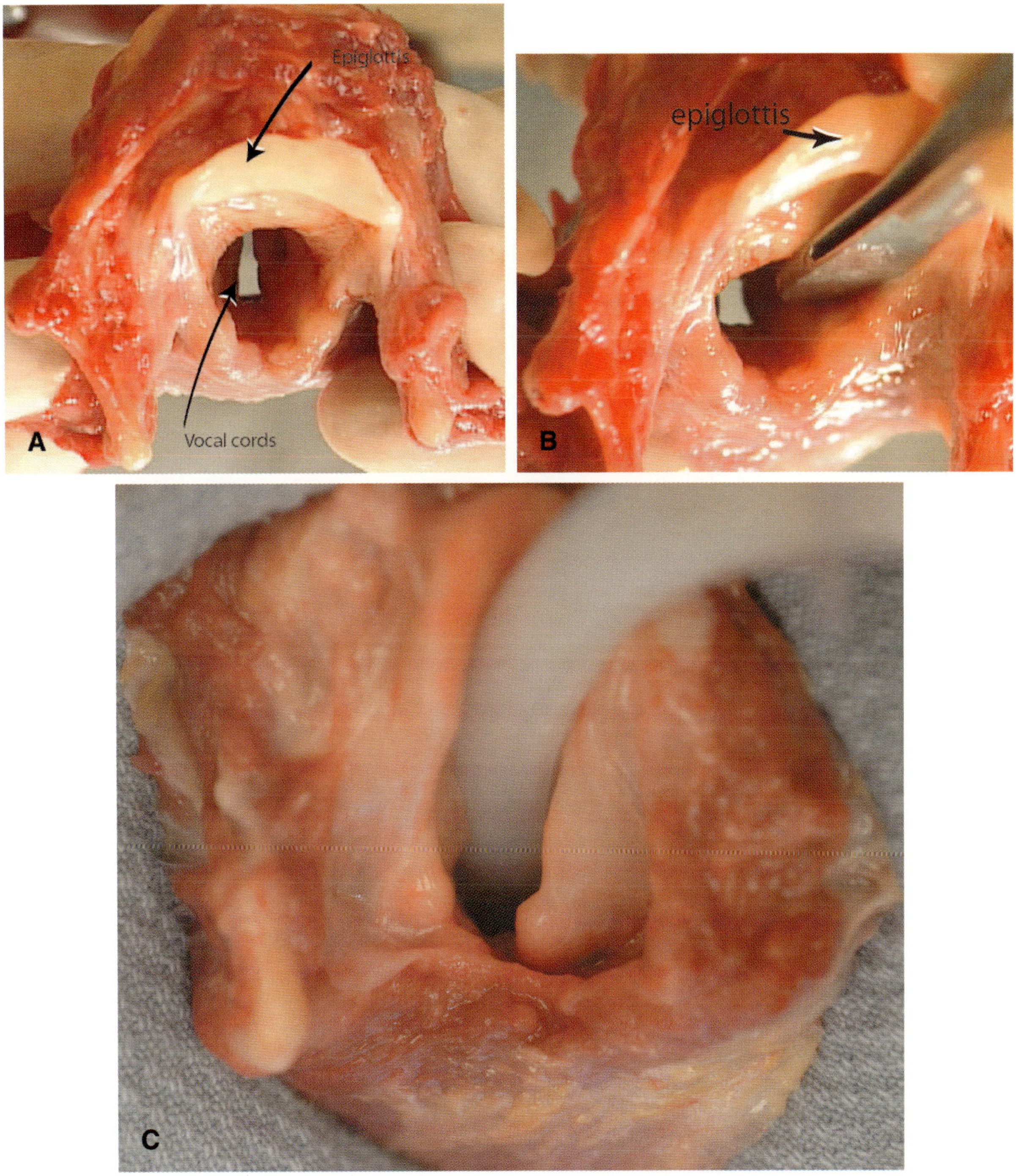

FIGURE 8.44 The epiglottis and vocal cords as seen during intubation. **(A)** Note the triangular opening in the middle of the pictures. The vocal cords border this opening. **(B)** The forceps trace the path where the endotracheal tube is placed during intubation. The epiglottis is pushed slightly upward out of the way as the device is inserted between the vocal cords. **(C)** The figure shows the relationship of the trachea and the endotracheal tube.

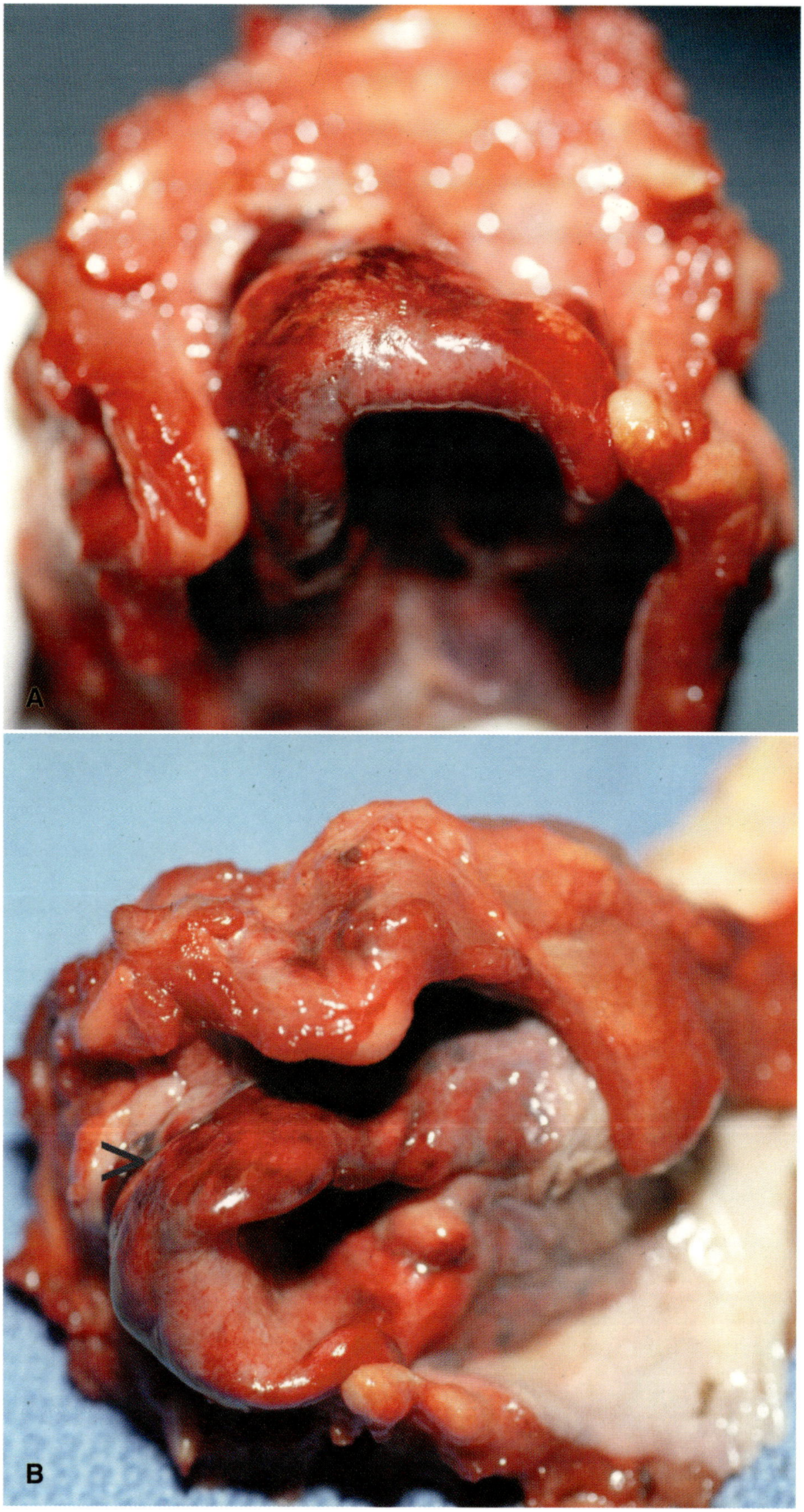

FIGURE 8.45 (A), (B) Epiglottitis. Edema and swelling of the epiglottis can cause occlusion of the airway and death. The rounded, meaty-red, swollen epiglottis shown here was the result of group B *Streptococcus* infection. The victim had trouble breathing and died suddenly after having a severe sore throat for several days.

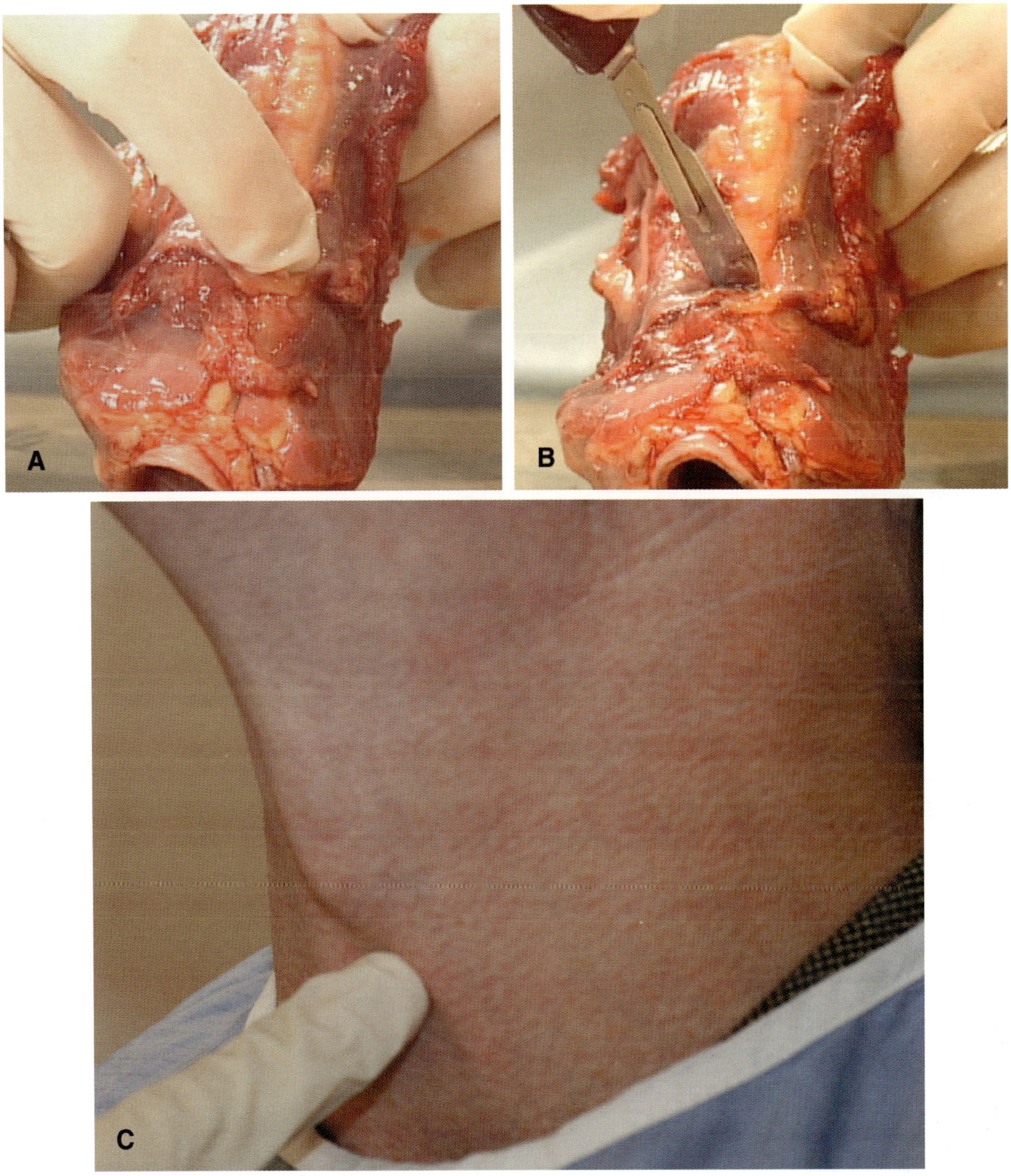

FIGURE 8.46 (A), (B) Cricothyroid membrane. (C) Cricothyroidotomy. To perform a cricothyroidotomy, the cricothyroid membrane, just below the thyroid cartilage, is palpated. One can feel this membrane as a break or cleft a little less than a finger's breadth below the "Adam's apple." Emergency cricothyroidotomies are done by physicians or trained emergency medical personnel when an airway cannot be established, such as with severe, traumatic facial injuries.

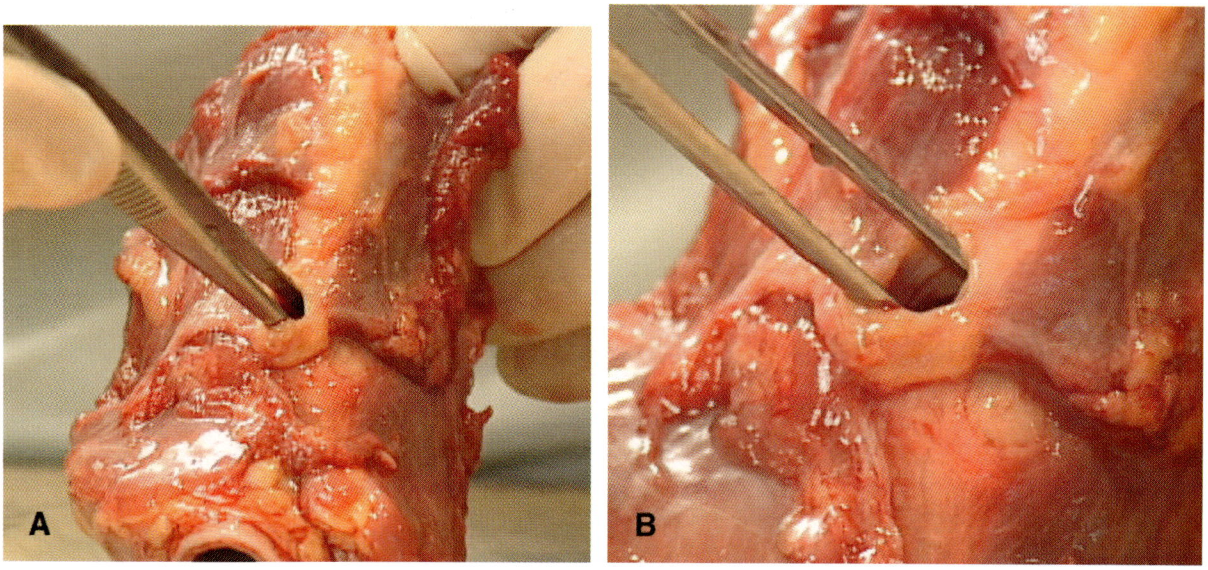

FIGURE 8.47 (A), (B) Opening the cricothyroidotomy. The opening is made and then must be kept open for ventilation of the patient.

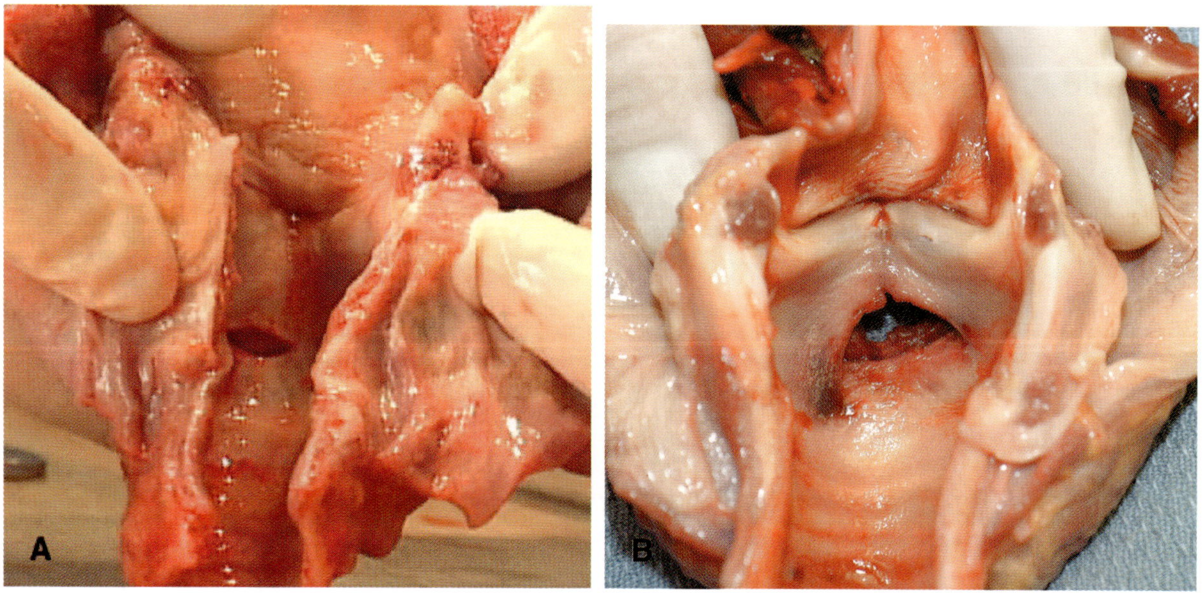

FIGURE 8.48 (A) Internal cricothyroidotomy site. The site of the cricothyroidotomy is seen well below the vocal cords. **(B) Proper cricothyroidotomy.** The figure shows an actual cricothyroidotomy properly performed in the field. The cut is below the vocal cords.

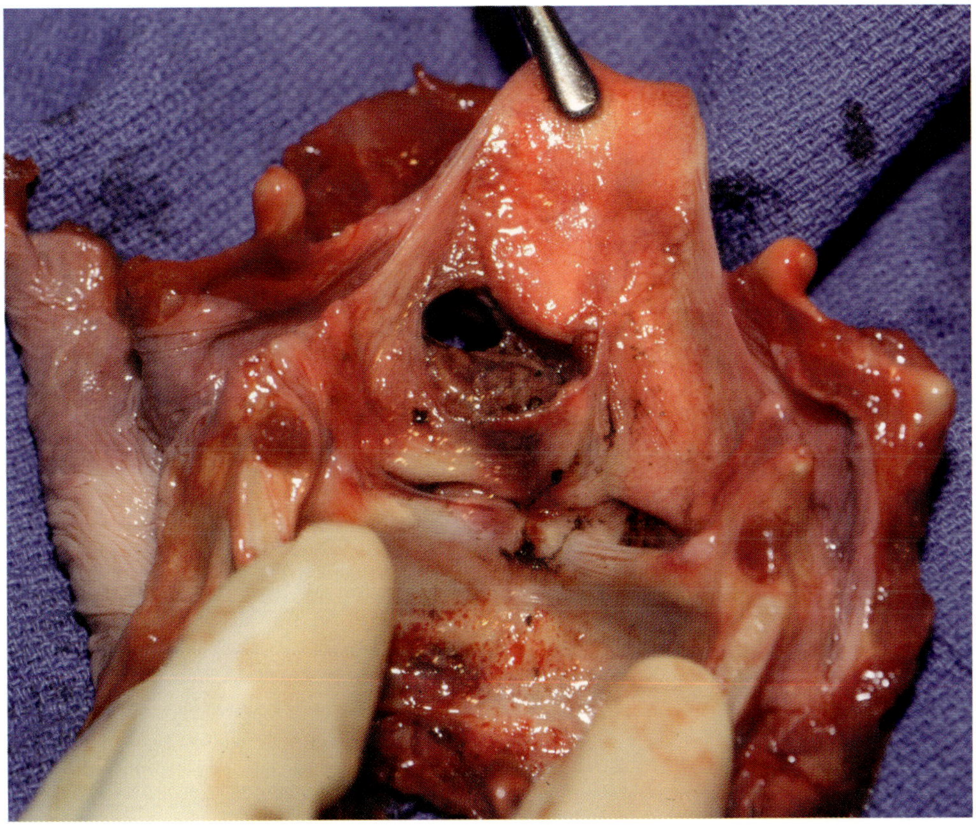

FIGURE 8.49 Improper cricothyroidotomy. This attempted cricothyroidotomy, performed in the field, was placed above the vocal cord, erroneously. Vocal cord damage might have resulted if the patient had survived.

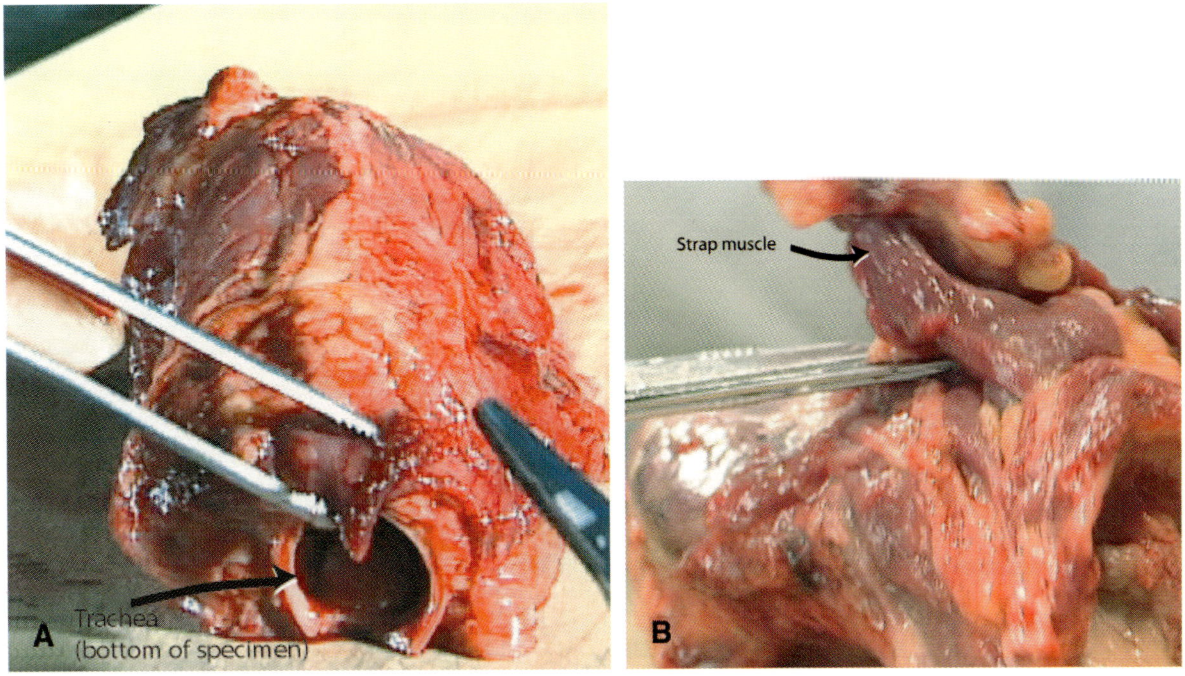

FIGURE 8.50 (A), (B) Strap muscle dissection. The strap muscles are in the anterior midline of the removed neck organs and are dissected away. During dissection, the pathologist is looking for hemorrhage.

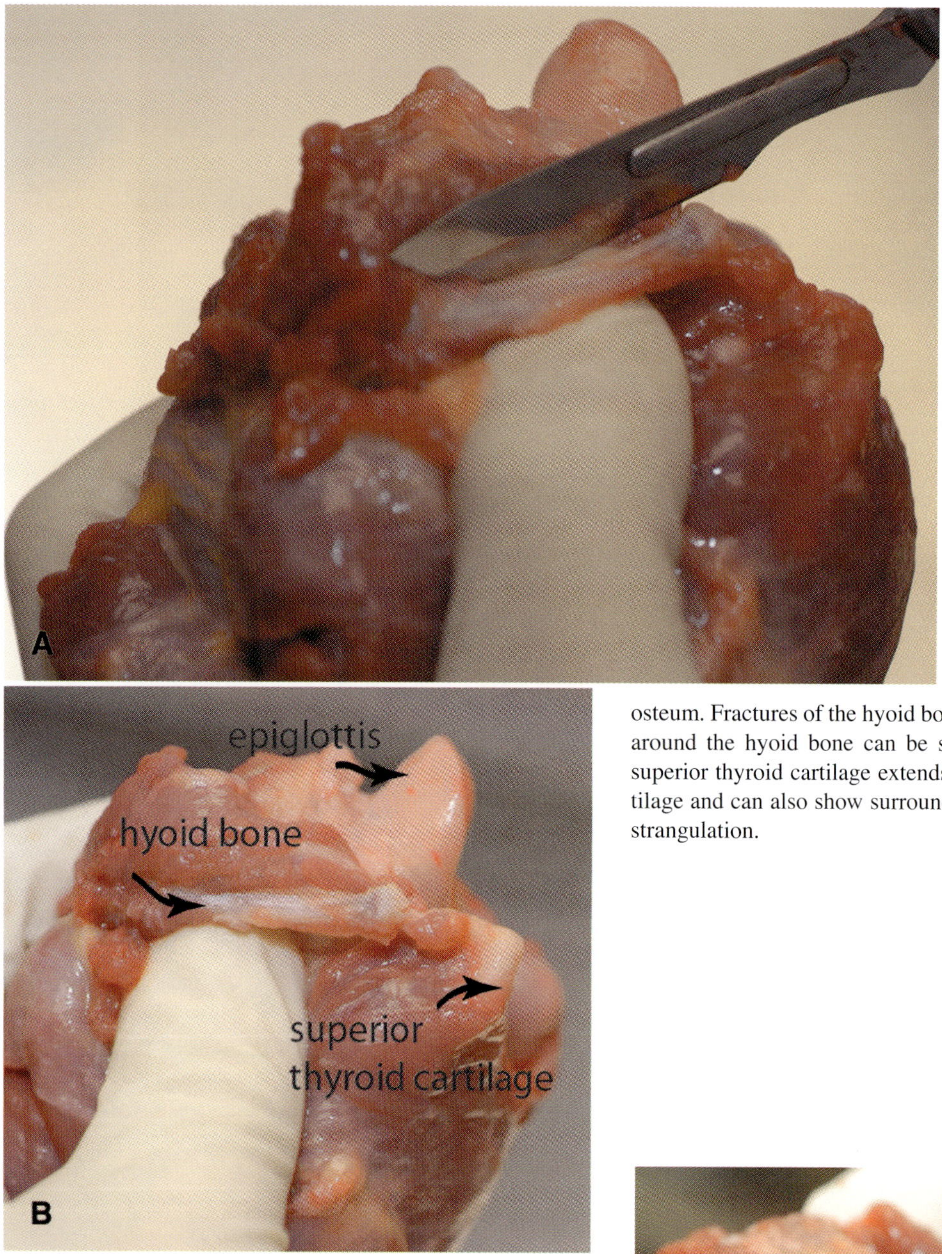

FIGURE 8.51 Examination of the hyoid bone for injury. **(A)** The hyoid bone is "cut down on," exposing the periosteum. Fractures of the hyoid bone or hemorrhage of soft tissue around the hyoid bone can be seen in strangulation. **(B)** The superior thyroid cartilage extends upward from the thyroid cartilage and can also show surrounding hemorrhage or fracture in strangulation.

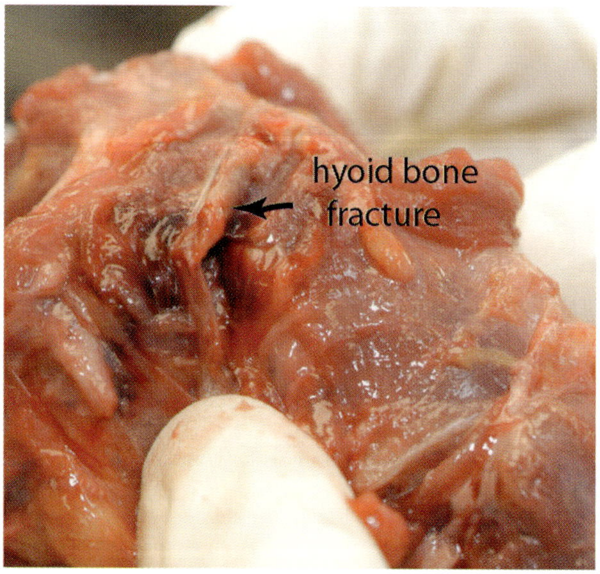

FIGURE 8.52 Hyoid bone fracture in strangulation. The hyoid bone is fractured, and hemorrhage surrounds this fracture.

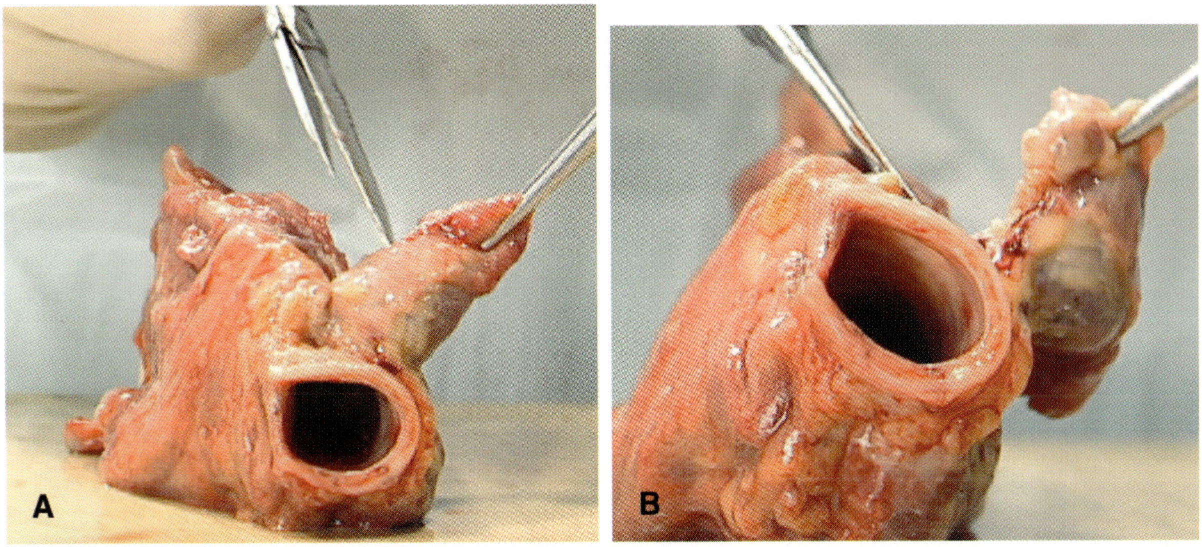

FIGURE 8.53 **(A), (B) Dissecting away the thyroid.** The thyroid gland is dissected away from the neck to look for hemorrhage or tumors.

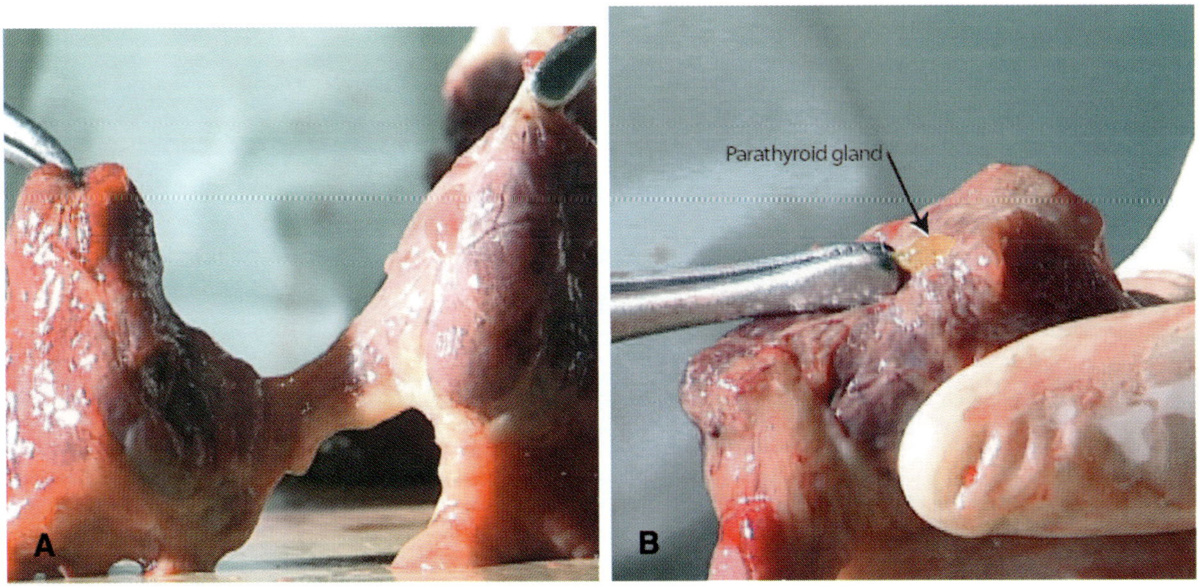

FIGURE 8.54 **Examination of the thyroid and parathyroid glands.** **(A)** The thyroid is held up to reveal two lobes and the connecting isthmus. **(B)** The small, round, yellow parathyroid gland can be seen just to the right of the forceps tip. The parathyroid gland mainly controls calcium levels in the body through a hormone called calcitonin.

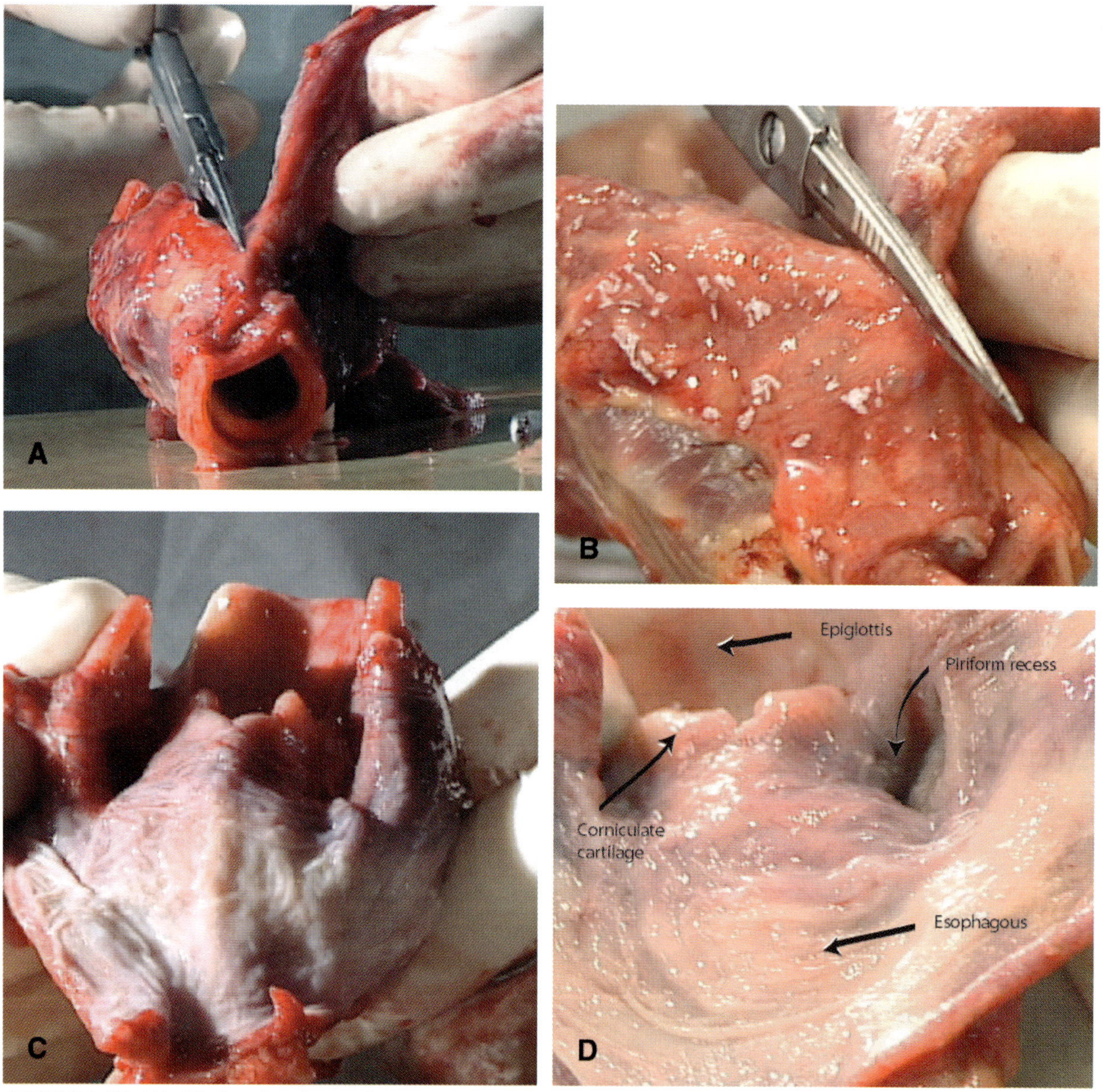

FIGURE 8.55 (A)–(D) Opening the esophagus. The neck specimen is turned around and the proximal portion of the esophagus is opened to reveal the smooth, white-pink mucosa. Foreign bodies can lodge at the origin of the esophagus and close off the trachea, resulting in asphyxia.

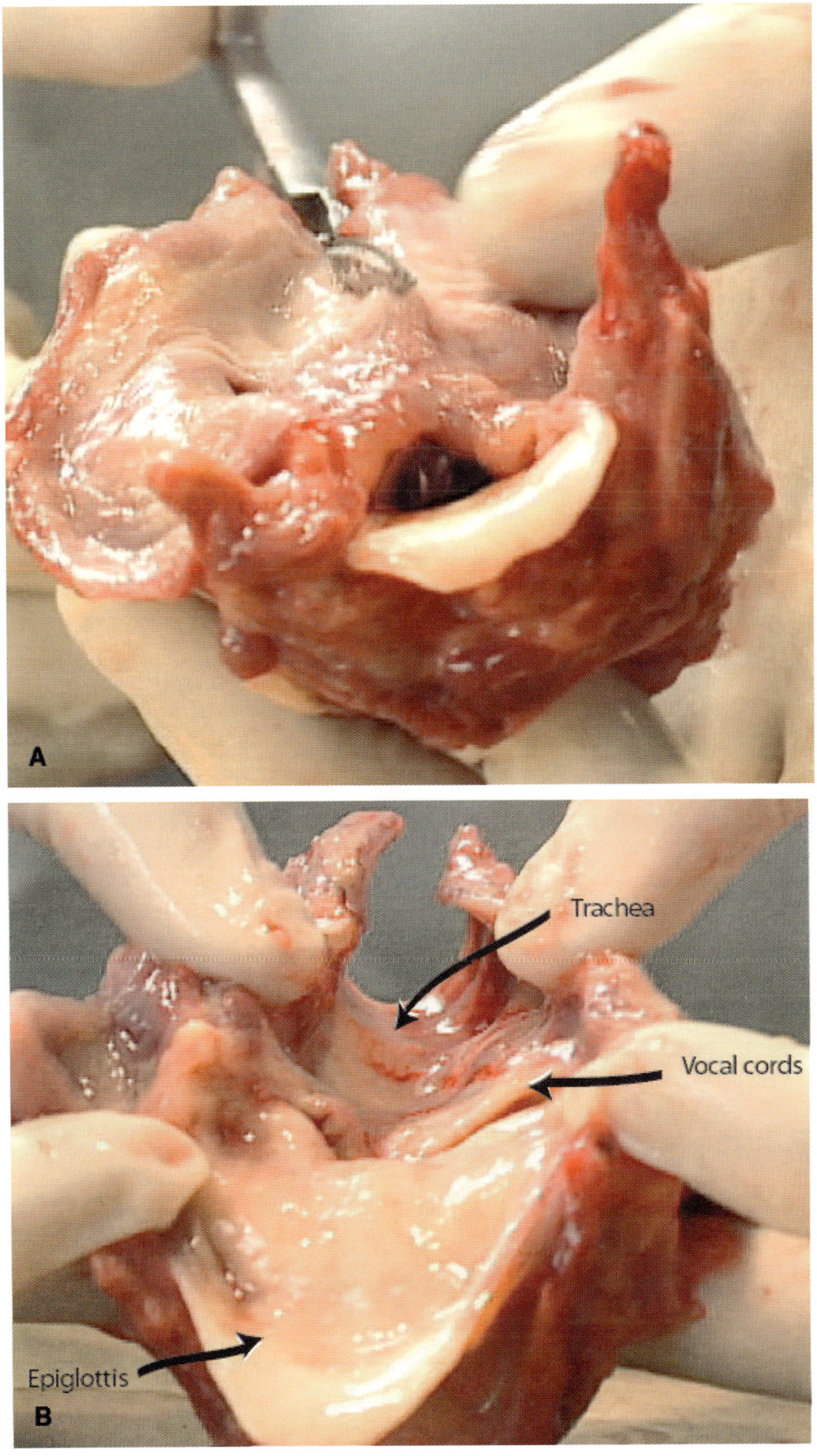

FIGURE 8.56 Opening the trachea. **(A)** The trachea is opened from the posterior aspect (back), where the anterior-lateral cartilaginous rings give way to soft tissue. **(B)** The trachea is opened to examine the vocal cords and mucosa.

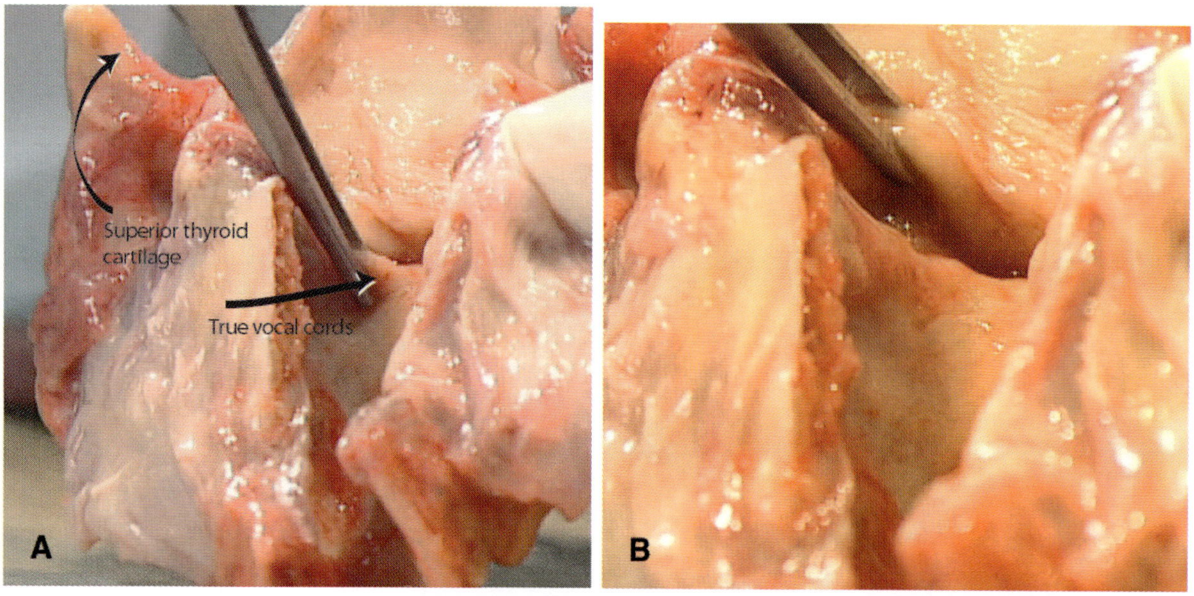

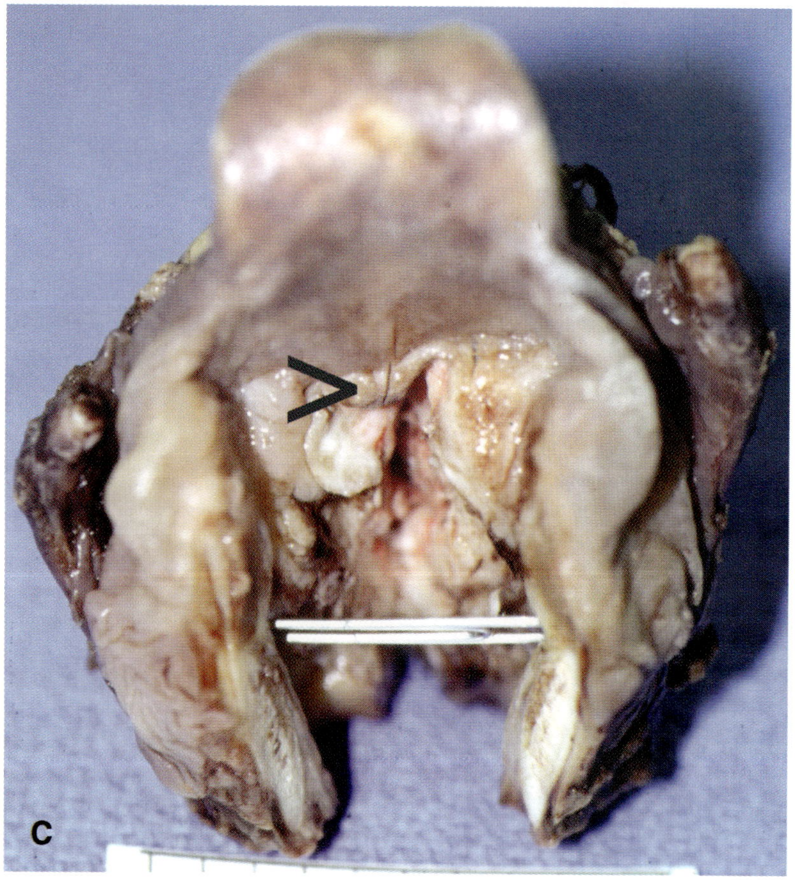

FIGURE 8.57 (A), (B) **True and false vocal cords.** The forceps are holding the true vocal cords, which are just below the false vocal cords, held by the forceps in the second figure. **(C) Squamous cell carcinoma.** The vocal cords are sites for squamous cell carcinoma (see arrow), especially in smokers, and polyps in those who abuse their voices.

LIVER

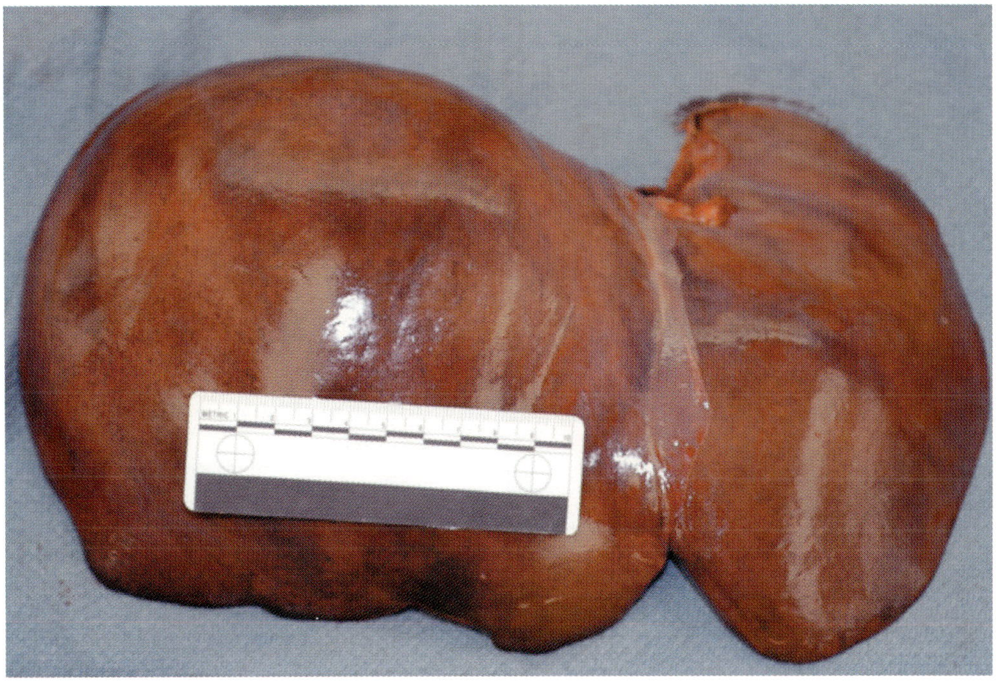

FIGURE 8.58 Normal liver. The liver is much larger than most autopsy neophytes realize. The liver depicted is about 25 cm (over 10 in.) wide. The average liver weighs about 1930 g (4.25 lb) in a 77-kg (170-lb) man. The liver performs many functions and is essential for life. Important functions of the liver include production of bile, production of blood coagulation proteins, breakdown of drugs and toxins, filtration of blood, and metabolism of fat proteins and carbohydrates.

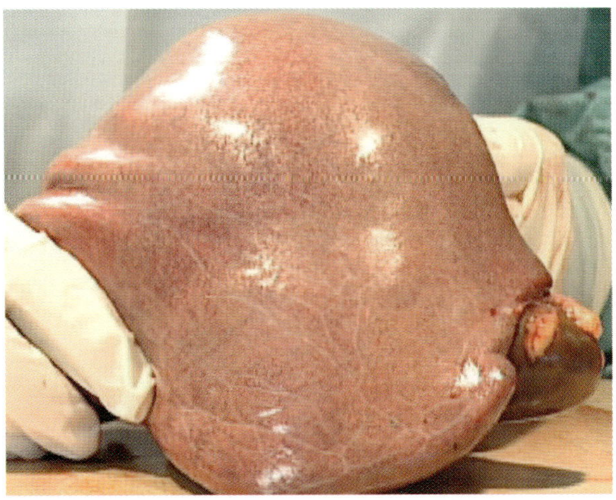

FIGURE 8.59 Examination of the liver capsule. The capsule of the liver is examined. The liver is dome-shaped, owing to its position in the body just under the right diaphragm. This liver shows chronic passive congestion (see Figure 8.63).

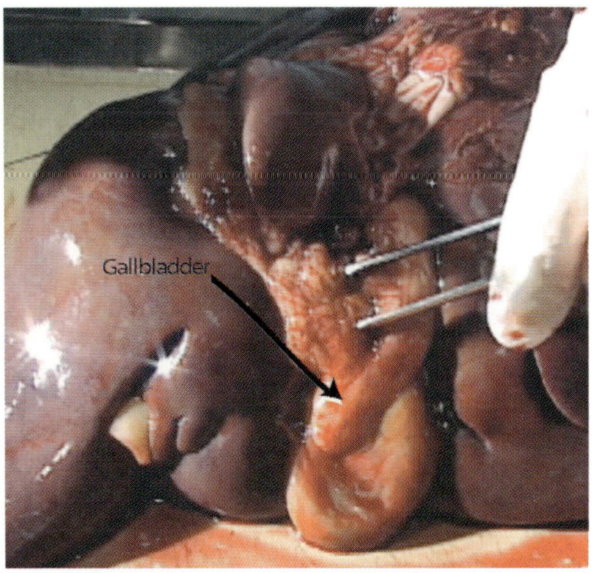

FIGURE 8.60 Porta hepatis examination. The liver is turned over to reveal the posterior–inferior side. The gallbladder can be seen below the forceps. The forceps is in the region of the porta hepatis, an area containing lymph nodes.

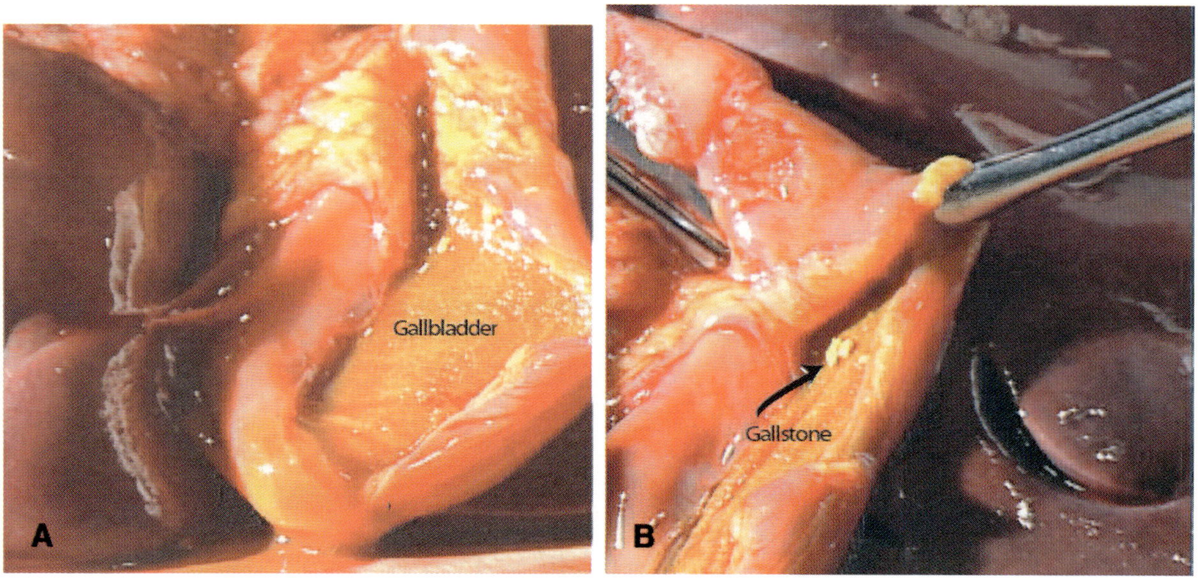

FIGURE 8.61 (A) Gallbladder. The gallbladder contains bile. **(B) Gallstones.** A closer examination of the opened gallbladder reveals greenish-yellow gallstones.

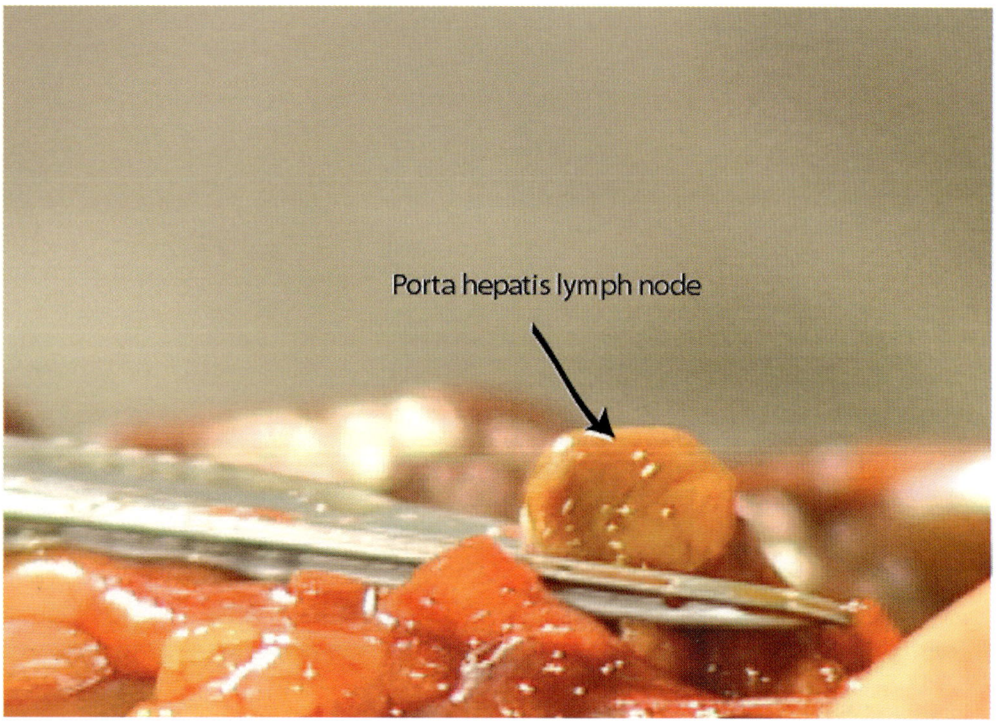

FIGURE 8.62 Porta hepatis lymph node. Examination of the porta hepatis reveals a large lymph node. These lymph nodes can contain metastatic cancers or granulomas, chronic reactive inflammations in drug addicts who inject drugs into their lower extremities.

FIGURE 8.63 **Sectioning the liver.** **(A)** The liver is serially sectioned, continuously inspected, and felt for tumors and other abnormalities. **(B)** A cut section shows a normal liver, which is a brown color. The large cavernous veins seen in the right lower part of the image are characteristic of the normal liver.

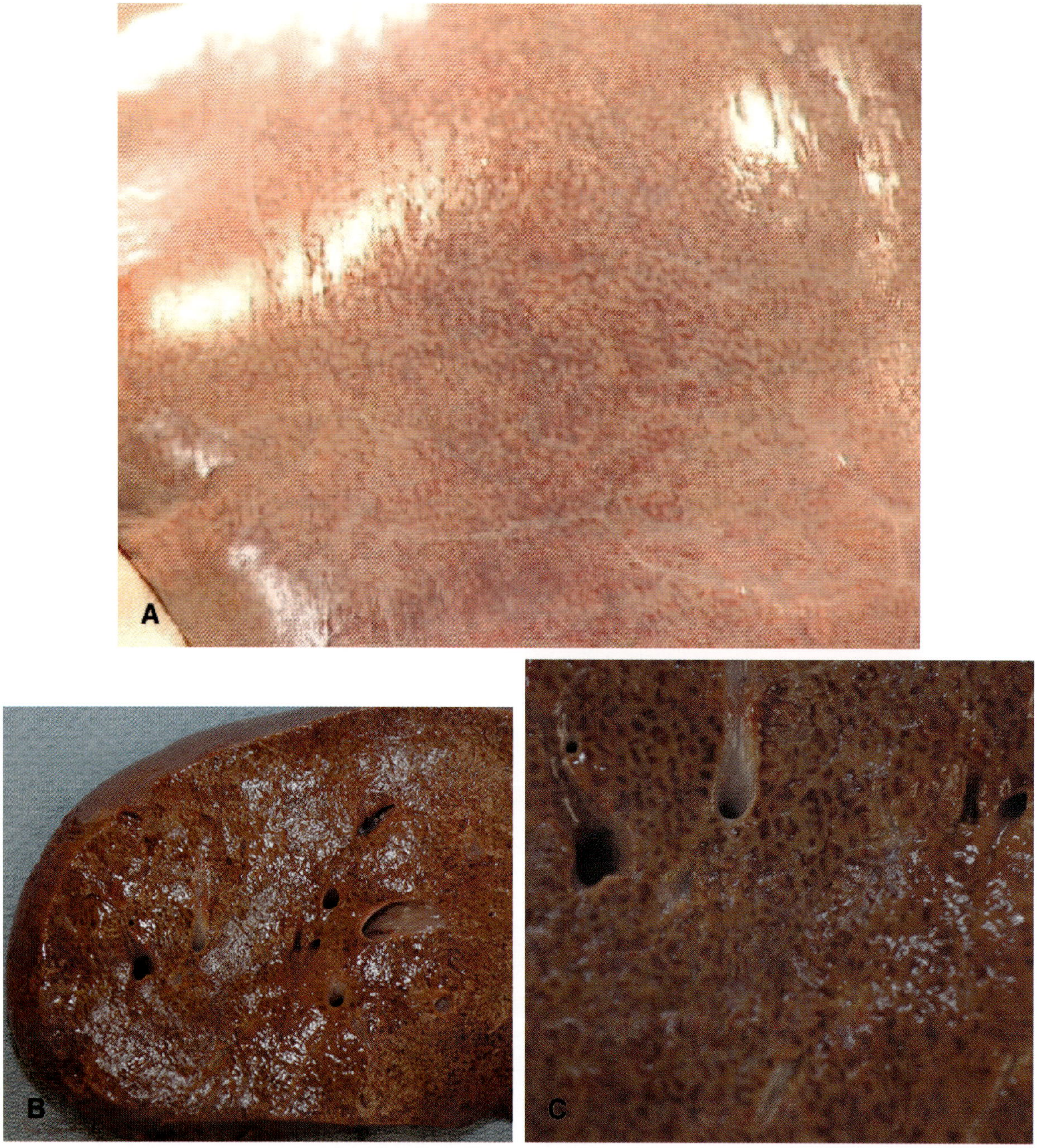

FIGURE 8.64 (A)–(C) Chronic passive congestion of the liver. A close-up of the liver shows chronic passive congestion of the liver, characterized by alternating light and dark contrasted areas. This appearance has been called "nutmeg liver," since the cut liver resembles a cut nutmeg. Gross descriptions in pathology occasionally reference food, drinks, and other common objects. The aim of gross descriptions is to communicate observations plainly. The gross appearance reflects the microscopic appearance. The dark areas are largely blood that has pooled around the central vein, or "draining area" of blood through the liver.

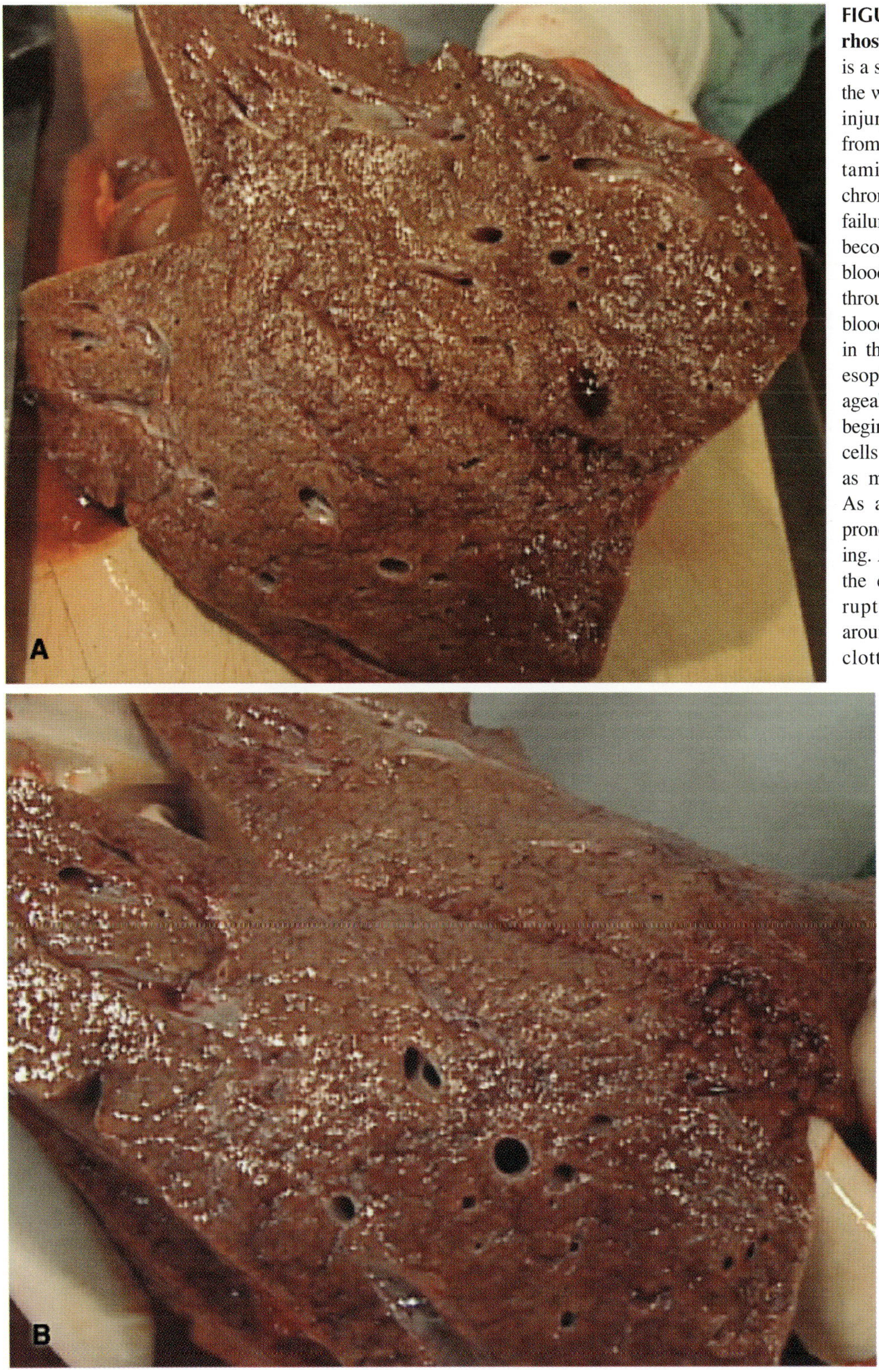

FIGURE 8.65 (A), (B) Cirrhosis of the liver. Cirrhosis is a scarring of the liver. It is the way the liver reacts to an injury. The injury can be from alcohol abuse, an acetaminophen overdose, or chronic ischemia due to heart failure. In cirrhosis, the liver becomes very hard so that blood cannot flow normally through it. This causes the blood to back up elsewhere in the body, such as in the esophagus (causing esophageal varices). Also, the liver begins to fail due to a lack of cells to perform work, such as making clotting factors. As a result, the patient is prone to spontaneous bleeding. A common problem for the cirrhotic patient is the rupture of dilated veins around the esophagus, and clotting is less likely to occur due to liver cell loss. When advanced, this condition is irreversible and very commonly fatal.

SPLEEN

FIGURE 8.66 Spleen capsule examination. The spleen is the largest collection of lymph tissue in the body. In addition to recycling aged red blood cells, the spleen helps the body fight some infections, like the encapsulated bacterium *Streptococcus pneumoniae*. The spleen is examined on the outer surface for lacerations or tumors. The capsule of the spleen is very thin and easily torn with trauma. Because a major function of the adult spleen is to recycle red blood cells, the spleen is vascular. Laceration of the spleen can cause extensive internal hemorrhage.

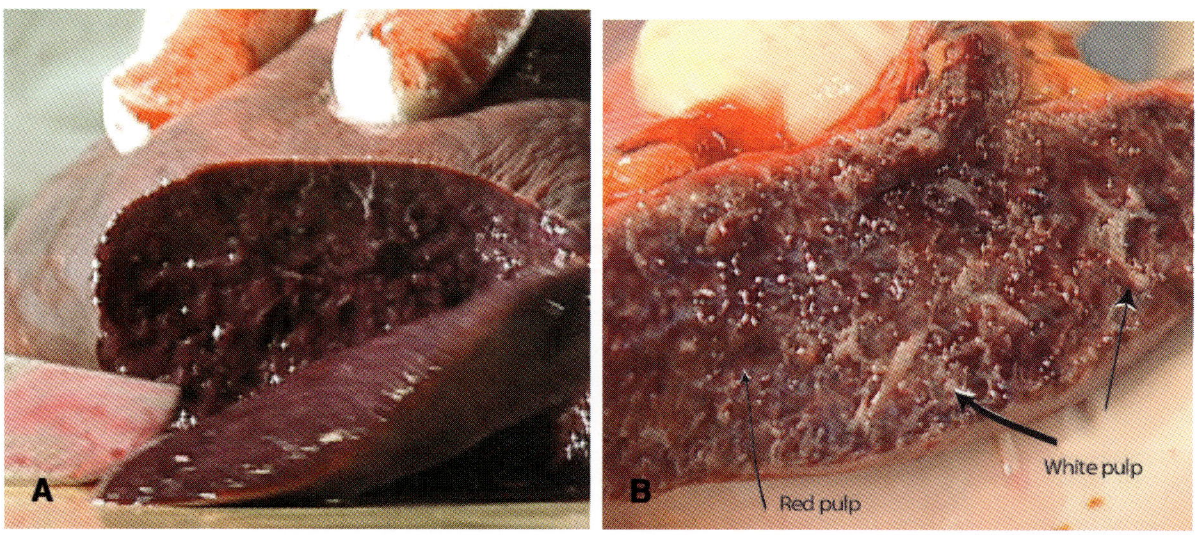

FIGURE 8.67 (A), (B) Spleen sectioning. On sectioning the spleen, one can see the aptly-named red pulp. The white dots are the white pulp. Red cells pool in the sinusoids of the red pulp. The capsule of the spleen is very thin, making it susceptible to rupture easily with trauma.

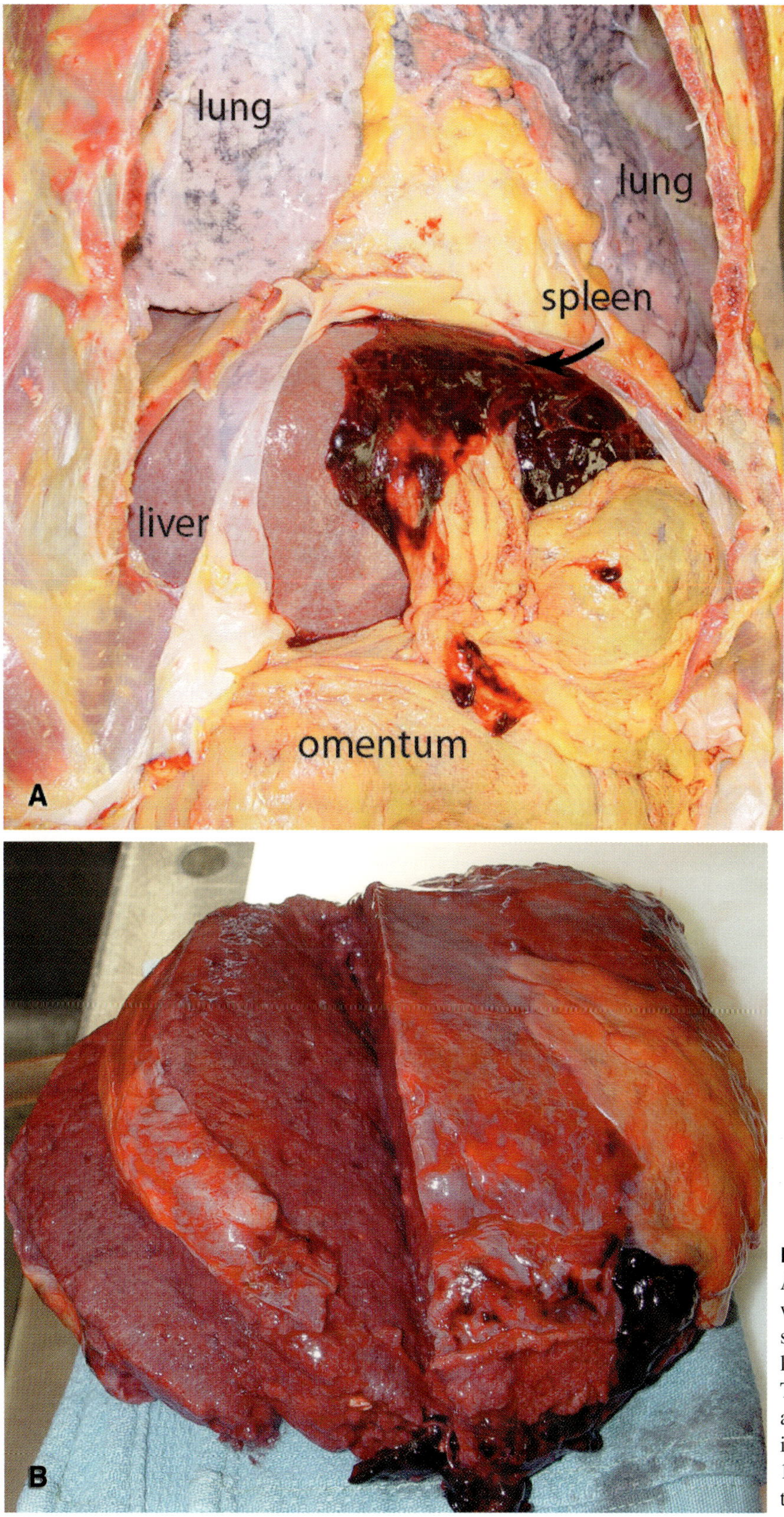

FIGURE 8.68 Ruptured spleen. (A) A hematoma can be seen in this patient who fell down the steps at home. The source of the hemorrhage is seen in the left upper quadrant of the abdomen. The spleen has a lacerated capsule with an attached hematoma. **(B)** The spleen is enlarged (over 600 g; normal is about 120 g), making it more susceptible to traumatic or even spontaneous rupture.

URINARY TRACT: KIDNEYS, BLADDER, URETER, PROSTATE

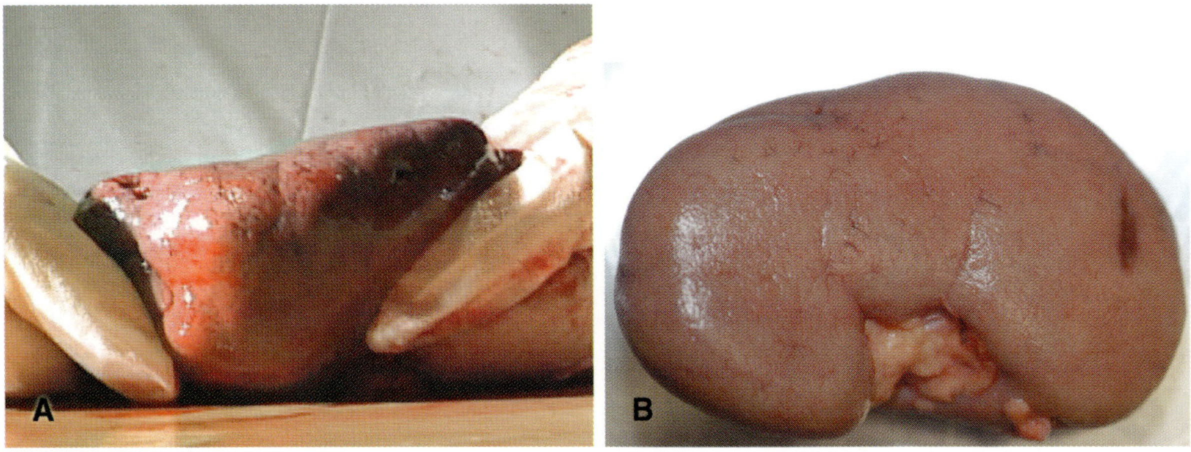

FIGURE 8.69 Left and right kidneys. **(A)** The pathologist is holding a normal left kidney, which has a delta or triangular shape. This shape is thought to result from the spleen molding the superior pole of the kidney. **(B)** The normal right kidney is bean-shaped and should have a smooth outer covering, or cortex. The main functions of the kidneys are to help regulate blood pH and blood pressure, filter blood, and remove excess salts, water, and products of protein metabolism. The waste product of these processes is, of course, urine.

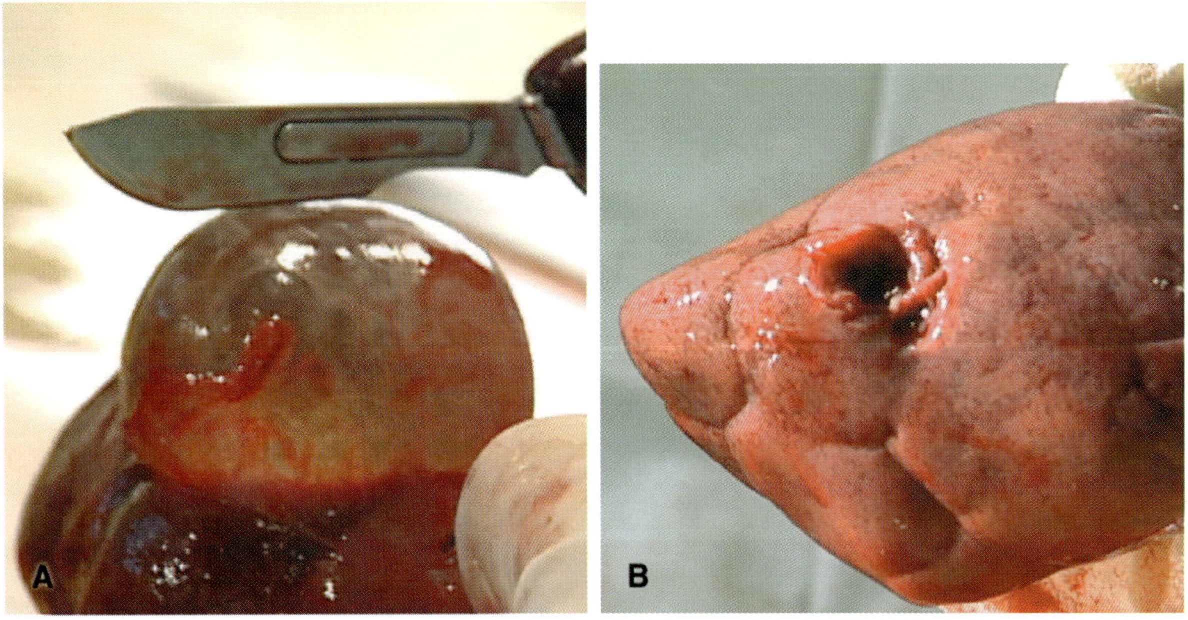

FIGURE 8.70 Cortical cyst of the kidney. **(A)** The cortex of this kidney has a large fluid-filled cyst. **(B)** This crater represents a cyst that burst open upon removal.

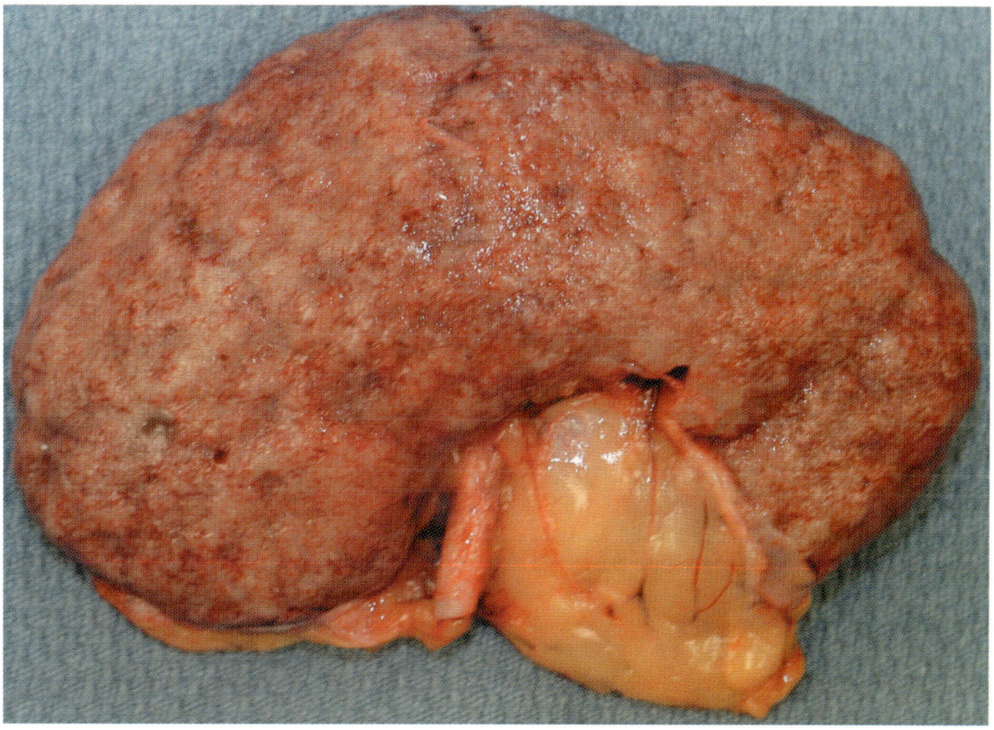

FIGURE 8.71 Renal arteriolosclerosis. This kidney has a pitted, granular surface. This condition is called arteriolosclerosis; it is a result of hypertension, which causes local ischemic changes in the small vessels near the outer surface, or cortex. Part of the outside of the kidney scars, while adjacent tissue survives, causing pitting of the surface (see Figure 10.19).

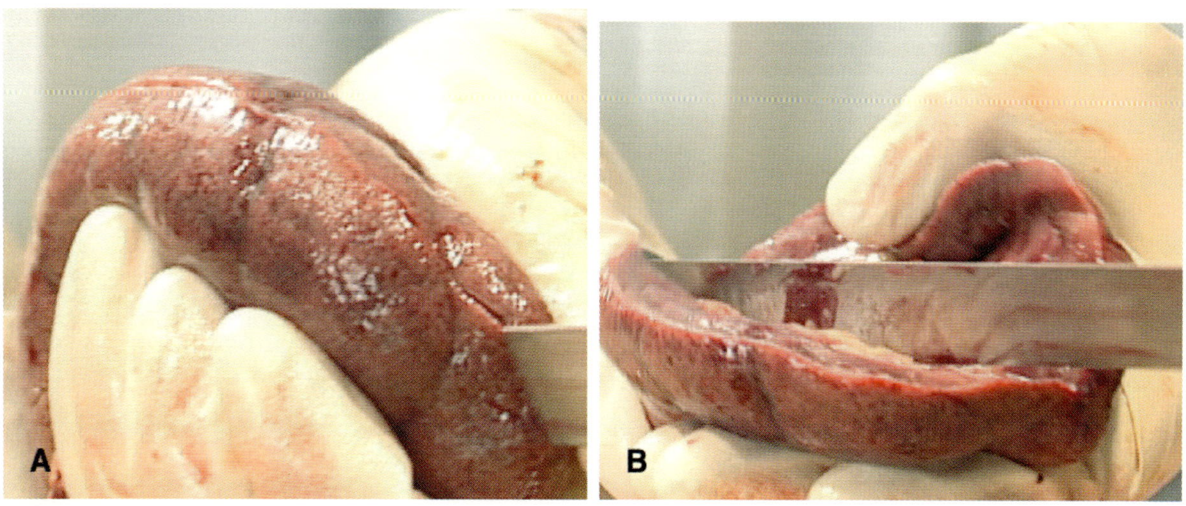

FIGURE 8.72 Dissection of the kidney. **(A)** The kidney is cut along the long axis, or "bivalved." **(B)** This type of cut allows a central view of the cortex (blood-filtering glomeruli), medulla (tubules), and calyces (urine-draining portions) of the kidney.

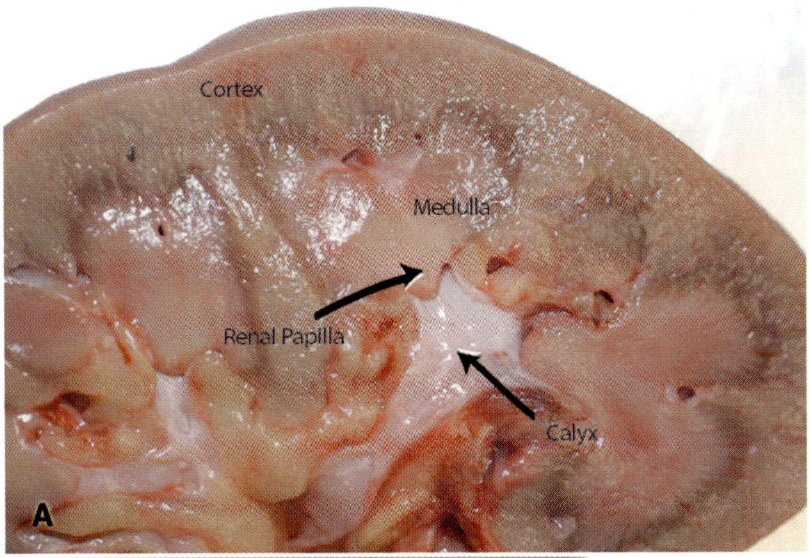

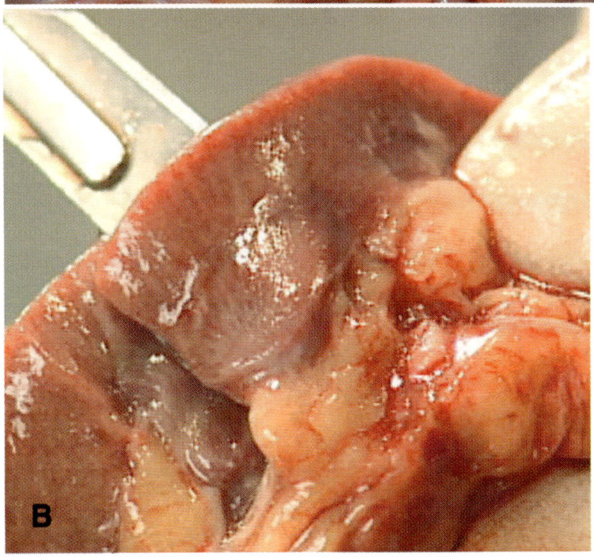

FIGURE 8.73 Cross section of the kidney. **(A)** The blood is filtered through the glomeruli, largely present in the cortex. In conditions such as diabetes and hypertension, these glomeruli can become sclerosed (scarred), and if significant numbers of glomeruli are sclerosed, renal failure can result. The medulla and papillary tip largely contain tubules, which drain the urine. Inflammation of this area is called pyelonephritis. **(B)** A section is taken of the outer cortex, medulla, and papillary tip for microscopic review.

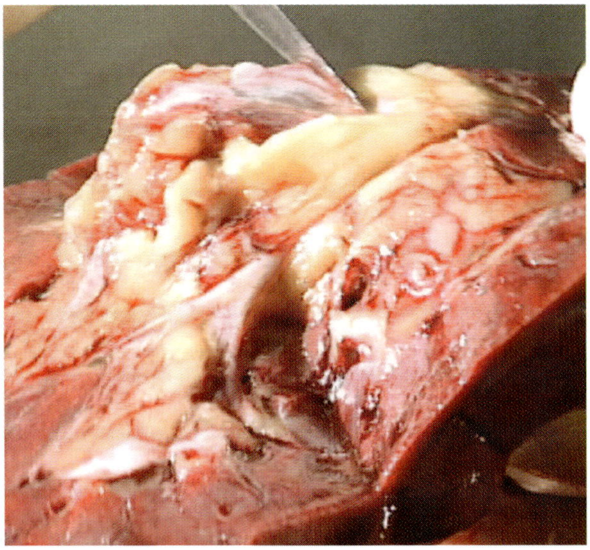

FIGURE 8.74 Opening the calyces. The papillary tips drain into a calyx, which, in turn, drains into the renal pelvis and then the ureter. The renal pelvis and calyces are opened. Tumors or stones can be found there.

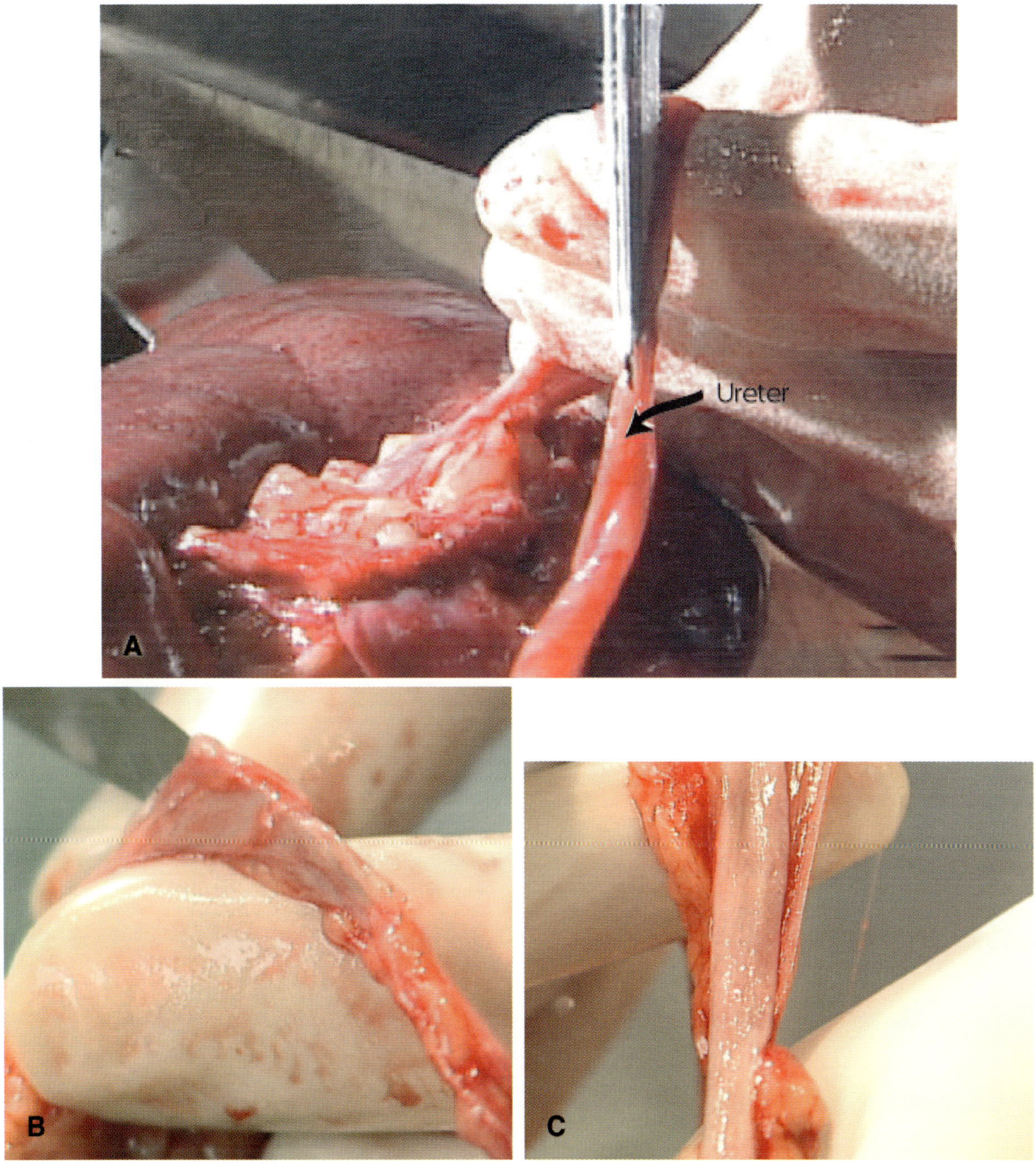

FIGURE 8.75 (A)–(C) Opening the ureter. The ureter is opened to look for stones, tumors, or inflammation.

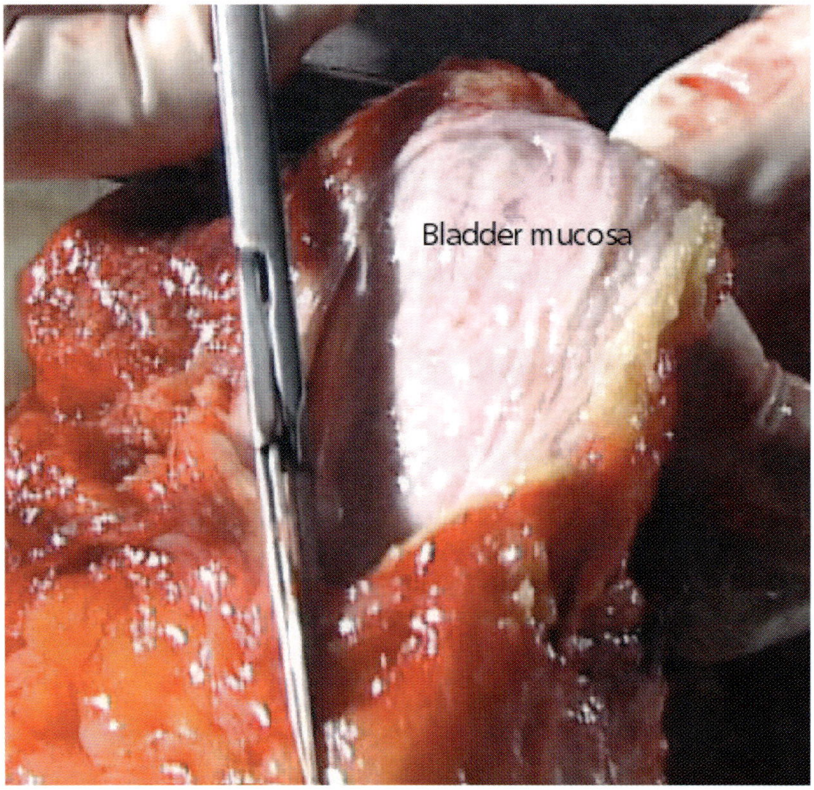

FIGURE 8.76 Opening the bladder. The dome of the bladder is opened, exposing the pink mucosa below. The urine has been removed.

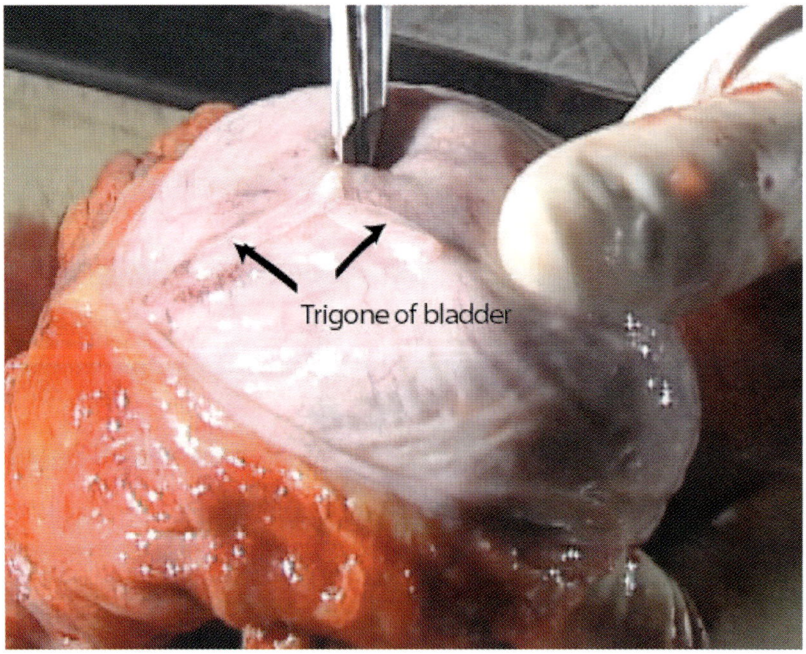

FIGURE 8.77 Bladder trigone. The scissors are in the urethra of the bladder. Note the triangular area, the trigone, just in front of the urethra (see arrows). The ureters empty into the bladder at the ends of the trigone.

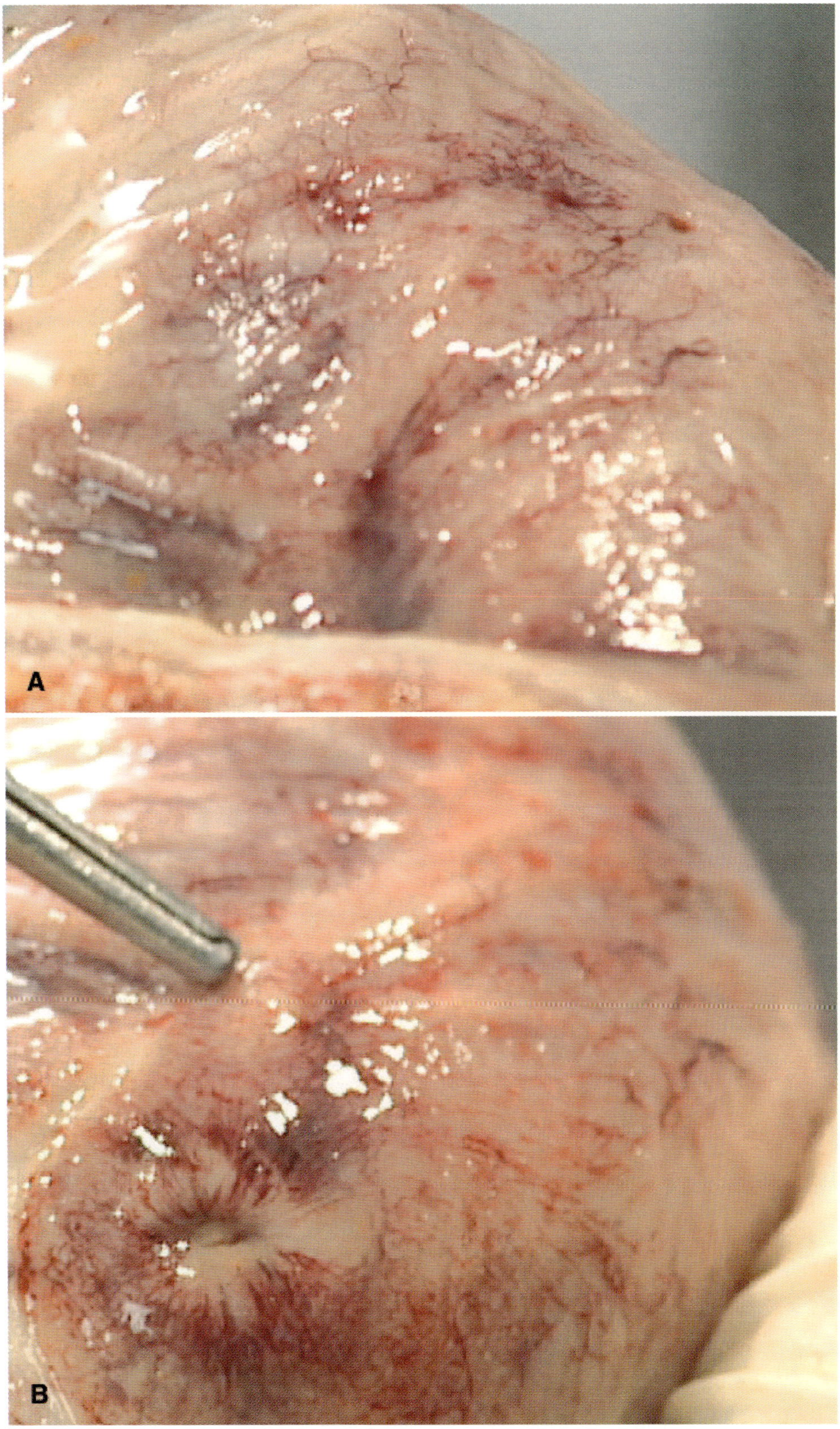

FIGURE 8.78 Bladder erythema and urethral opening. **(A)** This close-up of the bladder shows reddened mucosa, and multiple small blood vessels are prominent. This erythema can indicate inflammation. **(B)** The inflammation is particularly prominent near the urethral opening.

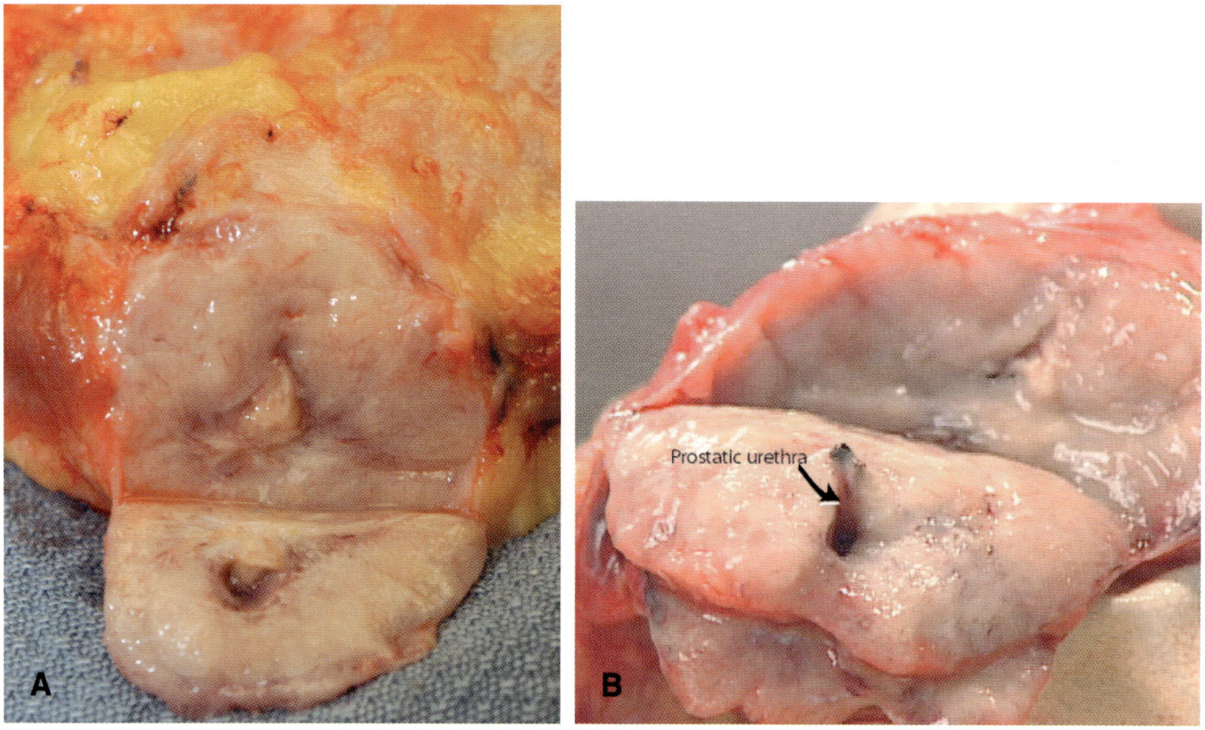

FIGURE 8.79 Prostate sectioning. **(A)** The base of the prostate is attached to the bladder. The prostate is serially sectioned. **(B)** The opening in the cut prostate is the portion of the urethra that courses through the prostate, or the prostatic urethra. The pathologist searches for carcinoma and inflammation.

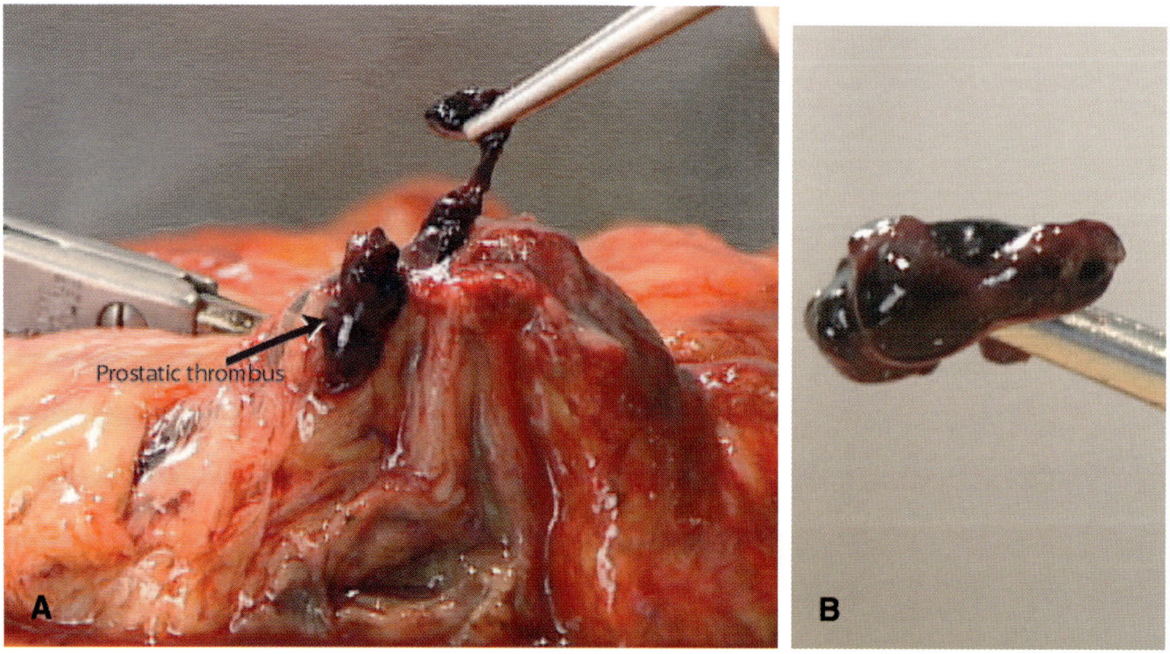

FIGURE 8.80 (A), (B) Prostatic thrombi. This prostate has a few thrombi which, when pulled out, retain their shapes. These are like premortem thrombi. This patient had lung cancer. Patients with many cancers are susceptible to thrombosis.

ESOPHAGUS AND STOMACH

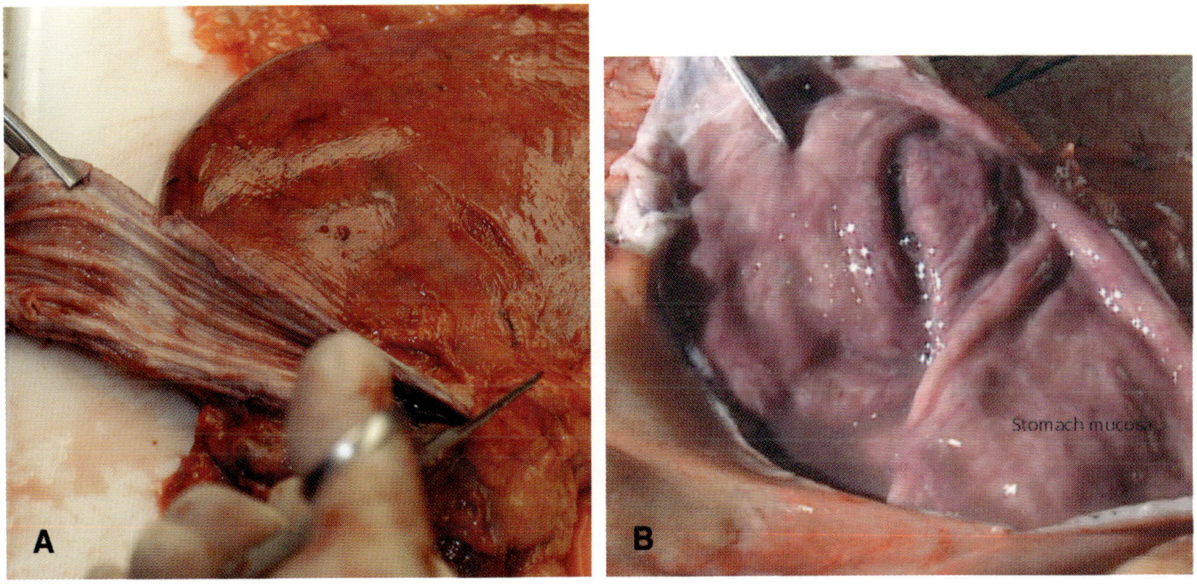

FIGURE 8.81 (A), (B) Opening of the esophagus and stomach. The esophagus is opened with the scissors to expose the stomach mucosa.

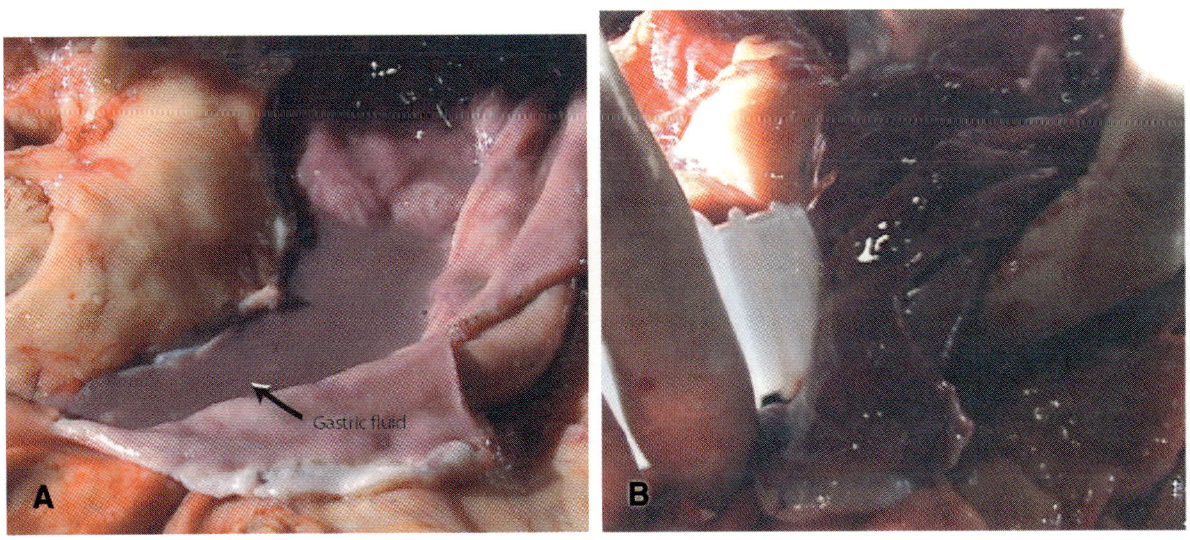

FIGURE 8.82 (A), (B) Obtaining gastric fluid. Gastric fluid is taken for analysis in a clean plastic container.

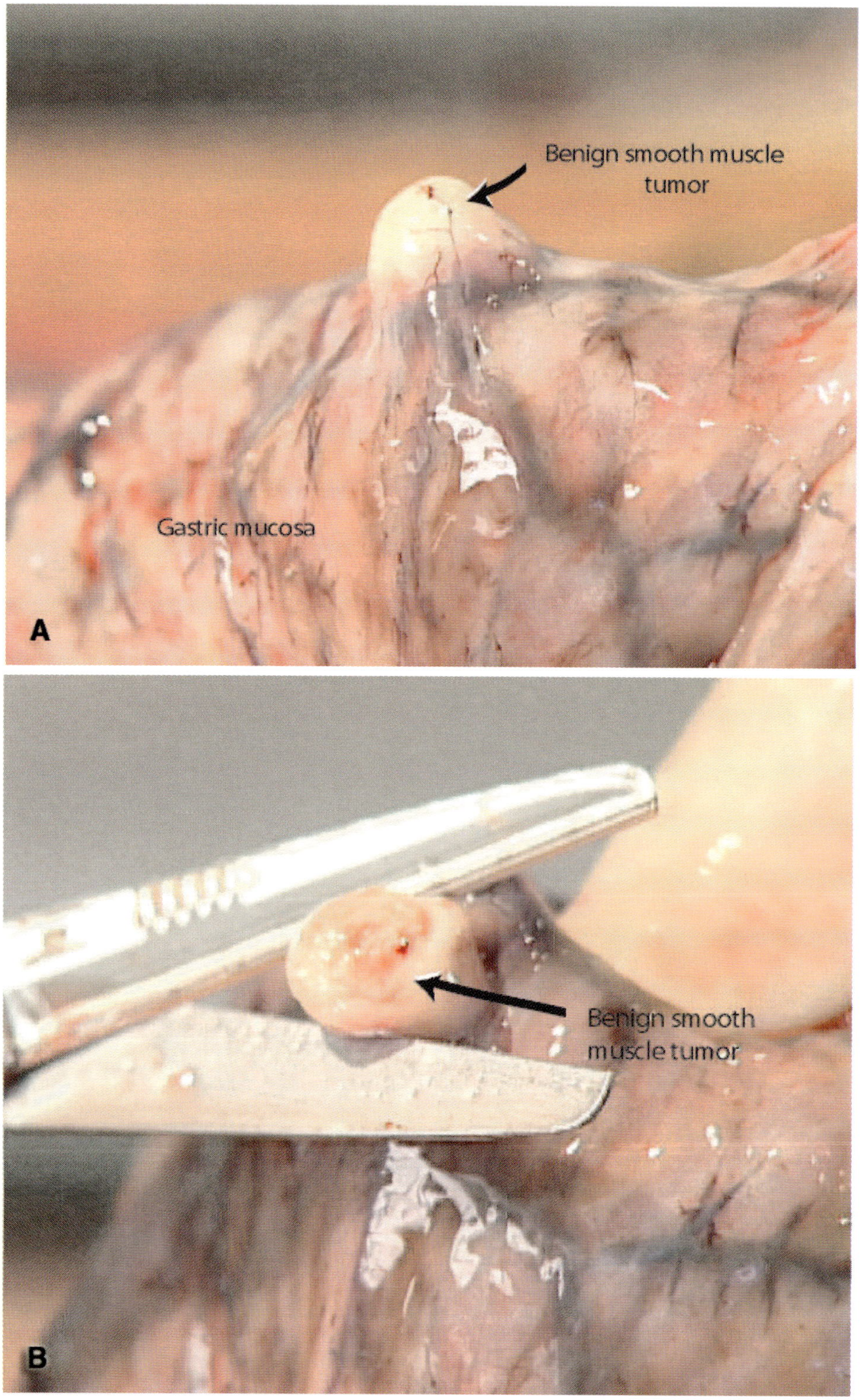

FIGURE 8.83 Benign stromal tumor of the stomach. **(A)** This nodule is seen in the mucosa. **(B)** Cutting the nodule shows that it is round and firm. This lesion is a benign gastrointestinal stromal tumor of smooth muscle origin.

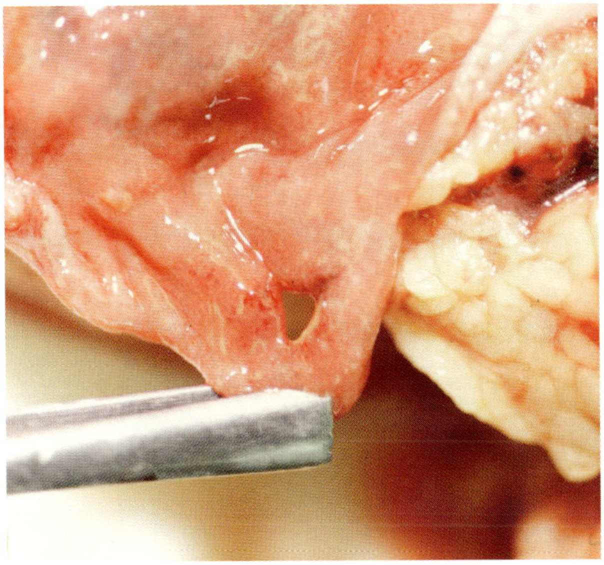

FIGURE 8.84 Perforated gastric ulcer. A gastric ulcer can be seen above the forceps. The ulcer has gone through the mucosa, muscular wall, and serosa (outer covering). The stomach contents then leaked into the peritoneal cavity, causing severe inflammation and infection (peritonitis). Prompt surgical repair of the stomach might have prevented the death.

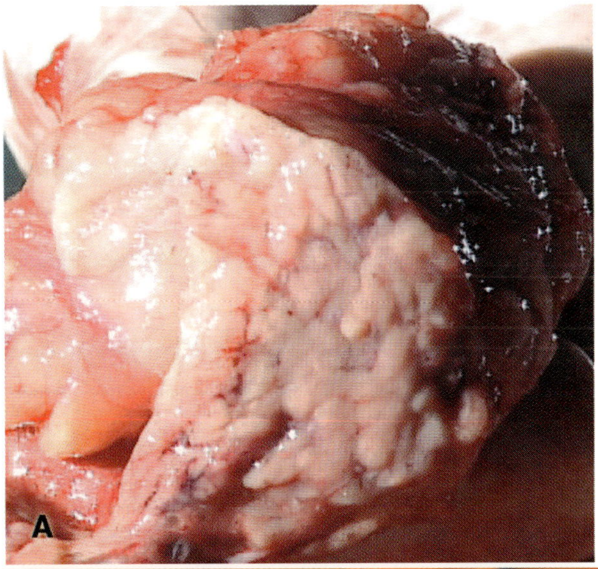

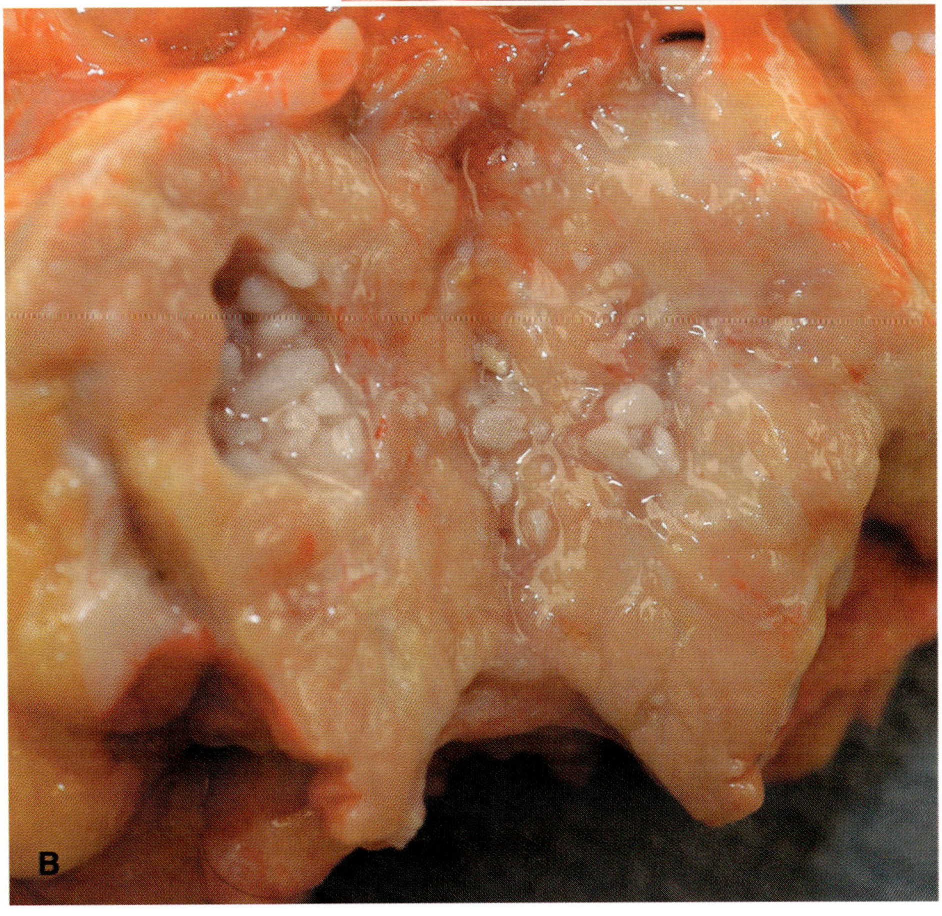

FIGURE 8.85 (A) Pancreas. The pancreas is sectioned to display the normal lobular appearance. The pancreas secretes enzymes used in digestion into the gastrointestinal tract and releases insulin, glucagon, and somatostatin into the blood. **(B) Chronic pancreatitis.** Pancreatitis is a condition commonly associated with alcohol abuse. In acute pancreatitis, the pancreas becomes inflamed and digestive enzymes can be released into the tissues, causing hemorrhage that sometimes results in shock or death. The figure depicts a hard, chronically inflamed pancreas with the formation of an inflammatory pseudocyst and calcification, as seen just left of center.

UTERUS AND OVARIES

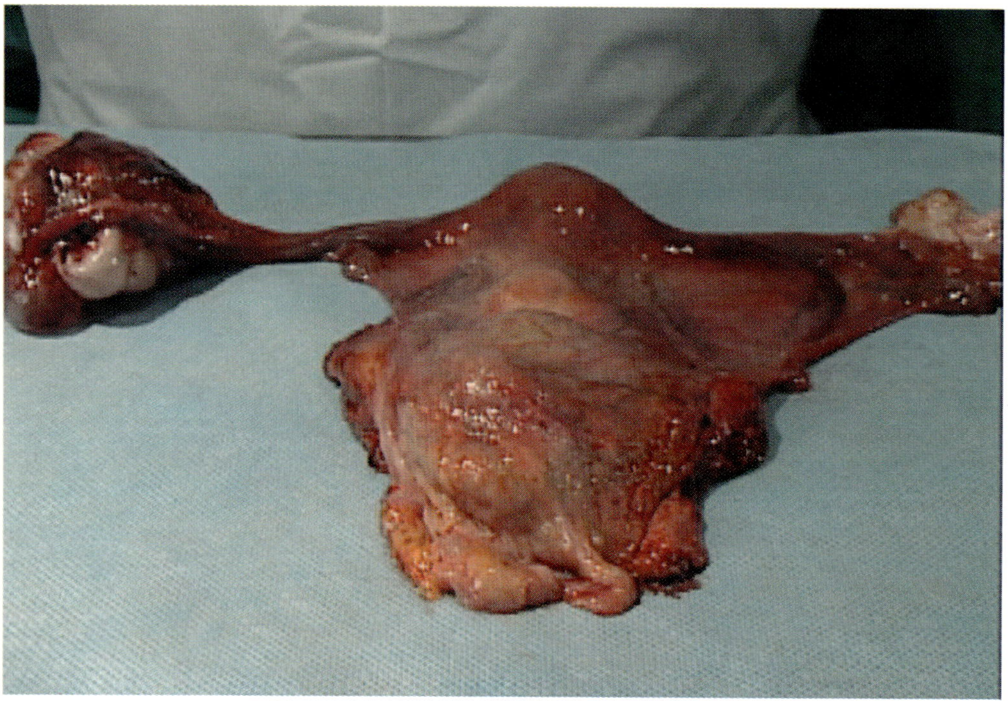

FIGURE 8.86 Uterus with ovaries and fallopian tubes. The uterus, ovaries, and fallopian tubes are displayed. Note the large ovary in the left corner of the figure (also seen in Figure 6.35A, Figure 6.35B, and Figure 7.46B).

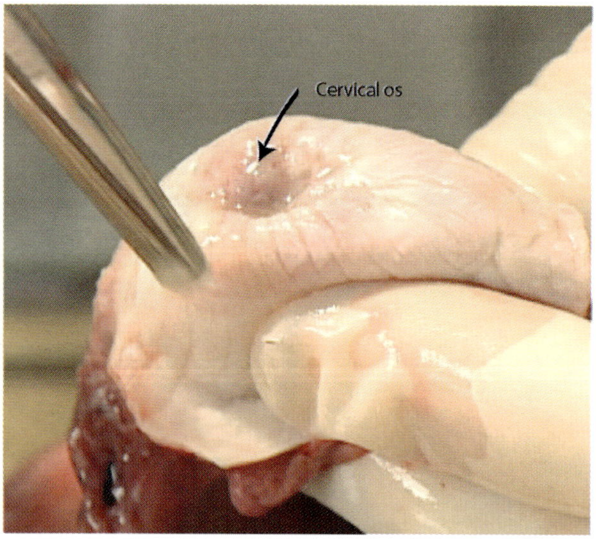

FIGURE 8.87 Cervix uteri. The cervix is displayed with the cervical opening or "os" in the center. This is the site where cervical dysplasia and carcinoma can occur.

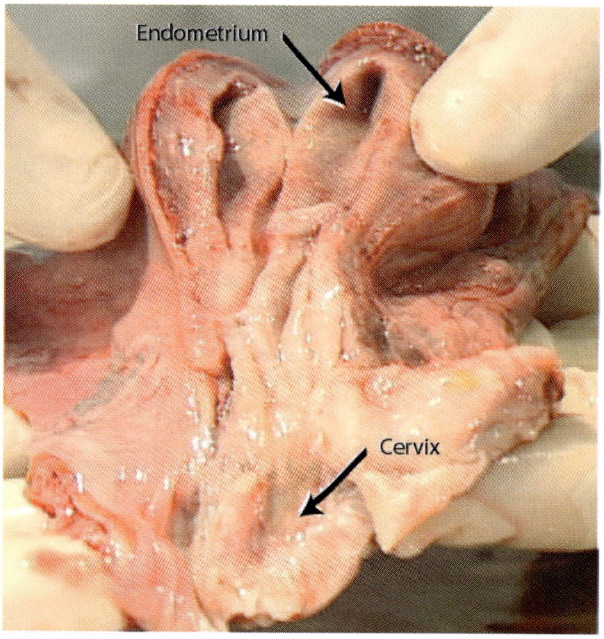

FIGURE 8.88 Uterus opened. The uterus is opened, exposing the endometrium. The endometrial cavity is examined for tumors. Presence or absence of pregnancy is noted. Samples can be taken from deceased fetal tissue to determine paternity.

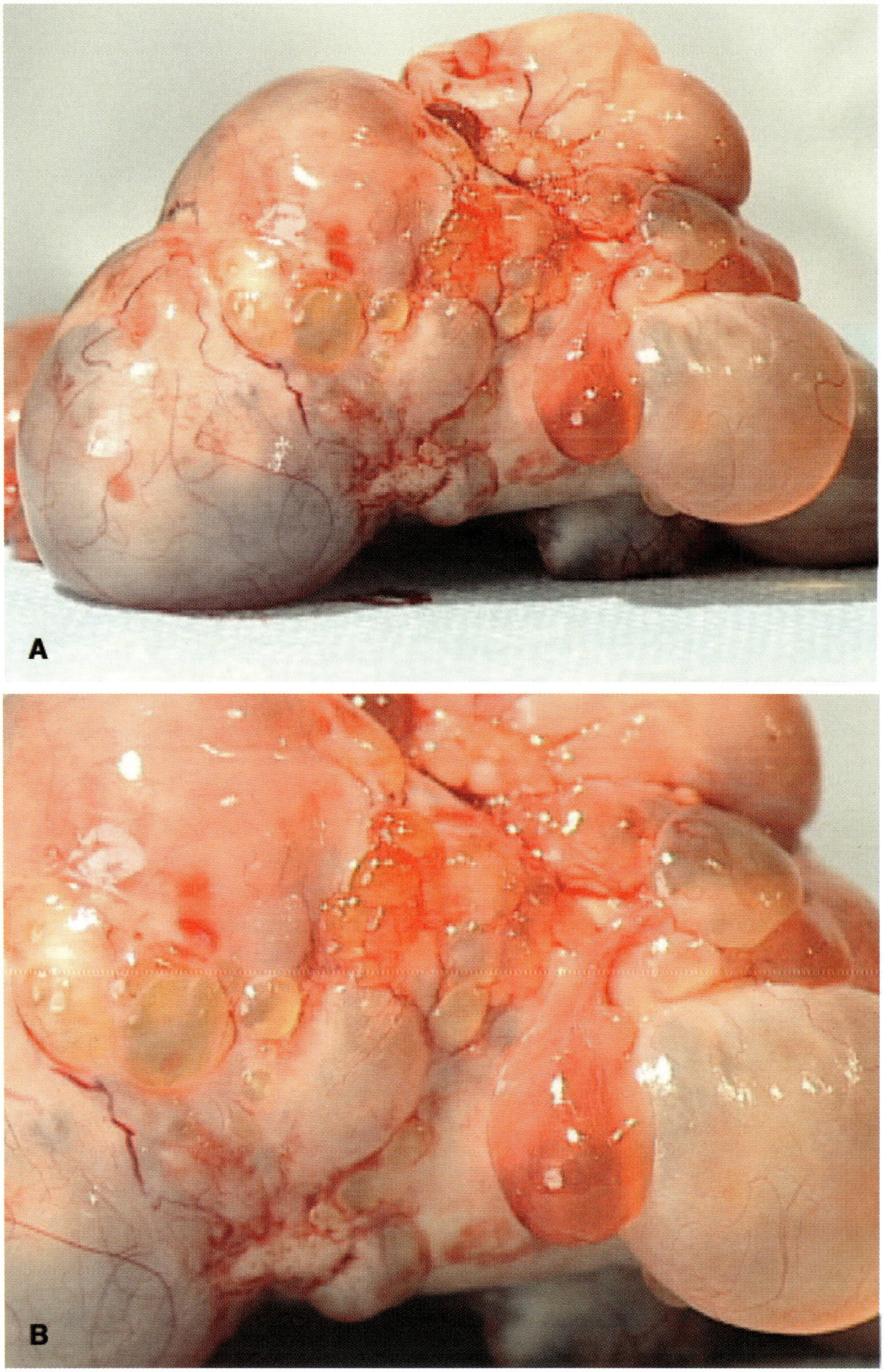

FIGURE 8.89 Ovarian serous cystadenoma. (A) This large cyst is about 8.0 cm (over 3 in.) in diameter and was likely to have caused pelvic pain and discomfort during life. **(B)** A close-up shows it to be a complex cyst with multiple smaller cysts attached to the larger cyst wall.

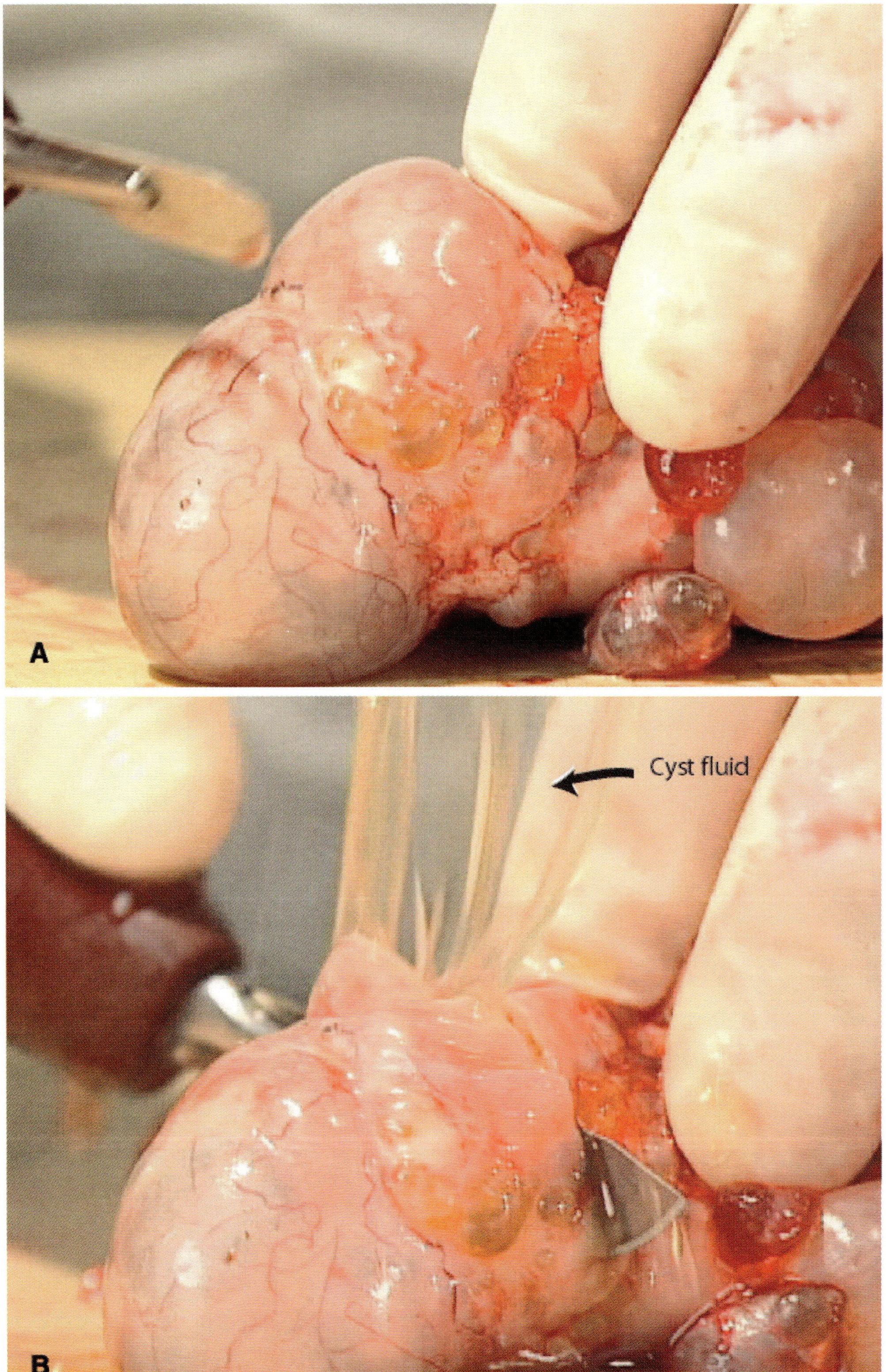

FIGURE 8.90 Dissecting ovarian serous cystadenoma. (A) The complex cyst has a smooth wall, although cavernous and complex. **(B)** When this cyst is cut, a yellow-colored fluid exudes from within. This fluid is under pressure and can squirt bystanders in the face (remember universal precautions). Microscopically, this cyst proved to be a serous cystadenoma, a benign tumor.

9 Examination of the Head, Skull, Brain, and Spinal Cord

All medical–legal examinations require the examination of the head, skull, and brain. This includes careful examination of the scalp, skull, and dura mater, the fibrous membrane that tethers the brain in place. Since the brain is the supreme organ system, giving orders to the rest of the body, no examination is complete without assessment of the brain and its coverings. At times this question is raised: "Why does the head need to be examined when the cause of death is obvious?" Aside from the reasons given in Chapter 2 for performing an autopsy when the cause of death is "obvious," additional reasons for examining the head are listed below:

- The scalp and hair can hide contusions and other injuries. Examining the scalp from the bottom side can make these injuries evident.
- Postmortem skull x-rays do not show small fractures.
- In the author's experience, computerized axial tomography (CAT) scans performed on the injured person can miss up to 10 cc of subdural blood.
- Unexpected tumors, old injuries, inflammation (e.g., meningitis), strokes, or other conditions are often found.
- A common injury seen in forensic pathology practice is the subdural hematoma. Often, the mechanism of sustaining a subdural hematoma is falling on a hard surface. Small blood vessels between the dural layer and the brain (bridging vessels) are severed, causing bleeding and hematoma. The brain must be examined for this injury.

SCALP EXAMINATION AND EXCISION OF THE BRAIN

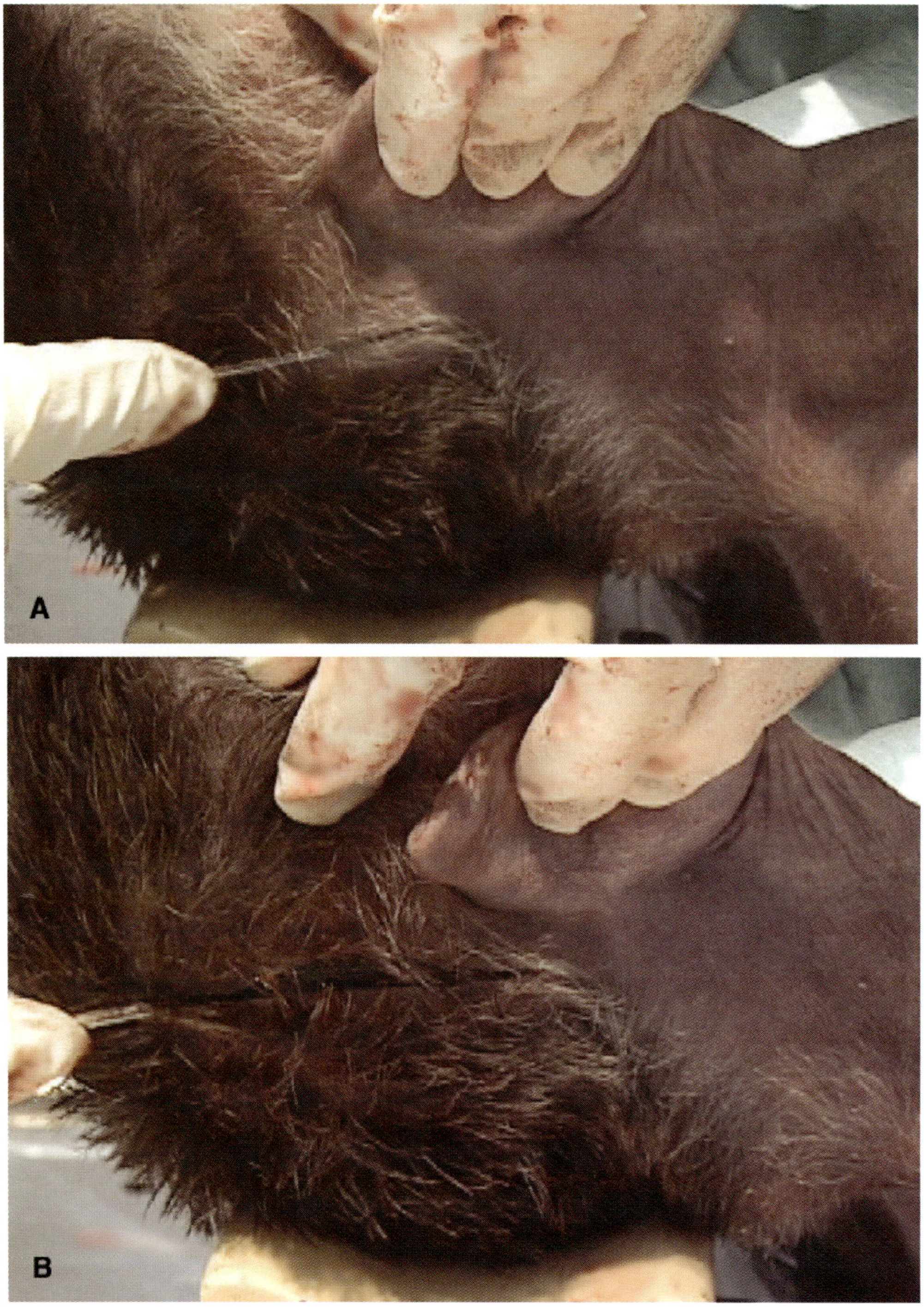

FIGURE 9.1 (A), (B) Incising the scalp. The scalp skin, subcutaneous tissue, and galea aponeurotica (thick fibrous layer) are cut down to the bone. The cut is started behind the ear, extended around the vertex (top of the head), and completed behind the other ear.

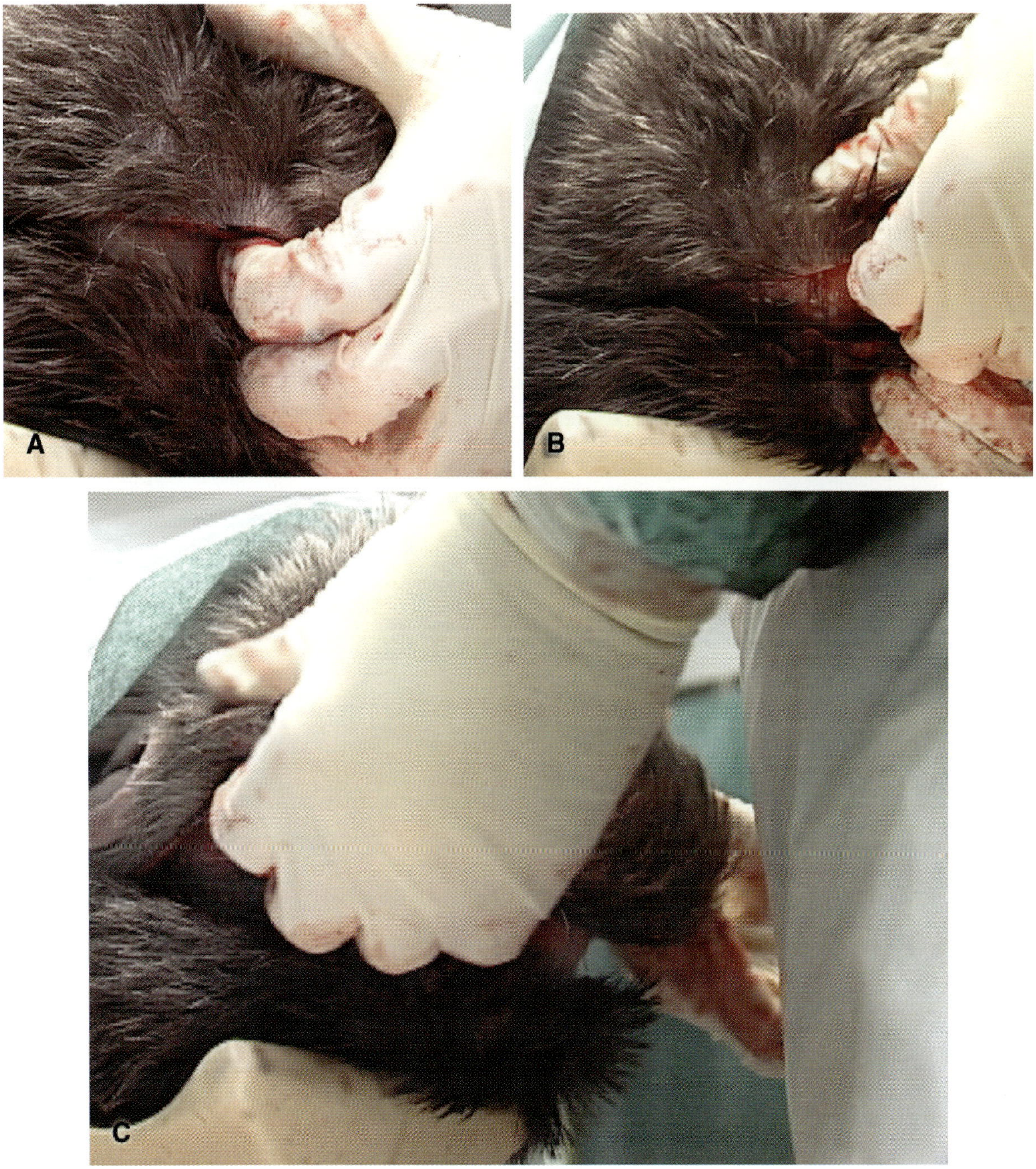

FIGURE 9.2 (A)–(C) Lifting the scalp and galea aponeurotica. The galeal layer is peeled from the periosteum of the bone.

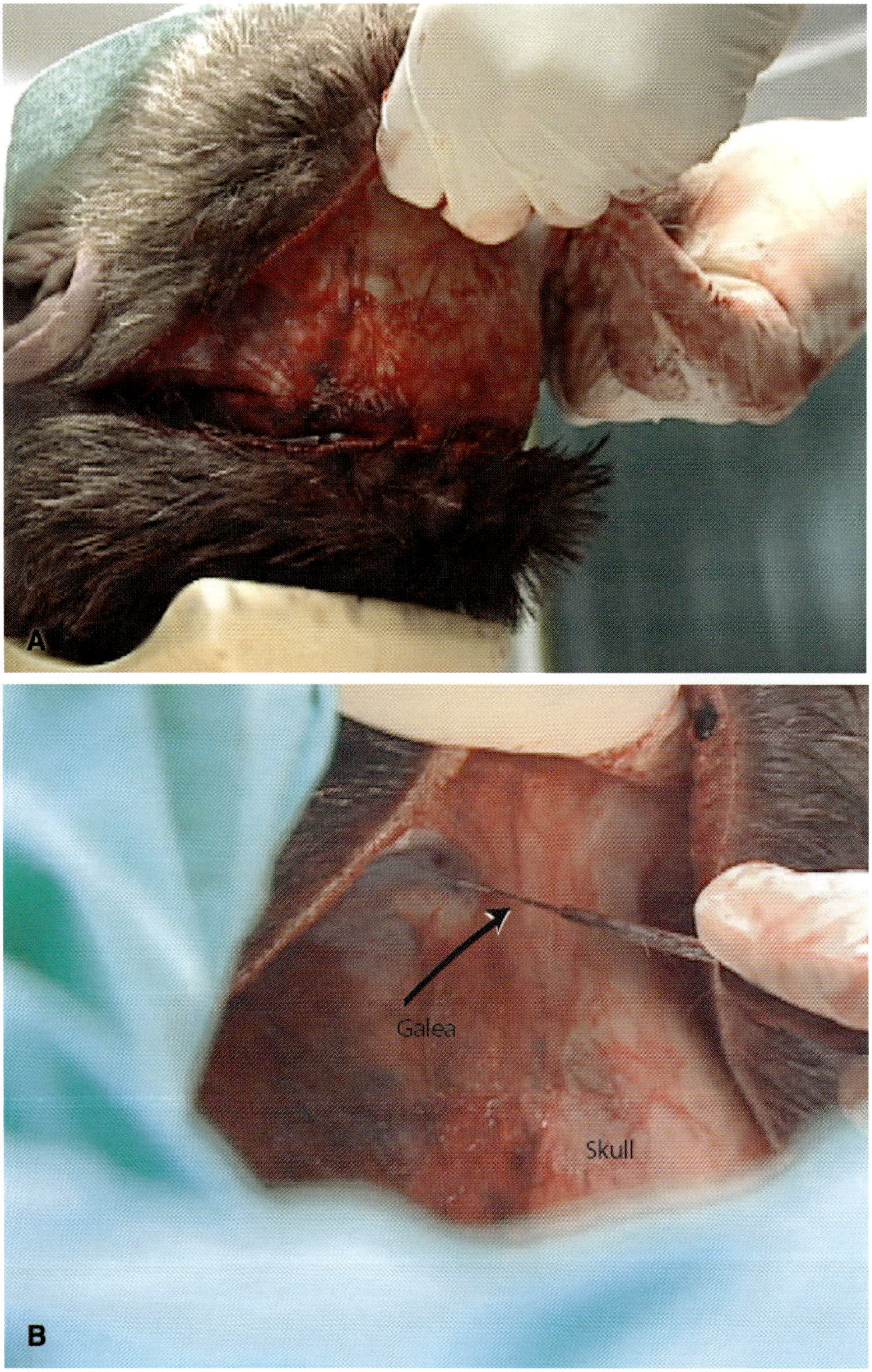

FIGURE 9.3 (A), (B) Reflecting the scalp back. Once the scalp is reflected back, a scalpel is used to dissect the attached fibrous soft tissue.

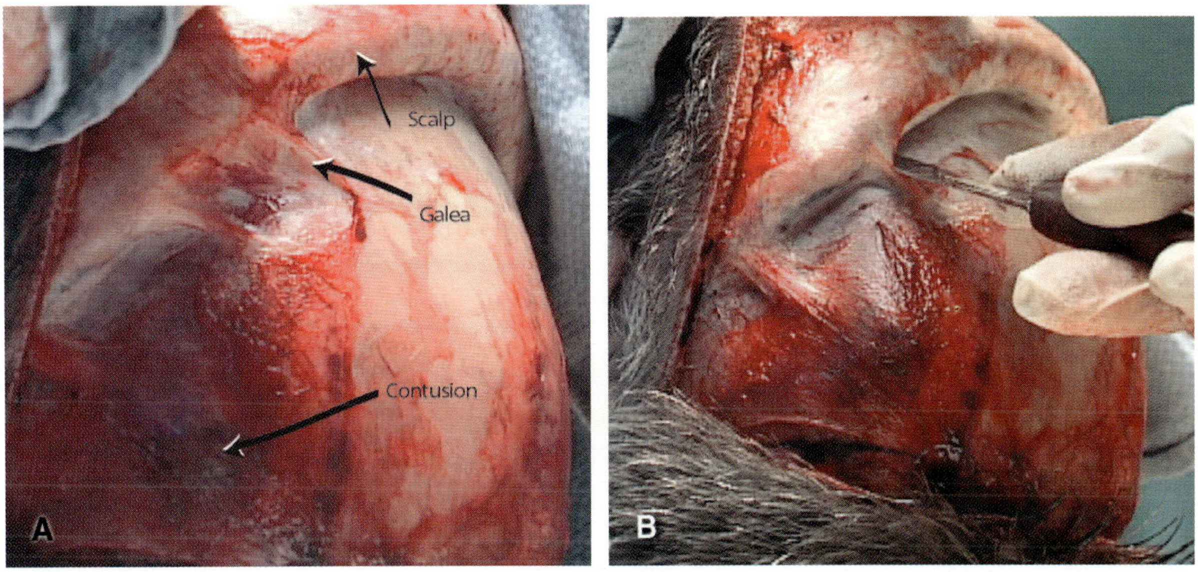

FIGURE 9.4 Scalp hemorrhage. (A) The scalp is reflected back as the remaining strands of soft tissue are cut. As the scalp is reflected back, a contusion is seen as a darkened area just below the scalpel. **(B)** The involved soft tissue is cut showing the underlying contusion hemorrhage.

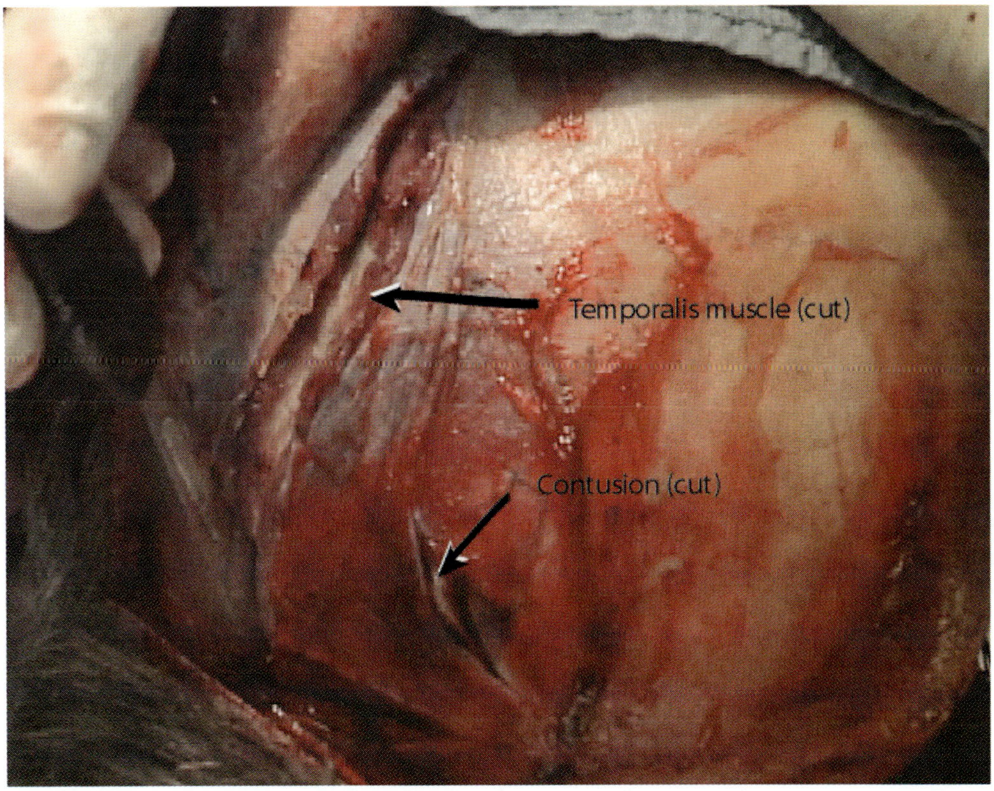

FIGURE 9.5 Cutting the temporalis muscle. The temporalis muscle is cut to prepare the skull for sawing. The saw blade does not cut soft tissue efficiently. A small contusion is seen at the arrow. This individual fell and then became unresponsive, having suffered a myocardial infarction.

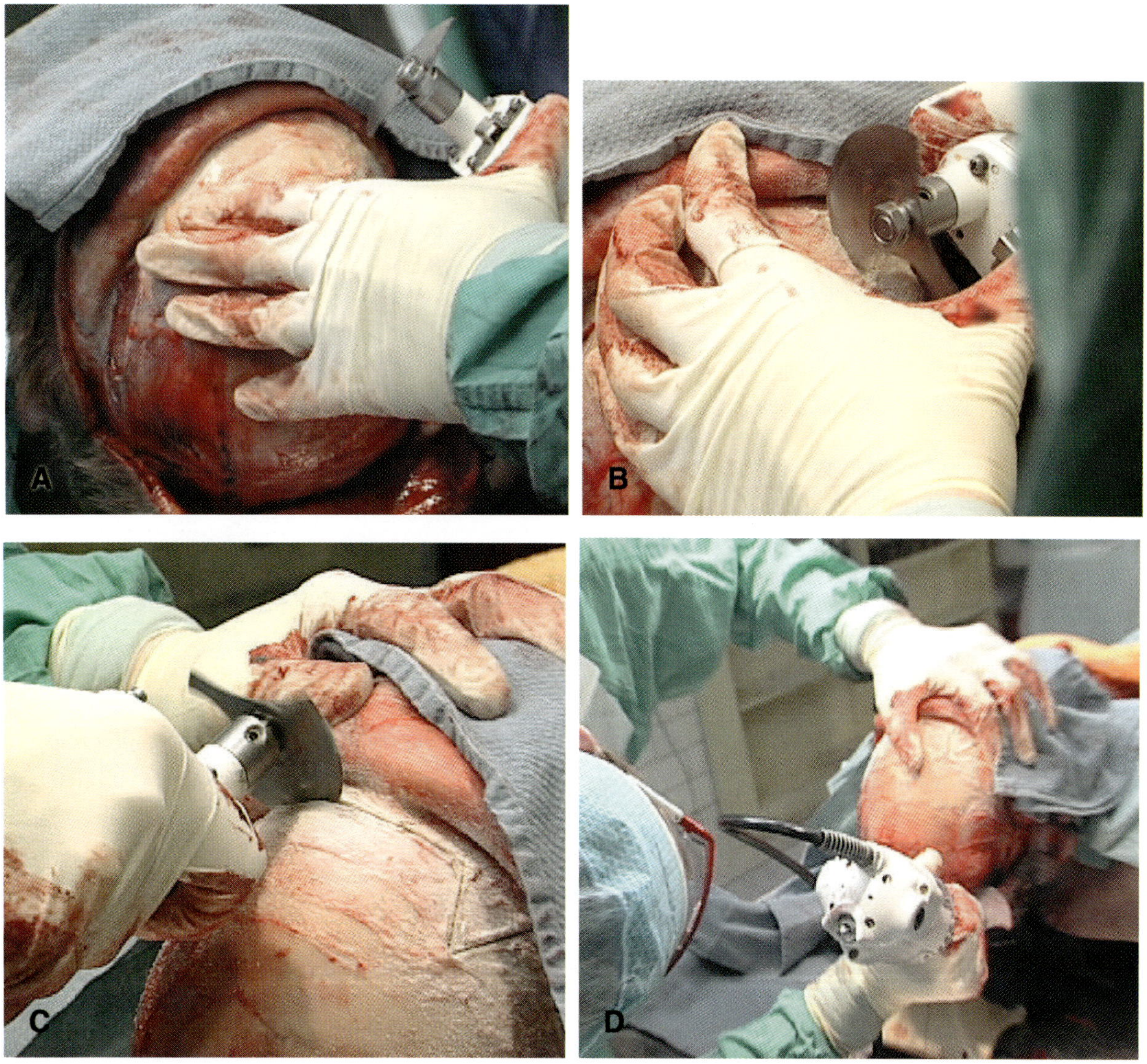

FIGURE 9.6 (A)–(D) Sawing the skull. The skull is sawed circumferentially. Care is taken not to saw too deeply, which could alter the brain surface.

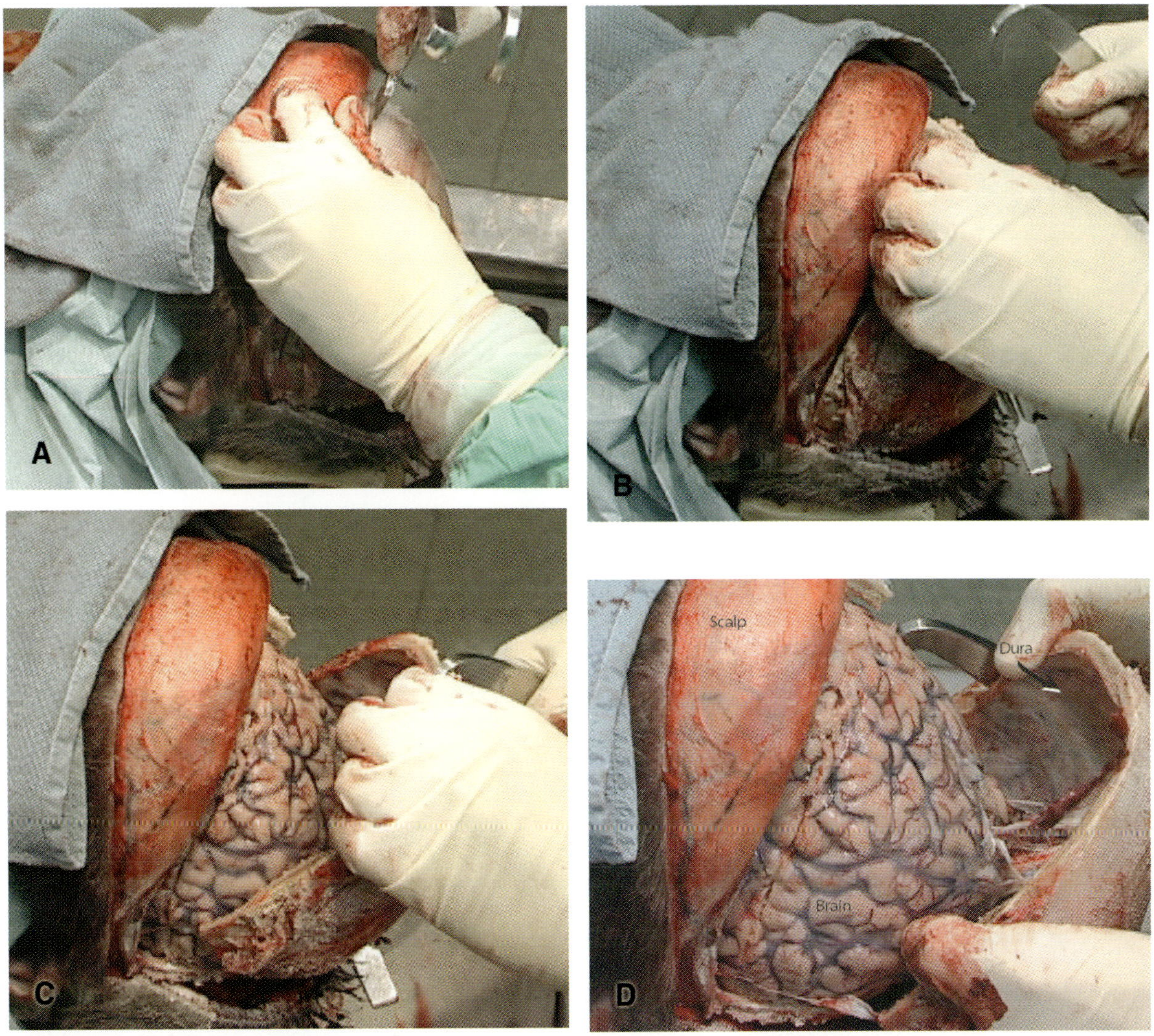

FIGURE 9.7 Opening the skull. (A)–(C) The opened portion of the skull (calvarium) is detached from the base. The pathologist is careful to look for hemorrhage above (epidural) or below (subdural) the dura mater. **(D)** The dura mater is the tough grey membrane outlined by the arrow.

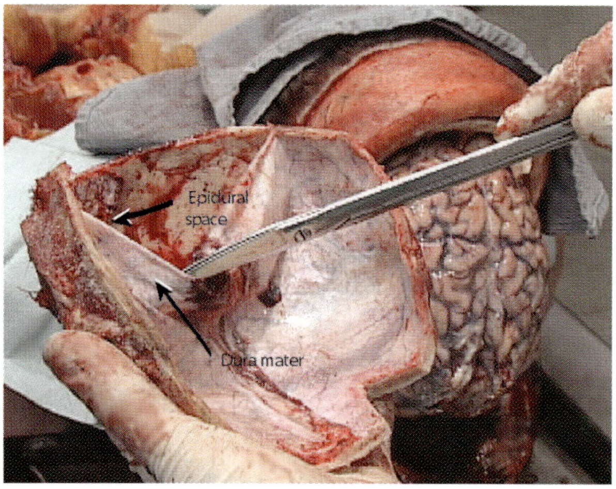

FIGURE 9.8 Examination of the dura. The top portion of the skull (calvarium) is examined here. The grey membrane is the dura mater. The dura mater has been partially stripped away from the skull. The tip of the scissors is in the epidural ("above the dura") region. The subdural space is the region below the dura.

FIGURE 9.9 (A)–(C) Subdural hematoma. A large hematoma can be seen between the brain and the dura, shown by the arrows. The pressure of the hematoma can affect the function of the brain, resulting in coma and death. This hematoma was produced by the deceased falling and striking his forehead. The small veins bridging the dura and the brain were torn during the fall, resulting in hemorrhage.

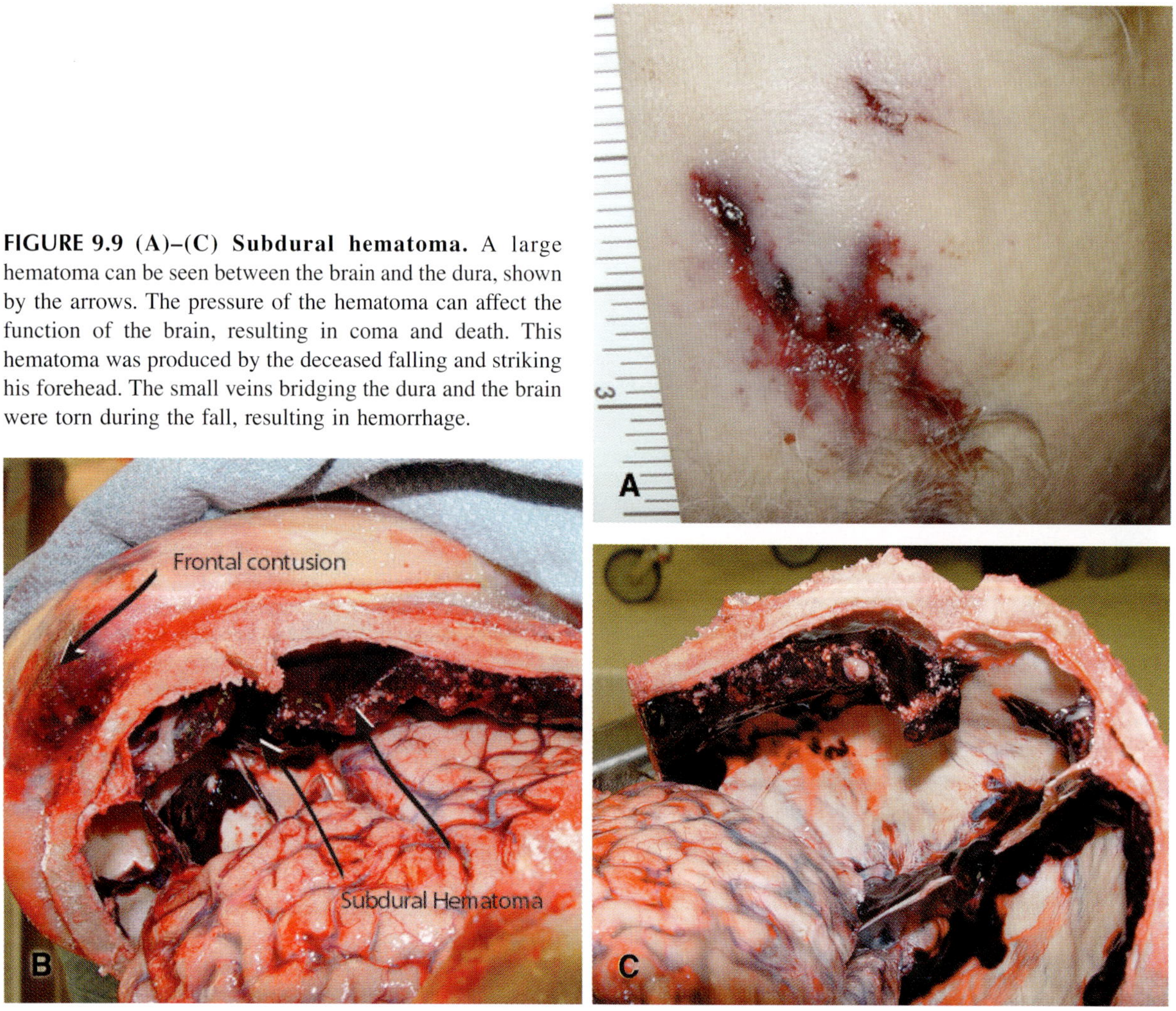

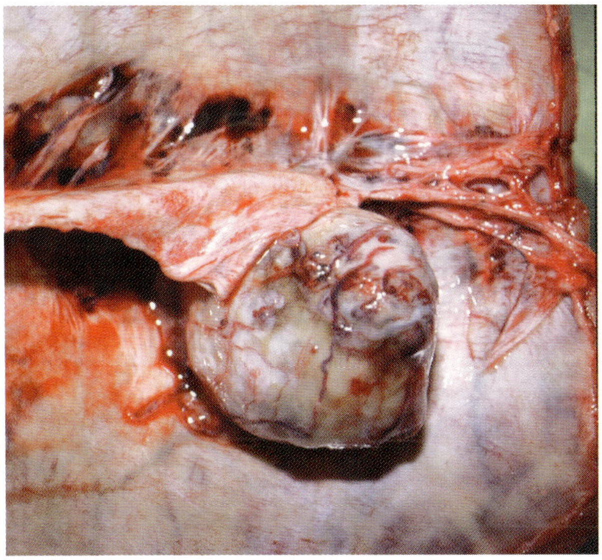

FIGURE 9.10 Meningioma. Tumors can be attached to the dura. The large, golf ball-sized tumor seen here is a benign tumor called a meningioma. Even though benign, the tumor occupies space in the closed area of the brain. As a result, the tumor can press on vital parts of the brain, causing symptoms related to these areas of the brain. Many of these tumors do not cause symptoms and are found incidentally at the autopsy.

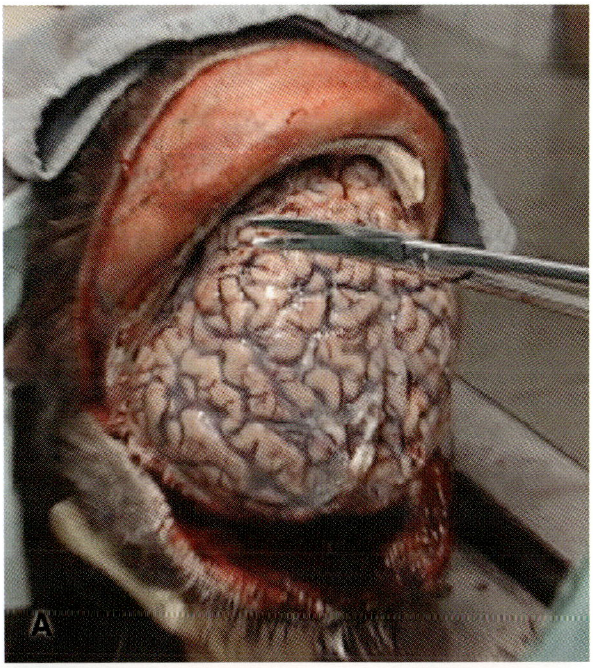

FIGURE 9.11 Brain *in situ*. (**A**) The frontal lobe is just below the scissors. (**B**) The frontal lobe is pulled back to expose the optic nerves. (**C**) The optic nerves are cut, exposing smaller nerves, the third cranial nerves (oculomotor), which are also cut.

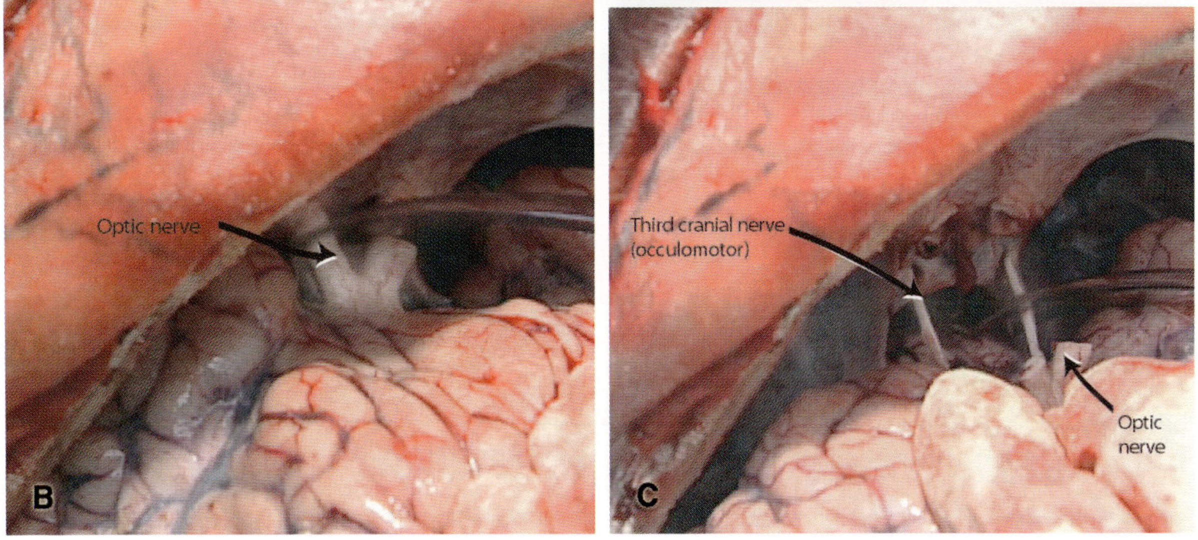

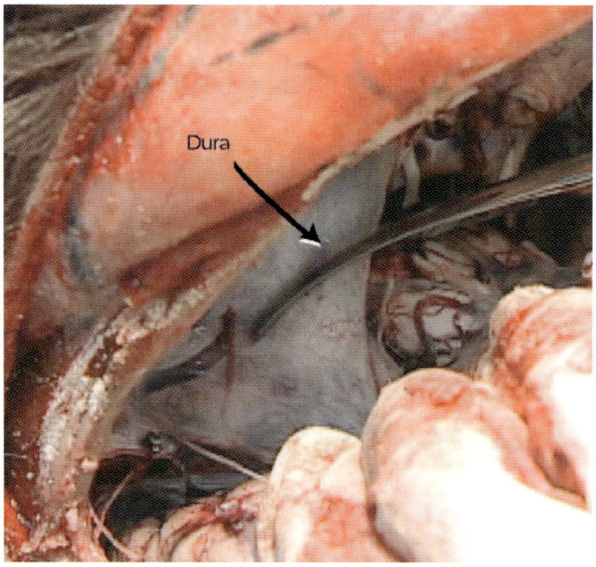

FIGURE 9.12 Cutting the tentorium cerebelli. The dural membrane covering the cerebellum is cut to reveal the cerebellum below. The cerebellum is an area of the brain dealing with coordination of muscles and balance.

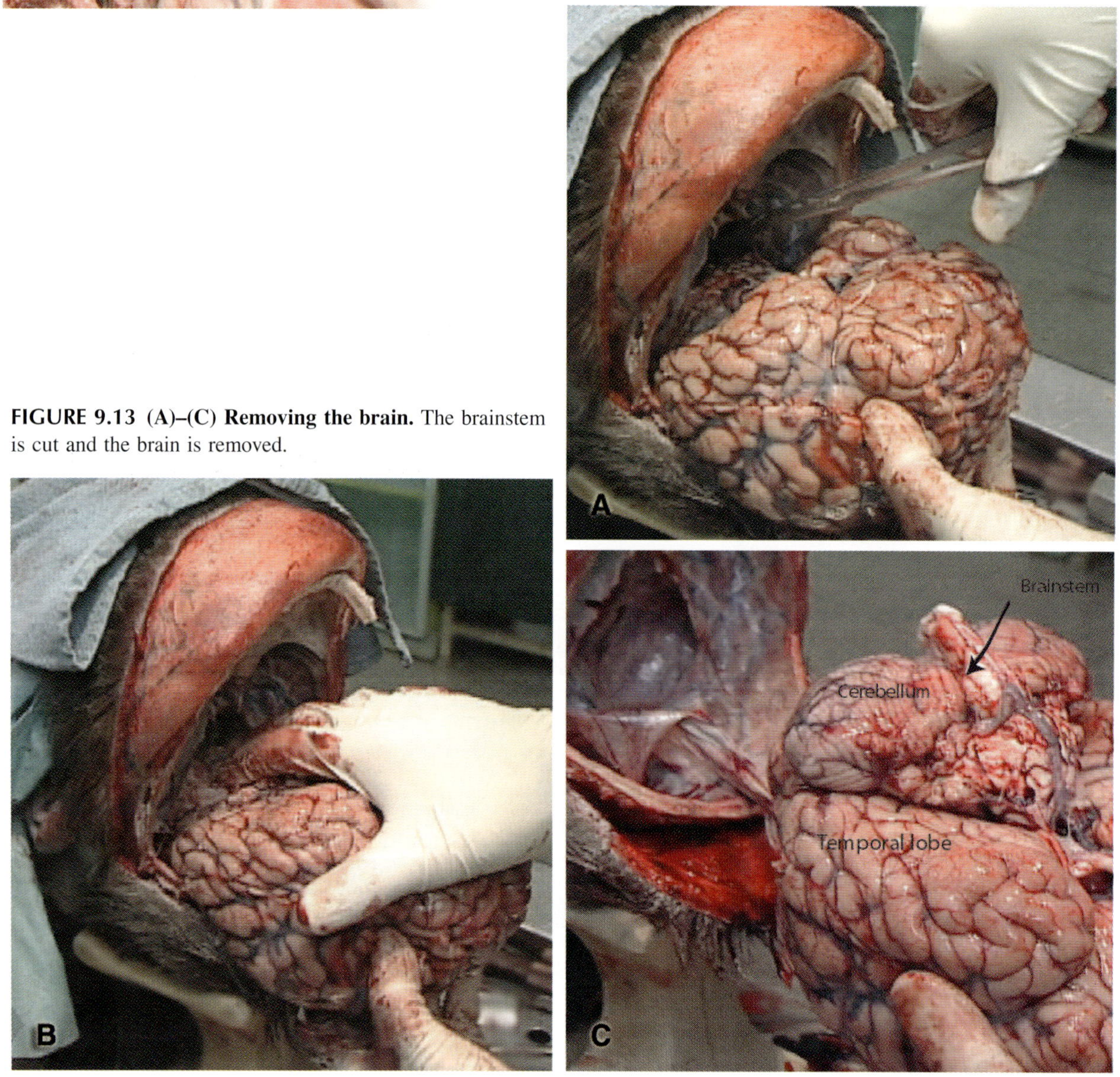

FIGURE 9.13 (A)–(C) Removing the brain. The brainstem is cut and the brain is removed.

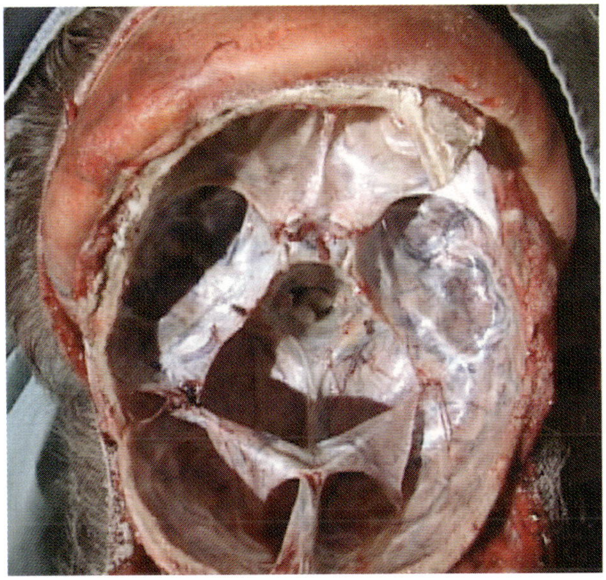

FIGURE 9.14 Base of the skull. The skull is seen with the dura attached. The dura is then peeled off to check the base of the skull for fractures. Direct examination of the base of the skull for fractures is often more effective than radiographs.

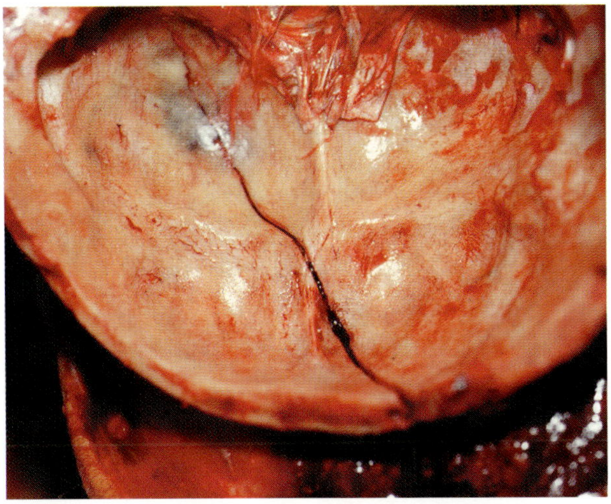

FIGURE 9.15 Fracture of the skull, occipital bone. The dura has been pulled from the base of the skull, revealing a fracture. This victim slipped, fell backward, and struck the head, suffering this fracture, subdural hemorrhage, brain swelling, and then death.

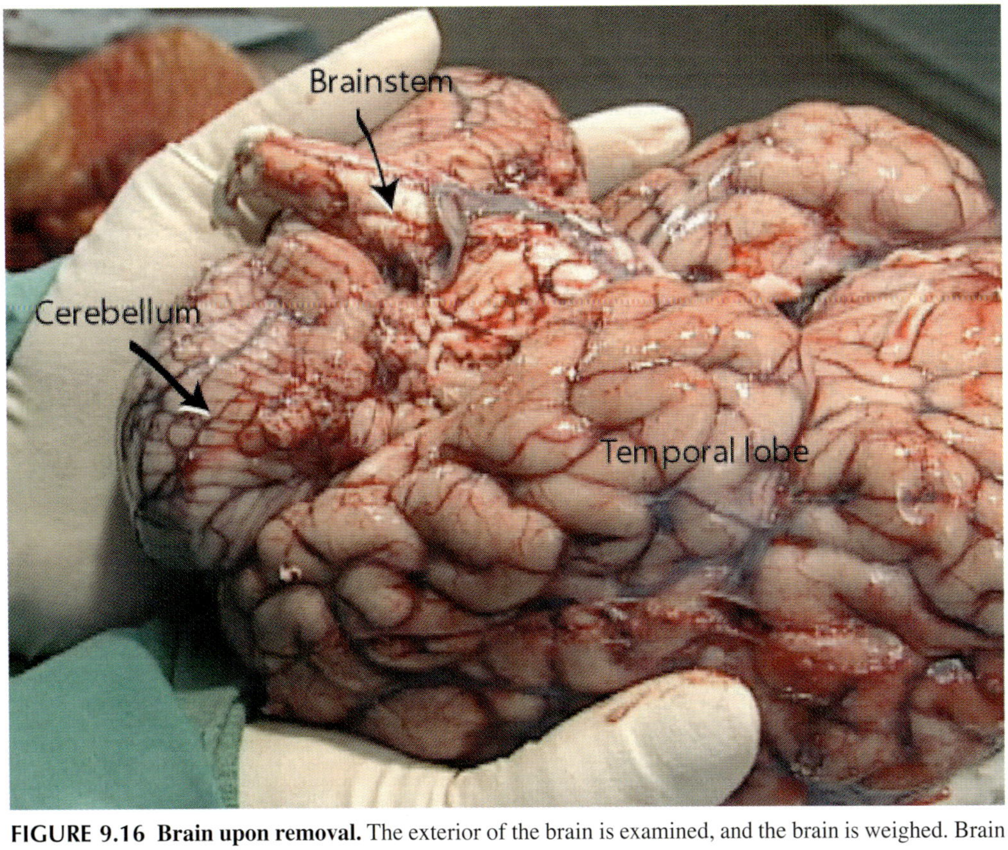

FIGURE 9.16 Brain upon removal. The exterior of the brain is examined, and the brain is weighed. Brain weight is generally 1.4% of body weight, or about 1100 g (2.4 lb) in a 77-kg (170-lb) person.

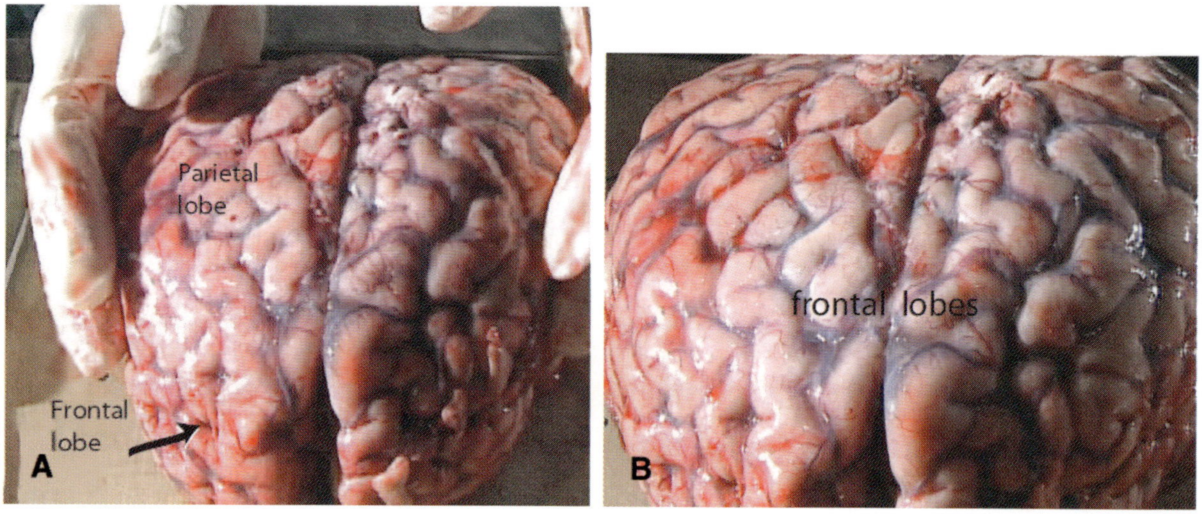

FIGURE 9.17 (A), (B) Frontal and parietal lobes of the brain. This view of the convexity of the brain shows the many convolutions of the cortex. The peaks are known as gyri and the grooves are sulci. Note the many blood vessels; the brain is very vascular.

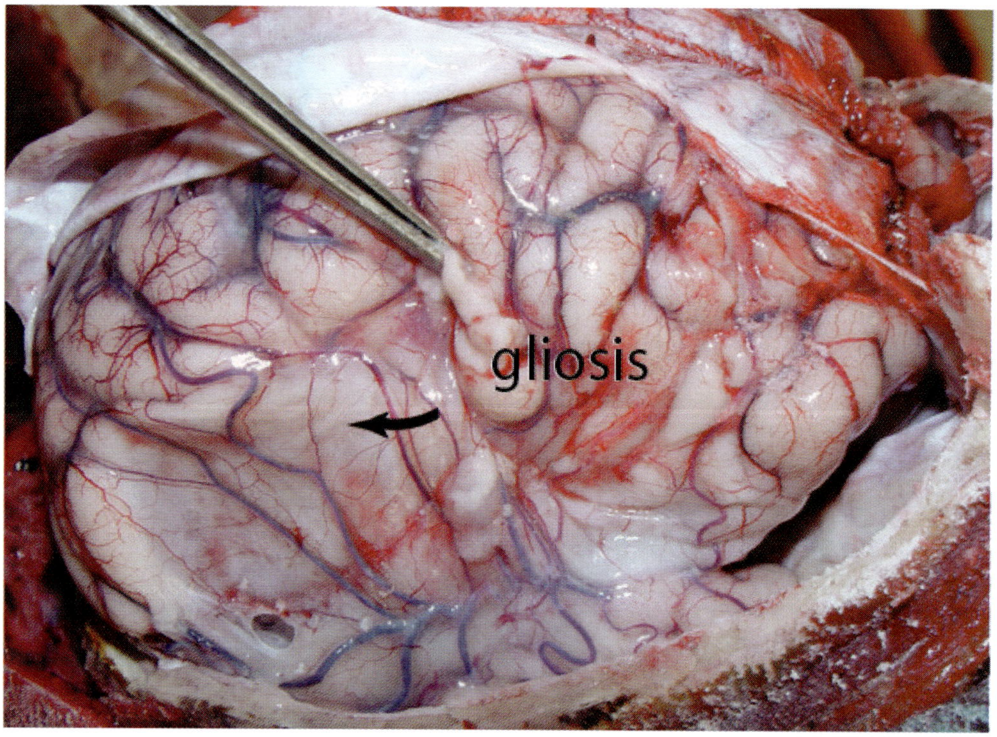

FIGURE 9.18 Gliosis. Injuries of the brain, such as scars or strokes, form a scarring called gliosis. The cortex of this brain is collapsed due to previous injury from a stroke.

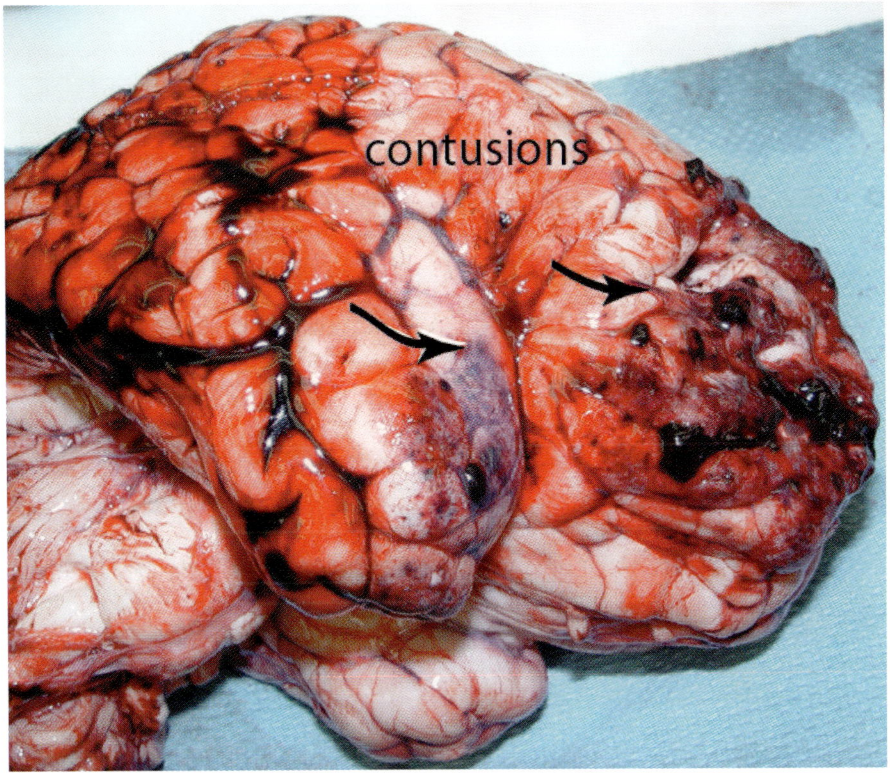

FIGURE 9.19 Contusions of the brain. The dark hemorrhagic areas of the brain display severe contusion from a motor vehicle crash. This contusion caused severe, fatal brain edema.

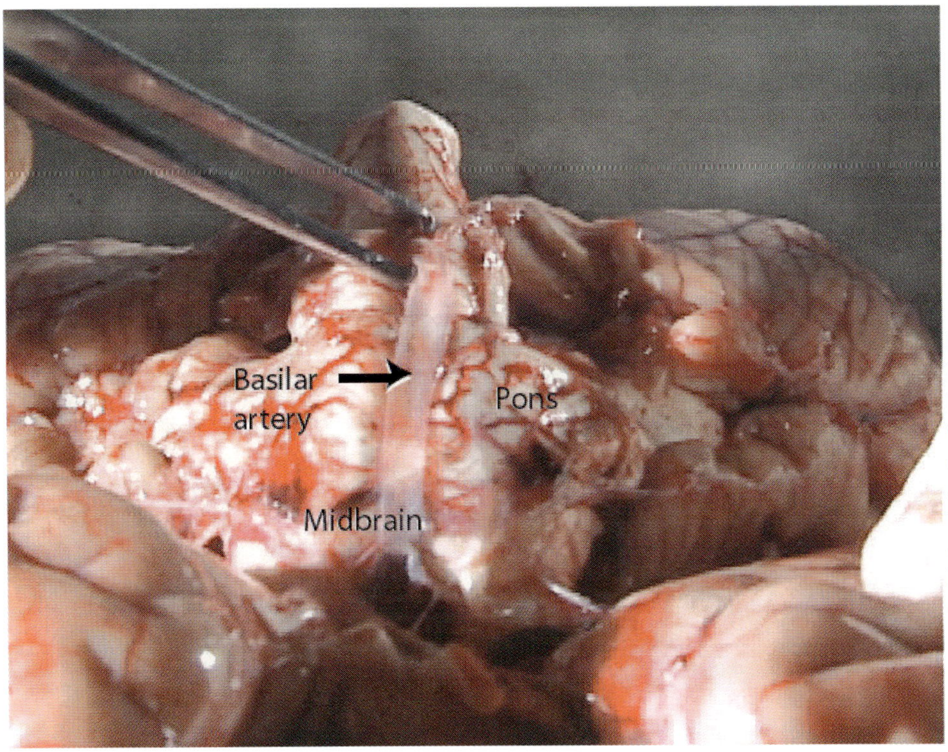

FIGURE 9.20 Vertebral basilar arteries at the brainstem. The arteries at the base of the brain are examined for atherosclerois and anomalies. Significant blockage of these arteries can cause infarction of the brain, known as a stroke. Aneurisms, or "outpouchings," of the wall (saccular or berry aneurisms) can rupture, causing serious, commonly fatal, hemorrhage.

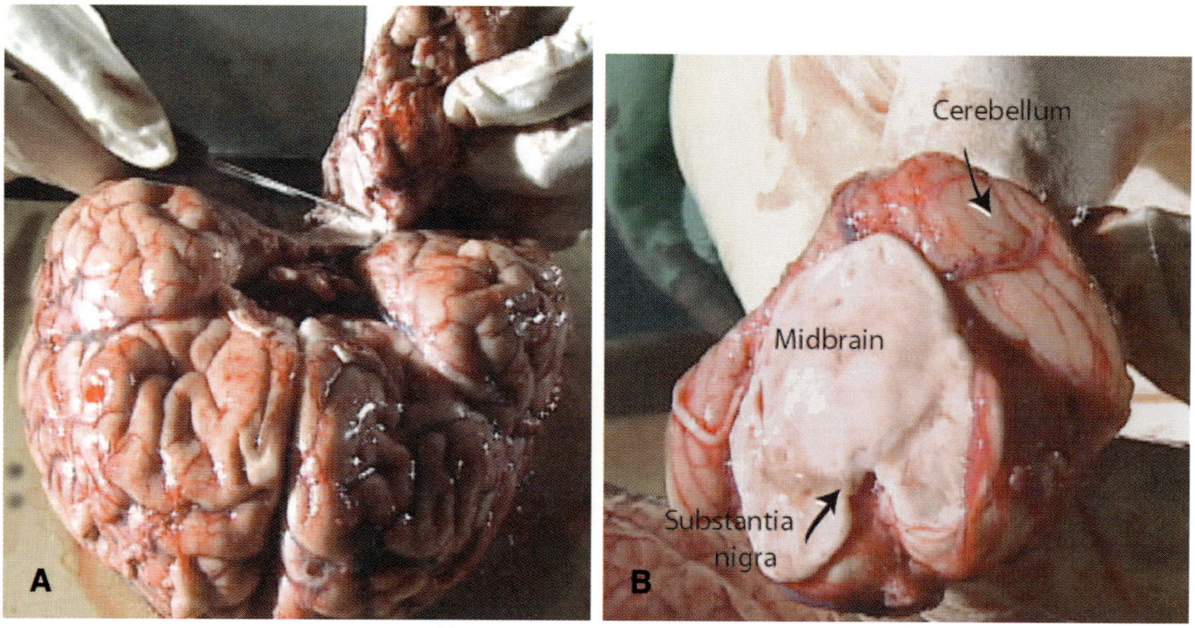

FIGURE 9.21 Examination of the midbrain. (A) The midbrain, brainstem, and cerebellum are removed. **(B)** This is a section of normal-appearing midbrain. Many vital functions are associated with this area.

FIGURE 9.22 Brainstem with hemorrhage. Hemorrhage in the midbrain, as seen here, is almost always quickly fatal.

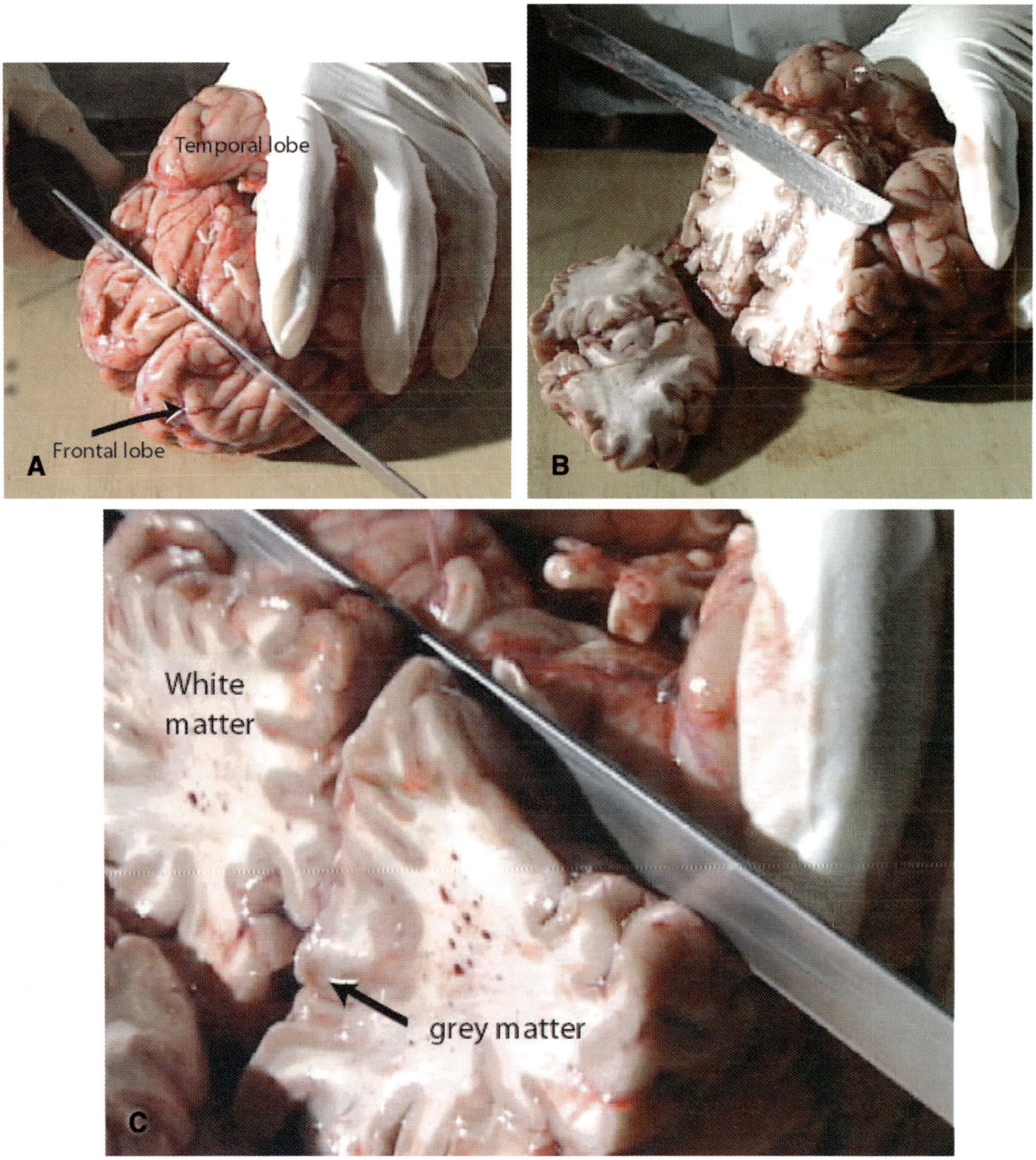

FIGURE 9.23 (A)–(C) Serial cutting of the brain. There are various methods for cutting the brain. One common method is cutting the brain perpendicular to the long axis, as shown here. The brain can be cut in the fresh state or, preferably, after fixation for about 1 month in formaldehyde. Hemorrhage and tumors are common findings.

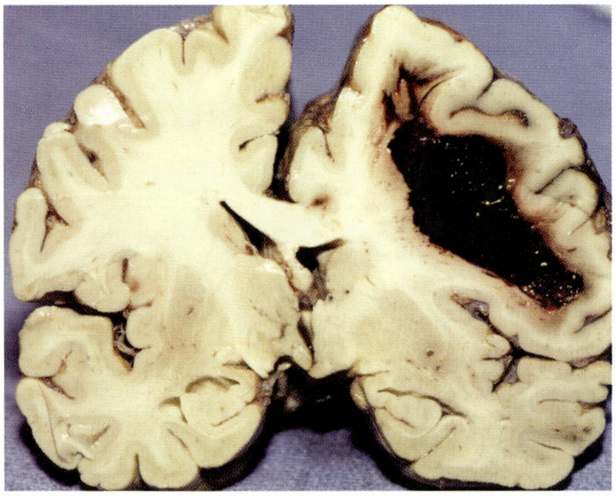

FIGURE 9.24 Cerebral infarct. This section of brain shows hemorrhage in the white matter. This patient had a history of hypertension.

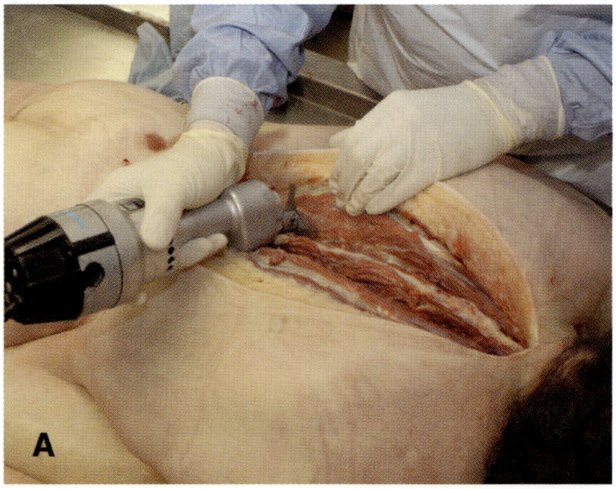

FIGURE 9.25 (A)–(C) Spinal cord examination. When spinal cord pathology or injuries are suspected, the cord is removed. The posterior method is depicted here. After exposing the spinal cord, the vertebral arches are cut up and down the spine, revealing the spinal cord below. The spinal cord is carefully removed. After removal of the spinal cord, the area is sewn together and sealed.

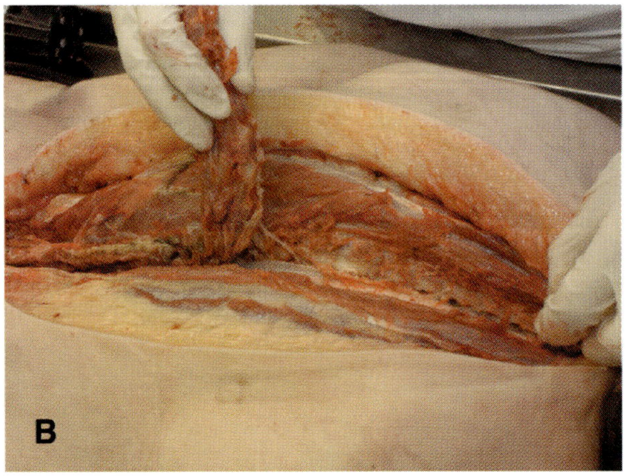

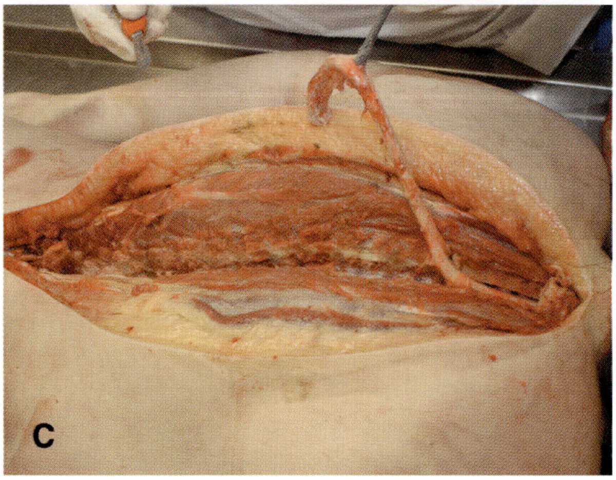

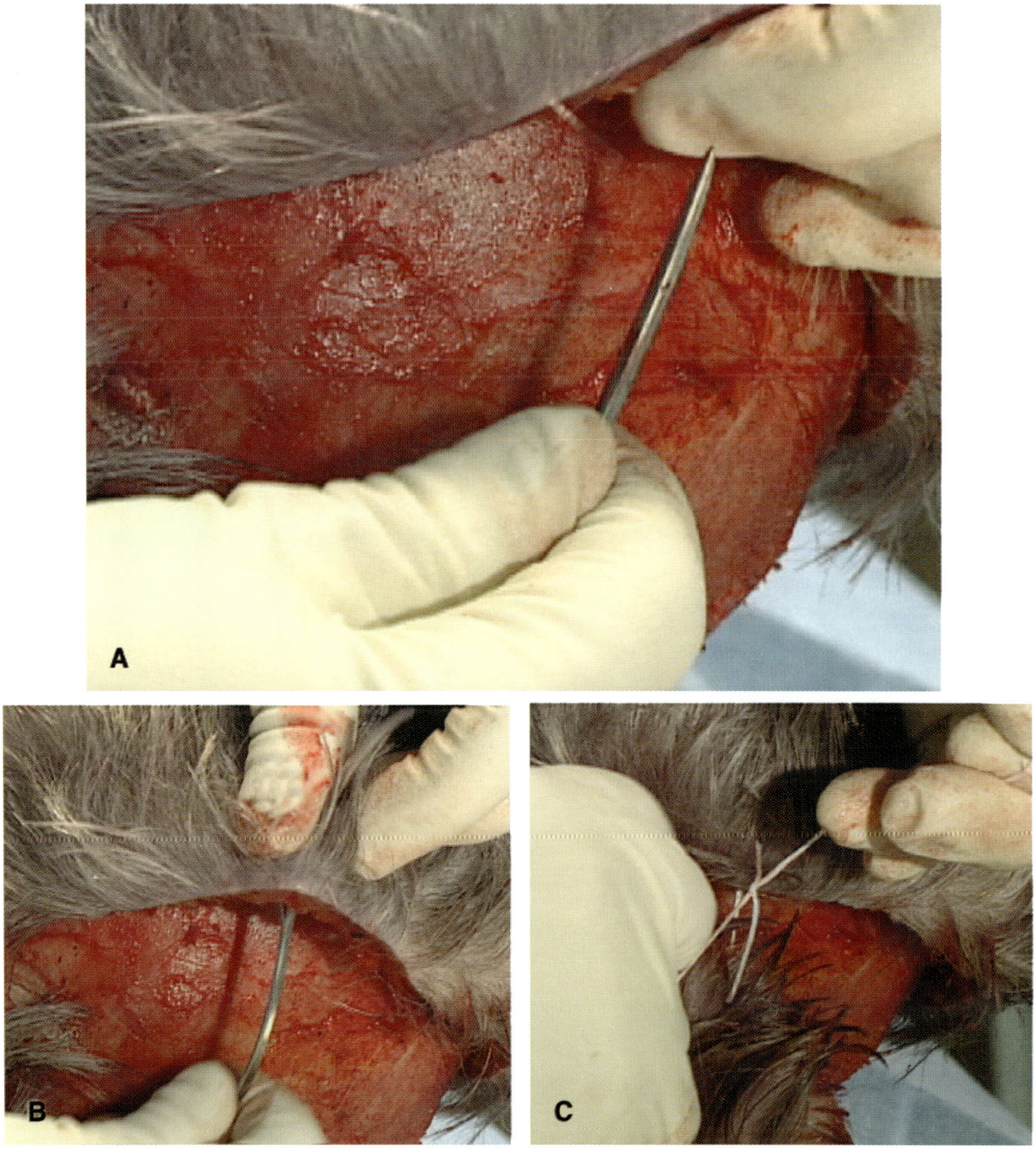

FIGURE 9.26 (A)–(C) Stitching the scalp. The skull is held together by stitching the scalp. The funeral director will tightly affix or glue the skull together. The incision will be hidden from view at the funeral.

10 Microscopic Examination

Making diagnoses using the microscope is the trade of most pathologists. If one has a breast biopsy or a tumor removed, the pathologist classifies the tumor and diagnoses the lesion as benign or malignant. The skill of making microscopic diagnoses is very useful in postmortem exams because the microscopic examination is used to support the gross findings in an autopsy.

The gross examination portion of the autopsy usually yields the cause and manner of death. That is, the pathologist normally walks away from the autopsy suite with a good idea of the major diagnoses and the cause and manner of death. For example, the pathologist does not need to look at microscopic slides to diagnose a contact gunshot wound of the head. However, he or she will take sections of the wound to confirm, microscopically, that there is heavy soot deposition in the wound. So the microscopic exam serves, in most cases, to supplement the autopsy.

In some cases, microscopic examination is pivotal in making a major diagnosis and in determining the cause and manner of death. These diagnoses include:

- Malignant tumors — lung, colon, and breast carcinomas; lymphomas
- Heart — myocarditis; myocardial infarction
- Lung — pneumonia vs. congestion, often difficult to differentiate grossly
- Liver — chronic hepatitis
- Spleen — splenitis, one sign of sepsis
- Kidneys — nephridites, leading to renal failure, e.g., lupus
- Infections — any tissue or organ; meningitis or inflammation of the coverings of the brain

The following figures are sample diagnoses of conditions and injuries that can be made by microscopic examination. These figures demonstrate how a pathologist uses the microscope to support, prove, or determine the cause or manner of death.

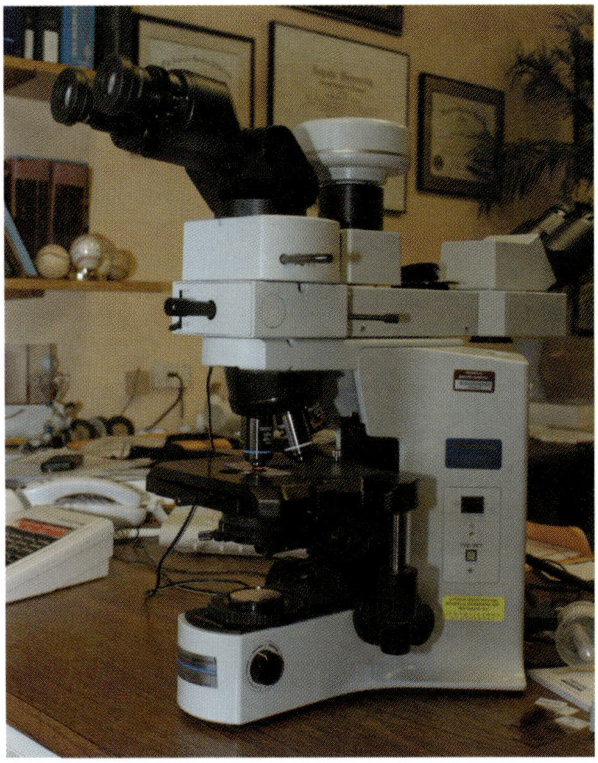

FIGURE 10.1 The microscope, the tool of the pathologist. Whether it is used to diagnose tumors or to study abnormal tissues seen grossly at autopsy, the microscope is the "stethoscope of the pathologist." Many findings cannot be diagnosed with the gross autopsy, and a few of these are seen in the following.

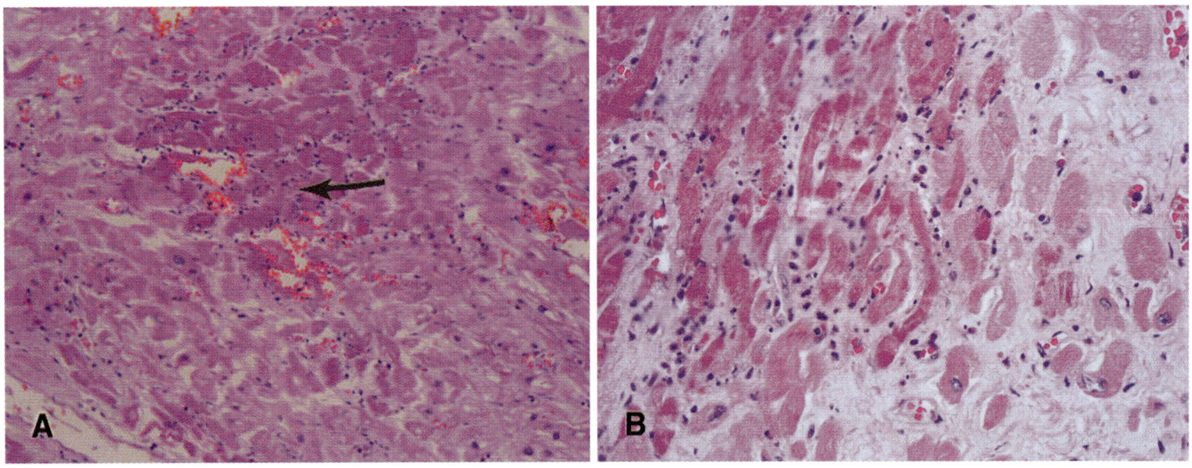

FIGURE 10.2 Acute myocardial infarction. (A) The arrow points to red, dead cardiac muscle cells. This cell death results from lack of blood flow (ischemia) as blood carries oxygen and other essential nutrients to the cells. The death of the cells invokes an inflammatory response. The small blue dots in the figure around the arrow are neutrophils, the sentinel of the acute inflammatory response. **(B)** This higher magnification shows the red serpentine fibers and the surrounding blue inflammatory cells.

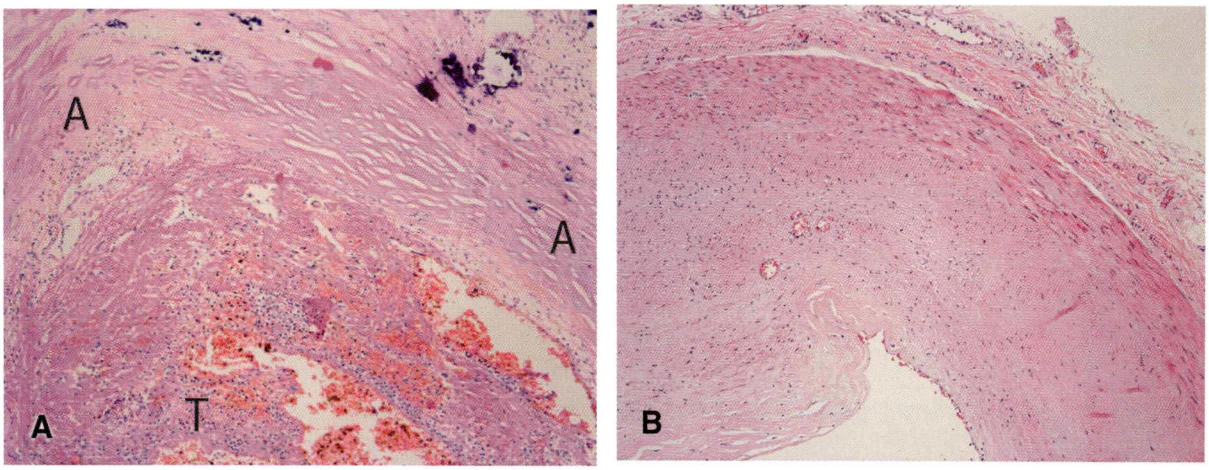

FIGURE 10.3 (A) Thrombosed (clotted) coronary. "A" is the arterial wall; "T" is the thrombus. The supply of blood to the cardiac muscle cells is carried out by the coronary arteries. Most commonly, as these arteries become clogged with atherosclerotic plaque or thrombi (clots), the myocardium dies, producing a myocardial infarction. **(B) Normal coronary.** The normal, open coronary artery is compared to the thrombosed artery.

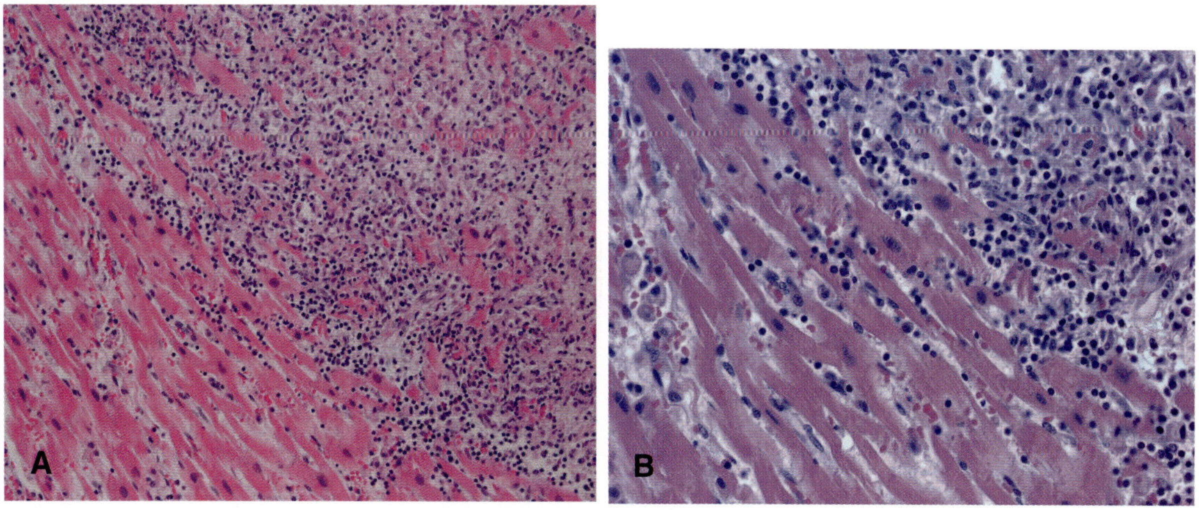

FIGURE 10.4 (A), (B) Myocarditis. These figures are microscopic examinations of the gross photos shown in Figure 8.19A and Figure 8.19B. The red myocardial fibers on the left are invaded by a diffuse lymphocytic and monocytic inflammatory response. Lymphocytes and monocytes indicate chronic inflammation. This type of inflammation most likely represents a viral origin of this myocarditis.

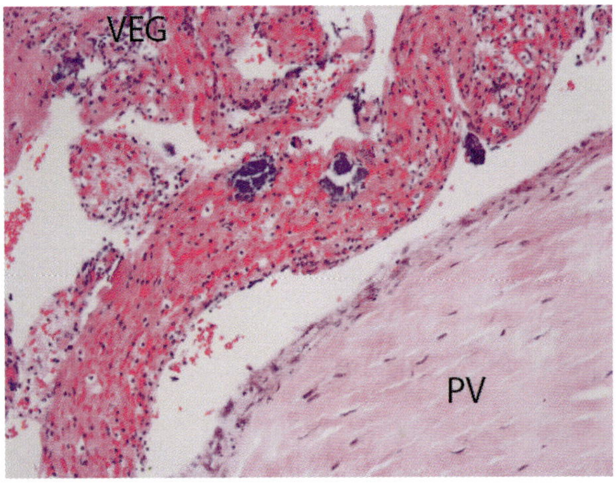

FIGURE 10.5 Vegetations of the pulmonic valve. "PV" is pulmonic valve; "VEG" is vegetation. Damaged or malformed valves can collect bacteria and thrombi (clots). These bacteria-laden clots can go to the lung, causing infection and infarction (septic emboli); in the case of the mitral and aortic valves, they can go to the brain, kidneys, and fingernails (also see Figure 5.15C and Figure 5.15D).

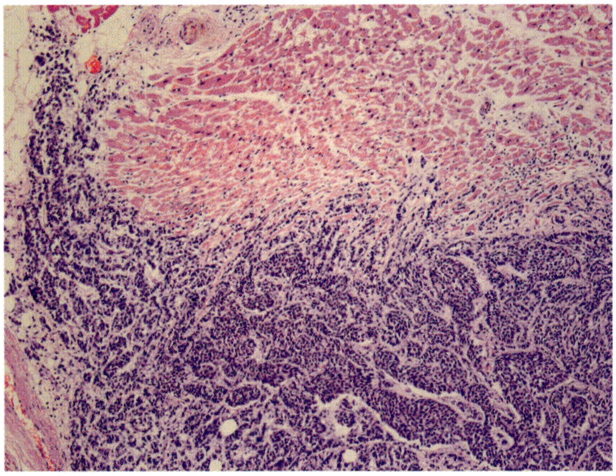

FIGURE 10.6 Carcinoma invading the heart. This patient had metastatic (spread outside the primary carcinoma) lung carcinoma. The carcinoma invaded the pericardium and then the heart (also see Figure 6.23).

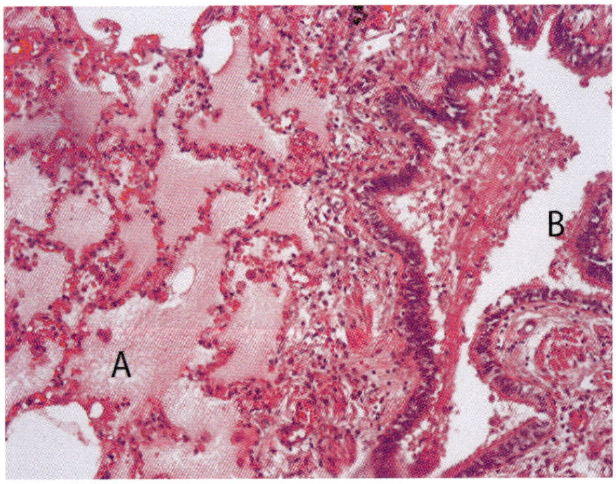

FIGURE 10.7 Pulmonary edema. "A" is alveolus; "B" is bronchus. Pink pulmonary edema is fluid in the airways, alveolus, and bronchus. This fluid comes from the rich vascular network in the lungs. If the heart does not pump properly or an excess of certain drugs is present (e.g., narcotics), fluid leaves these blood vessels and goes into the alveolar air space (also see Figure 8.43). There are many other causes of pulmonary edema. See the references for a detailed discussion.

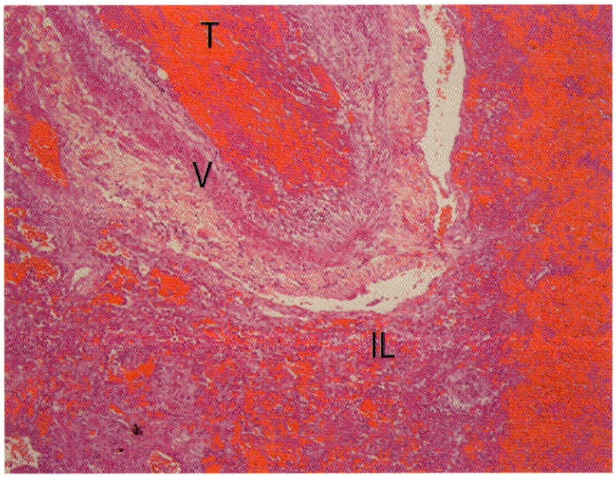

FIGURE 10.8 Pulmonary embolus with infarction. "T" is thrombus, "V" is pulmonary artery, and "IL" is infarcted lung. As with the heart, a clot stopping the blood flow causes infarction. In the lung, however, there is a dual blood supply, the bronchial arteries. Blood from these arteries pumps in, causing the bright red hemorrhage seen in the figure, called a hemorrhagic infarction.

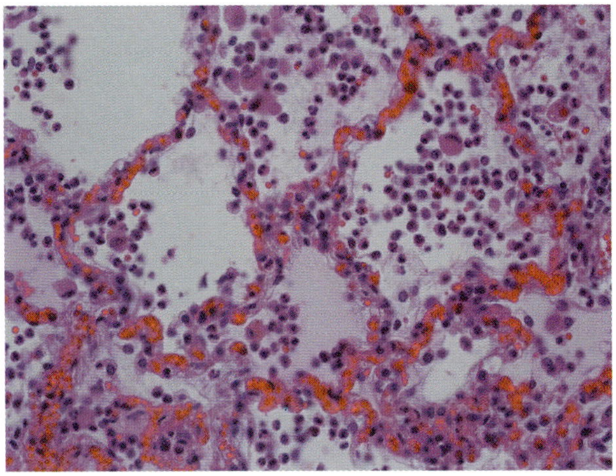

FIGURE 10.9 Lobar pneumonia. The alveolar spaces are filled with numerous inflammatory cells and other debris. This inflammatory material is usually the result of bacterial infection, and one can see how, in the alveolus, it can interfere with air exchange in the lung.

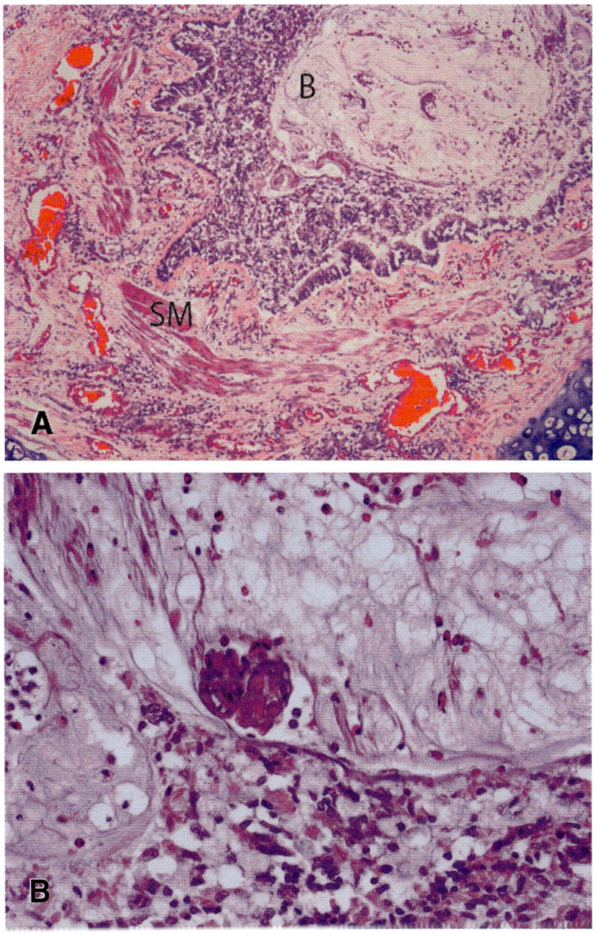

FIGURE 10.10 Asthmatic lung. (A) "SM" is smooth muscle; "B" is bronchus. In asthma, the airways are overreactive in reacting to allergins, for example. The bronchi, surrounded by smooth muscle, clamp down, decreasing air flow. Increased mucus is secreted, and the eosinophils are prominent. The result is wheezing, difficulty breathing, and in *status asthmaticus*, possible respiratory failure and death. The figure shows hypertrophied smooth muscle and mucous plugging in a patient who died of *status asthmaticus*. **(B)** Note the numerous red eosinophils, mucus, and a central red conglomerate of shed epithelial cells called Curschmann's spirals, an occasional microscopic finding in asthma.

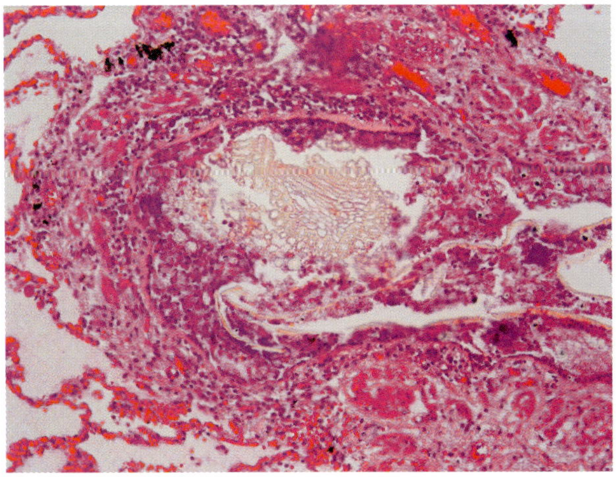

FIGURE 10.11 Plant matter in a bronchus. This unfortunate victim fell into a grain elevator. Grain is loose enough for a man to sink down into, as in quicksand. The grain surrounds the body eventually, not allowing the person to raise the chest wall to breathe. This victim was buried deep into the mountain of grain. At the same time, grain was inhaled into the mouth, causing aspiration into the lung.

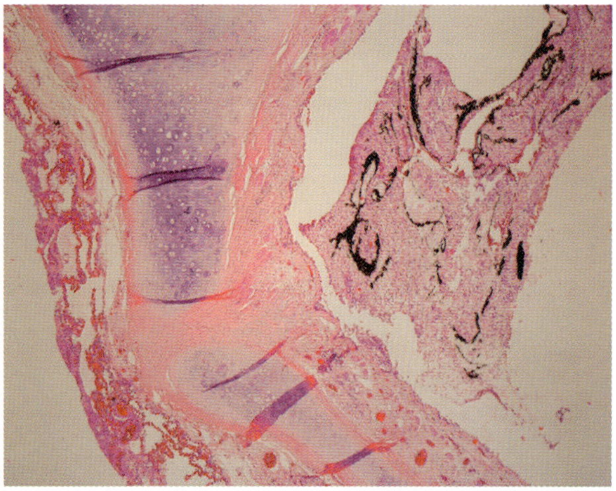

FIGURE 10.12 Soot in the trachea. In fire deaths, a great deal of soot (and hot air) can be inhaled. The figure shows black soot and mucus on the right. The trachea is seen on the left.

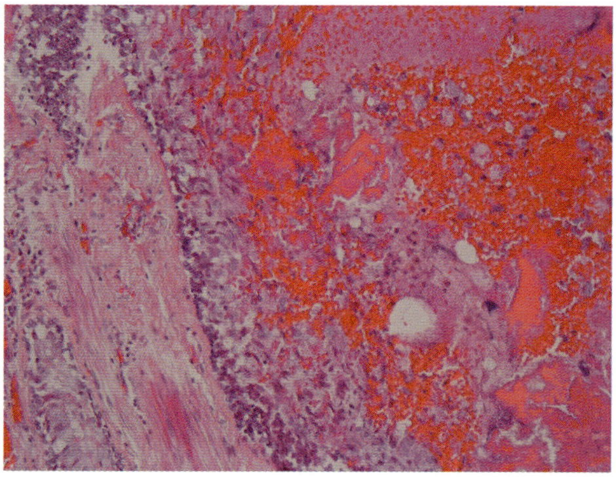

FIGURE 10.13 Aspirated blood. Many traumatic injuries of the head, face, mouth, and neck can cause blood to run into the bronchi. The blood can interfere with respiration and cause or contribute to asphyxia. Blood can be seen on the right side of the figure.

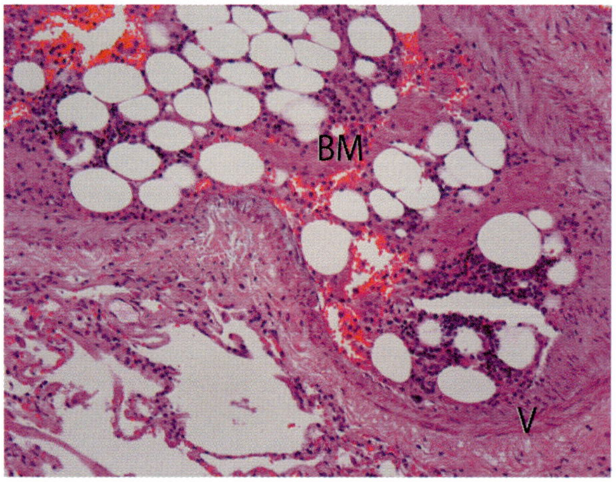

FIGURE 10.14 Bone marrow embolus in the lung. Even properly performed cardiopulmonary resuscitation (CPR) can break ribs, but only in adults (see Figure 6.5). At times, breaking of the ribs results in small bone fragments entering the bloodstream and, as in this case, stopping in the lungs. Fractures of large bones can also cause this phenomenon.

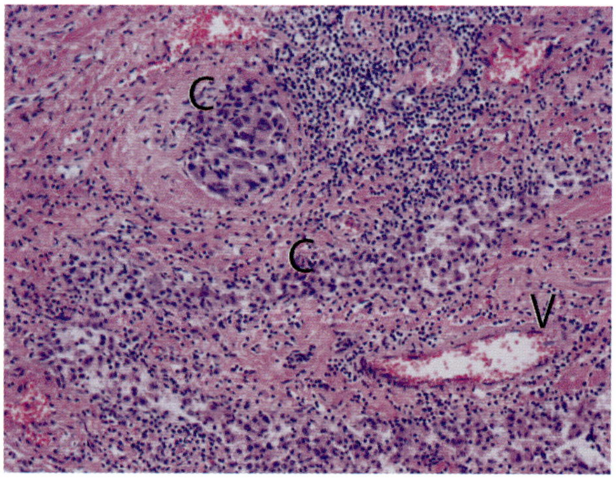

FIGURE 10.15 Invasive carcinoma of the lung. "C" is carcinoma; "V" is blood vessel. Any carcinoma, like this carcinoma of the lung, attacks the body by invading local and distant tissues. Carcinoma also invades the blood and lymph systems, as can be seen here. The large, malignant cells are highly and abnormally active, multiplying at an extreme rate and taking nutrients from the normal tissues.

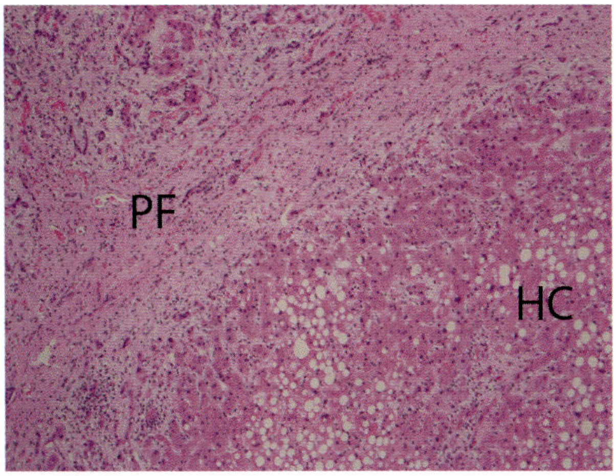

FIGURE 10.16 Cirrhosis of the liver. "PF" is portal fibrosis; "HC" are hepatocytes (liver cells). Cirrhosis is a reaction to damage to the liver. The damage can come from a virus (hepatitis), a toxic substance (ethyl alcohol), or a poison (carbon tetrachloride), among other causes. The resulting scarring or fibrosis bridges the portal areas. The end result of cirrhosis is liver failure. Clotting factors are not made; therefore, the patient is prone to bleeding. Also, since the fibrosis interferes with portal blood flow, veins around the esophagus and anus dilate and are prone to rupture.

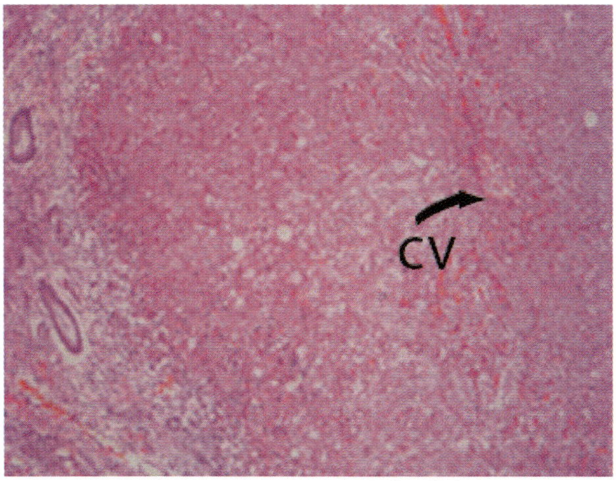

FIGURE 10.17 Central venous necrosis of the liver (shock liver). Prolonged shock can cause the part of the liver with less blood flow (central vein region) to die (necrotize). The right part of the figure demonstrates this necrosis, which causes liver failure. "CV" is central vein.

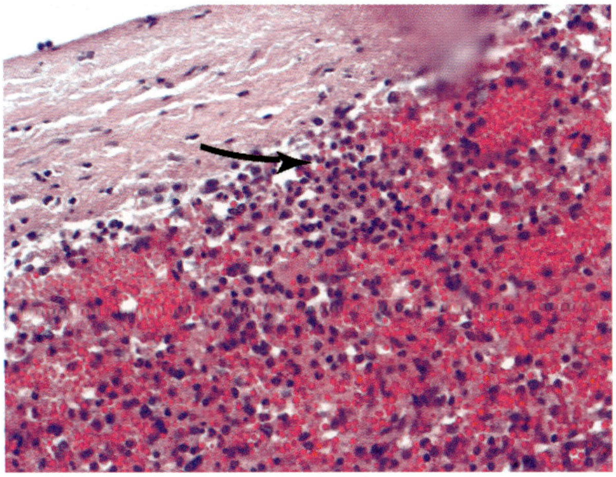

FIGURE 10.18 Splenitis. Neutrophils can be seen near the capsule (see arrow) of the spleen in this patient who died of sepsis. The red pulp is congested as well. Postmortem blood cultures and knowledge of premortem history of sepsis are the best ways to diagnose this condition. Occasionally splenitis is seen in sepsis.

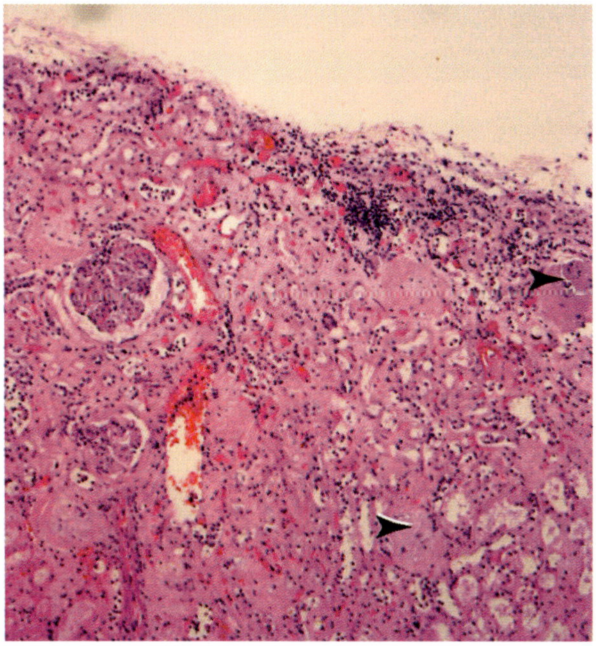

FIGURE 10.19 Renal arteriolosclerosis. The smooth outer cortex of the kidney is gone here. Hypertension has damaged the blood vessels supplying the glomerulus, causing sclerosis of the glomeruli (see arrows) and surrounding tubules and resulting in a pitting of the surface of the kidney (see Figure 8.71).

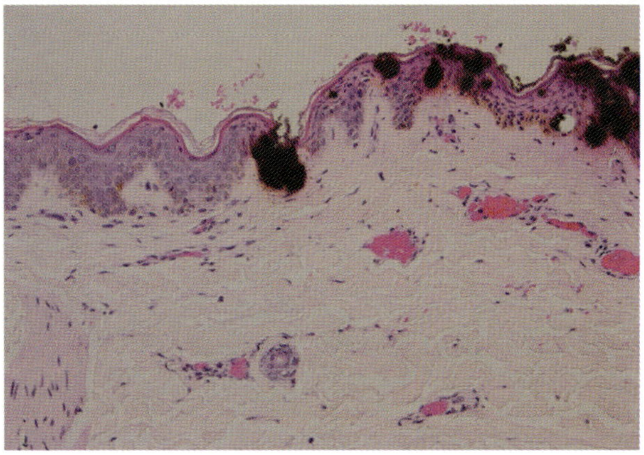

FIGURE 10.20 Soot deposited in the skin from a contact gunshot wound. Soot can be seen in the epidermis on the right side of the figure. The soot tattooed the skin because the barrel was close enough for the soot to be deposited. This microscopic section helps to substantiate the gross finding of soot on the skin in a gunshot wound (see Figure 2.1 and Figure 4.16A).

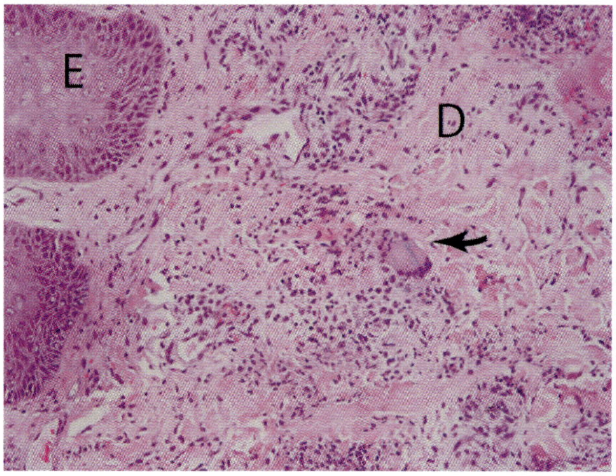

FIGURE 10.21 Skin granuloma in intravenous drug (IV) abuse. "E" is epidermis, "D" is dermis, and the arrow points at a granuloma. The chronic injection of the skin with drugs and their impurities like talc or baby powder forms a granulomatous reaction of the skin (see arrow). A bluish needlelike foreign object can be seen within the granuloma. This section helps to document the history of IV drug abuse. These granuolmas can also be seen in the lungs (see Figure 3.44).

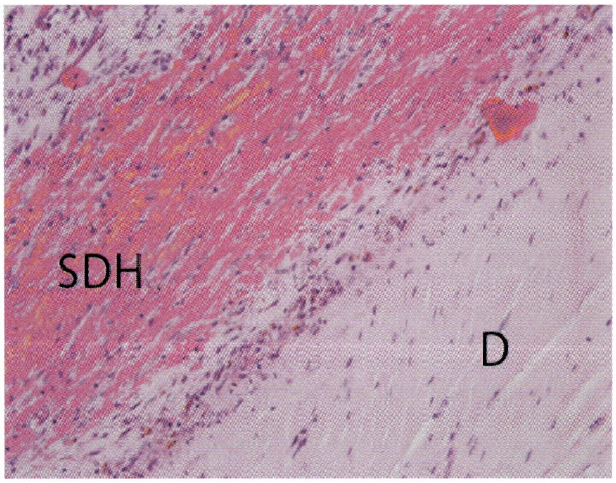

FIGURE 10.22 Chronic subdural hematoma. "D" is dura matter; "SDH" is subdural hematoma. A microscopic exam can give an idea of the age of injuries. This dating is not absolute. For example, this figure shows organized hemorrhage; therefore, the hemorrhage is at least 3 weeks old, i.e., it is not acute.

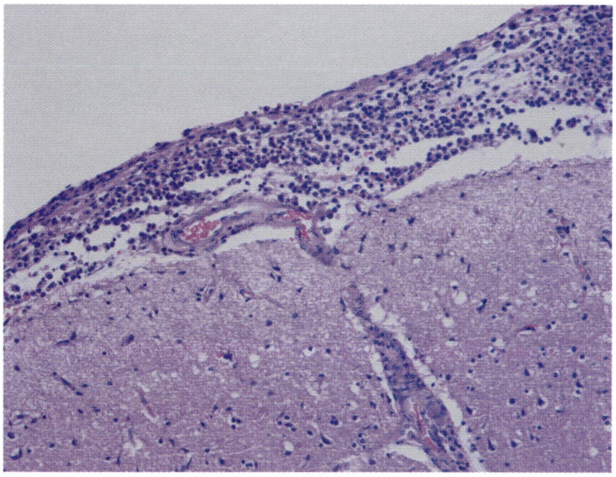

FIGURE 10.23 Meningitis. Meningitis is the inflammation of the meninges covering the brain. It can be caused by bacteria, viruses, fungi, or other sources. The result is the dark blue strip of inflammatory cells seen at the top of the figure. The specific organism that causes meningitis is best found by microbiologic culture.

11 Postmortem Laboratory Analysis of Drugs, Chemicals, and Microorganisms

The postmortem laboratory analysis of body fluids and tissues is an essential tool for the forensic pathologist. Toxicology studies are useful to help determine the cause and manner of death and to answer key investigative questions. This book has shown the power of visual gross microscopic findings in the autopsy. Drugs and chemicals, however, seldom leave characteristic or identifying visual findings at the autopsy. Even those substances that do leave visual findings, such as cyanide (causing pink livor) and carbon monoxide (causing red livor), must be confirmed and quantified. The specific drugs or chemicals found and their concentrations tell us a story about the death. The discovery of unexpected poisons can identify a perpetrator or even save a life. For example, finding a blood carbon monoxide of 50% in a person who died at home during the winter might save the life of the other occupants by implicating a faulty furnace.

The pervasive use and abuse of alcohol, cocaine, marijuana, amphetamines, and even prescription drugs in today's society necessitate determining whether these chemicals had any bearing on a death. The presence of these compounds is especially important if the death occurred on the job or as a result of a vehicle crash. Toxins and poisons in the environment, the home, and the workplace are increasingly common. The Occupational Safety and Health Administration (OSHA) investigates deaths involving toxins or poisons in the workplace. The Federal Aviation Administration and the National Transportation Safety Board require toxicology studies in many death investigations, such as those of pilots who died in airplane crashes.

Drug and alcohol analysis is part of a complete death investigation. To perform this analysis, the investigator, pathologist, and toxicologist must work together. The toxicologist heads up this team. Standard blood and urine screens are performed for commonly abused drugs and alcohol. These toxicology tests do not test for every possible drug or poison. If any drugs outside the standard screen are suspected, the toxicologist must be informed, since the method of analysis can depend on the compound suspected. In short, the investigator should say more to the toxicologist than simply, "Look for poison."

THE SCENE AND THE BODY

The search for drugs and poisons begins at the death scene. Prescription drugs should be logged and pills counted. One should be sure that the drug in the container is the same as that named on the label. Potentially fatal problems can arise when patients under therapeutic drug treatment by a physician take either less or more medication than prescribed. In accidental and suicidal overdoses, the number of pills present is much lower than it should be based on the last refill date. Patients with seizure disorders, for example, can succumb to *status epilepticus* (prolonged, violent seizure leading to respiratory arrest) if they stop taking prescribed seizure medication. As pointed out in Chapter 3, the types of medication present speak to the medical history. The medication bottles list the prescribing physician, who is a good source of further information about the victim. Pertinent hospital, clinic, and doctors' office records should be reviewed.

Alcohol is the most common drug found in medical examiners' cases. Searching the death scene for empty alcohol containers and counting these containers is the first step. In addition to searching for illicit drugs, the trappings of drug abuse (Figure 11.1) such as paraphernalia, whether the deceased was found in a known "drug house," and other observations should be noted. Often drugs, needles, and similar items can be found around or even on the body (Figure 11.2A, Figure 11.2B). In illicit drug deaths, witnesses commonly remove or dispose of the drugs. Searching arrest records can help uncover drug abuse history. Drug-oriented tattoos (Figure 11.3), clothing, and other materials can also alert the investigation team.

A well-publicized method of suicide involves tying a plastic bag over the head and taking a large amount propoxyphene, codeine, or other pain medication. These deaths can be recognized by the fact the bag is tied shut, presumably tied by the deceased (Figure 11.4). The mechanism of death in these cases is asphyxia, due to lack of oxygen in the bag, aided by the drugs acting as respiratory depressants.

Another sometimes fatal practice involves inhaling substances while placing one's head in a plastic bag. Figure 11.5A shows an adolescent who inhaled nitrous oxide from canisters, or "whippets," while his head was in a plastic bag (Figure 11.5B, 11.5C). The bag became a low-oxygen environment when the deceased breathed. This method concentrates the gas, giving a better "high." As the nitrous oxide was released, it replaced the oxygen in the environment even further, resulting in asphyxia. Note the belt used to cinch the bag closed.

The nose and mouth should be examined for drug residues. Crack cocaine smokers can have darker than usual oral mucosa. Glue sniffers or aerosol huffers can have residue around the mouth and nose. The hands and extremities should also be examined. Figure 11.6A shows the hand of an adolescent who was suspected of sniffing glue. A search of the house uncovered this compound (Figure 11.6B), the color of which matched the residue on the hand. The antecubital fossa, legs, and feet should also be searched for intravenous drug abuse needle marks or scars (see Figure 3.44).

Some poisons and drugs have unique odors. Cyanide, for example, smells of bitter almonds. The sickenly fruity smell of ethyl alcohol at autopsy is characteristic. However, one must be cautious in interpreting the odor of alcohol. The author has found that the strength of the odor does not necessarily correlate with the blood level. Also, other compounds such as acetone can smell like alcohol. In deaths due to diabetic ketoacidosis, acetone levels are elevated.

SPECIMENS TO OBTAIN AT AUTOPSY

Blood

Blood should be saved at all autopsies. Sodium fluoride tubes (or another preservative) should be used if the blood is to be saved for any period of time because they inhibit bacterial growth. At least 20 ml of blood should be obtained. Half of this blood should also be placed into plain tubes. Blood is the specimen of choice for alcohol analysis providing the result as a percentage. For example, 0.08% is the legal limit for operating a motor vehicle in many states. Care must be taken not to use contaminated blood samples. When the stomach is ruptured from a motor vehicle crash, for example, the contents could be admixed with heart blood. When the specific level of a drug is needed, blood concentrations are measured. Drug concentrations can vary depending on the collection site. In addition to taking heart blood, femoral artery and/or subclavian samples should be taken. At least one tube should be saved for future testing. The legal defense team might want to have the specimen tested in another lab because new questions might arise over time.

Urine

Urine is the ideal specimen for drug screening. When a drug is detected during screening, the drug can be quantified in the blood. At least 10 ml should be saved, or ideally 30 to 60 ml. A common problem is that very little or no urine is present at autopsy. In such cases, bladder washings can be performed.

Vitreous Humor

About 2 to 3 ml of clear vitreous fluid can be obtained from each eye and placed in a clean tube. Vitreous fluid is useful in confirming alcohol levels when contamination of blood is suspected. Drug analysis can also be done, and sodium, chloride, glucose, and blood urea nitrogen (BUN) can be reasonably analyzed. Since vitreous glucose decreases after death, the analysis is helpful only in hyperglycemia.

Gastric Contents

The stomach is tied off at the duodenum and esophagus for removal. About 50 ml of specimen is ideal. Any pills should be saved. Gastric analysis is very helpful for establishing intent in suicidal overdose cases.

Bile

Bile is useful in cocaine and narcotic analysis. These drugs are concentrated in the bile.

Tissues and Other Specimens

Liver, kidney, brain, heart, muscle, and fat can all be used in toxicologic analysis, especially when no liquid specimens are available. Many drugs are eliminated by the liver or kidneys. These specimens are useful if the deceased has been embalmed, decomposed, or if blood is not available. The type of specimen needed for each drug is variable. Consultation with a forensic toxicologist is very helpful before performing the autopsy.

Hair, nails (preferably toenails), bone, and even maggots can be used to detect drugs or poisons. These analyses are performed to detect the drug (qualitative analysis), not to determine the quantity of drug. Hair is the best specimen for detecting arsenic poisoning. Also, hair samples can be used to detect chronic drug abuse.

Finally, all specimens are submitted to the toxicology lab with a chain of custody form. This form indicates the type of specimen, the time and date collected, and the signature of the collector. All specimens are sealed, and the date, time, and collector's initials are written on the seal. All containers are marked with a unique name and case number. A chain of custody is maintained to reasonably demonstrate to the court that the analyses results match the person from whom specimens were taken.

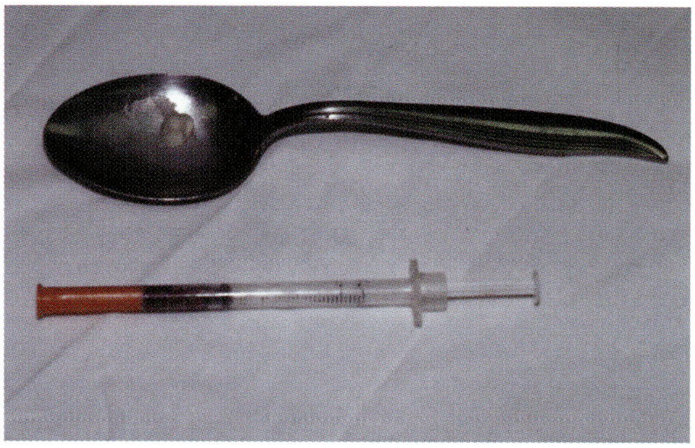

FIGURE 11.1 Needle and spoon. These trappings of intravenous drug abuse were found on an individual. The spoon is a "cooker" used to melt heroin into liquid form. The needle still contains the blood of the deceased, who died of a heroin overdose. The syringe can be analyzed for heroin.

FIGURE 11.2 (A) Crack cocaine, cigarette papers. These objects were found in the clothing of a homicide victim. Crack cocaine in the "rock" form shown here can be smoked from a pipe. **(B) Marijuana.** Marijuana is often rolled in cigarette papers, such as those seen in Figure 11.2A, to make marijuana cigarettes.

FIGURE 11.3 Syringe tattoo. Tattoos, clothing, jewelry, belt buckles, paraphernalia, and other personal items alert the investigator to a drug-related death.

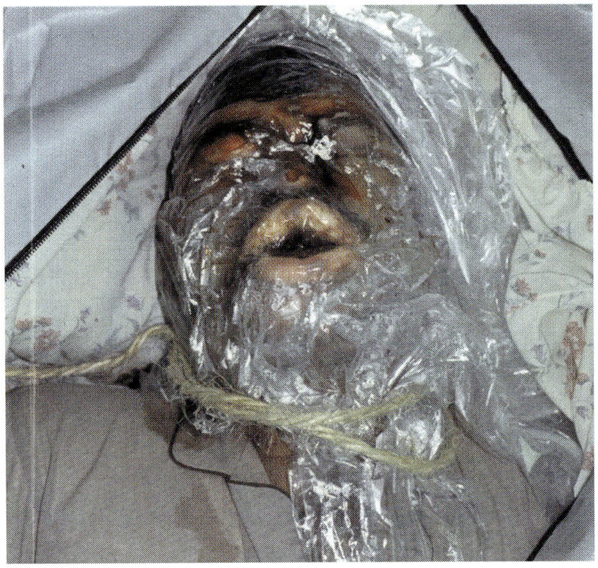

FIGURE 11.4 Suicide by suffocation. This individual took toxic levels of pain medication, placed the bag over his head, and then tied the rope. Published suicide literature was found nearby, instructing an individual how to commit suicide in this fashion. The deceased had not been seen for a few days and was beginning to decompose.

FIGURE 11.5 (A)–(C) Nitrous oxide use causing suffocation. This individual used the depicted nitrous oxide canisters from a whipped cream dispenser to release the gas into a plastic bag. This bag was placed over his head, as shown. Note the belt, which was used to cinch the bag closed. The nitrous oxide replaces the oxygen in the bag, causing asphyxia. Nitrous oxide is a recreational drug that causes euphoria, a floating feeling, and laughter.

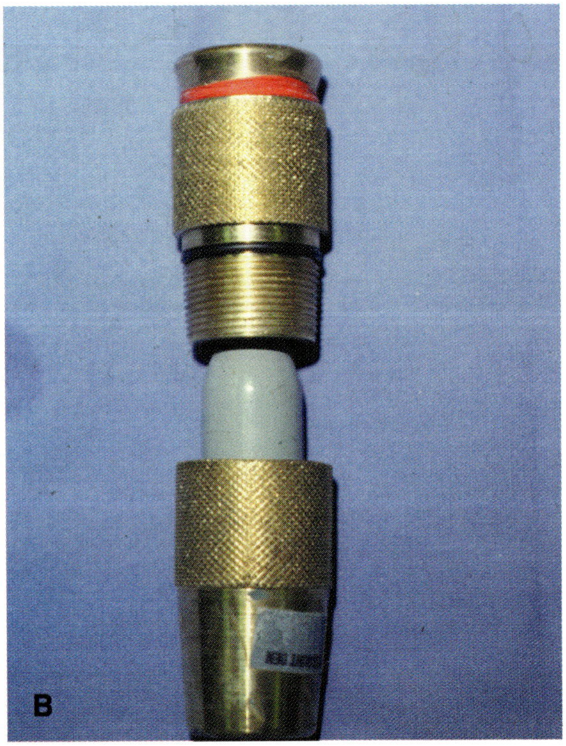

FIGURE 11.6 (A) **Glue residue on the hand.** This individual was found dead at his residence. He was seen sniffing glue previously. **(B) Glue container.** Search of the house revealed this glue container.

12 Review Questions: Putting It All Together

ANSWER THE FOLLOWING QUESTIONS. CHOOSE:

"A" if a, b, and c are true
"B" if a and c are true
"C" if b and d are true
"D" if d only is true
"E" if a, b, c, and d are true

1. The following types of deaths usually require an autopsy:
   a. Deaths of prisoners
   b. Deaths in the workplace
   c. Deaths within months of a traumatic accident
   d. Accidental deaths where there is no witness

2. The following are valid reasons for performing an autopsy in the case of an apparent homicide due to a single gunshot wound of the head:
   a. To confirm the cause of death
   b. To document the injuries
   c. To obtain adequate toxicology specimens
   d. To retrieve the bullet for further study

3. Reliable methods of identifying a badly burned body that would likely stand up to legal challenge include:
   a. DNA analysis
   b. Dental examination and records
   c. A uniquely numbered prosthesis
   d. Location; victim was sole resident of the home

4. The following statements about the external examination are true:
   a. Universal precautions should be observed in all autopsies.
   b. Nearly all trace evidence should be collected from the body at the scene.
   c. The clothing should not be cut off in homicides.
   d. All bodies must be x-rayed before an autopsy.

5. These facts related to the four signs of death are true:
   a. Rigor mortis is accelerated by cold conditions.
   b. Body temperature always drops at a rate of 1.5 degrees per hour.
   c. Livor mortis is permanently fixed after 12 hours.
   d. Decomposition rate is very dependent on environmental conditions.

6. The following statements about documentation of injuries are true:
   a. Many states have laws restricting the use of autopsy images.
   b. Both sketches and photographs are useful in documenting injuries.
   c. Injuries should be carefully cleaned to show wound configuration.
   d. Documentation of injuries is essential for other experts to review.

7. Radiographs are a useful supplement to the autopsy in the following ways:
   a. To find and enumerate bullets
   b. To identify remains by dental fillings
   c. To evaluate abusive fractures in children
   d. To diagnose pneumonia

8. Lacerations are defined by:
   a. Undermined margins
   b. Tissue bridging
   c. Abraded margins
   d. Jagged configurations

9. Blunt force injuries include:
   a. Lacerations
   b. Contusions
   c. Abrasions
   d. Cuts

10. Sharp force injuries include:
    a. Stab wounds
    b. Defense wounds
    c. Incised wounds
    d. Lacerations

11. The following statements about gunshot wounds are true:
    a. Intermediate gunshot wounds are defined by stippling.
    b. Contact wounds show soot deposition in and around the wound.
    c. Undetermined-range wounds show no soot or stippling.
    d. Hard contact wounds can show some marginal tearing.

12. The findings of the external examination direct the pathologist toward internal conditions, diseases, and injuries. Which of these external findings are matched with the appropriate internal findings?
    a. Laceration of scalp — Skull fracture
    b. Crepitus of chest wall — Pneumothorax
    c. Distended abdomen — Lacerated liver
    d. Contusions of neck and abrasions of mouth — Fracture of hyoid bone

13. The following statements are false:
    a. Pulmonary emboli are usually found in the pulmonary vein branches.
    b. The heart weight is less than normal in hypertension.
    c. The spleen's capsule is thin and easily torn on removal.
    d. The neck dissection is performed after the viscera are removed.

14. The following are important objectives of the individual organ examination:
    a. To perform gross and microscopic exams to diagnose disease
    b. To describe and record pertinent findings
    c. To document diseases and injury by photography, as appropriate
    d. To preserve key tissues for later examination

15. These statements concerning the neck tissue examination are true:
    a. Epiglottitis can cause fatal swelling and occlusion of the airway.
    b. An emergency airway is typically made in the thyroid cartilage.
    c. Hyoid and superior thyroid cartilage fractures are associated with strangulation.
    d. Cricothyroidotomies are made just below the hyoid bone.

16. Which of the following matches the correct disorder with the organ that most commonly displays the disorder?
    a. Anthracosis — Lung
    b. Chronic passive congestion — Liver
    c. Arteriosclerosis — Kidney
    d. Serous cystadenoma — Prostate

CHOOSE THE BEST ANSWER.

17. Which answer depicts the proper order of tissue layers of the head?
    a. Skin–Skull–Galea aponeurotica–Dura mater–Brain
    b. Skin–Dura mater–Skull–Galea aponeurotica–Brain
    c. Skin–Galea aponeurotica–Skull–Brain–Dura mater
    d. Skin–Galea aponeurotica–Skull–Dura mater–Brain

18. Why should the head and brain be subject to examination in all forensic autopsies?
    a. Most states require it by law
    b. For forensic research purposes
    c. Many injuries and conditions cannot be seen externally
    d. CAT scans miss many injuries

19. Which of the following is not a manner of death to be recorded on the death certificate?
    a. Homicide
    b. Suicide
    c. Natural
    d. Unnatural

20. The specimen of choice for determining possible hyperglycemia is:
    a. Blood
    b. Bile
    c. Vitreous fluid
    d. Urine

ANSWERS

1. E
2. E
3. A
4. A
5. D
6. E
7. A
8. A
9. A
10. A
11. E
12. E
13. B
14. E
15. B
16. A
17. D
18. C
19. D
20. C

References and Suggested Reading

Adelson, L.A., *The Pathology of Homicide,* Charles C Thomas Publisher, Springfield, IL, 1974.

Brogdon, B.G., *Forensic Radiology,* CRC Press, Boca Raton, FL, 1998.

Clark, S.C., et al. *Medicolegal Death Investigator,* Occupational Research and Assessment, Inc., Big Rapids, MI, 1996.

Collins, K.A. and Hutchins, G.M., *Autopsy Performance and Reporting,* 2nd ed., College of American Pathologists, Chicago, 2003.

Cotran, R.S., Kumar V., and Collins, T., *Robbins Pathological Basis of Disease*, 6th ed., W.B. Saunders Co., Philadelphia, 1999.

Di Maio, D.J. and Di Maio, V.J.M., *Forensic Pathology,* Elsevier, New York, 1989.

Di Maio, V.J.M., *Gunshot Wounds, Practical Aspects of Firearms, Ballistics and Forensic Techniques,* Elsevier, New York, 1990.

Dix, J., *Color Atlas of Forensic Pathology,* CRC Press, Boca Raton, FL, 2000.

Ellenhorn, M.J. and Barceloux, D.G., *Medical Toxicology, Diagnosis and Treatment of Human Poisoning,* Elsevier, New York, 1988.

Froede, R.C., Ed., *Handbook of Forensic Pathology,* 2nd ed., College of American Pathologists, Chicago, 2003.

Haglund, W.D. and Sorg, M.H., Eds., *Forensic Taphonomy – The Post Mortem Fate of Human Remains,* CRC Press, Boca Raton, FL, 1996.

Karch, S.B., *The Pathology of Drug Abuse,* CRC Press, Boca Raton, FL, 1993.

Ludwig, J., *Handbook of Autopsy Practice,* 3rd ed., Humana Press, Totowa, NJ, 2002.

Mortiz, A.R., Classical mistakes in forensic pathology, *Am. J. Clin. Pathol.*, 26, 1383, 1956.

Rohen, J.W. and Yokochi, C., *Color Atlas of Anatomy,* 3rd ed., Igaku-Shoin, New York, 1993.

Spitz, W.U., Ed., *Mediolegal Investigation of Death,* 3rd ed., Charles C Thomas Publisher, Springfield, IL, 1993.

Stimson, P.G. and Mertz, C.A., Eds., *Forensic Dentistry,* CRC Press, Boca Raton, FL, 1997.

Wetli, C.V., Investigations of drug-related deaths, an overview, *Am. J. Foren. Med. Pathol.,* 5, 2, 111, 1984.

Wetli, C.V., Mittleman, R.E., and Rao, V.J., *An Atlas of Forensic Pathology,* ASCP Press, Chicago, 1999.

Wetli, C.V., Mittleman, R.E., and Rao, V.J., *Practical Forensic Pathology,* Igaku-Shoin, New York, 1988.

Index

A

Abdomen
- examination of, 52, 62
- inflammation of, 91
- pus in, 74

Abdominal aortic aneurism, 134–135
Abdominal cavity, 72–73
Abdominal organs
- examination of, 87
- upper, 88

Abdominal panniculus, 87
Abdominal scar, 32
Abrasions, 37, 41–43, 57
Acanthosis nigricans, 51, 54
Accessory spleen, 112
Accidents, 4
Acute myocardial infarction
- gross anatomy findings of, 157
- microscopic findings of, 222

Adhesions, 81
Adrenal cortical adenoma, 124
Adrenal glands, 124
Alcohol use, 9, 187, 229
Algor mortis, 16
Anal examination, 53, 65
Aneurisms
- abdominal aortic, 134–135
- ascending aortic, 135
- coronary artery, 155

Anthracosis, 164, 169
Aorta
- dissection of, 135
- examination of, 151, 160
- excision of, 131–136
- laceration of, 136

Aortic valve, 162
Appendix, 117
Arteries
- basilar, 215
- carotid, 141, 144–145
- coronary, *see* Coronary arteries
- pulmonary, 101, 166
- renal, 134

Arteriolosclerosis, 191, 227
Ascending aortic aneurism, 135
Asthmatic lungs, 80, 225
Atherosclerosis, 133
Atherothrombotic occlusion, 155
Atrium
- left, 158, 160
- right, 159

Auricles, heart, 150–152
Autoerotic asphyxia, 4
Autopsy
- cases that require, 2–4
- definition of, 1
- elements of, 1
- homicide uses, 3–4
- hospital, 1–2
- medical–legal, *see* Medical–legal autopsy
- purpose of, 2
- Virchow method, 99

Autopsy permit, 1
Avulsion, 37, 44

B

Back examination, 52–53, 64
Bacterial endocarditis, 52
Bandages, 19, 35
Basilar artery, 215
Bile specimens, 96, 230
Bladder
- anatomy of, 96
- erythema of, 195
- examination of, 194–195
- excision of, 138–139
- trigone of, 194

Blood
- microscopic findings, 226
- specimen collection, 95, 230

Blood clot, 168
Blunt force injuries, 37, 41–44
Body
- identification of
  - dental identification, 8, 12
  - description of, 7
  - by family members, 7
  - fingerprints, 8, 11
  - objects in body, 8, 11
  - personal features for, 7, 10
  - radiographs for, 18, 29
- storage of, 16, 22
- tags on, 15

Body bag, 15, 20
Body temperature
- normal, 16
- postmortem, 16

Bone marrow embolus, 226
Brain
- cerebral infarct of, 218
- contusions of, 215
- cutting of, 217
- dura mater, 210
- exposing of, 209
- frontal lobe of, 214
- gliosis of, 214
- grey matter of, 217
- injuries of, 56
- *in situ* examination of, 211
- meningioma of, 211
- midbrain, 215–216
- parietal lobe of, 214
- removal of, 212–213
- subdural hematoma of, 210, 228
- temporal lobe of, 213
- tentorium cerebelli, 212
- weight of, 213
- white matter of, 217

Brainstem
- cutting of, 212
- hemorrhage, 216
- vertebral basilar arteries at, 215

"Breadloafing," of heart ventricles, 156
Breast(s), 52, 61
Breast cancer, 52, 61
Bronchial inflammation, 168
Bronchial pneumonia, 105, 171
Bruise, *see* Contusion
Bullet
- fragments of, 28
- path of, 39, 49
- removal of, 38

C

Carcinoma
- breast, 52, 61
- colon, 51, 54
- lung, 80, 169, 224, 226

Carotid artery, 141, 144–145
Cecum, 117
Celiac trunk, 132
Cerebral infarct, 218
Cervical vertebra fracture, 143
Cervix, 200
Charred remains, 29
Chest
- examination of, 52, 60
- puncture wounds of, 45
- scar of, 32
- skin dissections, 70–71

Chest cavity, 105
Chest plate, 77–78
Chief complaint, 7
Child abuse, 18, 29
Chopping wounds, 38, 46
Chordae tendineae, 161
Circumflex coronary artery, 154
Cirrhosis of liver, 187, 227
Clavicle fracture, 29
Clothing, 15, 21
Colon
- carcinoma of, 51, 54
- examination of, 79, 88
- sigmoid, 90, 114
- transverse, 89

Common bile duct, 107–108
Common iliac artery, 132
Congestion
- liver, 186

lung, 172
Conjunctival petechiae, 57
Contact gunshot wounds, 39, 48
Contrecoup injury, 56
Contusion
brain, 215
definition of, 37
illustration of, 43–44
orbital, 51, 57
Cooler, 16, 22
Coronary arteries
aneurysm of, 155
circumflex, 154
left, 152–153
left anterior descending, 153
right, 155
thrombosed, 223
Coronary ostia, 162
Coroner, 5
Crack cocaine, 230–231
Cricothyroid membrane, 175–176
Cricothyroidotomy, 19, 34, 175–177
Cuts
defense, 38, 45, 63
hesitation, 45
laceration vs., 37
Cyanide, 230
Cysts
ovarian, 92–93, 201–202
renal cortical, 190

D

Death
algor mortis, 16
decomposition, 17, 26
livor mortis, 16–17, 23–25
natural, 3
rigor mortis, 16, 23
signs of, 16–17, 23–25
unnatural, 3–4
Decomposition, 17, 26
Defense wounds, 38, 45, 63
Dental amalgam, 12
Dental cap, 10
Dental examination, 52, 58
Deoxyribonucleic acid, 8
Diaphragm, 83, 106
Dissection
aorta, 135
neck, 140–145
renal, 191
skin, 68–72
Distant-range gunshot wounds, 39, 49
Diverticulum, 114
Documentation
description of, 17–18
photography for, 31–32
video, 31–32
Drug abuse and use
intravenous site, 34
paraphernalia of, 229, 231
questions regarding, 9
scene investigation for, 229–230
Duodenum
description of, 94
excision of, 118, 120
illustration of, 107–108
Dura mater, 210

E

Electrical injury, 13
Embolus
bone marrow, 226
pulmonary, 101, 167, 171, 224
Entrance wound, 47
Environmental conditions, 17
Epiglottis, 173–174
Epiglottitis, 174
Esophagus, 121, 180, 197
Ethanol use, 9
Ethyl alcohol, 230
Examination
external, *see* External examination
internal, 67–72
microscopic, *see* Microscopic examination
Excisions
adrenal glands, 124
bladder, 138–139
heart, 100–102
kidneys, 123–130
large bowel, 113–122
liver, 106–110
lung, 103–105
ovaries, 137
small bowel, 113–122
spleen, 111–112
ureter, 125–126
uterus, 137
Exit wound, 47
Expert witness, 5
External examination
body bag, 15, 20
clothing, 15, 21
medical devices or artifacts, 19, 33–35
radiographs, 18, 28–30
trace evidence, 16, 23
universal precautions for, 15, 20
Extremities, 52, 63
Eyes, 51–52, 57

F

Face examination, 51, 57
Fact witness, 5
Fallopian tubes, 200
Family members, 7
Fingerprints, postmortem, 8, 11
Fingers, 52, 63
Fly larvae, 27
Forearm fractures, 30
Forehead laceration, 41
Forensic entomology, 17, 27
Forensic pathologist
definition of, 5
medical devices noted by, 19
Fractures
cervical vertebra, 143
clavicle, 29
forearm, 30
occipital, 56
radiography of, 18, 30
rib, 165
skull, 56, 213
Frontal lobe, 214

G

Galea aponeurotica, 204–205
Gallbladder, 96, 106–107, 184
Gallstones, 107–108, 184
Gas formation, 26
Gastric fluid specimen, 197, 230
Gastric ulcer, 199
Gastrocolic ligament, 116
Genitalia examination, 53, 65
Gestalt, 51
Gliosis, 214
Glue sniffing, 230, 233
Gohn method, 99
Grey matter, 217
Gun-induced laceration, 10
Gunshot wounds
bullet path, 39, 49
in clothing, 21
contact, 39, 48
description of, 38
distant-range, 39, 49
general images of, 10
hard contact, 38–39, 47
intermediate-range, 39, 48
pathologist's evaluation of, 38
radiographs for, 18, 28
suturing of, 35

H

Hair, 51, 55
Hands
bagging of, 15, 20
deformity of, 18, 33
examination of, 52, 63
Hanging, 145
Hard contact gunshot wound, 38–39, 47
Head examination
brain, *see* Brain
reasons for, 203
scalp, 204–207
skull, 208–209
Heart
anatomy of, 83, 135
aortic valve of, 162
auricles of, 150–152
examination of, 148–162
excision of, 100–102
in situ palpation of, 86
laceration of, 149
left atrium of, 158, 160
metastatic carcinoma of, 85
mitral valve of, 160–161

mottling of, 148, 157
myocarditis of, 158, 223
pulmonic valve of, 160, 224
right atrium of, 159
tricuspid valve of, 159
ventricles of, 156
weighing of, 102
Hemopericardium, 85
Hemorrhage
brainstem, 216
scalp, 207
splinter, 52, 63
Hesitation cuts, 45
Hilt mark, 44
Hilum of lung, 103–104
Homicides
autopsy in, 3–4
definition of, 3
"justifiable," 3
natural diseases in, 3
photographic documentation, 18
Hospital autopsy, 1–2
Hyoid bone, 141, 178

I

Identification
body, *see* Body identification
dental, 8, 12
deoxyribonucleic acid for, 8
Illicit drugs, 9
Incised wounds, 38, 45
Incisions
midline, 70
Y-shaped, 68–69
Infarction
cerebral, 218
myocardial, 3, 148, 157
pulmonary, 168
Inferior vena cava, 100, 109
Inflammatory bowel disease, 53, 65
Insects, 17, 27
Intermediate-range gunshot wounds, 39, 48
Internal examination
elements of, 67
overview of, 67
skin dissection, 68–72
Investigative questions
description of, 8
ethanol use, 9
illicit drug use, 9
law enforcement, 9
medical history, 8–9, 13
medications, 9, 13
occupation, 8, 13
types of, 8–9

J

Jugular veins, 144
"Justifiable" homicide, 3

K

Kidneys
arteriolosclerosis, 191
calyces, 192
cortical cyst of, 190
cross-sectional image of, 192
dissection of, 191
examination of, 190–192
excision of, 123–130
functions of, 190
perirenal fat, 126–127
polycystic, 130
renal cell carcinoma, 130
shape of, 190

L

Lacerations
aorta, 136
cardiac, 149
characteristics of, 37, 40
cut vs., 37
definition of, 37
forehead, 41
gun-induced, 10
heart, 149
illustration of, 40–41
lung, 165
scalp, 40, 55
spleen, 89
Large bowel excision, 113–122
Left anterior descending coronary artery, 153
Left atrium, 158, 160
Left auricle, 151–152
Left main coronary artery, 152
Lesser sac, 116
Ligature hanging, 145
Lines of Zahn, 135
Liver
cirrhosis of, 187, 227
congestion of, 186
description of, 79, 83, 88
examination of, 183–187
excision of, 106–110
"nutmeg," 186
porta hepatis, 183–184
sectioning of, 185
size of, 183
weight of, 110, 183
Livor mortis, 16–17, 23–25
Lobar pneumonia, 225
Lung(s)
adhesions, 81
anthracosis of, 164, 169
asthmatic, 80, 225
carcinoma of, 80, 169, 224, 226
congestion of, 172
examination of, 79, 163–172
excision of, 103–105
lacerations of, 165
masses, 82
metastatic carcinoma of, 80
pleural scar of, 82
sectioning of, 170
Lymph node, 184

M

Machete, 46
Marbling, 17, 26
Mediastinum, 122
Medical devices, 19, 33–35
Medical history, 8–9, 13
Medical–legal autopsy
definition of, 2
morgue analysis, 5
phases of, 4–5
postmorgue analysis, 5
premorgue analysis, 5
Medications, 9, 13
Meningioma, 211
Mental health history, 9
Mesentery, 119
Metastatic carcinoma
of heart, 85
of lungs, 80
Microscope, 222
Microscopic examination
acute myocardial infarction, 222
asthmatic lung, 225
blood, 226
bone marrow embolus, 226
cirrhosis of liver, 227
description of, 221
indications for, 221
lobar pneumonia, 225
lung carcinoma, 226
meningitis, 228
myocarditis, 223
pulmonary edema, 224
pulmonary embolus, 224
renal arteriosclerosis, 227
splenitis, 227
subdural hematoma, 228
thrombosed coronary arteries, 223
Midbrain, 215–216
Midline incisions, 70
Mitral valve, 160–161
Morgue analysis, 5
Mottling of heart, 148, 157
Mouth
examination of, 27, 52, 58
strangulation-related injuries, 58
Mummification, 27
Myocardial infarction, 3, 148, 157
Myocarditis, 158, 223

N

Nails, 52, 63
Natural death, 3
Neck
abrasions of, 59
contusions of, 44, 59
dissection of, 140–145
examination of, 52, 59
organs of, 173–182
strangulation injuries, 52, 59

Nitric oxide, 229–230
Nose examination, 52
"Nutmeg" liver, 186

O

Objects in body, 8, 11
Occipital fracture, 56
Occupation, 8, 13
Occupational Safety and Health Administration, 4, 15, 229
Oculomotor nerve, 211
Omentum, 88
Optic nerve, 211
Orbital ecchymoses, 57
Ovaries
  cyst of, 92–93, 201–202
  examination of, 200
  excision of, 137

P

Pancreas, 94, 120, 199
Pancreatitis, 199
Paraphernalia, drug abuse, 229, 231
Parathyroid glands, 179
Parietal lobe, 214
Pathologist, 5
Pattern abrasion, 37, 42
Pericardial air bubbles, 82
Pericarditis, 149
Pericardium
  anatomy of, 79, 83
  hemopericardium, 85
  opening of, 84
Perirenal fat, 126–127
Peritonitis, 74
Photography, 31–32
Pleura, 163
Pleural adhesions, 81
Pleural cavity, 79
Pleural scar, 82
Pneumonia
  bronchial, 105, 171
  lobar, 225
Polycystic kidneys, 130
Pons, 215
Porta hepatis, 183–184
Postmorgue analysis, 5
Postmortem fingerprints, 8, 11
Postmortem x-rays, 8, 12
Premorgue analysis, 5
Prescription drugs, 229
Pressure abrasion, 37, 42
Prostate gland, 196
Pulmonary artery, 101, 166
Pulmonary edema, 172, 224
Pulmonary embolus, 101, 167, 171, 224
Pulmonary infarction, 168
Pulmonary trunk, 160
Pulmonic valve
  gross anatomy of, 160
  vegetations of, 224
Puncture wounds, 38, 45

R

Radiographs
  body identified using, 18, 29
  child abuse evaluations, 18, 29
  dental, 12
  fracture evaluations, 18, 30
  gunshot wounds evaluated by, 18, 28
  objects in body, 11, 18, 29
  skull, 12, 28
  uses of, 18, 28–30
Rectum examination, 53, 65
Renal arteriolosclerosis, 227
Renal artery, 134
Renal cell carcinoma, 130
Renal cortical cyst, 128–129
Ribs
  fracture of, 165
  marking of, 74
  opening of, 75–76
Right auricle, 150
Right coronary artery, 155
Rigor mortis, 16, 23
Rokitansky method, 99

S

Scalp
  examination of, 51, 55–56, 204–207
  excision of, 204–207
  hemorrhage of, 207
  lacerations of, 40, 55
  reflection of, 206
  stitching of, 219
Scars, 18, 32
Scene investigation, 229–230
Scrape, *see* Abrasion
Seborrheic keratoses, 51, 54
Sexual assault kit, 53, 65
Sharp force injuries, 38–39, 44–49
Sigmoid colon
  description of, 90
  diverticuli of, 114
Skin
  decomposition-related changes, 17, 26
  discoloration of, 17, 26
  dissection of, 68–72
  examination of, 51, 54
  scars, 18, 32
  tattoos, 18, 33
  venous marbling of, 17, 26
Skin granuloma, 228
Skull
  base of, 213
  fracture of, 56, 213
  occipital fracture of, 56
  opening of, 209
  radiographs of, 12, 28
  sawing of, 208–209
Sliding abrasion, 37, 41
Small bowel
  description of, 88–89
  excision of, 113–122
Specimens
  bile, 96, 230
  blood, 95, 230
  chain of custody for, 230
  gastric fluid, 197, 230
  tissue, 230
  urine, 96, 230
  vitreous humor, 97, 230
Spinal cord examination, 218
Spleen
  accessory, 112
  anatomy of, 89
  examination of, 188–189
  excision of, 111–112
  laceration of, 89
  ruptured, 189
  sectioning of, 188
Splenitis, 227
Splinter hemorrhage, 52, 63
Squamous cell carcinoma, 182
Stab wounds, 31, 38, 44, 64
Status asthmaticus, 80, 225
Sternoclavicular joint, 75
Sternocleidomastoid, 140
Stomach, 83, 88, 121, 197–198
Storage of body, 16, 22
Strangulation injuries
  ligature, 145
  of mouth, 58
  of neck, 52, 59
Strap muscles, 177
Stromal tumor, 198
Subdural hematoma, 210, 228
Suffocation, 229, 232
Suicide
  accidents that appear as, 4
  autopsy after, 4
  definition of, 4
  hesitation cuts, 45
  intent, 3–4
  ligature hanging, 145
  methods of, 229–230
  nitric oxide inhaling, 229–230
  by suffocation, 229, 232
Sutures, 19, 35

T

Tattoos, 18, 33, 231
Temporalis muscle, 207
Temporal lobe, 213
Tentorium cerebelli, 212
Thromboembolus, 167
Thrombus, 196, 223
Thymus, 122
Thyroid gland, 179
Trace evidence, 16, 23
Trachea
  anatomy of, 142, 181
  soot in, 226
Transverse colon, 89
Traumatic injuries, 17–18
Tricuspid valve, 159

U

Universal precautions, 15, 20
Unnatural deaths, 3–4
Ureter
  examination of, 193
  excision of, 125–126
Urine specimens, 96, 138, 230
Uterus
  examination of, 200
  in situ anatomy of, 91
  removal of, 137

V

Vaginal examination, 53, 65
Valuables, 15, 22
Venous marbling, 17, 26
Ventricles, heart, 156
Video documentation, 31–32
Virchow autopsy method, 99
Vitreous humor specimens, 97, 230
Vocal cords, 173, 182

W

Water, body recovered from, 26
White matter, 217
Wounds
  chopping, 38, 46
  defense, 38, 45, 63
  gunshot, *see* Gunshot wounds
  incised, 38, 45
  puncture, 38, 45
  stab, 31, 38, 44, 64

Y

Y-shaped incision, 68–69